Case Problems in Finance

Case Problems in Finance

Edited by

J. KEITH BUTTERS, Ph.D.
Thomas D. Casserly, Jr., Professor of Business Administration
WILLIAM E. FRUHAN, JR., D.B.A.
Associate Professor of Business Administration
THOMAS R. PIPER, D.B.A.
Associate Professor of Business Administration

All of the
Graduate School of Business Administration
Harvard University

1975   Seventh Edition

RICHARD D. IRWIN, INC.   *Homewood, Illinois   60430*
IRWIN-DORSEY INTERNATIONAL   *Arundel, Sussex   BN18 9AB*
IRWIN-DORSEY LIMITED   *Georgetown, Ontario   L7G 4B3*

Seventh Edition

First Printing, October 1975
Second Printing, February 1976
Third Printing, August 1976

Case material of the Harvard Graduate School of
Business Administration is made possible by the
cooperation of business firms who may wish to remain
anonymous by having names, quantities, and other
identifying details disguised while basic relationships
are maintained. Cases are prepared as the basis
for class discussion rather than to illustrate either effective
or ineffective handling of administrative situations.

ISBN 0-256-01756-5
Library of Congress Catalog Card No. 75-3518

Printed in the United States of America

Acknowledgments

To the businessmen who contributed the material for the cases in this volume we express our sincere gratitude. In the development of these cases they gave liberally of their time and, in most instances, they made available to us facts about their businesses normally held confidential.

We wish to acknowledge our debt to Pearson Hunt, Charles M. Williams, James T. S. Porterfield, Leonard C. R. Langer, Robert F. Vandell, Alan B. Coleman, Frank L. Tucker, James E. Walter, Erich A. Helfert, and Victor L. Andrews, whose names have appeared as editors of the first four editions of this book. Their influence on the organization and objectives of the current edition will be obvious to anyone who has used the early editions of *Case Problems in Finance.*

The cases in this edition, or prior versions of these cases, were written or supervised by 28 different members of the senior faculty of the Harvard University Graduate School of Business Administration. Three cases were written or coauthored by members of the faculty of the Stanford University Graduate School of Business. Most of the cases appearing for the first time in this edition were written by one of the editors of this volume.

In addition to the editors of earlier editions of this volume we wish to thank Robert N. Anthony, M. Edgar Barrett, Lee Bodenhamer, Gordon Donaldson, Fred K. Foulkes, Bertrand Fox, Samuel L. Hayes, III, Leonard Marks, Jr., Robert L. Masson, John H. McArthur, John G. McDonald, Robert W. Merry, Ronald W. Moore, William W. Sihler, Lawrence E. Thompson, Richard F. Vancil, Louis T. Wells, Jr., and Harold E. Wyman for permission to use cases for which they are responsible as author or supervisor. We also wish to express our appreciation to the Stanford University Graduate School of Business for permission to reprint the Phoenix Aircraft Company, the Cal-Chem Corporation, and the Midwest Communications, Inc., cases in this volume.

We also wish to extend our thanks to the many instructors and research assistants of the Harvard University Graduate School of Business Administration and to Thomas Schiff of the Stanford University Graduate School of Business who wrote or assisted in the writing of many of the cases in this volume under the supervision of senior faculty members.

Most of all we should once again like to express our special appreciation to Carolyn Stubbs and Hedwig Pocius for their invaluable editorial assistance in the preparation of this volume and the accompanying Teacher's Manual. To the extent that errors and inconsistencies have been avoided, they deserve much of the credit.

The editors assume full responsibility for the contents of this edition, but they are keenly aware of their obligation to their predecessors and associates.

Graduate School of Business
Administration
Harvard University
September 1975

J. KEITH BUTTERS
WILLIAM E. FRUHAN, JR.
THOMAS R. PIPER

CONTENTS

vii

APPENDIXES

INDEX

Introduction

Many readers may be meeting the case method of instruction for the first time. More often than not the experience is a frustrating one, for cases typically end at the critical point—in the words of some, "just when they seem to be getting some place." At that point the reader is left to make his own way. It may be helpful, therefore, to know from the outset what case problems are and what advantages we believe can be gained from their use.

The heart of the case method of instruction is the use of problems to train the student to discover, and then to fix in his mind, *ways of thinking that are productive in the subject area.* Appropriate use of theory and the acquisition of factual material and procedural skills are also important goals, but the main objective is an ability to handle different types of managerial problems intelligently.

The word "decisional" is sometimes used to contrast the case method with "expository" teaching. The reader will find, for example, that most of the cases in this book are essentially descriptions of actual business situations. The facts are those which were known to some businessman; in total they present an immediate financial problem which that person had to decide. Some cases emphasize the preliminaries of decision making—the difficulty of isolating and defining the crucial problem or of determining whether enough information is at hand to make an intelligent decision. The great majority of cases, however, are "issue" cases; these present reasonable alternative courses of action which might have been followed in the given situation. Sufficient information is given for the reader to place himself or herself in the executive's position. From this vantage point the student is challenged to analyze the problem and to decide upon the course of action to be taken.

The cases themselves depict a wide variety of financial problems and business situations. Reference to the Table of Contents will show that problems have been drawn from most of the major areas covered in financial courses. Cases have been selected from a wide variety of industries and from different time periods. Cases are also included which illustrate different phases in the life cycle of business firms and problems of cyclical decline as well as of prosperity.

Twenty of the 48 cases in this edition are new. Of these 20 cases 13 are completely new and 7 represent updated, revised, and improved replacements for previous cases. The total number of cases has been reduced from 57 in the Sixth Edition to 48 in this edition. We have also substituted shorter cases for a number of the longer cases or case series in the Sixth Edition. As a consequence, this edition is about 150 pages shorter than the previous edition. We believe that this reduction in length has been accomplished without a major loss of content.

Inevitably, some instructors will find that some of their favorite cases have been omitted in this edition. The editors share this feeling. If an instructor is especially eager to continue to use one or more of the cases dropped from the Sixth Edition, they can be ordered separately from the Intercollegiate Case Clearing House, Soldiers Field Post Office, Boston, Massachusetts 02163.

No major changes have been made in the basic structure of the book. The effort has rather been to improve its overall quality by weeding out old, outdated cases and substituting more timely material. In our judgment, Part I of the Sixth Edition consisted of well-tested cases that provided a very teachable sequence of material offering a good opportunity for drill on fundamental techniques of analysis. The usefulness of a number of these cases had been impaired, however, by the fact that they were badly dated. Four of the cases in Part I of this edition, therefore, have been rewritten under different names to substitute more current data without altering the basic issues posed by these cases. Two entirely new cases have also been added in Part I. Science Technology, covering events occurring in 1974, provides an excellent opportunity to appraise a five-year financing plan under inflationary conditions. American Motors, dated in 1973, replaces the old National Motor Car case.

The general format of Part II has been carried over unchanged from the Sixth Edition. In most sections, however, some of the older cases have been replaced by new and more interesting cases. To cite some examples: We have decided with some regret to retire the classic Liquigas case. A newer case on the cost of capital, written by Professor McDonald of Stanford, the Cal-Chem Corporation, has been substituted for Liquigas. The old American Telephone and Telegraph Company case on debt capacity has been replaced by a new AT&T case dated in 1974. Several cases in the capital budgeting section are new. Perhaps of most interest is the Pertamina–Gulf Industrial Processing case which poses an interesting capital budgeting problem under inflationary conditions in an international setting. The Harrington case in the new ventures section presents an excellent opportunity for a discussion of the way in which different segments of the capital market can be tapped to enable the management of an established company to buy out the retiring owner despite the fact that the prospective purchasers have very little equity capital of their own to invest. As a final illustration, three new cases, all involving topical issues, have been substituted for badly dated materials in the "Problems in Public Issues" section. The Ling-Temco-Vought case poses the problem of a voluntary recapitalization under conditions of financial stress in the early 1970's. The Synerdyne case involves a major stock repurchase under current conditions. Finally, the Equitable Capital Fund case deals with a 1974 offer by Gulf & Western Industries to exchange a package of cash and debentures for its common stock. Among other things, this case provides an excellent opportunity for the student to discuss the problems associated with the valuation of a debt instrument under conditions of relatively high risk.

All of these cases are designed to provide a basis for class discussion; as such they are not intended to present either correct or incorrect illustrations of the solution of management problems. It need hardly be added that the discussion which they provoke will move along more realistic lines if students also have a standard finance text or reference book available and use it freely for background information not provided by this casebook. In addition, students will need to acquire proficiency in a number of analytical techniques useful in handling the quantitative aspects of cases.

Case problems confront students with the necessity of making decisions, and this is perhaps their greatest value. The student cannot stop with an understanding of the facts and a listing of items that deserve consideration. Mastery of these matters is merely the jumping-off point for class discussion. To be effective, the student must actually think the problem through to a decision, explain his analysis to his classmates, and defend it against their ideas. The need to choose among balanced alternatives and to discuss the decision intelligently is a great force in learning. It helps to provide that elusive quality of judgment that is often missed when learning is restricted to memorization of fact and views which others have codified.

Since the cases present business situations that pose debatable alternatives of action, they contain problems which can be narrowed but not settled by the usual techniques of financial analysis. Judgment must enter into the process of decision making, and therefore unanimous agreement as to the best decision is neither an expected nor a desired result of class meetings. This end result also contributes to the initial frustration of many students who have been working with scientific and technical problems; in the beginning phases of study in these areas a mechanistic approach can usually be counted on to yield a single "right" conclusion.

In developing a logical approach toward case problems, the reader should not overlook intangible human factors. The choice between financial alternatives in many, if not all, of the cases depends in part upon the principal's disposition for risk taking and other matters of judgment and taste.

In some instances, work with cases may require more of the student's time than would normal textbook reading assignments; however, the satisfaction of handling problems that bridge the gap between classroom study and business action, and the zest of independent thinking are usually adequate recompense for any extra time employed.

Part I

financing current operations

THE CASE OF THE UNIDENTIFIED INDUSTRIES (Revised)

Despite variations in operational and financial policies and practices and in operating results between firms in the same industry, the nature of the industry has an important impact on the general patterns of the need for funds (asset allocation), the methods of meeting these needs, and the financial results of most firms in the industry. Presented in Exhibit 1 are balance sheets, in percentage form, and selected ratios drawn from the balance sheets and operating statements of 12 firms in 12 different industries. Recognizing the fact of certain differences between firms in the same industry, each firm whose figures are summarized is broadly typical of those in its industry.

See if you can identify the industry represented. Then, be prepared as best you can to explain the distinctive asset structures and ratios of each industry.

1. Basic chemical company.
2. Electric and gas utility.
3. Supermarket chain.
4. Maker of name-brand, quality men's apparel.
5. Meat-packer.
6. Retail jewelry chain (which leased its store properties).
7. Coal-carrying railroad.
8. Automobile manufacturer.
9. Large department store (which owns most of its store properties).
10. Advertising agency.
11. A major airline.
12. Commercial bank (fitted into the most nearly comparable balance sheet and ratio categories of the nonfinancial companies).

Exhibit 1

THE CASE OF THE UNIDENTIFIED INDUSTRIES

Balance Sheet Percentages	A	B	C	D
Cash and marketable securities	4.0	7.6	5.1	15.7
Receivables	3.9	8.6	16.4	26.8
Inventories	...	24.9	11.0	23.2
Other current assets	0.9	3.5	...	1.2
Plant and equipment (net)	78.7	44.6	49.5	33.4
Other assets	12.5*	10.8†	18.0‡	0.7
Total assets	100.0	100.0	100.0	100.0
Notes payable	...	...	12.8	...
Accounts payable	2.9	23.9	5.3	29.3
Accrued taxes	2.6	3.6	1.9	1.4
Other current liabilities	0.6	4.9	5.7	...
Long-term debt	35.2	3.4	30.4	1.7
Other liabilities	3.8	6.4	...	1.6
Preferred stock	...	...	...	...
Capital stock and capital surplus	16.7	6.8	27.8	9.4
Retained earnings and surplus reserves	38.2	50.0	16.1	56.6
Total liabilities and stockholder equity	100.0	100.0	100.0	100.0
Selected Ratios				
Current assets/current liabilities	1.45	1.38	1.25	2.06
Cash, marketable securities, and receivables/ current liabilities	0.96	0.50	1.20	1.32
Inventory turnover (X)	...	6.4X	6X	23X
Receivables collection period (days)	20	19	64	18
Total debt/total assets	0.412	0.356	0.565	0.339
Long-term debt/capitalization	0.403	0.055	0.425	0.025
Net sales/total assets	0.32	1.61	0.69	5.40
Net profits/total assets	0.052	0.059	0.057	0.080
Net profits/total net worth	0.102	0.105	0.137	0.121
Net profits/net sales	0.167	0.037	0.083	0.015

* Includes 10.1% of investments in affiliated companies.
† Includes 9.2% of investments in affiliated companies.
‡ Includes 14.4% of investments in affiliated companies.
§ Includes 5.9% of investments in affiliated companies.

E	F	G	H	I	J	K	L
4.1	0.5	8.5	4.3	3.2	5.4	17.0	38.6
21.5	3.8	13.7	5.4	27.6	13.0	72.1	59.2
61.0	2.2	22.7	39.3	49.2	...	...	...
0.2	2.6	1.6	2.4	1.6	2.5	0.8	...
10.9	90.0	45.4	44.1	17.1	73.9	7.4	1.1
2.3	0.9	8.1§	4.5	1.3	5.2	2.7	1.1
100.0	100.0	100.0	100.0	100.0	100.0	100.0	100.0
5.1	3.1	0.8	5.2	2.0	...	...	...
12.6	2.6	10.0	25.3	10.5	8.3	50.3	84.4
6.6	1.4	2.7	2.4	3.1	...	...	...
1.2	2.6	12.0	10.4	5.8	7.7	2.6	...
5.8	43.3	25.6	3.8	20.6	45.6	3.3	1.6
1.0	1.8	7.5	8.2	...	10.9	1.0	5.9
2.2	9.4	4.9	...	0.1	...	...	...
31.0	25.3	11.9	12.0	17.4	8.4	6.8	5.1
34.5	10.5	24.6	32.7	40.5	19.1	36.0	3.0
100.0	100.0	100.0	100.0	100.0	100.0	100.0	100.0
3.41	0.92	1.85	1.19	3.81	1.29	1.44	...
1.62	0.44	0.33	0.22	1.44	1.13	1.24	...
2.1X	...	8.8X	12.8X	3.1X	...	...	...
64	44	30	4	66	69	42	...
0.313	0.530	0.510	0.471	0.420	0.619	0.663	0.918
0.078	0.490	0.382	0.078	0.262	0.628	0.090	0.191
1.30	0.32	1.65	5.03	1.51	0.69	5.33	0.06
0.085	0.048	0.077	0.056	0.065	0.026	0.081	0.008
0.124	0.107	0.211	0.125	0.112	0.095	0.240	0.112
0.065	0.153	0.047	0.011	0.043	0.037	0.015	0.131

THE HINTZ COMPANY

On May 10, 1967, Mr. Samuel Hintz, president of The Hintz Company, noted that the company's accounts receivable balance had increased to $93,000 as of April 30, 1967. Since this was $19,000 higher than it had been on March 31, 1967, Mr. Hintz decided to investigate the reasons for the increase to see whether it might have significance in determining the company's future plans.

The Hintz Company, located in New York City, manufactured baseball, basketball, and other athletic uniforms. The company's 20 employees cut and sewed fabrics to color and size specifications. The uniforms were sold directly to retail sporting goods shops in the New York metropolitan area. As there were several other small manufacturers of uniforms in New York City, competition for the business of these retail outlets was keen.

Since Hintz's founding in 1959 it had operated profitably, and sales volume had reached a peak of $350,000 in 1964. In the fall of 1965, sales failed to recover from the seasonal low of the summer months. In July, 1966, when a new sales manager, Mr. Katz, was employed, sales volume began improving. By May, 1967, Mr. Katz had secured 50 new accounts for the company.

After reading trade papers, Mr. Hintz believed that the prospects of the athletic uniform market looked promising for the remainder of 1967. It was reported that there were a large number of newly organized athletic teams in the New York area and that schools and other regular purchasers were buying new uniforms more frequently. Since Mr. Katz's more detailed experience in the market tended to confirm this information, Mr. Hintz was looking forward to the best year in the company's history. On this basis, he projected sales and profits by months for the remainder of 1967 as follows:

	Sales	Profit before Taxes
May	$ 50,000	$ 4,000
June	40,000	2,000
July	40,000	2,000
August	40,000	2,000
September	50,000	4,000
October	55,000	5,000
November	60,000	6,000
December	60,000	6,000
Total	$395,000	$31,000

Hintz's customers were for the most part small sporting goods stores. Of 450 accounts, only six purchased more than $10,000 worth of uniforms in a year. Most of the remainder made periodic purchases of approximately $100 per order. Hintz sold on terms of net 30, but only the large stores paid consistently within 60 days of billing. Bad debt losses were 2% of sales in 1966. A substantial portion of the retail stores' sales of athletic uniforms was made to schools that paid their accounts slowly, and Hintz's collections also tended to be slow. Mr. Hintz believed that many of the smaller stores were operated without adequate capital investment.

Mr. Katz received a salary of $10,000 and a 2% commission on his personal sales. He sold one third of the company's accounts as well as supervised the company's two other salesmen. Each salesman was paid a straight commission of 5%. No attempt was made to charge a salesman for bad debt losses resulting from his sales efforts.

Neither Mr. Hintz nor the company's bookkeeper, Mr. Stein, had abundant time to devote to credit management. As a result, the following general policies had been established for guidance in credit matters. Before selling to a new account, a company salesman was expected to appraise the storekeeper's character and abilities on the basis of his observations at the store, and to judge the financial condition of the store as best he could. If these appeared satisfactory, a line of credit of $200 was extended to the store. After a year, a salesman was authorized to increase the line of credit to $500 if the store had made all its payments within 90 days of billing. After two years of satisfactory credit experience, open lines of credit were granted when necessary. If a specific case warranted exception to these rules, Mr. Hintz reviewed the information available and made the final decision.

Billings were prepared by Mr. Stein when shipment was made. If payment was not received within 60 days, a form letter was sent to the customer calling his attention to this omission. After 90 days, a warning letter was sent, requesting payment within 10 days. Mr. Hintz telephoned all store owners who had not made payment within 100 days of billing; and unless he received a firm promise for immediate remittance, he threatened to turn the account over to his lawyer. If payment was not received after 120 days, the receivables were given to a law firm for collection, and the account was written off as a bad debt.

On April 30, 1967, $2,200 in outstanding receivables were in the hands of lawyers pending settlement. Legal fees on these collections amounted to 25% of the amount collected or $50, whichever was the larger. Mr. Hintz considered the company fortunate if it received as much as 50% on a receivable after it had been turned over to a law firm. In several instances, final settlement took as long as one year.

Although sales tended to fluctuate from month to month, Mr. Hintz maintained raw material and finished goods inventories at even levels. Since the company's production facilities were adequate to support a substantial increase in sales volume, no additions to fixed assets were contemplated. Mr.

Hintz noted that with the exception of the bank loan, current liabilities tended to remain relatively constant.

On May 10, 1967, when Mr. Hintz received the April 30, 1967, balance sheet shown in Exhibit 1, he was disturbed by the sharp increase in accounts receivable. He thought several questions important: (1) whether the increase indicated larger bad debt losses might be incurred in the future; (2) whether the current policies of credit administration needed alteration; and (3) whether the receivables balance might increase in the future to the point where the company would require more funds from the bank. To help answer these questions, he requested Mr. Stein to prepare the information contained in Exhibits 2 and 3. Profit and loss statements are given in Exhibit 4.

Exhibit 1

THE HINTZ COMPANY

BALANCE SHEETS, DECEMBER 31, 1965–66; APRIL 30, 1966–67

CHANGES IN BALANCE SHEET AMOUNTS, SELECTED PERIODS

(Dollar figures in thousands)

	Balance Sheets				Changes	
	Dec. 31, 1965	*April 30, 1966*	*Dec. 31, 1966*	*April 30, 1967*	*Dec. to April, 1966–67*	*April to April, 1966–67*
ASSETS						
Cash	$10	$10	$10	$ 4	$ −6	$ −6
Accounts receivable (net)	41	37	68	93	+25	+56
Inventory	23	22	25	22	−3	—
Total current assets	$74	$69	$103	$119	$+16	$+50
Machinery and equipment (net)	20	20	19	19	—	−1
Other assets	4	3	4	3	−1	—
Total assets	$98	$92	$126	$141	$+15	$+49
LIABILITIES						
Accounts payable	$20	$19	$ 21	$ 21	$ —	$ +2
Taxes payable	4	—	4	5	+1	+5
Accrued payroll	6	8	5	8	+3	—
Bank loan	—	—	25	32	+7	+32
Total current liabilities	$30	$27	$ 55	$ 66	$+11	$+39
Common stock	35	35	35	35	—	—
Surplus	33	30	36	40	+4	+10
Total liabilities and net worth	$98	$92	$126	$141	$+15	$+49

Exhibit 2

THE HINTZ COMPANY

SUMMARY OF TRANSACTIONS IN ACCOUNTS RECEIVABLE,
JANUARY, 1966–APRIL, 1967

(Dollar figures in thousands)

1966	Accounts Receivable Beginning	Sales (+)	Collections (−)	Bad Debts (−)	Accounts Receivable Ending	Collection Period (Days)
January	$41.5	$ 30.6	$ 30.7	$0.5	$40.9	
February	40.9	32.4	37.1	0.6	35.6	34*
March	35.6	24.1	21.4	0.6	37.7	40*
April	37.7	26.3	26.4	0.6	37.0	44*
May	37.0	25.4	24.7	0.6	37.1	43*
June	37.1	22.0	28.0	0.7	30.4	38*
July	30.4	24.6	22.7	0.5	31.8	41*
August	31.8	27.6	17.7	0.5	41.2	47*
September	41.2	24.6	23.1	0.5	42.2	49*
October	42.2	31.7	28.0	0.4	45.5	48*
November	45.5	30.1	13.3	0.5	61.8	60*
December	61.8	38.2	31.2	0.5	68.3	60*
Total	$41.5	$337.4	$304.3	$6.3	$68.3	73†
1967						
January	$68.3	$ 33.7	$ 40.8	$0.5	$60.7	51*
February	60.7	38.1	28.4	0.6	69.8	58*
March	69.8	45.8	41.0	0.5	74.1	53*
April	74.1	54.9	35.1	0.6	93.3	56*
Total 1967 to date	$68.3	$172.5	$145.3	$2.2	$93.3	65†

* Based on most recent 60-day sales period.
† Based on year, or year to date.

Exhibit 3

THE HINTZ COMPANY

ANALYSIS OF COLLECTIONS, APRIL, 1966–67, AND ACCOUNTS RECEIVABLE, APRIL 30, 1966–67

(Dollar figures in thousands)

Month of Sale	Age April 30 (Days)	Amount of Sales 1966	Amount of Sales 1967	Amount Collected in April 1966	Amount Collected in April 1967
Collections in April:					
April	0–30	$26.3	$54.9	$ 1.0	$ 2.7
March	31–60	24.1	45.8	2.1	5.5
February	61–90	32.4	38.1	22.7	26.3
January	91–120	30.6	33.7	0.6	0.5
Earlier	121+	....	....	0.0*	0.1*
				$26.4	$35.1

				Amount of Outstanding Receivables by Month of Sale %	
Age of accounts receivable on April 30:					
April	0–30	26.3	54.9	$25.3 68.4 $52.2	55.9
March	31–60	24.1	45.8	9.5 25.7 37.7	40.4
February	61–90	32.4	38.1	2.0 5.4 2.7	2.9
January	91–120	30.6	33.7	0.2 .5 0.7	.8
Earlier	....	....	....	0.0* 0.0*	
				$37.0 $93.3	

* Charged off, in hands of attorneys.

Exhibit 4

THE HINTZ COMPANY

PROFIT AND LOSS STATEMENTS

(Dollar figures in thousands)

	Year 1965	Year 1966	Four Months Jan.–Apr. 1966	Four Months Jan.–Apr. 1967
Sales	$335	$338	$114	$173
Cost of goods sold	213	215	75	120
Gross profit	$122	$123	$ 39	$ 53
General selling and administrative expenses	101	103	36	40
Bad debt loss	3	3	1	1
Operating profit	$ 18	$ 17	$ 2	$ 12
Provision for taxes	4	4	0	3
Net profit	$ 14	$ 13	$ 2	$ 9
Dividends	10	10	5	5
Retained earnings	$ 4	$ 3	$ (3)	$ 4

SUNSHINE TOY COMPANY

In early January, 1973, Mr. William Kincaid, president and part owner of Sunshine Toy Company, was considering a proposal to adopt level monthly production for the coming year. In the past, the company's production schedules had always been highly seasonal, reflecting the seasonality of sales. Mr. Kincaid was aware that a marked improvement in production efficiency could result from level production, but he was uncertain what the impact on other phases of the business might be.

Sunshine Toy Company was a manufacturer of plastic toys for children. Its product groups included billiard sets, automobiles, trucks, construction equipment, guns, rockets, spaceships and satellites, musical instruments, animals, and cartoon figures. Under most of the product categories, the company produced a wide range of designs, colors, and sizes. Dollar sales of a particular product item had sometimes varied by 30–35% from one year to the next.

The manufacture of plastic toys was a highly competitive business. The industry was populated by a large number of companies, many of which were short on capital and management talent. Since capital requirements were not large, and the technology was relatively simple, it was easy for new competitors to enter the industry. On the other hand, design and price competition was fierce, resulting in short product lives and a relatively high rate of company failures. A company was sometimes able to steal a march on the competition by designing a popular new toy, often of the fad variety. Such items generally commanded very high margins until competitors were able to offer a similar product. For example, Sunshine's introduction of moon rocket launcher sets in 1967 had contributed importantly to that year's profits. However, in 1968 eleven competitors had marketed a similar product, and the factory price of the Sunshine offering had plummeted. In recent years, competitive pressures on smaller firms had been intensified by the rise of a number of large, national toy manufacturers, which had comparatively ample financial resources to employ in elaborate product development and advertising programs.

Sunshine Toy Company had been founded in 1955 by Mr. Joseph Richardson after his release from naval service. Before the Korean War, Mr. Richardson had been employed as production manager by a large manufacturer of plastic toys. Mr. Richardson and his former assistant, Mr. William Kincaid,

12

established Sunshine Toy Company with their savings in 1955. Originally a partnership, the firm had been incorporated in 1956, with Mr. Richardson taking 75% of the capital stock and Mr. Kincaid, 25%. The latter served as production manager, and Mr. Richardson, as president, was responsible for overall direction of the company's affairs. After a series of illnesses, Mr. Richardson's health had broken down in 1970 and he had been forced to retire from active participation in the business. Mr. Kincaid had assumed the presidency at that time. In 1971, he had hired Mr. James Hardy, a recent graduate of a prominent eastern technical institute, as production manager. Mr. Hardy had worked during summers in the plastics plant of a large diversified chemical company and thus had a basic familiarity with plastics production processes.

Sunshine Toy Company had experienced relatively rapid growth since its founding and had enjoyed profitable operations each year since 1959. Sales were $3 million in 1972, and on the strength of a number of promising new products, were projected at $3.6 million for 1973. Net profits had reached $86,000 in 1972 and were estimated at $108,000 in 1973, under seasonal production, after taxes of 50%. Exhibits 1 and 2 present the latest financial statements for the company. The cost of goods sold had averaged 80% of sales in the past and was expected to maintain approximately that proportion in 1973 under seasonal production. In keeping with the company's experience, operating expenses were considered likely to be incurred evenly throughout each month of 1973 under either seasonal or level production.

Expanding operations had resulted in a somewhat strained working capital position for Sunshine Toy Company. The year-end cash balance of $140,000 in 1972 was regarded as the minimum necessary for the operations of the business. The company had periodically borrowed from its bank of account, Hood Trust Company, on an unsecured line of credit. A loan of $294,000 was outstanding at the end of 1972. Mr. Kincaid had been assured that the bank would be willing to extend a credit line of up to $850,000 in 1973, with the understanding that the loan would be completely repaid and "off the books" for at least a 30-day period during the year. Interest would be charged at a rate of 8%, and any advances in excess of $850,000 would be subject to further negotiations.

The company's sales were highly seasonal. Over 80% of annual dollar volume usually was sold during August–November. Exhibit 3 shows sales by months for 1972 and projected monthly sales for 1973. Sales were made principally to large variety store chains and toy brokers. Although the company quoted terms of net 30 days, most customers took 60 days to pay. Collection experience had been excellent, however.

The company's production processes were not complex. Plastic molding powder, the principal raw material, was processed by injection molding presses and formed into the shapes desired. The plastic shapes were next painted at "merry-go-round" painting machines. The final steps in the process were assembly of the toy sets and packaging in cardboard cartons or plastic bags. Typically, all runs begun were completed on the same day so that there was virtually no work in process at the end of the day. Purchases on net 30-day terms were made weekly in amounts necessary for estimated production in the forthcoming week. Total purchases in 1973 were forecast at $1,080,000. It was the company's policy to retire trade debt promptly as it came due.

Mr. Hardy, the production manager, believed the company would be able to hold capital expenditures during the coming year to an amount equal to depreciation, though he had cautioned that 1973's projected volume would approach the full capacity of Sunshine's equipment.

The company's practice was to produce in response to customer orders. This meant only a small fraction of capacity was needed to meet demand for the first seven months of the year. Ordinarily, not more than 25–30% of manufacturing capacity was used at any one time during this period. The first sizable orders for Christmas business arrived around the middle of August. For the rest of the year, the work force was greatly expanded and put on overtime, and all equipment was utilized 16 hours a day. In 1972, overtime premiums had amounted to $66,000. Shipments were made whenever possible on the day that an order was produced. Hence, production and sales amounts in each month tended to be equal.

As in the past, pro forma balance sheets and income statements based on an assumption of seasonal production had been prepared for 1973 and presented to Mr. Kincaid for his examination. These appear in Exhibits 4 and 5.

Having experienced a selling season at Sunshine, Mr. Hardy was deeply impressed by the many problems that arose from the company's method of scheduling production. Overtime premiums reduced profits. Seasonal expansion and contraction of the work force resulted in recruiting difficulties and high training and quality control costs. Machinery stood idle for seven and a half months, then was subjected to heavy use. Accelerated production schedules during the peak season resulted in frequent setup changes on the machinery. Seemingly unavoidable confusion in scheduling runs resulted. Short runs and frequent setup changes caused inefficiencies in assembly and packaging as workers encountered difficulty relearning their operations.

For these reasons, Mr. Hardy had urged upon Mr. Kincaid adoption of a policy of level monthly production in 1973. He pointed out that estimates of sales volume had usually proved to be reliable in the past. Purchase terms would not be affected by the rescheduling of purchases. The elimination of overtime wage premiums would result in substantial savings, estimated at $80,000 in 1973. Moreover, Mr. Hardy firmly believed that significant additional direct labor savings, amounting to about $94,000 would result from orderly production. A portion of the savings would be offset, however, by higher storage and handling costs estimated at $40,000 annually. Mr. Kincaid speculated upon the effect that level production might have on the company's funds requirements in 1973. He assumed that except for profits and fluctuations in the levels of inventories, accounts receivable, and accounts payable, funds inflows and outflows would be approximately in balance. To simplify the problem, Mr. Kincaid decided to assume that gross margin percentages would not vary significantly by months under either method of production.

Exhibit 1

SUNSHINE TOY COMPANY

CONDENSED INCOME STATEMENTS, 1970–72

(In thousands)

Seasonal

	1970	1971	1972	73
Net sales......................	$2,079	$2,380	$2,973	3600
Cost of goods sold..............	1,628	1,961	2,387	2880
Gross profit....................	$ 451	$ 419	$ 586	720
Operating expenses..............	304	376	416	504
Profit before taxes..............	$ 147	$ 43	$ 170	216
Federal income taxes............	71	16	84	108
Net profit.....................	$ 76	$ 27	$ 86	108

Exhibit 2

SUNSHINE TOY COMPANY

BALANCE SHEET, DECEMBER 31, 1972

(In thousands)

ASSETS

Cash...	$ 140
Accounts receivable...............................	1,051
Inventory..	212
Total current assets............................	$1,403
Plant and equipment, net..........................	428
Total assets....................................	$1,831

LIABILITIES

Accounts payable..................................	$ 102
Notes payable—bank...............................	294
Accrued taxes.....................................	60*
Current portion—long-term debt.....................	40
Total current liabilities.........................	$ 496
Long-term debt...................................	160
Shareholders' equity...............................	1,175
Total liabilities...............................	$1,831

* Taxes payable on 1972 income are due in equal installments on March 15 and June 15, 1973.

Exhibit 3

SUNSHINE TOY COMPANY

MONTHLY SALES, 1972

(In thousands)

January	$28	July	$ 39
February	35	August	469
March	39	September	556
April	36	October	648
May	35	November	711
June	38	December	340

PROJECTED MONTHLY SALES, 1973

(In thousands)

January	$43	July	$ 58
February	50	August	583
March	58	September	662
April	50	October	770
May	50	November	823
June	50	December	403

Exhibit 4

SUNSHINE TOY COMPANY

PRO FORMA BALANCE SHEETS, 1973 (SEASONAL PRODUCTION)

(In thousands)

	Actual Dec. 31, 1972	Jan. 31, 1973	Feb. 28, 1973	Mar. 31, 1973	Apr. 30, 1973	May 31, 1973	June 30, 1973	July 31, 1973	Aug. 31, 1973	Sept. 30, 1973	Oct. 31, 1973	Nov. 30, 1973	Dec. 31, 1973
ASSETS													
Cash (a)	$ 140	$ 392	$ 652	$ 579	$ 524	$ 500	$ 397	$ 361	$ 140	$ 140	$ 140	$ 140	$ 140
Accounts receivable (b)	1,051	383	93	108	108	100	100	108	641	1,245	1,432	1,593	1,226
Inventory (c)	212	212	212	212	212	212	212	212	212	212	212	212	212
Total current assets	$1,403	$ 987	$ 957	$ 899	$ 844	$ 812	$ 709	$ 681	$ 993	$1,597	$1,784	$1,945	$1,578
Net plant and equipment (d)	428	428	428	428	428	428	428	428	428	428	428	428	428
Total assets	$1,831	$1,415	$1,385	$1,327	$1,272	$1,240	$1,137	$1,109	$1,421	$2,025	$2,212	$2,373	$2,006
LIABILITIES AND NET WORTH													
Accounts payable (e)	$ 102	$ 13	$ 15	$ 17	$ 15	$ 15	$ 15	$ 17	$ 175	$ 199	$ 231	$ 247	$ 121
Notes payable—bank (f)	294	0	0	0	0	0	0	0	80	591	634	657	418
Accrued taxes (g)	60	44	28	(17)	(54)	(70)	(137)	(152)	(115)	(91)	(35)	26	24
Current portion—long-term debt	40	40	40	40	40	40	40	40	40	40	40	40	40
Total current liabilities	$ 496	$ 97	$ 83	$ 40	$ 1	$ (15)	$ (82)	$ (95)	$ 180	$ 739	$ 870	$ 970	$ 603
Long-term debt (h)	160	160	160	160	160	160	140	140	140	140	140	120	120
Shareholders' equity (i)	1,175	1,158	1,142	1,127	1,111	1,095	1,079	1,064	1,101	1,146	1,202	1,263	1,283
Total liabilities and net worth	$1,831	$1,415	$1,385	$1,327	$1,272	$1,240	$1,137	$1,109	$1,421	$2,025	$2,212	$2,373	$2,006

(a) Assumes maintenance of minimum $140,000 balance and includes excess cash in months when company is out of debt.
(b) Assumes 60-day collection period.
(c) Assumes inventories maintained at December 31, 1972 level for all of 1973.
(d) Assumes equipment purchases equal to depreciation expense.
(e) Assumed equal to 30% of the current month's sales and relates to material purchases of $1,080,000 for year as against sales of $3,600,000. This represents a 30-day payment period. Since inventories are level, purchases will follow seasonal production and sales pattern.
(f) Plug figure.
(g) Taxes payable on 1972 income are due in equal installments on March 15 and June 15, 1973. On April 15, June 15, September 15, and December 15, 1973, payments of 25% each of the estimated tax for 1973 are due. In estimating its tax liability for 1973, the company had the option of using the prior year's tax liability ($84,000) for its estimate and making any adjusting tax payment in 1974. Alternatively, the company could estimate its 1973 tax liability directly. Sunshine planned to use its prior year's tax liability as its estimate and to pay $21,000 in April, June, September, and December, 1973.
(h) To be repaid at rate of $20,000 each June and December.
(i) Adjusted for net profit from current month's operations, as per attached pro forma income statements.

Exhibit 5

SUNSHINE TOY COMPANY

PRO FORMA INCOME STATEMENTS, 1973 (SEASONAL PRODUCTION)

(In thousands)

	January	February	March	April	May	June	July	August	September	October	November	December	Total
Net sales	$43	$50	$58	$50	$50	$50	$58	$583	$662	$770	$823	$403	$3,600
Cost of goods sold (a)	34	40	46	40	40	40	46	467	530	616	659	322	2,880
Gross profit	$9	$10	$12	$10	$10	$10	$12	$116	$132	$154	$164	$81	$720
Operating expenses (b)	42	42	42	42	42	42	42	42	42	42	42	42	504
Profit (loss) before taxes	$(33)	$(32)	$(30)	$(32)	$(32)	$(32)	$(30)	$74	$90	$112	$122	$39	$216
Federal income taxes (c)	(16)	(16)	(15)	(16)	(16)	(16)	(15)	37	45	56	61	19	108
Net profit	$(17)	$(16)	$(15)	$(16)	$(16)	$(16)	$(15)	$37	$45	$56	$61	$20	$108

(a) Assumes cost of goods sold equal to 80% sales.
(b) Assumed to be same for each month throughout the year.
(c) Parentheses show tax credits from operating losses, and reduce accrued taxes shown on balance sheet.

Exhibit 2

WEL-BILT FURNITURE COMPANY

LLOYD'S INC.—INCOME STATEMENTS FOR YEARS ENDING JANUARY 31, 1965–67

(In thousands)

	1/31/65	1/31/66	1/31/67
Sales	$2,334	$1,900	$1,802
Less returns and allowances	210	223	146
Net sales	$2,124	$1,677	$1,656
Cost of goods sold	1,292	1,025	1,031
Gross profit	$ 832	$ 652	$ 625
Less operating expenses	714	618	598
Operating profit	$ 118	$ 34	$ 27
Other income	80	13	17
Net after other income	$ 198	$ 47	$ 44
Other deductions	48	49	51
Net profit (loss) before tax	$ 150	$ (2)*	$ (7)*
Dividends paid	42	42	—

* Parentheses denote losses.

Exhibit 3

WEL-BILT FURNITURE COMPANY

BARCLAY BROTHERS—BALANCE SHEETS AS OF JANUARY 31, 1966–67

(In thousands)

	1/31/66	1/31/67
ASSETS		
Cash	$ 148	$ 95
Notes and accounts receivable*	1,100	1,061
Inventory	1,074	985
Tax carryback claim	. . .	89
Total current assets	$2,322	$2,230
Fixed assets, net	293	265
Leasehold improvements, net	718	692
Cash value life insurance	56	55
Investments	11	11
Notes receivable—officers and employees	22	28
Prepaid and deferred items	29	31
Total assets	$3,451	$3,312
LIABILITIES AND NET WORTH		
Notes payable—Industrial Finance Corp.*	$1,062	$ 860
Accounts payable	488	532
Miscellaneous accruals	118	136
Total current liabilities	$1,668	$1,528
Common stock	684	684
Surplus	1,099	1,100
Total liabilities and net worth	$3,451	$3,312

* Receivables pledged to secure 30-day renewable notes to Industrial Finance Corporation.

Exhibit 1

WEL-BILT FURNITURE COMPANY

LLOYD'S, INC.—BALANCE SHEETS AS OF JANUARY 1, 1965–67

(In thousands)

	1/31/65	1/31/66	1/31/67
ASSETS			
Cash	$ 17	$ 13	$ 10
Accounts receivable, net	277	313	322
Inventory	365	364	365
Total current assets	$659	$ 690	$ 697
Land	71	71	71
Buildings, fixtures, and equipment	271	274	315
Less: Reserve for depreciation	38	58	79
Net buildings, fixtures, and equipment	$233	$ 216	$ 236
Investments	13	13	13
Due from stockholders	...	43	58
Deferred charges	8	4	4
Total assets	$984	$1,037	$1,079
LIABILITIES AND NET WORTH			
Accounts payable	$173	$ 174	$ 185
Notes payable—employees	14	16	16
Estimated federal income tax	13	...	...
Current maturities on long-term debts	31	72	44
Miscellaneous accruals	44	41	13
Total current liabilities	$275	$ 303	$ 258
Notes payable—bank*	109	180	175
Mortgage notes payable	452	450	526
Preferred stock—5% noncumulative	38	38	38
Common stock	72	72	72
Capital surplus	...	...	23
Earned surplus	38	(6)†	(13)†
Total liabilities and net worth	$984	$1,037	$1,079

* Secured by pledged accounts receivable.
† Deficit.

WEL-BILT FURNITURE COMPANY

In April, 1967, Mr. Richard Allan, an assistant credit analyst for Wel-Bilt Furniture Company, was concerned about changes in two of Wel-Bilt's accounts in Minnesota—Lloyd's, Inc. of Minneapolis and Barclay Brothers in St. Paul. He therefore brought the credit folders of these two customers to the attention of Mr. Watt Ralphson, the credit manager of the Wel-Bilt company. The Wel-Bilt company had its headquarters in Wheeling, West Virginia, and manufactured high-quality home furniture for distribution to department stores, independent home furnishing retailers, and regional furniture chains.

Lloyd's retailed quality home furnishings from four locations, one in the downtown section of Minneapolis and the others in nearby suburban areas. Sales were fairly steady throughout the year and were approximately 75% for cash and 25% by six-month installment terms. Installment terms called for 25% down and the balance in equal monthly payments over a six-month period.

The store had been established in 1927 as a partnership and was incorporated in 1953. In June, 1966, two of the four original partners sold their shares in the company to the two remaining owners.

Lloyd's had been a customer of the Wel-Bilt company since 1934 and had previously handled its affairs in a most satisfactory manner. Barclay Brothers was a comparatively new customer of Wel-Bilt's, having been sold since 1963. A medium-sized department store in downtown St. Paul, it was well-known for its extensive lines of home furnishings. Its account with Wel-Bilt had been satisfactory through 1966.

Both accounts were sold on terms of 1% 10, net 30 and, although not discounting, had been paying invoices promptly until December, 1966. Mr. Ralphson had previously established a $10,000 limit on Lloyd's and a $15,000 limit on Barclay Brothers.

The Wel-Bilt company advertised its lines nationally and attempted to maintain intensive coverage of trading areas by distributing through stores strategically located within a particular marketing area. Beginning in 1965, activity in the furniture market had become sufficiently spotty that quality of product and service were not the only bases for competition among manufacturers for outlets. Credit terms and financing of dealers became equally important; thus the Wel-Bilt company, in Mr. Ralphson's words, was "backed into the position of supporting numerous customers in order to maintain adequate distribution for its products." This was made somewhat more difficult because of the credit squeeze, which had meant higher interest rates on money borrowed by Wel-Bilt.

Because of this requirement for the extension of fairly liberal credit, Mr. Ralphson had since 1965 adhered strictly to a policy of obtaining current reports on the financial status of customers. These reports, obtained as annual balance sheets and profit and loss statements for customers that were considered satisfactory risks, were supplied directly by the customers. Under certain circumstances, wherein Wel-Bilt was working very closely with a particular customer who was trading actively on a small investment, Mr. Ralphson received quarterly and at times monthly statements in order "to keep on top" of the credit situation.

In early April, 1967, Mr. Richard Allan, an assistant credit analyst for the Wel-Bilt company, received the annual reports of Lloyd's and Barclay Brothers. After reviewing these statements and checking the accounts receivable ledger for both customers, Mr. Allan felt that the accounts should be reviewed by Mr. Ralphson. Accordingly, he furnished Mr. Ralphson with the information found in Exhibits 1 through 5.

When reviewing the accounts Mr. Allan kept in mind that 1966 had not been a particularly good year for retail furniture stores. It was generally known that stores such as Barclay Brothers, carrying low-priced furniture lines, were the first to suffer the declines which had come in the late summer and early fall. This situation was followed by signs of a relaxing demand for furniture of higher quality and higher price toward the end of 1966. The drop in volume and the subsequent price cutting hit the profit margins of some retailers to such an extent that the losses in the latter part of the year in some cases equaled or more than offset profits gained in the earlier part of the year.

In the early months of 1967 the "softness" of the furniture business continued. Although there was no severe drop in the buying of furniture at the retail level, retail stores reduced orders of new lines and reorders of established lines in February, March, and April because of a general feeling that there had been considerable "overbuying" by consumers which would result in a subsequent downturn in retail sales. Throughout the country, orders for shipment in April were down about 30% from March; March had itself shown a drop of about 10% from February. Thus credit managers among furniture manufacturing concerns were placed in the unhappy position of trying to please sales managers who wanted to maintain volume while they were aware that the shipment of furniture to customers who had already overextended their financial positions was potentially dangerous in such a period.

Exhibit 4

WEL-BILT FURNITURE COMPANY

BARCLAY BROTHERS—INCOME STATEMENTS FOR YEARS ENDING JANUARY 31, 1966–67

(In thousands)

	1/31/66	*1/31/67*
Gross sales	$6,253	$5,794
Less: Returns and allowances	574	443
Net sales	$5,679	$5,351
Cost of goods sold	3,570	3,677
Gross profit	$2,109	$1,674
Operating expenses	1,799	1,956
Operating profit	$ 310	$ (282)*
Adjustments:		
Elimination—reserves for inventory losses	. . .	174
Reduction—bad debt reserve	. . .	21
Tax carryback	. . .	89
Federal income tax	130	. . .
Net before dividends	$ 180	$ 2
Dividends paid	120	1
Net to surplus	$ 60	$ 1

* Deficit.

Exhibit 5

WEL-BILT FURNITURE COMPANY

AGING OF ACCOUNTS RECEIVABLE BALANCES
AS OF MARCH 31, 1967

	Prior	*Dec.*	*Jan.*	*Feb.*	*Mar.*	*Totals*
Lloyd's	$ . . .	$6,963.77	$1,095.96	$4,229.24	$ 1,233.61	$13,522.58
Barclay Bros.	457.01*	5,860.75	1,230.66	5,222.40	10,949.72	23,720.54

* Represents invoice on disputed shipment; customer claimed damaged merchandise.

THE CUNNINGHAM COMPANY

^^

In early September, 1967, Mr. Thomas Carr, assistant vice president and loan officer of the Farmers Union Bank of Kansas City, Missouri, was reviewing a loan request of $60,000 from Mr. Harry Cunningham, president of The Cunningham Company.

The Cunningham Company manufactured medical research and diagnostic equipment, and highly technical scientific instruments for industrial use. Its plant, located in rented space in a downtown area of Topeka, Kansas, was fully equipped with the latest type of electrically driven machinery.

The company, founded in 1947 by Mr. Cunningham, started as a small wholesaler of electrical appliances. Although this business was moderately successful, Mr. Cunningham showed more interest in experimenting with electronic equipment than in running the business. He devoted a substantial portion of his time to experimentation, and by 1956 had developed several electronic instruments, which appeared to have wide application in industry. When these models were sold successfully in 1957, Mr. Cunningham decided to manufacture them himself. Although demand for these instruments exceeded the limited production facilities from the start, Mr. Cunningham continued to spend much of his time experimenting with new equipment. All of the company's subsequent products were designed and developed by him.

In 1959 the company was incorporated with an initial capital of $34,000. Sales volume, which had grown continuously from the start, was always large in relation to the available capital, and as a result, there had always been heavy reliance on short-term credit to supply the expanding working capital requirements. Since incorporation, the company had never incurred a loss and all earnings had been retained in the business. Mr. Cunningham, the company's only officer, was 52 years old and drew a salary of $15,000.

On August 25, 1967, at the suggestion of his public accountant, Mr. Cunningham visited the Farmers Union Bank to discuss the possibility of securing a line of credit. He met with Mr. Carr, assistant vice president and loan officer of the bank. Mr. Carr explained that although he was unfamiliar with Cunningham's products, he had handled the accounts of several similar types of manufacturing companies. Exhibits 1 and 2 present the financial statements Mr. Cunningham had brought to the bank.

Mr. Cunningham was thoroughly dissatisfied with the company's current loan arrangement with the Topeka City Trust Company, from which it had been borrowing between $25,000 and $35,000 at an annual interest rate of 8% (7% interest fee plus 1% service charge) with accounts receivable pledged as security. He thought that Mr. Heath, the loan officer at the Topeka bank who handled the Cunningham account, made no effort to understand the company's problems, although he was constantly making suggestions that seemed inappropriate. Mr. Cunningham felt the bank had been quite arbitrary in selecting the receivables it would accept as collateral so that he never knew from one day to the next whether there would be sufficient funds to operate the company.

Mr. Cunningham thought that this restrictive attitude on the bank's part limited the company's ability to expand its sales volume. In the last few years the company had been unable to solicit new customers because of insufficient funds. Thus, increased sales volume, which had been financed internally, had come solely from expansion of existing accounts. Since Mr. Cunningham thought operations were currently just above the break-even point (he believed general, selling, and administrative expenses would remain fixed at an annual level of $130,000), any further increase in sales volume would increase profits before taxes by the amount of the gross margin, which was 36% in 1966. Because the plant was being operated at only 60% of capacity, Mr. Cunningham was eager to increase sales.

Mr. Cunningham was perfectly willing to pledge the company's accounts receivable or anything else that the bank thought would be desirable security so long as the arrangement was fair to the company and specific enough so that he could count on having the funds available when he needed them.

Mr. Carr explained that the bank was "pretty well loaned up" at the moment but that it was always interested in sound loan proposals from companies that showed promise of developing into good accounts. Mr. Carr promised to look into Mr. Cunningham's request and said he would plan to visit the company on August 28, 1967. He suggested Mr. Cunningham prepare an estimate of his cash requirements by that time. Mr. Cunningham seemed pleased with this arrangement; he said that although the Topeka bank was only 10 blocks from his plant, Mr. Heath had never visited the company.

Before going to the company, Mr. Carr telephoned Mr. Heath and learned that his experience with Cunningham had been thoroughly unsatisfactory. According to Mr. Heath, the company had maintained extremely low balances and on numerous occasions had overdrawn its account. The receivables pledged as security did not always measure up to the bank's standards of acceptable collateral. Although Mr. Cunningham seemed entirely competent from a technical standpoint, Mr. Heath thought he lacked financial and administrative ability. Mr. Cunningham had been promising for several years "to get his house in order" but had never accomplished it to the satisfaction of the bank. However, Mr. Heath believed that the company's products were well received by the trade and that with better management, Cunningham had good possibilities of developing into a sound business.

Upon visiting the Cunningham plant, Mr. Carr noted that although the production process included some fabricating, it was primarily an assembly operation. The instruments sold to the medical profession were all standard models and were produced in small lots. There was no apparent orderly flow of work, and a number of partially completed units were in storage awaiting further processing. It took an average of eight weeks to complete the processing of medical instruments. Industrial products, however, were manufactured on an individual basis and generally were designed to meet specific requirements of a customer. Because each unit required individual engineering modifications by Mr. Cunningham, the company accepted orders on a four-month delivery basis. Sales volume was equally divided between these two product lines. Mr. Carr was impressed with the company's products and thought that the company could increase its sales volume substantially without much difficulty.

Since the inventory of $168,000 on July 31, 1967, seemed excessive in relation to sales volume, Mr. Carr inquired into its composition. Finished goods inventory, which included only medical instruments, totaled $18,000; there were $30,000 of medical instruments and $36,000 of industrial equipment in process; the remaining $84,000 represented raw materials. Mr. Carr noted that the raw material inventory consisted of a large number of electronic and mechanical parts, ranging in value from a few cents each to several hundred dollars.

Mr. Cunningham agreed with Mr. Carr's comment that inventory was probably too large and said that he planned to reduce it to a total of $120,000 by the end of the year. Most of this reduction would be in raw materials inventory and would result from a recently installed inventory control system whereby all purchases were channeled through one man. Mr. Cunningham believed this action had already proved beneficial since purchases had dropped from an average of $14,000 per month at the beginning of the year to $6,000 in recent months despite a steady increase in sales volume. Terms of these purchases ranged from C.O.D. to net 30.

Sales to the medical profession were made through 120 surgical supply houses and doctors' equipment houses as well as directly to the Armed Service Medical Procurement Agency, a few hospitals, and, on occasion, individual doctors. These accounts had all been extended open lines of credit on net 30 terms without investigation, and in several instances credit balances ran as high as $8,000. Most accounts, however, purchased infrequently with orders ranging from $200 to $1,000. Although Mr. Cunningham believed that some wholesalers might be considered poor credit risks since they tended to be undercapitalized, he had never experienced a bad debt loss in the five or more years he had dealt with them.

Cunningham sold its industrial products directly to 20 large corporations, including General Motors, whose credit standings were above question. Orders by these companies, although infrequent, usually ranged between $2,000 and $10,000, and in all instances payments were made within the company's sales terms of net 30.

Accounts receivable on Cunningham's books as of July 31, 1967, were aged as follows:

Shipment	Age	Outstanding Receivables	Sales
July	0– 30 days	$36,000	$37,100
June	31– 60 days	12,000	43,600
May	61– 90 days	6,000	33,600
April	91–120 days	7,000	36,200
Total		$61,000	

Of the $7,000 representing accounts over 90 days old, $6,000 was due from the Armed Service Medical Procurement Agency, which was often slow in paying its accounts. The other $1,000 was owed by two surgical supply houses and one hospital. The remaining $18,000 in receivables over 30 days old were due from 28 other wholesalers. Mr. Carr noted that by August 28, 1967, collection had been made of all shipments prior to June and that only $8,000 of June shipments remained uncollected.

In investigating several disturbing aspects of the July 31, 1967, balance sheet, Mr. Carr learned that the accounts payable balance of $49,000 compared with total purchases of $70,000 during the first seven months of 1967. To ascertain the company's credit picture, Mr. Carr aged the trade debt on the company's books as of August 28, 1967, as shown below:

Purchase Month	Purchases	Trade Debt Payable
August	$ 6,100	$ 4,800
July	4,900	3,000
June	7,800	4,800
May	10,400	9,500
Prior		23,500
Total		$45,600

Mr. Cunningham said that the prior accounts included $3,000 in dispute and $3,500 payable to friendly creditors to whom payment could be postponed indefinitely.

The accrued taxes payable account on July 31 included delinquent withholding taxes totaling $22,000. Federal income taxes had been paid in March and June, 1967. Mr. Cunningham said the tax collector had been "after him" in August and all but $9,800 of these delinquent taxes were paid. Although no penalty was imposed on the company, a tax lien of $9,800 was filed against the company and Cunningham was put on a "pay as you collect" withholding tax basis. By arrangement with the tax collector, weekly payments of $350 were being made against the tax lien. After learning this, Mr. Carr said the bank would not consider making a loan unless the delinquent taxes were paid in full and maintained on a current basis in the future.

The company's public accountant, acting as trustee for a group of investors, had loaned Cunningham $35,000 at 17% interest secured by a chattel mortgage on the company's machinery and equipment. The note was payable on demand with no definite repayment schedule set, although it was originally intended that $1,500 be repaid monthly.

Mr. Cunningham estimated that sales in the last five months of 1967 would average $42,000, and his goal for 1968 was a monthly average of $50,000. Since a number of medical wholesaling houses had expressed continued interest in carrying Cunningham's instruments, and since the company's industrial products were almost without competition, Mr. Cunningham thought that with bank support there would be little difficulty in achieving these goals. In this respect, he estimated his needs as follows:

Repayment of present bank loan	$29,000
Additional working capital	31,000
Total requirement	$60,000

As the company had recently modernized its production facilities, no further expenditures for fixed assets were planned. Depreciation charges amounted to $400 per month. Mr. Cunningham did not expect the balances in the deferred asset account and the miscellaneous accrual account would change much in the next few months. In addition, he planned to maintain a cash balance of $3,000 in the future.

When Mr. Carr returned to Kansas City, he sent out letters of inquiry to a random list of Cunningham's suppliers. (Excerpts from the responses received by the bank are shown in Exhibit 3.) He also obtained a copy of the Dun & Bradstreet report on the company. Since the report was almost a year old and related to financial statements prior to 1966, it contained no additional information that was helpful to Mr. Carr. However, he noted that the company's credit rating was in the lowest category and that Mr. Cunningham had withheld from the Dun & Bradstreet reporter general financial information and in particular had declined to give information on payables and sales.

On September 1, 1967, Mr. Cunningham returned to the Farmers Union Bank to discuss the loan proposal further. He reported that the accounts receivable balance on August 31 was $67,000 (August sales totaled $41,000), and of this, $60,000 represented accounts less than 60 days old. Mr. Cunningham said he would invest an additional $2,000, the last of his personal resources, in subordinated debt and would agree not to pay dividends, increase his salary, or repay the loan he had made to the company until the bank debt had been cleared. Finally, Mr. Cunningham said he had discussed the chattel mortgage with his public accountant who suggested that his group might be willing to subordinate the chattel mortgage to the bank loan. On

September 1, the company's loan balance at the Topeka bank amounted to $29,000.

Mr. Carr agreed to consider this proposal further and promised to let Mr. Cunningham know the bank's decision within a few days.

Exhibit 1

THE CUNNINGHAM COMPANY

BALANCE SHEETS, DECEMBER 31, 1962–66, JULY 31, 1967

(Dollar figures in thousands)

ASSETS	12/31/62	12/31/63	12/31/64	12/31/65	12/31/66	7/31/67
Cash	..	..	$ 1	$ 5	$ 4	$ 1
Accounts receivable	$ 50	$ 36	38	43	71	61
Inventory	75	72	100	130	164	168
Total current assets	$125	$108	$139	$178	$239	$230
Fixed assets, net	22	20	18	21	22	45
Deferred assets	7	6	6	7	14	14
Total assets	$154	$134	$163	$206	$275	$289
LIABILITIES						
Overdraft—bank	$ 5	$ 4	..	..	..	..
Notes payable—bank	26	18	$ 31	$ 28	$ 37	$ 26
Notes payable—chattel mortgage	7	..	..	..	18	35
Accounts payable	21	17	17	44	47	49
Taxes payable	7	7	16	13	25	22
Miscellaneous accruals	6	7	8	10	19	20
Total current liabilities	$ 72	$ 53	$ 72	$ 95	$146	$152
Subordinated loan from officers	25	20	12	19	26	26
Total liabilities	$ 97	$ 73	$ 84	$114	$172	$178
Common stock	34	34	34	34	34	34
Surplus	23	27	45	58	69	77
Total liabilities and net worth	$154	$134	$163	$206	$275	$289

Exhibit 2

THE CUNNINGHAM COMPANY

INCOME STATEMENTS, 1962–66, JANUARY–JULY, 1967
(Dollar figures in thousands)

	1962	1963	1964	1965	1966	Jan.–July 1967	
Net sales	$206	$223	$259	$372	$396	$228	*1967*
Less cost of goods sold:							*438*
Material	67	71	77	120	127	75	*153*
Labor	31	32	36	59	63	41	*78*
Overhead	36	39	42	58	59	30	*58*
Depreciation	3	2	2	2	4	3	*5*
Total cost of goods sold	$137	$144	$157	$239	$253	$149	*294*
Gross profit	$ 69	$ 79	$102	$133	$143	$ 79	*144*
General, selling, and administrative expenses	63	74	78	115	127	71	*130*
Net profit before taxes	$ 6	$ 5	$ 24	$ 18	$ 16	$ 8	*14*
Taxes	1	1	6	5	5		*6*
Net after taxes	$ 5	$ 4	$ 18	$ 13	$ 11		*8*

Exhibit 3

THE CUNNINGHAM COMPANY

EXCERPTS FROM RESPONSES TO LETTERS OF CREDIT INQUIRY SENT OUT BY MR. CARR

. . . The firm in question is definitely undercapitalized but apparently has a good market for its products as they seem to be quite busy. Their available capital has always been small resulting in slow payments to their suppliers. From time to time we have had to hold orders pending a payment on account as is true at this writing. . . .

. . . . .

At times they are slow paying, but all amounts are paid. They are fine people to do business with.

. . . . .

At the present time the company owes us a low four-figure amount. In the past payments have all been met in approximately 60 to 90 days. The company appears to be a small, progressive, and expanding concern which we hope to develop into a good customer.

. . . . .

. . . We used to extend them credit, but their payments were so slow we now sell them only on C.O.D.

. . . . .

We have sold the company for several years. We have given credit up to a medium four-figure amount, but their payments have been continuously six months or more slow.

CUTRITE SHEARS, INC.

On April 28, 1970, Mr. Hamilton, Senior Loan Officer at the Fulton National Bank of New York, was reviewing the credit file of Cutrite Shears, Inc. in preparation for a luncheon meeting with the company's president and treasurer. Mr. Schultz, treasurer of Cutrite, had recently informed Mr. Hamilton that the company would be unable to liquidate its outstanding seasonal loan as initially anticipated. Mr. Hamilton, while agreeing to extend the outstanding $500,000 loan, had suggested that he would like to stop by and discuss the company's recent progress when he was next in the vicinity of Savannah, Georgia, where Cutrite's home plant and offices were located.

Cutrite Shears, Inc. manufactured a complete line of household scissors and shears. Its quality lines were distributed through jobbers to specialty, hardware, and department stores, located throughout the country. Its cheaper products were sold directly to large variety chains. Although competition, particularly from companies in foreign countries, was severe, Cutrite had made profits in each year since 1934. Sales and profits had grown fairly steadily, if not dramatically, throughout the postwar period.

Fulton National Bank had been actively soliciting the Cutrite account for several years prior to early 1969. Mr. Hamilton, after several unsuccessful calls, finally convinced the officers of Cutrite that association with a large New York bank offered several advantages not to be found with local banks. Mr. Hamilton was particularly pleased with the success of his efforts because Cutrite historically held fairly sizable deposit balances in its principal banks.

The company had sufficient capital to cover its permanent requirements over the immediate foreseeable future. Its short-term borrowings from banks were typically confined to the period July through December of each year, when additional working capital was needed to support a seasonal sales peak. As a matter of policy the company attempted to produce at an even rate throughout the year, and this accounted in good part for the sizable need for seasonal funds.

In June, 1969, Mr. Schultz arranged a line of credit of $1,200,000 with the Fulton National Bank to cover requirements for the fall. At the time, Mr. Schultz anticipated that the loan would be completely paid off by December, 1969. He gave Mr. Hamilton a pro forma estimate of the company's fund requirements over the forthcoming 12-month period to support his request.

31

(These estimates are shown in Exhibits 1 and 2.) In addition to the above requirements, the forecast showed a need for a new loan of approximately $600,-000 by June, 1970. Mr. Schultz attributed this increase in fund requirements (no funds were needed in June, 1969) to a plant modernization program. He explained that the program, requiring expenditures of $2,000,000, was approximately half completed and would be finished by August, 1969. Efficiencies resulting from the modernization program, once completed, were expected to save about $300,000 per year before taxes in manufacturing costs.

Mr. Schultz called Mr. Hamilton in early September, 1969 to let him know that the company would require $150,000 more than had been initially requested to cover peak seasonal needs. Mr. Schultz explained that the principal reason for the larger requirements was higher expenditures for modernization than had initially been estimated. Mr. Hamilton informed Mr. Schultz that the bank would be happy to accommodate the additional loan requirements.

In January, 1970, Mr. Schultz again contacted Mr. Hamilton. Mr. Schultz noted that sales had slackened considerably since his previous call. He attributed this decline largely to the economic recession then in progress, not to any special conditions affecting his company or the shear industry. Slackening in sales demand, however, had created a need for additional short-term borrowing. Mr. Schultz believed that additional funds would be required until the company could adjust to the new economic conditions. He envisioned that this adjustment probably would not occur until mid-April, 1970, or thereabouts. Once more, Mr. Hamilton agreed to extend the necessary loan funds to Cutrite.

In early April, 1970, Mr. Schultz telephoned Mr. Hamilton a third time to inform him that Cutrite would probably not be able to repay its outstanding short-term loan of $500,000 before the seasonal upturn in fund requirements in June. Mr. Schultz explained that a further sales decline, occasioned by the recession, was largely responsible for the company's inability to liquidate the loan as anticipated. Mr. Hamilton, in reply, noted that the bank preferred seasonal loans to be "off the books" for at least two months of the year, but saw no reason why he would not be willing to renew Cutrite's outstanding loan. He nevertheless thought it advisable to explore whether or not the inability to repay the seasonal loan in 1970 might be caused by a permanent change in the nature of the company's loan needs, such as might be occasioned by the modernization program. He consequently suggested a meeting for April 29 to discuss the company's recent progress.

In preparing for this meeting, Mr. Hamilton examined carefully the various profit and loss statements and balance sheets that Mr. Schultz had submitted to the bank over the course of the last nine months. (These data are shown in Exhibits 3 and 4.) He hoped this analysis might uncover the reasons for Cutrite's inability to repay its loan in accordance with original estimates.

Exhibit 1

CUTRITE SHEARS, INC.

PRO FORMA INCOME STATEMENTS BY MONTHS—FISCAL YEAR ENDING JUNE 30, 1970

(In thousands)

	Actual Year Ended June 30, 1969	1969						1970						Pro Forma, Year Ending June 30, 1970
		July	Aug.	Sept.	Oct.	Nov.	Dec.	Jan.	Feb.	March	April	May	June	
Sales	$10,079	$700	$900	$1,100	$1,500	$1,300	$1,100	$700	$700	$600	$500	$400	$500	$10,000
Less cost of goods sold:														
Materials and labor at 60% of sales	6,184	420	540	660	900	780	660	420	420	360	300	240	300	6,000
Overhead (includes depreciation of $50 per month)	1,191	100	100	100	100	100	100	100	100	100	100	100	100	1,200
Total costs	$7,375	$520	$640	$760	$1,000	$880	$760	$520	$520	$460	$400	$340	$400	$7,200
Gross profit	2,704	180	260	340	500	420	340	180	180	140	100	60	100	2,800
Selling and administrative expenses	1,033	90	90	90	90	90	90	90	90	90	90	90	90	1,080
Profit before taxes	$1,671	$90	$170	$250	$410	$330	$250	$90	$90	$50	$10	$(30)	$10	$1,720
Taxes at 50%	837	45	85	125	205	165	125	45	45	25	5	(15)	5	860
Profits after taxes	$834	$45	$85	$125	$205	$165	$125	$45	$45	$25	$5	$(15)	$5	$860
Dividends	500			100			100			100			200	500
Retained earnings	$334	$45	$85	$25	$205	$165	$25	$45	$45	$(75)	$5	$(15)	$(195)	$360
Cumulative retained earnings	...	45	130	155	360	525	550	595	640	565	570	555	360	

Exhibit 2

CUTRITE SHEARS, INC.

PRO FORMA BALANCE SHEETS BY MONTHS, FISCAL 1970

(In thousands)

	Actual June 30, 1969	1969						1970					
ASSETS		July 31	Aug. 31	Sept. 30	Oct. 31	Nov. 30	Dec. 31	Jan. 31	Feb. 28	March 31	April 30	May 31	June 30
Cash	$ 864	$ 400	$ 400	$ 400	$ 400	$ 400	$ 404	$ 894	$ 1,084	$ 759	$ 699	$ 539	$ 400
Accounts receivable*	697	950	1,250	1,550	2,050	2,050	1,750	1,250	1,050	950	800	650	700
Inventories (see below)	2,711	2,800	2,780	2,640	2,260	2,000	1,860	1,960	2,060	2,220	2,440	2,720	2,940
Total current assets	$ 4,272	$ 4,150	$ 4,430	$ 4,590	$ 4,710	$ 4,450	$ 4,014	$ 4,104	$ 4,194	$ 3,929	$ 3,939	$ 3,909	$ 4,040
Net plant	8,215	8,715	9,215	9,215	9,215	9,215	9,215	9,215	9,215	9,215	9,215	9,215	9,215
Total assets	$12,487	$12,865	$13,645	$13,805	$13,925	$13,665	$13,229	$13,319	$13,409	$13,144	$13,154	$13,124	$13,255
LIABILITIES AND NET WORTH													
Bank loans payable	$ 0	$ 327	$ 926	$ 1,151	$ 861	$ 271	$ 0	$ 0	$ 0	$ 0	$ 0	$ 0	$ 636
Accounts payable—trade†	288	249	260	260	260	260	260	260	260	260	260	260	260
Taxes payable‡	0	45	130	40	245	410	320	365	410	220	225	210	0
Miscellaneous other	90	90	90	90	90	90	90	90	90	90	90	90	90
Total current liabilities	$ 378	$ 711	$ 1,406	$ 1,541	$ 1,456	$ 1,031	$ 670	$ 715	$ 760	$ 570	$ 575	$ 560	$ 986
Mortgage at 6%	4,000	4,000	4,000	4,000	4,000	4,000	3,900	3,900	3,900	3,900	3,900	3,900	3,800
Common stock	4,000	4,000	4,000	4,000	4,000	4,000	4,000	4,000	4,000	4,000	4,000	4,000	4,000
Earned surplus	4,109	4,154	4,239	4,264	4,469	4,634	4,659	4,704	4,749	4,674	4,679	4,664	4,469
Total liabilities and net worth	$12,487	$12,865	$13,645	$13,805	$13,925	$13,665	$13,229	$13,319	$13,409	$13,144	$13,154	$13,124	$13,255

Inventory Subsidiary Data (FIFO)	July	Aug.	Sept.	Oct.	Nov.	Dec.	Jan.	Feb.	March	April	May	June
Raw Materials												
Opening balances.............	$ 271	$ 260	$ 260	$ 260	$ 260	$ 260	$ 260	$ 260	$ 260	$ 260	$ 260	$ 260
Plus purchases...............	249	260	260	260	260	260	260	260	260	260	260	260
Less transfers to work-in-process....	260	260	260	260	260	260	260	260	260	260	260	260
Closing balance.............	$ 260	$ 260	$ 260	$ 260	$ 260	$ 260	$ 260	$ 260	$ 260	$ 260	$ 260	$ 260
Work-in-Process												
Opening balance.............	$1,040	$1,040	$1,040	$1,040	$1,040	$1,040	$1,040	$1,040	$1,040	$1,040	$1,040	$1,040
Plus raw material additions.........	260	260	260	260	260	260	260	260	260	260	260	260
Plus labor additions.............	260	260	260	260	260	260	260	260	260	260	260	260
Transfers to finished goods.........	520	520	520	520	520	520	520	520	520	520	520	520
Closing balance.............	$1,040	$1,040	$1,040	$1,040	$1,040	$1,040	$1,040	$1,040	$1,040	$1,040	$1,040	$1,040
Finished Goods												
Opening balance.............	$1,400	$1,500	$1,480	$1,340	$ 960	$ 700	$ 560	$ 660	$ 760	$ 920	$1,140	$1,420
Plus additions from work-in-process....	520	520	520	520	520	520	520	520	520	520	520	520
Less cost of goods sold...........	420	540	660	900	780	660	420	420	360	300	240	300
Closing balance.............	$1,500	$1,480	$1,340	$ 960	$ 700	$ 560	$ 660	$ 760	$ 920	$1,140	$1,420	$1,640
Total closing inventory........	$2,800	$2,780	$2,640	$2,260	$2,000	$1,860	$1,960	$2,060	$2,220	$2,440	$2,720	$2,940

* Assumes collections lag sales by 45 days.
† Assumes 30-day payment period, in accordance with trade terms.
‡ Estimated taxes are paid in four equal installments of $215,000 each in September, December, March, and June based on pro forma earnings calculated the previous June.

Exhibit 3

CUTRITE SHEARS, INC.

ACTUAL BALANCE SHEETS BY MONTHS, JUNE 30, 1969–MARCH 31, 1970

(In thousands)

	1969							1970		
	June 30	July 31	Aug. 31	Sept. 30	Oct. 31	Nov. 30	Dec. 31	Jan. 31	Feb. 28	March 31
ASSETS										
Cash	$ 864	$ 474	$ 345	$ 388	$ 387	$ 432	$ 367	$ 533	$ 514	$ 385
Accounts receivable	697	949	1,219	1,470	1,890	1,848	1,864	1,324	1,060	882
Inventories	2,711	2,802	2,777	2,663	2,401	2,242	2,174	2,316	2,398	2,466
Total current assets	$ 4,272	$ 4,225	$ 4,341	$ 4,521	$ 4,678	$ 4,522	$ 4,405	$ 4,173	$ 3,972	$ 3,733
Net plant	8,215	8,730	9,255	9,314	9,317	9,312	9,326	9,312	9,301	9,287
Total assets	$12,487	$12,955	$13,596	$13,835	$13,995	$13,834	$13,731	$13,485	$13,273	$13,020
LIABILITIES AND NET WORTH										
Bank loans payable	$ 0	$ 424	$ 924	$ 1,300	$ 1,099	$ 699	$ 875	$ 575	$ 375	$ 500
Accounts payable—trade	288	264	259	282	293	279	229	234	220	172
Taxes payable	0	33	99	(33)	141	270	149	174	176	(46)
Miscellaneous other	90	92	106	95	97	92	90	89	87	86
Total current liabilities	$ 378	$ 813	$ 1,388	$ 1,644	$ 1,630	$ 1,340	$ 1,343	$ 1,072	$ 858	$ 712
Mortgage at 6%	4,000	4,000	4,000	4,000	4,000	4,000	3,900	3,900	3,900	3,900
Common stock	4,000	4,000	4,000	4,000	4,000	4,000	4,000	4,000	4,000	4,000
Earned surplus	4,109	4,142	4,208	4,191	4,365	4,494	4,488	4,513	4,515	4,408
Total liabilities and net worth	$12,487	$12,955	$13,596	$13,835	$13,995	$13,834	$13,731	$13,485	$13,273	$13,020

| | 1969 | | | | | | 1970 | | |
Inventory Subsidiary Data (FIFO)	July	Aug.	Sept.	Oct.	Nov.	Dec.	Jan.	Feb.	March
Raw Materials									
Opening balance	$ 271	$ 272	$ 253	$ 254	$ 265	$ 275	$ 260	$ 255	$ 252
Plus purchases	263	260	280	290	268	230	231	218	173
Less transfers to work-in-process	262	279	279	279	258	245	236	221	201
Closing balance	$ 272	$ 253	$ 254	$ 265	$ 275	$ 260	$ 255	$ 252	$ 224
Work-in-Process									
Opening balance	$1,040	$1,047	$1,069	$1,077	$1,078	$1,049	$1,015	$ 987	$ 929
Plus raw material additions	262	279	279	279	258	245	236	221	201
Plus labor additions	264	264	258	264	250	264	264	230	216
Transfers to finished goods	519	521	529	542	537	543	528	509	500
Closing balance	$1,047	$1,069	$1,077	$1,078	$1,049	$1,015	$ 987	$ 929	$ 846
Finished Goods									
Opening balance	$1,400	$1,483	$1,455	$1,332	$1,058	$ 918	$ 899	$1,074	$1,217
Plus additions from work-in-process	519	521	529	542	537	543	528	509	500
Less cost of goods sold	436	549	652	816	677	562	353	366	321
Closing balance	$1,483	$1,455	$1,332	$1,058	$ 918	$ 899	$1,074	$1,217	$1,396
Total inventory	$2,802	$2,777	$2,663	$2,401	$2,242	$2,174	$2,316	$2,398	$2,466

Exhibit 4

CUTRITE SHEARS, INC.

ACTUAL INCOME STATEMENTS BY MONTHS, JULY 1969–MARCH 1970

(In thousands)

	1969						1970		
	July	*Aug.*	*Sept.*	*Oct.*	*Nov.*	*Dec.*	*Jan.*	*Feb.*	*March*
Sales..........	$692	$871	$1,030	$1,360	$1,128	$936	$588	$581	$ 501
Less cost of goods sold:									
Materials and labor........	436	549	652	816	677	562	353	366	321
Overhead (includes depreciation of $50 per month).....	99	97	114	104	101	96	98	125*	108*
Total costs........	$535	$646	$ 766	$ 920	$ 778	$658	$451	$491	$ 429
Gross profit........	157	225	264	440	350	278	137	90	72
Selling and administrative expenses.....	91	93	98	93	92	90	87	86	86
Profit before tax........	$ 66	$132	$ 166	$ 347	$ 258	$188	$ 50	$ 4	$ (14)
Taxes at 50%........	33	66	83	174	129	94	25	2	(7)
Profits after tax........	$ 33	$ 66	$ 83	$ 174	$ 129	$ 94	$ 25	$ 2	$ (7)
Dividends........			100			100			100
Retained earnings........	$ 33	$ 66	$ (17)	$ 174	$ 129	$ (6)	$ 25	$ 2	$(107)
Cumulative retained earnings........	33	99	82	256	385	379	404	406	299

* Includes special costs for laying off personnel.

BROWNING LUMBER COMPANY

After a rapid growth in its business during recent years, the Browning Lumber Company in the spring of 1972 anticipated a further substantial increase in sales. Despite good profits, which were largely retained in the business, the company had experienced a shortage of cash and had found it necessary to increase its borrowing from the Suburban National Bank to $99,000 in the spring of 1972. The maximum loan that Suburban National would make to any one borrower was $100,000, and Browning had been able to stay within this limit in the spring of 1972 only by relying very heavily on trade credit. Mr. Roger Browning, proprietor of the Browning Lumber Company, was therefore actively looking elsewhere for a new banking relationship where he would be able to negotiate a larger loan.

Mr. Browning had recently been introduced by a personal friend to Mr. George Dodge, an officer of a much larger bank, the Northrup National Bank. The two men had tentatively discussed the possibility that the Northrup bank might extend a line of credit to Browning Lumber up to a maximum amount of $200,000. Mr. Browning thought that a loan of this size would more than meet his foreseeable needs, but he was eager for the flexibility that a line of credit of this size would provide. Subsequent to this discussion Mr. Dodge had arranged for the credit department of the Northrup National Bank to investigate Mr. Browning and his company.

The Browning Lumber Company had been founded in 1962 as a partnership by Mr. Browning and his brother-in-law, Mr. Henry Stark. In 1969 Mr. Browning bought out Mr. Stark's interest for $50,000 and continued the business as a sole proprietorship. Mr. Stark had taken a note for $50,000, to be paid off in 1970, in order to give Mr. Browning time to arrange for the financing necessary to make the payment of $50,000 to him. The major portion of the funds needed for this payment were raised by a mortgage of $30,000 on the company's buildings. This mortgage, negotiated in late 1969, carried an interest rate of 8%, and was repayable in quarterly installments at the rate of $3,000 a year over the next ten years.

The business was located in a growing suburb of a large city in the southern section of the Midwest. The company owned land with access to a railroad siding, and two large storage buildings had been erected on this land. The company's operations were limited to the wholesale distribution of lumber products in the local area. Typical products included plywood, moldings, and sash and door products. Quantity discounts and credit terms of net 30 days on open account were usually offered to customers.

Sales volume had been built up largely on the basis of successful price competition made possible by careful control of operating expenses and by quantity purchases of materials at substantial discounts. Much of the moldings and sash and door products, which constituted significant items of sales, were used for repair work. About 55% of total sales were made in the six months from March through August. No sales representatives were employed, orders being taken exclusively over the telephone. Annual sales of $314,000 in 1967 and $476,000 in 1968 gave profits of $40,000 and $49,000, respectively.[1] Comparative operating statements for the years 1969 through 1971 and for three months ending March 31, 1972, are given in Exhibit 1.

Mr. Browning was an energetic man, 39 years of age, who worked long hours on the job, not only handling management matters but also performing part of the clerical work. He was helped by an assistant who, in the words of the investigator of the Northrup National Bank, "has been doing and can do about everything that Mr. Browning does in the organization." Other employees numbered 12 in early 1972, 10 who worked in the yard and drove trucks and 2 who assisted in the office.

As a part of its customary investigation of prospective borrowers, the Northrup National Bank sent inquiries concerning Mr. Browning to a number of firms that had business dealings with him. The manager of one of his large suppliers, the Barker Company, wrote in answer:

The conservative operation of his business appeals to us. He has not wasted his money in disproportionate plant investment. His operating expenses are as low as they could possibly be. He has personal control over every feature of his business, and he possesses sound judgment and a willingness to work harder than anyone I have ever known. This, with a good personality, gives him an excellent turnover; and from my personal experience in watching him work, I know that he keeps close check on his own credits.

All the other trade letters received by the bank bore out the statements quoted above.

In addition to the ownership of his lumber business, which was his major source of income, Mr. Browning held jointly with his wife an equity in their home. The house cost $35,000 to build in 1963 and was mortgaged for $28,000. He also held a $30,000 life insurance policy, payable to Mrs. Browning. Mrs. Browning owned independently a half interest in a house worth about $30,000. Otherwise, they had no sizable personal investments.

---

[1] The profits figures for 1967 and 1968 are not comparable with those shown in Exhibit 1 for 1969–71. The 1967 and 1968 figures do not reflect the payment of salaries to either Mr. Browning or Mr. Stark. Their remuneration would constitute a "drawing by proprietors" rather than an operating expense. When Mr. Stark withdrew from the business in 1968, the employee who took his place was paid a salary which is shown in Exhibit 1 as a component of the "operating expense" account, not as a drawing by a proprietor.

The bank gave particular attention to the debt position and current ratio of the business. It noted the ready market for the company's products at all times and the fact that sales prospects were favorable. The bank's investigator reported: ". . . Sales are expected to reach $1,600,000 in 1972 and may exceed this level if prices of lumber should rise substantially in the near future." On the other hand, it was recognized that a general economic downturn or a return to the very tight credit conditions of 1969–70 with the resultant shortage of funds for residential mortgages might slow down the rate of increase in sales. Browning Lumber's sales, however, were protected to some degree from fluctuations in new housing construction because of the relatively high proportion of its repair business. Projections beyond 1972 were difficult to make, but the prospects appeared good for a continued growth in the volume of Browning Lumber's business over the foreseeable future.

The bank also noted the rapid increase in Browning Lumber's accounts and notes payable in the recent past, especially in the spring of 1972. The usual terms of purchase in the trade provided for a discount of 2% for payments made within 10 days of the invoice date. Accounts were due in 30 days at the invoice price but suppliers ordinarily did not object if payments lagged somewhat behind the due date. During the last two years Mr. Browning had taken very few purchase discounts because of the shortage of funds arising from his purchase of Mr. Stark's interest in the business and the additional investments in working capital associated with the company's increasing sales volume. Trade credit was seriously extended in the spring of 1972 as Mr. Browning strove to hold his bank borrowing within the $100,000 ceiling imposed by the Suburban National Bank.

Comparative balance sheets as of December 31, 1969–71, are presented in Exhibit 2. A detailed balance sheet drawn up for the bank as of March 31, 1972, and the change in proprietorship for the first quarter of 1972 appear as Exhibits 3 and 4.

The tentative discussions between Mr. Dodge and Mr. Browning had been in terms of a revolving, unsecured 90-day note not to exceed $200,000 in amount. The specific details of the loan had not been worked out, but Mr. Dodge had explained that the loan agreement would involve the standard covenants applying to such a loan. He cited as illustrative provisions the requirement that restrictions on additional borrowing would be imposed, that net working capital would have to be maintained at an agreed level, that additional investments in fixed assets could be made only with the prior approval of the bank, and that limitations would be placed on withdrawals of funds from the business by Mr. Browning. Interest would be set on a floating rate basis at 3 percentage points above the lowest rate charged by the bank on short-term loans. Mr. Dodge indicated that the initial rate to be paid would be approximately 10% under conditions in effect in early 1972. Both men also understood that Mr. Browning would sever his relationship with the Suburban National Bank if he entered into a loan agreement with the Northrup National Bank.

In addition to working out arrangements for increased bank credit, a second issue of concern to Mr. Browning was whether he should continue to operate as a proprietorship or whether it would be better for him to incorporate his business. As a proprietorship he paid taxes on the full amount earned by the business, the item shown as "net profit before taxes" in Exhibit 1. As explained in Exhibit 1, this figure was computed without any allowance for a salary for Mr. Browning. As the business became increasingly profitable, Mr. Browning was subject to increasingly severe individual income taxes.

Mr. Browning understood that if he were to incorporate his business he would be able to deduct a reasonable salary in computing his net profits subject to the corporation income tax. The salary so deducted would be taxable to him as an individual. Profits retained in the business would not be subject to the individual income tax if the business were incorporated. On the other hand, any dividends paid to Mr. Browning would be taxed twice, first as income to the corporation and then as personal income to the stockholder.

Exhibit 5 summarizes briefly the tax rates applicable to individuals and to corporations as of 1972.

$$\frac{319 - 259}{259} = 23$$

Exhibit 1

BROWNING LUMBER COMPANY

OPERATING STATEMENTS FOR THE YEARS ENDING DECEMBER 31, 1969
THROUGH 1971 AND FOR THE THREE MONTHS
ENDING MARCH 31, 1972

(In thousands)

	1969	1970	1971	First Quarter 1972
Net sales (after discounts)	$733	$869	$1,163	$310*
Cost of goods sold:				
Beginning inventory	$ 79	$103	$ 141	$180
Purchases	552	658	881	285
	$631	$761	$1,022	$465
Ending inventory	103	141	180	240
Cost of goods sold	$528	$620	$ 842	$225
Gross profit	$205	$249	$ 321	$ 85
Operating expenses†	160	194	249	68
Net profit before taxes†	$ 45	$ 55	$ 72	$ 17
Drawings by proprietor	$ 29	$ 37	$ 49	$ 12

* In the first quarter of 1971 sales were $252,000 and net profit was $13,000.
† No allowance for a salary for Mr. Browning is included in either of these items. For a discussion of the tax treatment of a proprietorship see the text and Exhibit 5.

Exhibit 2

BROWNING LUMBER COMPANY

COMPARATIVE BALANCE SHEETS AS OF DECEMBER 31, 1969–71

(In thousands)

	1969	1970	1971
ASSETS			
Cash	$ 26	$ 21	$ 18
Accounts receivable—net	74	96	137
Inventory	103	141	180
Total current assets	$203	$258	$335
Property—net	56	61	65
Total assets	$259	$319	$400
LIABILITIES AND NET WORTH			
Notes payable—bank	...	$ 61	$ 91
Notes payable—Mr. Stark	$ 50	...	...
Notes payable—trade	...	...	...
Accounts payable	52	83	110
Accrued expenses	10	13	17
Long-term debt—current portion	3	3	3
Total current liabilities	$115	$160	$221
Long-term debt	27	24	21
Total liabilities	$142	$184	$242
Net worth	117	135	158
Total liabilities and net worth	$259	$319	$400

Exhibit 3

BROWNING LUMBER COMPANY

BALANCE SHEET AS OF MARCH 31, 1972

(In thousands)

ASSETS

Cash...		$ 15
Accounts receivable.................................	$152	
Less reserve...	3	
Accounts receivable—net...........................		149
Inventory..		240
Total current assets.............................		$404
Land, buildings, and equipment......................	$ 75	
Less: Accumulated depreciation.....................	21	
Land, buildings, and equipment—net.................		54
Trucks and automobile...............................	$ 22	
Less: Accumulated depreciation......................	10	
Trucks and automobile—net..........................		12
Total assets...................................		$470

LIABILITIES AND NET WORTH

Notes payable—bank.................................	$ 99
Notes payable—trade................................	68
Accounts payable—trade.............................	102
Accrued expenses....................................	15
Long-term debt—current portion......................	3
Total current liabilities...........................	$287
Long-term debt..	20
Total liabilities.................................	$307
Net worth...	163
Total liabilities and net worth.....................	$470

Exhibit 4

BROWNING LUMBER COMPANY

CHANGE IN PROPRIETORSHIP, FIRST QUARTER, 1972

(In thousands)

Proprietorship, December 31, 1971......................		$158
Net profit, first quarter............................	$17	
Drawings by proprietor.............................	12*	
Balance...		5
Proprietorship (net worth), March 31, 1972.............		$163

* Drawings to cover living expenses and provision for payment of income taxes.

Exhibit 5

BROWNING LUMBER COMPANY

SUMMARY OF TAX RATES APPLICABLE TO A PROPRIETORSHIP AND TO A CORPORATION

Tax Rates Applicable to Individuals and Proprietorships

As noted in the text of the case the income of a sole proprietorship or a partnership is taxable to the owner(s) rather than to the business as such. Thus, the income of the Browning Lumber Company would be taxable in its entirety to Mr. Browning. It is probably reasonable to assume that the taxable income attributable to Mr. Browning from his company would be approximately equal to the amount shown as "net profit before taxes" in Exhibit 1. Since the case indicates that Mr. Browning and his wife have little or no income from sources other than his business, the figures shown in Exhibit 1 can be assumed to be Mr. Browning's sole (or principal) source of taxable income. In interpreting the following table, it should be recognized that the tax brackets and tax rates shown refer to "taxable income" in the legal sense. Mr. Browning, of course, would be entitled to any deductions and personal exemptions authorized by the Internal Revenue Code. Since Mr. Browning is married, he presumably would file a joint tax return and benefit from the lower rates applicable to married couples. The following table presents the tax brackets and corresponding tax liabilities applying to individual taxpayers filing joint returns for the tax brackets in which Mr. Browning's income might fall:

Taxable Income	Tax	Rate on Excess*
$ 20,000	$ 4,380	32%
24,000	5,660	36
28,000	7,100	39
32,000	8,660	42
36,000	10,340	45
40,000	12,140	48
44,000	14,060	50
52,000	18,060	53
64,000	24,420	55
76,000	31,020	58
88,000	37,980	60
100,000	45,180	62
120,000	57,580	64
140,000	70,380	66
160,000	83,580	68
180,000	97,180	69
200,000	110,980	70

Tax Rates Applicable to a Corporation

If the Browning Lumber Company were incorporated, Mr. Browning could, of course, deduct as an expense a reasonable salary for himself. This salary would then be taxable to him as personal income. Since Mr. Browning and his wife had little or no income other than his salary, he would not be subject to the top brackets of the individual income tax on his salary. If, for example, he paid himself a salary of $32,000 of which $28,000 was taxable, after deducting personal exemptions and other allowable deductions, his personal tax liability would be $7,100, as shown in the preceding tabulation.

The corporation income tax rates to which the Browning Lumber Company would be subject are as follows:

Taxable Income	Tax
$25,000 or less	22% of taxable income
Over $25,000	$5,500 plus 48% of taxable income in excess of $25,000

In 1972, after the deduction of a reasonable allowance for a salary, a large fraction of the income of Browning Lumber Company, if organized as a corporation, would be subject to the 22% tax rate.

Any dividends paid by the company would of course be taxable as ordinary income to its stockholders.

* The current tax law provides a "maximum tax on earned income." The top *marginal* tax rate under this provision applicable to an individual's *earned* taxable income is limited to 50%. A taxpayer engaged in a business where both services and capital are material income-producing factors may treat a reasonable amount (not more than 30% of his share of the net profits) as earned income. The provision with respect to the maximum tax supersedes those in the general schedule of tax rates.

It is unlikely that the "maximum tax" would have any bearing on Mr. Browning in the foreseeable future. Given the 30% limitation cited in the previous paragraph, the provisions of the "maximum tax" would not help Mr. Browning until the profits of the company taxable to him exceeded $173,333 ($52,000 divided by .30).

SCIENCE TECHNOLOGY COMPANY

^^

Early in April, 1974, Bill Watson, president of Science Technology Company (STC), was reviewing a "Five-Year Capital and Financing Plan" prepared for the company by Mr. Finson, STC's chief financial officer. Mr. Finson intended to discuss the Plan at a forthcoming board meeting. Presumably if the Plan and the premises on which it was drawn were endorsed by the board it would greatly influence the financial policies and indeed the total development of the firm in the coming years.

Mr. Watson had spent much of his 30 years at STC in various engineering and sales positions. His appointment as president in 1973 had followed several years of very disappointing performance by the company—years that had impaired STC's financial strength significantly. He knew that other members of the board would be keenly interested in his comments on the Plan, especially as indications of his willingness to relax the stringent controls imposed in 1973.

After some study, Mr. Watson identified several questions as important for his further consideration and resolution. Among these were the following:

1. In view of the uneven growth in sales, inventory and receivables, and earnings in the past, was Mr. Finson's use of averages for his projections a valid and useful approach?
2. What were the implications of forecasting that both volume and dollar sales would increase at 10% per year? More specifically, Mr. Watson wondered what impact inflation would have on STC and whether it should be factored into the financial forecasts.
3. What corporate sales and profit performance would be required over the next 3–5 years to secure financing and to allow STC to "go public"?
4. What should STC do?

STC was founded in 1915 and for the first 30 years of its existence pioneered the design, manufacture, and use of electronic measuring instruments. Until World War II the company faced very little serious competition and it successfully pursued a policy of self-financed, controlled growth.

The competitive situation changed dramatically during the 1950's. The explosive growth of the electronics industry encouraged the entry of a number of new firms eager to participate in large government contracts. STC, with its policy of self-financing all growth, watched its sales growth slip from 10% per year during 1945–55, to only 8% per year during 1965–72—well below the 20–25% annual growth rate of its prime competitor, Hewlett-Packard Company. The company also experienced a steady decline in its profitability, as price competition heightened.

STC Return on Net Worth   PROS₍

1935–45	1946–55	1956–65	1966–69	70-73	79-78
12%	11%	9%	6%		

It was apparent to management by 1969 that STC had not been keeping up with the dynamic electronics industry and that substantial changes were needed to convert it from a sedate, if not stodgy, company to an active, growing company responsive to the opportunities arising from new technology and new markets. For many in management, job security seemed assured and their interest was in establishing an exciting track record that might one day be converted into a high multiple for the stock.

Efforts to revitalize the company proceeded on two fronts. Research and development had always been a central part of STC's strategy. Approximately one third of its sales at any point in time were from products introduced within the most recent three years. Beginning in 1968, however, expenditures on research and development were increased from 9–10% of sales to 14% as STC began the development of its own minicomputer. It was felt that the minicomputer project was consistent both with the trend toward computer-linked, electronic testing systems and with management's interest in converting the image of the company.

Two acquisitions were also made in 1969–70 to position STC in several embryonic but potentially high growth areas. Both involved the application of sophisticated electronic measuring systems in areas requiring substantial customer education and custom design.

The results of the crash catch-up program were extremely mixed. By 1974 STC had positioned itself in a mix of growth areas and cash generating areas that would provide:

1. A satisfactory overall corporate growth rate of at least 10% per year (in constant dollars), in line with the company's past experience (see Exhibit 1).
2. Reasonable market and product diversification.
3. A balance of products in terms of their product-life cycles.
4. Challenging career opportunities for the engineering staff.
5. Concentration on a limited number of product-markets in which STC's expertise and competitive prospects should enable it to maintain a strong market position.

The company also strengthened its sales and distribution system to improve both geographic coverage and field servicing. By 1974 there were 10 sales engineering offices in North America, staffed by 45 sales engineers all of whom held degrees in electrical engineering or had equivalent technical experience. European operations, which accounted for 18% of total sales, were conducted through manufacturers' representatives.

Unfortunately, the catch-up program placed heavy financing pressures on STC. The company's control systems were inadequate and management lost control of operations. Profitability fell sharply and the company operated at a cumulative deficit of $0.2 million during the period 1969–73. (See Exhibit 1.) This low profitability, when combined with a 75% increase in sales, created a substantial financing need (see Exhibit 2). In addition, the cash acquisition of Acoustical Controls Company for $1.9 million in 1970 further strained STC's financial position.

Management had no alternative to meeting these needs with additional debt financing. One of the basic tenets of the company since its founding was the policy that the stock would be owned solely by the employees. Departing employees were not allowed to retain their stockholdings, but first were required to offer the shares back to the company at their then book value.[1] During the period 1963–72, stock repurchases by the company (net of stock sales to employees) had totaled $3 million. Beginning in 1973, however, STC ceased all stock repurchases in an effort to conserve cash.

The outstanding debt of STC rose from $400,000 in 1962 to $3 million in 1969 to $12 million by year-end 1973. Of the $12 million, $3 million represented a long-term mortgage bond secured by all of the company's real estate and the remainder represented short-term bank debt at a cost of 2½% over the prime rate and secured by all remaining assets.

It seemed clear to Mr. Watson that STC was approaching the prudent limit of debt financing in relation to its equity. Furthermore, the sale of stock seemed unattractive in 1974, both as a matter of policy and from the standpoint of market timing. The stock prices of small, publicly-traded electronics companies had been under substantial selling pressure in recent months. Price-earnings ratios had plummeted from 15–20 times in 1973 to only 6–7 times in early 1974. While Beckman Instruments, Inc. and Hewlett-Packard Company still commanded multiples of 18 and 40 times, respectively, their sales and earnings records were far superior to that of STC.

Mr. Watson was therefore encouraged by Mr. Finson's projections of reasonable sales growth financed without new equity issues. (See Exhibit 3.) The projections were based on an extensive 12-month study by a national consulting firm of each of STC's principal product-markets, completed in conjunction with STC's divisional managers. Exhibit 4 shows the consultants' characterization of each of STC's seven business units in marketing, financial, and strategic terms.

---

[1] With no public market for the stock, the book value seemed the least controversial measure of the stock's value and in 1974 was accepted without question by the employee-stockholders. At year-end 1973 book value per share was $51.

Exhibit 1

SCIENCE TECHNOLOGY COMPANY

CONSOLIDATED INCOME STATEMENTS, 1969–73

(Dollar figures in thousands)

	1969	1970	1971	1972	1973
Net sales	$25,780	$26,451	$29,411	$33,350	$44,991
Cost of goods sold	13,212	13,173	15,117	18,745	23,715
Gross profit	$12,568	$13,278	$14,294	$14,605	$21,276
Research and development expenses	3,239	3,777	4,271	4,870	4,195
Selling, administrative, and general expense	8,156	8,929	9,140	11,814	14,783
Interest expense	294	366	311	494	1,041
Other expenses	140	143	141	93	100
Profit before taxes	$ 739	$ 63	$ 431	$(2,666)	$ 1,157
Taxes	434	18	187	(839)*	82*
Profit after taxes	$ 305	$ 45	$ 244	$(1,827)†	$ 1,075
Earnings per common share (in dollars)	$ 0.94	$ 0.14	$ 0.75	$ (5.65)†	$ 3.30
# SHARES	32.4468	321929	325333	323363	325758

SELECTED FINANCIAL RATIOS

% of Sales:					
Cost of goods sold	51.2%	49.8%	51.4%	56.2%	52.7%
Research and development	12.6	14.3	14.5	14.6	9.3
Selling, administrative, and general	31.6	33.8	31.1	35.3	32.8
Interest	1.1	1.4	1.1	1.5	2.3
Profit after taxes	1.2	0.2	0.8	—	2.4

* The tax figures reflect tax loss carrybacks and carryforwards.
† The deficit in 1972 resulted in part from delays in production. Substantial shipments scheduled for 1972 were actually made in 1973. However, all of the expenditures programmed for 1972 were made in that year.

Exhibit 2

SCIENCE TECHNOLOGY COMPANY

CONSOLIDATED BALANCE SHEETS AT DECEMBER 31, 1969–73

(Dollar figures in thousands)

	1969	1970	1971	1972	1973
Cash.............................	$ 858	$ 1,304	$ 1,217	$ 436	$ 639
Accounts receivable.................	5,019	5,422	7,711	10,129	11,936
Inventories—at lower of cost (first-in, first-out) or market.......	9,400	10,396	9,833	12,820	13,918
Other.............................	43	66	—	905	754
Total current assets............	$15,320	$17,188	$18,761	$24,290	$27,247
Net fixed assets....................	5,923	5,744	5,289	5,129	4,991
Patents and trademarks.............	330	288	245	203	166
Goodwill..........................	457	904	911	911	931
Other.............................	603	842	742	642	430
Total assets.................	$22,633	$24,966	$25,948	$31,175	$33,765
Notes payable—banks..............	$ —	$ 1,110	$ 984	$ 6,346	$ 8,480
Accounts payable..................	1,140	1,012	1,580	4,349	3,154
Accrued expenses..................	441	540	622	711	1,614
Accrued payroll...................	339	282	659	400	610
Other.............................	644	537	483	29	436
Total current liabilities.........	$ 2,564	$ 3,481	$ 4,328	$11,835	$14,294
Long-term debt*...................	3,133	4,236	4,360	4,032	3,088
Other liabilities...................	111	132	26	—	—
Shareowners' equity...............	16,825	17,117	17,234	15,308	16,383
Total liabilities and net worth...	$22,633	$24,966	$25,948	$31,175	$33,765

SELECTED FINANCIAL RATIOS

% of Sales:					
Accounts receivable..............	19.5%	20.5%	26.2%	30.4%	26.5%
Inventories......................	36.5	39.3	33.4	38.4	30.9
Net fixed assets..................	23.0	21.7	18.0	15.4	11.1
Accounts payable.................	4.4	3.8	5.4	13.0	7.0
Notes payable, long-term debt, and equity..............	77.4	84.9	76.8	77.0	62.1

* To be repaid in semi-annual payments of $175,000.

Exhibit 3

SCIENCE TECHNOLOGY COMPANY

FIVE-YEAR CAPITAL AND FINANCING PLAN: 1974–78,

(Prepared by Mr. Finson, chief financial officer)

Permanent *new* capital requirements for STC depend almost entirely on sales growth, retained profits, and the efficiency with which corporate assets are employed. Our growth has been strong —15% per year compounded since 1969. Our net profits after taxes since 1969 have ranged from a deficit in 1972 to 2.4% of sales in 1973. Profits have not increased our equity rapidly enough to keep up with requirements, resulting in the necessary increase of $8.4 million in debt.

At the end of 1973 our capital (equity, bank notes, and long-term debt) totaled $28 million, or 62% of sales. The company has improved its asset turnover ratio in recent years as utilization of plant and equipment moved towards full capacity. Further improvement is anticipated as the new inventory control system comes on stream. I have used 56% of sales as a reasonable amount of capital on which STC can operate.

The accompanying table shows a 5-year projection of shipments at a 10% growth rate per year compounded, a 3.0% profit margin on sales, and the forecasted improvement in the turnover of total assets. The projections are based on the forecasts prepared by the divisional managers, with active consultation with International Consultants, Inc., earlier this year. The figures are in constant dollars; that is, both volume and dollar sales are projected to increase at a 10% annual rate.

From 1974 to 1978 shipments are projected to grow from $50 million to $74 million, and net profit from $1.4 million to $2.2 million. By 1978 total debt will be 39% of total capital—an improvement from the present 41% level and in line with our target level of 40%.

Earnings per share grow from $4.30 in 1974 to $6.75 and the possible market price of the stock, if the company goes public in 1978, reaches $74 (assuming a multiple of 11 times).

FINANCIAL PROJECTIONS, 1974–78

(Dollar figures in millions)

	1974	1975	1976	1977	1978	*Assumptions*
Net sales	$50	$55	$61	$67	$74	+10% per year
Gross profit	24.1	26.6	29.5	32.4	35.9	48% of sales
Research and development expenses	4.8	5.2	5.8	6.4	7.0	9½% of sales
Selling, administrative, and general expenses	15.5	17.1	18.9	20.8	22.9	31% of sales
Interest expense	1.0	1.1	1.3	1.4	1.6	10% rate
Profit before tax	$ 2.8	$ 3.2	$ 3.5	$ 3.8	$ 4.4	
Taxes	1.4	1.6	1.8	1.9	2.2	
Profit after tax	$ 1.4	$ 1.6	$ 1.7	$ 1.9	$ 2.2	

ASSETS						
Current assets	$29.0	$31.9	$35.4	$38.9	$42.9	58% of sales
Fixed assets	5.0	5.5	6.0	6.6	7.2	increase with sales
Other	0.5	0.6	0.6	0.7	0.7	1% of sales
Total assets	$34.5	$38.0	$42.0	$46.2	$50.8	

LIABILITIES AND NET WORTH						
Accounts payable	$ 4.1	$ 4.5	$ 5.0	$ 5.5	$ 6.0	60 days
Accrued expenses	1.5	1.7	1.8	2.0	2.2	3% of sales
Accrued payroll	0.5	0.6	0.6	0.7	0.7	1% of sales
Income taxes payable	0.9	0.4	0.6	0.5	0.7	
Total current liabilities	$ 7.0	$ 7.2	$ 8.0	$ 8.7	$ 9.6	
Debt (plug figure)	9.7	11.4	12.9	14.5	16.0	
Equity	17.8	19.4	21.1	23.0	25.2	
Total liabilities and net worth	$34.5	$38.0	$42.0	$46.2	$50.8	

(handwritten annotations: "10% of" next to Assumptions; "increase with sales 10% of"; "1/12 of sales"; "1/12 of sales" next to Accounts payable row)

Exhibit 3—Continued

It is extremely interesting to note the relationship to net profit of additional debt financing requirements, earnings per share, and market price per share.

Net Profit % Sales	5-Year Cumulative Profit ($ millions)	Net Worth 1978	Total Debt Needed	Total Capital	Debt as % of Total Capital	Earnings per Share 1978	Stock Price 1978
2%	$ 6.1	$22.5	$18.7	$41.2	45%	$4.54	$ 50
3%	8.8	25.2	16.0	41.2	39%	6.75	74
4%	12.3	28.7	12.5	41.2	30%	9.08	100

Obviously, the higher the profit rate, the lower the need for additional debt financing and the higher the earnings per share. This demonstrates the importance of the programs to reduce manufacturing costs by adopting assembly line techniques and to control expenditures on research. The 5% increase in product prices and sharp reduction in research expenditures in 1973 contributed to the improved operating results, and continuing review will be essential if inflation remains at a high rate.

The stock prices per share are based purely on 11 times earnings, and assume that STC goes public in 1978. It seems likely that the price-earnings ratio will be influenced by the growth rate of sales and earnings. The following table, based on a profit margin of 3% and a capital to sales ratio of .56, considers the implications for stock price of different levels of sales growth. While no one knows with certainty the price-earnings ratio at which a stock will sell five years hence, the table does suggest the importance of maintaining a strong sales pattern.

Annual Growth	Earnings per Share 1974	Earnings per Share 1978	Annual % Increase in Earnings per Share	Price/ Earnings Ratio 1978	Stock Price 1978	Debt as % of Total Capital
0%	$4.30	$5.06	4%	8	$ 40	11%
10	4.30	6.75	12	11	74	39
15	4.30	8.28	18	14	116	46

The implications for the stock are clear. Continued strong sales growth should help the price of the stock substantially. With almost 45% of the stock scheduled to be held by retired employees by 1978, it is important that both a source of liquidity and an attractive price be provided for them. By far the best possible operation is to generate profit at a rate sufficient to sustain strong internal growth while lowering our level of debt to total capital.

Exhibit 4

SCIENCE TECHNOLOGY COMPANY

MARKET/FINANCIAL DATA
(Dollar figures in millions)

Unit	Industry Data (Domestic) 1973 Market Size	Annual Growth Rate	1973 Unit Data Sales ($)	PBT* ($)	Net Assets ($)	Market Share (%)	(Trend)
1. Audiometry	$ 31	20%	5.4	(0.6)	2.8	17	Stable
2. High Frequency Test Equipment	91	25	13.6	1.9	7.7	15	Stable +
3. Vibration Analysis and Control Systems	11	10	3.0	0.2	1.1	27	Stable +
4. System Network Testers	25	8	4.1	(0.2)	2.6	16	Stable
5. Noise Measurement Equipment	119	2	3.4	0.4	2.2	3	Stable
6. Industrial Test Equipment	40	15	7.7	1.2	4.8	19	Stable
7. International Sales and Corporate Headquarters	—	10	7.8	0.3	12.6		
Total		15%	$45.0	$ 2.2	$33.8		

STRATEGIC DATA

Unit	Maturity	Competitive Position	Strategic Thrust	Principal Strategies	Risk
1. Audiometry	Growth	Favorable	Improve	Market penetration, new products, backward integration	Moderate/High
2. High Frequency Test Equipment	Growth	Strong	Improve	Market penetration, new products	Moderate/High
3. Vibration Analysis and Control Systems	Late growth	Strong	Maintain/Improve	Market penetration, new products	Moderate/High
4. System Network Testers	Mature	Favorable	Rationalize	Opportunistically milk	Low
5. Noise Measurement Equipment	Mature	Favorable	Improve	New products	Moderate
6. Industrial Test Equipment	Growth	Strong	Maintain/Improve	Market penetration, new markets, add capacity	Low/Moderate
7. International Sales and Corporate Headquarters			Improve	Market penetration, new products, new markets	Moderate/High

* Profit after allocation of corporate overhead but before taxes and interest.

AMERICAN MOTORS CORPORATION

During the fall of 1973, Mr. Alan Foster, treasurer of American Motors Corporation, was preparing recommendations to the Executive Committee regarding the company's large holdings of marketable securities. Three years of sharply improved profitability had resulted in the accumulation of over $100 million of excess cash. While the riskiness of automobile manufacturing seemed to warrant the maintenance of financial reserves, Mr. Foster questioned the need for such a high level. American Motors had a number of strategically important investment opportunities, several of which would have to be deferred for lack of funds. All excess cash not needed to ensure the company's solvency was needed to finance these major capital expenditures.

American Motors had been incorporated as Nash Motors Corporation in 1916 and, with the exception of a period during World War II, had been engaged in the manufacture and sale of passenger vehicles continuously. The company, with a 3% share of market, was dwarfed by GM, Ford, and Chrysler, which had market shares of 45%, 25%, and 14%, respectively. Imports accounted for the remaining sales. American Motors also produced utility and recreational vehicles, and military and special purpose vehicles.

The auto industry[1]

The auto industry was subject to cyclical fluctuations in sales. For most buyers, the purchase of a car represented a major expenditure which could be, and often was, deferred in times of adversity. Year-to-year swings in industry sales of 10–15% were not unusual. In addition, within any year there was a pronounced seasonal pattern with sales strong at the start of the model year in October and again in the spring.

Market shares of the four major producers varied quite widely, which tended to magnify the underlying cyclical changes inherent in the industry. (See Exhibit 1.) Consumer tastes often changed quickly and dramatically, and cars that sold well one year might miss totally the next. The Ford Falcon, for example, sold 482,000 units in 1961 and slid downhill thereafter to a level of only 110,000 units in 1967. The Chevrolet Corvair took an even steeper dive. Sales in 1965 were a respectable 209,000 units. By 1967, after Ralph

---

[1] Based in part on "Tiny American Motors Struggles to Survive as a Separate Concern," *The Wall Street Journal,* July 12, 1971, pp. 1, 13.

Nader's claims of the dangerous qualities of earlier Corvairs, sales fell to fewer than 25,000 units.

The volatility of consumer tastes, together with a long lead time for design and with heavy tooling and development expenditures, resulted in substantial risks for the auto manufacturers. Roughly three years were required from the initial design stage until the new model first reached the dealers' showrooms. Millions of dollars had to be invested in tooling and engineering long before any inkling of consumer reaction to the new product filtered in. As early as one year before delivery date, 40% of the new model costs was irretrievably sunk and the other 60% was largely committed unless the project was scrapped. The amounts of capital involved could be substantial. Ford, for example, spent $40 million on the development and tooling for the Mustang. And an estimated $250 million was invested in tooling, development, and plant capacity for the ill-fated Edsel before the car was ever unveiled.

Competition in the industry was largely on the basis of product design, price, promotion, and intensive distribution. Both to conserve space and to assure adequacy of dealer inventories, manufacturers normally shipped cars as soon as they rolled off the assembly line. Sales were made on a cash basis, but dealer financing was available from commercial banks and the manufacturer's own captive finance company. In addition to financial support, the companies also spent millions of dollars on advertising to maintain brand loyalty and to get potential buyers into the showrooms.

American Motors

The ability of a small producer to survive in the auto industry was a subject of almost continuous debate by industry observers. American Motors had lived under clouds of speculation about its viability and future ever since Nash-Kelvinator Corporation merged with Hudson Motor Car Company in 1954. The merged enterprise stumbled along with 2% or less of the U.S. auto market for the first four years of its existence, posting deficits each year. In fact, the only time the rumors ever really went away was during the small-car boom in the late 1950's after American Motors gambled everything on its ability to make and sell cheap, economical small cars. The gamble paid off handsomely.

Tiny AMC plunged into the small car market a year before its Big Three rivals, set low but reasonably profitable prices on its Ramblers, and roared off to its most profitable years, tripling its share of all cars sold to over 6%.

But the rumors started to swirl again in the early 1960's when the small-car boom began to fade. A number of importers were driven out of the market through the enormous economic and marketing clout of GM, Ford, and Chrysler, who then turned around and made their compacts bigger. AMC was left with the tough choice of sticking with its successful compact cars and battling for sales in a shrinking market, or augmenting its line with new, bigger cars to compete against the Big Three.

AMC chose the multicar approach, bringing out sporty cars to compete against Ford's successful Mustang and intermediate-sized cars to battle Chevelles, Fairlanes, and Belvederes. But the proliferation of models did not succeed. AMC's original sporty car, the Marlin, flopped and was killed after only three years. Its intermediates—the Rebel, now called Matador, and Ambassador—never caught fire. So AMC's share of all car sales shrank to under 3% again, plunging the auto maker into the red. Between 1967 and 1970, the company lost a total of $115 million. (See Exhibit 2.)

By 1971 many industry observers were forecasting imminent doom. Demand for small cars, which first showed up with a resurgence of imported-car sales in the mid-1960's, was growing even faster than expected. But AMC's marketing strategies were not panning out and its market share declined to only 2.5% in early 1971. Increasingly, the company was forced to turn to General Motors for help. To get emergency financing for some of its dealers, AMC worked out a special arrangement with General Motors Acceptance Corporation. (Unlike the Big Three, AMC did not have a captive finance subsidiary and its dealers were dependent upon banks and finance companies to finance their inventories.) To augment its limited research budget, AMC turned to GM for technical help to meet the goverment's new, more stringent standards on auto exhaust emissions. And to bolster its shrunken dealer network, AMC worked out a plan to sign up Pontiac and Oldsmobile dealers to also handle AMC cars in key markets.

Many marketing men in Detroit believed that AMC was floundering in the midst of the small-car boom because it had elected to continue selling many sizes of cars rather than revert to its successful one-car formula of the late 1950's. "AMC's big mistake was to toss aside the idea of one car, of selling to its strength," commented an official at a rival company. "The cost of proliferation has killed them. The costs of manufacturing and developing cars are very high and spread over too few car sales at American Motors."

Mr. Chapin, president of American Motors, agreed that competing in several markets, rather than just one, was difficult. But he stoutly defended AMC's basic multicar strategy as the only way a company its size could survive in the fiercely competitive, high cost auto industry. "We have an inherent structure as an automobile company where you have certain levels of fixed costs, and you have to get units to support it."

The results of the period 1971–73 seemed to substantiate the soundness of Mr. Chapin's strategy. They also attested to the powerful competitive advantage gained by AMC by the devaluation of the U.S. dollar. In 1971 American Motor's Gremlin was selling for about $150 more than the Volkswagen Beetle. By late 1973 it sold for $500 less, and in the meantime its price had gone up a couple of hundred dollars. AMC's sales rose 64%, from $1.1 billion in 1970 to over $1.7 billion in 1973. More importantly, the increased sales pushed AMC well beyond the $1.3 billion sales level at which it covered its fixed operating costs of approximately $260 million. Pre-tax earnings rebounded strongly from a deficit of $56 million in 1970 to a profit of $76 million in 1973.

Expansion plans and financial policies

Management of American Motors was committed to a strategy of capitalizing more fully on the scale economies inherent in the industry by expanding its domestic car sales from 380,000 units in 1973 to 500,000 units by 1977. (Exhibit 3 indicates the extent of potential scale economies.) Though the industry was heading into rough times as energy shortages cut into sales, management believed that the shift toward small cars that conserved on gas would allow AMC to increase its market share. It was also hoped that AMC's passenger car business, which accounted for two thirds of the company's sales in 1973, would decline to a 50% share by 1977 as the company moved into related businesses by acquisition.

Continued expansion within the auto and utility-trailer markets would require capital expenditures of $100 million per year during 1974–75, and could place the company under unexpected and substantial additional financing pressures. However, with renewed profitability, $100 million of marketable securities, and bank credit lines totaling $70 million, management felt confident that "We have the financial muscle to provide the products and facilities to meet these objectives." (See Exhibit 4 for a summary of AMC's financial condition.)

Mr. Foster questioned, however, the extent to which the holdings of liquid assets should be used to finance acquisitions or the expansion of either plant capacity or the dealer system. An important characteristic of the auto industry was that all the major manufacturers maintained large liquid balances (cash and marketable securities) to provide for operations and protect against wide fluctuations in funds needs. (Exhibit 5 provides financial information on the four auto manufacturers.) In line with industry practice, AMC had funded its peak seasonal and cyclical funds requirements internally insofar as possible rather than borrow such amounts externally as they were required. To give just one example of what this meant, the annual retooling and model changeover resulted in a period of weeks each summer during which there were no cash receipts from auto sales and sharply increased payments to suppliers and outside contractors. The cash deficit during this one short period often ranged up to $40 million. In addition to its seasonal need, the company also had significant cyclical financing pressures. (Exhibit 6 shows AMC's pattern of funds flows on an annual basis for the period 1963–73.) Clearly, any decision to reduce the level of marketable securities could only be made after first determining the magnitude of AMC's liquidity needs and reviewing alternative methods of meeting this need.

Exhibit 1

AMERICAN MOTORS CORPORATION

MARKET SHARE—U.S. AUTO SALES BY CALENDAR YEAR

(Units in thousands)

	GM		Ford		Chrysler		AMC		Foreign		
	Units	%	Units	%	Units	%	Units	%	Units	%	Total
1972	4,824	44.2	2,668	24.5	1,518	13.9	312	2.9	1,586	14.5	10,908
1971	4,654	45.6	2,377	23.3	1,388	13.6	257	2.5	1,533	15.0	10,209
1970	3,333	39.8	2,216	26.4	1,350	16.1	254	3.0	1,231	14.7	8,384
1969	4,420	46.8	2,291	24.3	1,428	15.1	240	2.5	1,062	11.3	9,441
1968	4,395	46.7	2,228	23.7	1,528	16.3	259	2.8	986	10.5	9,396
1967	4,139	49.5	1,851	22.2	1,341	16.1	238	2.8	781	9.4	8,350
1966	4,336	48.2	2,349	26.1	1,387	15.4	266	3.0	658	7.3	8,996
1965	4,663	50.2	2,372	25.5	1,366	14.7	325	3.5	569	6.1	9,295
1964	3,959	49.3	2,097	26.1	1,114	13.9	379	4.7	481	6.0	8,030
1963	3,857	51.5	1,880	25.1	935	12.5	428	5.7	386	5.2	7,486
1962	3,599	52.5	1,825	26.6	667	9.7	423	6.2	339	5.0	6,853
1961	2,724	47.2	1,670	28.9	632	10.9	371	6.4	379	6.6	5,776

Exhibit 2

AMERICAN MOTORS CORPORATION

Operating Highlights, Fiscal Years 1963–73

(In millions)

	1963	1964	1965	1966	1967	1968*	1969	1970†	1971	1972	1973
Operating Results											
Net sales	$1,144	$1,022	$998	$876	$778	$766	$747	$1,098	$1,240	$1,413	$1,739
Profit before tax	75	42	7	(31)	(71)	10	7	(56)	11	31	76
Taxes	37	16	2	(15)	0	6	2	0	6	15	31
Profit after tax and before extraordinary items	$ 38	$ 26	$ 5	$ (16)	$ (71)	$ 4	$ 5	$ (56)	$ 5	$ 16	$ 45
Shareholder Information											
Earnings per share	$ 2.01	$ 1.38	$ 0.27	$(0.82)	$(3.70)	$ 0.17	$ 0.26	$(2.28)	$ 0.22	$ 0.64	$ 1.65
Dividends per share	1.00	1.15	0.875	0	0	0	0		0	0	0
Stock price range	16–23	14–18	7–15	6–14	7–16	10–16	8–14	6–12	6–9	7–11	7–10
Price–earnings ratio	8–11	10–13	27–56			60–90	31–54		27–41	10–17	4–6
Financial Condition											
Current ratio	1.7	1.7	1.5	1.3	1.2	1.5	1.7	1.3	1.4	1.6	1.7
Long-term debt as % of capital	0	0	0	0	0	0	15%	18%	17%	22%	16%

* Reflects sale of the Kelvinator division.

† Reflects acquisition of Kaiser-Jeep Corporation, which contributed $390 million to sales in 1970.

Exhibit 3

AMERICAN MOTORS CORPORATION
SCALE ECONOMIES

I. In Car Production

Annual Production of a Model	*Relative Unit Cost*
50,000 units	120
100,000	110–115
200,000	103–105
400,000	100
800,000	99+

II. In Advertising

	1972 National Advertising Budgets	*Advertising Cost per Car Sold*
Ford	$115 million	$43
GM	111	23
Chrysler	63	42
American Motors	18	58
VW	28	N.A.
Toyota	17	N.A.

Exhibit 4

AMERICAN MOTORS CORPORATION

BALANCE SHEETS—YEARS ENDED SEPTEMBER 30

(In millions)

	1963	1964	1965	1966	1967	1968	1969	1970	1971	1972	1973
ASSETS											
Cash	$48	$29	$29	$17	$12	$8	$8	$11	$18	$101	$110
Marketable securities	48	16	6	3	9	51	62	12			
Receivables	53	59	70	68	64	72	56	106	123	105	108
Inventories	127	124	151	136	122	94	108	202	172	166	201
Prepaid expenses	4	5	9	7	4	3	3	5	6	7	9
Returnable federal taxes				23	10				5		23
Total current assets	$280	$233	$265	$254	$221	$228	$237	$336	$324	$379	$450
Investments and other assets	54	62	51	55	19	15	21	33	33	42	68
Property, plant, and equipment	192	221	252	274	264	219	239	330	330	333	379
Less: Accumulated depreciation	86	95	111	123	126	113	120	162	171	180	191
Net property, plant, and equipment	$106	$126	$141	$151	$138	$106	$119	$168	$159	$153	$188
Unamortized debt expense							8	8	7		
Goodwill								2	2	2	7
Total assets	$440	$421	$457	$460	$378	$349	$385	$547	$525	$576	$713
LIABILITIES AND NET WORTH											
Short-term debt			$52	$73	$66	$23		$30	$25	$25	
Accounts payable	$91	$86	85	90	82	85	$91	169	148	149	$184
Current portion of long-term debt								3	5	1	1
Income taxes	27	9	3	3	3	3	6	6	5	6	17
Accrued expenses	43	43	41	35	35	39	42	51	51	50	69
Total current liabilities	$161	$138	$181	$201	$186	$150	$139	$259	$234	$231	$271
Long-term debt							35	45	43	68	64
Other liabilities	6	4	6	2	11	8	7	39	34	33	34
Minority interest			3	2	2						
Stockholder equity	273	279	267	255	179	191	204	204	214	244	344
Total liabilities and net worth	$440	$421	$457	$460	$378	$349	$385	$547	$525	$576	$713

Note: The following restrictions and covenants were in effect under the various debt issues and credit lines outstanding at September 30, 1973: (1) Consolidated working capital must exceed $100 million; (2) Dividends may only be paid out of cumulative earnings subsequent to 9/30/72 in excess of $11 million; (3) The company may not create, guarantee or assume any new Funded Debt unless immediately thereafter consolidated net tangible assets exceed 200% of the total funded debt; (4) Sinking fund payments commence in 1978 and gradually increase from $2.1 million in 1978 to $4.5 million in 1991.

Exhibit 5

AMERICAN MOTORS CORPORATION

FINANCIAL COMPARISONS—AMC, GM, FORD, CHRYSLER
(Dollar figures in millions except per share data)

	AMC	GM	Ford	Chrysler
1972 Operating Results				
Sales.............................	$1,413	$30,435	$20,194	$ 9,759
Net income.......................	16	2,163	870	220
% Sales.........................	1.1%	7.1%	4.3%	2.3%
Earnings per share.................	.64	7.51	8.52	4.27
Dividends per share................	0	4.45	2.68	.90
Stock price range.................	7–11	71–85	61–80	28–42
Financial Position—Year-End 1972				
Cash and marketable securities.......	$ 101	$ 2,947	$ 1,469	$ 711
Total assets......................	576	18,273	11,634	5,497
Long-term debt as % of capital......	22%	6%	15%	24%
Cash and marketable securities as % of total assets...................	18%	16%	13%	13%

Exhibit 6

AMERICAN MOTORS CORPORATION

ANNUAL FUNDS FLOW ANALYSIS, 1963–73

(In millions)

	1963	1964	1965	1966	1967	1968	1969	1970	1971	1972	1973
Sources of Funds											
Net income (loss) before extraordinary items	$ 38	$ 26	$ 5	$(16)	$(71)	$ 4	$ 5	$(56)	$ 5	$ 16	$ 45
Depreciation and amortization	30	45	44	48	53	42	35	44	37	37	35
Funds from operations	$ 68	$ 71	$ 49	$ 32	$(18)	$ 46	$ 40	$(12)	$ 42	$ 53	$ 80
Tax credit from loss carryforward or carryback						19					41
Special credit (charges) to net income				4	(5)	(11)	8		5	14	
Decrease in receivables				2	4		16			18	
Decrease in inventories		3		15	14	28			30	6	
Decrease in other current assets					16	11				4	
Increase in accounts payable	16					3	6	78		1	35
Increase in other current liabilities	24			5		4	6	12			30
Total sources	$108	$ 74	$ 49	$ 58	$ 11	$100	$ 76	$ 78	$ 77	$ 96	$186
Uses of Funds											
Cash dividends	$ 19	$ 22	$ 17	$	$	$	$	$	$	$	$
Additions to property, plant, and equipment	47	65	59	58	40	10	48	93	28	31	70
Increase in receivables	3	6	11					50	17		
Increase in inventories	31		27				14	94			35
Increase in other current assets		1	4	21				2	6	1	25
Decrease in accounts payable		5	1		8				21		
Decrease in other current liabilities		18	8	6					1		
Other uses (sources)		10	(16)	9	(17)	1	15	(16)	4	2	30
Total uses	$100	$127	$111	$ 94	$ 31	$ 19	$ 77	$223	$ 77	$ 34	$163
Financing (need) surplus	$ 8	$ (53)	$(62)	$(36)	$(20)	$ 81	$ (1)	$(145)	$ 0	$ 62	$ 23
Financed by:											
Cash and marketable securities (decrease)	$ 8	$ (51)	$(10)	$(15)	$ 1	$ 38	$ 11	$ (47)	$ (5)	$ 83	$ 9
Short-term debt (increase)			(52)	(21)	7	43	23	(33)	3	4	25
Long-term debt (increase)							(35)	(10)	2	(25)	3
Sale of investment		(2)									
Issuance of common stock					(28)			(55)			(14)
	$ 8	$ (53)	$(62)	$(36)	$(20)	$ 81	$ (1)	$(145)	$ 0	$ 62	$ 23
Sales	$1,144	$1,022	$998	$876	$778	$766	$747	$1,098	$1,240	$1,413	$1,739
Stock price	16–23	14–18	7–15	6–14	7–16	10–16	8–14	6–12	6–9	7–11	7–10

ALLEN DISTRIBUTION COMPANY

On June 16, 1967, Mr. William McConnell of the mid-Atlantic office of the Allen Distribution Company was considering whether his company should extend a credit limit of $1,000 to the Morse Photo Company of Harrisburg, Pennsylvania. Mr. McConnell had recently transferred from his job as credit representative in one of the company's western branch offices to become credit manager of the mid-Atlantic branch office, where he assumed full responsibility for initiating and supervising the branch's credit policies. When he assumed this position, Mr. McConnell had asked the five credit representatives who had been handling the branch's accounts on their own to submit to him for review a few borderline credit accounts waiting the establishment of credit limits. Mr. McConnell believed that his decision and method of analysis might prove helpful in setting the tone of future operations in the credit department. Therefore, he planned to write out his analysis and decision so that it could be circulated.

The Allen Distribution Company, a subsidiary of the Allen Electric Company, one of the nation's largest manufacturers of electrical appliances and lighting equipment, was a national wholesale distributor of the parent company's products. Merchandise sold by the Allen Distribution Company ranged from refrigerators and television sets to electric light bulbs. Its competition included other nationally known wholesalers and small regional wholesalers of the Allen line as well as wholesalers of a number of competing product lines.

The parent company sold goods to the Allen Distribution Company on the same terms as to independent wholesalers. Allen Distribution in turn usually sold its merchandise at the wholesale prices and on the terms suggested by the parent company, as did most other wholesalers of the Allen line. However, Allen Distribution maintained the right to set its own prices, and occasionally, when price competition developed in local areas, prices were reduced for short periods.

Since wholesale prices for competing products tended to be uniform, the intense competition for retail outlets and intermediary wholesale houses handling the Allen line caused the company to give major attention to the services offered these customers, including cooperative advertising, store displays, inventory control, and credit arrangements. However, the slight differences in the quality of services rendered by the large wholesalers of Allen products were not fully appreciated by customers, and sales often depended more on the personal relationships developed between the customer and company salesmen. For this reason, Allen Distribution's salesmen tended to concentrate on maintaining current accounts and on expanding sales by securing outlets carrying competing product lines where brand differentials could be emphasized.

These salesmen were paid a straight commission of 1% for net sales in their territory. An additional 1% commission was given salesmen on net sales to new accounts during the first year. Salesmen were not held responsible for bad debt losses resulting from their sales efforts, although they sometimes helped in collecting overdue receivables.

Sales during the first four months of 1967 for the entire company, as well as the mid-Atlantic branch, had decreased 2% in comparison with the similar period in 1966 even though the number of customers serviced remained relatively unchanged. In late May, 1967, the president of Allen Distribution had called together the branch managers and announced an intensified sales campaign for new outlets to offset the sales decline. Sales quotas by branch and by salesmen were established, and a prize system was devised to reward sales personnel for successful efforts. Mr. McConnell knew that the mid-Atlantic branch manager was actively supporting the program and that he wanted the branch to make a good showing.

The mid-Atlantic branch office of Allen Distribution had net sales of $78 million in 1966. A percentage analysis of the branch's 1966 income statement is shown below:

Net sales........................	100.0%	
Cost of merchandise..............	92.0	(All costs variable)
Gross profit......................	8.0%	
Operating and other expenses:		
Warehouse.....................	4.1	(Variable portion: 1.2% of sales)
Selling.......................	1.4	(Variable portion: 1.1% of sales)
Administrative.................	1.1	(Variable portion: 0.1% of sales)
Bad debt loss..................	0.13	
Interest expense...............	0.27	
Total......................	7.0%	
Net profit before taxes............	1.0%	

Mr. McConnell found that throughout 1966 the branch's outstanding receivables had averaged $5.6 million, of which approximately $150,000 represented overdue amounts. The active accounts, numbering 15,000, were turning over approximately every 25 days. Twelve people were employed in the credit department, and its operating expenses (included in the administrative expenses above) were $150,000 per year. This did not include bad debt losses, which were 0.13% of sales in 1966 and had averaged 0.14% of sales in recent years. These bad debt losses derived principally from the marginal accounts and were, therefore, approximately 1.4% of sales to the marginal accounts.

In Mr. McConnell's belief, a credit department should have little difficulty in approving good accounts and rejecting the bad ones. The real core of the credit department's operation rested in the evaluation of marginal accounts. Although Mr. McConnell had not made a study of the branch's operation, it was his opinion that the good accounts covered Allen Distribution's total operating and overhead costs, whereas the selection and handling of marginal accounts made the difference between profit and loss. Furthermore, Mr. McConnell believed that the purpose of a credit department was not to minimize credit losses but rather to maximize profits. He thought it was significant to recognize that an increase in sales volume for Allen Distribution usually meant increased sales for the parent company.

In evaluating a marginal account, Mr. McConnell considered the cost of handling the account, the current and potential profitability of the account, and the inherent risks. Although Mr. McConnell did not know how much more it cost a credit department to maintain a marginal account, he knew the credit department spent at least twice as much time maintaining credit files and collecting overdue amounts on marginal accounts as on good accounts. He estimated that 20% of the branch's accounts, representing nearly 10% of sales, were marginal firms. Nevertheless, collections from these companies tended to be on the average only 5 to 10 days slower than collections from good accounts. Mr. McConnell had not determined an appropriate basis for distributing these costs to marginal firms, but he thought they should bear a substantial portion of the credit department's operating expenses. He also believed that the 7% interest charge on bank loans, which roughly paralleled the size of the accounts receivable balance, was a cost factor chargeable to his department. Although Mr. McConnell was not certain how it might apply, he knew that management of the parent company expected new investments to promise returns of 20% or more (before taxes) before the investment was considered acceptable.

Although Mr. McConnell hesitated to define a good account in specific terms, he generally considered that companies with a two-to-one current ratio and with an equity investment greater than outstanding debt fitted into this category. He also examined, when appropriate, acid test ratios, net working capital, inventory turnover, and other balance sheet and income statement relationships, but found it difficult to establish rules to cover every situation. Unsatisfactory credit requests were also difficult to define in terms of specific ratios. With experience, a good credit analyst was able to handle good and bad accounts in a routine manner. Real judgment, however, was required to select from the marginal applications those worthy of credit. In evaluating a marginal account, Mr. McConnell thought the principal's character, although difficult to ascertain, was as important as the company's financial status. In an analysis of a credit application, two factors were considered important: (1) the risk of losing all or part of the outstanding receivable balance through bankruptcy; and (2) the cost of having to carry the amount due beyond the net period. Since the credit department screened almost 1,000 new requests for credit annually, Mr. McConnell knew that the evaluative procedures would have to be streamlined.

Mr. McConnell thought that the most difficult aspect of his new job would be translating any changes in credit policy into appropriate action by the credit representatives. Consequently, he planned to analyze a few selected marginal accounts so he might set forth the reasons for accepting or rejecting the accounts as a step toward establishing new credit standards. The Morse Photo Company was the first situation he had decided to review.

A credit file on the Morse Photo Company had been established on the basis of the following memorandum, dated May 16, 1967, from the company's Harrisburg salesman:

Have sold Mr. Anthony W. Morse, president of Morse Photo Company, 280 Carlisle Avenue, Harrisburg, Pennsylvania, on the idea of switching from Oliver Electric Company's flash bulbs to ours. Sales would be $5,000 a year on current volume, and the Morse company is a real grower. Tony Morse is a terrific salesman and should sell a whale of a lot of bulbs for us. He wants $1,000 worth (net cost to him) of bulbs as a starter.

Photographic flash bulbs were not a major product item and for statistical purposes were grouped with electric lighting equipment, which accounted for 25% of Allen Distribution's sales volume. These electrical lighting supplies normally carried gross margins of 7% to 10% for Allen Distribution, but photo bulbs, one of the highest profit items sold by the company, had a gross margin of 17% after cash discounts. In addition, the parent company earned a "contribution" profit margin of 20% (before taxes) on its sales of photo bulbs.

The Morse Photo Company was similar to a number of Allen Distribution's customers. Almost half of Allen Distribution's 15,000 credit accounts purchased only lighting supplies from the company. Many of these accounts were small wholesale houses or regional chain stores whose annual purchases were in the $5,000 to $20,000 range.

Largely in order to control the retail price, photo bulbs were sold only on a consignment basis, but the practice had possible financial significance. Although a supply of bulbs was delivered to a customer, Allen Distribution remained the owner until the bulbs were sold by the consignee and, hence, was entitled to recover its bulbs at any time from the consignee's stock. To insure recovery, segregation of inventory was agreed to by the customer. This meant that his stock of Allen bulbs should be plainly marked and physically separated from the remainder of his inventory.

After a sale of bulbs, the consignee was supposed to keep the resulting receivables or cash separate from its other accounts or funds until payment was made to Allen Distribution. Therefore, if the prescribed procedures were followed, it was possible to identify, as Allen Distribution's, the total value of a consignment, either in inventory, receivables, or cash. Thus, in the event of liquidation, no other creditor could make claim against these items.

Owing to the inconvenience of keeping separate stocks, accounts, and funds, the safeguards associated with these consignment shipments were not often observed in practice. Allen Distribution made little effort to verify whether a separate inventory was actually maintained by its photo bulb customers. Nevertheless, it was believed that the company might have some protection in recovering consigned merchandise in the event of a customer's bankruptcy, since the bulbs carried the Allen brand name. More significantly, Allen Distribution made no effort to enforce segregation of funds after bulb sales were made by the customer. In consequence, it stood in the same general position as other creditors from the time the bulbs were sold by the consignee until remittance was made. Mr. McConnell, therefore, concluded that the consignment method afforded little financial protection in practice and appraised these accounts in the same way as open accounts.

At each month's end, the consignee inventoried the bulb supply and made payment in the amount of actual sales, less its 25% trade discount. Credit terms were 5% 10 E. O. M. All photo bulb consignees were on a one-year contract basis, whereby the customer agreed to sell Allen bulbs exclusively, and Allen Distribution agreed to supply the customer's needs up to a predetermined limit ($1,000 in the case of Morse Photo Company), provided payments were made within terms.

In the credit file Mr. McConnell found a credit report containing balance sheets and income statements of the Morse Photo Company (Exhibit 1) and four letters in reply to credit inquiries sent out by a branch credit representative (Exhibit 2).

Exhibit 1

ASSOCIATED CREDIT AGENCY REPORT, MAY 27, 1967

Company:	Morse Photo Company, 280 Carlisle Avenue, Harrisburg, Pennsylvania.
Rating:	Limited (unchanged from previous report).
Business:	Commercial developing and photographic finishing. Also does a small volume of wholesaling films and camera supplies. Its distribution includes about 300 drug and periodical stores within a 130-mile radius of Harrisburg.
Management:	Anthony W. Morse, president and principal stockholder.
History:	Business started as proprietorship in May, 1961, with limited capital. On November 12, 1962, present owner purchased the assets but did not assume the liabilities for a reported $11,000; $2,000 was derived from savings and the balance was financed through a bank loan. On April 30, 1965, the proprietorship was succeeded by the present corporation, which corporation took over assets and assumed liabilities of the predecessor business.
Sales terms:	2% 10 days, net 30.
Employees:	Twelve individuals of which three are salesmen.

Exhibit 1—Continued

BALANCE SHEETS FOR THE PERIOD ENDED APRIL 30, 1966, AND 1967
(Figured in even dollars)

ASSETS	April 30, 1966	April 30, 1967
Cash	$ 320	$ 439
Accounts receivable, net	11,503	16,201
Inventory at cost	12,712	12,681
Total current assets	$ 24,535	$ 29,321
Fixed assets:		
Cost	$ 58,331	$ 93,574
Depreciation	12,573	21,492
Net	$ 45,758	$ 72,082
Other assets	2,839	9,641
Total assets	$ 73,132	$111,044

LIABILITIES		
Accounts payable	$ 9,953	$ 22,311
Note payable—bank	5,136	9,360
Notes payable—other	9,127	15,158
Income tax	198	373
Other tax	3,123	2,546
Interest payable	...	96
Payroll payable	...	1,514
Total current liabilities	$ 27,537	$ 51,358
Other liabilities:		
Notes payable—officers	2,648	2,648
Notes payable—bank	764	...
Notes payable—other	...	810
Bond payable	...	14,000
Total liabilities	$ 30,949	$ 68,816
Net worth:		
Preferred stock	$ 10,000	$ 10,000
Common stock	32,100	32,100
Earned surplus	83	128
Total net worth	$ 42,183	$ 42,228
Total liabilities and net worth	$ 73,132	$111,044

Exhibit 1—Continued

INCOME STATEMENT FOR FISCAL YEARS 1966 AND 1967

(Figured in even dollars)

	April 30, 1966	April 30, 1967
Net sales	$162,898	$269,461
Less cost of goods sold:		
Material	$ 58,453	$ 88,079
Wages	33,963	65,263
Other	28,841	44,049
Total cost of goods sold	$121,257	$197,391
Gross profit	$ 41,641	$ 72,070
Administrative and selling expense:		
Officers' salaries	$ 12,000	$ 22,000
Office salaries	5,733	10,000
Sales commissions	...	3,568
Depreciation	7,848	10,071
Other	15,779	25,613
Total administrative and selling expense	$ 41,360	$ 71,252
Net earnings before tax	$ 281	$ 818
Income tax	198	373
Earnings	$ 83	$ 445
Dividends	nil	400
Earnings transferred to surplus	$ 83	$ 45

Analysis of Financial Statements:

This seven-year old concern has expanded rapidly since its founding. This has been accomplished by expanding from a local territory to a radius of 130 miles and by giving 24-hour service to its customers. In order to accomplish this, there has been a substantial increase in fixed assets and approximately a 60% increase during the last year under review. This has been made possible in part by acquiring the Meade Photo Company in September, 1966. While the net earnings transferred to surplus have been small, there has been an increase in capital. During 1965 an 8% preferred stock issue of $10,000 was made, and in 1967 bonds were issued for $14,000. In connection with the acquisition of the Meade Photo Company for $24,000, $7,000 was borrowed from the Harrisburg Fidelity and Trust Company and the seller was given a chattel mortgage for $17,000, payable $180 a week. In addition Meade receives a payment of 10% of the net sales which are transacted from their former customers for a period of five years. During the year more equipment was purchased with money obtained in the form of notes from the bank. The amount due the bank is made up of five installment notes, secured by various pieces of equipment. Other notes payable consist of $5,500 payable to a large film manufacturer; $8,500 payable to Meade Photo; and the balance to others. Notes payable after one year are due to Meade Photo. Mr. Morse, the president, estimates that sales during the fiscal year, 1968, will be $320,000.

Exhibit 1—Concluded

CREDIT RECORD, MAY 15, 1967

High Credit	Owes Currently	Past Due	Terms	Payments
3,000	0	0	Net 30	Prompt
2,693	0	0	2% 10 E.O.M.	Prompt
2,740	245	127	Net 30	Slow 8 months
582	0	0	2% 10	Prompt to slow 60 days
108	108	108	Net 10	Slow
2,518	2,518	0	Net 30	Prompt
582	61	0	2% 10	Prompt
9,308	8,854	4,601	2% 10, net 30	Slow 30 to 60 days
5,000	4,800	4,800	2% 10 E.O.M.	Slow 90 to 120 days
4,492	3,452	3,452	2% 10 E.O.M.	Slow 90 to 120 days
167	0	0	Net 30	Slow 60 days
118	118	118	Net 15	Slow 60 to 90 days

Exhibit 2

ALLEN DISTRIBUTION COMPANY

LETTER FROM THE HARRISBURG FIDELITY AND TRUST COMPANY

Allen Distribution Company   June 6, 1967
Philadelphia, Pennsylvania

Attention: Credit Manager

GENTLEMEN:

Morse Photo Company has maintained a satisfactory account with us for a number of years and such accommodation as we have extended them is cared for as agreed. It is our feeling that they are entitled to their reasonable trade requirements.

Yours very truly,

(*Signed*) GEORGE GRUBB
Assistant Vice-President
Harrisburg Fidelity and Trust Company

LETTER FROM A LARGE FILM MANUFACTURER

Allen Distribution Company   June 5, 1967
Philadelphia, Pennsylvania

Attention: Credit Manager

GENTLEMEN:

Re: Morse Photo Company

With reference to your inquiry regarding the above account, we wish to advise that we have been doing business with them since 1961.

Recently we have had a fair amount of trouble with them because of overexpansion in relation to their net worth. In the past, customer's promises for payment could not be depended upon, although there has been a decided improvement in the last six months. Around the first of the year we had to take notes totaling $7,500 for the past-due accounts. At the present time $2,500 is still outstanding, but the notes are not in default. In April, we extended them $2,700 worth of credit, $2,600 of which was under the term

Exhibit 2—Continued

⅓ payable every ten days. The last payment was not received until June 1, whereas it was due May 22. At the present time the concern owes us outside of the notes $115 of which $76.70 represents the April charge which is past due in our books.

To sum the whole thing up we are willing to extend credit up to $5,000 but must watch the account carefully.

Yours very truly.

(*Signed*) ALFRED WHITTIER
Credit Manager

LETTER FROM A LARGE CHEMICAL COMPANY

Allen Distribution Company   June 7, 1967
Philadelphia, Pennsylvania

Attention: Credit Manager

GENTLEMEN:

The following summary is the information you requested with respect to Morse Photo Company:

How Long Sold—May, 1965
Last Sale—June, 1967
Highest Credit—$700
Amount Owing—$700
Past Due—0
Terms—2% 10 days
Amount Secured—None
Manner of Payment—Previous sales C.O.D.

This is a trial order on restricted credit terms. Future policy will be determined by payment record.

Yours very truly,

(*Signed*) ARNOLD HEAD
Credit Manager

LETTER FROM OLIVER ELECTRIC COMPANY

Allen Distribution Company   June 9, 1967
Philadelphia, Pennsylvania

Attention: Credit Manager

GENTLEMEN:

Re: Morse Photo Company
How Long Sold—July, 1962
Date of Last Sale—April, 1967
High Credit—$1,600
Amount Owing—$630
Past Due—$630
Terms—2% 10 End of the Month

Other comments:

We would suggest watching this account carefully. It has been up to nine months slow with us.

Yours very truly,

(*Signed*) J. E. STEWART
Credit Manager

THE O. M. SCOTT & SONS COMPANY

∧∧

Between 1955 and 1961, management of The O. M. Scott & Sons Company launched a number of new programs aimed at maintaining and increasing the company's past success and growth. Largely in response to these activities, Scott's field sales force grew from 6 to 150 men, several entirely new and expanded production facilities went on stream, and the number of products in the company's product line tripled. Sales increased from about $10 million to $43 million. In late 1961, company officials were preparing to review the results of all these changes to ascertain how, if at all, Scott's plans and financial policies should be changed.

The O. M. Scott & Sons Company commenced operations in 1868, when it began processing the country's first clean, weed-free grass seed. Scott's early business came from a small but rapidly growing local market in central Ohio. Later, however, the company went through several stages in its growth. At about the turn of the century the company turned from supplying its local market to selling grass and other farm seeds over a wider geographic area by mail. As its success with its mail-order business increased, the company began to advertise extensively and in 1927 added a free magazine called *Lawn Care*, which has been widely distributed ever since. In all of these early promotional activities, the company sought to sell the Scott name and products as well as the idea of improved care of lawns. In the 1920's a special lawn fertilizer developed for home use was added to the company's product line. During the 1930's the company began to distribute its products on a small scale through selected retail stores and garden centers. Sales and profits grew steadily throughout these years. Scott continued to grow along these same general lines until 1945, by which time sales reached $2.7 million and net profits after taxes were about $30,000.

Over the decade immediately following the war, pioneering research by Scott led to the development and introduction of a wide range of new chemical weed and garden pest controls and special-purpose lawn fertilizers. In addition, the company's grass seed lines were upgraded and supplemented. Largely in response to the success of this research, sales increased to $11.4 million and profits to over $210,000 in fiscal 1955.

By 1955, however, despite the company's impressive postwar record of growth in sales and profits, management was convinced that neither Scott nor its competitors had begun to develop and tap the potential inherent in the national lawn care market. In Scott's own case this failure to develop and tap the national market was attributed to the fact that Scott's customers could not buy its products easily where and when they expected to find them. The company's distribution system had not evolved adequately in response to developing market opportunities, and in many instances the company's dealers either were poorly stocked or were not the right kind of dealer for the company's products.

Thus began a new stage in Scott's development. Early in 1955 the company launched a program to build a national field sales organization with the objective of increasing the number, quality, and performance of its distributors so as to capitalize more fully on the success of its product research and development efforts. When this program started, the company had six field salesmen. By 1960 Scott had a field sales force of 150 men serving almost 10,000 retail dealers across the country. These dealers were mainly department stores and small hardware stores and garden supply centers. The company's salesmen spent most of their time training the dealers how to do a better selling job with Scott products and were paid a salary plus a bonus based on factory shipments to dealers.

Scott's product development program continued apace with the buildup in the direct selling force so that by the end of the 1950's the company was engaged in the purchase, processing, and sale of grass seed, and the manufacture and sale of fertilizers, weed and pest control products, mechanical spreaders, and electric lawn mowers. In 1959 sales increased to $30.6 million and profits to $1.5 million. A large proportion of these sales comprised new products that had been developed and patented by the company within the past few years.

Reviewing the company's progress again in early 1959, management was still not satisfied that the company was marketing its products as effectively as possible. For one thing, it was estimated that an annual market potential of at least $100 million existed for Scott products. Another important consideration was that several nationally known chemical firms had either begun or were expected to begin competing against Scott in certain lines. These facts led management to conclude that the most effective way for Scott to preserve its preeminent market position would be to push for immediate further market penetration. If successful, such a strategy would enable Scott to eclipse competition as completely as possible before its competitors could establish a firm market position against the company. In this context an annual growth rate in sales and profits of up to 25% was thought to be a reasonable goal for the company over the next few years.

Apart from the need to continue strengthening the company's field sales force and dealer organization, management thought in early 1959 that the most important factor standing in the way of further rapid growth and market penetration was the inability of the typical Scott dealer to carry an adequate inventory of Scott products. Because of the highly seasonal character of sales at retail of the company's products, it was essential that dealers have enough inventory on hand to meet local sales peaks when they came. Experience showed that in many parts of the country a large percentage of dealer sales were made on a few weekends each season. Failure to supply this demand when it materialized most often resulted in a sale lost to a competitor, although sometimes a customer simply postponed buying anything. The problem of assuring adequate dealer inventories had become more of a problem in recent years. The effectiveness of Scott's product development program meant that the dealer was expected to carry many more products than in the past. In addition, Scott had shifted its marketing emphasis from selling individual products to one of selling complete lawn and garden programs. And in order to sell a full lawn maintenance program it was necessary that the dealer carry the complete Scott line and have it on hand when needed by the consumer.

Because of their small size and often weak working capital position, most of Scott's dealers could not realistically be expected to increase their inventory investment in Scott products. This meant that any desired buildup in dealer inventory levels would have to be financed in some way by Scott itself. In the past the company had extended generous seasonal datings to its dealers, as was industry practice. As a normal pattern, winter and early spring shipments became due at the end of April or May, depending on the geographical area. Shipments during the summer months were due in October or November. The purpose of these seasonal datings was to enable and encourage as many dealers as possible to be well stocked in advance of seasonal sales peaks. Anticipation at the rate of 0.6% a month was offered on payments made in advance of these seasonal dates, although few dealers availed themselves of this opportunity. With purchases made outside the two main selling seasons, dealers were expected to pay on the tenth of the second month following shipment.

The company's past experience with seasonal datings suggested certain changes in the event Scott proceeded to finance a higher level of dealer inventories. Because of the seasonal nature of the business and the fact that most dealers were thinly capitalized, payment was not often received by Scott until the merchandise involved was sold, irrespective of the terms of sale. This meant that many dealers were continually asking for credit extensions. Another problem inherent in the seasonal dating policy was that Scott retained little or no effective security interest in the goods involved. A final problem was that in the past Scott had followed a policy of not selling to dealers that could not be relied upon to maintain prices at reasonable levels. It was thought that widespread selling at discount prices would undermine the company and the market image it was trying to project. Thus, in any decision to expand dealer inventories, management hoped to contrive a procedure whereby Scott would retain the right to reclaim goods from third parties in the event any of its dealers began selling at wholesale to a discounter.

After considerable study it was decided to continue the traditional seasonal dating plan and to introduce a new trust receipt plan as well. This combination was thought to fulfill all of the requirements outlined in the previous paragraph. As the particular trust receipt plan adopted by Scott worked, a trust receipt dealer was required to sign a trust receipt that provided for (1) immediate transfer to the dealer of title to any Scott products shipped in response to a dealer order, (2) retention of a security interest by Scott in merchandise so shipped until sold by the dealer acting in his capacity as a retailer, and (3) segregation of a sufficient proportion of the funds received from such sales to provide for payment to Scott as billed. Among other things, these provisions made it possible for Scott to move in and reclaim any inventory held by third parties that had been sold by a trust receipt dealer acting illegally as a wholesaler. Exhibit 5 shows the trust receipt form used by Scott. In addition to obtaining the trust receipt from its dealers, the company also was required to file a statement of trust receipt financing with the secretary of state in each state where a trust receipt plan dealer was domiciled. Such a statement is shown in Exhibit 6. Dealers using the trust receipt plan were charged an extra 3% on the cost of purchases from Scott. They also had to place all purchase orders directly through Scott's field salesmen, inasmuch as these account executives were held responsible by the company for controlling dealer inventories in connection with the trust receipt plan.

This last-mentioned role of Scott's sales force was absolutely central to the proper functioning of the trust receipt plan. Apart from simply policing the level and character of dealer inventories, the account executives also periodically inventoried the trust receipt dealers so that Scott could bill the dealers for merchandise sold. During the two peak retail selling seasons these physical inventories were taken once a month, and even oftener in the case of large dealers. In the off seasons the inspections occurred much less frequently. In any event, the terms of payment associated with the trust receipt plan required that the dealer pay Scott within 10 days of receipt of an invoice from the company for goods sold since the last physical inventory date.

After introduction of the two payment plans in 1960, about half of Scott's sales were by seasonal dating and half by trust receipt. The trust receipt dealers were for the most part local garden centers and hardware stores, whereas the seasonal dating dealers were the larger chain garden centers and department stores. The company's overall collection experience with both plans was that about 75% of receivables were collected in the month due, another 16% in the following month, an additional 6% in the next month after that, and the balance thereafter.

The rapid growth in outstanding receivables resulting from the trust receipt program was financed largely by a combination of subordinated notes, a revolving line of bank credit, and increased use of supplier credit arising out of special deferred payment terms extended by the company's chemical suppliers. The company also retained almost all of its earnings each year as had been its policy in the past.

At the end of fiscal 1961 Scott and its subsidiaries had $16.2 million of long-term debt outstanding, of which $12 million comprised renewable five-year subordinated notes of the parent company held by four insurance companies and a trustee and $4.2 million was publicly held bonds owed by Scotts Chemical Plant, Inc., a wholly owned subsidiary. The key terms associated with the $12 million of subordinated notes are summarized in the footnotes to Exhibits 1 and 2. The governing loan indenture limited the unconsolidated parent company's maximum outstanding debt at any time to an amount not greater than three times what was termed the company's "equity working capital" as of the preceding March 31. What was meant by equity working capital and the calculation of maximum allowed debt are shown in Exhibit 7. The note indenture restricted outstanding subordinated notes to only 60% of maximum allowed debt as determined by the above equity working capital formula. The agreement also required that Scott be out of bank debt for 60 consecutive days each year and that the company earn before taxes $1\frac{1}{2}$ times its fixed financial charges including interest on funded and unfunded debt, amortization of debt discount, and rentals on leased properties.

In addition to the long-term debt just described, Scott also had a $12.5 million line of credit at the end of fiscal 1961 with a group of seven commercial banks. The purpose of this line was to provide for seasonal funds needs, and in recent years the maximum line had been used at some point during each year. An informal understanding covering this seasonal financing arrangement required that Scott maintain average compensating balances with the banks involved of 15% of the line of credit.

As far as accounts payable were concerned, Scott had negotiated an arrangement with its principal chemical suppliers whereby the company settled with these suppliers just once or twice a year. It had been possible to negotiate these favorable terms because the suppliers were persuaded that it was in their best interests to help Scott develop and expand the home lawn market. Generally, no interest or other charges were levied on these amounts.

As fiscal 1961 drew to a close, management was generally pleased with what appeared to have been the results of the trust receipt program, although final figures for the year just ending were not yet available. Company sales had increased from $31 million in 1959 to over $43 million in 1961. At this level of operations the company's break-even point was estimated at between $27.5 million and $30 million.

By the end of 1961, when company officials were reviewing the results of fiscal 1961 and preparing plans for the 1962 selling season, the audited statements shown in Exhibits 1 and 2 were available, as well as the unaudited and unconsolidated quarterly statements in Exhibits 3 and 4. In addition, on the basis of a physical inventory taken by the company's sales force, combined standard and trust receipt plan dealer inventories were estimated to be at a level of about $28 million at the end of calendar 1961. This compared with roughly $17 million at the end of 1960. On the basis of these and other data, Scott's sales department estimated that in terms of cost of sales, dealer sales in fiscal 1961 reached an all-time high of over $30 million. The recent record of earnings, dividends, and market price range is shown in Exhibit 8.

It was against this background that company officials began their review and evaluation of recent operations and current financial position. They were particularly anxious to formulate any indicated changes in company plans and financial policies before the new production and selling seasons were upon the company.

Exhibit 1

THE O. M. SCOTT & SONS COMPANY AND SUBSIDIARY COMPANIES

CONSOLIDATED BALANCE SHEETS AS OF SEPTEMBER 30, 1957–61

(Dollar amounts in thousands)

	1957	1958	1959	1960(a)	1961(e)
Cash	$ 533.9	$ 1,232.0	$ 1,736.4	$ 2,328.7	$ 1,454.3
Accounts receivable	2,640.0	4,686.5	5,788.4	15,749.7	21,500.5(f)
Inventories	2,340.3	3,379.8	6,993.2	3,914.3	5,590.5
Total current assets	$5,514.2	$ 9,298.3	$14,518.0	$21,992.7	$28,545.3
Land, buildings, equipment	$2,253.5	$ 2,439.5	$ 7,364.6	$ 8,003.4	$ 8,370.2
Less: Accumulated depreciation	544.0	650.0	1,211.3	1,687.1	2,247.1
Net fixed assets	$1,709.5	$ 1,789.5	$ 6,153.3	$ 6,316.3	$ 6,123.1
Investment in and advances to affiliates	1,165.6	28.9	232.3	462.0	133.6
Other assets	488.5	376.6	837.5	1,132.0	937.8
Total assets	$8,877.8	$11,493.3	$21,741.1	$29,903.0	$35,739.8
Accounts payable	$1,540.8	$ 2,134.6	$ 4,140.2	$ 2,791.0	$ 6,239.2
Notes payable—banks	300.0	. . .	1,000.0		
Accrued taxes, interest, and other expenses	674.3	1,437.7	1,900.7	1,941.2	1,207.7
Current sinking fund requirements	77.0	173.9	324.3	382.5	512.5
Total current liabilities	$2,592.1	$ 3,746.2	$ 7,365.2	$ 5,114.7	$ 7,959.4
Long-term debt:					
Of parent company (c) (b)	2,186.7	2,059.7	1,777.2	9,000.0	12,000.0
Of subsidiary (c) (b)	. . .	. . .	5,162.6	4,649.5	4,170.4
Total liabilities (d)	$4,778.8	$ 5,805.9	$14,305.0	$18,764.2	$24,129.8
Preferred stock (i)	1,757.2	2,432.2	2,392.5	2,347.5	2,254.3
Common stock and surplus	2,341.8	3,255.2	5,043.6	8,791.3 (b) (g)	9,355.7
Total liabilities and net worth	$8,877.8	$11,493.3	$21,741.1	$29,903.0	$35,739.8

See notes beginning p. 80.

Exhibit 2

THE O. M. SCOTT & SONS COMPANY AND SUBSIDIARY COMPANIES

CONSOLIDATED INCOME STATEMENTS FOR THE YEARS
ENDING SEPTEMBER 30, 1957–61
(Dollar amounts in thousands)

	1957	*1958*	*1959*	*1960(a)*	*1961(e)*
Net sales (*b*) (*g*)	$18,675.9	$23,400.2	$30,563.7	$38,396.4	$43,140.1
Cost of sales and operating expenses:					
Cost of products sold including processing, warehousing, delivery and merchandising (including lease rentals)	$15,500.9	$18,914.7	$24,119.5	$30,416.8(*d*)	$34,331.7
General and administrative, research and development expenses	1,817.2	2,134.1	2,499.3	2,853.6	3,850.7
Depreciation and amortization	263.2	185.9	377.6	584.2	589.6
Interest charges	199.8	212.7	410.6	881.6	1,131.5
Total cost of sales	$17,781.1	$21,447.4	$27,407.0	$34,736.2	$39,903.5
Earnings before taxes on income	$ 894.8	$ 1,952.7	$ 3,156.7	$ 3,660.2	$ 3,236.6
Federal and state taxes on income	443.5	1,051.6	1,671.2	1,875.2	1,665.9
Net income after taxes	$ 451.3	$ 901.1	$ 1,485.5	$ 1,785.0	$ 1,570.7

See notes following.

Exhibits 1 and 2—Continued

THE O. M. SCOTT & SONS COMPANY

NOTES TO FINANCIAL STATEMENTS

a) *1960 Auditor's Statement*

The Board of Directors
The O. M. Scott & Sons Company

We have examined the statement of consolidated financial position of The O. M. Scott & Sons Company and its subsidiaries as of September 30, 1960, the related consolidated statements of operations, capital surplus and retained earnings for the fiscal year then ended, and accompanying notes to financial statements. Our examination was made in accordance with generally accepted auditing standards, and accordingly included such tests of the accounting records and such other auditing procedures as we considered necessary in the circumstances.

In our opinion, the accompanying statements, together with the explanatory notes, present fairly the consolidated financial position of The O. M. Scott & Sons Company and its subsidiaries at September 30, 1960, and the results of their operations for the year then ended, in conformity with generally accepted accounting principles, except as described in note (*b*), applied on a basis consistent with that of the preceding year.

PEAT, MARWICK, MITCHELL & CO.

Columbus, Ohio
November 23, 1960

Exhibits 1 and 2—Continued

b) *Sales*

For several years the company has followed a prebilling system to obtain more efficient and economical control of production through the medium of unappropriated inventory. Under this system, the invoicing of customers pre-dates shipment. Consequently, both fiscal 1960 and 1959 sales stated in the operating statement include firm orders received, billed, and costed-out in late September which were shipped early in the immediately following October. Prior to September 30, 1960, the amounts involved were not significant, but toward the end of that month shipment was delayed by the company to facilitate the taking of physical inventories at storage warehouses as of the month end. The result of the foregoing is to include an additional amount of approximately $343,000 in net earnings for the year 1960. In management's opinion, the earnings on these sales are properly earnings of the year 1960.

c) *Long-Term Debt*

All long-term obligations of the parent company at September 30, 1959, were retired prior to December 31, 1959.

In fiscal 1960, the parent company sold five-year subordinated promissory notes, principally to certain insurance companies, at the principal amount of $9 million, maturing October 13, 1964. The notes bear interest to October 10, 1960, at $6\frac{1}{2}\%$ per annum and thereafter to maturity at (*a*) 6% per annum, or (*b*) the New York prime commercial rate plus $1\frac{1}{2}\%$, whichever is higher.

The loan agreement provides, among other things, that (*a*) payment of principal and interest on the notes is subordinated to repayment of bank loans due within one year, (*b*) new or additional notes may be sold on October 28th of each future year, and (*c*) any holder of the notes may, before October 15th of each year, require payment by October 10th of the immediately ensuing year of all or part of the notes held.*

All holders of the notes at September 30, 1960, surrendered the notes then held in exchange for new notes having exactly the same terms but maturing October 28, 1965, at an interest rate of 6% per annum to October 10, 1961. Interest after October 10, 1961, accrues at the rate determinable under the provisions of the loan agreement.

Long-term obligations of subsidiary outstanding on September 30, 1960:

20-year $5\frac{3}{4}\%$ first mortgage bonds due March 15, 1977	$1,026,000
18-year 6% secured sinking fund debentures due Feb. 1, 1977	2,840,500
10-year 6% sinking fund notes due March 15, 1967	178,000
10-year 6% subordinated debentures due Dec. 15, 1967	950,000
	$4,994,500
Less: Current sinking fund provision	345,000
	$4,649,500

---

* Such payments were to be made in four equal annual installments beginning on October 10 of the immediately ensuing year.

Exhibits 1 and 2—Continued

The above obligations of a subsidiary are secured by property mortgages, and/or assignment of lease rentals payable by the parent company.

d) Long-Term Leases

The main production, warehousing, and office facilities used by the company are leased from affiliated interests not consolidated, namely, the company's Pension and Profit Sharing Trusts, and also from a consolidated subsidiary, Scotts Chemical Plant, Inc. These leases, all having over 10 years to run, required minimum annual rentals in fiscal 1960 of $872,577. This represented less than 17% of net taxable profit before deduction for rentals, depreciation, and expenses based on net profits. It is anticipated that in fiscal 1961, the fixed rentals under these leases will approximate the same amount.

e) 1961 Auditor's Statement

Board of Directors
The O. M. Scott & Sons Company
Marysville, Ohio

We have examined the statement of consolidated financial position of The O. M. Scott & Sons Company and its subsidiaries as of September 30, 1961, and the related statements of consolidated operations, capital surplus, and retained earnings for the year then ended. Our examination was made in accordance with generally accepted auditing standards, and accordingly included such tests of the accounting records and such other auditing procedures as we considered necessary in the circumstances.

In our opinion, the accompanying statements of financial position, operations, capital surplus, and retained earnings present fairly the consolidated financial position of The O. M. Scott & Sons Company and its subsidiaries at September 30, 1961, and the consolidated results of their operations for the year then ended, in conformity with generally accepted accounting principles which, except for the changes (in which we concur) referred to in Notes (*f*) and (*g*), have been applied on a basis consistent with that of the preceding year.

ERNST & ERNST

Dayton, Ohio
January 6, 1962

f) Accounts Receivable

Accounts receivable are stated net after reserve of $740,000 for dealer adjustments, allowances, and doubtful accounts.

In 1959 the company adopted a plan of deferred payments for certain retail dealers. Accounts receivable include $16,033,093 for shipments under this plan which are secured by trust receipts executed by the dealers. The trust receipt arrangements provide for (1) immediate transfer to the dealers of title to the merchandise shipped in response to the dealers' orders, (2) retention by the company of a security interest in the merchandise until sold by the dealers, and (3) payment by the dealers to the company as the merchandise

Exhibits 1 and 2—Continued

is sold at retail. The dealers, whether trust receipt or other, do not have the right to return any part of merchandise ordered by them and delivered in salable condition, but they may tender merchandise in full or part payment of their accounts in the event of termination by the company of their dealerships. To provide for possible adjustments and allowances in the liquidation of dealer accounts receivable, the company has provided an increase in reserve by a charge to net earnings of the current year of $150,000 and a charge to retained earnings at October 1, 1960, of $530,000.

g) *Sales*

In the financial statements for the year ended September 30, 1960, attention was directed to the company's policy of including in the operating statement firm orders received, billed, and costed out in late September which were shipped early in the immediately following October. During 1961, this policy was discontinued. In order to reflect this change in policy prebilled sales at September 30, 1960, together with related costs and expenses included in operations of the year then ended, have been carried forward and included in the operating statement for the year ended September 30, 1961, with a resulting charge to retained earnings at October 1, 1960, of $429,600. This change in accounting principle did not have a material effect on net earnings for the year ended September 30, 1961.

h) *Long-Term Debt: Five-Year Subordinated Promissory Notes*

The notes bear interest to October 10, 1961, at 6% per annum and thereafter to maturity at a rate which is the higher of (a) 6% per annum, or (b) the New York prime commercial rate plus 1½%. The loan agreement provides, among other things, that (a) payment of principal and interest on the notes is subordinated to repayment of bank loans due within one year, and (b) elections may be exercised annually by the holders to (1) exchange the notes currently held for new notes having a maturity extended by one year, (2) purchase additional notes if offered for sale by the company, or (3) require payment of all or part of the notes held, such payments to be made in four equal annual installments beginning on October 10 of the immediately ensuing year.

All holders of the notes at September 30, 1961, except for $1 million, surrendered the notes then held in exchange for new notes having exactly the same terms but maturing October 28, 1966, at an interest rate of 6% per annum to October 10, 1962. Subsequent to September 30, 1961, arrangements have been made for the note for $1 million not exchanged to mature September 1, 1962, and to issue a note for $1 million to another lender maturing October 28, 1966.

Exhibits 1 and 2—Continued

Obligations of Subsidiaries:

5¾% first mortgage bonds, due March 15, 1977 ....$	964,000	
6% sinking fund notes, due March 15, 1967	147,500	
6% subordinated debentures, due December 15, 1967	819,000	
6% secured sinking fund debentures due February 1, 1977	2,620,500	
	$4,551,000	
Less classified as current liability...	414,000	$4,137,000
Real estate mortgage notes ($252 payable monthly for interest at 6% per annum and amortization of principal) ....$	34,383	
Less classified as current liabilities..	1,000	33,383
		$4,170,383

The above long-term obligations of subsidiaries are secured by mortgages on property, plant, and equipment, and/or assignment of lease rentals payable by the parent company.

i) Preferred Stock

Preferred stock is 5% cumulative, $100 par value.

Exhibit 3

THE O. M. SCOTT & SONS COMPANY

UNCONSOLIDATED QUARTERLY BALANCE SHEETS OF PARENT COMPANY FOR
FISCAL YEAR 1961*

(Dollar amounts in thousands)

	12/31/60	3/31/61	6/30/61	9/30/61
Cash	$ 1,810	$ 2,140	$ 1,760	$ 2,070
Accounts receivable:				
Standard plan	$ 1,500	$ 6,540	$ 3,110	$ 4,400
Trust receipt plan	8,660	15,880	11,890	16,830
Total receivables	$10,160	$22,420	$15,000	$21,230
Inventories:				
Finished goods	$ 7,390	$ 5,850	$ 6,420	$ 4,040
Raw materials and supplies	2,380	2,520	1,890	1,460
Total inventories	$ 9,770	$ 8,370	$ 8,310	$ 5,500
Total current assets	$21,740	$32,930	$25,070	$28,800
Land, buildings, equipment	$ 2,130	$ 2,190	$ 2,270	$ 2,290
Less: Accumulated depreciation	800	830	870	910
Net fixed assets	$ 1,330	$ 1,360	$ 1,400	$ 1,380
Other assets	$ 1,990	$ 1,730	$ 1,720	$ 1,240
Total assets	$25,060	$36,020	$28,190	$31,420
Accounts payable	$ 1,390	$ 3,680	$ 3,150	$ 7,040
Notes payable—bank	6,250	12,000	5,750	—
Accrued taxes, interest, and other expenses	(390)	950	110	1,170
Total current liabilities	$ 7,250	$16,630	$ 9,010	$ 8,210
Subordinated promissory notes	9,000	9,000	9,000	12,000
Total liabilities	$16,250	$25,630	$18,010	$20,210
Net worth:				
Preferred stock	2,380	2,380	2,350	2,250
Common stock and surplus	6,430	8,010	7,830	8,960
Total liabilities and net worth	$25,060	$36,020	$28,190	$31,420

* Excluding items relating to certain nonoperating subsidiaries. Unaudited and unpublished. For these reasons Exhibit 3 does not correspond exactly with Exhibit 1. In particular, the cash account in Exhibit 3 is not consistent with that in Exhibit 1.

Exhibit 4

THE O. M. SCOTT & SONS COMPANY

UNCONSOLIDATED QUARTERLY INCOME STATEMENTS OF PARENT COMPANY
FOR THE YEAR ENDING SEPTEMBER 30, 1961*

(Dollar amounts in thousands)

	Quarter Ending 12/31/60	Quarter Ending 3/31/61	Quarter Ending 6/30/61	Quarter Ending 9/30/61	Year
Net sales.............................	$ 1,300	$15,780	$9,570	$14,740	$41,390
Cost of sales and operating expenses: Cost of products sold including processing, depreciation, warehousing, delivery and merchandising..........	$ 3,250	$11,730	$8,670	$10,790	$34,440
General and administrative, research and development expenses...........	660	800	940	1,000	3,400
Interest charges.....................	150	240	260	200	850
Total cost of sales...............	$ 4,060	$12,770	$9,870	$11,990	$38,690
Earnings (losses) before taxes on income...............................	$(2,760)	$ 3,010	$ (300)	$ 2,750	$ 2,700
Federal taxes on income................	(1,440)	1,570	(160)	1,390	1,360
Net income (loss) after taxes...........	$(1,320)	$ 1,440	$ (140)	$ 1,360	$ 1,340

* Excluding items relating to the operations of certain nonoperating subsidiaries. Unaudited and unpublished.

Exhibit 5

THE O. M. SCOTT & SONS COMPANY

TRUST RECEIPT

The undersigned Dealer, as Trustee, and Entruster agree to engage in Trust Receipt financing of the acquisition by Trustees of seed, fertilizer, weed controls, pest controls, applicators, mowers and other lawn and garden products, all bearing the brands and trade marks of The O. M. Scott & Sons Company. Entruster will direct said company to deliver said products from time to time as ordered by Dealer.

  a) Dealer agrees to hold said products in trust for the sole purpose of making sales to consumers, functioning as a retailer and not as a wholesaler.

  b) Dealer agrees to hold a sufficient proportion of the funds received from such sales for payment to Entruster as billed.

  c) Either party may terminate this Trust Receipt on notice. In such event Dealer will surrender to Entruster his complete stock of The O. M. Scott & Sons Company products, proceeds thereof to be credited to Dealer.*

Official Business Name
of Dealer as Trustee:

Accepted at Marysville, Ohio

_____, 19__

Street & No._____
City_____Zone___State_____

THE O. M. SCOTT & SONS COMPANY
(Entruster)

Authorized
Signature_____.
Date_____Title_____

President

* This statement differs from the statement quoted in footnote (f) to Exhibits 1 and 2. Presumably the statement in Exhibit 5 is correct.

Exhibit 6

THE O. M. SCOTT & SONS COMPANY

STATEMENT OF TRUST RECEIPT FINANCING

The Entruster, The O. M. Scott & Sons Company, whose chief place of business is at Marysville, Ohio, and who has no place of business within this state, is or expects to be engaged in financing under trust receipt transactions, the acquisition by the Trustee whose name and chief place of business within this state is:

of seed, fertilizers, weed controls, pest controls, applicators, mowers and other lawn and garden products, all bearing the brands and trade marks of The O. M. Scott & Sons Company.

Entruster: The O. M. Scott & Sons Company Date_____, 19__
 For the Trustee (Dealer)
By :_____ By :_____
 President

Exhibit 7

THE O. M. SCOTT & SONS COMPANY

EXAMPLE SHOWING CALCULATION OF EQUITY WORKING CAPITAL AND MAXIMUM ALLOWED DEBT OF PARENT COMPANY FOR THE TWELVE MONTHS FOLLOWING MARCH 31, 1961*

(Dollar amounts in millions)

Calculation of equity working capital:
Current assets... $32.9
Current liabilities...$16.6
Long-term debt.. 9.0
Total debt...$25.6 25.6
Equity working capital... $ 7.3

Calculation of maximum allowed parent company debt:
300% of equity working capital................................. $21.9
Actual parent borrowings—March 31, 1961....................... 21.0
Available debt capacity.. $ .9

Calculation of maximum allowed subordinated debt of parent:
60% of maximum allowed total debt ($21.9 million × 60%)........ $13.1

 * Calculations based on figures taken from Exhibit 3.

Exhibit 8

THE O. M. SCOTT & SONS COMPANY

RECORD OF EARNINGS, DIVIDENDS, AND MARKET PRICE RANGE, 1958–61

Fiscal Year	Earnings per Share	Dividends per Share	Market Price Range*
1958	$0.69	10% stk.	6⅛– 1½
1959	1.15	10% stk.	32⅞– 6⅛
1960	1.21	10% stk.	51 –31⅞
1961	0.99	10¢ + 5% stk.	58¾–30

* Calendar year; bid prices. Closing prices September 29 and December 29, 1961 were $49 and $32¼ respectively. Stock first sold publicly in 1958 and has traded over-the-counter since then. The company had about 4,100 common shareholders in 1961.

KOEHRING COMPANY

^^^

The Koehring Company is a Milwaukee-based manufacturer of heavy non-electrical industrial equipment, primarily construction machinery. Koehring is known as the most widely diversified company in its industry. Early in 1958 it comprised seven manufacturing divisions; two nonmanufacturing divisions, which constituted Koehring's world-wide marketing apparatus handling products of all the manufacturing divisions; and still another division, which was essentially a field servicing organization for the western states. Plants were located in four midwestern states and one Canadian province. An illustrative product listing included "commercial-sized"[1] power cranes, trench diggers, small motorized concrete mixers, concrete handling equipment used at mass pouring installations such as the St. Lawrence Seaway, road rollers and compactors, pulp and paper making machinery, hydraulic presses, plastic injection molding machinery, mining machinery, and water well drilling rigs. Of these products, earthmoving and excavating equipment were the primary revenue producers. Replacement parts typically amounted to about one fourth of annual sales.

Substantial growth had taken place during the 1950's by acquisition of existing companies. Waterous Ltd., a Canadian producer, was added in 1952 as Koehring-Waterous Ltd., a subsidiary, and in 1956 the Buffalo-Springfield Roller Company and Hydraulic Press Manufacturing Company were acquired, and subsequently operated as divisions. Other manufacturing divisions had been a part of the company since at least the early 1930's.

In January, 1958, Koehring's vice president–finance, Mr. Orville Mertz, was pondering a proposal from the marketing department for the institution of a schedule of terms on installment sales and a policy declaration of credit practices. Until then, divisional credit managers had evaluated each request for installment sales financing individually. No company-wide policy on down payments, length of payment period, and financing charge had been employed, and final decisions on these terms were made at the divisional level. In essence, special terms had been granted in each instance. Bad debts had never exceeded 2/100 of 1% in a single year after World War II. During the capital

---

[1] Up to three cubic yards capacity when used as a shovel and up to four cubic yards when used as the power for a dragline. Giant shovels, not produced by Koehring, have capacity as high as 60 cubic yards.

goods boom of 1955 through 1957, the number of requests for deferred payment sales contracts increased in number, and requests for more liberal terms grew increasingly common. The combination threatened to dangerously weaken managerial control of both marketing policy and, in turn, financial policy through its indirect impact on the length and size of notes receivable. If the vice president–finance concurred with marketing's proposal, a series of meetings were to be held with the general, sales, and credit managers of each of the divisions, and the new policy on terms quickly implemented. Administration was to remain in the hands of divisional credit managers.

A few days previously the company's president had issued a letter to the vice presidents of marketing and finance relating in part to this subject (Exhibit 1). Consequently, Mr. Mertz welcomed a review of procedure and an establishment of policy; but because of its possible effects on company financing, he held serious reservations about the advisability of a loosening of credit terms. His apprehension about the impact of the proposed installment sales program arose partly because recent rapid asset expansion had occasioned resort to substantial amounts of debt and preferred stock, and partly because the company's liquidity was low. Rapidly expanding receivables would force the firm to use outside fund sources. More debt, he feared, would raise risk in the firm through the fixed cash drain it would add to the existing fixed interest, sinking fund, and preferred stock dividend cash outflows. (See footnotes to the balance sheets in Exhibit 4.) He was also unsure of his banks' and long-term creditors' reaction. Although his company's relations were secure with both of these classes of its creditors, Mr. Mertz was aware that the cyclical variability of capital goods sales led to a preference on the part of institutional lenders for moderate use of debt by heavy equipment makers. Although no more mergers were contemplated presently, a policy of expansion by this means inclined Mr. Mertz to hedge against commitments that might make the company's capital structure inflexible in the face of unforeseeable demands for funds.

Market structure

While many of its competitors concentrated in relatively narrower product lines, diversification internally and through acquisition had led Koehring to straddle a broad segment of the nonelectrical machinery market. Because of this great diversity Koehring probably faced a broader array of product competitors than any other single firm. A representative cross-classification of Koehring's major competitors with its major construction machinery lines appears in Exhibit 2.

A substantial part of the marketing apparatus for these equipment lines was the domestic and foreign distributorship network. Since low unit volume prevailed, most of the industry's sales were made directly through distributors, and few retail outlets were maintained. Most distributors handled more than one manufacturer's product line, and many handled several. It was common, however, for individual distributors to market only part of a single manufacturer's product line. Koehring distributed through 450 distributors, for example, but only 70 handled equipment produced by all of its manufacturing divisions. Competition among manufacturers was intense for priority in inventory stocking and in the sales efforts by distributors.

Koehring customarily made some sales on special order directly from its factory to ultimate purchasers, but much the greater part of sales was made via the company's distributors, who sold mostly off the shelf. Open account sales, possibly with a discount for short-term payment but net 30 days, were the dominant type of distributor sales. In the few years preceding 1958, however, installment sales had grown relatively. These were financed (1) by the dealer, who carried the resulting installment receivable on his own books; or (2) by a lender such as a sales finance company or local commercial bank with or without the endorsement of the distributor; or (3) by Koehring, which absorbed the installment receivable and carried it for the life of the sales contract. Installment receivables resulting from sales to ultimate purchasers were known as "retail financing." Also, distributors frequently required assistance in financing inventories. Thus, for many years Koehring had made a practice of lending to its distributors through inventory-secured loans, known as "wholesale financing" or "floor planning." Koehring's product competitors typically extended this kind of financing to distributors. In part, the readiness of the manufacturers to extend wholesale financing stemmed from a desire on the part of each company to have its product line prominent among the offerings of distributors at point of sale. Manufacturers competed too in another sense. Individual distributors possessed a limited capacity to finance receivables from deferred payment retail sales, and there was a strong tendency for each to allocate it to what he considered his prime product line. Installment sales of other manufacturers would be financed as the distributors or buyers could find available funds elsewhere.

Competition in Koehring's product lines in recent years had centered at least as much around the terms of financing offered dealers and buyers by manufacturers as around equipment prices. After sharp rises in the post–World War II decade, prices had stabilized and been virtually uniform for machines of comparable capacity.

Proposed schedule of terms of sale

The schedule of terms of sales and credit policies proposed by the marketing department essentially constituted a four-point statement of company policy with respect to retail and wholesale financing. After a reiteration of the desirability of cash and open account sales, the draft document presented to Mr. Mertz addressed itself to the following points:

1. The Koehring "Buy-Back" Plan.
2. Retail financing through notes and rental purchase plans.
3. Special retail financing through distributors.
4. Floor planning.

The proposed Buy-Back Plan would essentially be Koehring's guarantee of a bank-financed installment sale. If a distributor negotiated bank financing and endorsed the sale contract upon which the buyer ultimately defaulted, Koehring guaranteed to repurchase the repossessed machine from the distributor. Similarly, if the buyer negotiated a bank loan directly, Koehring would guarantee repurchase from the bank. In both types of transactions the agreed repurchase price scaled downward with time to parallel loss of value.

Repurchase agreements would be offered on bank-financed sales, but not on sales financed by commercial or sales finance companies.

The retail financing and rental purchase plans would commit Koehring's financial resources. If neither a distributor nor banks and finance companies could or would finance a deferred payment sale when more than enough machines were available for cash or open account sales, Koehring would accept a note signed by the purchaser under the installment sale plan, or, alternatively, the rental purchase plan would allow a customer to, in effect, rent machinery with a purchase option. The two plans differed primarily in the terms of payment, length of contract, and interest rate. The terms to be offered were as follows:

Plan	Down Payment	Interest Rate	Maximum Time
Retail note	25% of purchase price	4½% per annum add-on*	24 months, 12 months preferred with equal monthly payments
Rental purchase plan	One monthly payment for each year the loan is to run	5% per annum add-on	36 months maximum with equal monthly payments

*The draft document explained computation of payment terms with add-on interest in this way. For example if a 24-month deal had been made with the amount to be financed $10,000, the payments would be:

Amount to be financed	$10,000.00
4½% add-on per year	900.00
Total	$10,900.00
24 monthly payments of	$ 454.17

Incentive prepayment terms were to be offered with both plans. It was anticipated that the retail note financing would be the more heavily used of the two plans.

The special retail financing through distributors scheme was envisaged as an exception program applying only "when inventory liquidation is considered necessary" and was "to be limited to good credit risks." It would have no-down-payment provisions and enable the customer to defer monthly payments in slack periods. It would be "in effect only when specifically so stated by the division management and then only for the products or models designated."

The floor planning arrangement would continue the distributor inventory financing policy of the past. Terms proposed were:

1. The distributor takes a 2% cash discount in paying for the machine 10 days after he sells it, net 30 days after the sale or 90 days after shipment from Koehring Company, whichever comes first.

2. If he has not paid by then, he may defer payment of the total amount, plus 6% simple interest, for up to an additional 90 days.

During the financing period inventory was secured by a trust receipt, chattel mortgage, or other title retention device.

Sales situation in December, 1957

When Mr. E. B. Hill, vice president–marketing, had first presented a draft of the new sales financing policies, he emphasized several conditions current in industry competition. He pointed to what he thought were signs of imminent recession in the economy generally and more particularly in the capital goods industries. Mr. Hill's research staff maintained a chart of the Department of Commerce's monthly data on inventories, sales, new orders, and order backlogs in the nonelectrical machinery industry. It appears as presented to Mr. Mertz in Exhibit 3. Mr. Hill pointed out that monthly sales for the industry had been falling off steadily in the latter half of 1957, and new orders had dropped behind sales. He compared this situation with that of late 1953, which had preceded the 1953 to 1954 recession. In support of his argument for a liberalization of credit terms, Mr. Hill said that competition in the industry would be worsened by a sales decline during the recession he felt "was in the cards." He was even more certain about "the near term prospects for dog-eat-dog sales competition" because he felt the industry had added greatly to its productive capacity during the 1955 through 1957 period, and he feared there would be strong efforts by individual companies to maintain sales above the resulting higher break-even points. By 1957 annual expenditures on new plant and equipment by the nonelectrical machinery industry had almost doubled at a yearly rate from the total of $694 million compiled in the recession year 1954. Mr. Hill "had a hunch" that the expansion of capacity may have been more excessive in the construction machinery industry than elsewhere because of rosy anticipations about the Federal Highway Program, which had not been met.

Though sympathetic with Mr. Hill's view about the likelihood of a recession and its probable effects on the industry, Mr. Mertz had questioned the need for liberalized sales terms. In reply, Mr. Hill had said that although he could not produce figures to buttress the point, he was certain that Koehring's competitors had been using progressively liberalized payment terms as a sales weapon in the last few years. This feeling came from field feedback, but also from Mr. Hill's observation that a number of the competitors had formed and had begun operating captive finance companies. He pointed out that these captives had been used to absorb the growing installment receivables produced by looser credit rationing and longer payment terms.[2] Moreover, it was

---

[2] The receivables accounts of Koehring's largest competitors consolidated with their captive company receivables are shown in Exhibit 6 with the exception of Euclid Division of General Motors, which used the facilities of Yellow Manufacturing Acceptance Corporation, a captive of General Motors.

common knowledge that many commercial banks had become loaned up in the tight money period of 1956 and 1957. This had placed a premium on manufacturer financing of installment sales. If Koehring failed to meet its competitors' deferred sales terms in the intense competition during the recession and beyond, Mr. Hill said, "sales will be 15% to 20% below" the level otherwise attainable.

At the conclusion of their conversation Mr. Mertz promised to return his views on the proposal within a few days.

Effects upon company financing

After this conversation, Mr. Mertz retained a number of doubts about the need for liberalization of sales terms, and also held reservations about Koehring's ability to meet the financial demands implied by such a program. On the other hand, he found the prospect of supporting sales at a high level to be most attractive because of its presumably beneficial effects on profits and cash flows (see Exhibits 4 and 5). Under the stimulus of booming sales, Koehring had participated in the industry's fixed asset expansion, and now a falling volume of production might prove awkward.

He asked a staff assistant to gather information on the credit terms currently offered by Koehring's competitors. Although confidential treatment by many companies made it impossible to assemble these data directly, the assistant returned the information in Exhibit 6 relating to a sample of competitors' accounts and notes receivable. Mr. Mertz noted some contrasts in sales results and receivables behavior between size classes of firm, product types, and time periods. These disparities reinforced his ambivalence about lengthening payment terms.

In view of these uncertainties Mr. Mertz reflected on a counter suggestion that would play upon the interest rates offered on installment financing and deemphasize the time period. If a competitive interest rate concession could be substituted for lengthy deferred sales contracts, it would minimize the cash committed to receivables. By the same token, however, the rate of return on the investment in installment receivables would be sliced, and Mr. Mertz noted that the add-on interest rates hypothesized in the proposed sales terms already were not high by industrial standards for cutoff rates of return applied to investment projects. Also, a reduction in interest rates below market was tantamount to a price cut, and to him not patently better than a forthright reduction of a gross margin. Also, since the company's president had recently voiced the need for intensified surveillance of the credit worthiness of Koehring's accounts, Mr. Mertz wondered whether the investment of funds in data processing equipment for centralized credit management might not be more profitable than investment in longer receivables.

A worrisome facet of the program was its effect on the company during the business recovery that would follow the recession. Even with liberalized terms, it was unlikely that the effect of the recession on sales could be stemmed altogether. Falling sales would result in liquidation of inventory and generation of cash, but commitment of this block of funds to a portfolio of lengthening receivables during the recession would pose a problem of financing inventory expansion in the ensuing upswing. The modest sales decline of 1954 had led to more than proportionate inventory reduction, but resurgent sales in 1955 resulted in considerable absorption of cash into inventory. With this experience fresh in mind, Mr. Mertz was particularly concerned about the problems of cash management entailed by the program over the next two years.

Exhibit 1

KOEHRING COMPANY

January 4, 1958

E. B. Hill
O. R. Mertz

SUBJECT: CREDIT

Dear Ed and Orville:

The recent experience with [name withheld] emphasizes what we have known for some time, namely that the low profit situation prevailing in the contracting industry will inevitably lead to some distributor failures and has already resulted in an extraordinary high level of contractor bankruptcies. At the same time these conditions make it necessary for us to engage in an increasing amount of credit business if we are to maintain anything like a normal level of market penetration and anything like the sales volume that is necessary to support our fixed overhead. We need, therefore, to take every precaution in our granting of credit to protect ourselves through title retention and other means against the contingency of customers or distributors failing financially.

One of the fundamental procedures that we need to follow is a greater degree of liaison between our divisions on credit matters. The way we have operated in the past it has been entirely possible, and in fact has happened, that one division would grant credit to a distributor who was currently in financial difficulties and not meeting payments to another division. We could reduce the possibility of this happening by having the various division credit managers check with all other divisions before granting credit. The time and expense involved in such a precedure would be substantial and the method quite cumbersome.

While we want to avoid as much as possible having reports sent here to the Central Office, I believe the circumstances make it necessary for us to require each division to make up a monthly credit report and send it to the Central Office where the various reports will be collated and danger spots pinpointed and reported back to the various divisions.

In addition we should undertake to set out for the divisional credit managers (many of whom operate in this capacity on a part-time basis only) those procedures which will minimize our possibilities of loss even in the event of a distributor or customer bankruptcy.

Exhibit 1—Continued

I would like to emphasize the responsibility for credit determination will still rest with the division but we must undertake to give them every assistance possible and see to it that they can carry out this responsibility with maximum effectiveness.

Yours truly,
KOEHRING COMPANY
(Signed) JULIEN
President

JRS/dz
cc: All Gen. Mgrs.

Exhibit 2

KOEHRING COMPANY

CROSS-CLASSIFICATION OF PRODUCERS AND PRODUCTS
IN CONSTRUCTION EQUIPMENT MANUFACTURING
1958

	Commercial-Sized Power Shovels and Cranes	Earthmoving and Other Construction Equipment*	Concrete Handling Equipment †
Large companies			
(Sales over $500 million)			
International Harvester		x	
Caterpillar		x	
Allis-Chalmers		x	
Euclid Division of General Motors		x	
Le Tourneau-Westinghouse		x	
Medium-sized companies			
(Sales $100–500 million)			
Baldwin-Lima-Hamilton	x	x	x
Worthington			x
Blaw-Knox			
Link-Belt	x	x	
Clark Equipment	x	x	
Small-sized companies			
(Sales less than $100 million)			
Harnischfeger	x		
Bucyrus-Erie	x	x	
Chain Belt		x	x
Thew Shovel	x	x	
Universal Marion	x		
American Hoist & Derrick	x		
Northwest Engineering	x	x	
Jaeger Machine			x
Unit Crane and Shovel	x		
Schield Bantam	x		
Gar Wood Industries	x	x	
Manitowoc Shipbuilding & Engin.	x		
Pettibone Mulliken		x	
Koehring	x	x	x

* Includes trench diggers, tandem road rollers, compactors, conveyor loaders, smaller earth dumpers, and other off-highway construction equipment.
† Includes primarily mixers, pavers, and spreaders.

Exhibit 3

KOEHRING COMPANY

SALES, NEW ORDERS, INVENTORIES, AND ORDER BACKLOGS IN
NONELECTRICAL MACHINERY MANUFACTURING, 1953–57

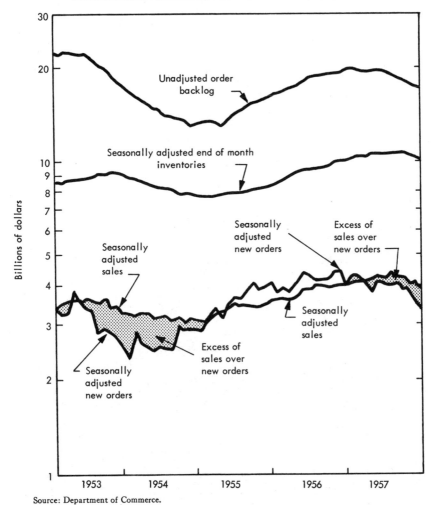

Source: Department of Commerce.

Exhibit 4

KOEHRING COMPANY

CONDENSED BALANCE SHEETS, 1953–57

(Dollar figures in thousands)

	Nov. 30, 1953	Nov. 30, 1954	Nov. 30, 1955	Nov. 30, 1956	Nov. 30, 1957
Current assets:					
Cash	$ 1,323	$ 1,024	$ 1,546	$ 1,412	$ 2,288
Notes and accounts receivable:					
Installment and deferred notes*	520	1,382	1,434	2,676	3,921
Trade accounts	1,661	2,070	2,435	3,718	4,075
Miscellaneous	28	46	82	86	152
Less: Allowance for doubtful accounts	(92)	(101)	(99)	(160)	(178)
Net receivables	$ 2,117	$ 3,397	$ 3,852	$ 6,320	$ 7,970
Inventories	11,385	9,707	12,991	22,510	26,259
Other	434	350	437	578	572
Total current assets	$15,259	$14,478	$18,826	$30,820	$37,089
Investments	$ 67	$ 44	$ 41	$ 267	$ 187
Property, plant, and equipment:					
Land	$ 538	$ 327	$ 335	$ 408	$ 504
Buildings, machinery and equipment, and construction in progress	11,339	11,388	12,210	19,019	22,087
Gross fixed assets	$11,877	$11,715	$12,545	$19,427	$22,591
Less: Accumulated depreciation	(6,009)	(5,770)	(6,577)	(10,049)	(11,407)
Net fixed assets	$ 5,868	$ 5,945	$ 5,968	$ 9,378	$11,184
Other assets	$ 39	$ 50	$ 46	$ 14	$ 13
Total assets	$21,233	$20,517	$24,881	$40,479	$48,473
* Including installment notes due after one year:	n.a.	$ 168	$ 188	$ 241	$ 460

NOTES FOR BALANCE SHEET

A. Of the $4\frac{1}{4}\%$ notes payable to insurance companies, $2,728,000 are payable in quarterly installments of $62,500 and the remaining $812,000 are payable in annual installments of $83,000. In addition, the conformed loan agreements covering these notes provide for annual sinking fund payments equal to 25% of the excess of consolidated net income, as defined, over $500,000, provided that such payments shall not exceed a calculated amount approximating $129,000 in any year.

The $5\frac{1}{4}\%$ notes payable to insurance companies are payable $250,000 on December 1, 1965, and $500,000 annually thereafter to December 1, 1973, when the remainder is due.

Among other provisions, the various loan agreements and amendments offered by the insurance companies covering the foregoing notes contain certain restrictions and requirements, which are summarized as follows: (1) the company is required to maintain consolidated net working capital of $20,000,000; (2) additional long-term borrowings are restricted to purchase money borrowings up to $200,000; (3) short-term borrowings are limited to $12,000,000 with the further requirement that the company be free of such borrowings for a period of 90 days annually.

The $4\frac{3}{4}\%$ first mortgage sinking fund bonds issued by the Canadian subsidiary, Koehring-Waterous Ltd., mature June 30, 1974, but the subsidiary is to provide a sinking fund sufficient to redeem $25,000 principal amount of the bonds annually beginning June 30, 1956.

Exhibit 4—Continued

	Nov. 30, 1953	Nov. 30, 1954	Nov. 30, 1955	Nov. 30, 1956	Nov. 30, 1957
Current liabilities:					
Notes payable: Secured	$ 1,177	$ 910	$ 841	$ 1,153	0
Unsecured	1,600	0	1,900	6,550	$ 6,990
Long-term debt due within one year	300	272	376	489	488
Trade accounts payable	937	885	1,705	2,115	1,289
Other accounts payable	0	0	0	1,127	830
Accrued payments to employees	515	527	546	1,084	854
Taxes on income	1,465	871	1,844	3,047	1,701
Miscellaneous	519	519	789	721	605
Total current liabilities	$ 6,513	$ 3,984	$ 8,001	$16,286	$12,757
Long-term debt—Note A:					
4¼% notes payable insurance companies	$ 1,800	$ 3,078	$ 2,928	$ 3,540	$ 3,078
5¼% notes payable insurance companies	0	0	0	0	4,500
3½% notes payable bank	550	350	150	0	0
4¾% first mortgage bonds	0	513	487	461	436
Total long-term debt	$ 2,350	$ 3,941	$ 3,565	$ 4,001	$ 8,014
Stockholders' investment:					
5% cumulative convertible Series A	0	0	0	$ 2,639	$ 2,618
preferred:* Series B	0	0	0	0	1,699
Common stock† and paid-in capital	$ 5,372	$ 5,374	$ 5,398	$ 6,527	$12,124
Retained earnings	6,998	7,218	7,917	11,026	11,261
Total net worth	$12,370	$12,592	$13,315	$20,192	$27,702
Total liabilities and net worth	$21,233	$20,517	$24,881	$40,479	$48,473

	1953	1954	1955	1956	1957
Common stock price trading range‡					
High	10	9⅞	14¾	25	25¼
Low	7⅞	7½	9¾	14½	13½

	Series A ($50 par)	Series B ($50 par)
* Preferred shares outstanding at year-end: 1956	52,777	0
1957	52,369	33,987
Basic conversion price per share of common stock:		
Prior to July 1, 1958	$23.06	$38.92
July 1, 1958 to June 30, 1961	24.51	46.13
After June 30, 1961	25.95	60.54

† Common shares outstanding at year-end:

1953	348,719
1954	348,761
1955	349,624
1956	1,206,290
1957	1,481,740

‡ Adjusted for splits and stock dividends.

Exhibit 5

KOEHRING COMPANY

Condensed Operating Statements, 1953–57

(Dollar figures in thousands)

	Nov. 30, 1953	Nov. 30, 1954	Nov. 30, 1955	Nov. 30, 1956	Nov. 30, 1957
Income					
Net shipments	$26,157	$25,197	$30,181	$51,765	$55,668
Royalties and service fees	226	234	283	401	377
Interest income	41	51	70	131	177
Other income	23	73	38	86	172
Total	$26,447	$25,555	$30,572	$52,383	$56,394
Expenses					
Cost of product sold	$22,962*	$23,123*	$26,154*	$39,385	$43,101
Selling, administrative, and general expenses				5,255	6,582
Depreciation	633	812	893	1,472	1,657
Interest expense	161	271	237	536	660
On long-term borrowings				196	290
Other				340	370
Employee profit sharing and retirement trusts	119	38	147	303	227
Income taxes	1,342	526	1,673	2,883	2,230
Other expenses	32	0	0	0	0
Total expenses	$25,249	$24,770	$29,104	$49,834	$54,457
Net earnings	$ 1,198	$ 785	$ 1,468	$ 2,549	$ 1,937
Dividends paid: Common†	$ 657	$ 767	$ 768	$ 900	$ 1,480
Preferred				66	222

* Including selling, general, and administrative expenses.
† Dividends per share were $0.72 in 1953–56 and $1.00 in 1957.

Exhibit 6

KOEHRING COMPANY

RELATIONSHIP OF RECEIVABLES TO SALES IN THE CONSTRUCTION
MACHINERY MANUFACTURING INDUSTRY, 1955–57

(Dollar figures in millions)

	Finance Subsidiary	Net Sales to Dealers			Accounts and Notes Receivable*			Accounts and Notes Receivable as % of Net Sales		
		1955	1956	1957	1955	1956	1957	1955	1956	1957
Large										
International Harvester	1949	$947.2	$1,008.5	$969.9	$251.1	$332.9	$380.9	26.5%	33.1%	39.3%
Caterpillar	1954	523.9	685.9	649.9	51.4	64.5	63.5	9.8	9.4	9.8
Allis-Chalmers	1956	535.1	547.4	534.1	118.6	133.5	145.7	22.2	24.4	27.3
Medium										
Worthington	no	140.9	170.2	191.5	27.0	35.1	41.2	19.2	20.4	21.5
Baldwin-Lima-Hamilton	no	160.3	195.3	184.4	31.3	38.9	38.9	19.5	19.7	21.0
Blaw-Knox	no	109.2	167.0	182.7	17.9	25.9	26.5	16.3	15.5	14.5
Link-Belt	no	129.5	163.9	163.5	19.4	20.6	21.2	15.0	12.6	13.0
Clark Equipment	1954	131.3	145.4	143.1	35.4	44.8	44.6	26.9	30.8	31.2
Small										
Harnischfeger	1956	66.3	81.1	87.5	9.7	10.0	11.2	14.7	12.2	12.9
Bucyrus-Erie	no	71.7	86.6	87.5	8.0	10.8	8.9	11.1	12.5	10.1
Chain Belt	no	45.2	56.8	59.6	5.7	7.1	7.8	12.6	12.5	13.1
Koehring	no	30.2	51.8	55.7	3.9	6.3	8.0	12.7	12.2	14.3
Gar Wood Industries	no	29.9	41.0	43.4	4.5	4.9	3.2	15.0	12.0	7.4
Pettibone Mulliken	no	24.0	34.5	41.8	3.6	4.9	5.9	15.0	14.2	14.1
Thew Shovel	no	34.7	46.3	36.4	3.8	3.8	2.3	11.1	8.3	6.3
American Hoist & Derrick	1955	21.4	30.8	35.6	2.9	4.3	6.3	13.5	13.9	17.7
Jaeger Machine	no	12.6	16.5	15.9	1.7	1.7	1.8	13.5	10.5	11.5
Schield Bantam	no	9.3	10.2	7.9	0.7	0.9	0.9	7.5	9.0	11.5

* The accounts and notes receivable figures reflect the consolidation of a finance subsidiary where this is appropriate, except for Harnischfeger and American Hoist & Derrick, whose finance subsidiary balance sheets were unavailable. Accounts and notes receivable carried net of reserves and unearned finance charges.

Part II

long-term financing

BURKE CANDY COMPANY

In October, 1949, after a dispute between stockholders of the Burke Candy Company, Mr. A. K. Martin, a St. Louis businessman, agreed to act as chairman of a committee to establish a value for 1,000 shares of the common stock. At the time, there were 10,000 shares of common stock outstanding; these were owned by various descendants of Jeremiah Burke, who had founded the company in 1860. A majority of the shares were held by three grandsons of Jeremiah Burke, each of whom was active in the management of the company. The board of directors of the company included the grandsons, the company's lawyer, and a commercial banker.

A cousin, Mrs. Richard Wilson, who owned 1,000 shares, over a period of time had expressed sharp dissatisfaction with the policies and results of the majority's management. After protracted discussion the majority stockholders agreed to buy Mrs. Wilson's shares at "a fair price." However, the ideas of the management group and Mrs. Wilson and her lawyer as to "fair value" were very different. Finally, each group agreed to the appointment of a three-man committee to establish the value of the shares. Each group named one man to the committee, and the two nominees together selected Mr. Martin as the third member and chairman of the committee.

Realizing that his views as to the value of the stock might well prove decisive, Mr. Martin undertook an inquiry into the affairs and financial status of the company.

He learned that the Burke Candy Company had long operated as a "general-line house," that is, it manufactured a wide variety of candies with no one type of candy predominating. While most candy houses had started in this way, by 1948 most confectionery manufacturers had specialized in one or more lines, so that general-line houses accounted for only some 11% of total industry sales. Burke products included five-and-ten-cent specialty items, such as packages of mints and caramels; package goods, chiefly in the less than one dollar per pound retail category; bulk goods, such as hard "Christmas candy" and unpackaged chocolates; penny goods, such as small marshmallow eggs; and candy bars. The company was generally acknowledged as the first American manufacturer of one of the popular types of chocolate bars. This candy was first marketed about 1900 in the form of large blocks, which the retailer cut apart to sell. The Burke company then furnished the retailer with small glassine bags in each box of blocks so the retailer could cut the bar from the block and slip it into a bag as he gave it to the customer. A change in manufacturing was next introduced so that each bar was a separate piece of candy. This change was enthusiastically received, and the company then decided to wrap each bar separately and label each wrapper "Burke's Best-Bet Bar."

Despite its early success with the Best-Bet Bar the company did not go along with a general tendency in the industry toward specialization in bar goods or other types of candy, and sales of Best-Bet Bar did not grow relatively to competitive products. During World War II, however, the company did sell large quantities of Best-Bet Bar and other bar items to the Army and Navy for sale in PX's and Ships' Stores. As military demand fell off, postwar sales returned to the prewar pattern of wide distribution among product lines.

Like most candy manufacturers, Burke owned no retail outlets. The company's products were marketed through brokers and by the company's own sales force. Direct sales effort was concentrated in Missouri and adjoining states and primarily on candy and tobacco jobbers and on grocery, variety, and drug chains. Sales through brokers were primarily made to candy jobbers. In an effort to compensate for declining military sales, the sales manager in 1946 and 1947 had expended substantial amounts in national magazines and in trade-paper advertising and other efforts to gain national distribution through brokers. Almost half of 1948 sales had been through brokers, many in distant areas. One broker in Texas had been particularly effective in producing volume. On the other hand, the advertising expense involved had been substantial, and the company was forced to absorb almost all the freight in order to compete successfully in distant states. Further, the brokers, who operated on a 5% commission, appeared to concentrate their efforts on standard product items, which were easy to sell but carried a very low margin to the manufacturer.

In general, competition among manufacturing confectioners was keen, except during World War II when sugar rationing limited production and demand was strong. Competition was particularly keen in unbranded candies, and with the exception of its candy bars, most of the Burke products were unbranded or had brands that meant very little to buyers. Two other candy manufacturers located in St. Louis competed directly with the company in the metropolitan area, and manufacturers in Chicago and Indianapolis also competed strongly in the St. Louis market area.

Reviewing the financial records of the company, Mr. Martin found that operations had been profitable during the 1920's. Severe competition had developed during the 1930's, and recurring losses were suffered owing to declining sales and an apparent tendency to change too slowly with the times. The company had entered the depression in strong financial condition, however, and had successfully withstood the drain of cash caused by unprofitable operations. Operations proved profitable in 1939, and the development of a sellers' market during World War II contributed to very profitable years. Management officials pointed out, however, that the lack of profits during prewar years had given the company an unfavorably low base of "normal" earnings for purposes of excess profits taxation. Consequently, Burke's excess profits taxes were higher than those of its competitors with similar earnings *before* taxes. As is indicated in Exhibit 2, postwar operations were also profitable until 1948.

Mr. Martin talked at length with the management regarding the large losses suffered in 1948 and in the first eight months of 1949. The management explained that a large portion of the losses in 1948 had resulted from a very sharp and unexpected decline in the market prices for chocolate, sugar, and other major raw materials. The cost of raw materials accounted for almost 80% of total cost of sales, and the purchasing officer had made heavy forward commitments at fixed prices during 1947 and early 1948. At the same time that the market prices of these commodities were falling rapidly, a decline in the company's own physical volume of sales set in. For competitive reasons it was necessary to reduce the company's selling prices substantially. Further, management at first had diagnosed the decline in sales as a temporary development. Consequently, appropriate retrenchment measures were not taken for some months after sales declined.

By August, 1949, a number of steps had been taken to remedy the situation, and operations in August were profitable for the first time in many months. Purchasing methods had been revised so as to minimize the risks of further inventory price decline. Steps had also been taken to strengthen the management of the company through employment of a young and aggressive man with an excellent educational background, who had been highly successful during a business career of some 10 years. This man, the son of one of the majority stockholders, had been established as executive vice president and given substantial responsibilities for the overall direction of the company. In addition, major changes had been made in the company's sales methods and personnel. The sales force had been strengthened and major efforts had been made to improve the company's sales effort in the home St. Louis area.

Painstaking analysis had been made of the profitability of various product items and lines. As a result, a number of unprofitable items were dropped and sales effort was shifted to particularly promising and profitable items. New product development was also being pushed aggressively.

In general, management officials were convinced that the new policies were well advised and would produce results.

In the summer of 1948 the board of directors voted to suspend the dividend payments. It was then that Mrs. Wilson, whose only income from the company was in the form of dividends, expressed particular concern and sought the advice of her lawyer, Mr. L. K. Eagle, regarding her investment. Dividend payments since 1938 are shown in Exhibit 2.

Since the stock was held only by members of the Burke family and all transfers had been among various members of the family, no market for the shares of the company existed. Investigation showed that there was no active market in the shares of any confectionery manufacturing company of comparable size and nature in the Midwest, so that no closely comparable market quotations were available as guides to the value of the Burke stock.

Acting in anticipation of difficulty in arriving at a satisfactory valuation, Mr. Roger Burke, the new executive vice president of the company, in September requested the Midwestern Company, local investment bankers, to undertake an appraisal of the value of the stock. Largely on the basis of the summary data given in Exhibits 1 and 2, along with personal discussion of the firm's affairs and policies with its officers, the Midwestern Company had arrived at a maximum valuation of $12 per share. Their report took the form of a letter, attached as Exhibit 3.

Mr. Martin talked at some length with officials of the Burke company regarding the financial statements as of August 31, shown in Exhibits 1 and 2. He first sought to establish the validity of the book value of the stock as shown on the balance sheet. He was told that the accounts receivable consisted entirely of receivables from the trade for merchandise sold. The amount of receivables shown was net of a reserve for bad debts of $30,000. This reserve had been accumulated over several years and was considered more than ample to cover expected bad debt losses. The raw material inventory consisted primarily of cornstarch and syrup, chocolate, sugar, and nuts. Mr. Martin satisfied himself that the company maintained accurate inventory records and that the material concerned was in good physical condition. Inventories were valued at the lower of cost or market. Prepaid expenses consisted largely of prepaid insurance premiums. Company officials explained that the large investment in United States bonds represented a temporary investment of funds earmarked to pay for machinery soon to be ordered. This machinery was needed to modernize several of the company's manufacturing operations, and management believed that the machines would pay for themselves in a few years by lowering costs.

In the opinion of company officials the fixed assets of the company were very conservatively valued. Operations were carried on in a multistory concrete building, which with an annex building occupied an entire city block in the center of an industrial area. Advanced construction ideas had been incorporated in the construction of the main building in 1909, and the building was considered in excellent condition and entirely adequate for the needs of the company. With the land it stood on, the annex building, carried in the balance sheet at $182,914 (net of the reserve for depreciation), was also of concrete construction and of multipurpose type. This building had housed certain operations of the company discontinued in 1938. At that time the building was leased to a bakery company that was expanding its operations. When the 10-year lease expired in 1948 a shortage of factory buildings in the area existed, and the company was able to lease the 84,000 square foot building for one year at $0.55 a square foot, or $46,200. The lessee assumed all costs of the building except property taxes, which were about $10,000 a year. In September, 1949, it was expected that a five-year lease would be signed at about $0.45 a square foot per annum, or $37,800 before taxes.

The multistory building in which the operations of the company were conducted provided a total floor area of 133,400 square feet. Current construction costs of similar buildings were approximately $8 a square foot. The management believed that with an unhurried sale of the main building, it could realize approximately $3.50 a square foot or approximately $466,900 for the building. The newer annex building was thought to have a normal resale value of about $4.50 a square foot.

The equipment of the company was considered fairly efficient, although much of it had been in use for many years. It was believed that depreciation rates had been appropriate, so that the balance sheet values represented reasonable values from the accounting point of view.

When Mr. Martin raised the question of realizable values in the event the company was liquidated, the officials of the company appeared reluctant to discuss the subject. They commented that many of the 175 employees of the company had been with the concern for many years, that they had faith in the business, and that management had no intention of terminating the business. Finally, they did agree to discuss the value in liquidation of each major asset. It was believed that the net value of receivables could be collected completely, with perhaps a 10% excess of collections over the amount shown net of the unusually large reserve. The liquidating value of the inventory was regarded as hinging on the speed of liquidation. It was felt that in an unhurried liquidation the inventory could be completely worked off at between 60% and 80% of its book value. Much of the value of prepaid expenses would be lost in liquidation, so that an estimate of 25% was given as the realizable value. The value of the fixed assets in liquidation was regarded as particularly problematical. If a willing buyer was available, as indicated above, the two buildings probably could be sold at approximately $3.50 and $4.50 per square foot. If no buyer was anxious to have the space for immediate use, distress sale could be expected to attract buyers only at a very much lower price. Currently, the market for industrial real estate in the area was active, and it was thought that a willing buyer could be found within a few months.

The value of the equipment in liquidation was highly uncertain. It was thought of most value to a candy manufacturer who would take over the entire plant. In 1947, the company had received and rejected informal inquiries from two large manufacturers regarding the possibility of sale of the company to them for operation as a branch plant. No inquiries had been received since that time. Much of the equipment would be next to valueless in a hurried liquidation, and the total proceeds from equipment under such circumstances would probably be no more than 30% of the book value.

Exhibit 1

BURKE CANDY COMPANY

BALANCE SHEET, AUGUST 31, 1949

ASSETS

Cash..		$ 13,396
Accounts receivable, net............................		32,673
Inventory:		
Raw materials..................................	$101,665	
Candies in process..............................	13,833	
Finished candies.................................	84,209	
Packaging materials.............................	32,002	
Other supplies..................................	8,183	239,892
Prepaid expenses....................................		25,606
U.S. bonds..		145,172
Total current assets......................		$456,739
Factory building and land, net.......................		61,868
Annex building and land, net........................		182,914
Equipment, net......................................		200,072
Total assets................................		$901,593

LIABILITIES

Accounts payable—trade and commissions.............		$ 51,944
Notes payable—bank................................		75,000
Accrued expense.....................................		28,080
Total current liabilities......................		$155,024
Common stock ($11.50 par)..		115,000
Reserve for contingencies............................		65,856
Paid-in surplus.....................................		562,092
Earned surplus January 1, 1949......................	$ 14,060	
Plus tax refund to company..........................	108,844	
Less loss since January 1, 1949......................	119,283	
Earned surplus August 31, 1949......................		3,621
Net worth August 31, 1949..........................		$746,569
Total liabilities.............................		$901,593

Exhibit 2

BURKE CANDY COMPANY

SELECTED DATA

	Net Sales	Net Profit or (Loss) before Taxes	Net Profit or (Loss) after Taxes	Dividends
1938.....................$	975,714	$ (38,934)	$ (38,934)	.....
1939....................	930,942	(27,493)	(27,493)	.....
1940....................	956,425	(25,647)	(25,647)	.....
1941....................	1,175,383	27,007	27,007	.....
1942....................	1,423,455	136,456	86,027	$23,000
1943....................	1,679,869	220,755	76,002	34,500
1944....................	1,917,260	193,343	45,169	40,250
1945....................	1,914,799	216,427	61,464	40,250
1946....................	2,073,594	201,531	89,915	46,000
1947....................	2,636,122	316,302	143,802	80,500
1948....................	1,769,103	(212,806)	(117,791)	23,000
1949—8 months.........	700,495	(119,283)	(119,283)†	.....

Exhibit 2—Continued

	Net Profit or (Loss) after Taxes as Percentage of Net Sales		Net Profit or (Loss) after Taxes as Percentage of Net Worth	
	Industry*	Burke	Industry*	Burke
1938	1.5%	(4.0)%	3.8%	(5.5)%
1939	2.1	(3.0)	5.9	(4.0)
1940	2.2	(2.7)	6.5	(4.0)
1941	2.8	2.3	8.6	4.0
1942	4.1	6.0	15.8	11.5
1943	4.7	4.5	16.0	9.7
1944	5.2	2.4	20.1	5.8
1945	2.9	3.2	13.5	7.5
1946	7.9	4.3	11.8	9.7
1947	7.0	5.5	19.2	15.7
1948	6.5	(12.0)†	13.9	(28.1)†

Comparison of Selected Ratios, 1948

	Industry*	Burke
Turnover of net worth	2.68	2.34
Turnover of working capital	5.32	4.92
Average collection period	15 days	15 days
Current ratio	3.48	2.50
Fixed assets to net worth	41.5%	58.6%
Total debt to net worth	35.8%	27.6%

* Figures are the median figures reported by 45 firms.
† Before tax refund credit, which can be carried back against prior year's earnings.

Exhibit 3

BURKE CANDY COMPANY

LETTER FROM THE MIDWESTERN COMPANY

September 20, 1949

Mr. Roger Burke
Burke Candy Company
203 West Illinois Street
St. Louis 6, Missouri

DEAR MR. BURKE

We have made an examination of the Burke Candy Company based principally upon financial statements furnished us by you, and other information which you have given us; and we have also examined the markets of stocks and financial statements of other companies in similar lines of business, so as to arrive at an opinion as to a fair value for the stock of the Burke Candy Company.

As I told you over the phone today, this is a very difficult question for us to answer, principally because the pattern of sales and earnings of your company does not justify its comparison with the history of the other companies with which you compete. These other companies in general have profits for most of the years, if not all of the years, under review; while your company has made money only during the war and the first year or two after the war, and during 1948 and the first eight months of 1949 has lost a substantial amount of money. The stock of the Burke Candy Company, therefore, could not be valued on the same basis as the other stocks, being intrinsically more speculative.

Exhibit 3—Continued

The speculative aspects of the stock are increased by the fact that your company is now evidently changing its type of business and has not yet indicated any earnings possibilities from the new type of business. In addition, the change-over requires a relatively substantial capital expenditure which has depleted and will probably continue to deplete your working capital position.

The company has some real estate holdings which might be used as a source of additional working capital if sold; but you have not indicated any such intention, and therefore I assume that the company will have to get along for capital expenditures and current operations on its present working capital position, augmented by profits in the future, if any.

As I told you, there is usually no relationship between market value and book value when valuing common stocks; in fact, any study of such relationship leads to such wide disparities that the only conclusion from such a study can be that there is no connection between market value and book value.

I believe the only likely buyer of stock of your company would be some person familiar with the type of business you are in, who would be willing to buy control at a sacrifice price and take over the management of the company in the hopes of making operations profitable and therefore of making himself a substantial profit by entering into the management. I do not believe it would be possible to sell the stock to investors in this area, because the company's record does not justify such an offering.

We are of the opinion that the stock of the Burke Candy Company, based largely on the previous comments, is not worth over $12.00 per share.

I am sure that you will appreciate that the comments made above are not in any way a reflection on the management of the company, but are made from the point of view of an outsider looking at the figures and the company's course of business in an effort to arrive at an impartial valuation of the stock.

Very truly yours,
MIDWESTERN COMPANY

(Signed) JOHN K. GRIMES

Vice President

UPSTATE CANNING COMPANY, INC.

During the period following his graduation from a business school in 1950, Mr. Nelson Shields had attempted to prepare himself for the opportunity of becoming the manager and sole or part owner of a company with real growth possibilities. Because he lacked financial resources, he had sought employment offering substantial immediate income as well as managerial experience that would be useful in later years. This search led him successively through positions in three distinctly different businesses, in each of which experience was largely concentrated in the sales and sales management areas. By 1956 he had accumulated personal savings of $15,000, which added to some family money placed at his disposal gave him an investment fund of $35,000.

At this point, Mr. Shields had begun an active search for opportunities to purchase an existing business. In the course of the year he looked into about 25 possibilities that came to his attention. Some of these were quickly rejected; others involved the expenditure of considerable time and some money before a negative decision was reached. While looking for business possibilities, Mr. Shields also sought to develop contacts with business and professional men who might be induced to invest equity capital in an attractive opportunity, should one be found requiring more capital than he possessed. By the end of 1956 he was still investigating business leads, but with no real prospect in sight. Meanwhile, the pressure to settle on a business was increasing. He had given up employment in October in order to devote full time to his search, and he realized that he could not afford many months of unemployment without eating into the sum set aside for investment.

In February, 1957, a business broker called Mr. Shields to advise him that a small cannery had just come up for sale. The property consisted of two plants, equipped for the canning of fruits and vegetables, which were located close to the source of supply in rural towns in New York State. The business, known as the Upstate Canning Company, Inc., was owned and managed by Mr. A. C. Fordham. Mr. Fordham's health was uncertain and at 55 he had decided to sell out because he had no relatives to take his place in the business. The broker urged Mr. Shields to investigate this opportunity because it looked as though it might fit his circumstances.

Mr. Shields immediately set out to learn what he could about the fruit and vegetable canning industry in general and this business in particular. The

113

broker arranged a meeting with Mr. Fordham; and from this and subsequent meetings and telephone conversations, Mr. Shields assembled a picture of the business.

In general, Mr. Fordham was very cooperative in providing the information requested from him. He was reluctant, however, to disclose the financial details of operations for the three years prior to 1956. During 1952 Mr. Fordham had brought in a general manager on a three-year employment contract as a means of easing himself out of the day-to-day responsibilities of the business. The new man had not worked out well, and sales and profits had suffered as a result. Upon the termination of this contract, Mr. Fordham had again assumed full management responsibilities, and results in 1956 improved substantially over those of 1953, 1954, and 1955. Mr. Fordham argued that these years were not representative of the earnings potential of the business and that 1956 should be taken as the most accurate measure of its possibilities. From what Mr. Shields had been able to find out about the business from other sources, he was inclined to accept Mr. Fordham's explanation and to base his estimates on the figures for 1956.

The physical plant of the business appeared to be in very good condition. The two buildings had been kept in excellent repair, and the canning equipment was modern. The combined plant and equipment had recently been appraised for insurance purposes, and their value had been placed at $200,000. Mr. Shields was assured that no major repairs would be necessary over the next few years.

Mr. Fordham had been accustomed to operating the plants only during the limited harvest season for the fruits and vegetables that he canned. The season lasted for four months, from July through October, with August and September normally accounting for two thirds of the company's total production. At times, Mr. Fordham had considered stretching out the production period with other canning operations, but he had never taken any action on the idea. During the 1956 season Upstate had produced canned fruits and vegetables with a total value of $850,000 (valued at Upstate's selling price). This production represented only about 50% of combined productive capacity of the plants during the production season. Excess capacity was attributed to the substantial expansion of facilities that had been undertaken to meet wartime demands.

The vegetables and fruits canned by Upstate were bought on a contract basis from farmers in the surrounding area; farmers were paid cash on delivery on the basis of prevailing market prices at the time of delivery. The quantities canned by Upstate varied to some extent with the crop conditions from year to year; normally, output could be increased considerably, however, by noncontract purchases if good marketing opportunities existed. The production process was almost entirely mechanical, and the towns and surrounding areas offered an ample supply of seasonal labor sufficiently skilled to perform the various operations in the plant. Labor was paid on a weekly basis.

The products of the Upstate Canning Company were marketed primarily under the Upstate brand through jobbers. It was the normal practice to sell the entire season's pack before the next canning season began, so that little inventory would be carried over from one year to the next. Sales tended to be concentrated during and immediately following the production period. Mr. Fordham indicated that about 50% of the pack would normally be sold by the end of the canning season (October) and 70% by the end of December. The rest of the sales were customarily spread rather evenly over the remaining months through June.

Mr. Shields was particularly attracted by the marketing opportunities of the business. It was his impression that Mr. Fordham had not been aggressive in sales promotion—that much better use could be made of the company's productive capacity. Mr. Shields believed that he could greatly increase the scale of operations by undertaking an active but relatively inexpensive sales program. He had in mind direct sales to supermarket chains of both Upstate and private brands, to be obtained largely through his own efforts with no significant increase in present selling costs.

Relying on these expectations, Mr. Shields prepared a five-year sales program (see Exhibit 1) which he planned to use as the basis of his estimates of profits and working capital requirements. He was informed by Mr. Fordham that collections on accounts receivable caused little trouble in this business; bad-debt losses were rare, and accounts were normally collected within 30 days. Mr. Shields expected that the planned expansion would not affect this collection period and might even improve it, because he would be increasing direct sales to large accounts.

In examining the cost aspects of the business, Mr. Shields soon became aware of the high proportion of variable costs. The principal items were the fruits and vegetables and other ingredients, cans, and direct labor. As previously indicated, fruits and vegetables were bought on a cash basis, labor was paid weekly at fixed hourly rates, and cans and "other ingredients" were purchased on normal terms of 2/10, net 30 days. The details of revenues and costs for 1956 are shown in Exhibits 2 and 3.

As negotiations proceeded, it became evident that Mr. Fordham was anxious to sell the business as soon as possible. The new crop season was coming on; and Mr. Fordham felt that if he were to operate the business for another year, it would soon be necessary to sign contracts with farmers for the year's production. After three weeks, during which Mr. Shields was gathering and studying information and talking to bankers, can company officials, government agencies, and others, Mr. Fordham came forward with a specific proposal for the sale of the business (see Exhibit 4).

The plan anticipated that Mr. Shields would organize a new company and purchase certain Upstate assets, namely, its plant and equipment, a small amount of finished goods inventory, and the right to use the Upstate brand names. Current assets (other than the inventory mentioned above) and liabilities of the old company would not pass to the new company. It was apparent from the plan that Mr. Fordham had guessed that Mr. Shields had very limited resources and, accordingly, had provided for an installment purchase of Upstate assets through the gradual redemption of $300,000 of income bonds to be issued to Mr. Fordham. By this time, Mr. Shields had become convinced that this business was sufficiently promising to justify a full and detailed study of Mr. Fordham's proposal.

Before accepting the proposal or making a counterproposal, it was necessary for Mr. Shields to determine how the new company was to be financed. His best lead for additional equity capital was a professional man who had indicated that he was prepared to invest as much as $100,000 if the right opportunity came along. This man was 50 years of age, and his investment goal appeared to be capital appreciation over the years rather than immediate income.

Mr. Shields was determined that the plan for the new company would include a means by which he could become the owner of 51% of the voting stock as soon as possible. More specifically, he hoped to obtain control within five years, and hence was intent on arranging a compensation plan for himself as manager that would enable him to accomplish this objective. Mr. Shields's plan, as tentatively formulated, provided for a basic salary of $15,000 plus 5% of profits before taxes; these figures took account of his estimate that roughly 60% of his annual income would be absorbed by living expenses and tax payments. His plan also included an option to buy enough additional shares—either new shares to be issued by the company or outstanding shares held by his associate(s)—to raise Mr. Shields's holdings to 51% of all outstanding voting stock. It was clear, however, that the exact details of the final plan would have to be worked out with the other shareholder or shareholders before arrangements could be completed with Mr. Fordham.

As part of his program to assure an adequate supply of capital, Mr. Shields obtained an introduction, through a mutual friend, to one of the officers of a medium-sized bank in a nearby city. This officer indicated that it was the bank's normal policy to avoid substantial loans to new enterprises, but that exceptions were occasionally made where there was adequate security. Canning operations were important to the surrounding area, and he suggested that the bank might consider a secured loan to the new company if it looked promising on closer examination. From further conversation, Mr. Shields concluded that the best possibility would be a loan of up to 75% of the cost of finished goods inventory under a field warehousing arrangement. The cost of this kind of financing, including field warehousing expenses, which would not otherwise have been incurred, would be about 6% per annum. In addition to the bank loan, Mr. Shields also believed that it might be possible to stretch the payment period on cans to 60 days without creating serious credit problems.

In considering his preliminary calculations, Mr. Shields planned to make a detailed study of the year 1957–58 and to use this as a basis for approximating the necessary figures for the fiscal years 1958–59 through 1961–62. He had in mind a fiscal year beginning July 1.

Mr. Shields was aware that the next move was up to him. As he saw it, there were three obvious courses of action: (1) accept Mr. Fordham's proposal as presented; (2) reject the proposal and look for another business; or (3) propose a compromise plan that would have a reasonable prospect of meeting the objectives of all interested parties.

Exhibit 1

UPSTATE CANNING COMPANY, INC.

PLANNED SALES VOLUME, 1957–62

1957–58...........................	$ 850,000
1958–59...........................	1,050,000
1959–60...........................	1,250,000
1960–61...........................	1,450,000
1961–62...........................	1,650,000

Exhibit 2

UPSTATE CANNING COMPANY, INC.

INCOME STATEMENT FOR YEAR ENDED DECEMBER 31, 1956

(Dollar figures in thousands)

		Amount	Percent of Sales
Sales (net after returns and allowances).......................		$850	100%
Less: Cost of goods sold			
Beginning inventory, January 1, 1956...................	$257		
Add: Cost of goods manufactured......................	630		
	$887		
Ending inventory, December 31, 1956..................	254	633	74
Gross profit on sales..		$217	
Less: Selling and administrative expense			
Selling and delivery...................................	$ 64		8
Administrative and general (including salary to			
Mr. Fordham of $20,000)..........................	56	120	7
Profit before taxes..		$ 97	
Less: Federal income tax*...................................		45	5
Net profit after taxes.......................................		$ 52	6

* Federal income tax was computed on the basis of 30% of the first $25,000 of taxable income plus 52% of income in excess of $25,000. For companies of this size the tax was payable in the succeeding fiscal year as follows: 50% on the 15th day of the 3d month following the end of the tax year and 50% on the 15th day of the 6th month following.

Exhibit 3

UPSTATE CANNING COMPANY, INC.

STATEMENT OF COST OF GOODS MANUFACTURED FOR
YEAR ENDED DECEMBER 31, 1956

(Dollar figures in thousands)

		Amount	Percent of Total Cost of Goods Manufactured
Direct costs:			
Vegetables and fruit	$232		
Labor	138		
Cans	112		
Other ingredients	36	$518	82%
Variable overhead:			
Fuel oil	$ 17		
Electricity and water	7		
Factory supplies	5		
Payroll taxes	7		
Truck and auto expenses	2		
Gas and oil	5	43	7
Fixed overhead:			
Repairs and maintenance	$ 18		
Insurance	12		
Property taxes	10		
Depreciation—plant and equipment	24		
Machinery rental	5	$ 69	11
Total cost of goods manufactured		$630	100%

Exhibit 4

UPSTATE CANNING COMPANY, INC.

INITIAL PROPOSAL BY MR. FORDHAM FOR THE PURCHASE OF CERTAIN ASSETS OF
THE UPSTATE CANNING COMPANY, INC., BY MR. SHIELDS AND ASSOCIATE(S)

1. New corporation to be formed with capitalization of $400,000 and with a capital structure as follows:
   a) $100,000 of common stock, $1 par, one vote per share, to be issued to Shields and associate(s) for $100,000 cash. Cash to be retained in new corporation.
   b) $300,000 of income bonds due on June 30, 1967; 3% interest per annum, payable semiannually (June 30 and December 31) if and when earned, cumulative, to be issued to Fordham in exchange for all plant and equipment of Upstate Canning Company, $50,000 of salable finished goods inventory, and the right to use the brand names of the Upstate Canning Company. (Prior to the exchange, the Upstate Canning Company will be liquidated and the assets distributed to Fordham as sole owner.)
2. Repayment provisions of income bonds:
   a) Company to repurchase $50,000 of income bonds on or before June 30, 1958.
   b) In succeeding years, company to repurchase income bonds equivalent in par value to 50% of the net profit after taxes, provided that the amount in any year will be no less than $15,000. The $15,000 will be due on June 30, and any balance within 30 days after the close of the fiscal year.
   c) Company to have the option of purchasing any amount of income bonds in excess of the minimum requirements according to a schedule of discounted prices as follows: in the first year at 80% of par, in the second year at 82½% of par, in the third year at 85% of par, and so on.

Exhibit 4—Continued

3. No fixed assets to be sold or encumbered in any way without the consent of the income bondholders.
4. Control of the company to be divided equally between the income bondholders and the common shareholders until the income bonds have been completely retired. Each group will elect two directors to a four-man board.
5. Fordham to act as chairman of the board and receive compensation for whatever time he spends on operating matters, beyond board meetings, on a basis to be determined in further negotiations.
6. Shields to act as president and general manager.
7. New company to be incorporated and assets of Upstate to be acquired on or about June 30, 1957. In the meantime, it is to be understood that Fordham and Shields will work together in negotiating contracts with farmers and arranging for an orderly transfer of ownership.

CENTRAL EXPRESS CORPORATION

In May, 1973, Mr. Thorp, treasurer of Central Express Corporation, was considering the relative advantages and disadvantages of several alternative methods of financing Central's acquisition of Midland Freight, Incorporated. At a recent meeting of the board of directors, there had been substantial disagreement as to the best method of financing the acquisition. After the meeting Mr. Thorp had been asked by Mr. Evans, president of Central, to assess the arguments presented by the various directors, and to outline a position to be taken by the management at the June directors meeting.

Central Express was a regulated general commodities motor carrier whose routes ran the length of the Pacific Coast, from Oregon and California to the industrial Midwest, and from Chicago to several Texas points. Founded in 1932 by three brothers, the firm had experienced little growth until the early 1960's. At that point Mr. Evans had joined the firm as president after many years as an executive of a major eastern carrier. Mr. Evans had first concentrated his efforts on expanding Central's revenues on existing routes through an intensive marketing effort and a renewed emphasis on improving service. In 1967, utilizing the proceeds of Central's initial public offering of common stock, Mr. Evans had begun a program designed to reduce operating costs through a combination of extensive computerization of operations and improvement in terminal facilities. As a result of these changes, Central had become a large and profitable concern, widely respected in the industry for its aggressive management.

In 1973, Mr. Evans and the directors of the firm had come to the conclusion that the key to continued expansion in revenues and income was a policy of selected acquisitions. After a study of potential candidates for acquisition, negotiations had begun with Midland Freight, Inc., a common carrier serving Michigan and Indiana from Chicago. The owners of Midland had agreed to sell the firm to Central for $10,000,000 in cash. Mr. Evans felt that Midland was an outstanding acquisition in that it would expand Central's route system and seemed well suited for the type of marketing and cost reduction programs that had fostered Central's growth. The board had unanimously approved the merger.

Central's lawyers felt that no difficulty would be encountered in gaining the approval of the Interstate Commerce Commission for the merger, and the closing date for the acquisition was set for October 1, 1973. Mr. Evans realized that the funds for the Midland acquisition would have to be raised from outside sources. Given that Midland would add $1,680,000 in earnings before interest and taxes (EBIT) to Central on an annual basis, he felt that such external financing would not be difficult to obtain.

The management had followed a consistent policy of avoiding long-term debt. The company had met its needs through use of retained earnings supplemented with the proceeds of the 1967 stock offering and infrequent short-term bank loans. As of 1973, Central's capitalization consisted of common stock and surplus with no fixed debt of any kind. The common stock was held in large amounts by the management. While the stock was widely distributed, there was no real dominant interest other than management. The shares were transferred infrequently and were traded over the counter. Discussions with an investment banker led Mr. Thorp to believe that, barring a major market decline, common stock could be sold to the public at $26.50 a share. After underwriting fees and expenses, the net proceeds to the company would be $25.00 a share. Thus, if common stock was used, the acquisition would require issuance of 400,000 shares.

For the past few years, Mr. Thorp and Mr. Evans had been disappointed in the market performance of Central common stock (Exhibit 1). Thus, they had decided to reconsider the firm's policy of avoiding long-term debt. It was felt that such a change might be justified by the anticipated stability of Central's future earnings. Mr. Thorp had determined that the firm could sell $10,000,000 in bonds to a California insurance company. The interest rate on these bonds would be 8% and they would mature in 15 years. An annual sinking fund of $500,000 would be required, leaving $2,500,000 outstanding at maturity. Although the bond terms would create a sizable need for cash, Mr. Thorp felt that they were the best that could be obtained.

In addition, Mr. Thorp had calculated that, given the tax deductibility of bond interest and Central's current effective tax rate of 50%, the 8% rate was the equivalent of 4% on an after-tax basis. In contrast, he felt that the stock at $25 a share and a dividend of $2.00 a share would cost Central 8%. This cost comparison made the debt alternative seem desirable to Mr. Thorp.

At the May directors meeting, the Midland acquisition received enthusiastic approval. Mr. Thorp then decided to sound out the board as to their sentiments regarding the possibility of financing the acquisition with long-term debt, rather than with common stock. He presented the cost calculations given above. To Mr. Thorp's concern, an acrimonious debate broke out among all the directors concerning financing policy.

Mr. Thorp was immediately questioned as to the cost of the debt issue since his figures did not include the annual payment to the sinking fund. One director argued that this represented 8% of the average size of the bond issue over its 15-year life, and he felt that the stock issue had a smaller cost than the bonds. In addition, he emphasized the cash outlay called for in the bond alternative and the $2,500,000 maturity, especially in view of Central's already existing lease commitments. He felt that the use of debt thus added risks to the company, making the common stock more speculative and causing greater variation in market price.

Another director argued for the issuance of common stock because "simple arithmetic" showed that Central would net 8.4% or $840,000 a year after taxes from the acquisition. Yet, if an additional 400,000 shares of common stock were sold, the dividend requirements, at the current rate of $2.00 a share, would be only $800,000 a year. Since management was not considering raising the dividend rate, he could not see how the sale of the common stock would hurt the interests of present stockholders. Further, if there were any immediate sacrifice by existing shareholders, he argued that it would be over-come as expansion of the firm continued. Under these circumstances, he argued that the bond issue should be rejected, given the cash demands it would place on the firm.

On the other hand, one director became very agitated in arguing that the stock was a "steal" at $26.50 a share. He pointed out that Central's policy of retaining earnings had built the book value of the firm to $45.00 a share as of December, 1972. In addition, he felt that the true value of the company was understated since book value of Central's assets was considerably below cur-rent replacement cost. This director was also worried by the substantial dilu-tion of management's voting control of Central that was implicit in the 400,-000 share offering. Thus, he concluded that the sale of common stock at this time would be a "gift" to new shareholders of the substantial value held by current stockholders.

Two directors agreed that sale of stock would dilute the stock's value, but they measured this dilution in terms of earnings per share instead of book or replacement value. These directors anticipated that postacquisition earnings would equal $6,800,000 before interest and taxes. If common stock was sold, earnings per share would be diluted to $2.62. In contrast, the directors argued that the sole use of debt would increase earnings per share to $3.33. The two directors felt that it was not important that the sinking fund equaled $0.56 a share each year.

Finally, a director spoke about some personal observations he had made about financing in the trucking industry. First, he noted that Central was one of the few major common carriers that had no long-term debt in their capital structures, while Central's price-earnings ratio was among the lowest in the industry. Second, he wondered whether Mr. Thorp had given consideration to the possibility of issuing preferred stock. This director had determined that Central could sell 100,000 shares of preferred stock bearing a dividend rate of $8.25 and a par value of $100. The director criticized Mr. Thorp for failing to deal with the issues he had raised.

This debate had caused the directors meeting to run over its scheduled conclusion and no signs of agreement had developed. Mr. Thorp asked that the discussion of financing alternatives be held over until the June meeting to allow him time to prepare additional material. Now, as the date for the meeting approached, Mr. Thorp once again turned his attention to the issues raised at the board meeting. He realized that a considerable number of issues raised by the directors needed to be considered, and he had designed a chart to aid in the comparison of the debt and stock alternatives (shown as Exhibit 3).

Exhibit 1

CENTRAL EXPRESS CORPORATION

SELECTED INCOME AND DIVIDEND DATA, 1967–73

(In thousands except per share data)

	Operating Revenue	Income before Taxes	Income after Taxes	Income per Share	Dividends per Share	Market Prices per Share of Common Stock	
						High	Low
1967	$126,000	$2,898	$1,449	$1.61	$1.00	19¼	11¼
1968	138,750	3,330	1,665	1.85	1.20	24	14¾
1969	147,461	3,834	1,917	2.13	1.20	25½	15
1970	171,692	4,464	2,232	2.48	1.20	27¼	17⅜
1971	185,333	5,004	2,502	2.78	2.00	38¾	22¼
1972	205,714	5,760	2,880	3.20	2.00	34	25½
1973 Est.*	216,000	5,120	2,560	2.85	2.00†	28¾‡	23½‡

* Excluding the proposed acquisition and its financing.
† Annual rate.
‡ To May 1 (May 1 prices were 28⅜-28⅛).

Exhibit 2

CENTRAL EXPRESS CORPORATION

SUMMARY BALANCE SHEET AS OF DECEMBER 31, 1972

(In thousands)

ASSETS

Cash	$ 3,800	
Accounts receivable	7,690	
Inventory	1,620	
Prepaid expenses	1,820	
Current assets		$14,930
Carrier operating property (cost)	47,330	
Less: Accumulated depreciation	17,820	
Net carrier operating property		29,510
Other assets		6,180
Total assets		$50,620

LIABILITIES AND STOCKHOLDERS' EQUITY

Accounts payable	$ 5,060	
Miscellaneous payables and accruals	4,050	
Taxes payable	1,010	
Current liabilities		$10,120
Common stock ($1 par)	900	
Paid-in surplus	8,000	
Retained earnings	31,600	
Stockholders' equity		40,500
Total liabilities and stockholders' equity		$50,620

Exhibit 3

CENTRAL EXPRESS CORPORATION

ANALYSIS OF FINANCIAL ALTERNATIVES

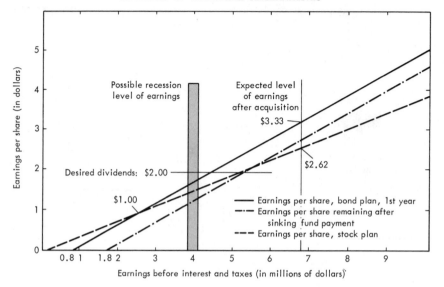

CALCULATION OF POINTS TO DETERMINE LINES

(In thousands except per share data)

	Bonds	Stock	Bonds	Stock
EBIT............................	$2,600	$2,600	$6,800	$6,800
Interest, 1st year...................	800	...	800	...
Taxable earnings..................	1,800	2,600	6,000	6,800
Tax at 50%......................	900	1,300	3,000	3,400
After-tax earnings.................	900	1,300	3,000	3,400
Earnings per share				
÷ 900,000.....................	$ 1.00		$ 3.33	
÷ 1,300,000....................		$ 1.00		$ 2.62
Annual sinking fund...............	500	...	500	...

Note: The effects of leverage and dilution are indicated by the differing slopes of the lines, and can be expressed:

"For each million change of EBIT, the bond plan brings a change in earnings per share which is $0.17 greater than the stock plan. Leverage is favorable from EBIT of $2.6 million upward."

WESTERN FABRICATING CORPORATION

In January, 1954, Mr. Rhodes, vice president and treasurer of the Western Fabricating Corporation, was preparing a report for the company's board of directors. At their last meeting the directors had discussed several methods of financing the first $3 million of a long-term expansion program and had narrowed the choice to two alternatives: (1) an offering of common stock to the public, and (2) private placement of a bond issue with an insurance company. The meeting had been adjourned at this point, with a request that Mr. Rhodes analyze these alternatives and recommend a course of action for the board to consider at its next meeting.

Western Fabricating Corporation (Westfab) was a medium-sized manufacturer of aircraft components and substructures. The company had originally been organized in 1925 to produce automotive parts and had operated successfully in this field until the depression. In 1932 most of the company's subcontracts with major auto manufacturers were lost, with the result that the company had been forced into a search for new products. Losses experienced between 1932 and 1936 drained off nearly half of the company's accumulated capital, but with miscellaneous sales to a variety of industries and recovery of a part of its automotive parts business the company had managed to weather the depression.

The search for new products was continued during the recovery period, and in 1939 the company entered its first successful bid to subcontract parts for a leading aircraft manufacturer. During the next four years of rearmament and war, aircraft production doubled each year, and Westfab grew with the industry. The company was awarded the Navy E in three successive years and by the end of World War II had established a reputation as a reliable fabricator of a wide variety of airframe subassemblies. These products accounted for 95% of the company's total sales of $29 million in 1945.

In the immediate postwar period, sales declined abruptly to $7 million, and a small loss was experienced in 1947. Although sales remained roughly constant at this level in 1948 and 1949, the company was able to report a profit of approximately $350 thousand in each year. Government orders for aircraft were greatly increased in 1950 as a result of the Korean crisis, and by 1953 Westfab's sales and profits had climbed to record levels of $48 million and $3 million, respectively. Selected data from the company's postwar operating statements are shown in Exhibit 1.

The 1950–53 increase in sales created extremely heavy working capital requirements. Cost and inventory controls were tightened to conserve funds, and from time to time the company was able to secure advances from prime contractors; in spite of such measures, however, the company was forced to rely heavily on short-term bank loans and a large increase in tax accruals to meet its increased requirements. By the end of 1953 the bank loans had been repaid, but the tax liability (income and excess profits tax) had increased to $9.1 million, an amount slightly less than the company's entire net worth. Comparative balance sheets for these years are shown in Exhibit 2.

Westfab's financial plight was further complicated during the postwar period by its plant and equipment requirements. At the end of World War II the company's officers had concluded that extensive equipment replacements were needed if the company was to retain its efficiency and reputation for quality output in the coming period of costlier, more complex aircraft. Equally important, it was thought that an effort should be made to diversify the company's production and decrease its dependence on the aircraft industry. Funds were invested in new equipment between 1946 and 1950, as they could be spared, but the profits of this period had not permitted modernization of the company's aircraft plant to the extent visualized or the hoped-for entry into new markets. Larger capital expenditures became imperative after the Korean war began, but the working capital squeeze limited plant and equipment additions to items that were considered essential for the company's immediate military contracts.

By the end of 1953, management had become convinced that its reequipment and diversification plans should be delayed no longer. The cost of the full program, it was estimated, might run as high as $10 million. Since this was more than the company could either finance or absorb at one time, a decision was made to undertake the program in two phases.

The first half of the program, budgeted at $5.25 million, was limited to projects that would directly increase the company's efficiency as an aircraft parts manufacturer. The largest single item, for example, was an expansion of the tool and die shop.

Under its contracts with aircraft manufacturers, Westfab had been obliged to change dies and machine setups at frequent intervals, and its own shop was neither large enough nor adequately equipped to supply the company's needs. The problems created by the shop's limited capacity had not been serious in the immediate postwar period, but experience during recent years of high demand had persuaded management to enlarge the shop at the earliest opportunity. Since 1950, Westfab had found that the cost of purchasing dies and carbide tools of suitable quality had increased tremendously and, also, that it was difficult if not impossible to get deliveries on schedule. Delays were apt to be critical because the company's contracts with aircraft manufacturers often contained severe penalty clauses for the protection of the prime contractor against subcontractor delays. The new shop was expected to support a sales volume of roughly $30 million.

Other projects included in the first part of the program were regarded as equally important. In total the projects were expected to produce annual savings of $1.2 million before taxes assuming Westfab was able to maintain an annual sales volume of $30 million or more after completion of the projects in early 1955.

Diversification projects made up a large part of the second half of the program. Though their immediate return was more problematical, they too were considered highly important.

Westfab's immediate sales outlook was favorable, judged by past standards, but Mr. Rhodes knew that a substantial portion of the estimated sales for 1954 represented carry-forward orders. With the return of peacetime conditions, it was expected that defense spending would be cut, perhaps drastically, and this in turn would affect Westfab's sales. When aircraft production declined, prime contractors often undertook many of the manufacturing operations previously awarded to subcontractors. This invariably created more intense competition among subcontractors for new orders, and both volume and profit margins tended to suffer.

To reduce Westfab's vulnerability to this cycle, management planned to diversify into new products for other industries. Several products with more stable earnings prospects had been investigated, but expenditures of at least $4.75 million appeared necessary to purchase new equipment and adapt current facilities to their production requirements. Mr. Rhodes did not believe that the diversification program could be started much before early 1955, even if the financing were completed before then, since the program would require the new tool and die shop and other facilities scheduled for purchase in 1954.

The decision to raise $3 million externally for the initial part of the program was based on the belief that the company could provide no more than $2.25 million from internal sources. This figure reflected estimates of $1.65 million for retained earnings in 1954 and $600 thousand for depreciation.

The directors were aware that it had been impossible in the past to predict Westfab's net earnings with much accuracy beyond a one-year period. For this reason they had been unwilling to look beyond 1954 earnings and depreciation for funds to finance the first stage of the program. Estimates for 1954 indicated that sales would probably decline to about $37 million and profits (before tax) to $6.9 million. However, with the repeal of the excess profits tax (effective for tax years beginning January 1, 1954) the company's effective tax rate would drop from approximately 75% to 52%, leaving a net profit of about $3.3 million. In view of the variable nature of the company's earnings, the directors had followed the policy of paying substantial dividends during favorable years. With a 50% dividend planned for 1954, retained earnings would amount to approximately $1.65 million. Depreciation of $600 thousand would make up the balance of the $2.25 million to be secured from operations.

At the end of 1953 the company held substantial liquid assets, including almost $1.2 million of tax anticipation notes and short-term government securities and $3.5 million of cash. These funds, above a minimum working balance of $2.0 million, plus funds released by an adjustment of inventories and accounts receivable to a $37 million sales level, would be needed for tax payments in 1954 and hence were not considered available for the expansion program.

As the first step in his investigation of the financing alternatives, Mr. Rhodes had attempted to determine the approximate terms under which each issue could be sold. After discussions with representatives of several investment banking houses and insurance companies, it appeared that the possibilities were approximately as follows:

1. *Common Stock.* An underwriter had indicated to Mr. Rhodes that the company could probably float an issue of common stock to the public at a price 6.7% below the market price existing a few days before the date of the offering. In Westfab's case, this relatively large discount appeared necessary to assure the successful sale of such a large block of stock relative to shares currently outstanding. Thus, if the present market price of $22.50 held, the issuing price would be set at $21 per share. At a price of $21 Mr. Rhodes planned to issue 150,000 shares to gross $3,150,000 before underwriting fees of 2% or $63,000. Westfab would also incur legal and other similar expenses of approximately $50,000, so that net proceeds to the company would amount to $3,037,000. These estimates were all subject to revision in the event market conditions changed significantly during the three-month period preceding final registration of the issue with the Securities and Exchange Commission.

2. *Debentures.* Unsecured debentures placed with an insurance company would have to carry an interest rate of 4.5% and be amortized in equal installments over a 10-year period. It also appeared that any lender who bought the issue would insist on an acceleration clause which would make the full loan due and payable within one month of default on any one of the following restrictions:

a) A minimum net working capital limit of $4.5 million.

b) A maximum limit of approximately $5 million on bank loans and long-term debt, including the present debentures.

c) A ban against the creation of senior long-term debt.

d) Restriction of dividend payments to earnings accumulated after the date of issuance of the debentures plus $150,000.

While the terms of the debt issue seemed fairly definite, Mr. Rhodes had thought it necessary to collect additional information on the market behavior of the company's common stock, since the price of the issue would be a crucial consideration. This information—annual price ranges, per share earnings and dividends, and volume of shares traded in recent years—is shown in Exhibit 3. Mr. Rhodes attributed much of the recent rise in the market price to the fact that the company had increased its regular quarterly dividend from $0.50 to $0.75 in December, 1953. In announcing the increase, the directors had stated that it was their intention to maintain the $0.75 quarterly payment insofar as future earnings permitted.

The figures in Exhibit 3 have been adjusted for a 2 for 1 stock split in late 1952. The stock, which was listed on the American Stock Exchange, had been split at that time to increase the number of shares available for trading and, also, to bring the price into a range where it might interest a broader group of investors. In the following year the volume of trading increased, as did the number of individual shareholders and joint accounts (currently 2,700). On the other hand, the percentage of shares registered in the name of individuals and joint accounts decreased, and the percentage registered in the name of stockbrokers, security dealers, and nominees increased; by the end of 1953 the holdings of the latter group amounted to almost one third of the 550,000 shares outstanding (Exhibit 3). Heavy purchases (25,000 shares) by two dealers who had never before been interested in Westfab's stock had given rise to rumors that some group might be seeking control of the company, but the principals of such a group, if any, were still unknown to Mr. Rhodes and the directors. At the current time Westfab's management owned or controlled beneficially approximately 10% of the shares outstanding.

Exhibit 1

WESTERN FABRICATING CORPORATION

SELECTED OPERATING DATA

(Thousands of dollars)

Year	Net Sales	Operating Profit	Net Income (after Taxes and Provision for Renegotiation)
1945	$29,211	$ 3,468	$ 943
1946	10,068	275	236
1947	7,011	(258)	(64)
1948	6,642	622	326
1949	7,416	717	391
1950	9,419	1,263	657
1951	24,545	5,379	1,149
1952	42,876	12,350	1,839
1953	48,464	13,947	3,003

Exhibit 2

WESTERN FABRICATING CORPORATION

COMPARATIVE BALANCE SHEETS, AS OF DECEMBER 31

(Thousands of dollars)

ASSETS	1950	1951	1952	1953
Cash	$ 551	$ 2,515	$ 5,160	$ 3,528
U.S. government securities	177	182	188	1,185
Accounts receivable	1,514	3,981	5,630	5,699
Inventories	4,225	7,527	9,432	8,761
Prepaid expenses	145	212	353	378
Total current assets	$6,612	$14,417	$20,763	$19,551
Net plant and equipment	3,052	3,495	3,692	4,358
Total assets	$9,664	$17,912	$24,455	$23,909

LIABILITIES				
Accounts payable	$ 378	$ 969	$ 1,606	$ 1,070
Notes payable	1,275	2,925	1,500	...
Customers' deposits	88	1,471	701	182
Reserve for federal income taxes and renegotiation	606	4,230	10,511	10,944
Other accruals	450	848	1,716	1,591
Total current liabilities	$2,797	$10,443	$16,034	$13,787
Reserve for employees' benefits	433	404	343	283
Common stock*	2,750	2,750	2,750	2,750
Earned surplus	3,684	4,315	5,328	7,089
Total liabilities and net worth	$9,664	$17,912	$24,455	$23,909

* Common stock—$5 par, 550,000 shares currently outstanding. In September, 1952, the previous $10 par stock was split 2 for 1.

Exhibit 3

WESTERN FABRICATING CORPORATION
SELECTED FINANCIAL DATA*

	Common Stock Price Range		Number of Shares Traded (000's)	Earnings per Share	Dividends
	High	*Low*			
1945	14¾	7	110	$1.71	$0.85
1946	17⅝	7	114	0.43	0.55
1947	8⅞	5⅜	97	(0.12)	nil
1948	8⅛	4¾	107	0.59	0.20
1949	7	4⅝	105	0.71	0.65
1950	11⅛	6⅞	103	1.19	0.65
1951	12	8⅞	113	2.09	0.95
1952	15	12½	390	3.34	1.45
1953	23⅞	13⅛	650	5.46	2.25

1953—BY QUARTERS

1st	18⅞	13⅛	174		0.50
2d	18⅛	14¾	86		0.50
3d	19¼	14¼	176		0.50
4th	23⅞	18¾	214		0.75
Jan. 1–10, 1954	23⅛	22			

DISTRIBUTION OF STOCK OWNERSHIP, DECEMBER 31, 1953

	Number of Shareowners	Number of Shares Owned
By type of owner:		
Individuals and joint accounts	2,682	361,542
Stock brokers, security dealers, and nominees	170	176,213
Fiduciaries, institutions, foundations, and others	45	12,245
Total	2,897	550,000
By size of holding:		
1 to 99 shares	1,960	94,372
100 to 999 shares	892	282,619
1000 or more shares	45	173,009
Total	2,897	550,000

* Adjusted for 2 for 1 split in 1952.

CROWN CORPORATION

^^

In February, 1969, Mr. Walter Bennett, treasurer of Crown Corporation, was considering several financing alternatives. Crown's decision to integrate backwards into the production of primary aluminum ingot had resulted in very heavy capital expenditures. Its need for funds for working capital and for completion of a large aluminum plant now outstripped the company's internal cash generation and it would be necessary to raise $30 million within the next six months to cover capital needs for 1969. Mr. Bennett hoped to develop a financing program that would meet the immediate and the longer-term needs without jeopardizing Crown's seventy-cent dividend rate.

Company description

A series of acquisitions and divestitures during the 1960's had totally transformed Crown Corporation from a mining company into a manufacturer of superalloy castings for aircraft and industrial uses and aluminum products for the building, packaging, and aircraft industries. Sales were evenly divided between castings and aluminum products.

Crown's castings were for the most part designed for operation in the "hot part" of the gas turbine engine. The company worked from designs prepared chiefly by aircraft engine manufacturers. These manufacturers, in their endeavor to obtain greater thrust, designed parts that would function at engine operating temperatures ranging to 2,150 degrees Fahrenheit. The high temperatures required the use of precision castings for blades and vanes. The techniques and know-how involved in casting operations were important and the commercial success of such an operation was in large measure dependent upon achieving a low ratio of rejects. Crown's constant emphasis on quality and technical excellence had established a high level of confidence among its customers. For adherence to a rigid standard of performance and quality, it had been selected to participate in the majority of United States jet engine programs in the past ten years. (Exhibit 1 provides information on jet engine production in the United States.)

The other half of Crown's sales comprised aluminum products, including a broad product line for the building and construction industry. Major efforts had been made to increase the company's captive source of primary aluminum ingot for consumption by its fabricating operations. To assure a steady and

132

economical source, Crown had become a producer of primary aluminum in 1966 through participation with American Metal Climax, Inc. in a project known as Intalco. Crown's share of Intalco's output was 130 million pounds, roughly 81% of its total need.

In 1967 the decision was made to build a second aluminum ingot plant, named Eastalco, at a cost of $50 million. Eastalco was expected to start operations in mid-1970, providing Crown with additional primary aluminum capacity of 85 million pounds a year and increased net income of $3–4 million. A planned addition of 85 million pounds in 1972 would raise Eastalco's capacity to 170 million pounds and would meet the company's objective to be a fully-integrated producer.

	Actual (Millions of Pounds)				Estimates (Millions of Pounds)		
	1965	1966	1967	1968	1969	1970	1973
Consumption of primary aluminum by Crown's fabricating divisions.......	94	107	116	135	160	185	290
Production of primary aluminum:							
at Intalco..............	0	16	69	88	130	130	130
at Eastalco.............	0	0	0	0	0	85	170
Purchases (sales) of primary aluminum by Crown..................	94	91	47	47	30	(30)	(10)

Company performance[1]

Crown's sales had risen sharply from $60 million in 1958 to $230 million in 1968 on the strength of 23 acquisitions, strong internal growth, and a firming of aluminum prices. The company's earnings had been considerably more erratic, however, with the volatility the result largely of instability in its aluminum business. After reaching a peak of $1.13 in 1959, earnings per share fell to $0.34 in 1963 as overcapacity developed in the aluminum business and prices of fabricated products were eroded. (Crown's operating results are shown in Exhibit 2.) The "great growth potential" of aluminum had encouraged major capacity additions by established producers and entry by new producers during the 1950's. Domestic industry capacity rose by 79% between 1954 and 1960. American producers were also faced with a tremendous buildup in capacity elsewhere in the world. After a decade of generally rising prices, excess capacity began to take its toll in 1958. In April of that year, the producer price for American ingot was lowered from 26 to 24 cents a pound to match a similar reduction initiated by Canadian firms in the world market. By December, 1962, the quotation had dropped to 22.5 cents a pound.

In the fabricated products market, where the relative ease of entry had

---

[1] The history of the aluminum industry is drawn in large part from *Aluminum: Past and Future*, by Yvonne Levy (San Francisco: Federal Reserve Bank of San Francisco, 1971).

brought in many small and medium-sized independent concerns, competition for the available business was even keener and price erosion more severe. List prices of fabricated products dropped on the average about 20% between late 1961 and late 1963. (Exhibit 3 provides data on aluminum shipments and prices.) The decline in actual market prices undoubtedly was even sharper because of a method of discounting—called "commodity pricing"—that was undertaken in order to penetrate new markets. This method, most prevalent in sheet, strip, coil, and plate products, involved selling a product for a specific application at a price lower than the published price. The seller then attempted to confine the lower price to specific product areas so as not to reduce revenues. However, in the late 1950's, the whole price structure came tumbling down and profits came tumbling after. Profits of the three major aluminum companies collapsed from $175 million in 1956 to a low of $88 million in 1960.

Demand–supply conditions in the industry finally improved in the early 1960's and with the improvement came sharply higher earnings for Crown and other aluminum producers. Over the 1961–66 period, industry shipments of aluminum increased by 14% annually. Despite increases in supply, the price of ingot went up four times between October, 1963 and November, 1964, from a low of 22.5 cents a pound to 24.5 cents a pound. But price weakness continued at the fabricating level during this period. The hundreds of small fabricators lowered prices to obtain business for their idle machinery, while consumers increasingly came to disregard published mill prices.

Prices of fabricated products remained weak until 1965, when strike-anticipation hedge buying bolstered demand and pushed up operating rates. Producers raised prices several times early in the year, and then again after a new three-year labor contract was signed in June. For the next three years shipments of aluminum products continued to rise 8–10% annually and prices firmed further. Shortly after a new three-year labor contract was signed in 1968, producers raised the price of ingot by 4%, to 26 cents a pound, and the price of fabricated products by a comparable amount. After a brief period of discounting in the wake of the labor settlement, the new list prices apparently took hold. In January, 1969, producers raised the price of ingot from 26 to 27 cents a pound and prices on a wide range of mill products by an average of 5%, and further price increases were anticipated.

The strong price situation improved industry profitability dramatically. Profits of the three major aluminum firms rebounded from the 1960 low of $88 million to $230 million in 1966. (See Exhibit 4.) Crown's record was no less dramatic. Rising from a low of $0.34 a share in 1963, Crown's earnings reached $2.03 a share in 1967. Its stock, which had sold at less than $5 a share in 1963, reached a high of $51 in mid 1968 on the strength of record earnings and an increased dividend rate.

Surpluses of the seventies?

The improved industry price structure in the late 1960's encouraged aluminum producers to move forward to meet the demands and the opportunities of the 1970's. Throughout the world, producers began to build new smelters and enlarge older ones. In the United States the expansion in capacity contemplated over the next three years seemed moderate in terms of past trends in demand. American producers were scheduled to boost their primary production potential from almost 4.2 million tons in 1970 to 5 million tons by 1973, or at a 6.4% annual rate. This rate of expansion, although substantial, was below the 10% rate of growth of domestic aluminum consumption during the 1960's.

In reducing their rate of expansion, U.S. producers recognized that they were facing the strongest counterattack from other materials in their history. Aluminum's success in penetrating the territory staked out by other metals had been phenomenal. Shipments of aluminum ingot and mill products grew at more than twice the rate of durable goods output and construction activity over the 1960's. The industry was successful, through research and development and aggressive marketing techniques, in creating new uses for the metal and in displacing traditional materials in older applications.

The steel industry, the giant of the metal field with 1968 ingot production of 130 million tons as against aluminum's 3 million tons, had initiated a strong fight to ward off the lightweight metal's further advances. In particular, steel was fighting hard to protect its position in the $3.5 billion can market and in the rapid transit market, which could evolve into a $10 billion outlet over the 1970's. The copper industry was also fighting to protect its markets and the plastics industry was challenging aluminum in each of aluminum's principal markets—construction, transportation, and packaging.

However, the most effective dampening influence on the domestic industry was the huge increase in aluminum capacity abroad. Plans in 1969 called for capacity elsewhere in the non-Communist world to rise at well over double the U.S. rate between 1970 and 1973, as major European and Asian nations built up their own production in an effort to reduce their dependence on imports. With almost 4.4 million tons of new capacity—3.5 million tons overseas plus 0.9 million tons in the United States—scheduled to come on stream in the 1970–73 period, world capacity could rise from about 9.4 million to 13.7 million tons, or at a 14% annual rate.

This expansion in capacity would exceed the anticipated growth in demand, since most industry analysts expected that world aluminum consumption would not exceed the 9% rate of growth registered during the 1960–68 period. If all the capacity programmed was brought in on schedule, growth in consumption at the 9% level over the next several years could result in as much as 2 million tons of excess capacity by 1973, representing about 15% of the industry's total production capability.

Before jumping to the conclusion that the industry's price structure was in danger of weakening, however, Mr. Bennett realized that the major aluminum producers might stretch out their expansion projects over a longer period, especially where expansion was scheduled through incremental additions to existing plants. Projects not yet started might be postponed or canceled.

Furthermore, he did not underestimate the ability of the industry to boost consumption above anticipated levels by imaginative research and development and marketing programs.

Crown's expected growth

Mr. Bennett expected that Crown's sales would increase at 6–8% annually, exclusive of acquisitions, over the foreseeable future. No growth was forecast through 1974 in the precision castings business as sharp reductions in defense procurement needs would offset the 15% per year increase in commercial sales. However, sales of aluminum products were expected to rise by 15–20% annually as the company broadened its penetration of major aluminum consuming markets. This sales growth would necessitate heavy spending on aluminum reduction facilities and fabricating capacity. Total capital expenditures, including the Eastalco project, were forecast at $39 million in 1969, $32 million in 1970, $7 million in 1971, and $50 million in 1972. The heavy capital spending would require that Crown raise $30 million in 1969, $22 million in 1970, and $30 million in 1972.

Financing alternatives

Several alternatives were open to Crown to meet its financing needs in 1969. (See the balance sheets for 1965–68 shown in Exhibit 5.) The company's investment bankers believed that a $30 million common stock issue was possible and pointed to the future financing flexibility afforded by the use of equity financing. On the other hand, the dilution of earnings per share that would result from sale of additional stock was a matter of concern to Mr. Bennett. Crown stock had fallen from $51 a share in May, 1968 to a level of $30 a share as investors reacted to disappointing earnings in 1968. (Comparative industry stock price data are provided in Exhibit 6.) Further near-term price weakness seemed likely as earnings per share remained depressed as Crown absorbed heavy start-up costs for the production of the main landing gear for the McDonnell Douglas DC–10 in 1969. Under these conditions, announcement of a large equity issue would drive the stock price down to the low twenties, at which price it would be necessary to sell 1.4 million shares to raise the $30 million net to the company. Mr. Bennett wondered whether equity financing should be deferred until the company resumed its pattern of earnings gains.

As an alternative to equity financing, a consortium of commercial banks had agreed to lend the company up to $30 million at 7¼% interest. The term loan would be repayable at an annual rate of $5 million beginning in 1970 and ending in 1975. Under the provisions of the loan agreement, net working capital must exceed $55 million, dividend payments were restricted to earnings accumulated after the date of the loan agreement, and additional funded debt was limited to $20 million.

It would also be possible to place a $30 million subordinated convertible debenture issue privately with the Northern Life Insurance Company. The debentures would carry a coupon of 6% with annual debt retirement of $2 million in years six through twenty. The issue would not be callable for ten years, except at par for mandatory debt retirement, and would be convertible into common stock at $31.50.

Mr. Bennett was interested in the debt alternatives. Although the company's use of debt had increased sharply and coverage ratios had narrowed, its coverage of interest costs was still considered adequate. On the other hand, the flexibility afforded by use of equity financing could be valuable in future years.

Exhibit 1

CROWN CORPORATION

AIRCRAFT ENGINE PRODUCTION

(Number of engines)

Year	Total	Military			Civil		
		Total Military	Recip-rocal	Jet	Total Civil	Recip-rocal	Jet
1946	43,407	2,585	1,680	905	40,822	40,822	...
1947	20,912	4,561	2,683	1,878	16,351	16,351	...
1948	14,027	4,988	2,495	2,493	9,039	9,039	...
1949	11,972	7,990	2,981	5,009	3,982	3,982	...
1950	13,675	9,361	3,122	6,239	4,314	4,314	...
1951	20,867	16,287	6,471	9,816	4,580	4,580	...
1952	31,041	25,659	8,731	16,928	5,382	5,382	...
1953	40,263	33,616	13,365	20,251	6,647	6,647	...
1954	26,959	21,440	7,868	13,572	5,519	5,519	...
1955	21,108	13,469	3,875	9,594	7,639	7,639	...
1956	21,348	9,849	2,663	7,186	11,499	11,499	...
1957	21,984	11,087	2,429	8,658	10,897	10,859	38
1958	18,869	8,121	1,452	6,669	10,748	10,233	515
1959	17,162	4,626	661	3,965	12,536	11,152	1,384
1960	16,189	3,673	756	2,917	12,516	10,891	1,625
1961	15,832	5,172	417	4,755	10,660	9,669	991
1962	15,919	5,441	241	5,200	10,478	9,921	557
1963	17,185	5,390	155	5,235	11,795	11,322	473
1964	19,585	5,380	175	5,205	14,205	13,346	859
1965	23,378	5,191	92	5,099	18,187	17,018	1,169
1966	30,810	7,548	45	7,503	23,262	21,324	1,938
1967	28,858	8,046	...	8,046	20,812	18,324	2,488
1968	29,761	8,542	...	8,542	21,219	17,806	3,413

Source: *Aerospace Facts and Figures 1973/1974* (New York: Aerospace Industries Association of America, Inc., 1973), p. 48.

Exhibit 2

CROWN CORPORATION

SELECTED OPERATING DATA, 1963–68

(In millions except per share data)

	1962	1963	1964	1965	1966	1967	1968
Net sales	$ 110	$ 122	$ 122	$ 141	$ 176	$ 213	$ 230
Operating profit*	8.3	4.6	5.5	9.1	18.5	27.8	28.5
Other income (expense)†	(0.4)	(0.6)	(0.3)	(0.8)	(0.1)	(0.7)	(1.0)
Income before taxes	$ 7.9	$ 4.0	$ 5.2	$ 8.3	$18.4	$27.1	$27.5
Federal income taxes	3.7	1.5	2.3	3.6	7.6	12.3	13.8
Net income	$ 4.2	$ 2.5	$ 2.9	$ 4.7	$10.8	$14.8	$13.6

Per Share Data

	1962	1963	1964	1965	1966	1967	1968
Earnings	$0.57	$0.34	$0.42	$0.66	$1.50	$2.03	$1.87
Dividends	0	0.20	0.20	0.23	0.40	0.60	0.70
Market price:							
High	9	7	7	11	27	51	51
Low	5	5	5	6	10	22	32
Price-earnings ratio:							
High	16	21	17	17	18	25	27
Low	9	15	12	9	7	11	17

* After deduction of depreciation expense ($5 million in 1968).
† Other income and other expenses including interest expense are offset against each other.

Exhibit 3

CROWN CORPORATION

STATISTICS ON INDUSTRY SHIPMENTS AND PRICES:
TOTAL ALUMINUM INDUSTRY SHIPMENTS, 1942–69
(Millions of pounds, net shipments)

Year	Total	Ingot	Domestic Mill Products	Imported Mill Products
1942	1,452.7	507.4	933.6	11.7
1943	2,217.2	724.6	1,492.4	0.2
1944	2,566.4	952.0	1,613.0	1.4
1945	1,886.4	549.2	1,329.8	7.4
1946	1,672.4	529.2	1,140.8	2.4
1947	2,040.1	631.8	1,408.2	0.1
1948	2,282.0	629.8	1,640.2	12.0
1949	1,654.1	479.9	1,158.1	16.1
1950	2,460.6	724.6	1,713.4	22.6
1951	2,506.6	709.8	1,756.2	40.6
1952	2,694.5	811.2	1,850.4	32.9
1953	3,276.8	982.9	2,228.2	65.7
1954	3,036.0	920.2	2,086.6	29.2
1955	4,035.1	1,205.4	2,791.8	37.9
1956	4,154.6	1,223.5	2,885.8	45.3
1957	3,880.1	1,161.6	2,677.6	40.9
1958	3,631.2	974.0	2,597.1	60.1
1959	5,061.0	1,575.0	3,386.1	100.1
1960	4,732.5	1,608.6	3,049.1	74.8
1961	4,970.1	1,536.6	3,345.1	88.4
1962	5,772.5	1,858.6	3,811.3	102.7
1963	6,377.0	2,032.6	4,257.2	87.2
1964	7,171.3	2,228.6	4,834.9	107.8
1965	8,150.2	2,337.3	5,679.4	133.5
1966	9,031.6	2,340.1	6,457.5	234.1
1967	8,946.4	2,486.4	6,350.6	109.5
1968	9,977.4	2,694.8	7,167.0	115.6
1969f	10,825.0	3,050.0	7,660.0	115.0

Notes: f = forecast.
Detail may not add to totals due to rounding.
Sources: Ingot and mill products, domestic: 1942–45—Aluminum and Magnesium Division, War Production Board; 1946 to date—U.S. Department of Commerce, Bureau of the Census, Industry Division, and Bureau of Domestic Commerce, Aluminum and Magnesium Industries Operations, Facts for Industry 1946–1959, and Current Industrial Report Series M33–2, 1960 to date.
Mill products, imported: U.S. Department of Commerce, Bureau of the Census, Foreign Trade Division, and CIR Series M33–2.

Exhibit 3—Continued

PRICE CHRONOLOGY

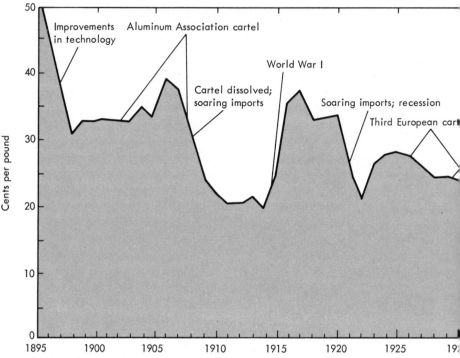

Little over a century ago, aluminum was still a rare metal, costing $545 a pound in 1852. Yet after several decades of technological advance, the price dropped to $8 a pound in 1885. Then, with the development of the electrolytic process for producing aluminum, the metal began to come within the reach of the average consumer . . . On the eve of World War I, aluminum was selling for 19½ cents a pound, thanks to the growth of a technologically advanced industry in Europe and North America—and despite the efforts of producers' cartels to maintain a high price structure for the metal. As a consequence of this price decline, aluminum markets were no longer confined to specialty items in the cooking, military, and surgical fields, but had spread also to tonnage items in the fast-growing electrical and automotive industries . . . During World War I, prices practically doubled despite the rapid expansion of production facilities. But by the end of 1921, prices were back to prewar levels as producers here and abroad fought to find peacetime markets for wartime-swollen supplies . . . During the next several decades, aluminum prices trended down-

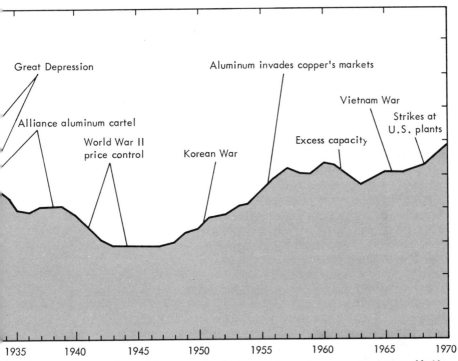

Great Depression

Aluminum invades copper's markets

Vietnam War

Strikes at
U.S. plants

Alliance aluminum cartel

World War II
price control

Korean War

Excess capacity

1935   1940   1945   1950   1955   1960   1965   1970

wards. In the 20's and 30's, industry cartels set prices and imposed output restrictions worldwide
in an attempt to manage markets that had been unsettled by lagging demand and increasing capacity. In the 40's, as the domestic industry expanded rapidly to meet insatiable wartime demands,
the government held the price line by setting the ingot price at 14 cents a pound . . . Prices have
generally moved upward since World War II. The surprisingly high level of civilian reconversion
demand, plus the heavy Korean-war and strategic-stock-pile demand, helped push prices from 14
to 25½ cents a pound between 1947 and 1957. But then prices slumped, reaching 22½ cents a
pound in 1963, as military and civilian demand turned sluggish in the face of a tremendous buildup
in capacity throughout the world. Finally, with the industrial expansion and the war boom of
the late 60's, prices increased again.

Source: *Aluminum: Past and Future*, by Yvonne Levy (San Francisco: Federal Reserve Bank of San Francisco,
1971).

Exhibit 4

CROWN CORPORATION

CHARTS SHOWING IMPROVEMENT IN PROFITS OF THE THREE MAJOR
ALUMINUM FIRMS IN THE LATE 1960's
ALONG WITH RISING PRICES

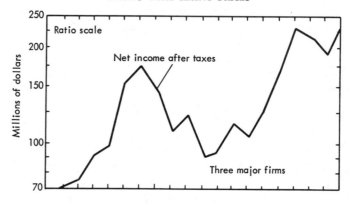

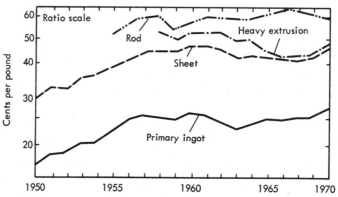

Source: *Aluminum: Past and Future*, by Yvonne Levy (San Francisco: Federal Reserve
Bank of San Francisco, 1971).

Exhibit 5

CROWN CORPORATION

BALANCE SHEETS AS OF DECEMBER 31, 1965–68

(In millions)

	1965	1966	1967	1968
ASSETS				
Cash..	$ 3	$ 3	$ 5	$ 4
Marketable securities.........................	7	10	23	6
Accounts receivable..........................	20	23	35	42
Inventories.................................	28	38	45	50
Other......................................	0	0	1	1
Total current assets.....................	$ 58	$ 74	$109	$103
Investments in aluminum plants				
Intalco.................................	32	29	34	36
Eastalco................................	0	0	0	4
Other net property, plant and equipment........	28	31	34	42
Other......................................	3	4	4	4
Total assets..........................	$121	$138	$181	$189
LIABILITIES				
Accounts payable............................	$ 8	$ 10	$ 13	$ 14
Accrued liabilities..........................	6	7	7	10
Accrued taxes.............................	4	8	8	6
Dividends payable..........................	1	1	1	1
Current maturities—long-term debt............	2	2	2	4
Total current liabilities...................	$ 21	$ 28	$ 31	$ 35
Long-term debt*.............................	30	28	56	52
Deferred federal taxes.......................	1	2	3	3
Stockholders' equity (7,273,000 shares outstanding at year-end 1968).................	69	80	91	99
Total liabilities and net worth..............	$121	$138	$181	$189

* Crown Corporation placed a $56 million debt issue directly with several life insurance companies in 1967. Of the proceeds, $26 million represented a refinancing of existing debt and the balance of $30 million represented new money to the company. The debentures have a coupon of 6% with debt retirement of $4 million annually beginning in 1968 and ending in 1981.

Exhibit 6

CROWN CORPORATION

COMPARATIVE DATA ON ALUMINUM COMPANIES

	Alcan	*Alcoa*	*Harvey*	*Crown*	*Braun**	*Standard & Poor's 425 Industrials*
Earnings per share:						
1962...............	$1.14	$2.52	$1.19	$ .57	$1.74	$3.87
1963...............	1.01	2.27	.90	.34	1.23	4.24
1964...............	1.57	2.72	.77	.42	1.55	4.83
1965...............	1.93	3.41	.53	.66	2.14	5.51
1966...............	2.41	4.83	2.24	1.50	3.30	5.89
1967...............	1.94	4.93	2.36	2.03	3.00	5.66
1968...............	2.14	4.75	2.16	1.87	2.81	6.15
1969 est...........	2.30	5.40	1.75	1.85†	3.00	6.25
Price-earnings ratio:						
1962...............	15–25	18–27	13–25	9–16	14–21	17
1963...............	20–28	23–31	20–27	15–21	25–34	18
1964...............	17–21	22–30	22–29	12–19	18–27	18
1965...............	13–17	18–23	34–44	9–17	13–19	17
1966...............	10–18	14–20	9–13	7–18	9–16	15
1967...............	12–17	14–19	11–25	11–25	13–20	18
1968...............	10–13	13–17	15–25	17–27	15–17	18
Feb. 1969..........	13	14	20	16	13	18
1968 sales (in millions)..........	$1,081	$1,353	$177	$230	$850	
Book value per share (1968)............	$23	$49	$20	$13	$25	
Current dividend rate..............	$1.10	$1.80	$1.20	$0.70	$1.00	$3.21
Long-term debt as % of total capital.....	46%	39%	41%	34%	55%	
Times interest earned..	5.2	6.6	6.7	9.1	4.8	
Debt rating: Senior debt.........	A	A	. . .	not rated	not rated	
Convertible subordinated debt...	. . .	BBB	BBB	. . .	. . .	

* Affiliated with Braun Industries.
† Before any new financing.

PHOENIX AIRCRAFT COMPANY*

In May, 1966, Mr. John Larson, president of Phoenix Aircraft Company, was preparing a proposal to present at the June meeting of the board of directors concerning how to finance $40 million in long-term funds needed for working capital, plant expansion, and other purposes over the next several years. After conferring with his senior vice president of finance, he had narrowed the possible sources of funds down to debt instruments, but the questions of what form this debt should take and the date of issue were yet to be decided.

The past three years had brought spectacular growth to Phoenix, with dollar sales doubling in the period from 1963 to 1966 (estimated), thereby creating pressing new needs for additional funds. A larger pool of long-term money was needed to support rising working capital requirements. This would allow the retirement of substantial short-term bank borrowing. Outstanding short-term bank loans had risen to $8.4 million as of the fiscal year ended September 30, 1965, and the combination of short-term bank loans and commercial paper had risen to $16 million by March 31, 1966 (Exhibit 1). The company was also engaged in an expansion program to enlarge the plant and equipment needed to meet increased sales demands and to introduce new production models. Expansion plan commitments for 1966 and 1967 alone entailed the addition of nearly one million square feet of plant space to existing facilities in Columbus at a cost of $11 million, in addition to new machinery and equipment costing about $12 million. Part of these funds would be provided from profits (profits had nearly tripled in four years, going from $5.1 million in 1963 to an estimated $14 million in 1966, as shown in Exhibits 2 to 4), but outside sources were needed to supplement flows into retained earnings. In his latest evaluation of these needs, Mr. Larson had decided that a total of $40 million of long-term capital within two years would be adequate to finance this growth.

Management believed that the company's outlook for the future was bright. The company's main thrust was in the general aviation market, which included all civil flying except that of public air carriers. The total time ac-

* Reprinted from Stanford Business Cases 1969 with the permission of the publishers, Stanford University Graduate School of Business, © 1969 by the Board of Trustees of the Leland Stanford Junior University.

cumulated in general aviation flying in the United States had grown very rapidly in the postwar years, to the point that general aviation averaged nearly four times the total scheduled flying time each year of domestic airline transports. Total industry sales of general aircraft had spurted in recent years, rising from $125 million in 1961 to nearly $320 million in 1965, with projections pointed steadily upward. Phoenix officers foresaw in the future a continued strong economy, with rising discretionary incomes and increased leisure time, all of which would contribute to expanding demands for business and pleasure flying.

In 1966, Phoenix was one of the top three manufacturers of general aviation aircraft for the 21st consecutive year. Out of all the light aircraft flying in the United States in 1966, Phoenix claimed nearly one fourth of the total small aircraft. Phoenix had first been incorporated in Ohio in the 1920's. Prior to World War II the company had manufactured several types of small aircraft, principally the Skychief, a single-engine, four-place cantilever-wing plane. During World War II, the company produced twin-engine trainer aircraft for the United States government. After the war, Phoenix reentered the private and business aircraft fields, retaining some government business while at the same time starting to diversify.

The company's marketing strategy was to maintain a balanced mix of commercial and military business to hedge against any downturn in defense expenditures. The company had also been able to diversify through acquisitions of existing companies. For example, Phoenix had acquired manufacturers of aircraft accessories, airborne communication and navigation equipment, and fluid power components for industrial equipment. By 1965, two thirds of sales resulted from commercial aircraft, 15% were in government business, and the rest came from other lines of manufacture.

In looking at its future business mix the Phoenix management foresaw a continued rapid increase in government orders due to the war in Vietnam. The company's policy in the past with respect to government contracts had been to bid only on work that could be performed with existing engineering and manufacturing facilities. As a result, sales to the United States government and to foreign governments over the past few years, which had been substantial, were regular commercial aircraft models. By May, 1966, the backlog on government work had grown to $21 million and was rising rapidly, with approximately 75% of this backlog in prime contracts and 25% in subcontracts.

Phoenix maintained a centralized manufacturing center, producing all its aircraft in company plants near Columbus, Ohio. Most component parts of the aircraft were fabricated by Phoenix. Those components that were not company-produced were purchased from independent sources.

Phoenix maintained a separate marketing division for commercial aircraft. Made up of 300 employees, the division conducted marketing research and established sales promotion and advertising programs for the network of distributors and dealers. Generally, sales were made directly to franchised distributors who had developed some 460 dealers in the United States and 110 in foreign countries. These dealers sold aircraft as well as providing flight instruction, servicing, and other ground support services. The company's capable marketing organization, which had conducted such successful promotional campaigns as the $5 first flight lesson, helped Phoenix meet active competition in the production and sale of general aviation aircraft. In addition to this strong network of distributors and dealers, the company had developed a reputation for producing quality products, with good engineering and design, all of which contributed to maintaining its prominent position in the industry.

From 1962 to 1966, Phoenix produced about one third of the industry's total unit output and dollar value. The other two large competitors together accounted for one half of unit output and one half of dollar volume for the industry. Phoenix also encountered strong competition in government business, where many of its competitors were corporations with total sales and resources far in excess of those of Phoenix. These competitors were at the same time customers buying various Phoenix products.

In order to assist dealers in financing its inventory and to provide retail financing, Phoenix established in 1957 a wholly owned unconsolidated finance subsidiary, Phoenix Finance Company, Inc. P.F.C. contributed greatly to Phoenix's aircraft sales and was growing rapidly. At fiscal year-end 1965, P.F.C.'s net notes receivable were $14.9 million, up 45% from the prior year (Exhibit 5). By the spring of 1966 these notes receivable had risen to about $25 million. Phoenix's investment in P.F.C., stated at cost plus undistributed earnings, totaled $3.3 million on September 30, 1965, and was expected to rise by more than $2 million by September 30, 1966, to support P.F.C.'s rapid rate of growth. In late 1965, after the close of the 1965 fiscal year, P.F.C. had negotiated with two insurance companies a 12-year $5.5 million unsecured loan, which was not guaranteed by Phoenix. In 1965, P.F.C.'s net earnings rose by 40% to $180,000.

P.F.C.'s earnings growth in 1966 was expected to be interrupted because of a temporary lag in realizing the benefits from increased rates charged by P.F.C. and from the higher level of receivables as compared with the more immediate effect of recent high money costs to P.F.C. and greater acquisition costs.

In the examination of alternative methods of financing the $40 million long-term capital needs a new issue of common stock was considered, but it was generally agreed that at existing stock prices the dilution of earnings per share would be prohibitively high. The two most promising alternatives remaining were some form of long-term debt, either straight debt or convertible debt.

After discussion of these issues with Kidder, Peabody & Co., Incorporated, the investment bankers with whom the Phoenix management had built up a close relationship over the years, the following possibilities stood out as the best alternatives for the board of directors to consider:

A. The sale in 1966 of either:
 1. A straight debt issue of $20 million taking the form of:
    a) A private placement with a New York insurance company, or
    b) A public issue underwritten by a syndicate headed by Kidder, Peabody & Co.
 2. A $20 million public issue of convertible debt, convertible into common stock at a price 20% above the common price at the time of the offering, to be sold by the syndicate.
B. An issue next year for $20 million in the form of the instrument not used this year.

Members of the Phoenix management appreciated the possible advantages of these different financial methods, and it was planned to present the alternatives to the board of directors for their consideration. Several persons who had studied this problem and discussed the alternatives with Kidder, Peabody & Co. felt that a $20 million straight debt issue should be sold immediately, to be followed by a $20 million convertible issue to be sold approximately one year later. Other company officers, backed by the opinion of a different investment banking house, believed the company should reverse the order. That is, Phoenix should sell the convertible debt now and wait one year before issuing the $20 million of straight debt. Another possibility raised was to issue the entire $40 million package in one bundle, either immediately or in one year.

Several points of speculation about future conditions concerned Mr. Larson as he grappled with these strategic timing questions. Sales and earnings had grown rapidly over the past few years, with profits after taxes projected to increase more than 250% over 1963 profits. In projecting these sales and earnings into the future, Mr. Larson was trying to determine whether the slope of the earnings line would be a straight extension of the trend, would increase faster than the recent past performance, or would increase less rapidly. As president of the company, his outlook for the future was generally very optimistic, with continued increases foreseen in sales demand. But Phoenix would encounter several special operating problems in the near future. The company was planning to introduce three new small aircraft models over the next two years, possibly involving high start-up production and marketing costs. Capacity production levels were being approached in nearly every facility, causing increases in overtime hours and shortages in strategic components. Moreover, the completion of the new Columbus plant was slated for the coming year, possibly involving high moving expenses and initial costs. On the other hand, aggregate disposable income within the economy had continued to post strong gains in the past few months, which normally would mean higher demand for Phoenix airplanes. Government orders due to the Vietnam War were also being stepped up, thus expanding Phoenix's sales of trainers and light observation aircraft.

Exhibit 4 presents management's projected increase in sales through 1968.

In this exhibit earnings were projected to expand in proportion to sales. As a first approximation, changes in current assets and liabilities were also projected to increase proportionately to sales. The other items shown seemed reasonable in the light of management plans. For the reasons indicated in the preceding paragraph there was considerably more uncertainty with respect to the earnings estimates than to the anticipated increase in sales and consequent changes in current assets and current liabilities.

Mr. Larson was also concerned about whether the price of the company's common stock would increase in proportion to the anticipated rise in earnings. He did not know the degree to which the current stock price already reflected the outlook for improved earnings. Recent stock prices and price-earnings ratios are given in Exhibit 6. In any event, Mr. Larson knew that continued increases in stock prices would be essential to the success of a convertible issue. A higher market price for the common stock at the time the convertible was issued would mean less dilution when the bonds were ultimately exchanged for stock, as is illustrated by Exhibit 7. Moreover, a further increase in the common stock price after the convertible issue would permit early retirement of the outstanding debt, thereby reducing interest payments by Phoenix and, more importantly, lowering the relatively high debt ratio. Mr. Larson tried to consider all these factors and their implications in determining the timing and sequence in which to issue the straight and the convertible debt.

Phoenix's debt policy had been discussed many times before by the board of directors, and Mr. Larson knew that several questions concerning the new capital proposal would be raised at the coming meeting. The outstanding long-term debt had never exceeded $10 million. The projected $40 million in new debt issues would therefore represent a major shift in capital structure policy. As additional information, Kidder, Peabody & Co. had provided the ratios of similar companies that had recently sold new debt issues (Exhibit 8). The high debt position of the unconsolidated finance subsidiary, P.F.C., made the burden of the proposed $40 million of new debt financing seem even heavier. As of September 30, 1965, P.F.C. had $11 million of bank debt and commercial paper outstanding (Exhibit 5). These obligations had grown somewhat during 1966; and in addition, P.F.C. had negotiated the $5.5 million term loan, previously described, in late 1965.

In the light of these facts Mr. Larson knew that he would be called upon to demonstrate the need for the planned large increase in external capital and to justify the reasons for raising it in the form of debt. He planned to emphasize the rapid past and projected increase in sales, which would have the effect of raising the sales-to-debt ratio and of diminishing the relative burden of the proposed debt issues in comparison with historical figures. Mr. Larson could see no other means of meeting the financial needs created by expanding sales without a very large dilution of earnings per share. More plant and equipment and a greater working capital base clearly were required. Mr. Larson also knew that the stockholders would expect dividends on the common stock to be maintained at their present level of $1.15 per share and to be increased if earnings rose as projected.

The additional leverage provided by debt in raising future earnings per share seemed attractive to Mr. Larson. Nonetheless, he remained concerned about the question of excessive risk due to high debt obligations and the burden of mandatory interest and sinking fund payments. This risk was further compounded by the possibility of a "frozen convertible" if the stock price failed to perform as hoped.

The crucial nature of timing the company's entry into the bond market brought up the question of future interest rates. The total dollar interest cost of the proposed debt over the next 20 to 25 years would vary depending upon the rate demanded in the money markets at time of issue. (See Exhibit 9.) Interest rates on a convertible debenture normally ran about 1% less than the rate paid on straight debt. Since interest costs would affect company earnings up until conversion, thereby affecting the company's stock price, the Phoenix management was attempting to anticipate the direction and movement of interest rates in the relatively near term future. Corporate bond yields were rising steadily in the months preceding May, 1966, and were approaching record levels. Whether interest rates would continue to climb or had already reached their peak seemed uncertain. A survey of capital spending plans reported in *The Monthly Economic Letter* of the First National City Bank of New York showed that business outlays were slated to increase on new plant and equipment in the near future and that backlogs of unfilled orders for durable goods were lengthening. These pressures had tended to reverse the decline in interest rates that occurred in mid-March of 1966, causing rates to climb during April. Mr. Larson was well aware that the current rate of about 5.8% on corporate bonds of a quality similar to the prospective Phoenix issue was the highest he had encountered in the last 35 years, but the prospect of still higher rates in the future made the postponement of the debt issue seem even less attractive.

In addressing himself to the remaining question of whether the straight debt issue should be publicly or privately placed, Mr. Larson outlined the differences in terms of the two debt issues. Since the analysts at Kidder, Peabody & Co. were most familiar with the acceptable design of debt instruments under the latest market conditions, Mr. Larson asked for an appraisal of the most important differing features between a public offering of senior debentures and a private placement of senior notes. Assuming that both these debt issues would be for the same amount, i.e., $20 million, the maturity of the private placement would probably be 20 years, whereas the maturity date of the public offering of senior debentures would be 25 years. The coupon interest rates would be nearly the same, about 5¾%, plus or minus ⅛%–¼%, depending on the immediate market conditions, with the slight possibility that the public offering might be somewhat less than the private placement. The spread by the investment banker would be ⅜% on the private placement and 1¼% on the public issue. The length of nonrefundability at a lower interest cost on the debentures would be 5 years, whereas the privately placed notes would be nonrefundable for 10 years. The private issue with a financial institution might involve some restrictions on the amount of subordinated debt and on working capital balances, whereas the public issue would not carry such restrictions.

Several other relevant considerations were raised by Mr. Larson in deciding between the private placement and the public debt. Since the company was considering two separate issues of $20 million each, the prospectus covering an initial public offering of debt would be made available to analysts, allowing them to become familiar with the company's current situation and thereby helping to prepare the investment community for a later security offering. Sinking fund payments on the debentures would be set at $800,000 per year starting at the end of the fifth year. Debt retirement on the private placement would be at the rate of $1.2 million per year beginning at the end of the fourth year. Credit against mandatory sinking fund requirements for debentures acquired by the company on the open market in advance of the specified date would be permitted under the public issue, but this same flexibility would not be available under the private placement. In the case of the public issue Phoenix would probably be able to buy its own debentures on the open market at less than par if interest rates continued to rise, thereby realizing savings on its debt retirement. The timing of the issue was extremely important since the period was one of rapidly changing interest rates. In this respect the private placement had the advantage in that it could be consummated one month sooner than the public issue.

The debt retirement provisions of the convertible debentures would be considerably more lenient than those of either form of straight debt. Under the convertible issue it was proposed that debt retirement start at the end of the 11th year at the rate of 5.9% of the amount of the issue, or $1,180,000 annually. Credit would be given for converted debentures or for debentures acquired on the open market.

With these data before him, Mr. Larson was preparing to present his conclusions to the board of directors, recommending a specific course of action and asking for prompt board ratification so that the financing decision could be promptly implemented.

The following quotation summarized key economic trends at this time:

The economy continues to push ahead into high ground with undiminished vigor. While the physical volume of goods and services produced and consumed has expanded—and will no doubt continue to expand—this expansion has been accompanied increasingly by price advances, as pressures on the economy's resources have mounted. . . . The rate of growth in spending for business fixed investment continued to exceed the rate of increase in over-all GNP in the first quarter. The latest survey of business plans by McGraw-Hill clearly supports earlier indications that the remainder of this year will see further strong advances in outlays for new plant and equipment.

Exhibit 1

PHOENIX AIRCRAFT COMPANY

COMPARATIVE STATEMENTS OF FINANCIAL POSITION

AS OF SEPTEMBER 30, 1961–65, AND MARCH 31, 1966

(In millions of dollars)

	September 30					March 31,
	1961	1962	1963	1964	1965	1966
ASSETS						
Cash..................................	$ 2.6	$ 1.7	$ 1.9	$ 2.4	$ 2.1	$ 4.5
Notes and accounts receivable............	8.2	7.9	9.2	10.6	12.6	17.8
Inventories............................	26.6	28.0	30.4	36.8	53.7	55.1
Prepaid expenses.......................	0.2	0.2	0.3	0.2	0.2	0.4
Total current assets.................	$37.6	$37.8	$41.8	$50.0	$68.6	$ 77.8
Investments and other assets.............	$ 5.7	$ 6.1	$ 5.4	$ 4.9	$ 5.4	$ 5.5
Property, plant, and equipment..........	$30.1	$29.3	$31.5	$33.2	$37.1	$ 40.8
Less: Accumulated depreciation........	17.8	18.0	19.2	20.6	22.9	24.0
Net fixed assets....................	$12.3	$11.3	$12.3	$12.6	$14.2	$ 16.8
Deferred charges.......................	3.5	4.1	3.4	4.0	3.5	3.4
Total assets......................	$59.1	$59.3	$62.9	$71.5	$91.7	$103.5
LIABILITIES						
Accounts payable.......................	$ 3.8	$ 3.2	$ 4.4	$ 5.3	$ 7.7	$ 6.2
Federal income taxes...................	3.4	3.1	2.9	5.3	6.7	7.0
Other taxes...........................	0.6	0.6	0.7	0.8	1.1	0.8
Accrued and other liabilities.............	1.7	1.5	1.9	3.1	4.0	4.5
Bank notes payable....................	4.1	5.1	—	0.5	8.4	16.0*
Long-term debt—current portion........	0.5	0.5	0.4	0.4	0.4	—
Total current liabilities..............	$14.1	$14.0	$10.3	$15.4	$28.3	$ 34.5
Long-term debt.......................	4.3	3.3	9.6	8.8	8.4	8.4
Stockholders' equity...................	40.7	42.0	43.0	47.3	55.0	60.6
Total liabilities and net worth........	$59.1	$59.3	$62.9	$71.5	$91.7	$103.5

* Includes $5 million of commercial paper outstanding.

Exhibit 2

PHOENIX AIRCRAFT COMPANY

COMPARATIVE STATEMENTS OF OPERATIONS FOR YEARS ENDED SEPTEMBER 30, 1961–65

(Dollar figures in millions)

	1961	1962	1963	1964	1965
Sales	$87.7	$89.8	$96.4	$122.9	$148.4
Other income	0.5	0.5	0.6	0.6	0.7
	$88.2	$90.3	$97.0	$123.5	$149.1
Manufacturing and engineering costs	$67.1	$69.8	$75.4	$ 94.4	$110.5
Depreciation	2.1	1.8	1.6	1.6	2.4
Sales and administrative expenses	6.4	6.8	6.9	9.2	11.2
Taxes other than federal income	1.6	1.8	2.1	2.6	2.9
Interest	0.3	0.5	0.5	0.5	0.6
	$77.5	$80.7	$86.5	$108.3	$127.6
Earnings before taxes	$10.7	$ 9.6	$10.5*	$ 15.2	$ 21.5
Provision for federal taxes	5.5	4.9	5.4	7.7	10.5
Earnings after taxes	$ 5.2	$ 4.7	$ 5.1*	$ 7.5	$ 11.0

(As percentage of net sales)

	1961	1962	1963	1964	1965
Sales	100.0%	100.0%	100.0%	100.0%	100.0%
Other income	0.6	0.5	0.5	0.4	0.4
	100.6%	100.5%	100.5%	100.4%	100.4%
Manufacturing and engineering costs	76.5%	77.7%	78.2%	76.8%	74.5%
Depreciation	2.4	2.0	1.6	1.3	1.7
Sales and administrative expenses	7.3	7.6	7.2	7.5	7.5
Taxes other than federal income	1.8	2.0	2.2	2.1	1.9
Interest	0.4	0.5	0.5	0.4	0.4
	88.4%	89.8%	89.7%	88.1%	86.0%
Earnings before taxes	12.2%	10.7%	10.8%*	12.3%	14.4%
Provision for federal taxes	6.2	5.5	5.5	6.2	7.0
Earnings after taxes	6.0%	5.2%	5.3%*	6.1%	7.4%

* Before special charge of $900,000 (after taxes) from discontinuance of helicopter program in 1963.
Note: Figures may not add due to rounding.

Exhibit 3

PHOENIX AIRCRAFT COMPANY

COMPARATIVE STATEMENT OF OPERATIONS FOR THE SIX MONTHS ENDED MARCH 31, 1965, AND 1966

(In millions of dollars)

	1965	1966
Sales	$70.5	$ 99.4
Other income	0.5	0.7
	$71.0	$100.1
Manufacturing and engineering costs	$53.9	$ 76.9
Depreciation	0.8	1.2
Sales and administrative expenses	5.3	6.9
Interest	0.3	0.5
	$60.3	$ 85.5
Earnings before taxes	$10.7	$ 14.6
Provision for income taxes	5.4	7.1
Earnings after taxes	$ 5.3	$ 7.5

Exhibit 4

PHOENIX AIRCRAFT COMPANY

PROJECTIONS AS OF MAY, 1966, OF SELECTED FINANCIAL ACCOUNTS
FOR YEARS ENDED SEPTEMBER 30

(In millions of dollars)

	Actual 1964	Actual 1965	Projected 1966	Projected 1967	Projected 1968
Sales	$122.9	$148.4	$189.0	$225.0	$252.0
Depreciation	1.6	2.4	2.5	3.6	3.9
Net profit after taxes*	7.5	11.0	14.0	16.7	18.6
Dividends	3.3	3.8	4.9	5.8	6.5
Retained earnings	4.2	7.2	9.1	10.9	12.1
Increase in current assets			19.2	16.7	12.5
Increase in investments and other assets†			5.7	3.5	—
Outlays on fixed assets			11.5	11.5	6.0
Increase in current liabilities‡			5.9	4.8	3.6
Reduction of long-term debt			0.4	0.7	0.7

* In this projection, allowance is made for interest payments on the outstanding bank loans, estimated at $8.4 million (the September 30, 1965, level) and for the existing long-term debt of $8.4 million, less the scheduled reduction of the existing long-term debt. As a crude approximation these interest payments on existing indebtedness are estimated at $1.0 million a year. No allowance is made for any new borrowing that may be needed to finance the projected expansion during the years 1966–68.

† This item consists primarily of an allowance for anticipated investments in Phoenix Finance Company and in unconsolidated foreign subsidiaries.

‡ Increases in current liabilities as shown here are for all current liabilities *except* short-term bank loans. One of the decisions confronting the Phoenix management was whether to replace its short-term bank loans with long-term debt.

Exhibit 5

PHOENIX FINANCE COMPANY, INC.
FINANCIAL STATEMENTS, 1964–65
(In thousands of dollars)

STATEMENT OF FINANCIAL POSITION
(As of September 30)

	1964	1965
ASSETS		
Cash	$ 319	$ 1,018
Notes and contracts receivable	10,272	14,889
Accrued interest and other receivables	129	203
Repossessed aircraft, at estimated realizable value	—	4
Prepaid expenses	37	83
Depreciable assets—net	44	29
Total assets	$10,801	$16,226
LIABILITIES		
Short-term notes payable:		
Banks and commercial paper	$ 6,400	$11,000
Phoenix Aircraft Company	900	750
Accounts payable:		
Phoenix Aircraft Company	49	675
Other	107	186
Federal income tax	100	148
Other	144	187
Total liabilities	$ 7,700	$12,946
Stockholders' equity	3,101	3,280
Total liabilities and net worth	$10,801	$16,226

STATEMENT OF OPERATIONS AND EARNINGS REINVESTED IN BUSINESS
(Years ended September 30)

	1964	1965
Income:		
Interest	$ 765	$ 1,072
Service	23	31
	$ 788	$ 1,103
Expenses:		
Interest	$ 318	$ 458
General and administrative	170	211
Provision for doubtful items	34	83
Depreciation	10	10
Other	3	2
	$ 535	$ 764
Earnings before federal income tax	$ 253	$ 339
Provision for federal income tax	125	159
Net earnings	$ 128	$ 180
Earnings reinvested in business at beginning of year	722	850
Earnings reinvested in business at end of year	$ 850	$ 1,030

Exhibit 6

PHOENIX AIRCRAFT COMPANY
PRICES OF COMMON STOCK, EARNINGS PER SHARE,
AND PRICE-EARNINGS RATIOS, 1959–66

Year Ended September 30	Stock Prices* High	Low	Close	Earnings per Share	Price-Earnings Ratio†
1959.........................	$30	$13	$26	$2.47	10.5
1960.........................	35	28	29	2.24	12.9
1961.........................	46	26	37	1.58	23.4
1962.........................	38	16	18	1.41	12.7
1963.........................	26	16	21	1.55	13.5
1964.........................	31	21	29	2.27	12.8
Period Indicated					
October–December, 1964........	32	28	32		14.1
January–March, 1965...........	35	31	32		14.1
April–June, 1965...............	36	29	32		14.1
July–September, 1965...........	43	31	41	3.30‡	18.1
October–December, 1965........	51	37	50		15.2
January–March, 1966...........	57	44	49		14.8
April, 1966....................	58	49	53		16.1
May, 1966.....................	54	42	49		14.8

* Stock prices are rounded to the nearest dollar.
† Price-earnings ratios for annual data are computed on the basis of closing prices and earnings per share for the current year. Price-earnings ratios for quarterly and monthly intervals are computed on the basis of the earnings per share of the preceding fiscal year.
‡ Earnings per share for the year ended September 30, 1965.

Exhibit 7

PHOENIX AIRCRAFT COMPANY
POTENTIAL EFFECT OF DELAYED CONVERTIBLE OFFERING
ON NUMBER OF SHARES OF COMMON STOCK ISSUED

Price of Common Stock	Price-Earnings Ratio*	Conversion Price†	Total Common Shares Issuable‡ (In Thousands)	Net Savings in Number of Shares Issuable§ Number (In Thousands)	Percentage
May, 1966:					
$46..............	13.9	$55.20	362		
May, 1967:					
$42..............	10.0	50.40	397	−35	−9.7%
46..............	11.0	55.20	362	0	0.0
50..............	12.0	60.00	333	29	8.0
54..............	12.9	64.80	309	53	14.6
58..............	13.9	69.60	287	75	20.7
66..............	15.8	79.20	253	109	30.1
74..............	17.7	88.80	225	137	37.8
82..............	19.6	98.40	203	159	43.9

* The price-earnings ratio in May, 1966, was computed on the basis of the earnings per share of $3.30 for the year ended September 30, 1965. The price-earnings ratio for May, 1967, was based on earnings per share of $4.18, computed from the figure for net profit after taxes projected in Exhibit 4 for the year ended September 30, 1966.
† Computed at a 20% premium over the price of the common stock.
‡ $20 million divided by the conversion price.
§ Amount by which the total number of shares issuable if the convertible was offered in 1967 at indicated prices differs from the 362,000 shares issuable if the convertible was issued immediately.

Exhibit 8

PHOENIX AIRCRAFT COMPANY
COMPARATIVE CAPITALIZATION RATIOS

	Senior Debt	Subordinated Debt	Preferred Stock	Minority Interest	Common and Surplus
*Certain companies recently offering convertible debentures by rights offerings:**					
Stauffer Chemical..................	18.3%	11.4%	1.1%	—%	69.2%
R. H. Macy.......................	10.7	12.6	13.4	—	63.3
American Airlines.................	49.0	16.9	0.5	—	33.6
International Silver...............	8.2	18.5	2.3	—	71.0
Celanese Corporation..............	37.1	8.9	10.9	—	43.1
United Air Lines..................	41.2	12.9	2.7	—	43.2
W. R. Grace......................	34.5	13.4	1.6	2.4	48.1
Cluett, Peabody..................	27.0	11.7	2.1	—	59.2
*Certain companies recently offering convertible debentures directly to the public:**					
Great Northern Paper..............	38.8%	5.6%	9.4%	—%	46.2%
Reynolds Metals...................	41.5	7.2	8.7	—	42.6
Chicago Musical Instrument........	10.0	29.5	—	1.2	59.3
Rockwell-Standard................	17.4	16.7	—	1.0	64.9
Reeves Brothers...................	17.3	20.6	—	—	62.1
International Minerals & Chem......	37.0	15.0	3.0	—	45.0
General Instrument................	1.5	25.5	—	—	73.0
United Merchants & Mfrs..........	20.9	14.4	—	—	64.7
Beaunit..........................	27.5 (*a*)	18.1	—	—	54.4
W. T. Grant.....................	15.0	15.0	6.4	—	63.6
J. P. Stevens.....................	24.3	7.6	—	—	68.1
*Certain companies recently offering senior debentures publicly:**					
Weyerhaeuser.....................	23.8%	—%	—%	0.3%	75.9%
Allied Chemical..................	35.6	—	—	—	64.4
Anheuser-Busch...................	35.1	—	—	—	64.9
Rockwell-Standard................	17.4	16.7	—	1.0	64.9
Hooker Chemical..................	29.5	—	3.8	—	66.7
Sun Oil..........................	15.3	1.2	—	0.4	83.1
Texas Instruments................	29.3	—	—	—	70.7
Magnavox........................	28.5	—	—	—	71.5
General Mills.....................	35.8	—	—	—	64.2
Lone Star Cement.................	31.9	—	—	—	68.1
Burlington Industries.............	33.2	3.5	—	0.9	62.4
Champion Papers.................	27.4	7.5	3.8	—	61.3
Times Mirror.....................	37.7	—	—	—	62.3
Deere............................	21.7	8.4	—	—	69.9
Ralston Purina...................	22.6	0.9	—	—	76.5
Honeywell.......................	27.0	—	7.2	—	65.8
Firestone Tire & Rubber...........	17.8	—	—	0.3	81.9

* Based on pro forma capitalization in prospectus.
a) Includes commitment.

Exhibit 9

PHOENIX AIRCRAFT COMPANY
EFFECT OF DECLINE IN INTEREST RATE
(BASED ON PROJECTED NET INCOME FOR 1968)
(In thousands except for per share data)

| | Financing Alternative | |
	No. 1	No. 2
Net income......................................	$18,600	$18,600
Less: After-tax interest cost........................	575	475
	$18,025	$18,125
Common shares now outstanding....................	3,350	3,350
Plus: Common shares issued in conversion............	315	378
Pro forma common shares.........................	3,665	3,728
Pro forma earnings per share.......................	$4.92	$4.87

Financing Alternative No. 1:
   Direct offering of $20 million of senior debentures at 5¾% now, and $20 million of subordinated debentures convertible at $63.40 (120% × $52.90—projected 1967 common price) in one year.

Financing Alternative No. 2:
   Rights offering of $20 million of subordinated debentures convertible at $52.90 (115% × $46—approximate current price) now and $20 million of senior debt at 4¾% in one year.

CAL-CHEM CORPORATION*

For several months, Mr. Jay Cochran, vice president for finance of Cal-Chem Corporation, had been considering two methods for measuring proposed capital expenditures: The net present value (NPV) method and the internal rate of return (IRR) method.[1] Mr. Cochran had become convinced that, once he had obtained reliable estimates of project cash flows, his biggest problem would lie in choosing the appropriate discount rate to use with the NPV method or in selecting the proper cutoff rate to use with the IRR method of evaluating projects. According to Mr. Cochran, it would be unwise to consider a discount rate or cutoff rate for Cal-Chem without first discussing the company's cost of capital. As chairman of the Finance Committee, he planned to present an estimate of the company's cost of capital at the next meeting of the committee on January 20, 1965. This estimate would serve as a discount rate or cutoff rate by which the acceptability of proposed investments could be determined.

At Cal-Chem's headquarters in Los Angeles, company officials directed the operations of three large manufacturing facilities, two in Southern California and one in Akron, Ohio. During World War II Cal-Chem had pioneered in the development and production of organic polymers. In 1955, Mr. James Semester, corporation president, had remarked in a speech before the New York Security Analysts that Cal-Chem was "first in fibers, films and foams"— a phrase later used in Cal-Chem advertising. In addition, the company manufactured a large number of chemical products for industrial, agricultural, and consumer use. Cal-Chem had concentrated its research efforts on the development of new products with widespread commercial use. The company's sales and after-tax earnings had grown steadily since World War II, reflecting both Cal-Chem's success and the overall expansion of the chemical industry in the postwar period. In Mr. Cochran's opinion, the company's earnings growth curve was reaching a plateau in the mid 1960's.

* Reprinted from Stanford Business Cases 1965, with the permission of the publishers, Stanford University Graduate School of Business, © 1965 by the Board of Trustees of the Leland Stanford Junior University.

[1] The net present value of a project equals the discounted present value of cash inflows minus the discounted present value of cash outflows. The internal rate of return is the discount rate at which the net present value of a project is zero.

While they had been sympathetic with Mr. Cochran's interest in the theory of capital budgeting, several Cal-Chem officials had some reservations about the value of quantitative analysis in evaluating proposed projects. Mr. Semester had made the following comments in December, 1964:

> Capital budgeting and the evaluation of capital projects in a large company are not, and cannot be, the precise jobs that textbooks seem to imply that they are. There are literally hundreds of projects considered every year, and responsibility for approval is delegated downward depending upon the size of the expenditure. Our overall policy is to maintain or improve the rate of return on investment for the company. Most projects can only be appraised as a matter of judgment under this policy and precise numerical evaluation is relatively seldom possible.
>
> I don't want to give you the impression that we don't make detailed economic analyses of specific projects—we do, and will probably do more in the future. But the use of quantitative techniques for analyzing many of our investments would not only waste time and money on a fruitless search, but would tend to give a spurious impression of accuracy. The problem seems, to me, to be the same as that faced in introducing other quantitative techniques into business use; you want to retain the overriding protection of experience and judgment.

The executive vice president, a member of the Finance Committee, Mr. Richard Bergeron, had this to say about the company's existing policy regarding capital investment decisions:

> The company does not set a firm cutoff rate which is applied automatically to all investment proposals. However, required minimum rates of return are set as a guide in considering proposed investments for which a rate of return analysis is applicable. These cutoff rates differ among proposals for (1) construction of new facilities and (2) improvement of existing facilities. However, a particular project that does not meet the required minimum rates of return will be considered if there are sufficient collateral considerations. Also, there are certain types of projects which are not susceptible to rate of return analysis, such as those involving power, service and office facilities, air and water pollution abatement, and employee safety and welfare.
>
> When individual projects are submitted for final approval, we use the discounted-cash-flow rate of return technique when this technique is applicable. In a large company such as ours, however, I feel this technique is applicable for relatively few projects—probably fewer than 20%. The cash flow technique is most useful down at the research-engineering level, where there are always many alternatives to consider. These are sifted out in the planning stage, however, and seldom become an issue when a decision is made as to whether or not to undertake the project.

On January 14, 1965, Mr. Cochran and Mr. Bergeron joined Mr. Semester in his office for a preliminary discussion of the topics on the agenda for the Finance Committee meeting scheduled for January 20.

COCHRAN: As I mentioned before, we've been doing some work with our staff people on improving our capital budgeting procedures. Next Wednesday

I'd like to present to the committee my estimates of our costs of debt and equity capital, so that we can get an idea what our cutoff rate or discount rate should really be.

SEMESTER: Those academic guys really got through to you last summer, didn't they, Jay?

COCHRAN: Well, frankly, I think that's the big value in a management program like that. You get back to the campus for a few weeks and get some new ideas on the old problems.

SEMESTER: O.K., shoot, Jay.

COCHRAN: First of all, we have come up with estimates of initial investment and future cash flows for *all* the projects proposed by the divisions in November. It was a little painful on some of the R & D and safety projects, but at least we have some numbers to look at and compare. Here are the ten major projects in our new budget.

Project	Initial Investment	Project Life	Net Present Value (at 10%)	Internal Rate of Return
A	$ 400,000	8	$ 460,000	37%
B	1,000,000	20	1,400,000	28%
C	1,200,000	10	560,000	20%
D	200,000	2	22,000	18%
E	800,000	15	190,000	14%
F	600,000	6	36,000	12%
G	100,000	5	(Negative)	9%
H	400,000	20	(Negative)	4%
I	800,000	4	(Negative)	3%
J	50,000	(?)	(Negative)	(−)
	$5,550,000			

BERGERON: How do you come up with the internal rate of return again?

COCHRAN: Actually, we find it by trial and error, Dick. For example, with Project D we estimated that an investment of $200,000 will give us a net cash inflow after taxes of $128,000 a year for two years. We found that 18% is the discount rate at which the present value of the two $128,000 inflows is equal to the initial investment of $200,000.

BERGERON: And all your figures are net of taxes?

COCHRAN: Right.

SEMESTER: What's the rate of return on Project J?

COCHRAN: That's the safety program I mentioned before. It's almost impossible to estimate the cash flows, but when we did the rate of return was less than zero. It's just one of those projects that we have to take even though the numbers alone don't justify it. The projects are ranked by rate of return, but obviously, other factors affect their acceptability.

This year we will have internally generated funds of about $3 million available for capital investments as you can see in this chart:

	Millions
Profit before taxes	$7.2
Taxes (overall tax rate of 50%)	3.6
Profit after taxes	3.6
Depreciation	0.6
Cash flow	4.2
Dividends[2]	1.2
Internally generated funds available	$3.0

So the cost of funds is particularly important, I feel, since we'll either have to obtain outside capital, or limit our capital spending to the amount available internally.

SEMESTER: If we were to limit our capital budget to $3 million, we wouldn't need a cutoff rate.

COCHRAN: Right, if we were using the IRR method. But we'd still have to choose an appropriate discount rate if we were evaluating new projects by the NPV method.

BERGERON: We could sell debentures at 3 to 3½% ten years ago, but those days are gone forever.

COCHRAN: There's no doubt about that. New issues with an "A" rating are going at about 4½ right now. I have talked with David Towers and a few other underwriters, and the consensus seems to be that we could add about $5 million in debt at a little over 4½. That would raise our debt ratio to 30%, pretty close to the industry average. The next $5 million issue would probably cost closer to 5%.

SEMESTER: We'll be working toward that industry average as a long-run goal, but I'd hate to have Moody's revise our rating.

COCHRAN: Well, if we went to $15 million in debt with our present equity position, we might slip to a "Baa".

SEMESTER: It seems to me that there is a hidden cost in new long-term debt. The increase in financial risk may have an effect on the market price of our stock.

BERGERON: With these bonds, are you talking about coupon rate or effective yield, Jay?

COCHRAN: Either one. The difference is small.

SEMESTER: Are you sure about that? I heard last week the *Times* received only 98 on their issue of 4½'s, so their cost must have been something over 4½.[3]

COCHRAN: O.K., O.K., right. But the difference is still small.

SEMESTER: How about a sinking fund?

COCHRAN: I think we can bank on it. It'll probably be the standard trustee

---

[2] Dividends include $180,000 on preferred stock and $1,056,000 on common stock.

[3] Mr. Semester referred to a recent Times Mirror Company offering of 4½% sinking fund debentures, due January 1, 1990 (Rating A). *Moody's Bond Survey* reported on January 11, 1965, "These debentures reached the market on January 7, priced to the public at 99 to yield 4.57% to maturity. Price to the company was 98, or the equivalent of an interest cost of 4.64%."

arrangement. With a 20-year maturity, the first payment to the trustee could probably be deferred for five years. This would mean retiring the full amount of the issue over 15 equal annual payments.

SEMESTER: Doesn't the sinking fund provision increase our net cost?

COCHRAN: Well, I don't know, Jim. There are obviously some trustee's fees to pay, but beyond that, I can't think of any other costs involved.

SEMESTER: There must be some opportunity costs involved in these sinking fund payments.

COCHRAN: I don't think so. As the trustee retires the bonds, it opens up the top for new debt.

BERGERON: What about a preferred issue?

SEMESTER: We've been over that a dozen times, Dick. Preferred issues are a thing of the past. They've got all the disadvantages of debt and common.

BERGERON: I don't want to beat a dead horse, but it still seems to me that with preferred we can avoid the risk of debt without diluting our common equity.

SEMESTER: Yes, I know, Dick, we've been through all that before. The big thing is that bond interest is deductible[4] and preferred dividends aren't. As long as we can sell bonds at any reasonable price, we're better off than with preferred. Our existing preferred probably cost us nearly 5% when you consider all the issue costs, and I'll bet that new preferred would cost at least that much. Don't talk to me about more preferred; tell me how to get rid of the $4 million we already have on our books.

COCHRAN: We could always recapitalize it, but it would be an expensive proposition.

SEMESTER: Right, and that day will come. As soon as the time is right, we'll eliminate the preferred from our balance sheet. But let's face it, it's a devil of a job to refinance a noncallable issue.

COCHRAN: Well, I guess maybe the cost of preferred isn't too relevant to our present budget. How about the cost of the new common?

BERGERON: We'd have to maintain our dividend on the new shares. So our annual cost would be at least a dollar a share.[5]

SEMESTER: What could we realize from a new issue, Jay?

COCHRAN: Well, the market price has been running around 51 to 53. I think we could net at least $50 a share after issue costs on a new offering.

BERGERON: Then that's cheaper than debt. We get $50 a share and pay out only a $1 a share each year. That's 2% money. You can't beat that.

COCHRAN: This is one thing I wanted to discuss. Last summer at the management program, the consensus seemed to be that the cost of common equity was equal to the earnings-price ratio.

BERGERON: Do you mean the price-earnings ratio?

---

[4] The company's tax rate was approximately 50%. A recent survey of Cal-Chem stockholders revealed that the "average stockholder," taking into account number of shares owned, had a marginal tax rate of 36%.

[5] Cal-Chem had paid a cash dividend of $1 per share each year for the past six years.

COCHRAN: No. One divided by the price-earnings ratio.

BERGERON: I don't follow you.

COCHRAN: Well, it has to do with diluting present earnings per share. If you don't earn a return on the new funds of at least the earnings-price ratio, then you dilute the earnings of the old stockholders.

SEMESTER: I wonder if we should look at present earnings or future earnings.

COCHRAN: Well, that gets into the fine points of the calculations. As a rough cut, I think we can use present earnings. It looks like competition will be tougher and our product prices will be weaker in the foreseeable future, so our earnings will probably level off for a few years.

SEMESTER: At any rate, this would be a good one to bring up at the meeting. Is there anything else we should talk about now?

COCHRAN: I'd like to hit one more point, briefly. How should we figure our overall cost of capital? The big trend seems to be toward using a weighted average cost of capital as a cutoff rate or discount rate.[6]

SEMESTER: I've read about that, Jay, and I've wondered about this weighting business.

COCHRAN: Well, the cost of each type of capital is weighted by its proportion of the total capital structure.

SEMESTER: Using book values, right?

COCHRAN: Right.

SEMESTER: That's one point I've wondered about. Our common stock is selling for more than book value, so why not use the market value of the securities instead of book values in weighting the cost?

BERGERON: I can't see why you go through this weighting business at all. It's a simple matter of economics. You just match the cheapest source of capital with the best available return on investment. For example, start with retained earnings: since they are already available for investment, the cost is effectively nil. Then debt might be the next cheapest source, and so on.

Mr. Bergeron's Sketch

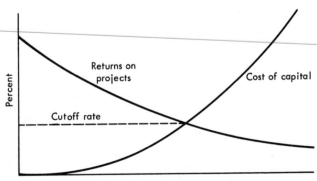

------

[6] See Exhibit 1 for the capital structure of the company at the end of 1964.

When you get to the point where your cost of capital is greater than your expected return, you stop investing. It's as simple as that.

SEMESTER: I think we'd better get our ideas firmed up before the full committee meets next week.

Exhibit 1

CAL-CHEM CORPORATION

CAPITAL STRUCTURE AS OF DECEMBER 31, 1964

(In millions)

Long-term debt
$3\frac{1}{2}\%$ debentures due 1975........................ $10.0
Preferred stock
   Cumulative, noncallable, $100 par value, $4\frac{1}{2}\%$
   Series, 100,000 shares authorized, 40,000
   shares outstanding........................... 4.0
Common stock
   No par, 3,000,000 shares authorized, 1,056,112
   shares outstanding.......................... 12.1
Retained earnings............................. 23.8
                                              $49.9

AMERICAN TELEPHONE AND TELEGRAPH
COMPANY—1974

^^

Early in 1974, the treasurer of the American Telephone and Telegraph Company[1] was reviewing the company's major financial policies. One major concern was the company's debt position, which had risen in recent years to a level that put the company's triple-A bond rating in jeopardy. For years, AT&T had carefully maintained the highest credit rating and the treasurer was hesitant to adopt a financing plan that might lead to its loss. However, a depressed stock price made common equity financing undesirable.

The company

The American Telephone and Telegraph Company and its 21 principal operating telephone subsidiaries furnished local and toll telephone service to over 80% of the telephones in the United States. Other communication services included data transmission, private line teletypewriter service, and the transmission of radio and television programs. A subsidiary, the Western Electric Company, manufactured telephone equipment and apparatus for the company and its telephone subsidiaries. Another affiliate, the Bell Telephone Laboratories, conducted scientific research and development work for AT&T and Western Electric.

Characteristics

Several characteristics distinguished AT&T from most other private enterprise in the United States. The company was the world's largest utility and the nation's largest private employer, with over one million employees. Its assets at the end of 1973 exceeded $67 billion and were greater than the combined assets of General Motors Corporation, Exxon Corporation, International Business Machines Corporation, and General Electric Company. In 1973, it spent $9.3 billion on construction, which exceeded the total assets of General Electric and approached those of IBM. Western Electric by itself was the nation's tenth largest manufacturing company and Bell Telephone Laboratories was the largest corporate research organization in the world.

As a regulated public utility, the size and profitability of its investments

---

[1] Although AT&T is the parent company, AT&T, as used herein, refers to the consolidated operation of AT&T and its subsidiaries.

were determined in large measure by forces not fully under the control of management. The company and its telephone affiliates were typically required to provide whatever level of service the public demanded at prices set by the regulatory bodies.

The communications business, moreover, was capital-intensive, i.e., large quantities of capital were required to meet service demands. For AT&T, over $2.60 of capital was required to produce $1.00 of annual revenue (sales); by contrast, the average manufacturing company needed $0.60 to produce a dollar of annual revenues.

In addition, the communications business was becoming more competitive. The Federal Communications Commission had adopted the policy of fostering competition. Customer owned devices were permitted to be connected to the telephone network through protective interconnecting devices. In addition, some firms had been authorized to provide specialized intercity services, and open competition appeared to be the policy with respect to domestic satellite communications.

Recent operating results

Demand for communication services had grown throughout the period following World War II at a rate almost twice that of the economy overall. The number of AT&T telephones quintupled from 22 million in 1945 to 110 million in 1973 and the total number of conversations (toll and local) rose in each consecutive year from 30 billion to an estimated 143 billion. Total revenues increased steadily from $1.9 billion in 1945 to $23.5 billion in 1973.

Beginning in 1969, the company experienced some service problems. Demand for telephone service had temporarily outpaced the company's capacity in a few large metropolitan areas and service quality had suffered. In these areas, public criticism had quickly mounted and the issue of quality of telephone service had become a political football for some regulators, politicians, and consumer groups. As a result of these service problems, the company spent large sums of construction dollars to expand its plant capacity. By the end of 1973, most of the service problems had been corrected.

The second half of the 1960's also saw the company's earning rate begin to fall. Inflation had caused a sharp rise in operating and capital costs, which could not be fully offset by productivity gains. For the first time in years, AT&T needed numerous rate increases to maintain its profitability and to insure access to the capital markets. For the remainder of the decade, appreciation of the need for rate relief in an inflationary environment by the various regulatory bodies was essential if the company was to achieve the earnings level necessary to finance its construction program on reasonable terms.

Construction and financing needs

As a result of the growth in the demand for service, AT&T's capital expenditures had been large. In 1973, the company spent $9.3 billion on new construction: $6.0 billion was spent to expand service; another $2.1 billion resulted from customer movement and plant relocations; and $1.2 billion was needed to modernize the system. For the rest of the 1970's, assuming inflation would not be greater than 3–5%, the construction program was expected to grow somewhat below the 1960–73 average of 9.3%.

On average, only 50% of the construction program had been financed internally. In recent years the deferred taxes from the normalization of the investment tax credit and accelerated depreciation had become an important source of internal funds, and by 1973, along with higher reinvested earnings, the internally-generated funds were 61% of the construction program. For the remainder of the decade, the percentage of internal sources was expected to increase further. However, the external financing requirement was expected to remain in the $3.5–4.0 billion range annually.

Financial policy

The company had always recognized the importance of the dividend to its shareowners. Since 1885, AT&T had never passed a dividend payment or lowered its dividend rate, even during the depression. In recent years, the dividend policy had been to increase the dividend when warranted by increased reinvested earnings and when the increase could be maintained at that level. This resulted in a payout rate in the range of 60–65%. The management felt that this policy maximized the attractiveness of the stock by achieving a reasonable mix between dividend income and capital gain.

The company's debt policy was designed to maintain a strong financial structure. The strong financial structure entitled AT&T's debt to the highest credit rating and maximized the access to all major sources of new capital. Public statements by the company continually stressed the intention of maintaining an appropriate capital structure to assure an ongoing top-quality rating for its bonds.

Until the late 1950's, the company's debt ratio objective had been between 30–40%. In the late 1950's, it became generally accepted that depression-boom swings in the economy could be prevented or at least mitigated and that a higher debt level could be safely carried by the company. At the same time, however, the company's stock price was very favorable. Accordingly, the company issued common stock in 1961 and 1964. Beginning in 1965, the company's debt ratio moved steadily upward from 32% in 1965 to 47.6% in 1973, the latter being somewhat above its long-term objective. During this time, debt was used almost exclusively to raise outside money except for the issuance of $3 billion of preferred stock. The rapid increase in the debt ratio beyond 40% since 1970 also reflected the substantial decline in the company's stock price. The sale of common stock between 1970–73 would have been below book value, which was undesirable because it would inhibit the growth rate in earnings per share.

Even though interest coverage stabilized in 1971–73, the precipitous decline from 1966 to 1971 had not gone unnoticed. Standard & Poor's had recently downgraded the bonds of three companies to a double-A rating—The

Southern New England Telephone Company, New England Telephone and Telegraph Company, and The Pacific Telephone and Telegraph Company. The reduction had been attributed to a steady downward trend in interest coverage and the continuing need for considerable external financing. Additional downgradings of other subsidiaries seemed probable unless the unsatisfactory trends were reversed.

At the end of 1973, the company was somewhat below the borderline for a triple-A rating and the treasurer believed that it was essential to maintain the triple-A rating. He said:

> It is most important that any company determine its capital structure on the relevant business and financial characteristics of the business. A company's capital requirement is one important characteristic. The frequency and volume of our debt issues to be marketed in the years ahead require that we maintain a top-flight credit standing. This is *not* simply a provincial wish on the part of the financial officers to have things comfortably in hand, but rather, it is a very practical need. Both debt ratio and interest coverage impinge on the credit rating. The credit rating of a bond is a major determinant in both the cost and availability of long-term debt. Lower-rated bonds pay more in interest charges because the risk is judged greater, and these cost differentials can be substantial, particularly in difficult markets.[2] Perhaps more importantly, lower-rated firms can find money difficult and perhaps impossible to obtain in periods of financial trauma such as we experienced in 1970.[3]

The treasurer also recognized that the company's heavy external financing needs during the rest of the 1970's would necessitate the sale of common stock and an improved stock price would reduce the number of shares that would have to be sold. It was within this context that he embarked upon a review of AT&T's financial policies. Exhibits 1–9 provide information on AT&T's operating results, financial needs, and policies. Exhibits 10–13 provide background information on bond ratings and on the capital markets.

---

[2] In 1973 yields on seasoned Public Utility bonds averaged 7.60%, 7.71%, 7.84%, and 8.17% for bonds rated AAA, AA, A, and BBB respectively. For AT&T, an increase of 10 basis points (one-tenth of one percent) in its average borrowing cost would mean increased interest expense of $28 million per year. [Footnote added.]

[3] Interview with casewriter.

Exhibit 1

AMERICAN TELEPHONE AND TELEGRAPH COMPANY—1974
GROWTH IN TELEPHONES IN THE UNITED STATES*

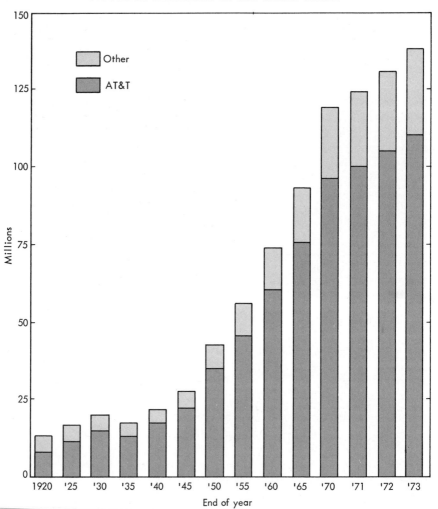

* Excluding Alaska and Hawaii.

Exhibit 2

AMERICAN TELEPHONE AND TELEGRAPH COMPANY—1974

RECENT OPERATING HISTORY

(Dollar figures in billions except per share data)

	1960	1965	1966	1967	1968	1969	1970	1971	1972	1973
Operating revenues—total	$ 7.9	$11.1	$12.1	$13.0	$14.1	$15.7	$17.0	$18.5	$20.9	$23.5
Local	4.5	6.0	6.4	6.7	7.2	7.8	8.5	9.2	10.4	11.4
Toll	3.0	4.6	5.3	5.7	6.3	7.3	7.9	8.7	9.8	11.3
Other	0.4	0.5	0.4	0.6	0.6	0.6	0.6	0.6	0.7	0.8
Net income	1.20	1.80	1.98	2.05	2.05	2.20	2.19	2.20	2.53	2.99
Return on average equity	10.0%	9.5%	9.9%	9.7%	9.3%	9.5%	9.2%	8.7%	9.4%	10.47%
Return on average total capital	7.7%	7.7%	7.9%	7.8%	7.5%	7.7%	7.6%	7.4%	7.7%	8.3%
Earnings per share	$ 2.77	$ 3.41	$ 3.69	$ 3.79	$ 3.75	$ 4.00	$ 3.99	$ 3.92	$ 4.34	$ 5.06
Dividends per share	1.65	2.05	2.20	2.25	2.40	2.45	2.60	2.60	2.70	2.87
Stock price range	39–54	60–70	49–63	49–62	48–58	48–58	40–54	41–54	41–54	46–55
Median price-earnings ratio	17	19	15	15	14	13	12	12	11	10
Telephones in service (millions)	61	76	80	84	88	93	97	100	105	110
Average conversations per day (millions)	219	280	295	307	323	350	368	388	410	N.A.
Toll messages (millions)	2,844	4,278	4,798	5,206	5,794	6,522	7,154	7,734	8,554	9,461
Revenues per message	$ 1.05	$ 1.08	$ 1.10	$ 1.10	$ 1.09	$ 1.13	$ 1.10	$ 1.12	$ 1.14	$ 1.19

Note: N.A. = not available.

Exhibit 3

AMERICAN TELEPHONE AND TELEGRAPH COMPANY—1974

Cost and Rate Information

	1960	1961	1962	1963	1964	1965	1966	1967	1968	1969	1970	1971	1972	1973
Applications for rate increases..	2	0	1	1	2	1	1	3	10	11	13	33	19	15
Amount requested (in millions).								$ 191	$ 257	$ 500	$ 898	$1,594	$1,315*	$357*
Amount granted (in millions)..								...	$ 56	$ 83	$ 396	$ 788	$ 792	$854
Telephone rates index (1960 = 100)														
Local...............	100	100	100	100	100	100	99	99	100	101	106	111	117	N.A.
Long distance............	100	100	99	98	98	95	94	92	93	93	92	95	98	N.A.
Wage and other employee benefits per telephone.............	$48.07	$47.69	$47.48	$47.13	$48.96	$49.99	$51.74	$52.99	$53.86	$59.26	$64.73	$69.99	$76.75	N.A.

* Some applications still pending.
Note: N.A. = not available.

Exhibit 4

AMERICAN TELEPHONE AND TELEGRAPH COMPANY—1974

INSTABILITY OF RATE EARNED ON TOTAL CAPITAL

(Measured by change from year to year)

Percent of
average rate earned

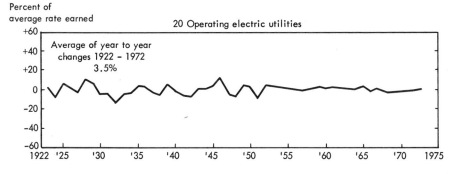

20 Operating electric utilities

Average of year to year
changes 1922 - 1972
3.5%

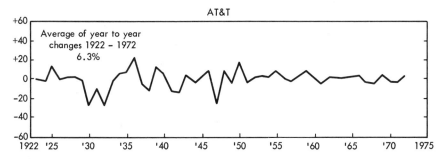

AT&T

Average of year to year
changes 1922 - 1972
6.3%

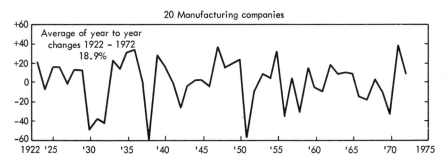

20 Manufacturing companies

Average of year to year
changes 1922 - 1972
18.9%

Exhibit 5

AMERICAN TELEPHONE AND TELEGRAPH COMPANY—1974
CONSTRUCTION EXPENDITURES AND NEW MONEY REQUIREMENTS

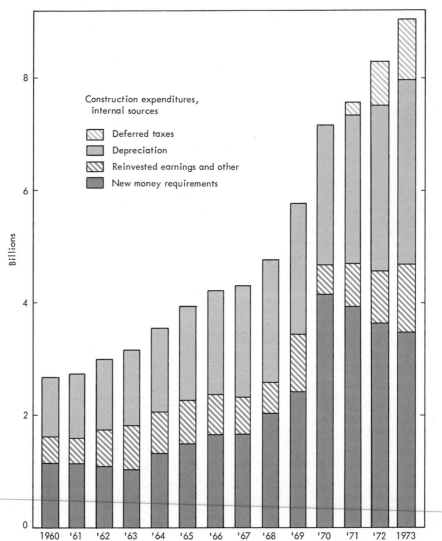

Exhibit 6

AMERICAN TELEPHONE AND TELEGRAPH COMPANY—1974

DEBT RATIO

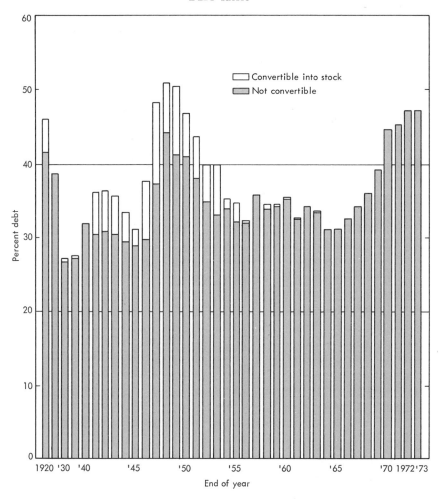

Exhibit 7

AMERICAN TELEPHONE AND TELEGRAPH COMPANY—1974

INTEREST COVERAGE

(Pre-tax)

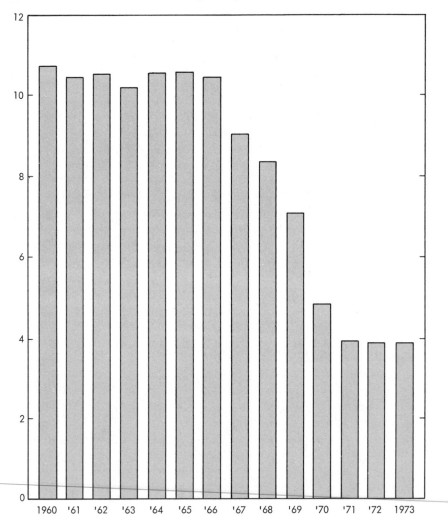

Exhibit 8

AMERICAN TELEPHONE AND TELEGRAPH COMPANY—1974

MARKET PRICE AND BOOK VALUES

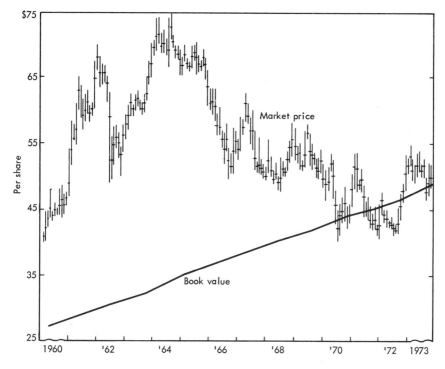

Exhibit 9

AMERICAN TELEPHONE AND TELEGRAPH COMPANY—1974

IMPACT OF VARIOUS DEBT POLICIES ON INTEREST COVERAGE, EARNINGS PER SHARE, AND DIVIDENDS

Bond
Rating

	1973	1974	1975	1976	1977
Debt = 48% Capital by 1977					
Debt ratio...........................	48%	48%	48%	48%	48%
Interest coverage (pre-tax)............	3.90	3.84	3.83	3.82	3.81
Earnings per share..................	$ 5.06	$ 5.36	$ 5.69	$ 6.03	$ 6.39
Dividends per share.................	$ 2.87	$ 3.08	$ 3.40	$ 3.60	$ 3.80
Payout ratio........................	57%	58%	60%	60%	60%
Return on equity...................	10.47%	10.59%	10.77%	10.93%	11.06%
Debt = 40% Capital by 1977					
Debt ratio...........................	48%	45%	43%	42%	40%
Interest coverage (pre-tax)............	3.90	4.07	4.25	4.43	4.60
Earnings per share..................	$ 5.06	$ 5.28	$ 5.46	$ 5.65	$ 5.89
Dividends per share.................	$ 2.87	$ 3.08	$ 3.25	$ 3.35	$ 3.50
Payout ratio........................	57%	58%	60%	60%	60%
Return on equity...................	10.47%	10.44%	10.35%	10.28%	10.26%
Debt = 55% Capital by 1977					
Debt ratio...........................	48%	50%	52%	54%	55%
Interest coverage (pre-tax)............	3.90	3.72	3.52	3.35	3.21
Earnings per share..................	$ 5.06	$ 5.43	$ 5.92	$ 6.44	$ 6.99
Dividends per share.................	$ 2.87	$ 3.08	$ 3.55	$ 3.85	$ 4.15
Payout ratio........................	57%	57%	60%	60%	60%
Return on equity...................	10.47%	10.73%	11.18%	11.61%	12.02%

AA (handwritten, beside Debt = 48% block)
AAA (handwritten, beside Debt = 40% block)
A (handwritten, beside Debt = 55% block)

Note: These forecasts are based on estimates and assumptions by the casewriter about future capital expenditures, interest rate levels, and the allowed return on capital. Assumed cost of debt for 48% capital = 8% for 1974–77.

Exhibit 10

AMERICAN TELEPHONE AND TELEGRAPH COMPANY—1974

BOND RATING GUIDELINES FOR INDUSTRY GROUPS

	AAA	AA	A	Baa	Ba
Telephone (Senior)					
Debt ratio.............................	43%	48%	53%	60%	70%
Pre-tax interest coverage.................	4.50X	4.00X	3.50X	3.00X	2.00X
Electric (Senior)					
Debt ratio.............................	49%	52%	55%	58%	60%
Pre-tax interest coverage.................	4.50X	3.50X	3.00X	2.50X	2.0X
Industrial—Manufacturing *(Sinking Fund Debentures)*					
Debt ratio.............................	15%	20%	30%	40%	50%
Pre-tax interest coverage.................	11.0X	9.0X	7.0X	4.0X	2.5X
Industrial—Retail (Sinking Fund Debentures)					
Debt ratio.............................	40%	50%	60%	68%	75%
Pre-tax fixed payment coverage............	5.00X	3.50X	2.50X	2.00X	1.75X
Finance Companies (Sinking Fund Debentures)					
Debt ratio.............................	...	75%	77%	82%	85%
Pre-tax interest coverage.................	...	2.25X	1.80X	1.60X	1.30X

Source: Internal memorandum of the Pacific Mutual Life Insurance Company, May, 1972.

Exhibit 11

AMERICAN TELEPHONE AND TELEGRAPH COMPANY—1974

TOTAL CASH OFFERINGS OF NEW CORPORATE SECURITIES

(Dollar figures in billions)

	1967	1968	1969	1970	1971	1972	1973e	1974e
Corporate stock issues (Common and preferred)	$ 2.6	$ 4.1	$ 7.2	$ 7.6	$12.0	$11.9	$ 8.3	$ 9.0
Corporate bonds								
Public straight debt	10.8	8.1	9.5	23.1	21.3	15.7	12.6	23.0
Privately placed straight debt	5.9	5.6	4.0	3.5	6.9	9.0	9.0	10.0
Convertible debt	4.4	3.3	4.0	2.7	3.6	2.3	0.4	1.0
Total corporate bonds	$21.1	$17.0	$17.5	$29.3	$31.8	$27.0	$22.0	$34.0
Total gross new cash offerings*	$23.7	$21.1	$24.7	$36.9	$43.8	$38.9	$30.3	$43.0
AT&T external financing needs	$ 1.6	$ 2.0	$ 2.4	$ 4.2	$ 3.9	$ 3.7	$ 3.5	$ 3.7
AT&T as percent of total gross new cash offerings	7%	9%	10%	11%	9%	10%	12%	9%

Note: e = estimate.
* Gross offerings including refinancing of maturing debt.
Source: Salomon Brothers, *Supply and Demand for Credit in 1974* (New York: Salomon Brothers, 1974).

Exhibit 12

AMERICAN TELEPHONE AND TELEGRAPH COMPANY—1974

PORTFOLIO INVESTMENTS OF SELECTED FINANCIAL INSTITUTIONS AND INDIVIDUALS IN THE UNITED STATES

AMOUNTS HELD AS OF DECEMBER 31, 1972

(In billions)

	U.S. Government Securities	Federal Agency Securities	Commercial Paper	State and Local Bonds	Corporate and Foreign Bonds	Corporate Stocks*	Mortgages	Loans	Total Credit†	Annual Net Increases in Amounts of Total Credit 1967–72		
										High	Low	Average
Mutual savings banks	$ 3.5	$ 4.2	$ 0	$ 0.9	$ 14.2	$ 4.1	$ 67.6	$ 1.8	$ 96.3	$10.6	$ 2.8	$ 6.1
Savings and loan associations	13.8	10.5	0.2	0	0	0	206.4	1.8	232.7	35.8	9.1	17.9
Life insurance companies	3.7	0.6	3.2	3.3	86.8	27.3	77.3	...	202.2	12.5	6.1	6.3
Fire and casualty companies	5.0	0.6	...	23.9	9.1	20.4	0	...	59.0	6.2	2.0	4.2
Private noninsured pension funds	3.1	0.6	0.5	...	27.4	107.1	3.0	...	141.7	7.2	5.8	6.4
State and local retirement funds	2.6	1.1	0.5	1.7	42.2	15.4	7.2	...	70.7	7.2	3.7	5.7
Open-end mutual funds	0.6	...	1.5	...	5.2	52.9	...	...	60.2	3.4	(1.4)	1.2
Commercial banks	67.0	21.8	10.1	89.8	5.5	...	99.3	280.5	574.0	70.0	15.6	41.1
Finance companies	...	...		...	...	...	11.1	59.8	70.9	7.9	0.6	4.5
Credit unions	3.0	...		...	...	...	1.0	16.7	20.7	3.4	0.8	2.0
Business corporations	6.2	3.1	19.6	5.4	...	...	...	34.5	68.8	7.6	(1.8)	3.8
State and local governments	19.1	3.5	0.6	...	...	...	...	...	23.2	4.1	(1.5)	1.6
Foreigners	55.5	3.8	3.7	...	2.9	26.8	...	...	92.7	27.7	.9	9.3
Individuals and miscellaneous	77.6	10.5	1.7	53.3	59.6	966.0	46.3	...	1,214.4	18.1	(9.8)	1.8
Total privately held	$260.7	$60.3	$41.6	$178.3	$252.9	$1,220.0	$519.2	$395.1	$2,927.5			
Federal agencies‡	189.1	3.2					45.3		237.6			
Total outstanding	$449.8	$63.5	$41.6	$178.3	$252.9	$1,220.0	$564.5	$395.1	$3,165.1			

* At market.
† Including holdings of corporate stock at market.
‡ U.S. trust funds, federal agencies, Federal Reserve banks.
Source: Salomon Brothers, op. cit.

Exhibit 13

AMERICAN TELEPHONE AND TELEGRAPH COMPANY—1974

TOTAL CORPORATE EXTERNAL FINANCING REQUIREMENTS* (1971–85)

(In billions)

Electric power industry.................	$ 175
Fossil fuel industry......................	200
Communications.......................	100
Metal industries........................	75
All other..............................	550
Total..........................	$1,100†
Average annual 1967–71.................	28
Average annual 1971–85................	73

* Net new issuance excludes refinancing of maturing debt.
† In constant 1971 dollars.
Source: Economic Report, "Financial Implications of Material Shortages," Manufacturers Hanover Trust
Company, November, 1973.

CYCLOPS CEMENT COMPANY (Abridged)

On May 27, 1965, Mr. Clinton Howe, a director of the Cyclops Cement Company, received from the president of the company a copy of the consultant's report on cash flows in recession conditions, a summary of which is reproduced as an Appendix to this case. Mr. Howe had been present at the directors meeting on March 15, when the scope and methodology to be used in the study had been discussed. Therefore he knew that the consultant planned to use his analysis of recession cash flows as a basis for recommendations on the company's future debt policy. Mr. Howe also knew that the president, Mr. Patrick Dean, had a number of proposals for expansion (by acquisition as well as internally) under study, and that he was prepared to consider an increase in Cyclops' borrowing ratio rather than issue stock at its currently depressed level. Mr. Dean had assured the directors, however, that he would not consider a debt/capitalization ratio of over 50%.

The report was likely to be discussed at the next meeting of the board of directors on June 5, and Mr. Howe undertook a study of the consultant's recommendations.

The Cyclops Cement Company had been established in the upper Mississippi Valley area in the late 19th century, and approximately 50% of company sales still came from this area. The remaining sales were evenly distributed among three widely separated areas: the Southwest, the Southeast, and New England, which Cyclops had entered through mergers with three smaller companies. In terms of production volume, Cyclops ranked among the top 15 companies in the industry in 1965, with six plants and a total productive capacity of 18,200,000 barrels a year.

The cement industry

The broadly based use of cement and concrete products in most types of construction provides the industry with considerable stability. The historical record has demonstrated this. The only exceptions have been the major depression of the 1930's and World War II (see Chart I in the Appendix).

The production of cement is very capital intensive, utilizing a highly mechanized process involving very old, well-established, and well-known technology. Significant reductions in unit production costs are possible from the operation of large plants, since coordination requires no more effort for

182

large fixed costs

large- than for small-scale operations. The cost of a barrel of production capacity also declines with increased plant size.

Plant size is limited, however, by the high cost of transport of cement— a bulky, low-value product. Since the raw materials used in cement production are readily available in most regions of the country, it is generally less expensive to operate a number of regional plants close to cement users than to incur high transport costs by shipping cement long distances from a few very large plants. Ninety percent of total U.S. cement production is shipped less than 160 miles, with the primary exceptions being the output of some new and very large plants where ready access to low-cost water transportation permits competitive pricing in markets up to 1,300 miles away. Competition, therefore, is generally on a regional basis, with three or four producers operating plants in the region and accounting for the great majority of total cement sales. The plants are small, but the relatively high production costs are offset by low distribution expense.

The ruinous trade conditions of the 1930's produced chronic overcapacity in the cement industry and made most companies reluctant to expand their facilities.[1] The 10-year period ending in 1955 saw very little increase in productive capacity despite strong gains in construction activity and use of cement. The resulting rise in operating rates combined with firm product prices to yield profit rates considerably above the average for manufacturing as a whole. By 1955 the industry was operating at 94% of capacity and was earning almost 19% on net worth. This high return resulted in part from the use of fully depreciated plant. Exhibit 1 provides data on this period.

Exhibit 1

CYCLOPS CEMENT COMPANY

OPERATING RATES, PRICES, AND PROFITS IN THE CEMENT INDUSTRY, 1950–55

	1950	1951	1952	1953	1954	1955
Industry capacity (mil. bbls.)	268	282	284	292	298	315
Cement production (mil. bbls.)	226	246	249	264	272	297
Percent capacity utilization	84	87	88	90	91	94
Annual increase in capacity (mil. bbls.)		14	2	8	6	17
Annual increase in production (mil. bbls.)		20	3	15	8	25
Bureau of Mines cement price index (1950 = 100)	100	108	108	114	117	122
Profit after tax as % of net worth:						
All manufacturing companies	17.1	14.4	12.3	12.7	12.3	14.9
Cement industry	17.8	14.5	14.3	15.0	17.6	18.6

Source: Standard & Poor's *Trade and Securities Statistics*.

The prosperity was short-lived, however. A number of factors spurred companies to invest heavily in new capacity in the years 1955–62, most important of which were (*a*) the high operating rates and profits of the industry,

---

[1] Shipments of Portland cement fell from 170 million barrels in 1929 to 81 million barrels in 1932, while the average realized price of cement at the mills fell from $1.48 per barrel in 1929 to $1.01 in 1932.

(*b*) inauguration of the federal highway program, and (*c*) a favorable ruling on depletion allowance (reversed by legislation in 1960). Existing cement producers expanded their facilities and entered new regional markets both by acquisition and by construction of new plants. In addition, a number of new companies entered the cement business during this period. By 1962 the industry's operating rate had declined to 72% under the pressure of substantial additions to capacity and a slowdown in cement consumption (see Exhibit 2).

Exhibit 2

CYCLOPS CEMENT COMPANY

OPERATING RATES, PRICES, AND PROFITS IN THE CEMENT INDUSTRY, 1956–62

	1956	1957	1958	1959	1960	1961	1962
Industry capacity (mil. bbls.)	349	380	403	420	433	443	469
Cement production (mil. bbls.)	316	298	312	339	319	324	337
Percent capacity utilization	91	78	77	81	74	73	72
Annual increase in capacity (mil. bbls.)	34	31	23	17	13	10	26
Annual increase in production (mil. bbls.)	19	−18	14	27	−20	5	13
Bureau of Mines cement price index							
(1950 = 100)	130	135	138	140	143	141	140
Profit after tax as % of net worth:							
All manufacturing companies	13.8	12.9	9.8	11.7	10.6	9.9	10.9
Cement industry	18.5	14.2	14.7	14.3	11.2	10.2	9.8

Source: Standard & Poor's *Trade and Securities Statistics*.

Despite the decline in operating rates, product prices were reasonably well maintained until 1960. Typically, the largest producer in each regional market set the base price, subject to the right to meet any lower price quoted by a competitor. The base prices were announced quarterly and were generally followed by the other competitors.

The combination of excess capacity, high fixed costs, and new entrants eager to secure a share of the market eroded the oligopolistic competitive structure in the early 1960's and producers adopted several strategies to offset the heightened competition. Financial support was provided by some cement producers to ready-mixed concrete companies in the form of lengthened payment periods and guarantees of bank loans. Typically short on capital, the ready-mix companies accounted for 60% of the cement industry's sales, and their business was essential to the profitable operation of a cement plant.

"Off-list" price reductions in the form of larger discounts for prompt payment, special "competitive" discounts, and "phantom delivery point" billing increased sharply. The average realized mill price of cement, which had risen in each year since 1940, fell in each year from 1961 through 1964.

AVERAGE REALIZED MILL PRICE PER BARREL

1955	1956	1957	1958	1959	1960	1961	1962	1963	1964
$2.86	$3.05	$3.18	$3.25	$3.28	$3.35	$3.32	$3.29	$3.20	$3.19

Customer service was improved by the establishment of distribution terminals that could insure prompt delivery of cement to users, thereby reducing the importance *to the user* of buffer inventories. The terminals also permitted the adoption of separate pricing policies for each terminal, in place of the historical reliance on a single policy for an entire region.

NUMBER OF NEW DISTRIBUTION TERMINALS

1950–59	1960–61	1962	1963	1964
69	32	42	44	43

By 1964 profitability of the cement industry had fallen to a 15-year low as product prices continued to erode (see Exhibit 3). Heavy investments in

Exhibit 3

CYCLOPS CEMENT COMPANY
OPERATING RATES, PRICES, AND PROFITS IN THE CEMENT INDUSTRY, 1963–64

	1963	1964
Industry capacity (mil. bbls.)	478	479
Cement production (mil. bbls.)	353	369
Percent capacity utilization	74	77
Annual increase in capacity (mil. bbls.)	9	1
Annual increase in production (mil. bbls.)	16	16
Bureau of Mines cement price index (1950 = 100)	136	136
Profit after tax as % of net worth:		
All manufacturing companies	11.6	12.7
Cement industry	8.9	8.8

Source: Standard & Poor's *Trade and Securities Statistics.*

plant modernization and automation and in distribution terminals were widespread in the industry and resulted in little competitive advantage for any one company. Rather than being a source of higher reported earnings, the savings merely offset (and possibly contributed to) price cuts. There was, however, one encouraging sign; namely, industry investment in capacity additions was low in 1963 and 1964 and, on the basis of announced investment plans, it seemed likely that the low level of capacity additions would continue into 1966. Some industry observers hoped that rising operating rates might permit a firming of product prices and a recovery in profits.

Financial history of Cyclops Cement Company

Cyclops did not escape the industrywide competitive pressures. Earnings plummeted by 35% in the two-year period 1959–60 and then rebounded in 1962–64 (see Exhibit 4 for a summary of operations). Capital expenditures were very heavy, and the company sold an issue of $15 million 5% debentures in 1958. The restriction in this issue that funded debt was not to exceed 33⅓% of net tangible assets was suggested by the company's investment bankers, who stated that this was in line with recent issues by other firms in a variety of industries. At the time, the provision seemed to allow for a

Exhibit 4

CYCLOPS CEMENT COMPANY
SEVEN-YEAR STATISTICAL AND FINANCIAL SUMMARY
(Dollar figures in millions except per share data)

	1958	1959	1960	1961	1962	1963	1964
Sales	$44.2	$49.4	$45.3	$48.9	$55.5	$54.3	$53.1
Net earnings after tax	4.7	4.4	3.1	3.3	4.35	3.8	4.75
Capital expenditures	12.0	13.3	7.1	5.5	5.7	9.7	11.8
Net working capital	11.0	2.0	8.0	9.1	12.2	9.2	5.8
Total assets	70.5	74.5	85.2	79.6	83.4	88.9	88.0
Long-term debt	15.0	15.0	19.75	19.75	19.75	19.75	19.3
Preferred stock	4.5	4.5	9.2	9.2	9.2	9.2	9.0
Common stockholders' equity	38.6	39.7	39.8	41.0	43.4	44.9	47.3
Cement capacity (mil. bbls.)	13.9	15.9	15.9	16.8	16.8	16.8	18.1
Employees	1,457	1,503	1,491	1,470	1,498	1,489	1,421
Common shareholders	5,600	6,300	6,700	7,200	7,300	7,300	7,400
Earned per share	$2.75	$2.57	$1.81	$1.93	$2.54	$2.22	$2.77
Dividends per share	2.00	2.00	1.60	0.90	0.80	0.95	1.00

10.9   10.0   6.3   6.6   8.3   7.0   8.4

considerable increase in the company's funded debt and had been accepted without comment by the officers and directors of Cyclops.

In 1960, however, the company's large plant-rebuilding programs and an adverse tax ruling forced Cyclops to go to the market for additional long-term funds. The 33⅓% restriction limited borrowing to an issue of $4.75 million of 5% debentures, and it was necessary to raise an additional $4.7 million by means of 6% cumulative preferred stock. Both issues were placed privately with groups of insurance companies.

Exhibit 5 presents the capitalization ratios of several cement companies. Except for Cyclops the list is in the order of debt ratio, with the highest ratio at the top. Companies A, B, and C are "captives" of larger companies whose financial strength in a sense guarantees their solvency. Consequently, their very high debt ratios cannot be considered as typical of the industry. With the exception of these three companies Cyclops is near the median position in this listing.

Future financing needs

Cyclops had a number of proposals for expansion under study. Capital expenditures were expected to average $7–$7.5 million over the next few years, although technological changes in the industry might make major investments necessary at some stage if Cyclops was to remain cost competitive. The directors were also interested in further mergers and acquisitions including the possibility of diversifying outside the cement industry. They wished to develop financial policies that would give the company sufficient flexibility to take advantage of any opportunities that might arise.

However, it was clear that there would be considerable resistance from the board of directors to any reduction in the current dividend rate to finance

Exhibit 5

CYCLOPS CEMENT COMPANY
TYPICAL CAPITALIZATION RATIOS IN THE CEMENT INDUSTRY

	Total Capitalization 100%		
	Debt	Preferred	Common
Cyclops Cement Company..............	25%	13%	62%
A†..................................	78	11*	11
B†..................................	82	—	18
C†..................................	79	—	21
D..................................	33	18	49
E..................................	33	30	37
F..................................	31	—	69
G..................................	30	—	70
H..................................	27	12	61
I..................................	24	—	76
J..................................	24	—	76
K..................................	22	3	75
L..................................	20	—	80
M..................................	11	—	89
N..................................	11	20	69
O..................................	—	—	100
P..................................	—	—	100
Q..................................	—	—	100

* Subordinated notes.
† These companies were captives of larger corporations so that their financial structures cannot be taken to be representative of independently owned companies in the cement industry.

the planned expansion. In Mr. Dean's words, "The board would take a hard and long look before cutting or omitting a dividend." Dividends had nevertheless been cut substantially in recent years from $2.00 a share in 1958 to $0.80 in 1962. The rate had been increased slightly to $1.00 in 1964. A recent study by the company had indicated that the stock prices of publicly owned cement companies were very closely correlated with dividend yields, and Mr. Dean had decided that the cash dividend should be increasd to $1.20 a share and had instructed the consultant to use this figure in his projections of future cash flows. It was hoped that the increased dividend rate would raise the stock price from its recent range of $25–$28.

APPENDIX

CYCLOPS CEMENT COMPANY
SUMMARY OF CONSULTANT'S REPORT

Introduction

In this section we shall explain briefly the importance of cash flows in any appraisal of the risk of default in a recession period. We shall make use of the recent history of Cyclops to indicate the advantages of cash flow analysis over income statements and balance sheets in an analysis of this kind.

The ability of a firm to meet its financial obligations in any given period or set of circumstances can only be determined after a study of each and every one of the sources and uses of funds expected to arise during that period. Attention to income and expense is not enough. Many profitable firms suffer temporary shortages of funds. For example, in the year 1964 Cyclops reported a net profit of $4.750 million; yet the net cash gain available for common and preferred dividends was a *negative* figure of $3.604 million. The disparity between these figures alone is sufficient evidence that profitability by itself is no guarantee of solvency. Other firms remain safely solvent during periods in which losses are being experienced. Some firms have enjoyed an adequate cash flow to keep them solvent through long periods of unprofitability.

Financial obligations are undertaken in order to obtain funds to be used to create income (and therefore value) in the firm. Properly used, low-cost senior securities add to the value of the common stock equity position by increasing the earnings available per common share. But the degree to which the fixed-charge burden associated with these senior securities may be accepted depends not on income but on cash flows. If the sources of cash provide a flow sufficient to meet all uses, *including the demands of the financial obligations,* without exhausting the organization's cash balances, then solvency is assured. If not, even if profits are earned, then there will be default unless either new sources of cash are found or uses are reduced.

To determine what financial burden is acceptable, it is necessary to examine the flows likely to arise during a recession period, making a realistic assessment of these flows on the basis of the organization's past experience in recession conditions. Only then can a debt-financing policy safely be made part of the company's long-range plans. In this study, therefore, the sources and uses of funds in Cyclops Cement Company will be forecast under various sets of assumptions about business recession, and under each set of assumed conditions the total burden of proposed financial obligations will be compared with net funds changes arising from other activities. Where the difference is positive—that is, the net positive cash flow from all other sources exceeds the financial burden—then that burden will be safely covered, whatever the reported earnings may be.

This method may be illustrated by examining the experience of Cyclops during the period 1961–64 in terms of funds movements. These data are presented in Table 1. In terms of the method of analysis we are here introducing, solvency was in fact threatened in 1964, but the reserves available in the form of cash balances were more than adequate to overcome the threat.

It should be noted that the financial burden sections of the "uses" columns are further subdivided between "contractual" and "policy" burden. Contractual burden includes those financial obligations, like bond interest and sinking fund payments, that are matters of contract and so must not be defaulted. Policy burden is made up of those obligations, such as dividends, that are at the discretion of the board of directors. The annual retirement of $225,000 of the 6% cumulative preferred issue is considered discretionary in view of the mild penalties for failure to do so.

penalties would add up

Table 1

CASH FLOWS, 1961–64
(Dollar figures in millions)

	1961	1962	1963	1964
Reported earnings after taxes..............	$ 3.3	$ 4.4	$ 3.8	$ 4.8
Sources of funds:				
Operations before lease payments, interest, noncash charges, and taxes............	$ 12.1	$ 13.2	$ 12.8	$ 12.8
Working capital excluding cash.........	8.3*	—	3.6	—
Total sources.......................	$ 20.4	$ 13.2	$ 16.4	$ 12.8
Uses of funds—operating:				
Working capital excluding cash and accrued taxes......................	—	$ (0.6)	—	$ (0.8)
Plant and equipment..................	$ (5.0)	(4.7)	$ (8.4)	(11.7)
Other needs.........................	(1.2)	—	(0.7)	(0.4)
Total operating uses.................	$ (6.2)	$ (5.3)	$ (9.1)	$(12.9)
Available for financial uses...............	$ 14.2	$ 7.9	$ 7.3	$ (0.1)
Uses of funds—financial:				
Income tax payments..................	$ (5.0)	$ (2.1)	$ (0.8)	$ (0.5)
Contractual burden:				
Lease payments.....................	$ (0.5)	$ (0.6)	$ (0.7)	$ (0.7)
Interest............................	(1.2)	(0.9)	(1.0)	(1.0)
Debt reduction......................	(3.8)	—	(0.8)	(0.8)
Total contractual burden............	$ (5.5)	$ (1.5)	$ (2.5)	$ (2.5)
Policy burden:				
Preferred dividends...................	$ (0.6)	$ (0.6)	$ (0.5)	$ (0.5)
Preferred redemption.................	—	—	(0.2)	(0.4)
Common dividends...................	(1.6)	(1.4)	(1.6)	(1.7)
Total policy burden..................	$ (2.2)	$ (2.0)	$ (2.3)	$ (2.6)
Total financial uses.................	$(12.7)	$ (5.6)	$ (5.6)	$ (5.6)
Balance—change in cash.................	$ 1.5	$ 2.3	$ 1.7	$ (5.7)

= –.2

* Primarily reduction of receivables by use of new financing.

The choice of a recession to be studied

The risks arising from debt-servicing burden are often too vaguely presented. Any debt increases the risk of default by some degree, however small. The question should be not whether there is or is not some abstract risk but whether or not there is a real risk of cash inadequacy in any foreseeable depression. To answer this question it is necessary to specify, after study of the economic conditions of the industry, the dimensions that a depression might assume.

Volume. The cement industry trends shown in Chart 1 (which is drawn on a semilogarithmic scale to emphasize relative changes) demonstrate a generally stable upwards tendency in both consumption and cement prices. The only major interruptions in this trend occurred during the depression of the 1930's and in World War II. Only two declines in volume have been experienced since World War II, neither of them involving a drop of more than 7% from the previous peak or lasting more than three years. The recession of 1936–38 was of similar magnitude.

NO!

INDUSTRY!

Cyclops Cement Company has experienced a greater fluctuation in post-war volume than that shown in the industry trends. No decrease experienced by the company has involved a decline of more than 17% from the previous peak, however, and no division has experienced a volume decline greater than 18%. It did take Cyclops five years to return to 1956 volumes after the 1957 decline. The author has concluded, therefore, that a recession of four years' duration with a return to previous volumes in the fifth year is for this company a conservative but not unrealistic basis for this study of recession cash flows. Volume levels during the five-year period are assumed to be:

Year preceding................	100%
Year 1.......................	90
Year 2.......................	85
Year 3.......................	80
Year 4.......................	80
Year 5.......................	100

Chart 1

CEMENT INDUSTRY TRENDS

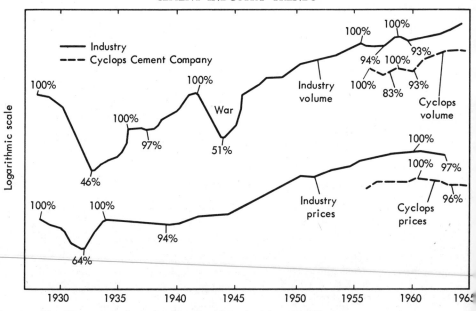

Note: The percentage figures show the peaks and troughs of the major declines.

In Chart 1 the upper long, unbroken line represents total industry volume plotted on a semilogarithmic scale and the lower unbroken line represents industry prices similarly plotted. The shorter dashed lines to the right of the chart represent Cyclops' actual volume and price performance for the years 1956–65. It is clear from these data that the author's assumptions concerning possible recession conditions and Cyclops' response to these conditions reflect more severe fluctuations than have actually been experienced since World War II.

Price. Cement prices have fallen surprisingly little in view of the severe competition in the industry in recent years. Certain areas have experienced marked fluctuations in prices, but the general pattern is one of considerable stability. The average industry price has fallen only twice since the 1930's: by 6% after 1934 and by 5% in the early 1960's. For the purposes of this study, however, since we are studying a particular company, a price decline of up to 10% of the prerecession price is assumed to be possible, distributed over the recession period as follows:

Year preceding	100%
Year 1	100
Year 2	95
Year 3	90
Year 4	90
Year 5	95

These assumptions as to the volume and price declines likely to be experienced in the recession period have been used as the basis for the analysis that follows. Although prices of delivered products were assumed to fall, there has been no adjustment for the reduction of prices of the elements of cost.

The recommendations concerning financial policy, which will be made in the final section of this study, will be designed to insure that the company is able to survive a recession of the dimensions specified above without appreciable danger of being unable to meet its contractual financial burdens and without contraction of the common stock dividends.

Forecast of cash movements related to operations

The information presented in Table 2 was obtained from detailed studies made by the divisions of Cyclops and coordinated by the headquarters staff. This table shows the cash receipts and expenditures arising from operations for each year of the recession as deliveries fall below 1965 levels. In each year except recession year 4 the assumption is made that this year is the first at that particular volume: the fourth-year column demonstrates the results of stabilizing volume for a second year at 80% of the 1965 level. Deliveries are assumed to return to their prerecession level in year 5.

Table 2 seeks to show the cash flow effects of changes in volume separately from those of changes in price. Thus, in the upper part of the table, cement prices are assumed to remain constant at their 1965 levels ($3.76 per barrel, delivered) so that the effect of volume changes may be seen in isolation. The slow decline in net operating inflow as a percentage of receipts is strikingly portrayed and demonstrates that the cash elements in the cost of production are dominated by variable costs. This fact is overlooked when one thinks of cost as including the heavy depreciation charges of a capital-intensive company such as Cyclops.

In the lower part of Table 2 the results of price declines of various

Table 2

FORECAST OF CASH FLOWS FROM OPERATIONS AT VARIOUS PRICE LEVELS
(Dollar figures in millions)

20% dr (handwritten)

	Year Preceding Recession	Recession Year				
		1	2	3	4	5
Shipments (mil. bbls.)..........	13.7	12.3	11.6	11.0	11.0	13.7
As % of 1965 levels..........	100	90	85	80	80	100
As % of capacity.............	77	69	65	62	62	77
Receipts at 1965 prices..........	$ 51.43	$ 46.29	$ 43.22	$ 41.15	$ 41.15	$ 51.43
Other income.................	0.58	0.52	0.49	0.46	0.46	0.58
	$ 52.01	$ 46.81	$ 43.71	$ 41.61	$ 41.61	$ 52.01
Cash operating expenditures*....	(35.17)	(33.60)	(31.37)	(30.27)	(28.51)	(35.17)
Net operating inflow:	*52.625*	*47.18*	*44.07*	*42.*	*42.26*	*52.625*
At 1965 prices...............	$ 16.84	$ 13.21	$ 12.34	$ 11.34	$ 13.10	$ 16.84
As % of receipts.............	32%	28%	28%	27%	31%	32%
Net operating inflow:						
Assuming 5% price decline....	$ 14.24	$ 10.87	$ 10.18	$ 9.28	$ 11.04	$ 14.24
Assuming 10% price decline...	11.64	8.53	8.02	7.22	8.98	11.64
Assuming 15% price decline...	9.04	6.19	5.86	5.16	6.92	9.04
Net operating inflow under assumed recession volumes and price levels.................	$ 16.84 *52.625*	$ 13.21 *47.18*	$ 10.18 *36.36*	$ 7.22 *26.74*	$ 8.98 *22.97*	$ 14.24 *44.5*

* Does not include headquarters expenditures, pension fund contributions, interest and lease payments, and taxes.

51.51   46.25   41.44   37.22   37.22   48.94 (handwritten)

magnitudes are superimposed on the volume changes and the effects on net operating inflows are shown. Whenever the consequences of a price change are being considered, it is necessary to take into account the change in income tax liability consequent on this reduction in revenues. Finally, the table shows the net operating inflows likely to be experienced under the combination of volume and price changes selected by this report as the dimensions of the recession to be studied. These inflow figures will be used in Table 5 below.

Forecast of other cash flows (excluding taxes on income and financial burden)

All nonoperating cash flows that may be expected under recession conditions, with the exception of changes in the company's cash balances, income taxes, and financial obligations, are set out in Table 3.

After discussion with company officers it was decided that it would be reasonable to assume that the onset of a recession would not bring about immediate adjustments in any items other than those directly related to volume. There are two reasons for this. First, it is unlikely that the recession will be recognized as such immediately, especially as short-term fluctuations of as much as 10% may be encountered in a normal year. Second, there will be considerable pressure to continue normal investment expenditures. The column representing the first year of the recession in Table 3 therefore uses "normal" levels of expenditure. Further columns depict the flows in years 2 and 3 and thereafter as investments are reduced in response to the continuing recession.

Table 3
FORECAST OF NONOPERATING FLOWS
(Dollar figures in millions)

	Year Preceding Recession	Recession Year 1	Recession Year 2	Recession Year 3	Subsequent Severe Years	Recovery to Prerecession Volumes
Headquarters expenditures*...	$(1.97)	$(1.95)	$(1.83)	$(1.79)	$(1.33)	$(1.87)
Plant and equipment.........	(7.50)	(7.50)	(2.50)	(1.00)	(1.00)	(5.00)
Subtotal..............	$(9.47)	$(9.45)	$(4.33)	$(2.79)	$(2.33)	$(6.87)
In-house resources:						
Reduction in pension fund contributions...........	0	0	0.20	0.20	0.20	0
Reduction of cash balances..	0	0.87	0	0	0	0
Special market expenditures.	0	0	(0.43)	0	0	0
Reduction (increase) in non-cash working capital (below)................	0	(1.00)	0.18	0.21	0	(0.80)
Total................	$(9.47)	$(9.58)	$(4.38)	$(2.38)	$(2.13)	$(7.67)

DETAILS OF CHANGES IN NONCASH WORKING CAPITAL ACCOUNTS

Volume as percentage of base (prerecession) year.......	100	90	85	80	80	100
Accounts receivable..........	$ 5.36	$ 6.04	$ 5.70	$ 5.36	$ 5.36	$ 6.77
Inventories (direct cost portion)................	1.43	1.28	1.21	1.13	1.13	1.44
	$ 6.79	$ 7.32	$ 6.91	$ 6.49	$ 6.49	$ 8.21
Accounts payable............	4.68	4.21	3.98	3.77	3.77	4.69
	$ 2.11	$ 3.11	$ 2.93	$ 2.72	$ 2.72	$ 3.52
Change in working capital account from previous year.		(1.00)	0.18	0.21	0	(0.80)

* Nonfinancial cash expenditures excluding leases.

It is clear that the dominant factors affecting these flows are, on the outflow side, the plant and capital equipment budget, and on the other side, the amount of liquid reserves that are quickly available. The December 31, 1964, cash level of $3.12 million is probably a minimum for the next several years, and even this figure is well in excess of management's comfortable assessment of minimum operating cash requirement of $2.25 million. It is assumed, therefore, that excess cash of $0.87 million is available and is used in year 1 of the recession.

The lower portion of Table 3 shows the amounts forecast for those working capital items that fluctuate with volume. An explanation of the amounts chosen and of other items in Table 3 follows.

Detailed discussion of Table 3

Headquarters expenses. An estimate was made by company officers of the needs to support the central office. They were made at four possible recession levels, keyed to earnings rather than to cash flow. Therefore, with a one-year lag, from the onset of the recession, the level of Headquarters Expense has been reduced according to plan.

Plant and equipment. At the beginning of 1965 the company projected $7.5 million for capital expenditures during the year. Although $11.7 million (net funds) was spent in 1964 and $8.5 million in 1963, management believes that no further major modernization expenditures will be required for several years and that an average of $7.5 million would be a generous allowance for normal years in the next decade. The five-year plan, already adopted, shows lower levels of expenditure than those in the last two years.

In recession, a much less ample program can be anticipated, but there will always be an important time lag before cutbacks can become a reality. Many projects require one to two years for construction, and it seems unlikely that they would be halted prior to completion in response to a recession. The author has been assured that the lower figures used in recession years are feasible, without any damage to the company's need to return to high levels of production in the recovery period. The figure of $5.0 million is used in the year of recovery, because it is believed that this is all that could be spent effectively in the first year following a period of retrenchment.

In-house resources. Most companies possess considerably more capacity to produce funds under the pressure of need than is apparent at first glance. The following in-house resources have been considered in picturing the funds flow of Cyclops Cement Company in a recession period.

Use of accumulated contributions to pension reserve: Since the company has built up $0.6 million above the legally required minimum, it is estimated by company officers that the present outflow of about $0.3 million annually could be reduced to $0.1 million for three years, without creating any need for higher levels of payment than previous levels when prosperity is restored. This estimate has been used with a one-year time lag. The saving appears in each of three years because the full pension charge was taken as an operating expense.

Liquidation of outside investments: Although there is a considerable investment in real estate that could be liquidated, the policy given to us by management is not to rely on this source of funds.

Use of cash reserves: The $3.12 million of cash funds shown at December 31, 1964, is well in excess of operating needs, which have been estimated at $1.3 million by a careful study recently made. A larger figure, $2.25 million, has been chosen on the authority of management, which feels that it is desirable to maintain liberal balances in the company's banks. So a reduction of only $0.87 million is taken.

Drawing down the liquid position as indicated would require the increased use of short-term credit to meet seasonal requirements. This credit is certainly available under present conditions, but the author's forecast that it would also be available under recession conditions should be checked.

Since the company manifests a large cash-generating capacity in normal years, the idea of recession use of the present cash reserves does not present the risk of permanent reduction of the firm's strength.

Special promotion fund: At the request of management, a special fund of

$0.43 million is appropriated in the second recession year, to permit special sales efforts and the absorption of bad debts beyond normal figures.

Working capital items related to sales volume. Significant changes would also occur in certain working capital items.

Accounts receivable: These are currently 10.3% of 1965 estimated sales volume. Since it is known that the granting of liberal credit terms is an important source of sales in a buyer's market, an increase of the collection period by 25% (about $1.5 million at current volume) is assumed.

Accounts payable: Since the maintenance of a strong credit position requires prompt payment, the "last ditch" resort to slowness on the part of Cyclops is rejected, and payables are maintained at 9% of sales, the recent average level.

Inventories: The nature of the production process and the present inventory control systems should permit the maintenance of inventories at approximately a constant relationship to shipments. This relationship is assumed here. Consistent with the objective of this analysis only the cash costs of production are reflected in Table 3.

Financial burdens

The year 1967 was chosen as the source of the figures for financing burden in the year preceding the recession, because in that year all the sinking fund requirements rise to their fullest amounts. They are presented in Table 4. The amounts are shown on a pretax basis. The tax deductibility of interest and lease payments is included in calculating the estimated tax payments shown in Table 5.

The "Contractual Burden," strictly defined, is the sum of interest and lease

Table 4

FINANCIAL BURDENS
(Dollar figures in millions)

	As in 1967	Recession Year				
		1	2	3	4	5
Contractual:						
Interest, debentures (5%)	$0.82	$0.76	$0.71	$0.67	$0.60	$0.54
Lease payments	0.56	0.56	0.56	0.56	0.56	0.56
	$1.38	$1.32	$1.27	$1.23	$1.16	$1.10
Debenture sinking funds	1.07	1.07	1.07	1.07	1.07	1.07
Total contractual	$2.45	$2.39	$2.34	$2.30	$2.23	$2.17
Policy:						
Preferred sinking fund*	$0.45	$0.23	$0.23	$0.23	$0.23	$0.23
Preferred dividend (6%)	0.49	0.47	0.46	0.44	0.43	0.42
	$0.94	$0.70	$0.69	$0.67	$0.66	$0.65
Total contractual and preferred burdens	$3.39	$3.09	$3.03	$2.97	$2.89	$2.82
Common dividend ($1.20)	2.07	2.07	2.07	2.07	2.07	2.07
Total burden	$5.46	$5.16	$5.10	$5.04	$4.96	$4.89

* It is assumed that Cyclops will exercise its option to retire an additional $225,000 of preferred stock in the year prior to the downturn.

payments and debenture sinking funds, but the author feels that Cyclops will always plan to meet the dividend and sinking fund requirements on the preferred stock. Not only is it in the spirit of a preferred stock agreement to pay dividends as long as possible, but also an accumulation of preferred dividends has disastrous effects on the value of the common stock. Therefore, the author proposes that the figures in Table 4 be interpreted to show a continuing burden of approximately $3.1 million, of which $1.3 million represents deductions due to sinking fund operations.

By making sinking fund payments, Cyclops is regularly restoring its borrowing power. Perhaps in recession this fact is not important, but it is a matter of long-run importance which will enter the final recommendations of this report. Debt of $5.36 million is scheduled for retirement in the five years shown.

A forecast of recession cash flows

Table 5 combines the cash flow patterns developed in Tables 2–4 and indicates the impact of the selected recession on the borrowing needs of Cyclops. The financial burdens are based on the present capital structure and on an increase to $1.20 in the dividend rate on the common stock.

The following conclusions seem important.

1. The pattern of changes in cash is very different from the pattern of reported earnings.[2] In contrast to net earnings, which decline through year 3, peak borrowing needs are reached in the first year of the recession.

2. Sharp curtailment in investment in plant and equipment by the second year of the recession is a key influence on the company's low borrowing needs during the recession. In view of the long construction period for many of Cyclops' projects, this assumes quick perception of, and response to, the onslaught of a recession.

3. Even at low levels of volume and price, and after maintaining the $1.20 annual dividend on the common stock, there is not a cash deficit after the volume of investment in new assets is reduced. Income tax carry-backs are important contributors to this result. [The tax calculations are not included in the report but are available from the vice president–finance.]

4. In interpreting Table 5 the reader should keep in mind that several additional elements of conservatism are built into the calculations. The cash balance is set at a level $1.0 million above operating needs. A four-year recession with declines in volume and in price below the experience of any recession since the 1930's has been assumed. While prices of delivered goods have been assumed to decline, no decline has been assumed in the prices of the elements of cost. Finally, Cyclops has an excellent credit standing. The

---

[2] The consultant and the Cyclops management elected to omit the earnings figures from the report to ensure that the board of directors would focus on the critical numbers —namely, the cash flow figures. The tax payment figures provide some insight, however, into the pattern of earnings. The differences between earnings and cash flow patterns are also shown in Table 1, which provides historical data for the 1961–64 period.

Table 5

A FORECAST OF RECESSION CASH FLOWS
(Dollar figures in millions)

SUMMARY OF OPERATIONS	Year Preceding Recession	Recession Year 1	2	3	4	5
Shipments (mil. bbls.)...........	13.7	12.3	11.6	11.0	11.0	13.7
Percent of base year..............	100	90	85	80	80	100
Percent of capacity...............	77	69	65	62	62	77
Price per barrel..................	$ 3.76	$ 3.76	$ 3.57	$ 3.38	$ 3.38	$ 3.57
Percent of base year..............	100	100	95	90	90	95
SUMMARY OF CASH FLOWS*						
Operating inflows (from Table 2)	$ 16.84	$ 13.21	$10.18	$ 7.22	$ 8.98	$ 14.24
Headquarters expenditures (from Table 3)..............	(1.97)	(1.95)	(1.83)	(1.79)	(1.33)	(1.87)
Investment in plant and equipment (from Table 3).........	(7.50)	(7.50)	(2.50)	(1.00)	(1.00)	(5.00)
Reduction (increase) in working capital (from Table 3).......	0	(0.13)	0.18	0.21	0	(0.80)
Reduction in pension fund contributions (from Table 3)	0	0	0.20	0.20	0.20	0
Special marketing expenditures (from Table 3)..............	0	0	(0.43)	0	0	0
Contractual financial burden (from Table 4)..............	(2.45)	(2.39)	(2.34)	(2.30)	(2.23)	(2.17)
Tax (payments) or refunds........	(2.25)	(1.03)	(0.29)	1.02	0.46	(1.91)
Subtotal..................	$ 2.67	$ 0.21	$ 3.17	$ 3.56	$ 5.08	$ 2.49
Preferred burden (from Table 4)...	(0.94)	(0.70)	(0.69)	(0.67)	(0.66)	(0.65)
Common dividend at $1.20.......	(2.07)	(2.07)	(2.07)	(2.07)	(2.07)	(2.07)
Total cash flow............	$ (0.34)	$ (2.56)	$ 0.41	$ 0.82	$ 2.35	$ (0.23)
Effect on cash, excluding preferred burden and common dividend....................	2.67	0.21	3.17	3.56	5.08	2.49
Cumulative effect, excluding preferred burden and common dividend....................	2.67	2.88	6.05	9.61	14.69	17.18
Effect on cash, including preferred burden and common dividend	(0.34)	(2.56)	0.41	0.82	2.35	(0.23)
Cumulative effect, including preferred burden and common dividend†..................	(0.34)	(2.92)	(2.66)	(1.97)	0.28	0.05

* Figures in ( ) are cash outflows.
† The cumulative effect includes interest on the prior-year cash deficit.

company obviously has an untapped source of short-term funds not shown in Table 5.

Recession cash flows and various debt policies

It seems desirable to expand the recession cash flow analysis to include a range of possible capital structures. Three specific capital structures are considered:

1. The present capital structure, which includes debt, 25%; preferred stock, 12%; common stock, 63% (based on book values).

2. The capital structure that would result from refinancing the two preferred issues with a new debt issue and would include debt, 37%; common stock, 63%.

3. An increase in debt to 50% of total capitalization, with the balance as common stock.

The implications of each of the three capital structures for Cyclops' cash flows and cyclical borrowing needs are shown in Table 6 and are discussed in the recommendations that follow.

Table 6

CASH FLOWS UNDER VARIOUS CAPITAL STRUCTURES
(Dollar figures in millions)

	Year Preceding Decline	Recession Year				
		1	2	3	4	5
Current Policy: debt, 25%; preferred, 12%; common, 63%:						
Effect on cash, excluding preferred burdens and common dividend	$ 2.67	$ 0.21	$ 3.17	$ 3.56	$ 5.08	$ 2.49
Cumulative effect, excluding preferred burdens and common dividend....................	2.67	2.88	6.05	9.61	14.69	17.18
Effect on cash, including preferred burdens and common dividend	(0.34)	(2.56)	0.41	0.82	2.35	(0.23)
Cumulative effect, including preferred burdens and common dividend*..................	(0.34)	(2.92)	(2.66)	(1.97)	0.28	0.05
Capital Structure: debt, 37%; common, 63%:†						
Effect on cash, excluding common dividend.....................	1.94	(0.51)	2.47	2.86	4.40	1.82
Cumulative effect, excluding common dividend.............	1.94	1.43	3.90	6.76	11.16	12.98
Effect on cash, including common dividend ($2.07 million).......	(0.13)	(2.58)	0.40	0.79	2.33	(0.25)
Cumulative effect, including common dividend*............	(0.13)	(2.72)	(2.46)	(1.79)	0.45	0.20
Capital Structure: debt, 50%; common, 50%‡ (and repurchase of common):						
Effect on cash, excluding common dividend.....................	1.18	(1.24)	1.74	2.16	3.69	1.14
Cumulative effect, excluding common dividend.............	1.18	(0.06)	1.68	3.84	7.53	8.67
Effect on cash, including common dividend ($1.72 million).......	(0.54)	(2.96)	0.02	0.44	1.97	(0.58)
Cumulative effect, including common dividend*............	(0.54)	(3.53)	(3.64)	(3.38)	(1.58)	(2.24)

Handwritten annotations in left margin: I, II, III. Handwritten values in the table: (2.90), (-2.49), (-1.67).

* The cumulative figures include interest on the prior year's deficit cash position. The preferred burden and common dividend in the year preceding the decline are $0.94 million and $2.07 million respectively.
† Assumes funding the retirement of the preferred issues with 20-year debt issue at 5½% on which sinking fund payments start immediately.
‡ Assumes a negotiated increase of ¼% in the rate on the existing debt in exchange for relaxation of the restriction on debt and issuance of an additional $18.6 million of 20-year debt at 5¾% (sinking fund payments start immediately). The proceeds from the $18.6 million debt issue are used to retire the preferred stock and to repurchase 300,000 shares of common stock at $30 per share. The common stock dividend in each year is $1.72 million. The reduction reflects the smaller number of shares outstanding as a result of recapitalizing the company. It is recognized that the company would probably not repurchase its stock but would use its newly discovered borrowing power in a series of steps through acquisitions to reach the desired goal over a period of years.

Recommendations

1. Since the first recession year shows large drains because of the continuation of expenditures for plant and equipment, it is recommended that the company maintain reserves in liquid funds or assured credit in amounts roughly equivalent to the capital commitments that are considered irreversible. Such an arrangement as a banker's commitment for a term loan might be considered and would bolster the certainty of the common dividend rate.

2. Since there appears to be no reason to pay the high cost of preferred stock, because the reduction of preferred dividends is not required to preserve solvency, it is recommended that this type of security be eliminated from the capital structure by the use of (a) funds generated in prosperous years and (b) increased long-term indebtedness.

On December 31, 1964, total long-term debt amounted to $19 million, or 25% of net tangible assets ($76 million). The ratio of 33⅓% imposed under the terms of the 5% debentures of 1958 permitted long-term debt of $25 million with net tangible assets at this level. Unused debt capacity of $6 million was therefore available without offending existing contracts. The extent of the funds available from operations for the retirement of the preferred stock was dependent upon the size of new capital investment projects being undertaken. In a year of normal sales volume in which investment in new plant and equipment did not exceed $5 million (e.g., 1961–62) approximately $2 million might be expected to be available for preferred retirement. The total sum required to accomplish the retirement of both preferred issues as of June 30, 1965, is $9 million.

3. Since dividend payments are an important key to value of the common stock of cement companies, it is recommended that the net savings of retiring preferred stock be passed on in the form of increased dividends on the common stock.

4. At present Cyclops Cement Company's flexibility in financial policy is greatly constrained by the existing indentures and preferred stock agreements. Thus, at the moment the only major available reductions in expenditures to meet recessions (other than in the control of operations) are in the budget for plant and equipment or the common dividend.

It is recommended that the company study its present indentures and consider how they might be changed to introduce needed flexibility. Raising the debt limit to make unnecessary the use of preferred stock is one goal. Another is to arrange an alternative to the sinking fund in the form of investment in approved types of assets. A third is the introduction of flexibility by specifically authorizing that advance payments could be made on sinking fund payments with the provision that an equal amount of later payments could be skipped over in times of stress if necessary. All these changes might be arranged by amendment of the existing indentures, and this step should be attempted first. But in the long run, if calling the present issues is necessary, it is a step worth taking.

WINN-DIXIE STORES, INC. (A)

In October, 1968, Mr. Stephen Darcie, a security analyst employed by a large mutual fund, was preparing to evaluate the dividend policy of Winn-Dixie Stores, Inc. The information about Winn-Dixie that he had assembled from his firm's research files is summarized below. Mr. Darcie realized that Winn-Dixie's long-standing policy of paying monthly cash dividends to stockholders and of increasing the dividend annually was unique among major American corporations.

Mr. Darcie decided to begin his analysis by considering the rationale for Winn-Dixie's unusual dividend policy. He wanted to determine the likely advantages and disadvantages of the dividend policy from the viewpoints of both the corporation and its stockholders. He then planned to try to anticipate Winn-Dixie's future dividend policy and the effect it might have on future common stock values.

The company

Winn-Dixie Stores, Inc., was a regional food chain located in the southeastern portion of the United States, with headquarters in Jacksonville, Florida. It operated a network of 746 modern retail supermarkets which dealt in all types of foods and other items usually sold in general retail food businesses. Winn-Dixie ranked seventh in the industry in terms of sales volume and number of stores operated.

Winn-Dixie had been incorporated in 1928 and had grown by expansion and acquisition from a sales level of about $10 million in 1939 to over $1 billion in fiscal 1968. In 1944 the company had operated 118 retail stores in Florida and southern Georgia with total sales of $35 million. From 1945 to 1964 Winn-Dixie had added, by acquisition, 406 retail grocery stores located in Kentucky, Florida, North Carolina, South Carolina, Louisiana, and Alabama. The acquisition of a chain of 35 stores in Alabama in 1962 had resulted in antitrust action by the Federal Trade Commission, and Winn-Dixie signed a consent order in 1966 giving up its acquisition rights for 10 years unless prior FTC approval could be obtained. No divestiture was required, however. During this period of growth by acquisition, the company had aggressively pursued a policy of internal expansion through the opening of new stores and the closing of older facilities. For example, of the 406 stores added by acquisition between 1945 and 1964, only 159 (accounting for 20% of the company's sales and net earnings) were in operation at the end of fiscal 1964. Average weekly sales per store increased by 175% between 1950 and 1960 as the company replaced older units with large, modern supermarkets. This transition was largely completed by 1960, and average sales per store had remained relatively constant since that time.

In recent fiscal years, changes in the number of stores were as follows:

	1962	1963	1964	1965	1966	1967	1968
New stores opened...........	40	41	31	55	44	38	40
Stores acquired..............	9	36	9	4	2	0	0
Less: Stores closed............	−24	−29	−18	−22	−18	−13	−15
Net increase in number of stores.............	25	48	22	37	28	25	25

Fifty-four new stores were budgeted for opening during the 1969 fiscal year. Construction had begun on a new distribution center in metropolitan Atlanta which was scheduled to open in the spring of 1969. Contractual obligations for construction and purchase of plant and equipment at June 29, 1968, amounted to approximately $6,000,000.

Practically all retail stores and wholesale units were in leased premises. Winn-Dixie retained title to all movable equipment installed by it at leased locations. In most instances alterations or additions to the premises were made, and their costs were carried as leasehold improvements and amortized over the life of the particular lease.

Because of occasional shifts in population and traffic patterns, the company preferred to negotiate leases for terms of not more than 10 or 12 years, although it entered into longer term leases in some key locations and shopping centers. The relatively short lease period gave the company the flexibility to shift its store locations periodically to new facilities. As of June 29, 1968, leases were in effect on locations for 746 retail stores, 7 wholesale units, and 11 other facilities (warehousing and distribution centers, bakeries, and processing plants). Rent expense on long-term leases for 1968 totaled $15,949,073.

In addition to the marketing flexibility resulting from the company's policy of leasing its facilities, the company reported in 1965 that its leasing policy contributed greatly to its high rate of return (21%) on average invested capital (i.e., long-term debt and stockholders' equity).

The company competed in its trading area with a number of national and regional food chains, including Colonial Stores Incorporated, Food Fair Stores, Inc., The Grand Union Company, IGA stores, The Kroger Co., National Tea Co., and Safeway Stores, Incorporated. However, Winn-Dixie had a larger concentration of stores in the Southeast than any other retailer, and it ranked first or second in most of the market areas in which it operated.

The geographical scope of the company's operations proved to be a significant advantage. While disposable income per capita in the South and Southeast was still among the lowest in the nation, income levels had increased more rapidly in this geographical area during the past 15–20 years than in many other parts of the United States. Furthermore, the State of Florida had shown, in the previous 15 to 20 years, a higher percentage growth in population than any other state. Both of these factors contributed to making Winn-Dixie the most profitable and one of the fastest growing of the major food retailers.

Winn-Dixie was controlled by, and for many years operated under the leadership of, four brothers: Mr. A. D. Davis, vice chairman of the board; Mr. James E. Davis, chairman of the board; Mr. M. Austin Davis, senior vice president; and Mr. Tine W. Davis, senior vice president. In 1968, the Davis brothers were still active in the company's management, but three of them were devoting less than full time to their duties for reasons of health. Approximately 29% of the 12,568,907 outstanding shares of common stock was owned by the Davis family. Approximately 233,000 shares were held by institutional investors, and the remaining shares were owned by about 33,000 stockholders.

The company dealt with its employees directly rather than through labor unions, and avoided labor problems that plagued some other companies in the industry. In addition to paying competitive wage rates, the company provided employees with a number of fringe benefits, including a profit-sharing retirement plan, a stock purchase plan, a contributory group life and hospitalization insurance program for employees and their families, and a college scholarship program for children of employees.

The purpose of the stock purchase plan for employees was to promote increased interest among the company's employees in its affairs, growth, and development and to foster an identity of interest between employees and management. The first stock purchase plan was instituted in 1952; and by June 29, 1968, employees had purchased a total of 923,848 shares of the company's stock.[1] Under the plan in effect in 1968, eligible employees could buy stock at a price not less than 85% of the fair market value on the date when a specified number of shares were offered for sale under the plan. Such stock offerings in recent years had been substantially oversubscribed by employees, and about 40% of the company's 13,000 full-time employees were Winn-Dixie stockholders at the end of fiscal 1968.

Dividend policy

Mr. Darcie's research had indicated two major distinctive features of Winn-Dixie's dividend policy. First, fiscal 1968 was the 25th consecutive year in which cash dividends had been increased and the 36th consecutive year in which cash dividends had been paid. The long history of annual dividend increases was unusual among merchandising and industrial companies. Second, dividends had been paid on a monthly basis since January, 1953. Most dividend-paying American corporations pay dividends quarterly; only a handful make monthly payments.

The record of annual dividend increases was made possible by Winn-

---

[1] Winn-Dixie purchased treasury stock to offset the sale of stock to employees.

Dixie's earnings history and financial condition. The company had earned a profit in every year since its incorporation in 1928. With the exception of fiscal 1967, when earnings dipped slightly, per share earnings had increased each year since 1942. The company's sales increased every year from 1928. Sales surpassed the $1 billion level in 1967, a sales level never before achieved by a southern-based retailer.

At June 29, 1968, the company's net working capital was $81,832,206, and the ratio of current assets to current liabilities was 3.17 to 1. Cash and marketable securities exceeded current liabilities by $814,958. Long-term debt amounted to $5,400,000, and sinking fund requirements for fiscal 1969 had already been met. Indentures relating to the long-term debt imposed certain restrictions on the amount of cash dividends that might be paid; however, at June 29, 1968, $92,824,760 of retained earnings was not so restricted and was available for dividends. Cash dividends averaged 71% of net earnings in the five years ended June 29, 1968. Financial statements of the company appear in Exhibits 1, 2, and 3.

One of Winn-Dixie's main objectives, according to a brokerage house study which Mr. Darcie had reviewed, was to be a "blue-chip" growth company. The company's annual cash dividend payment since 1934 and annual cash dividend increases since 1944 appeared to be part of its plan to achieve this goal.

For many years, Winn-Dixie had had a policy of paying dividends on a month-to-month basis. Mr. Darcie understood that the purpose of monthly payments was to interest as many as possible of Winn-Dixie's employees and customers in becoming stockholders. The company believed that most stockholders favored the monthly dividend payments and that the monthly budget tie-in appealed to housewives and resulted in more stockholder-customers. A housewife who became a Winn-Dixie stockholder was expected to become a loyal customer. Furthermore, the monthly payments were believed to appeal to employees of the company; and the company believed that stock ownership helped bridge the gap between labor and management, provided other personnel policies were fair.

Winn-Dixie's 1968 annual report indicated that management expected record sales and profits in fiscal 1969 and that further dividend increases would be dependent upon the company's ability to overcome rising taxes and increasing operating costs. As he began to think about future dividend prospects, Mr. Darcie decided to assume that per share earnings would continue to grow at the rate experienced during the last five years.

Exhibit 4 shows a 20-year history of per share earnings and dividends. Selected financial data for Winn-Dixie and other companies in its industry are presented in Exhibit 5. A record of market price changes in Winn-Dixie's stock for the period 1949–68 appears in Exhibit 6.

Exhibit 1

WINN-DIXIE STORES, INC. (A)
STATEMENT OF CONSOLIDATED EARNINGS, FISCAL YEARS 1964–68
(In millions)

	Fiscal Year Ended:				
	June 27, 1964	June 26, 1965	June 25, 1966	July 1, 1967	June 29, 1968
Net sales...........................	$871.8	$915.3	$982.5	$1,020.3	$1,082.1
Cost of sales........................	700.4	731.7	780.5	813.4	860.6
Gross profit........................	$171.4	$183.6	$202.0	$ 206.9	$ 221.5
Operating and administrative expenses..	137.0	146.8	162.0	168.1	178.8
Other income (net)..................	6.3	6.9	7.8	7.2	5.8
Income before taxes.................	$ 40.7	$ 43.7	$ 47.8	$ 46.0	$ 48.5
Federal income taxes................	20.3	20.9	23.0	22.5	24.0
Net income.........................	$ 20.4	$ 22.8	$ 24.8	$ 23.5	$ 24.5
Lease rental expense included above.....	$ 12.9	$ 13.9	$ 15.2	$ 15.9	$ 15.9

Exhibit 2

WINN-DIXIE STORES, INC. (A)
CONSOLIDATED BALANCE SHEETS, 1964–68
(In millions)

ASSETS	June 27, 1964	June 26, 1965	June 25, 1966	July 1, 1967	June 29, 1968
Cash and marketable securities.....................	$ 30.5	$ 25.0	$ 32.2	$ 38.7	$ 38.5
Receivables.......................................	2.0	3.0	1.9	1.9	2.4
Inventories.......................................	62.8	67.9	67.5	69.3	74.9
Prepaid expenses.................................	2.4	2.9	3.0	2.2	3.8
Total current assets...........................	$ 97.7	$ 98.8	$104.6	$112.1	$119.6
Plant and equipment, at cost......................	$ 76.7	$ 85.4	$ 92.9	$ 97.0	$104.7
Less: Reserve for depreciation and amortization....	48.4	50.6	53.5	58.0	64.4
Net plant and equipment..........................	$ 28.3	$ 34.8	$ 39.4	$ 39.0	$ 40.3
Other assets......................................	5.3	4.5	4.2	4.9	4.5
Total assets...............................	$131.3	$138.1	$148.2	$156.0	$164.4
LIABILITIES AND STOCKHOLDERS' EQUITY					
Current liabilities................................	$ 25.7	$ 28.3	$ 29.6	$ 34.1	$ 37.7
Sinking fund debentures..........................	9.6	6.6	6.6	5.8	5.4
Stockholders' equity..............................	96.0	103.2	112.0	116.1	121.3
Total liabilities and stockholders' equity..........	$131.3	$138.1	$148.2	$156.0	$164.4

Exhibit 3
WINN-DIXIE STORES, INC. (A)
SOURCE AND APPLICATION OF FUNDS, 1964–68
(In millions)

	June 27, 1964	June 26, 1965	June 25, 1966	July 1, 1967	June 29, 1968
SOURCE OF FUNDS					
Net income	$20.4	$22.8	$24.8	$23.5	$24.5
Depreciation and amortization	9.5	9.1	9.9	10.6	11.3
	$29.9	$31.9	$34.7	$34.1	$35.8
APPLICATION OF FUNDS					
Cash dividends	$13.7	$15.2	$16.7	$18.1	$18.8
Expenditures for plant and equipment (net)	7.5	15.0	14.0	9.7	12.1
Reduction of long-term debt	2.2	3.0	—	0.8	0.4
Other	0.4	0.5	(0.5)	2.5	0.6
Increase (decrease) in working capital	6.1	(1.8)	4.5	3.0	3.9
	$29.9	$31.9	$34.7	$34.1	$35.8

Exhibit 4
WINN-DIXIE STORES, INC. (A)
SELECTED FINANCIAL DATA, 1949–68

Fiscal Year Ended	Earnings per Share*	Dividend per Share*	Dividend Payout
June 25, 1949	$0.12	$0.04	33%
June 24, 1950	0.19	0.05	26
June 30, 1951	0.20	0.08	40
June 28, 1952	0.23	0.10	43
June 27, 1953	0.25	0.13	52
June 26, 1954	0.31	0.14	45
June 25, 1955	0.41	0.22	54
June 30, 1956	0.73	0.35	48
June 29, 1957	0.85	0.42	49
June 28, 1958	0.98	0.48	49
June 27, 1959	1.11	0.54	49
June 25, 1960	1.26	0.60	48
July 1, 1961	1.36	0.71	52
June 30, 1962	1.39	0.85	61
June 29, 1963	1.49	0.97	65
June 27, 1964	1.62	1.08	67
June 26, 1965	1.81	1.21	67
June 25, 1966	1.98	1.32	67
July 1, 1967	1.87	1.44	77
June 29, 1968	1.95	1.50	77

* Based on shares outstanding (12,568,907) at end of fiscal 1968.

Exhibit 5

WINN-DIXIE STORES, INC. (A)
COMPARATIVE FINANCIAL DATA FOR LEADING GROCERY CHAINS

	Acme Markets, Inc.	Allied Super- markets, Inc.	Colonial Stores, Inc.	First National Stores, Inc.	Food Fair Stores, Inc.
Latest statement date	4/1/68	6/29/68	12/31/67	3/30/68	4/27/68
Total assets (in millions)	$275	$196	$104	$123	$291
Long-term debt as % of total capitalization	8%	65%	20%	5%	37%
Long-term debt + leases as % of adjusted capitalization[1]	58%	79%	65%	57%	73%
Profit after taxes as % of sales (latest year)	0.64%	0.48%	1.32%	d1.03%	0.79%
Return on common equity (latest year)	5.1%	7.0%	12.0%	d7.8%	9.2%
Book value per share	$55.11	$12.64	$20.64	$52.77	$15.82
Sales (latest year, in millions)	$1,294	$756	$552	$640	$1,372
Annual growth[2] of sales:					
Last 3 years	3.7%	19.7%	4.8%	−3.3%	7.0%
Last 7 years	3.2%	10.4%	3.1%	2.5%	7.3%
Earnings per share (latest year)	$2.81	$0.84	$2.48	d$4.14	$1.49
Annual growth[2] of e.p.s.:					
Last 3 years	−13.1%	−13.1%	7.0%	deficit	4.9%
Last 7 years	−5.6%	−5.5%	17.5%	deficit	−1.9%
Dividends per share (latest year)	$1.91	$0.60	$1.40	$1.00	$0.90
Annual growth[2] of d.p.s.:					
Last 3 years	5.0%	−0−	16.9%	−26.4%	−0−
Last 7 years	5.0%	2.7%	8.3%	−12.3%	1.7%
Dividend payout (latest year)	68%	71%[4]	57%	*	61%
Average annual payout:					
Last 3 years	59%	55%	53%	*	55%
Last 7 years	45%	51%	49%	*	59%
Average dividend yield (latest year)[3]	4.9%	3.2%	5.9%	3.9%	5.6%
Average dividend yield:					
Last 3 years	4.1%	3.4%	5.1%	5.9%	4.6%
Last 7 years	3.2%	4.0%	4.4%	5.1%	4.0%
Average price-earnings ratio (latest year)[3]	13.7	22.6[4]	9.6	†	10.7
Average price-earnings ratio:					
Last 3 years	14.2	15.6	10.6	†	12.2
Last 7 years	14.0	12.9	11.4	†	15.9

d Deficit.
[1] "Adjusted capitalization" consists of long-term debt, stockholders' equity, and capitalized value of lease obligations. The capitalized value of leases has been estimated, for purposes of this exhibit, by capitalizing annual lease rentals at a 10% rate.
[2] Growth rates shown are the compound average rate of increase from the beginning of the time period indicated to the current year. Negative figures represent compound rates of decline.
[3] Dividend yields and price-earnings ratios are based upon average market price (i.e., mean of high and low prices) for the year. Prices are New York Stock Exchange prices, with the exception of Colonial Stores, Inc., which is traded over-the-counter.
[4] High payout and price-earnings ratio for Allied Supermarkets, Inc., is the result of a 32% decline in e.p.s. in fiscal 1968 without a corresponding change in dividend payments and average market prices.

Grand Union Co. 3/2/68	Great Atlantic & Pacific Tea Co. 2/24/68	Jewel Companies Inc. 2/3/68	The Kroger Co. 12/31/67	Lucky Stores, Inc. 1/28/68	National Tea Co. 12/31/67	Red Owl Stores, Inc. 1/27/68	Safeway Stores, Inc. 12/31/67	Von's Grocery Co. 12/31/67	Winn-Dixie Stores, Inc. 6/29/68
$195	$884	$313	$548	$120	$205	$67	$654	$72	$164
12%	0	36%	10%	41%	15%	28%	8%	1%	4%
61%	60%	57%	58%	70%	61%	69%	65%	25%	58%
1.22%	1.02%	1.41%	0.92%	1.83%	0.81%	0.79%	1.51%	2.26%	2.26%
10.7%	8.9%	7.9%	10.1%	29.9%	7.6%	7.9%	12.6%	11.0%	20.2%
$17.12	$25.28	$20.86	$18.52	$7.49	$15.48	$19.65	$15.71	$17.19	$9.48
$936	$5,459	$1,244	$2,806	$627	$1,147	$313	$3,361	$268[5]	$1,082
8.1%	2.4%	16.5%	6.4%	26.5%	0.7%	1.0%	6.1%	1.3%	5.7%
6.5%	3.6%	13.6%	6.0%	18.6%	4.3%	1.9%	4.5%	5.8%	5.0%
$1.90	$2.25	$2.63	$1.98	$2.17	$1.18	$1.63	$2.00	$1.89[5]	$1.95
4.0%	2.3%	8.0%	−2.6%	31.3%	−1.9%	−7.2%	1.0%	–0–	2.5%
5.6%	−2.1%	9.1%	0.8%	21.4%	−0.6%	−0.2%	5.7%	7.6%	5.3%
$0.60	$1.60	$1.25	$1.30	$0.84	$0.80	$1.00	$1.10	$1.20	$1.50
4.9%	3.1%	5.3%	4.8%	30.3%	–0–	1.7%	5.8%	6.3%	7.4%
3.6%	8.6%	5.5%	2.4%	15.3%	–0–	3.2%	6.5%	17.8%	11.3%
32%	71%	48%	66%	38%	68%	61%	55%	63%	77%
30%	69%	48%	59%	45%	62%	69%	51%	55%	74%
34%	64%	52%	63%	52%	65%	55%	50%	56%	69%
3.4%	5.2%	4.1%	5.7%	3.4%	5.7%	5.5%	4.4%	4.7%	4.8%
2.9%	4.6%	3.5%	4.5%	3.8%	5.3%	5.1%	3.6%	4.0%	4.5%
2.8%	3.8%	3.0%	4.1%	3.7%	4.9%	4.1%	3.3%	3.7%	3.7%
9.2	13.6	11.7	11.6	11.3	11.9	11.2	12.4	13.5	16.0
10.3	15.3	14.2	13.5	12.0	11.8	14.4	14.4	14.2	16.5
13.4	17.4	17.8	15.7	13.8	13.5	14.7	15.6	15.5	19.2

[5] Sales of Von's Grocery Co. do not include $51.5 million sales of 40 supermarkets which were divested in 1967 pursuant to a decision of the U.S. Supreme Court. E.p.s. for 1967 is before an extraordinary gain (equivalent to $2.97 per share) on the sale of divested stores.
* Cash dividend payments exceeded net income for the time periods indicated.
† Price-earnings ratios not computed because of negative e.p.s. in the last two years.
Sources: *Moody's Industrial Manual* and *Moody's Handbook of Common Stocks.*

Exhibit 6

WINN-DIXIE STORES, INC. (A)
MARKET PRICES AND STOCK MARKET INDEXES, 1949–68

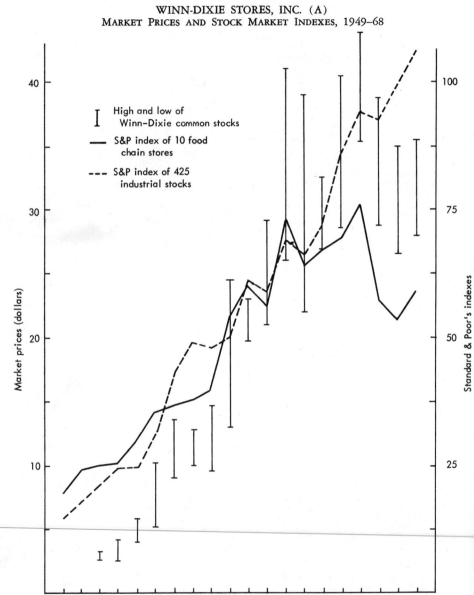

SCM CORPORATION (A)

In October, 1965, Mr. Paul Elicker, vice president and treasurer of SCM Corporation, was considering possible changes in SCM's dividend policy. He knew that this topic would be discussed at the December meeting of the board of directors, and he wanted to be adequately prepared to make a sound recommendation on this matter to Mr. Mead, president of SCM, and to the board of directors.

Earlier in October, Mr. Elicker had received a comprehensive report on dividend policy for SCM from the Corporate Services Division of Irving Trust Company (see Appendix). This report recommended that SCM resume paying cash dividends in December and eliminate its stock dividend at the same time. After reviewing this recommendation, Mr. Elicker had asked Mr. Anthony H. Meyer of Irving Trust Company for his opinion about the implications of deferring the resumption of cash dividend payments until a later time. Mr. Meyer's reply is contained in Exhibit 5.

SCM's business had been founded in 1903 to manufacture and sell typewriters. In the early 1950's the company, then known as the Smith-Corona Typewriter Company, had two main product lines. Office typewriters were expected to provide a fairly stable earnings base regardless of swings in the business cycle. Portable typewriters were thought to be more subject to consumer whims and economic conditions, and thus were expected to contribute to the company's profits primarily during periods of prosperity. On a cash basis, sales of office typewriters (with relatively short collection periods) were expected to provide a steady net inflow of cash throughout the year. Portables, on the other hand, were subject to a pronounced seasonal sales pattern, which required a seasonal buildup of inventories, and were sold through dealers who were often slow in paying SCM for the typewriters, necessitating a seasonal swing in receivables.

Because of the stability of the office typewriter line, and because many of the 300,000 shares of common stock then outstanding were held by a family group who had special dividend interests, the company had adopted what it considered to be a fairly liberal cash dividend policy in the early 1950's. For example, the dividend payout ratio ranged from 36% to 64% in the 1951–53 period.

During the 1950's, however, sales of manual office typewriters proved to be unstable for SCM, and as IBM electric typewriters began to command an increasing share of the office typewriter market, SCM's manual typewriter line began to generate large losses. Portable typewriter sales grew rapidly during this period and proved to be relatively insensitive to general business conditions. While SCM's share of the market for portables increased from 30% in 1953 to 35% in 1960, this growth of sales plus the seasonal pattern of inventories and receivables for this line created a growing need for funds at a time when losses on office typewriters were also consuming funds. By the late 1950's, these developments had created a severe cash shortage.

Despite the cash squeeze and the necessity for additional debt financing in the late 1950's, cash dividends were continued. Earnings declined to $0.30 per share in fiscal 1959, but SCM maintained its dividend payment of $0.85 per share in the hope that earnings would improve in the following year. In addition, the company planned to force conversion of its outstanding convertible debentures in fiscal 1959 to strengthen its equity base in anticipation of future debt financing, and an adverse market price reaction to a dividend cut could have made it impossible to force conversion of the debentures. In fiscal 1960, however, when SCM reported a loss of $0.24 per share, the directors voted—in a close vote—to eliminate the cash dividend payment entirely. Modest earnings of $301,747 (or $0.16 per share) were reported in fiscal 1961, but special charges and write-offs of $2,398,000 were made directly to Earned Surplus.

SCM's management had begun taking steps in the late 1950's to improve the company's long-range prospects. The acquisition of Kleinschmidt Laboratories (1956) and Marchant Company (1958) added teletype equipment and calculators to the product line; and by 1965 other product lines, such as office supplies, photocopy machines, peripheral data processing equipment, electronic calculators, adding machines, and accounting machines, had been developed or acquired.

This restructuring of SCM's business began to show results in fiscal 1962 as earnings improved to $2,592,000 ($1.35 per share), and a 2% stock dividend was paid. Management's rationale for the 2% stock dividend was that it should enable stockholders to benefit from the improving earnings outlook. Cash dividends were not considered appropriate at that time because of the company's continuing cash squeeze.

Earnings in 1963 and 1964 were somewhat below the 1962 level, but stock dividends of 3% were paid in each of these years. In fiscal 1965 earnings had increased to $3,815,477 ($1.47 per share) and management was very optimistic about the outlook for SCM's photocopy equipment, particularly a new model of the Coronastat electrostatic office copier scheduled for introduction in fiscal 1968. The directors had discussed resuming cash dividend payments during fiscal 1965; but the company's cash needs were still considerable, and additional external financing was planned to raise additional cash. As a result of the optimistic earnings outlook during a period of continuing cash stringency, the directors declared a 5% stock dividend during fiscal 1965.

As Mr. Elicker approached the study of the Irving Trust Company material in October, he had certain additional data available for consideration. SCM's annual report for fiscal 1965 had recently been sent to stockholders; so Mr. Elicker knew that investors were aware of the company's improved situation. (Exhibits 1 and 2 contain financial data about the company.) The cash situation was still tight in view of SCM's projected need for funds, but he felt that the worst part of the cash squeeze was past. (Exhibit 3 shows an historical record of sources and uses of funds; Exhibit 4 is the company's forecast of sources and uses of funds for a four-year period, based upon the assumption that SCM adopts Irving Trust Company's recommendation of a $0.10 cash dividend per quarter.)

Mr. Elicker's own research had suggested that "glamour companies" which paid modest cash dividends might have higher price-earnings ratios than those in the nondividend-paying group, but he was not sure whether the apparent difference in price-earnings ratios was due to dividend policy differences or to other factors. It was possible, but not certain, that a cash dividend might help maintain the current high market price of SCM's stock or push it up even further.

Since external financing was contemplated in the future, Mr. Elicker desired to take legitimate steps to create a better and more solid market value for the common stock. On the other hand, SCM had not paid a cash dividend for five years, the image of the company had changed significantly during that time, and SCM's stock was actively traded. The market price had risen from $25¾ to $51⅝ during September, and the shares had been trading in late October between $44 and $52 per share. Consequently, Mr. Elicker doubted whether SCM's present shareholders really cared very much about cash dividends.

Since Mr. Elicker expected dividend policy to be a main topic for discussion at the December meeting of directors, he planned to review the Irving Trust Company report again and then decide what type of dividend action he would recommend. If he decided that resumption of cash dividends was desirable, he would have to decide on a recommendation about the amount of the cash dividend as well as whether a stock dividend should also be declared.

Exhibit 1

SCM CORPORATION (A)
CONSOLIDATED BALANCE SHEETS AS OF JUNE 30, 1964–65
(In millions)

ASSETS	1964	1965
Current assets:		
Cash	$ 1.2	$ 2.1
Accounts receivable	25.0	28.0
Inventories	41.2	41.5
Total current assets	$67.4	$71.6
Fixed assets, net	22.5	23.9
Other assets	1.8	1.4
Total	$91.7	$96.9
LIABILITIES		
Current liabilities	$18.0	$20.7
Long-term debt	23.3	21.9
Deferred income taxes	0.5	1.4
Stockholders' equity	49.9	52.9
Total	$91.7	$96.9

Notes:

1. Under the provisions of the long-term debt, approximately $2.5 million of retained earnings was available for cash dividends at June 30, 1965.

2. In June, 1965, the company announced that it would redeem for cash any shares of its convertible preferred stock still outstanding on July 8, 1965. As a result of this announcement, over 99% of the outstanding preferred stock was converted into common stock in June and early July.

3. At June 30, 1965, 2,694,178 shares of common stock were issued and outstanding, and an additional 235,445 shares were reserved (and subsequently issued) for conversion of the preferred stock.

Exhibit 2

SCM CORPORATION (A)
EIGHT-YEAR STATISTICAL SUMMARY
FISCAL YEARS ENDED JUNE 30, 1958–65

	1958	*1959*	*1960*	*1961*	*1962*	*1963*	*1964*	*1965*
Net sales (in thousands)	$ 87,146	$ 90,411	$ 93,359	$ 96,476	$103,165	$117,343	$ 124,704	$ 149,657
Net income (loss) (in thousands)	2,244	482	(455)	302	2,592	1,656	2,437	3,815
Earnings per common share*	$ 1.22	$ 0.23	$ (0.21)	$ 0.14	$ 1.21	$ 0.57	$ 0.83	$ 1.47
Dividends paid on common stock:								
Cash dividends per share	$ 0.77	$ 0.75	—	—	—	—	—	—
Stock dividends	—	—	—	—	2%	3%	3%	5%
Market price of common stock (calendar years)	$13¼–20¼	$11–19½	$9⅞–16¼	$10¾–26⅞	$8⅞–24⅞	$9⅛–15	$12½–19⅛	$15⅞–52½†
Price-earnings ratio‡								
SCM Corporation	14.5	66.3	—	134.4	13.9	21.2	19.0	23.3
Dow-Jones Industrials	18.2	18.3	19.4	21.5	17.3	17.2	17.8	16.8

* 1965 on average shares outstanding after stock dividend; prior years adjusted for subsequent stock dividends.
† Range for year to October 25, 1965.
‡ Based on midpoint of price range.

Exhibit 3

SCM CORPORATION (A)
SOURCE AND USE OF FUNDS
FISCAL YEARS ENDED JUNE 30, 1958–65
(In millions)

	1958	1959	1960	1961	1962	1963	1964	1965
Beginning cash balance	$ 2.4	$ 4.2	$ 4.0	$ 3.2	$ 3.2	$ 2.3	$ 3.9	$ 1.0
Add:								
Income after taxes	2.2	0.5	(0.5)	0.3	2.6	1.7	2.4	3.8
Depreciation	1.2	1.6	2.0	2.0	2.3	2.7	2.4	2.5
Other increases (decreases) in current liabilities	1.0	(2.0)	(0.5)	1.5	1.7	(0.1)	1.9	1.9
Borrowings from (repayments to) banks	(3.1)	(6.7)	7.4	2.4	0.9	(10.7)	0.5	1.6
Debentures	4.2	7.4						
Other long-term debt	9.7	6.0						
Increases (decreases) in stockholders' equity	0.2	4.9†	(1.7)‡	(2.0)§	(0.6)¶	11.4**	0.1	0.1
Total available	$17.8	$15.9	$10.7	$ 7.4	$10.1	$ 7.3	$11.2	$10.9
Less:								
Increase (decrease) in accounts receivable	$ 5.0	$(4.0)	$ 3.0	$ 0.6	$ 1.1	$ 1.0	$ 1.1	$ 3.0
Increase (decrease) in inventories	1.0	4.8	(0.2)	2.8	2.2	(0.9)	4.8	0.3
Capital expenditures*	6.2	3.7	3.0	2.5	2.2	1.4	2.8	3.8
Long-term debt repayments	—	4.9†	1.5	1.1	2.6	1.4	1.5	1.4
Other increases (decreases) in assets	—	1.0	0.2	(2.8)‖	(0.3)	0.1	(0.7)	(0.4)
Cash dividends paid	1.4	1.5	—	—	—	0.4††	0.7††	0.7††
Total cash employed	$13.6	$11.9	$ 7.5	$ 4.2	$ 7.8	$ 3.4	$10.2	$ 8.8
Ending cash balance	$ 4.2	$ 4.0	$ 3.2	$ 3.2	$ 2.3	$ 3.9	$ 1.0	$ 2.1
Interest expense—long-term debt*	$ 1.2	$ 1.5	$ 2.0	$ 2.2	$ 2.0	$ 1.7	$ 1.4	$ 1.6

* Casewriter's estimate, based upon analysis of published financial statements.
† Increase in equity in 1959 represents conversion of outstanding 6% convertible subordinated debentures into 229,128 shares of common stock. An equivalent reduction in long-term debt is included in "debt repayments" for 1959.
‡ Net special charges to retained earnings amounted to $1,737,349 in 1960, and represented provision for nonrecurring costs and write-downs of assets (less estimated reduction in U.S. income taxes).
§ Reduction in equity in 1961 was due to special charges to retained earnings ($2,144,850), less proceeds from issuance of common stock for acquisitions and stock options.
‖ Includes write-offs and sales of assets.
¶ Due primarily to change in accounting method in one corporate division.
** Represents net proceeds from sale of $12,002,200 (par value) 5½% convertible preferred stock, after issuance and distribution expenses of $561,050.
†† Dividends paid on 5½% convertible preferred stock.

Exhibit 4

SCM CORPORATION (A)
SOURCE AND USE OF FUNDS FORECAST
FISCAL YEARS ENDED JUNE 30, 1966–69
(In millions)

	1966	1967	1968	1969	Total
Beginning cash balance..............	$ 2.1	$ 4.8	$ 4.7	$ 5.0	$ 2.1
Add:					
Income after taxes *...............	8.6	10.9	11.9	18.7	50.1
Depreciation....................	2.1	5.6	8.1	10.4	26.2
Borrowings—banks and payables...	15.5	4.3	(20.5)	5.5	4.8
Debentures......................	—	—	33.0	—	33.0
Other long-term debt..............	—	10.0	—	—	10.0
Increase in equity†	1.9	5.5	—	—	7.4
Total available..............	$30.2	$41.1	$ 37.2	$39.6	$133.6
Less:					
Increase in accounts receivable......	$ 6.0	$ 5.3	$ 5.7	$ 7.5	$ 24.5
Increase in inventories.............	6.1	7.5	8.0	10.5	32.1
Increase in lease inventories........	1.3	6.7	7.0	9.2	24.9
Capital expenditures..............	5.0	8.5	6.7	3.9	24.1
Debt repayments†	3.0	6.9	1.9	1.9	13.7
Other increases in assets...........	3.4	0.2	0.8	0.2	4.6
Cash dividend‡	0.6	1.3	1.4	1.4	4.7
Total cash employed.........	$25.4	$36.4	$ 32.2	$34.6	$128.6
Ending cash balance................	$ 4.8	$ 4.7	$ 5.0	$ 5.0	$ 5.0
Interest on long-term debt at 7%§.....	$ 1.4	$ 1.6	$ 3.1	$ 4.2	$ 10.3

* The reader may assume an income tax rate of 50% in his study of this exhibit.
† Increases in equity in 1966 and 1967 represent anticipated conversion of $7,441,900 of outstanding 5¼%
convertible subordinated debentures for 377,378 shares of common stock. An equivalent reduction in long-term
debt is included in "debt repayments" for 1966 and 1967.
‡ Assuming dividends of $0.10 per quarter (two quarters in fiscal 1966) on outstanding shares (including shares
issued for conversion of convertible preferred stock in fiscal 1966 and shares expected to be issued for conversion of
the 5¼% convertible subordinated debentures in fiscal 1966 and 1967).
§ Casewriter's estimate.

Exhibit 5

SCM CORPORATION (A)
IRVING TRUST COMPANY
ONE WALL STREET
NEW YORK, N.Y.   10015

Anthony H. Meyer
Assistant Vice President

Telephone: LL3–3283

October 20, 1965

Mr. Paul Elicker
Vice President and Treasurer
SCM Corporation
410 Park Avenue
New York, New York

Dear Paul:

You asked me to comment on our dividend policy recommendations for SCM with respect to what the results might be if you decide to defer the resumption of cash dividends
for the time being.

Short range, we would not expect any very significant reaction. As we stated in our report,
SCM's shareholders at this point are not likely to be dividend oriented. Even if they were,
no reasonable dividend would provide a yield of any consequence.

However, you'll recall that Mr. Mead's remarks at the New York Society of Security
Analysts last summer implied that the time to resume dividends was not too far distant.
The market may be looking for a dividend declaration, not for yield but as an ex-
pression of management's confidence in the future, and may expect it to come when the

Exhibit 5—Continued

stock dividend is usually declared. To avoid any possible adverse reaction, SCM should make it clear if dividends are deferred that this decision is in no way a reflection of management's thinking about earnings prospects.

We would also have to recommend that you pay a stock dividend again this year if you don't reinstitute a cash payout. Again we are considering short-range market effect. As you know we don't believe there are any permanent market effects from stock dividends, but you could get an unfavorable temporary reaction by taking no dividend action whatever in December.

Long range, we are back in never-never land because of the difficulty of relating payout policy to price-earnings ratio. We do believe that the ultimate effect of a regular cash dividend policy is to enhance a stock's investment quality, thereby broadening its ownership base and improving both its price-earnings ratio and its price stability. If SCM defers the resumption of cash dividends, it is doing no more than deferring the time when it begins to acquire the improved investment quality a regular dividend record would give it.

If current cash needs merit a higher priority than enhancing your image a bit sooner, we would see no serious objection to delaying the dividend. At the same time, we would hate to see a "cash needs" argument marshaled against dividends year after year. There is a positive value to a cash dividend record, even if the dividend is modest. On the other side of the coin, the difference between retaining 75% of earnings and retaining them all is relatively minor in terms of helping to meet SCM's capital needs.

You sometimes hear people say that dividends can't matter for growth companies because there are nondividend-paying growth companies whose stocks sell at very fancy earnings multiples. What this argument overlooks is that there is no way of knowing where these stocks would sell if they did pay a dividend. Statistics can't tell us much, but just to take a couple of examples:

	Year	% Increase in Earnings per Share over Prior Year	Average Price-Earnings Ratio	Payout Ratio
Litton Industries	1962	56	34X	0
	1963	40	31X	0
	1964	25	25X	0
IBM	1962	19	40X	27%
	1963	19	34X	31
	1964	18	36X	39

There are a great many differences between Litton and IBM, and dividends aren't likely to be the most important one—but the devil can quote scripture to his purposes, and someone could argue from these figures that Litton should adopt a dividend policy like IBM's. I hope some of these thoughts will be useful to you. Let me know if we can do anything more.

With best regards,

Sincerely,
(*Signed*) Tony

APPENDIX

SCM CORPORATION (A)
DIVIDEND POLICY FOR SCM CORPORATION [1]

I. Summary

In this report we set forth what we consider the underlying principles on which to base an effective dividend policy and then apply these criteria to

---
[1] A report prepared by Corporate Services Division, Irving Trust Co., Oct., 1965.

SCM. Briefly stated, we believe an effective dividend policy involves:

1. The establishment of a consistent dividend record on which investors can reasonably base their future dividend expectations; and
2. The selection of an appropriate dividend payout ratio based on earnings expectations, earnings volatility, the nature of investment interest in the company's stock, and in some cases credit considerations.

Applied to SCM, all criteria point to the resumption of cash dividends with a low payout target. Our recommendation is that the company resume cash dividends at an initial $0.40 annual rate and eliminate its stock dividend at the same time.

II. Introductory Comments

The ultimate goal of corporate financial policy is to maximize the stock-holder's return on investment in the long run. Return on investment usually takes only two forms—dividends and capital appreciation. Dividend policy is an important aspect of overall financial policy because it influences, directly and significantly, both forms of return.

A simple example can be used to highlight the main elements in the dividend policy problem. Assume that two companies, A and B, both earn a steady 12% on equity. Equity in each case consists of one share of stock with a book value of $100. Company A elects to pay out 25% of its earnings in dividends, and Company B pays 75%. The results would be as follows:

Company A

Year	Equity	Earnings at 12%	Dividends Paid (25%)	Earnings Retained (75%)
1	$100.00	$12.00	$3.00	$ 9.00
2	109.00	13.08	3.27	9.81
3	118.81	14.26	3.56	10.70
4	129.51	15.54	3.89	11.65
5	141.16	16.94	4.24	12.70

Company B

Year	Equity	Earnings at 12%	Dividends Paid (75%)	Earnings Retained (25%)
1	$100.00	$12.00	$ 9.00	$3.00
2	103.00	12.36	9.27	3.09
3	106.09	12.73	9.55	3.18
4	109.27	13.11	9.83	3.28
5	112.55	13.51	10.13	3.38

Effect on dividend return

The differing dividend payout policies of A and B clearly result in radically differing dividend returns to their owners. B's dividend is initially three times as great as A's. As time goes on, however, A's dividend will overtake and pass B's, since A's dividend, in keeping with its earnings, is growing at 9% annually, whereas B's is growing at only 3%. The effect of any payout policy on future dividend returns is easily measurable to the extent that future earnings can be predicted.

Effect on appreciation return

The impact of dividend policy on future capital gains is more nebulous and more complex. On the one hand a cash dividend is a certain, current return compared with the uncertain, future return offered by potential capital gains. Therefore, investors like cash dividends, and a stock which pays a higher dividend, all other things being equal, will command a higher price.

However, all other things are not equal. The effect of dividend payout policy on earnings growth shows up very clearly in the Company A–Company B illustration. Simply stated, the higher the payout the slower the growth. More precisely, the rate of internal growth in earnings per share can be expressed as the percentage return on equity times the percentage of earnings retained. 12% return × 25% retained = 3% growth. 12% return × 75% retained = 9% growth. Since investors like earnings growth, they will pay a higher price for a stock if its earnings are growing more rapidly.

Moreover, a fast earnings growth obviously implies higher earnings per share in the future than slow earnings growth, starting from the same earnings base. Companies A and B each earned the same amount in the first year. In the fifth year A's earnings were 25% greater than B's. And earnings are a major determinant in stock market prices.

To summarize, payout policy affects appreciation return in three ways. Payout exerts pressure on the price-earnings ratio (the rate at which earnings are capitalized) in one direction because of investor interest in dividends. It exerts pressure in an opposite direction because of investor interest in earnings growth. Finally, it affects the future earnings to which the capitalization rate will be applied.

Combined effect on overall return

Clearly a low payout policy, because it accelerates earnings growth, will produce a higher stock price eventually. However, this does not necessarily argue for a low payout in all cases. A higher eventual capital gain return resulting from a low payout may be more than offset by a lower dividend return in the meanwhile.

Even if management can make a reasonably close estimate of future earning power, it is left with the problem of what capital gain returns would result from various payout policies. If a correlation between price-earnings ratio and payout ratio could be found, the capital gain question could be answered and the effect of dividend policy on overall return to investors could be determined with some fairly simple mathematics.

However, the market prices of industrial common stocks are a reflection of so many factors that the long-range effect of payout on price-earnings ratio is usually impossible to isolate. It is equally difficult to find the precise payout ratio which is sure to produce the highest overall return to investors. Nevertheless, careful evaluation of a number of relevant factors can direct a company toward a payout range appropriate to its particular circumstances.

III. DIVIDEND PATTERN

Before selecting a target payout ratio it is necessary to consider what constitutes an effective dividend pattern, since the company's goal with respect to pattern will influence its decision on payout.

The importance of dividend pattern cannot be overstressed. The company's dividend record influences the future dividend expectations of investors, and these expectations in turn affect the market price of the company's stock. Investors learn about a company's dividend policy primarily by looking at its dividend history. A regular pattern in the past implies a regular pattern in the future. A dividend cut in the past makes future payments less certain. And the more certain investors feel about future dividends, the more they will pay for them.

With this in mind, what is the most effective dividend pattern a company can hope to achieve?

A regular dividend increasing regularly would be highly effective, but a record like this can be established only by companies which enjoy extremely stable and predictable earnings growth. Many public utilities are in this category, but most industrial companies are not.

A regular dividend increasing irregularly as earnings permit is probably the best pattern which can be accomplished by typical industrial companies, subject as they are to fairly wide earnings fluctuations.

A regular dividend is somewhat less desirable, since it implies flat earnings. Unless a company suffers from a steadily declining return on equity, earnings retention should result in earnings and dividend growth.

Variable dividends offer an investor little on which to base his future dividend expectations, so they are unlikely to exert much influence on the market price of the stock.

The same is true of *irregular extra dividends.* As for *regular extras,* most analysts feel that companies which can pay them would do more for their stock by incorporating the extra amount into the regular dividend rate. Extra dividends may in some cases be a perfectly sound way of disposing of excess cash, but they probably have no appreciable effect on stock prices.

Stock dividends were the subject of an exhaustive and rigorous statistical analysis by C. Austin Barker, a partner at Hornblower & Weeks, Hemphill Noyes & Co. He reported on his work in a *Harvard Business Review* article, "Evaluation of Stock Dividends," which appeared in the July–August, 1958, issue. Barker's principal finding was that stock dividends have no lasting effect on stock prices. This being the case, and bearing in mind that stock dividends are costly[2] and tend to confuse a company's record, it is hard to

---

[2] Note also that stock dividend issuing costs are not deductible for tax purposes.

see much merit in a policy of paying stock dividends either to supplement or to replace cash dividends.

Credibility of pattern

No dividend record, however regular, will have a favorable long-run market effect if the dividend pattern is clearly unsustainable. To illustrate:

	Company A			Company B		
Year	Earnings per Share	Dividend	Payout Ratio	Earnings per Share	Dividend	Payout Ratio
1.................	$1.15	$0.60	52%	$1.05	$0.60	57%
2.................	1.35	0.60	44	0.92	0.60	65
3.................	1.60	0.80	50	1.10	0.80	73
4.................	1.73	0.80	46	0.93	0.80	86
5.................	2.05	1.00	49	1.00	1.00	100

Company A's dividend policy is right in line with its earnings growth. Investors will feel fairly certain about a continuation of orderly dividend increases if they believe the company has good prospects for continued earnings growth. For Company B, the same dividend record makes no sense in terms of its earnings record. If no earnings improvement is in sight, investors will expect no dividend increases in spite of the past pattern—in fact they will recognize that the future of the $1.00 dividend is in jeopardy. The future of A's dividend is therefore very much more valuable than the future of B's, even though the patterns are identical.

Payout ratio and pattern

Since corporate earnings tend to fluctuate from year to year around the line of their long-term trend, the maintenance of a precise payout ratio every year would result in a variable cash dividend. It is usually necessary, and entirely in order, to take liberties with the payout target in any given year in order to maintain an effective dividend pattern.

IV. PAYOUT RATIO

The question of payout for most industrial companies can be approached by thinking in terms of three broad payout categories:

	Payout Percentage
Small payout.........................	25
Average payout.......................	50
Full payout..........................	75

The factors which would govern the choice of one of these payout areas are discussed below.

Payout and return on equity

The rate of return a company earns on its equity investment is an extremely important element in the payout decision. A few mathematical relationships are worth reviewing to bring out the points involved:

1. *Return to investors through yield and growth.* If a stock is bought and later sold at the same price-earnings ratio and the dividend payout ratio remains constant, the total return to investors is the sum of the dividend yield when the stock is bought and the annual rate of growth in earnings per share. For example, suppose a stock's cash dividend yield on its market price is 3%, and earnings per share are growing at 7% annually. With a constant price-earnings ratio, the price of the stock will appreciate at 7% per year in keeping with earnings, thereby giving the investor a 7% appreciation return when he sells it. Meanwhile he will have been receiving another 3% return from dividends, or a total of 10%.

2. *Price-earnings ratio, payout, and yield on market value.* Dividend yield on market value is entirely unaffected by return on equity. It is a function of only two things—price-earnings ratio and payout ratio.

3. *Earnings retention, rate of return, and rate of growth.* Earnings growth is directly affected by return on equity. As we noted in the Introductory Comments, the rate of growth in earnings per share is the percentage return on equity times the percentage of earnings retained.

With these relationships in mind we can examine how varying rates of return on equity and varying payout ratios will tend to affect overall return to stockholders.

Table 1 illustrates the returns to investors which would result from various payout ratios at various rates of return on equity, assuming the investor buys and sells at the same price-earnings ratio. Appreciation return on this basis is always percentage earned on equity times percentage of earnings retained. Since yield return is affected by price-earnings ratio, we show a range of possible price-earnings ratios in the table, and the range of yields and overall returns these price-earnings ratios would produce.

Although it isn't possible to pinpoint price-earnings ratios, it is likely that Company A, whose earning power is low, would tend to sell at closer to 10 times earnings than 25. Company C, with its substantially greater earnings potential, would tend to sell at closer to 25 times earnings than 10. This being the case, high payout adds up to higher overall return for Company A, while

Table 1

PAYOUT AND RETURNS TO INVESTORS

| | | | | Range of Percentage Returns to Investors | | | |
| | | | | From Yield, Assuming Price-Earnings Ratios of | | Overall | |
Company	% Return on Equity	Payout %	From Appreciation	10×	and 25×	At 10× Earnings	At 25× Earnings
A	5	25	3.75	2.50	1.00	6.25	4.75
		50	2.50	5.00	2.00	7.50	4.50
		75	1.25	7.50	3.00	8.75	4.25
B	10	25	7.50	2.50	1.00	10.00	8.50
		50	5.00	5.00	2.00	10.00	7.00
		75	2.50	7.50	3.00	10.00	5.50
C	15	25	11.25	2.50	1.00	13.75	12.25
		50	7.50	5.00	2.00	12.50	9.50
		75	3.75	7.50	3.00	11.25	6.75

low payout produces higher overall return for Company C. At 10 times earnings, A gains 5% in yield and loses only 2½% in appreciation if its payout is 75% rather than 25%.[3] At 25 times earnings, C gains 7½% in appreciation and loses only 2% in yield if its payout is 25% rather than 75%.

This seems to suggest that companies like A should pay out all their earnings in dividends, and companies like C should pay none. However, several factors are present which would make this unwise.

For low-earning, low price-earnings ratio companies like A, the higher the payout, the better, *provided* an effective pattern of well-protected dividends can be maintained. A payout of 75% pushes very hard at the upper limit of what would be considered well protected. Investors would have serious doubts about the company's ability to maintain a dividend rate which represented a higher payout. Moreover, investors might well be proved right. Several years of poorer earnings might force the company to cut its dividend, which would hurt its dividend record and the price of its stock.

For high-earning, high price-earnings ratio companies like C, the question of why pay dividends at all is a hard one to answer, but the major factor is the degree of uncertainty investors feel about appreciation return. Our illustrations have assumed steady earnings growth and a constant price-earnings ratio. However, investors are properly uncertain about both these assumptions. Earnings growth, particularly when it reflects a high return which will tend to attract competition, may decelerate. The future price-earnings ratio may decline, either because earnings fall short of expectations or because of a generally poorer stock market period. Moreover, investors recognize that stocks which sell at a high multiple of earnings are particularly vulnerable to market fluctuation. Cash dividends, on the other hand, are a more certain return to investors. Even a small one is to some extent an anchor to windward.

A final consideration is that some investors, particularly institutions and fiduciaries, restrict their common stock investments to dividend-paying securities.[4] Omitting cash dividends would deprive a company of this pool of potential investment interest in its stock.

Payout and stability of earnings

Because of the importance of dividend pattern, a company must choose a dividend rate which it can sustain. If earnings are volatile, a low target pay-

---

[3] Actually, A would be unlikely to sell as low as 10 times earnings with a 75% payout, since the resulting 7½% yield is extremely high. Analysts tend to think of a well-protected dividend yield of 4½ to 5% as quite attractive, and the market price of a stock with a higher yield would tend to rise until the yield declined to this level. With a 75% payout A's stock would probably sell at 15 times earnings so as to yield 5%. This tendency of dividends to put a floor on a stock's market price is a very significant consideration for companies which earn a low return on equity.

[4] For example, a stock which does not have a 10-year uninterrupted cash dividend record does not qualify as a legal investment for insurance companies under New York State insurance law.

out ratio is indicated, since this would produce a dividend rate which could be sustained even during a period of sharply reduced earnings. If earnings are stable, on the other hand, a high target payout ratio can be set if other factors make high payout desirable. Several factors influence earnings stability. The major ones are these:

Level of earnings. In our economy, a company which earns an abnormally high return tends to attract competition which will force earnings down to an average level sometime in the future. Conversely, when a company is earning a low return, chances are good that this condition will remain stable or improve as time goes on. New competition is unlikely to rush into an essentially unpromising area, and companies with poor earnings are likely to be very active in seeking ways to improve profits.

Nature of the business. By their nature some companies are far more stable than others. A company supplying parts to one auto manufacturer runs a higher risk of earnings fluctuation than a chain of department stores. Electronics companies are less predictable than electric utilities.

Debt leverage. The stability of a company's earnings is also affected by the percentage of debt in its capital structure. Debt leverage magnifies fluctuations in operating earnings into larger fluctuations in common stock earnings. For this reason, a decision on capital structure should normally be made before a decision is reached on dividend policy.

Payout and the nature of investment interest

Stockholders differ on the returns they seek on their investments. They may be seeking cash dividends, or growth in market price, or both. Each company must decide, in the light of the nature of its business, what sort of investment interest it is likely to attract. At one end of the spectrum is the investor in a new and speculative venture, hoping for market gain. He is not particularly interested in receiving dividends. He wants earnings to be plowed back into the business and feels that a large dividend would limit the company's internal growth rate. At the other end of the spectrum is the investor in a stable, low-growth company who plans on income from cash dividends.

The speculative investor is unlikely to pay a premium price for stock in consideration of its dividend, but the income-seeking investor probably will.

Summary—selection of a payout ratio

In selecting a payout ratio, we would suggest that potential return on retained earnings be used as a starting point. On this basis, a 25% payout would constitute a sound preliminary target for companies which visualize a future return of 15% or better on new investment. The payout target should move up toward the 50% area if future return expectations range down toward 10%. A payout of up to 75% would produce the best overall results if future earnings expectations are substantially lower than 10%.

The target area selected on the basis of potential earnings on equity should then be reviewed and perhaps modified in the light of (1) the earnings stability factor and (2) the probable nature of investment interest in the company's stock.

As a matter of interest, the average payout ratio of Moody's 125 Industrials during the 1960–64 period declined from 63% to 53%, averaging 59%. Return on equity during this period climbed from 11% to 14% and averaged 12%.

Special situations—nominal payout or none

Companies which are financially strong can consider their capital needs aside from their dividend policy, since strong companies can raise capital externally on a reasonable basis. Weaker companies are forced to subordinate dividend policy to their capital needs to the extent that avenues for raising capital externally on a satisfactory basis are closed to them.

Typically, new companies have a very thin equity base; their growth potential is high; and raising capital externally is a considerable problem for them. The success of these companies may well depend on the reinvestment of every dollar of earnings they can generate, and their stockholders are almost certain to have no interest whatever in dividends. Cash dividends would make no sense for these companies.

A policy of paying nominal cash dividends is one into which a young company might evolve temporarily. The company would presumably still need virtually all of its earnings for reinvestment in the business. However, a nominal dividend payout would establish a basis for eventual purchases of the company's stock by institutional investors who prefer or require a dividend record. Nominal payout would also accord recognition to the belief of many investors that a cash dividend is an indication of some measure of investment quality.

Payout and changing the dividend

Since investors know that most seasoned companies do in fact have a target payout ratio, a change in the dividend rate carries with it strong implications about management's future earnings expectations. In raising the rate, for example, management is saying that earnings will rise, or have risen already to a sustainable new plateau high enough to justify the increase. Holding the rate if earnings go off implies management's faith that previous earnings levels will be restored. Cutting the dividend implies a permanent downtrend. The market for the company's stock will react accordingly. Since one of the objectives of financial management is to minimize fluctuations in the price of a stock, it is important to change the dividend rate only when future expectations warrant such a change. Increasing the dividend capriciously can give the stock a short-term lift, but in the long run will tend to undermine investor confidence.

Payout and tax considerations

The personal income tax treatment of dividend income as distinguished from capital gains is well known to us all. Stated briefly, dividend income is taxed at full income tax rates, which range up to a current maximum of 70%, while capital gains are taxed at either half the income tax rate or 25%, whichever is less. Consequently, the argument is sometimes advanced that dividend payout should be minimized so as to permit investors to receive most of their return on a capital gains basis.

For companies with great earning capacity, selling at high price-earnings ratios, the personal income tax aspect reinforces other powerful arguments for a low payout. However, for companies with poor earnings the tax factor does not, on careful examination, justify disregarding other arguments for high payout. Consider what might happen to investors in Company A in Table 1 if it changed its payout from 75% to 25%. It will be recalled that Company A earned 5% on equity, and we suggested that a 75% payout might cause it to sell at 15 times earnings so as to yield 5%. Assume a personal income tax rate of 40%, which would mean a captial gains rate of 20%.

Payout %	Price-Earnings Ratio	Percentage Gross Return			Percentage Return to Investors after Payment of Personal Income Taxes		
		Yield	Appreciation	Total	Yield	Appreciation	Total
75	15×	5.0	1.25	6.25	3.0	1.0	4.0
25	15×	1.67	3.75	5.42	1.0	3.0	4.0

In spite of tax savings, net return has not improved in amount. Moreover, it has declined in quality, since the return now has a larger component of appreciation, which is relatively uncertain, and a smaller component of dividends, which are relatively certain. Finally, a stock yielding 1⅔% and expected to grow in earnings at 3¾% is unlikely to sell at 15 times earnings. It might well drop to 10 times or below. At that level yield will be somewhat improved, but the stockholder will have sustained a capital loss of a third or more of his investment.

A final aspect of the personal income tax question is the fact that not all investors are taxed at the same rate. Speculative investors are likely to be in a higher bracket than income-seeking investors, and some income-seeking investors—charitable trusts, pension funds, etc.—are entirely tax-free. Differences in the extent to which investors are taxed will thus tend to coincide with other factors favoring high payout with low earnings and low payout with high earnings.

V.   DIVIDEND POLICY FOR SCM

A review of SCM's present situation convinces us that a low payout target is the company's best dividend policy for the time being. Each factor in this decision is discussed below.

Return on common equity

SCM's historical return on common equity has been subnormal in recent years, but has shown marked improvement which the company expects to continue. The following returns for 1963–65 and an estimated return for 1966 are based on the company's equity at the beginning of each year and its net income for that year. Equity includes preferred equity in each year and net income has not been reduced by the preferred dividend. This gives us a good comparative performance measure.

Fiscal Year	Return on Equity
1963	4.6%
1964	5.1%
1965	7.6%
1966	9.0%–10.0% (est.)

Since these are overall returns which are partially a reflection of losses in the Data Processing Systems Division and unsatisfactory results in some other areas, opportunities clearly exist in the more profitable sectors of SCM's business to invest retained earnings at potential returns substantially greater than the 10% which is average for American industry. Moreover, SCM is currently selling at a high price-earnings ratio. Earnings retained might add considerably to future appreciation return; earnings paid out wouldn't constitute a very significant yield return. It is difficult to pin down SCM's price-earnings ratio because of the stock's recent market behavior; but our analysis suggests that a 20× price-earnings ratio is, on the average, a reasonable expectation for SCM. A price-earnings ratio of 20× would result in the following yields:[5]

Payout Ratio	Yield
25%	1.25%
50	2.50
75	3.75

On the basis of our return-on-equity criterion, a low payout appears to be indicated.

Earnings stability

SCM's management is in a better position than we are to judge how stable its business is, but we would be inclined to classify it as relatively unstable. Factors we would cite are strong competition in those sectors of its business which are actually or potentially highly profitable, a market demand subject to cyclical fluctuations, heavy dependence on continuously productive R & D, and the risks associated with capital commitments abroad and reliance on foreign sales.

---

[5] Yield on current market of about $44⅛ (October 5, 1965, closing price) would of course be somewhat lower.

Debt leverage is also present to a significant extent, and increases the potential for variance in earnings available for common. SCM's 1966 budgeted figures indicate interest coverages will be just under seven times pretax and just under four times after-tax—rather low, although they represent a substantial improvement over recent years' results.

All told, the stability factor also suggests a low payout policy.

Nature of investment interest in SCM

SCM's stock has been extremely volatile this year, ranging from $16¼ to $51⅝ so far. Most of the move occurred during the month of September, when the stock rose from $25¾ to $51⅝ and then backed off to $42. There is little doubt that recent interest in SCM is concentrated on the company's Coronastat line, principally the Model 55, and the potential for future earnings growth arising from this source. Under the circumstances, we believe SCM investors are almost entirely seekers of capital gains, and we would not anticipate that any cash dividend the company could reasonably pay would have an appreciable effect on the price of SCM stock. Consequently, we don't think the company should penalize its rate of internal earnings growth at this point by paying out a substantial part of its earnings in dividends.

Financial strength

We suggested above that financially strong companies can consider dividend policy apart from capital needs because they are able to raise capital externally on a reasonable basis. However, SCM's budgeted capital requirements, at least for the coming year, are very substantial indeed. Its 1966 budget indicates capitalization will be as follows:

	Millions of Dollars	Percent
Current bank loans*.........................	14	15
Senior long-term debt......................	14	15
Conv. subordinated debt....................	7	8
Common equity............................	58	62
Total...............................	93	100

* Included because they appear to represent permanently needed capital.

This compares with debt of about 20% of total capital for typical major industrial companies, whose earnings records are generally better than SCM's. We note also that the company's convertible debentures are rated double B by two rating agencies, and single B by the third, indicating that there is not a great deal of extra long-term borrowing capacity. We do not know if management is considering an equity financing. However, an offering of normal proportions would still leave SCM somewhat short on equity in terms of its growth expectations. Consequently, we believe that credit considerations suggest the minimization of cash dividends.

Statistical correlations

As we stated earlier, there are so many elements present in the market's appraisal of an industrial common stock that the effects of dividend policy are usually impossible to isolate. However, we did examine the office equipment industry, as well as a group of other companies which have some of the characteristics of SCM, to see if any significant correlations could be found between price-earnings and payout ratios. As we anticipated, the results did not show any clear relationship. Consequently, we are basing our dividend policy recommendations for SCM strictly on the general principles reviewed in this report.[6]

Recommendations

1. We believe that the establishment of a regular cash dividend would add to SCM's investment quality and would begin to lay the groundwork for eventual ownership of SCM stock by institutional investors with a dividend requirement or a dividend preference. We recommend that cash dividends be instituted in December coinciding with the time when the stock dividend is usually declared.
2. We recommend a $0.10 dividend—a $0.40 annual rate—as a starter. Our reasons for suggesting this low payout are: (1) our assumption that reinvestment of retained earnings offers a high potential return; (2) the fact that current interest in the stock is not dividend-oriented; and (3) SCM's need for capital.
3. We do not believe that stock dividends result in any real benefits to stockholders and recommend that SCM's stock dividend policy be dropped.

Comparable situations

[This section of the Report states that the record of listed stocks was studied to try to find situations comparable to SCM. Three companies were located that had eliminated cash dividends, switched to stock, and then switched back. A study of the data for these companies, the Irving Trust Report states, fails to show any significant change in market price as an immediate result of replacing stock dividends with cash. The Irving Trust Report states, however, that the experience of these companies "says nothing about the possible long-range benefits of such a transition."]

Dividend policy—long range

We believe that a long-range dividend policy for SCM can be designed on the basis of the principles reviewed in this report. There are several important factors we are not able to evaluate at the present time—the company's potential earning power and its capital structure goal—and we would be glad to review these points with SCM's management if this would be of interest. At the same time, we are satisfied that a low payout target is in order for the time being.

---

[6] Note: The full Irving Trust Report contained about 10 pages of supporting data and charts. This portion of the report is omitted from the case since the results, as anticipated, were inconclusive.

GENERAL PUBLIC UTILITIES
CORPORATION (A)

^^

The dividend decision

In January, 1968, Mr. William Kuhns, president of General Public Utilities Corporation (GPU), was considering both the merit of a new dividend policy and the wisdom of inviting shareholder participation in deciding whether or not to adopt the policy. The dividend proposal which Mr. Kuhns was analyzing would eliminate three of the company's four quarterly cash dividends and substitute in their place stock dividends with a market value equal to the eliminated cash dividends. A large increase in the capital requirements of GPU prompted Mr. Kuhns to consider this policy in lieu of raising equity capital through rights offerings to GPU's stockholders.

Prior financing of capital needs

Over the period 1959 through 1967 GPU had issued common stock in 1960 and 1966. In each case, the shares were sold through rights offerings and the amount of new stock issued represented about 5% of the number of shares previously outstanding. Rights for over 50% of the shares in each instance were exercised by the individuals who initially received them.

Over the same nine-year period, the percentage of long-term debt in GPU's capital structure grew from 51.5% to 60.2% while preferred stock shrank from 9.9% to 5.4% (Exhibit 1). GPU had been able to provide the capital needed to support growth in customer electric power requirements mainly through a combination of internal cash throw-off and long-term debt additions. In 1967 the company began taking on significant amounts of short-term debt in addition to its traditional long-term borrowings. The Securities and Exchange Commission[1] gave the company authority to borrow up to $75 million by issuing commercial paper, and the company had sufficient bank lines of credit to give it a short-term borrowing capacity (including commercial paper) up to $150 million. So long as GPU wished to maintain a capital structure consisting of 60% debt, 5% preferred stock, and 35% common equity, the corporation had to limit long-term debt additions to

---

[1] The SEC held this authority under the Public Utility Holding Company Act of 1935.

170% of earnings retentions plus any new funds raised by the sale of common stock (i.e., 0.60/0.35 = 1.70).

According to Mr. George Schneider, financial vice president of GPU, a 60% long-term debt fraction was close to the limit that industry lenders and regulatory authorities would allow. Furthermore, certain states required that long-term debt be held below 60% of total capitalization if the securities of the company were to qualify as legal investments for savings banks and other regulated financial institutions. Although there was no formal regulation to establish this debt ceiling, few public utilities attempted to exceed it. A move in the direction of higher debt utilization could endanger a utility's bond rating (causing the interest rate to be higher on all its future debt issues) and/or invite additional regulation at the state and federal government levels.

Growing capital demands for the industry

Mr. Schneider outlined the reasons for a sudden surge in the capital-raising burden facing the electric utility industry.

While the electric utilities as a group have been able to get by with occasional small stock issues in the past, in the immediate future and out as far as three to five years, we all face a dramatic acceleration in the needs for capital to finance our growth. This expansion in the need for capital has come about for six reasons.

First, and perhaps most importantly, the rate of growth in electric power consumption is accelerating. Take "all electric"[2] homes as an example. These homes use almost five times as much electric power as comparable homes without this feature. Construction of "all electric" homes is increasing substantially.

Second, the electric utility industry is becoming even more capital intensive than it has been in the past. The construction cost of a nuclear powered generating plant lies between $160 and $180 per kilowatt of installed capacity versus $135 per kilowatt for a fossil fired plant.

Third, since the failure of the Northeast power grid at the end of 1965,[3] there has been a good deal of pressure for additional spending on redundant facilities to enhance system reliability.

Fourth, the utilities face longer lead times in constructing power-generating facilities than we did 8 or 10 years ago. There used to be a four-year lead time on plant construction. Now it's six years. Since we make progress payments equal to 90% of the project's total price, a longer lead time substantially increases the size of our "plant under construction" account.

Fifth, inflation has eroded the purchasing power of the dollar so that we're paying more for a unit of power-generating capacity than we were 10 years ago.

Finally, expenditures for beautification such as wire-burying within cities add substantially to our needs for capital.

---

[2] "All electric" homes were built and sold with many electrical appliances, including oven, range, water heater, and furnace incorporated into the original home design.

[3] Early in the evening of November 9, 1965, a massive electric power failure threw most of the eastern seaboard of the United States and Canada into darkness. The blackout stretched from Toronto to Washington and lasted for more than 10 hours in some affected areas.

The future capital expenditures of GPU

Mr. Kuhns spoke specifically of the capital-raising burden in terms of its impact on GPU.

Relating capital requirements more specifically to GPU, in the late 1950's and early 1960's, we expended an average of $80 million per year for new facilities. As late as 1964 we spent only $90 million. From 1968 through 1970, our capital spending will be in excess of $200 million annually, and at this time I cannot really foresee much of a letup after 1970.

GPU's capital requirements made it clear to us that given our current dividend policy the company would have to raise additional equity capital through annual rights offerings to our shareholders for at least the next few years. Coincidentally, it appeared that the amount of equity financing required each year would approximate three quarters of the cash dividends which the company expected to pay out to its shareholders.

Exhibit 2 shows projections of GPU's sources and uses of funds through 1972. Since the elimination of three quarters of GPU's cash dividend would permit the company to meet its capital needs without resorting to additional annual equity financing (line 20 versus line 35 of Exhibit 2), the company began seriously to examine the feasibility of a dividend policy that would make this earnings retention possible.

Meeting the shareholders' needs for cash

The officers of GPU were sure that many of the company's shareholders preferred regular cash income. Any new GPU dividend plan would thus have to deal effectively with the shareholders' demands for regular cash payments. The company felt that this demand could be met if *stock* dividends equal in market value to the projected *cash* dividends were paid for the first three quarters of each year. By simply checking an IBM card, GPU shareholders would be able to specify anew each quarter whether they wished to sell their stock dividend for cash or receive certificates representing the number of GPU shares paid out as a dividend. Shareholders could round a fractional interest to a full share by either selling or buying the necessary fractional share. GPU was willing to absorb all transaction expenses (except brokerage commissions equal to about $33 per 100 shares) involved in selling dividend shares for cash.

A comparison—the old plan versus the new plan

When compared with a cash dividend payout ratio equal to 68% of earnings—coupled with an annual rights offering—the stock dividend alternative plus one quarterly cash dividend presented substantial tax savings to the investor (Exhibit 3).

A shareholder in the 20% federal income tax bracket[4] who normally *exercised* his rights would receive $312 after taxes per 1,000 shares of GPU

---

[4] As of 1967, the minimum marginal federal income tax rate for a married taxpayer was 14%. For taxable income between $4,000 and $8,000, the rate rose to 19%. For taxable income over $200,000, the marginal rate rose as high as 70%.

owned if the stock dividend plan were adopted, an increase of $234 over the $78 that would be received if the old cash dividend plan were continued. (See Basis A of Exhibit 3.)

The shareholder in the same tax bracket who normally *sold* his rights would receive $1,519 after taxes per 1,000 shares of GPU owned if the stock dividend plan were adopted, an increase of $117 over the $1,402 that would be received if the old cash dividend plan were continued.

Exhibit 4 shows that for shareholders in higher federal income tax brackets, the favorable impact of the stock dividend plan would be substantially greater. A shareholder in the 70% tax bracket would increase his after-tax cash receipts by more than $500 regardless of whether he chose to exercise or to sell his rights.

Comparative cost of administering the plan

The benefits of the stock dividend plan to the shareholders of GPU were fairly clear. In terms of the cost to the corporation, bank charges for each quarterly cash dividend payment were roughly $25,000. A single rights offering would cost the company about $450,000. A combination of four quarterly cash dividends plus one rights offering would thus cost the company $550,000. The stock dividends would cost roughly $175,000 each. The combination of three quarterly stock dividends and one cash dividend would thus cost GPU approximately $550,000. On balance, then, the cost to GPU of the two plans would be about the same provided that GPU anticipated a rights offering each year.

Some possible drawbacks in the stock dividend plan

GPU's dividend proposal was quite attractive from the standpoint of cash flow to any shareholder subject to income taxes. It was neutral from the standpoint of GPU's corporate administrative costs. Finally, the plan did have some drawbacks at both the shareholder and corporate levels. For example, GPU's officers were uncertain about the period of years during which heavy earnings retentions might be necessary. Comparatively speaking, quarterly stock dividends would be very expensive to administer unless the company faced an equally costly annual rights offering. Should GPU's capital requirements stabilize in the early 1970's, the company would rapidly increase the equity percentage in its overall capital structure under the stock dividend plan. Mr. Kuhns mentioned that another large utility had frozen the level of its per share cash dividend in 1952 to conserve cash for a large capital expenditure program. The utility in question had 35% equity in its capital structure in 1952. By 1962, the reduced cash payout coupled with stable capital expenditures had raised the equity percentage to 50% of total capital, and the frozen-dividend plan was finally abandoned. Mr. Kuhns did not want to make a fundamental change in GPU's dividend policy unless it could be justified by long-term benefits.

Other potential problem areas were evident in the new dividend policy proposal.

First, if a shareholder received cash in lieu of fractions of a share in a stock dividend, according to law these cash payments would be taxable to the recipient as ordinary income. A holder of 60 or less GPU shares would probably receive less than a single share in each quarterly stock dividend distribution. If this small holder wished to sell this fractional share, the cash received would have to be treated as ordinary income. The small GPU stockholder would thus gain no tax saving benefit from the stock dividend plan, and would in fact have to bear a small charge for selling the fractional share. This charge would have been avoided with a straight cash dividend. Since only about 4% of GPU's stock was held in lots of less than 60 shares (Exhibit 5), this drawback of the dividend plan did not appear to be a serious problem. However, some of the large holdings registered in the names of brokers might have been actually owned by a large number of small holders.

Second, since GPU would be establishing a convenient marketing mechanism for shareholders with the stock dividend plan, the company might have to maintain an effective registration statement continuously with the SEC on the theory that this was an indirect form of marketing shares of GPU. While this would not be a serious drawback (most mutual funds were in perpetual registration), it was inconvenient in that it would limit what GPU's management could report to the financial press regarding earnings projections or favorable company developments.

Finally, the most troublesome problem involving the proposed new dividend plan might arise with respect to shares held by estates and trusts. A conflict with regard to stock dividends could arise when the income beneficiary of a trust was not the same person as the beneficiary of trust principal (the remainderman). In such a situation, stock dividend shares were regarded as a distribution of principal in some states such as Massachusetts, while in other states such as New York and Pennsylvania they were treated as income. Where banks expected a conflict of interest between the income beneficiary and the remainderman, they might resolve the problem by selling their shares of GPU stock. GPU's officers were uncertain about how much selling pressure this problem might engender. The normal volume of GPU shares traded annually on the New York Stock Exchange totaled about 1.5 million shares. GPU's officers felt that if an extra million shares of selling pressure arose over a one-year period under normal circumstances the company's stock might have to decline 5% or more in order to attract the required number of new buyers.

If any such selling should develop, however, GPU's officers felt that the beneficial aspects of the new dividend plan might encourage new buyers to take up the extra available stock without any reduction in market price. GPU's managers examined the company's stockholder list to determine the number of shares held in trust accounts at Massachusetts banks, but they had no way of knowing how many of these shares were held in trusts where the income beneficiary and the remainderman were different persons (Exhibit 5). In addition they had no way of knowing the amount of buying interest which the new dividend plan might engender among existing GPU shareholders or investors as yet unknown to the company.

Checking shareholder reactions

Before making a decision on the new dividend plan, the officers of GPU felt that it might be useful on an informal basis to explore with some interested parties the acceptability of the new dividend proposal. GPU's officers were particularly concerned that some of the company's shares held by Massachusetts banks might have to be sold if the new dividend proposal was adopted. GPU's management was reluctant to make contact with Massachusetts bankers, however, since if the company were to do so, GPU's entire stockholder group would have to be simultaneously informed that the proposal was under consideration. A new ruling by the New York Stock Exchange Board of Governors[5] had made such disclosure necessary even though in the past companies had often sought out the opinions of major shareholders and others outside the management group—without such disclosure—before making financial policy changes.

If the shareholders were informed of the proposal, a logical extension of this action might be to ask the shareholders to vote on the matter. Since dividend policy had traditionally been determined at the level of the board of directors, Mr. Kuhns was somewhat wary of setting a new precedent by involving the shareholders in the dividend policy question.

Required decisions

In January, 1968, Mr. Kuhns thus faced the twin problems (1) of deciding whether the benefits of the proposed dividend plan were sufficiently attractive to merit an attempt to put them into practice, and (2) of deciding whether or not to involve the shareholder group in the making of this decision.

---

[5] Part of the text of the NYSE ruling follows:

"Negotiations leading to acquisitions and mergers, stock splits, the making of arrangements preparatory to an exchange or tender offer, changes in dividend rates or earnings, calls for redemption, new contracts, products or discoveries, are the type of developments where the risk of untimely and inadvertent disclosure of corporate plans is most likely to occur. Frequently, these matters require discussion and study by corporate officials before final decisions can be made. Accordingly, extreme care must be used in order to keep the information on a confidential basis.

. . . . .

"At some point it usually becomes necessary to involve persons other than top management of the company or companies to conduct preliminary studies or assist in other preparations for contemplated transactions, e.g., business appraisals, tentative financing arrangements, attitude of large outside holders, availability of major blocks of stock, engineering studies, market analyses and surveys, etc. Experience has shown that maintaining security at this point is virtually impossible. Accordingly, fairness requires that the company make an immediate public announcement as soon as confidential disclosures relating to such important matters are made to 'outsiders.'"

Exhibit 1

GENERAL PUBLIC UTILITIES CORPORATION (A)

INCOME AND BALANCE SHEET ITEMS FOR YEARS ENDED DECEMBER 31, 1959–67

(Dollar figures in millions except per share data)

	1959	1960	1961	1962	1963	1964	1965	1966	1967
INCOME ITEMS									
Revenues	$196.0	$204.8	$214.3	$227.2	$240.0	$253.2	$270.0	$289.3	$310.9
Net profit after taxes	33.1	35.1	36.5	40.7	41.6	44.1	46.4	48.7	51.9
BALANCE SHEET ITEMS									
Current assets	$55.1	$45.8	$47.1	$60.2	$59.8	$62.4	$60.4	$62.4	$75.4
Property, plant, and equipment	859.8	832.0	886.5	933.4	982.7	1,042.6	1,117.2	1,241.9	1,365.3
Other assets	21.0	53.0	52.9	82.0	77.3	72.3	66.5	60.6	68.9
Total assets	$935.9	$930.8	$986.5	$1,075.7	$1,119.8	$1,177.3	$1,244.1	$1,364.9	$1,509.6
Current liabilities	$55.3	$45.7	$51.1	$57.1	$75.0	$71.2	$52.6	$54.2	$50.6
Long-term debt	437.6	442.6	480.9	522.4	534.8	576.8	654.9	732.2	862.0
Preferred stock	84.2	84.2	84.2	84.2	84.2	83.7	79.7	77.5	77.5
Common equity	328.6	341.9	354.0	394.7	407.2	420.3	434.3	477.2	491.5
Other liabilities	30.2	16.4	16.3	17.3	18.6	25.3	22.6	23.8	28.0
Total liabilities	$935.9	$930.8	$986.5	$1,075.7	$1,119.8	$1,177.3	$1,244.1	$1,364.9	$1,509.6
Long-term debt/total capital	51.5%	50.9%	52.2%	52.2%	52.0%	53.4%	56.0%	56.8%	60.2%
Preferred stock/total capital	9.9	9.7	9.2	8.4	8.2	7.7	6.8	6.1	5.4
Common stock/total capital	38.6	39.4	38.6	39.4	39.8	38.9	37.2	37.1	34.4
	100.0%	100.0%	100.0%	100.0%	100.0%	100.0%	100.0%	100.0%	100.0%
Common shares outstanding (in millions)	22.6	23.7	23.8	23.8	23.8	23.8	23.8	23.9	24.8
PER SHARE ITEMS									
Earnings per share	$1.46	$1.48	$1.53	$1.71	$1.75	$1.85	$1.95	$2.04	$2.09
Dividends per share	$1.05	$1.09	$1.13	$1.15	$1.22	$1.30	$1.37	$1.42	$1.52
Average price per share	$24.20	$24.20	$30.30	$29.70	$33.30	$35.90	$37.20	$31.10	$29.70
Average price-earnings ratio	16.5	16.3	19.8	17.4	19.0	19.4	19.1	15.2	14.2
Average dividend yield	4.4%	4.5%	3.7%	3.7%	3.6%	3.6%	3.7%	4.6%	5.1%

Exhibit 2

GENERAL PUBLIC UTILITIES CORPORATION (A)
ESTIMATED FUNDS FLOW, 1967–72
(In millions)

		Actual 1967	1968	1969	1970	1971	1972
					Pro Forma		
1	Use of funds:						
2	Additions to plant including invest-						
3	ments in nuclear fuel...........	$176.5	$203.1	$250.9	$246.3	$235.0	$235.0
4	Working capital additions and						
5	other uses....................	13.6	4.0	4.0	4.0	4.0	4.0
6	Total funds applied.........	$190.1	$207.1	$254.9	$250.3	$239.0	$239.0
				New Dividend Plan			
11	Source of funds:						
12	Net income plus tax deferrals*......	$ 55.3	$ 59.8	$ 64.6	$ 69.8	$ 75.5	$ 81.5
13	Less dividends (17%)†..........	37.6	10.2	11.0	11.9	12.9	13.8
14	Income retained...............	$ 17.7	$ 49.6	$ 53.6	$ 57.9	$ 62.6	$ 67.7
15	Depreciation.....................	37.8	40.7	46.1	51.0	56.0	61.0
16	Total internal cash generation.	$ 55.5	$ 90.3	$ 99.7	$108.9	$118.6	$128.7
17	Additions to short-term debt........	27.8	24.4	55.3	34.0	4.2	(15.3)
18	Additions to long-term debt‡.......	106.8	85.3	92.3	99.1	107.2	116.0
19	Additions to preferred stock‡.......	—	7.1	7.6	8.3	9.0	9.6
20	Extra equity capital needed........	—	—	—	—	—	—
21	Total funds available.........	$190.1	$207.1	$254.9	$250.3	$239.0	$239.0
				Old Dividend Plan			
26	Source of funds:						
27	Net income plus tax deferrals*.......	$ 55.3	$ 59.8	$ 64.6	$ 69.8	$ 75.5	$ 81.5
28	Less dividends (68%)†..........	37.6	40.0	44.0	47.5	51.3	55.5
29	Income retained...............	$ 17.7	$ 19.8	$ 20.6	$ 22.3	$ 24.2	$ 26.0
30	Depreciation.....................	37.8	40.7	46.1	51.0	56.0	61.0
31	Total internal cash generation.	$ 55.5	$ 60.5	$ 66.7	$ 73.3	$ 80.2	$ 87.0
32	Additions to short-term debt........	27.8	24.4	55.3	34.0	4.2	(15.3)
33	Additions to long-term debt‡........	106.8	85.3	92.3	99.1	107.2	116.0
34	Additions to preferred stock‡........	—	7.1	7.6	8.3	9.0	9.6
35	Extra equity capital needed........	—	29.8	33.0	35.6	38.4	41.7
36	Total funds available.........	$190.1	$207.1	$254.9	$250.3	$239.0	$239.0

* Assumes that net income plus tax deferrals would increase about 8% each year over the base year 1967.
† GPU's annual dividend payments had historically amounted to 68% of reported earnings and tax deferrals. Under the proposed stock dividend plan, one quarter of this amount (17%) of earnings and tax deferrals would be paid out in cash. An amount equivalent to 51% of earnings and tax deferrals would be declared in the form of stock dividends.
‡ Assuming a capital structure with 35% common equity, 5% preferred stock, and 60% debt, long-term debt additions equal to 0.60/0.35 = 1.70 times retained earnings could be made each year. Preferred stock additions equal to 0.05/0.35 = 0.143 times retained earnings could also be made annually.
Source: The company was unable to provide or substantiate data relating to income and dividend projections because of SEC regulations. GPU had a security in registration when the case was being prepared. Projections were thus made by the casewriter.

Exhibit 3

GENERAL PUBLIC UTILITIES CORPORATION (A)

CASH EFFECTS OF NEW DIVIDEND POLICY ON HOLDER OF 1,000 GPU SHARES AND ON GPU AS A CORPORATE ENTITY

I. CASH EFFECTS OF NEW DIVIDEND POLICY ON HOLDER OF 1,000 GPU SHARES

	Shares	Amount per Share	Cash Dividend	Stock Dividend	20% Income Tax	Net Receipts Stockholder
Basis A—Shareholder Maintains Position by Exercising Rights or Accumulating Stock Dividends:						
Old dividend plan (use rights offering):						
Cash dividend received	1,000	$ 1.56	$1,560.00		$312.00	$1,248.00
Cash outlay to exercise rights to 50 shares	50	$23.40a				(1,170.00)
Total	1,050					$ 78.00
New stock dividend plan:						
Cash dividend received	1,000	$ 0.39	$ 390.00		$ 78.00	$ 312.00
Stock dividend accumulated	43⅓	$27.00		$1,170.00		
Total	1,043⅓					$ 312.00
Basis B—Shareholder Does Not Subscribe to Rights Offering or Sells Stock Dividend:						
Old dividend plan (use rights offering):						
Cash dividend received	1,000	$ 1.56	$1,560.00		$312.00	$1,248.00
Proceeds from sale of rights to 50 shares		$ 3.43f	171.50		17.15	154.35
Total	1,000		$1,731.50		$329.15	$1,402.35
New stock dividend plan:						
Cash dividend received	1,000	$ 0.39	$ 390.00		$ 78.00	$ 312.00
Proceeds from sale of stock dividend		$ 1.17c,e		$1,170.00	117.00	1,053.00
Proceeds from sale of additional shares	(61⅓)	$27.00b,c,d,e		171.50	17.15	154.35
Total	993⅓				$212.15	$1,519.35

Exhibit 3—Continued

II. CASH EFFECTS OF NEW DIVIDEND POLICY ON GPU AS A CORPORATE ENTITY
(IN THOUSANDS)

	Shares	Stock Dividend	(Disbursements)
Old dividend plan (use rights offering):			
Cash dividend paid out............	24,805 @ $ 1.56		$(38,696)
Cash received from exercise of rights........	1,240 @ $23.40		29,016
Total............	26,045		$ (9,680)
New stock dividend plan:			
Cash dividend paid out............	24,805 @ $ 0.39		$ (9,680)
Stock dividend............	1,075	$29,016	—
Total............	25,880		$ (9,680)

	Total Shares (In Thousands)	Shareholder's Holdings	Shares	Shareholder's Equity
Initial.............	24,805	1,000		0.00403%
Rights offering..........	26,045	1,050		0.00403
Sell rights............	26,045	1,000		0.00384
Initial............	24,805	1,000		0.00403
Stock dividend	25,880	1,043⅛		0.00403
Sell stock............	25,880	1,000		0.00386
Sell additional shares............	25,880	993⅞		0.00384

[a] Assumes market value of common stock equals $27.00 and that one right is issued for each share of common stock held. One thousand rights entitle their owner to purchase 50 shares of GPU common stock at $23.40 per share. The 1,000 rights received by the GPU shareholder would thus have a total value equal to approximately $50 \times (\$27.00 - \$23.40) = \$180.00$.

[b] Additional holdings are sold to maintain same equity position as under a rights offering wherein the rights are sold. In other words:

[c] Assumes stock has a cost basis for tax purposes of zero, the most conservative possible assumption.

[d] Under the stock dividend plan, the GPU shares retained by the shareholder would continue to have a zero tax basis. With cash dividends, the shareholder who exercised his rights would slowly build up a small tax basis for his stock. For this reason, the calculations assume that the shareholder does not sell his GPU holdings during his lifetime.

[e] All calculations assume that the GPU shareholder has owned his shares for at least six months and that capital gains are therefore taxed at reduced rates.

[f] The ex-rights price of the common stock should be $[(\$27 \times 20) + \$23.40]/21 = \$26.83$. The proceeds from the sale of the rights would thus be $50 \times (\$26.83 - \$23.40)$.

Exhibit 4

GENERAL PUBLIC UTILITIES CORPORATION (A)
INCREASED CASH IN HAND TO SHAREHOLDER UNDER STOCK DIVIDEND PLAN AS COMPARED WITH EXISTING DIVIDEND POLICY

| | Extra Cash per 1,000 GPU Shares Owned | |
Shareholder's Marginal Income Tax Bracket	*Basis A**	*Basis B†*
20%	$234	$117
30%	351	176
40%	468	234
50%	585	293
60%	702	410
70%	819	527

* Basis A—assumes that the shareholder would (1) subscribe to the rights offering under the old dividend plan or (2) accumulate his stock dividends under the new plan. Either action would leave his percentage equity interest in GPU intact.

† Basis B—assumes that the shareholder would (1) sell his rights under the old dividend plan or (2) sell his stock dividend and a small number of his common shares under the new plan. Either action would reduce slightly his percentage equity interest in GPU.

Exhibit 5

GENERAL PUBLIC UTILITIES CORPORATION (A)
COMMON SHAREHOLDERS OF GPU AT DECEMBER 31, 1967

I. DISTRIBUTION BY SIZE OF HOLDINGS

Size of Holdings	Number of Holders	Percent	Number of Shares	Percent
1 to 20 shares	17,089	22%	153,775	1%
21 to 60 shares	17,328	22	679,113	3
61 to 100 shares	11,152	14	949,203	4
101 to 300 shares	23,820	30	4,072,560	16
301 to 1,000 shares	7,469	10	3,680,096	15
1,001 shares and over	1,853	2	15,270,349	61
Total	78,711	100%	24,805,096	100%

II. INSTITUTIONAL HOLDERS

	Number of Shares (In Millions)
Bank trust departments:	
Pennsylvania	3.0
New York	2.9
Massachusetts	1.6
Other states	2.1
Mutual funds	1.5
Insurance companies	1.0
Pension funds	0.2
Total	12.3

Note: Some shares held by bank trust departments and insurance companies were beneficially owned by pension funds.

MIDWEST COMMUNICATIONS, INC.*

^^

In June, 1974, the management of Midwest Communications, Inc. decided to acquire $1 million in new broadcasting equipment for one of its television stations. Various means of financing this acquisition had been considered during the past several months. Mr. Jonathan Stone, vice president of finance of Midwest Communications, Inc., had narrowed the financing decision to two alternatives: (1) a seven-year lease proposed by the manufacturer of the equipment to be acquired, Audionics Corporation, or (2) a seven-year term loan for $1 million from a major insurance company. Mr. Stone knew that a final choice between these two alternatives would have to be made within a matter of days.

Midwest Communications and the broadcasting industry

Prior to 1960, Midwest Communications was a privately-held business engaged in magazine publishing and distribution. The corporation raised external equity capital in 1960 with an initial public issue of common stock. In 1961, Midwest purchased its first radio station and embarked on a program of investment in the broadcasting industry. A second radio station was acquired in 1963, and in the period 1963–66 both stations produced operating losses.

As a result of management changes and significant promotional work, the two radio stations were profitable in every year of the period 1967–73. Several additional radio and television stations were purchased in the late 1960's and early 1970's, and by 1973 operating revenues from broadcasting had grown to $9.7 million, representing 28% of Midwest's total operating revenues of $34.6 million. A five-year summary of income statements is shown in Exhibit 1, and balance sheets for 1971–73 are summarized in Exhibit 2.

Midwest ranked in the "second tier" of the broadcasting industry in terms of total broadcasting revenues, as the company was significantly smaller than the ten major broadcasters in the United States. The largest independent companies in the radio and television broadcasting industry were Columbia Broadcasting Systems, Inc. (sales revenues of $1.5 billion) and American Broadcasting Companies, Inc. ($880 million).

* Reprinted from Stanford Business Cases 1974 with the permission of the publishers, Stanford University Graduate School of Business, © 1974 by the Board of Trustees of the Leland Stanford Junior University.

Early in 1974, observers of the broadcasting industry noted widespread Wall Street pessimism about rising operating costs (reflecting an 8% increase in costs reported for 1973) with only modest increases in total advertising revenues. One prominent New York Stock Exchange member firm anticipated that advertising revenues to broadcasters would grow at only 3% to 5% in 1974, down from a 9% increase in 1973. Under these industry conditions the price of the common stock of most major broadcasters had dropped 50% from the market highs of 1973, and Midwest's stock price had declined from its 1973 peak of $31 a share to around $10 by mid-1974. In the light of this development the management of Midwest had ruled out a new issue of common stock as a source of financing capital expenditures so long as the price of the company's common stock remained depressed.

The lease proposal

The seven-year lease under consideration had been proposed by the manufacturer of the new equipment to be acquired, Audionics Corporation. Audionics Corporation was a leading manufacturer of audio and video broadcasting equipment with total sales of several hundred million dollars. Audionics had recently organized a new financial subsidiary, Audionics Finance Corporation (AFC), whose purpose was to extend lease financing to customers interested in acquiring Audionics equipment. AFC customarily retained new leases in its portfolio, but it reserved the right to place some of its leases with third-party institutions.

The principal terms of the seven-year lease proposed to Midwest by Audionics to cover the acquisition of the $1 million of Audionics equipment were as follows:

1. *Annual lease payment for duration of lease.* Midwest would be obligated to pay AFC seven equal annual lease payments of $166,611 a year, payments to be made at the end of each year.[1]
2. *Maintenance, taxes, and insurance.* All payments for maintenance of the equipment and any taxes and assessments thereon would be the responsibility of Midwest. Midwest would also be obligated to carry a specified level of insurance on the equipment. (Mr. Stone estimated that Midwest's outlays for these purposes would be the same whether the equipment was leased or purchased.)

The annual lease payments quoted by AFC were computed so as to amortize the full $1 million sales price of the equipment over the seven-year period at an implicit interest rate of 4%. At the end of the seven-year period ownership of the equipment would, of course, reside in the hands of AFC. If Midwest desired to continue to use the equipment beyond the expiration of the lease, it would have to negotiate a renewal of the lease or a purchase of the equipment from AFC as of the expiration of the lease in 1981.

---

[1] Actually, most leases provide for monthly or quarterly rental payments, with payments due at the beginning of the period. The terms as here stated have been modified to simplify the analysis of the case.

In the course of his investigations of possible financing arrangements for the new equipment Mr. Stone had read an article in *Fortune* magazine on "Leveraged Leasing." This article, a portion of which is reproduced in Exhibit 3, described a leveraged lease of Anaconda Company on the plant and equipment of a new aluminum reduction mill. Mr. Stone had inquired of AFC whether a leveraged lease might be an attractive means of financing the equipment that Midwest was acquiring. The representative of AFC had responded that leveraged leases were seldom used in transactions of less than $5 million because of sizable legal and administrative costs involved. He advised Mr. Stone that a leveraged lease would not be appropriate in a $1 million transaction. He recommended instead a standard lease such as that described above.

The loan proposal

The only practical alternative to the lease proposal was for Midwest to buy the new equipment outright from Audionics and to finance it from available funds or by new borrowing. Since all of Midwest's internal funds were fully committed to projects previously undertaken, a decision to purchase the $1 million of equipment from Audionics would necessitate a new loan of $1 million. After investigating a number of loan possibilities Mr. Stone had decided that a seven-year term loan from a major insurance company was the most attractive source of additional debt available to Midwest.

The provisions of this loan were straightforward. Interest on the loan would be set at a rate of 12% on the outstanding balance of the loan for the duration of the loan. Repayments of principal would be made in equal annual installments at the rate of $142,857 a year, the payments to be made on each anniversary date of the loan. The loan proposal contained standard covenants on the usual subjects such as the maintenance of a required minimum level of working capital, incurrence of additional indebtedness, and repurchases of stock. All such provisions were regarded as reasonable by Mr. Stone.

Additional considerations relevant to lease versus buy-borrow decision

One of the considerations important in the decision as to whether to lease or buy the Audionic equipment was the tax consequences of the two transactions. Mr. Stone had been advised by his tax counsel that under the lease proposal the full amount of the annual lease payments would be deductible for income tax purposes as rental payments. In the event the property was purchased the tax consequences would be as follows: (1) Midwest would be entitled to an investment tax credit in the year of purchase equal to 7% of the purchase price, or $70,000; (2) the full $1 million purchase price could be depreciated on an accelerated basis over an eight-year life. Under the sum-of-the-years-digits method the depreciation allowances to which Midwest would be entitled would be:

Year	Allowable Depreciation
1	$222,222
2	194,444
3	166,667
4	138,889
5	111,111
6	83,333
7	55,556
8	27,778

In addition, under the purchase alternative the interest payments on the term loan obtained to finance the purchase would be deductible.

A second consideration involved in the decision was whether the equipment would have continued usefulness to Midwest at the end of the seven-year lease period, either for use within the company or for resale purposes. Mr. Stone estimated that under normal conditions the Audionics equipment package would be worth $200,000, or 20% of its initial value, at the end of seven years, even though the equipment would be fully depreciated by the end of the eighth year. Mr. Stone recognized, however, that technological developments might render the equipment obsolete sooner than he anticipated. On the other hand, a sustained rapid rate of inflation over the next seven years might mean that the dollar value of the equipment at the end of seven years would substantially exceed Mr. Stone's estimate of $200,000.

A third consideration that troubled Mr. Stone was the appropriate discount rate or discount rates to use in comparing the cash flows involved in the lease versus the buy-borrow alternatives. Mr. Stone had asked his assistant, Mr. Young, a recent MBA graduate, to prepare a memorandum for him discussing this issue. Mr. Young's memorandum, which is reproduced as Exhibit 4, did not fully resolve Mr. Stone's uncertainty on this point.

The decision

In order to obtain a better feel for the merits of the two alternatives Mr. Stone gave Mr. Young another assignment. First, he requested Mr. Young to lay out precisely the cash flows involved under the two alternatives. Where uncertainties were involved, such as the residual value of the equipment at the end of the seven years, Mr. Stone asked Mr. Young to prepare multiple estimates that would bracket the reasonable range of probable outcomes. Finally, Mr. Stone asked Mr. Young to compute the present value of the lease versus the buy-borrow alternative over the range of discount rates that might conceivably be justified on the basis of his earlier memorandum (Exhibit 4). Mr. Stone hoped that this additional information would resolve the uncertainty regarding the relative attractiveness of the two alternatives. In any event, he knew that he had to make a firm decision on the appropriate method of financing within the next two or three days.

Exhibit 1

MIDWEST COMMUNICATIONS, INC.

INCOME STATEMENTS FOR YEARS ENDING DECEMBER 31, 1969–73

(In millions except for per share data)

	1969	1970	1971	1972	1973
Newspaper operating revenues	$10.6	$17.1	$18.2	$19.7	$22.1
Broadcasting operating revenues	6.8	7.1	7.4	7.8	9.7
Other operating revenues	0.2	1.5	2.3	2.6	2.8
Total operating revenues	$17.6	$25.7	$27.9	$30.1	$34.6
Operating expenses	12.3	17.8	19.5	20.9	23.9
Depreciation	0.7	1.1	1.1	1.2	1.4
Interest expense	...	1.3	1.2	0.5	0.3
Other income	0.1	0.3	0.1	0.1	...
Net income before taxes	$ 4.7	$ 5.9	$ 6.2	$ 7.6	$ 9.0
Provision for income taxes	2.6	3.2	3.2	3.7	4.3
Net income after taxes	$ 2.1	$ 2.7	$ 3.0	$ 3.9	$ 4.7
Earnings per share (in dollars)	$ 0.57	$ 0.67	$ 0.73	$ 0.89	$ 1.06

Note: Figures may not add because of rounding.

Exhibit 2

MIDWEST COMMUNICATIONS, INC.

BALANCE SHEETS AS OF DECEMBER 31, 1971–73

(In millions)

	1971	1972	1973
ASSETS			
Cash and marketable securities	$ 2.7	$ 2.1	$ 2.0
Accounts receivable	2.7	2.8	3.6
Inventories	0.5	0.5	0.4
Other current assets	0.5	0.4	0.6
Total current assets	$ 6.3	$ 5.8	$ 6.7
Land and land improvements	1.1	1.1	1.8
Buildings	6.7	7.0	8.9
Equipment and fixtures	12.9	13.7	17.5
	$20.7	$21.8	$28.2
Less: Accumulated depreciation	9.4	10.1	11.1
Net fixed assets	$11.3	$11.7	$17.1
Intangible assets	16.6	16.6	18.7
Other assets	1.0	1.0	1.3
Total assets	$35.3	$35.0	$43.8
LIABILITIES			
Long-term debt due within one year	$ 1.2	$ 1.2	$ 1.3
Accounts payable	0.7	0.9	0.8
Dividends payable on common stock	...	...	0.3
Accrued income taxes	0.9	1.0	0.5
Film contracts, payments due in one year	0.1	0.2	0.4
Accrued expenses and other current liabilities	0.9	1.0	1.1
Total current liabilities	$ 3.9	$ 4.3	$ 4.4
Long-term debt	11.0	3.5	7.8
Film contracts, payments due after one year	0.1	0.1	0.6
Deferred income taxes	0.5	0.5	0.8
Total liabilities	$15.4	$ 8.4	$13.5
Convertible cumulative preferred stock	9.1	8.5	...
Net common equity	10.8	18.1	30.2
Total liabilities and net worth	$35.3	$35.0	$43.8

Note: Figures may not add because of rounding.

Exhibit 3

MIDWEST COMMUNICATIONS, INC.

LEVERAGED LEASING: HOW TO SAVE $74 MILLION, MAYBE

Leasing deals tend to be complicated, and Anaconda Company's new Sebree plant—an aluminum reduction mill—is an interesting example. Fourteen other companies were involved in the deal that raised $110.7 million and brought the plant into being. (Anaconda itself financed another $28 million not involved in the lease.)

Two of the companies did a lot of consulting and arranging for Anaconda. U.S. Leasing (upper left of the diagram), a company that specializes in "packaging" leasing deals, helped to design this one after it outbid another packager and several banks.

First Boston (upper right in the diagram), which has served for many years as Anaconda's investment banker, arranged for 65 percent of the financing by lining up three insurance companies, Prudential, Metropolitan, and Aetna Life (lower right), which together agreed to lend $72 million. The insurance companies will earn 9⅛ percent on this investment, with interest and principal coming out of Anaconda's annual lease payments.

The other 35 percent is "equity capital," put up by those six banks and Chrysler (lower left). In return for putting up $38.7 million, the seven get the rest of the lease payments. They also get to own the plant itself, which means that they receive the tax benefits from depreciation and the federal investment tax credit on the plant.

The property is held in the banks' name by First Kentucky Trust Company (center of the diagram), which took in both the debt and equity capital needed for construction and paid it out to the builder-contractor, the Aluminum Company of America. In addition, First Kentucky will funnel the lease payments from Anaconda to the insurance companies and banks. (The banks, as owners of the property, pay the trustee's expenses, which will be deducted from those lease payments.)

The point of this involved exercise, from Anaconda's point of view, is to reduce the cost of financing the plant. The company has calculated that over the twenty-year term of the lease, its lease payments will total some $74 million less than would the cost of interest payments on bonded debt. This calculation assumes, however, that Anaconda's effective tax rate, which has been extremely low recently (because of heavy losses in 1971), will stay low. If the company's tax rate should rise sharply, then it will miss the tax shelter it has given up by forgoing ownership of the plant.

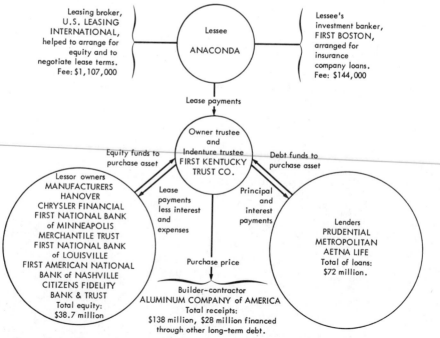

Source: *Fortune* (November 1973), p. 133.

Exhibit 4

MIDWEST COMMUNICATIONS, INC.

MEMORANDUM

June 15, 1974

TO: Mr. Stone

FROM: Mr. Young

SUBJECT: *Discount Rate to Use in Computing Present Values in Lease versus Buy-Borrow Decisions*

There seems to be a big difference of opinion these days about the right discount rate to use in computing present values in lease versus buy-borrow decisions. As you know, we have always used Midwest's (weighted average) cost of capital in *all* discounted cash flow calculations, in the interests of consistency. Our target debt ratio is 0.30 (long-term debt to total long-term capital), and in 1973 we were comfortably below that figure (0.23).

Under the term-loan alternative, with a 12% interest rate, the cost of debt to us currently would be about 6% on an after-tax basis. The cost of equity capital represents one number on which we have never had total agreement. The fundamental point is that this figure should reflect the basic business and financial risk of the company. Nearly everyone would agree that the broadcasting industry is subject to above-average risk—a look at our current stock price versus the high of last year will confirm that assessment. We assume the average public corporation in this country has a cost of equity of about 12%. Adding a 3% margin for additional risk would place our cost of equity in the area of 15%. Under current conditions in the capital markets even these figures may be too low.

At a level of abstraction commonly found in academic finance journals, it seems to make sense to discount each item of cash flow in a project at a rate commensurate with its risk. The problem is that any one project has many individual components of cash flow, all more or less risky, so that some degree of aggregation must be used in practice. The traditional approach has been to apply a single rate to the whole company as a "risk class" as well. At a practical level, we have to decide whether to apply one rate, our (weighted average) cost of capital, in all discounted cash flow calculations, or to use a higher or lower rate depending on some judgment of the risk of future cash flows in each specific instance in Midwest.

A case can be made for discounting lease payments at a rate lower than our cost of capital, on grounds that the payments are legal commitments that we certainly intend to honor. In this sense a lease payment is very similar to a loan payment. Both are legal obligations which can be treated as virtually certain over the term of the lease or loan. On the other hand, our estimates of residual equipment values are subject to all the obvious uncertainties concerning the state of new technology, new competing products, and demand for used audio/video broadcasting equipment. The argument for discounting everything at our cost of capital is based on simplicity. It has the great virtue of being workable and understandable, although it seems to be less elegant from a conceptual standpoint than applying different rates to different cash flows of different risk.

I.C.A. CORPORATION

^^^

On February 6, 1968, Mr. Simon Greenspan, president of I.C.A. Corporation, was considering whether his company should own outright or lease a new manufacturing facility. A new plant was needed by the company to meet the level of production required by a rapidly expanding backlog of orders. The directors of I.C.A. had recently approved in principle Mr. Greenspan's proposal to have a new manufacturing facility built to the company's specifications. Now Mr. Greenspan had to decide whether to (1) finance the new plant with a mortgage loan or (2) lease the plant from a group of private investors who would own and finance the property themselves.

Corporate history of I.C.A.

In October, 1958, Mr. Greenspan and two friends, who later became senior vice presidents, founded I.C.A. (then called Instruments Corporation of America) to conduct research and development for profit in technologically based industries. From its early days the company grew rapidly in terms of sales, profits, and assets, as evidenced by Exhibits 1 and 2. To sustain its early growth, the company raised capital in 1960 by offering to the public 50,000 shares of common stock. This security was not actively traded until 1965, when I.C.A. issued an additional 450,000 shares, this time to raise the cash necessary to finance an acquisition. The price behavior of the company's common stock after the 1965 offering is shown in Exhibit 3.

As the company grew, its profit-making activity, which was initially limited to contract research, soon expanded to include the manufacture of scientific instruments. I.C.A.'s entry into the field of instrument manufacture came about as a result of four highly profitable acquisitions between 1960 and 1966. By 1967 the company had diversified to the extent that its equipment was being used for precision measurement, integrated circuit production, and vacuum processing and joining of metals. Sales of laboratory apparatus and industrial equipment accounted for 77% of the company's revenue in 1967, while the revenues from contract research, a less profitable activity, declined to 23% of the combined corporate total.

In late 1967, I.C.A. markedly stepped up the pace of its merger activity. In November and December of that year I.C.A. and three privately owned companies signed merger agreements, which called for the issuance of a minimum of 330,000 and a maximum of 430,000 shares of I.C.A. common stock. The total number of shares ultimately issued would vary between these limits depending on the price of I.C.A.'s stock during a period of time immediately preceding the effective date of each particular merger. When consummated, the three mergers would substantially boost I.C.A.'s sales and profits.

Rapid growth causes shortage of facilities

By mid-1967 it was clear to Mr. Greenspan that I.C.A. was going to need an increase of 75% in its instrument manufacturing capability within the next two years simply to keep pace with internal growth opportunities. I.C.A. was already cramped for space in its two existing manufacturing facilities; a new plant would be needed to meet future production requirements. A plant of sufficient size would provide about 150,000 square feet of manufacturing floor space.

In August, 1967, Mr. Greenspan hired an architect to draft plans for a new plant and set out to locate a large plot of land for the new facility. Mr. Greenspan and the architect agreed on an ideal location for the plant and determined that the cost of suitable acreage would be $535,400. After the architect's plans had been drafted and approved, the treasurer of I.C.A. obtained construction bids from two building contractors. The lower bid was $2,464,600. The cost of the land and building together would amount to $3,000,000, and the treasurer calculated that the interest on interim loans used to finance construction would add an additional $185,400 to the project's total cost before the building could be occupied.

Financing via direct loan

In order to line up long-term financing for the proposed new plant, the treasurer had spoken at some length with the mortgage loan officers at the First National Bank. He found that I.C.A. could borrow the entire cost of construction by mortgaging both the proposed plant and one other plant, which the company owned outright. The bank offered an interest rate of 6%. No principal was to be payable on the loan of $3,185,400 in the first year. Thereafter the loan was to be amortized over a 30-year period in equal quarterly payments of $57,396 (equal to $229,584 annually), which included both principal and interest.

Financing via lease

Before hiring the architect, Mr. Greenspan had informally discussed the need for a new facility with some of the company's directors. During the course of one of these conversations he learned that a number of investment banking firms were offering a relatively new type of financial service. The partners of these firms or wealthy clients would put up the money needed to construct an office or factory tailored to the needs of a company such as I.C.A. On a property like the one under consideration, the investor group would put up a small fraction of the cost themselves and mortgage the property for the remaining amount. The company would then rent the property under a long-term noncancellable lease.

If I.C.A. financed by this method, it would pay a lease rate sufficient for the owners to recover the full cost of the building plus interest on their mortgage in 31 years, the initial term of the lease. At the end of the initial lease term the investor group would have recovered all of its original investment, and it would also own the building free and clear of any mortgage. I.C.A. could then renew the lease at a substantially reduced rate.

Mr. Greenspan decided to follow up the financing information he had received from the director, and shortly thereafter he asked the investment banking firm of Fare, Supple & Smarte, Inc. (FS&S), for a specific proposal under which I.C.A. could lease its new manufacturing facility. The representatives of FS&S appeared to be quite interested in submitting a lease proposal, and they offered to do a substantial part of the analysis necessary to enable the management of I.C.A. to make the lease versus ownership decision. Mr. Greenspan supplied them with the details of the financing package offered by the First National Bank, and the FS&S group returned three weeks later with their analysis and a proposal. Appendix A presents the FS&S analysis.

Exhibit 1

I.C.A. CORPORATION

CONSOLIDATED STATEMENT OF INCOME, 1962–67*

(In thousands)

	Years Ended September 30†					Nine Months Ended	
	1962	1963	1964	1965	1966	July 3, 1966	June 30, 1967
Net sales	$5,576	$7,308	$9,495	$9,973	$19,511	$14,301	$16,702
Cost of sales	4,751	6,172	7,906	8,049	14,523	10,533	12,203
Selling, general, administrative	391	498	793	979	2,373	1,804	2,100
Interest	33	42	57	117	375	282	305
Income before federal income tax	$ 401	$ 596	$ 739	$ 828	$ 2,240	$ 1,682	$ 2,094
Federal income tax	213	312	364	403	1,054	808	977
Net income	$ 188	$ 284	$ 375	$ 425	$ 1,186	$ 874	$ 1,117
Average number of shares outstanding	431	466	492	497	948‡	948	952
Income per common share§	$ 0.44	$ 0.61	$ 0.76	$ 0.85	$ 1.25	$ 0.92	$ 1.17

* This statement was prepared on the following basis:
On October 5, 1965, I.C.A. purchased all the outstanding stock of Instrumentation Company for approximately $10,300,000. The transaction was treated as a purchase, and accordingly the consolidated statement of income includes the operations of Instrumentation since the date of acquisition.

† Audited.

‡ Includes 450,000 shares issued in a public offering incident to the acquisition of the Instrumentation Company.

§ No dividends have been paid.

Exhibit 2

I.C.A. CORPORATION

CONSOLIDATED BALANCE SHEET AS OF JUNE 30, 1967

(Dollar figures in thousands)

ASSETS

Cash	$ 1,806
Accounts receivable	4,730
Inventories	5,356
Prepaid expenses	245
Total current assets	$12,137
Land and buildings	$ 2,772
Machinery and equipment	2,813
Less: Accumulated depreciation	(1,224)
Total property, plant, and equipment	$ 4,361
Excess of cost of investments in subsidiaries over net tangible assets acquired	6,269
Total assets	$22,767

LIABILITIES AND STOCKHOLDERS' EQUITY

Notes payable	$ 2,852
Accounts payable	1,126
Other accruals	2,038
Total current liabilities	$ 6,016
Long-term debt	4,239
Deferred taxes	106
Common stock: 1,500,000 shares authorized; 957,104 shares issued and outstanding	$ 545
Capital in excess of par value	7,948
Retained earnings	3,913
Total stockholders' equity	$12,406
Total liabilities and stockholders' equity	$22,767

Exhibit 3

I.C.A. CORPORATION

PRICE PERFORMANCE OF I.C.A. CORPORATION
COMMON STOCK

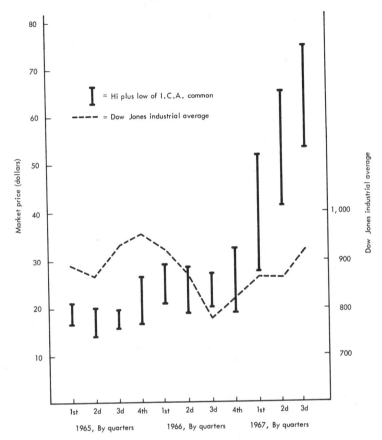

APPENDIX A

LEASE FINANCING PROPOSAL AND ANALYSIS PREPARED FOR I.C.A. CORPORATION BY THE FS&S INVESTOR GROUP

Proposal

FS&S Investor Group will build and lease to I.C.A. Corporation the proposed manufacturing facility, costing $3,185,400, under the following terms:
(1) I.C.A. Corporation will execute a noncancellable 31-year lease with FS&S Investor Group calling for quarterly rental payments of $54,159 (equal to $216,636 annually) except during the first year of the basic term.

During the first-year the quarterly rent will be $45,651 (equal to $182,604 annually).

(2) No rents will be payable by I.C.A. Corporation during construction.

(3) I.C.A. Corporation may, but is not required to, renew the lease at an annual rent equal to:

a) $53,067 from year 32 through year 46.

b) $37,798 from year 47 through year 52.

c) $26,535 from year 53 through year 62.

Analysis

The following discussion shows how the lease versus buy decision facing I.C.A. can be analyzed in terms of two important criteria. Part I of this report discusses the impact of the two possible decisions on I.C.A.'s earnings as reported to shareholders. Part II of the report discusses the impact of the two possible decisions on the net present value of I.C.A.'s cash outlays.

Part I. Effect of financing on corporate earnings as reported to shareholders

Exhibit A compares the effect of lease financing with that of ownership-debt financing on the annual income of I.C.A. over the 31-year basic term of the lease. Column 1 presents the years commencing when the plant construction is completed. Column 2 shows the expenses incurred under the leasing financing alternative. This expense amounts to $182,604 in the first year and $216,636 for each of the 30 years thereafter.

Columns 3, 4, and 5 of the exhibit show the cost of ownership-debt financing as it would be reflected in I.C.A.'s shareholder income statements. The interest expense on the mortgage loan is shown in column 3. This figure is naturally a declining amount since part of each mortgage payment reduces the principal outstanding on which the interest is computed. Straight-line depreciation calculated over a 45-year life is shown for each period in column 4. This building life and method of depreciation was chosen to reflect the most favorable way of reporting shareholder net income. If a shorter life or an accelerated method of depreciation were used, an already convincing argument in favor of the lease financing would become even more compelling. Column 5 sums the total cost of ownership-debt financing, i.e., the sum of columns 3 and 4.

Column 6 of Exhibit A shows for shareholder reporting the difference between the cost of ownership-debt financing (column 5) and the cost of lease financing (column 2). A positive figure indicates that lease financing will result in higher stated profits. For example, in the first year of plant occupancy, I.C.A.'s pretax profit would be higher by $67,485 if lease financing were chosen over ownership-debt financing. This differential would decline slowly until the 13th year, when I.C.A.'s profit would be higher if the building had been completed with ownership-debt financing. Since in a rapidly growing company current earnings are far more valuable than deferred earnings, we feel that if this analysis were made solely from the standpoint of reported earnings, I.C.A. should choose the lease financing over the ownership-debt financing alternative.

Part II. Effect of financing on net present value of cash outlays

Obviously I.C.A. will not want to make the lease versus buy decision based only on considering the implications for shareholder earnings. I.C.A. must also carefully weigh the impact of cash outflows arising under the two alternative choices.

In analyzing the lease versus buy decision according to net present value criteria, we need to choose a discount rate or opportunity cost of capital and apply that rate to the cash outflows associated with the ownership-debt financing and lease financing alternatives. Since we are dealing with the present value of a stream of cash *outflows* rather than *inflows,* in every case the alternative course of action with the *lower* net present value will be favored.

We in the FS&S Investor Group do not know what opportunity cost of capital I.C.A.'s management feels is appropriate for use in the company's investment decisions. Thus in our remaining calculations the present value of cash outlays will be computed with a number of possible discount factors ranging from 5% to 15%.

Exhibit B shows the actual cash outlays incurred in connection with ownership-debt financing and lease financing for the first quarter in each year of the initial lease term. Only the first quarter is shown for each year in order to limit the exhibit to a single page. To minimize the cash outflow under ownership-debt financing, depreciation in column 6 is calculated by double declining balance until the 22d year, at which point a switch to straight-line becomes advantageous.

Exhibit C, columns 2 and 3 respectively, show the net present value of all the cash outflows for 31 years associated with the ownership-debt financing and lease financing alternatives. The outflows discounted include all those shown in Exhibit B plus the intermediate quarterly flows that were omitted from Exhibit B in order to conserve space.

Column 4 of Exhibit C shows the net present value of the cash outflows associated with ownership-debt financing if no principal is repaid over the 31-year period. While in practice I.C.A. will have to repay principal, the impact of this cash outflow could be offset if I.C.A. were to borrow on a short-term basis amounts equivalent to the annual mortgage amortization. The total debt of I.C.A. would remain unchanged, but some long-term debt would shift into the short-term category. If this shift from long to short-term debt should prove bothersome, I.C.A. could increase its mortgage to the original amount after five or six years and use the cash made available from this transaction to repay short-term borrowings. Ownership-debt financing without debt amortization (column 4, Exhibit C) is clearly favored over the lease financing alternative presented in column 2 of Exhibit C. This comparison neglects, however, one major advantage of entering into a lease financing. The advantage is that lease financing does not use up as much of the borrowing capacity of a corporation as ownership-debt financing. (See attached excerpts from Alvin Zises' speech, "Equipment Leasing: Its Place in the Corporate Financial Design.") For example, assume that I.C.A. could borrow only about $3,000,000 within its present debt structure. If I.C.A. should enter into the lease financing, the company would still be able to borrow some additional funds. This would be true because lending institutions do not seem to weight the effects of lease financing as heavily as the effects of a direct loan. Columns 5 through 8 of Exhibit C take into account the value of additional borrowing power available to I.C.A. under the lease financing alternative. For instance, if I.C.A. should enter into the lease financing arrangement and could

1. Borrow an additional 25% of $3,185,400 @ 6% interest and
2. Invest that borrowing at an opportunity rate of 10%, then if we assume no debt amortization the lease financing alternative represents a net present value saving at $153,000. (Row 6, column 4, versus row 6, column 5, of Exhibit C.)

Residual values under two alternatives

To this point the analysis has assumed that I.C.A.'s "end position" 31 years after the plant construction is completed would be the same under the ownership-debt financing and lease financing alternatives. Since I.C.A. would *own* the facility under one alternative and merely have the option to renew the lease under the other alternative, the two "end positions" are not equivalent unless the plant has no value at the end of the initial lease term. Since this outcome is highly unlikely, additional adjustments are needed to make the end positions under the two alternatives equivalent.

At the end of 31 years, the market value of the land and building being considered by I.C.A. could be substantial. If this were the case, the rentals that could be charged on an "arm's length" lease might also be substantial. Assume that at the end of 31 years I.C.A.'s planned facility could be sold for exactly its original cost, $3,185,400. If I.C.A. owned the property, on its sale the company would realize a pretax gain of $1,959,856, an amount equal to the total depreciation taken on the property over the first 31 years of its life. Taxes of $489,964 would be due on the gain from the sale, leaving I.C.A. with a lump sum cash inflow of $2,695,436 at the end of 31 years (Table 1).

If I.C.A. leased the plant and the property retained its market value of $3,185,400 over 31 years of life, then the "arm's length" rental value would probably remain about equal to that amount paid by I.C.A. during the initial lease term. Since I.C.A. has the right to renew its plant lease at a large discount after 31 years, I.C.A. could exercise this option and sublease the plant to a third party, or continue to occupy the property itself at a "below

Table 1

Sale price	$3,185,400
Book value	1,225,544
Pretax gain	$1,959,856
Capital gain tax	489,964
After tax gain	$1,469,892
Add book value	1,225,544
Cash inflow	$2,695,436

market" cost. If the property were subleased, I.C.A. would receive a substantial cash inflow. If I.C.A. continued to occupy the property itself, however, the company could "impute" to this choice, for comparison purposes, a cash inflow equivalent to that which would have been received under a sublease. If a third party sublessee could be found who would be willing to pay $216,636 rent per year under a sublease, I.C.A. would realize an actual (or imputed) after-tax profit of $81,784 for 15 years, followed by a profit of $89,419 for 6 years, followed by $95,050 for 10 more years (Table 2).

Table 2

	Years 32–46	Years 47–52	Years 53–62
Lease revenue	$216,636	$216,636	$216,636
Lease cost	53,067	37,798	26,535
Pretax profit	$163,569	$178,838	$190,101
Income tax	81,785	89,419	95,051
Profit after tax	$ 81,784	$ 89,419	$ 95,050

If the lump cash inflow relating to the sale of I.C.A.'s plant 31 years in the future were discounted back to the present, the net present value of the cash outlays associated with ownership-debt financing, as shown in columns 2 and 4 of Exhibit C, would be reduced by $593,000 at the 5% opportunity rate (Exhibit D). If the after-tax cash flows from subleasing were similarly discounted at 5%, the net present value of the cash outlays associated with lease financing, as shown in columns 3 and 5–8 of Exhibit C, would be reduced by $293,000 (Exhibit D). By using Exhibit C and Exhibit D together, I.C.A.'s management can roughly test the impact of various assumed future plant values on the net present values of the ownership-debt financing and lease financing alternatives.

We, the FS&S investor group, feel that I.C.A. could not borrow much more than the $3,185,400 cost of the plant's construction on its present equity base. We also feel that if I.C.A. accepts the lease financing proposal, the company will still have borrowing power equal to at least 25% of $3,185,400. The value of this extra borrowing power is so substantial (as shown in Exhibit C) that if we ignore residual values the lease financing alternative is favored at every opportunity rate from 5% to 15%. At the upper end of this opportunity rate range, the lease financing alternative would still be favored under any reasonable assumption regarding plant residual values.

Since the analysis under criteria of (1) earnings and (2) present value of cash outflows both indicate that the lease financing is favored, we feel I.C.A. should accept our proposal.

Exhibit A

I.C.A. CORPORATION

COMPARISON OF THE LEASE FINANCING AND THE DIRECT LOAN
AS TO THEIR EFFECT ON CORPORATE EARNINGS
REPORTED TO STOCKHOLDERS

(1)	(2)	(3)	(4)	(5) = (3) + (4)	(6) = (5) − (2)
	Lease Plan Cost of Lease	—Ownership-Debt Plan—		Total	Difference between Cost of
Year	Financing	Interest Expense	Depreciation Expense	Cost of Direct Loan	Direct Loan and Lease Financing
1....................	$182,604	$191,124	58,965	$250,089	$ 67,485
2....................	216,636	190,248	58,965	249,213	32,577
3....................	216,636	187,836	58,965	246,801	30,165
4....................	216,636	185,274	58,965	244,239	27,603
5....................	216,636	182,553	58,965	241,518	24,882
6....................	216,636	179,667	58,965	238,632	21,992
7....................	216,636	176,604	58,965	234,569	18,933
8....................	216,636	173,355	58,965	232,320	15,684
9....................	216,636	169,905	58,965	228,870	12,234
10....................	216,636	166,242	58,965	225,207	8,571
11....................	216,636	162,354	58,965	221,319	4,683
12....................	216,636	158,229	58,965	217,194	558
13....................	216,636	153,852	58,965	212,817	−3,819
14....................	216,636	149,205	58,965	208,170	−8,466
15....................	216,636	144,270	58,965	203,235	−13,401
16....................	216,636	139,035	58,965	198,000	−18,636
17....................	216,636	133,479	58,965	192,444	−24,192
18....................	216,636	127,584	58,965	186,549	−30,087
19....................	216,636	121,323	58,965	180,288	−36,348
20....................	216,636	114,681	58,965	173,646	−42,990
21....................	216,636	107,628	58,965	166,593	−50,043
22....................	216,636	99,846	58,965	159,111	−57,525
23....................	216,636	92,202	58,965	151,167	−65,469
24....................	216,636	83,772	58,965	142,737	−73,899
25....................	216,636	74,826	58,965	133,791	−82,845
26....................	216,636	65,228	58,965	124,293	−92,343
27....................	216,636	55,251	58,965	114,216	−102,420
28....................	216,636	44,553	58,965	103,518	−113,118
29....................	216,636	33,198	58,965	92,163	−124,473
30....................	216,636	21,147	58,965	60,112	−136,524
31....................	216,636	8,355	58,965	67,320	−149,316

Exhibit B

I.C.A. CORPORATION

COMPARISON OF AFTER-TAX CASH OUTFLOWS OF LEASE FINANCING AND DIRECT LOAN FINANCING

(1)	(2)	(3) = 0.5 x (2)	(4)	(5)	(6)	(7) = (4) − .5((5) + (6))	(8) = (7) − (3)
	— Lease Plan —		— Ownership-Debt Plan —				
Quarterly Rent Payment Number	Lease Rentals	After-Tax Cash Outflow of Lease	Loan Payment	Loan Interest	Depreciation	After-Tax Cash Outflow of Loan	Amount by Which Cash Outflow with Direct Loan Exceeds Cash Outlay with Lease
1	$45,651	$22,827	$47,781	$47,781	$29,481	$ 9,150	$−13,677
5	54,159	27,078	57,396	47,781	28,170	19,419	−7,659
9	54,159	27,078	57,396	47,190	26,919	20,340	−6,738
13	54,159	27,078	57,396	46,566	25,722	21,252	−5,826
17	54,159	27,078	57,396	45,900	24,579	22,155	−4,923
21	54,159	27,078	57,396	45,195	23,487	23,055	−4,023
25	54,159	27,078	57,396	44,445	22,443	23,952	−3,126
29	54,159	27,078	57,396	43,650	21,447	23,952	−2,232
33	54,159	27,078	57,396	42,807	20,493	25,746	−1,332
37	54,159	27,078	57,396	41,913	19,584	26,649	−429
41	54,159	27,078	57,396	40,962	18,711	27,558	480
45	54,159	27,078	57,396	39,954	17,880	28,479	1,401
49	54,159	27,078	57,396	38,883	17,085	29,412	2,331
53	54,159	27,078	57,396	37,749	16,326	30,360	3,279
57	54,159	27,078	57,396	36,543	15,600	31,326	4,245
61	54,159	27,078	57,396	35,262	14,907	32,310	5,232
65	54,159	27,078	57,396	33,903	14,244	33,321	6,243
69	54,159	27,078	57,396	32,463	13,611	34,359	7,281
73	54,159	27,078	57,396	30,933	13,005	35,427	8,349
77	54,159	27,078	57,396	29,310	12,429	36,528	9,450
81	54,159	27,078	57,396	27,585	11,877	37,665	10,587
85	54,159	27,078	57,396	25,755	11,349	38,844	11,766
89	54,159	27,078	57,396	23,814	10,845	40,068	12,987
93	54,159	27,078	57,396	21,753	10,599	41,220	14,142
97	54,159	27,078	57,396	19,566	10,599	42,315	15,234
101	54,159	27,078	57,396	17,244	10,599	43,476	16,395
105	54,159	27,078	57,396	14,781	10,599	44,706	17,028
109	54,159	27,078	57,396	12,165	10,599	46,014	18,936
113	54,159	27,078	57,396	9,390	10,599	47,403	20,222
117	54,159	27,078	57,396	6,444	10,599	48,876	21,795
121	54,159	27,078	......	3,318	10,599	50,436	23,358

Exhibit C

I.C.A. CORPORATION

COMPARISON OF THE NET PRESENT VALUE OF CASH OUTFLOWS UNDER LEASE FINANCING VERSUS THE NET PRESENT VALUE OF CASH OUTFLOWS UNDER DEBT FINANCING

(Dollar figures in thousands)

(1) After-Tax Discount Rate	(2) Present Value of Outflows Associated with 31-Year Loan Assuming Amortization	(3) Present Value of Outflows Associated with 31-Year Lease	(4) Present Value of Outflows Associated with 31-Year Loan with No Amortization	(5) Present Value of Outflows Associated with 31-Year Lease Assuming Borrowing — Power of I.C.A. Is Increased by: 25%	(6) 50%	(7) 75%	(8) 100%
5%	$1,812	$1,686	$1,575	$1,434	$1,185	$936	$684
6	1,575	1,503	1,284	1,170	864	498	162
7	1,380	1,350	1,059	948	546	144	−258
8	1,218	1,221	885	768	312	−144	−597
9	1,080	1,110	747	615	117	−371	−879
10	996	1,017	639	486	−45	−579	−1,110
11	870	936	555	375	−183	−744	−1,302
12	789	864	486	282	−300	−882	−1,464
13	717	801	429	201	−399	−1,002	−1,602
14	657	747	384	129	−486	−1,104	−1,719
15	603	699	348	69	−561	−1,191	−1,824

Exhibit D

I.C.A. CORPORATION
PRESENT VALUE ADJUSTMENTS FOR PLANT'S RESIDUAL VALUE
(Dollar figures in thousands)

After-Tax Discount Rate	*Present Value of Lump Cash Inflow from Plant Sale—Ownership-Debt Financing*	*Present Value of Cash Inflows from Sublease of Plant—Lease Financing*
5%	$593	$293
6	443	194
7	331	130
8	248	88
9	186	60
10	140	41
11	106	28
12	80	20
13	60	14
14	46	10
15	35	7

APPENDIX B

EXCERPTS FROM "EQUIPMENT LEASING: ITS PLACE IN THE CORPORATE FINANCIAL DESIGN"[1]

by Alvin Zises

Attitude of investment community

Does the investment community recognize the junior nature of chattel leasing and its effect upon the equity and debt capital of a company if the lease is used prudently?

One of the largest banks in the United States in its credit analysis manual makes the following policy statement:

Leases . . . are not necessarily similar to debt; nor are the properties assets since there is no ownership. These commitments are in the nature of contingent liabilities, similar to management contracts, purchase obligations, and the like . . . in bankruptcy or reorganization lease obligations and long-term debt are dissimilar. The lessor is limited to an award of damages which he must prove. . . .

Bennett R. Keenan of New England Merchants National Bank of Boston in his paper, "Financing a Leasing Corporation," circulated by the bank writes, "A lease is not debt . . . a lease has, to be sure, certain elements also found in debt . . . it lacks, however, one feature of debt, at least, that to a creditor should explode any notion that a lease is debt. In the event of bankruptcy of the debtor, debt is normally recognized in full as a claim; in bankruptcy of a lessee, this is not the case."

Frederick R. H. Witherby, Associate Counsel of New England Mutual Life Insurance Company, in "Personal Property Lease Financing," warns The

---

[1] Privately printed speech. Most footnotes omitted.

Association of Life Insurance Counsel that, "Since uncertainties in the enforceability of rental obligations militate against their ranking on the same level, in the hierarchy of priorities, as direct promises to pay . . . life insurance companies . . . [should be] . . . alert to the risks inherent in the enforceability of their position as creditors. . . ."

Ralph L. Gustin, Jr., Vice President of the John Hancock Mutual Life Insurance Company in his paper, "Financing by Contract and by Lease," stresses "the difference in the creditor position of the lender in [lease] financings from that of the lender in ordinary loan transactions . . ."

Gordon D. Brown, Vice President of The Bank of New York, stated:

Going back through the history of finance, you will find that questions were asked about the conditional sales contract when the straight mortgage was a more common security form. Only a few years ago the term loan was not considered sensible for a business or a bank. The lease is filling a current need for supplemental financing and is probably in about the same status as consumer financing and the term loan were some 15–20 years ago.

Attitude of regulatory commissions

To learn the attitude of regulatory commissions, we asked a former chairman of the Securities and Exchange Commission what had been the attitude of the S.E.C. We were informed that where chattel leasing was used in amounts that were not material, the public had little interest in the transactions. We were referred to the S-X regulations.

To our best knowledge, whenever public service commissions regulating utility companies were requested to authorize approval of lease-back of equipment for utility companies, such agencies or their staffs after studying the economic effect have indicated such action as being in the interests of the company and the public. The commissions of Massachusetts, New Hampshire, Pennsylvania, Connecticut, New York, and California are among such regulatory bodies.

Statements of rating services

We wrote three security rating services to learn their attitude on fleet leasing. We quote excerpts from their replies:

Standard and Poor's Corporation wrote: "We would be inclined to agree that vehicle leasing would not ordinarily be a significant factor."

Fitch Investors Services wrote:

. . . it is not our practice to regard this as an adverse factor where the amounts involved are not material to the assets of a utility or a sizeable industrial concern. It might even happen that we might regard such an arrangement as a favorable factor in the light of the advantages and freeing of capital for other purposes.

Moody's Investors Service stated:

One analyst who has had close acquaintance with vehicle leasing programs was of the opinion that some such programs were indicative of astute management. We go along with this observation, particularly from the point of view of equity owners, since we know of one situation where a company effected substantial savings per common share by changing over from ownership to leasing.

Harvard's survey of investment community's attitude

Probably the most extensive survey of the attitude of the investment community was conducted during 1959 for the *Harvard Business Review*. 512 of the largest financial institutions of the United States and Canada and the 1300 largest industrial and utility companies were solicited for information. Insurance company respondents represented 77% of total life insurance assets. Respondent banks represented 42% of total bank resources.[40]

Differences in negative covenants in debt agreements

In a study of negative covenants in formal debt agreements, it was disclosed that 50% of all such agreements placed no ceilings on the incurrence of additional lease commitments; such ceilings, if imposed, are far more prevalent in regard to realty than equipment leasing and applicable almost entirely to long-term noncancelable leases; such covenants are less restrictive and more flexible than limitations on debt. One conclusion of the study was:

By far the most common restriction is one which establishes a fixed dollar or percentage limitation on annual lease payments. This . . . restriction, while serving to control the amount of lease financing, suggests that the lender considers a certain amount of such financing permissible in addition to the stated limits on long-term debt.[41]

Expanding the total financing pool

The final paragraph of the study which summarized the attitude of analysts and corporate officers, but only as to long-term and material leases, stated:

90% of the respondents to the analysts' survey and 65% of the respondents to our corporate survey state that the use of long-term, noncancelable leases makes it possible for a company to obtain a greater amount of credit than would be possible if debt financing were used. This may mean that they do not regard—or do not believe others regard—leasing as being exactly comparable with debt financing.[42]

It is an interesting commentary that lenders and investors hold to this doctrine in greater degree than do treasurers, controllers and financial vice presidents.

Because the lease offers to an investor a security position inferior to that of bonds or debentures, the other side of the coin enables the lessee to expand, through reasonable use of the lease, his total pool of financing.

. . . .

---

[40] R. F. Vancil and R. N. Anthony, "The Financial Community Looks at Leasing," *Harvard Business Review*, November–December, 1959, pp. 120 and 121.

[41] See (40) supra.

[42] See (40) supra.

Cost related to incremental debt

Each increase in the ratio of a company's senior debt likewise increases the comparative cost of incremental debt. The treasurer of a major oil company informed us that because his firm had not made sufficient use of junior financings like leasing, his company's ratio of senior debt securities was higher than that of comparable companies and consequently, he claimed, the interest rates on his company's incremental debt securities were also higher. His conclusion was that his company, by paying a higher rate on incremental debt, was paying the rate equivalent for junior financing but did not have its benefit in the capital structure. The prudent use of equipment leasing, according to institutional investors and financial analysts, will not be treated as a debt burden because of its junior nature.[54]

To a growing corporation the preservation of its capacity to borrow term debt at the lowest possible cost may be important if sizeable opportunities for future expansion present themselves. To the extent that a company uses the lease in prudent manner, it conserves such capacity.

.   .   .   .

Comparison with total cost of alternatives

Before leasing or any form of financing should be acceptable, the total economic cost should be competitive with alternatives available to the company under the individual circumstances. To the extent that economical leasing extends the total pool of all capital and incurs a rate lower than that of earnings or of the required rate of return—and, more significantly, lower than the total cost of available alternatives—leasing is in the interest of the company, its shareholders, and customers.[65] Again, it is important to bear in mind that the interest rate on debt is not the total cost of alternatives.

---

[54] See (40) supra.

[65] Joel Dean, "Measuring the Productivity of Capital," *Harvard Business Review*, January, 1954.

NOTE: COMPUTER LEASING INDUSTRY

∧∧∧

The electronic data processing industry can be broken down into five major segments which include (1) main frame hardware[1] manufacturers, (2) peripheral equipment manufacturers, (3) supporting services (programming consultants, etc.), (4) computer utilities (sellers of computer time), and (5) computer leasing companies. This note will focus on the independent computer leasing industry. Since the policies of computer manufacturers play a key role in determining the operating environment of the computer leasing companies, introductory information will also be provided on the producers of main frame hardware.

BACKGROUND—COMPUTER HARDWARE MANUFACTURERS

Structure of industry

Only nine U.S. companies are significantly involved in the manufacture of main frame hardware. Most of these manufacturers decline to release the information necessary to determine market shares within the industry. For this reason, the statistics cited in the financial press relating to competitive positions are based on uncertain estimates. In spite of this uncertainty, it is clear that International Business Machines Corporation (IBM) is far and away the industry leader.

According to an article in *Forbes* magazine, IBM had, through 1965, installed 75% of the dollar value of computer equipment in use within the United States and 67% of the value of such equipment in use throughout the world.[2] Another trade source estimated the value of computers shipped by manufacturers during 1966 as shown in Exhibit 1.

Regarding IBM's share of the total computer market, the *Forbes* article went on to state:

IBM dominates the world computer business in a way no other giant industrial dominates any other major market. General Motors has about 52% of the U.S.

---

[1] "Main frame hardware" refers to the central processing units of a computer where numerical calculations are actually performed. This is distinct from input and output devices (peripheral equipment) such as card readers and tape drives.

[2] "International Business Machines," *Forbes*, September 15, 1966, p. 46.

265

Exhibit 1

COMPUTER LEASING INDUSTRY

ESTIMATED VALUE OF COMPUTERS SHIPPED BY MANUFACTURERS DURING 1966

(Dollar amounts in millions)

	Amount	% of Total
IBM	$2,500	68.3%
Honeywell	270	7.4
Control Data	200	5.5
Univac	195	5.3
General Electric	190	5.2
National Cash	95	2.6
Radio Corporation	95	2.6
Burroughs	60	1.6
Scientific Data	30	0.8
Others	25	0.7
Total	$3,660	100.0%

Source: "EDP Industry and Market Report," International Data Publishing Co.

auto business. . . . U.S. Steel has only about 25% of the domestic steel market, . . . [and] Standard Oil (N.J.) . . . [has] about 15% of the Free World crude production.[3]

Market growth

The estimated value of general-purpose computers shipped annually since 1955 and future demand projected through 1970 are shown in Exhibit 2. Between 1960 and 1965 industry shipments grew at a compounded rate of more than 25% annually. With deliveries of IBM's third-generation[4] "System/360" equipment beginning in earnest late in 1965, the 1965–66 annual rate of growth swelled to over 45%.

Computer manufacturers face financial problems similar to those of any industrial company experiencing rapid growth. Accounts receivable and in-process inventories of growing companies often jump sharply in response to rising sales levels. Plant and equipment expenditures may simultaneously increase if capacity must be expanded to bring production into a more reasonable balance with sales demand. In addition to the normal problems accompanying rapid growth, computer manufacturers face one additional financial problem that is *not* characteristic of most companies in fast-growing industries. That problem arises from the fact that computer users have traditionally leased rather than purchased more than 80% of the computer equipment they have accepted for installation.[5]

---

[3] *Ibid.*

[4] The "generation" of computer equipment is determined by the state of advancement in its electronic circuitry. First-generation equipment employed thousands of vacuum tubes in its circuitry. These relatively slow and inefficient machines were superseded in 1960 by second-generation equipment (such as IBM's 1401) employing transistors. The System/360 machines represent a third generation, which relies on integrated circuits (IC's) and hybrids of IC's and transistors.

[5] Barton M. Biggs, "Numbers Game," *Barron's*, July 24, 1967, p. 3.

Exhibit 2

COMPUTER LEASING INDUSTRY

ESTIMATED ANNUAL VALUE OF COMPUTER EQUIPMENT SHIPPED
BY U.S. MANUFACTURERS

(In millions of dollars)

	General-Purpose Digital Computers	Total*
1955	$ 75	$ 339
1960	720	2,225
1965	2,300	4,800
1966	3,660	6,535
1967	4,200–4,400	7,250– 7,640
1968	4,600–4,900	8,010– 8,660
1970	5,300–5,800	9,180–10,360

* Total includes general-purpose digital computers, special-purpose computers, independent peripheral equipment, software service bureau and consultants, and supplies and supporting services.
Source: "EDP Industry and Market Report," International Data Publishing Co.

Cash flow implications of leasing

The practice of leasing rather than selling a rapidly growing product line can place a terrific strain on a corporation's cash resources. A typical computer selling for $1,000,000 has a manufacturing cost of about $400,000. All other corporate operating expenses, such as engineering, selling, and administrative overhead, add another $300,000 to the machine's cost, leaving a pretax profit of $300,000 for the manufacturer if the machine is sold outright.[6,7] The same computer installed under a manufacturer's standard lease contract would produce annual revenues of about $238,000, but the expenses associated with earning this revenue would amount to $460,000 during the first year as shown in Exhibit 3.

Exhibit 3

COMPUTER LEASING INDUSTRY

FIRST-YEAR FINANCIAL STATEMENT RELATING TO THE LEASE OF A
COMPUTER WITH A SALES PRICE EQUAL TO $1,000,000

Revenue		$ 238,000
Depreciation	$160,000	
Other costs	300,000	
Total costs		460,000
Pretax profit (loss)		$(222,000)
Income tax (credit)		(111,000)
After-tax profit (loss)		$(111,000)
Add: Depreciation		160,000
Cash inflow from lease		$ 49,000
Cash outflow to manufacture		400,000
Net cash outflow in first year		$ 351,000

---

[6] *Ibid.*
[7] Annual Report, 1967, Digital Equipment Corp.

If the computer's basic manufacturing cost of $400,000 is depreciated over four years using the sum-of-the-years'-digits method, the depreciation expense for the first year would be $160,000. This depreciation method is reported to be general industry practice for tax accounting.[8] The previously mentioned corporate operating expenses of $300,000 are not capitalized. Instead they are immediately charged off as an expense. This leads to a first year loss on the leased machine amounting to $222,000. If corporate income from other sources is available to offset the loss on this lease transaction, tax savings eliminate half of this loss, or $111,000. Adding depreciation, a noncash expense, to the after-tax loss gives $49,000 as the first year cash inflow from the leased computer. Since the manufacturer incurred an initial cash outflow of $400,000 to produce the machine, the lease transaction during the first year causes a net cash drain of $351,000. From this analysis it is easy to see why a large volume of computer shipments placed out on lease can be very damaging to a manufacturer from a cash standpoint.

Short-term leasing as a competitive weapon

Widespread leasing of equipment has long been a custom in the computer industry. Prior to 1956, this phenomenon could be explained by IBM's refusal to offer its data processing equipment for sale. As a result of a legal action in that year IBM must now "offer for sale all equipment which it offers for lease and must establish a sales price for such equipment which will have a commercially reasonable relationship to its lease charges for the same equipment."[9]

While the Consent Decree made the outright purchase of equipment possible, most users of IBM equipment still favor the one-year lease contract. A short-term lease frees the user from any risk of technological obsolescence and makes "trading-up" a simple matter if the user's data processing needs outgrow the capacity of the machine in question.

Almost through an accident of corporate history the popularity of one-year lease contracts has given IBM a strong competitive advantage within the computer industry. IBM enjoys the unique advantage of cash revenues in excess of a billion dollars annually from rentals of items such as punch card accounting equipment and typewriters placed in the field many years ago.[10] Other manufacturers without this cash flow have considerable difficulty meeting the huge cash drain that necessarily accompanies short-term leases. Cash shortages force manufacturers such as Honeywell to encourage outright sales or long-term leases (three to five years) against which they can immediately borrow almost the total value of future lease payments. Inability to offer one-year leases places a computer manufacturer such as Honeywell at a

[8] Biggs, op. cit.

[9] United States v. International Business Machines Corporation, 1956 Trade Cas. 71, 117 (S.D.N.Y. 1956).

[10] "Data Processing Equipment Leasing," Equity Research Associates, August 19, 1966.

competitive disadvantage since many lessees favor the one-year contract in order to avoid obsolescence risk and the necessity of showing a large future lease obligation in a footnote to their balance sheets.

Theoretically IBM assumes the risk of massive annual equipment returns since the company is protected only by one-year leases. In practice, however, a lessee rarely returns a piece of equipment in less than three to four years because of the considerable expense and time lost in converting existing programs to a new system. Lessees simply continue their contracts on a 90-day notification basis once they expire. Returned machines present only minor marketing problems. If the returned computer is new enough so that the model is still in production, IBM's large sales force will usually be able to place it with another lessee at the full rental rate enjoyed by a comparable piece of new equipment.

IBM cash shortage

Although the ability to offer a one-year lease contract represents a strong competitive weapon for IBM, customer acceptance of the System/360 line of computers was so great that in 1966 the company became a victim of its own success. The cash throw-off from operations, which amounted to $1,258,000,000 in 1966,[11] was no longer sufficient to sustain internally IBM's growth rate. Whereas in 1964 the corporation could boast of cash balances totaling nearly one billion dollars, the situation had changed markedly by 1966 and the company found it necessary to raise the money from external sources. Since IBM avoids debt of any consequence in proportion to equity, in 1966 its shareholders were called upon to supply the company with over $350,000,000 in new equity capital. It is clear that IBM's cash shortage in 1966 was unanticipated, since in 1964 the company had *prepaid* $160,000,000 of loans bearing 3½% interest to The Prudential Insurance Company. By 1966, however, in addition to raising the new equity capital already mentioned, the company had to establish new bank lines of credit equal to $160,000,000, this time at an interest rate of 5½%. In light of this fact, the Prudential prepayment decision ". . . stands as one IBM decision about which there is, in retrospect, no controversy—it was a mistake."[12]

The lease-sales ratio

System/360 was dramatically successful for IBM in terms of market acceptance, but the high percentage of shipments placed on a lease basis drained the corporation financially. Exhibit 4 presents estimates of IBM's cash requirements arising *solely* from shipments of System/360 equipment placed on lease.

In September, 1966, IBM moved to bring its lease-sales ratio down to a level consistent with the company's ability to finance its leases through

---

[11] Annual Report, IBM, 1966.

[12] T. A. Wise, "The Rocky Road to the Marketplace," *Fortune,* October, 1966, p. 206.

Exhibit 4

COMPUTER LEASING INDUSTRY

ESTIMATED IBM CASH FLOW ARISING SOLELY FROM SHIPMENTS
OF SYSTEM/360 EQUIPMENT PLACED ON LEASE

($ Millions)

	1966	1967	1968	1969	1970
Total lease revenue.................	$518.3	$1,130.7	$1,800.3	$2,510.7	$3,272.5
Depreciation expense................	348.4	673.0	933.2	1,108.2	1,198.3
Other costs........................	653.3	771.9	844.1	895.5	960.1
Pretax income......................	−483.4	−314.3	23.1	507.1	1,114.0
After-tax net.......................	−241.7	−157.1	11.5	253.5	557.0
Total inflow from operation.........	106.7	515.9	944.7	1,361.7	1,755.3
Total equipment investment.........	871.1	1,029.2	1,125.4	1,194.0	1,280.2
Cash inflow-outflow................	−764.4	−513.3	−180.7	167.7	475.1

	1966	1967	1968	1969	1970
Assumptions:					
1. Sales value of total industry computer shipments (billions) from Exhibit 2.	$3.66	$4.40	$4.90	$5.30	$5.80
2. IBM's share of above from Exhibit 1, plus casewriter's estimates.	0.70	0.68	0.66	0.64	0.62
3. IBM's lease-sales ratio from page 311, plus casewriter's estimates.	0.85	0.86	0.87	0.88	0.89

4. According to this exhibit, in 1966 IBM could expect to place out on lease System/360 computer equipment with a sales value of $2.18 billion. This figure can be derived by multiplying together three numbers: the sales value of industry shipments ($3.66 billion); IBM's share of total industry shipments (0.70); and IBM's lease-sales ratio (0.85).

Exhibit 3 shows the first-year cash flow relating to a leased computer with a sales price equal to $1,000,000. To arrive at IBM's 1966 cash flow arising from leasing equipment with a sales value of $2.18 billion, we simply multiply the figures in Exhibit 3 by 2,180.

Source: Publicly available estimates and casewriter's projections.

internal cash generation. IBM reduced the sales price of its computers by 3% and shortly thereafter raised its lease rental rates by 3%. The expectation of trade sources was that this new pricing schedule would stop and perhaps reverse the rising trend in IBM's lease-sales ratio. When the new pricing decision was announced, the value of shipments made on a lease basis was estimated to exceed the value of shipments sold outright by a very wide margin. If the new pricing schedule would reduce the lease to sales ratio significantly from its estimated level of 85%,[13] the immediate cash inflow would be substantial, and the downward pressure on corporate earnings implied by Exhibit 3 would be reduced. Since the heavy placements of leased systems were depressing earnings in 1966, this price change presumably helped the company maintain its historical uptrend in earnings per share.

INDEPENDENT COMPUTER LEASING INDUSTRY

Enter the financial entrepreneur

The cash squeeze at IBM, coupled with the fact that an entirely new generation of computers was being introduced, created a clear profit opportunity for financial entrepreneurs. IBM had widened substantially the spread between the revenues available to computer lessors and the cost of purchasing

---

[13] Biggs, op. cit.

computers to be placed on lease. Financial middlemen could purchase computers from IBM at standard prices and place them with lessees at rental rates ranging from 10% to 20% lower than those charged by IBM. If the machines were depreciated over 8 or 10 years in contrast to the manufacturer's practice of using 4 years, reported profits could be substantial even during the first year that the equipment was placed in service. Since the System/360 represented an entirely new computer generation when it was introduced in late 1965, the economic life of these machines was expected to extend well into the 1970's, limiting an early buyer's risk of premature technological obsolescence. Experience showed that second-generation equipment such as IBM's 1400 series was actively manufactured and marketed for as long as six years (1960–66), and the continued rental of existing equipment in this series was expected to remain profitable for a number of years to come.

Short-term versus long-term leases

While four or five publicly owned computer leasing companies were in existence prior to 1966 (Exhibit 5), the majority of the companies were created to take advantage of the profit opportunity afforded by IBM's pricing decision of September, 1966. With two exceptions the companies concentrate on writing leases of short duration, the average being about two years. Pricing policy among the companies is quite uniform, with the lessee usually paying the leasing company 90% of the standard manufacturer's rental rate on a two-year lease.

The rental rates charged by computer manufacturers allow them to recover the full sale price of their computers after about 47 months of continuous rental receipts. Since the independent computer leasing companies charge at most 90% of the manufacturer's rental rate, it takes the leasing companies at least 52 months to recover the full purchase price. With a purchase price payback of at least 52 months and an average lease term of 24 months, the computer leasing companies are obviously concerned with future marketability of returned machines. Concern with this problem leads most of the companies to restrict their computer purchases to models with proved market acceptance. Machines with large order backlogs or a large number of existing installations (such as IBM's System/360–30) are favored for purchase by the leasing companies. This is true because every user renting a System/360–30 from the manufacturer represents a potential future customer should the leasing company find itself with a returned machine of the same model. The concern with future marketability has led computer leasing companies to deal almost exclusively in IBM System/360 equipment.

Leasco Data Processing Equipment Corporation, the one company specializing in non-IBM equipment, writes only noncancellable full payout leases. In such a lease the entire purchase price plus interest is recovered during the initial lease term. Because Leasco carries essentially no obsolescence risk, its business is substantially different from that of the other computer leasing companies, which specialize in leases with much shorter terms. First, Leasco's

Exhibit 5

COMPUTER LEASING INDUSTRY

COMPARISON OF COMPUTER LEASING COMPANIES

Computer Leasing Companies	Computer[1] Investment	Type of Computers	Type of Leases	Service	Marketing	Principals
GC Computer Corp. (1966)	$73.1 MM gr. $51.1 MM net (12/31/66) 96 leases	IBM's ⅔—1400's 7000's ⅓—360's	Length: Most 1–3 yrs. Range: 1 mo.—8 yrs. Rental: 90% of IBM's. Costs recovery: 70–78 mos. (all costs)	No repair, maintenance, or programming.	Own marketing organization with five sales offices around the U.S.	Owned by Greyhound.
Randolph Computer Corp. (1965)	$35.9 MM gr. (2/10/67) 68 systems 31 lessees	IBM 360's Cost $225 M—$747 M	Length: 2–5 yrs. Rental: 90% of IBM's. (all costs) Cost recovery: 6 yrs. (all costs) 4–5 yrs. (machine cost) Options: Purchase options at 7½% per annum discount (purchase price always slightly above book value)	No repair or maintenance. In April, acquired United Data Processing, Inc., to add software capability.	The eight officers find most leasing opportunities. Work out of NY office.	Randolph (Pres.) from Boothe Leasing. Arbour (EVP) marketing man from IBM.
Levin-Townsend Computer Corp.	$20.5 MM gr. (3/10/67) 35 leases	IBM 360's	Length: Most 1 year. Rental: About 90% of IBM	No maintenance or repair. Programming and systems consulting for a fee.	Own marketing force (about five men). Also representatives who find deals for commission. 67 employees.	Levin (Pres.) is former math professor and founded L-T as consulting firm in data processing.
Data Processing Financial & General Corp. (1961)	$18.2 MM gr. (11/30/66)	IBM's Cost $85 M—$2.3 MM	Length: 1 mo.—5 yrs. About 20% are monthly, about 40% are 1 yr. Rental: n.a. Options: A few leases have options at fair market value—exercisable any time.	No repair, maintenance, or programming.	Uses some brokers on commission basis. Has 10 full-time salesmen. (12/1967).	Harry Goodman (Pres.) data processing expert—formerly in IBM market forecasting.
Leasco Data Processing Equipment Corp. (1961)	$20–25 MM gr. (4/30/67 est.)	CDC and others	Length: 2–8 yrs. full payout leases. Rentals: About 80% of manufacturers'. Options: A few have purchase option at fair market—end of lease. Most provide for renewal at lower rental.	No repair or maintenance. Plans to acquire Documentation, Inc., to provide software capability.	Has 37 salesmen among its 71 employees. Also trains manufacturer's salesmen in lease techniques. Manufacturer then sells lease package with machine. Has exclusive contract for CDC payout leases.	Steinberg Family controls. They are leasing, not computer experts. VP Sweetbaum is former accounting machine salesman.
Standard Computer Corp.	$8.2 MM gr. (2/28/67)	IBM's Cost $171 M—$3.9 MM	Length: 1 mo.—8 yrs. most 2 yrs. Cost recovery: 5–7 yrs. Options: None except in the case of an 8-yr. lease	No repair, maintenance, or programming.	Uses brokers and Lease Finance Co. (parent) to find deals.	Formed by: Auerbach (Tech. consulting firm which evaluates deals); Lease Finance Co. (management consultant which puts together deals); Blair & Co.; Pres. Affel is an engineer from Auerbach.

(1) Amounts shown are gross. "Net" amount is nearly as large in all cases. Most machines are less than 2 years old and are depreciated over an 8- to 10-year life.

sharply limited risk allows it to command a 4 to 1 debt to equity ratio, to be compared with about a 2 to 1 debt to equity ratio for its "short-term" counterparts. Second, Leasco has arranged its pricing policy to insulate the company from possible future increases in the cost of maintaining its computer equipment. Leasco accomplishes this by offering its lessees the standard 10% discount and adding to this amount a second deduction equal to the cost of the equipment manufacturer's full service maintenance contract at the time the lease is signed. The lessee must then assume the cost of a separate maintenance contract, which normally amounts to about 10% of the cost of renting the machine from its manufacturer. The companies specializing in short-term leases almost always assume the cost of maintenance contracts. While their higher rental charges offset this cost, the short-term leasing companies shoulder all the risk involved in future cost increases for the maintenance service.

Leasco enjoys the advantages of reduced risk and increased financial leverage, but these benefits do not come without cost. Leasco must give up a substantial part of the residual value in the equipment it leases in order to induce lessees to accept a longer term. "At the end of the initial lease term . . . , lessees may then renew the term at a negotiated rental rate which frequently ranges between 30% and 50% of the rental . . . originally charged."[14]

Importance of remarketing

Leasco's approach to computer leasing leaves the company practically immune from the problem of remarketing returned equipment. In contrast, the companies writing shorter leases face problems in two areas: (1) that of avoiding equipment inventories and (2) that of providing programming assistance to "second users."

1. It is of critical importance to these companies to keep all machines productively utilized since the average lease contract involves over $500,000 worth of computer equipment. Because the System/360 line of computers is so new, through 1967 no leasing company has yet had to remarket a returned machine in this series. Levin-Townsend Computer Corporation, a leasing company that occasionally purchases second generation equipment (at a considerable discount from its original purchase price), has had some experience with returns of this older equipment. Regarding the importance of rapidly remarketing equipment returns the company's president, Howard S. Levin, has said, "We hold sales contests with the salesman who places the computer keeping his job."[15] Presumably the comment was not made entirely with tongue in cheek. Leasing companies never purchase equipment for inventory: a lease agreement is always simultaneously executed. In fact, two simultaneous transactions generally occur in closing a deal. The leasing

---

[14] "Leasco—A Study for Institutional Investors," Goodbody and Co., February 1967.

[15] "Computer Leasing Stocks," *Fortune*, July, 1967, p. 171.

company signs a purchase agreement with the equipment manufacturer for a computer already chosen by company A. Company A simultaneously signs a contract with the leasing company to rent the machine for a period of from one to five years.

2. At present, it is IBM's policy to provide education, systems assistance, and other services to customers who are "first users" of its equipment but not necessarily to subsequent users. Through 1967 all System/360 lessees renting through leasing companies have been first users, but in future years as equipment is returned and remarketed, this will not continue to be the case. At some future time, therefore, computer leasing companies may be forced to furnish software support. Otherwise they might face a serious competitive disadvantage in the remarketing of equipment to second and later users.

Ease of growth

The growth rate of a manufacturing company is often constrained by the need for comparable expansion of such factors as capital resources, physical facilities, top-management talent, and a trained force of production employees. For the computer leasing business, available capital is the principal factor restricting growth. The "people" and "facilities" factors are far less critical. Indeed, Data Processing Financial & General Corporation was purchasing equipment at an annual rate of $50 million in September, 1967, with a staff of 10 people including the office secretaries.[16]

The computer leasing companies have purchased equipment at a spectacular rate since the end of 1965. Probably the only factor restraining even faster growth is the companies' limited cash resources. Yet even in the area of raising equity capital the companies have had few problems. Rapid price appreciation and growth in earnings per share have given the stocks in this industry a large market following. If we ignore the sharp general market setback between February and October, 1966, prices of the companies' common stocks have risen as dramatically as their equipment holdings, as shown in Exhibits 6 and 7. Almost everyone buying the securities of computer leasing companies has made money, a factor that greatly contributes to the ability of these corporations to keep coming to the market for additional financing.

Exhibit 7 shows the public financing pattern of three companies in the computer leasing industry. Each new security issue has been larger in absolute terms, and in many cases successive issues have grown larger and larger as a percentage of total computer equipment previously owned.

Accounting policies boost earnings

Corporate growth depends on the availability of funds and the availability of funds for computer leasing companies depends in large measure on a rising stock price. Price appreciation is the only return a common shareholder can

---

[16] *Preliminary Prospectus*, Data Processing Financial & General Corp., August 22, 1967.

Exhibit 6

LEVIN-TOWNSEND COMPUTER CORPORATION

STOCK PRICES AND VALUE OF EQUIPMENT OWNED

DECEMBER, 1965–SEPTEMBER, 1967

Exhibit 7

COMPUTER LEASING INDUSTRY

AMOUNTS AND PRICES OF PUBLIC SECURITY ISSUES OF SELECTED COMPANIES

Company	Date of Public Security Issue	Amount of Security Issue	Computer Equipment Owned	Elapsed Time Since Previous Security Issue	Common Stock Price $
		⌐In Thousands of Dollars ¬			
Standard	April, 1966	2,500	6,000	. . . .	5
Computer	March, 1967	4,000	12,143	11 mos.	15¾
Corporation	June, 1967	8,000	14,476	3 mos.	19½
Randolph	April, 1966	1,800	3,057	. . . .	20
Computer	March, 1967	5,000	35,945	11 mos.	41¼
Corporation	July, 1967	10,000	44,913	4 mos.	46
Data Processing	December, 1965	3,300	6,000	. . . .	11
Financial &	March, 1967	12,000	18,183	15 mos.	41⅛
General Cor-	September, 1967	50,000	38,941	6 mos.	73¼
poration					

expect for a number of years since loan covenants accepted by these companies severely restrict and generally prevent dividend payments.

Perhaps in an effort to provide the rising stock price necessary for growth in computer leasing, the companies in this industry have adopted accounting policies allowing them to report the highest possible current earnings. Thus, even though IBM depreciates a System/360–40 computer over 4 years using accelerated depreciation in its financial statements to its shareholders, most of the leasing companies depreciate the identical machine over 10 years using straight-line depreciation for shareholder reporting. To reduce their income tax liability, however, the companies use sum-of-the-years'-digits depreciation and an eight-year life for tax reporting. In a similar vein, leasing companies "flow through" the 7% investment tax credit as rapidly as possible rather than spreading the credit evenly over the life of the asset in question.

Automatic growth in reported earnings

Exhibit 8 shows pro forma financial statements relating to a typical short-term lease for a $1,000,000 computer system placed in service on January 1, 1966. The upper half of the page, lines 1–21, shows pro forma income statements as reported for purposes of calculating the annual federal income tax liability. The lower half of the page, lines 22–32, shows how the income statements would appear in a leasing company's shareholder reports.

Although the complexity of Exhibit 8 may at first appear overwhelming, detailed study of the numbers presented is unnecessary. Careful examination of a very few lines (those relating to depreciation expense and after-tax income) will provide most of the information needed for a thorough understanding of the importance of management accounting choices in the earnings reports of companies operating in this industry.

Lines 9 and 27 project the annual pretax profit for tax and shareholder reports, respectively. It is important to note that except for the depreciation charge, all the revenue and expense items used to calculate pretax profit in the tax and shareholder reports are exactly the same each year. Although tax loss carryforwards and the investment tax credit play a major role in determining after-tax income (lines 12 and 30), the striking numerical differences found in these two lines result entirely from the variation in depreciation charges.

While the importance of accounting policy in determining earnings is highlighted by Exhibit 8, two other key factors can be gleaned from the figures. First, net income for shareholder purposes (line 30) has a built-in increase of at least 15% per year during the first four years of the computer's life. This is caused by decreasing interest payments as the debt outstanding is reduced. Second, the first-year return on equity equals 10% ($32,799/$334,000). So long as equity for new equipment purchases is sold at a price exceeding 10 times current earnings, future earnings per share will be enhanced by simply buying and leasing additional equipment with the proceeds from new common stock issues. With leasing company equities selling at well above 20 times current earnings, the enhancement in earnings arising from simply selling additional stock to purchase and lease more computer equipment is dramatic.

The industry's future

While reported profits are currently moving even higher, a number of factors weigh heavily on the future prospects of the computer leasing indus-

Exhibit 8

COMPUTER LEASING INDUSTRY

FINANCIAL STATEMENTS RELATING TO A $1,000,000 COMPUTER PLACED UNDER A TWO-YEAR LEASE CONTRACT

BOOK VERSUS TAX ACCOUNTING FOR A TYPICAL COMPUTER LEASING COMPANY

#	Item	1966	1967	1968	1969	1970	1971	1972	1973	1974	1975	
1	IBM rental rate	256,000	256,000	256,000	256,000	256,000	256,000	256,000	256,000	256,000	256,000	Leasing Company Tax Reports
2	(1) Discount allowed	25,600	25,600	30,720	35,840	40,960	46,080	51,200	56,320	61,440	66,560	
3	Overtime premium	7,680	7,680	7,680	7,680	7,680	7,680	7,680	7,680	7,680	7,680	
4	Gross rentals	238,080	238,080	232,960	227,840	222,720	217,600	212,480	207,360	202,240	197,120	
5	Maintenance expense (10% of line 1)	25,600	25,600	25,600	25,600	25,600	25,600	25,600	25,600	25,600	25,600	
6	(2) Depreciation expense	188,889	165,278	141,667	118,056	94,444	70,833	47,222	23,611	....	....	
7	(3) Interest (9% of line 18)	59,940	48,354	35,726	22,375	8,238	....	....	....	....	....	
8	Selling, general, and administrative	23,808	23,808	23,296	22,784	22,272	21,760	21,248	20,736	20,224	19,712	
9	Pretax profit (loss)	(60,157)	(24,960)	6,672	39,025	72,166	99,407	118,410	137,413	156,416	151,808	
10	Taxes (before investment credit)	....	....	....	....	16,373	49,703	59,204	68,706	78,208	75,904	
11	(4) Investment credit used	....	....	....	....	8,186	24,851	29,602	7,359	....	....	
12	Net profit	(60,157)	(24,960)	6,672	39,025	63,979	74,555	88,807	76,066	78,208	75,904	
13	Add depreciation	188,889	165,278	141,667	118,056	94,444	70,833	47,222	23,611	....	....	
14	Total cash inflow	128,732	140,318	148,338	157,081	158,424	145,388	136,030	99,677	78,208	75,904	
15	Debt repayment	128,732	140,318	148,338	157,081	91,531	....	....	....	....	....	
16	Available for equity holders	....	....	....	....	66,893	145,388	136,030	99,677	78,208	75,904	
17	(5) After-tax cash flow from liquidation	....	....	....	....	....	....	....	....	....	275,000	
18	Debt outstanding (start of yr.)	666,000	537,268	396,950	248,612	91,531	....	....	....	....	....	
19	Equity invested (start of yr.)	334,000	334,000	334,000	334,000	334,000	267,107	121,719	(14,311)	(113,988)	(192,196)	
20	Remaining investment credit	70,000	70,000	70,000	70,000	61,813	36,962	7,359	....	....	....	
21	Tax loss carry-forward	60,157	85,117	78,445	39,420	....	....	....	....	....	....	
22	Gross rentals	238,080	238,080	232,960	227,840	222,720	217,600	212,480	207,360	202,240	197,120	Leasing Company Shareholder Reports
23	(2) Depreciation	85,000	85,000	85,000	85,000	85,000	85,000	85,000	85,000	85,000	85,000	
24	Maintenance	25,600	25,600	25,600	25,600	25,600	25,600	25,600	25,600	25,600	25,600	
25	(3) Interest	59,940	48,354	35,726	22,375	8,238	....	....	....	....	....	
26	Selling, general, and administrative	23,808	23,808	23,296	22,784	22,272	21,760	21,248	20,736	20,224	19,712	
27	Pretax profit	43,732	55,318	63,338	72,081	81,610	85,240	80,632	76,024	71,416	66,808	
28	Taxes (before investment credit)	21,866	27,659	31,669	36,040	40,805	42,620	40,316	38,012	35,708	33,404	
29	(4) Investment credit used	10,933	13,829	15,834	18,020	11,384	....	....	....	....	....	
30	Net profit	32,799	41,488	47,503	54,061	52,189	42,620	40,316	38,012	35,708	33,404	
31	(5) After-tax cash flow from liquidation	....	....	....	....	....	....	....	....	....	275,000	
32	Remaining investment credit	59,067	45,238	29,404	11,384	....	....	....	....	....	....	

Assumptions:

(1) Discount: 10% of the IBM rate through 1967; increasing by 2 percentage points per year thereafter to 26% in 1975.

(2) Depreciation: 8 yrs. sum of years' digits, 15% residual value for tax purposes; 10 yrs., straight line, 15% residual for shareholders.

(3) Interest: 9% rate on outstanding balance which is reduced each year by the full cash flow.

(4) Investment credit: 7% investment credit deducted from tax liability as fast as possible rather than evenly amortized over the life of asset.

(5) Cash flow from liquidation: The computer is sold for 40% of original cost at the end of 1975; taxes paid at the corporate rate (0.50).

try. In the short run, the industry is threatened by the fact that it is dependent on the pricing strategy adopted by computer manufacturers. Should these manufacturers find their cash positions improving substantially in the next few years, they might wish to finance a higher proportion of computer shipments themselves. Higher computer sale prices relative to lease rental charges would tend to raise the manufacturers' lease to sales ratio. Higher computer maintenance fees would also tend to reduce the leasing companies' profit margins, thus slowing their growth and raising the manufacturers' lease to sales ratio.

Over the longer term, computer leasing companies are threatened by the obsolescence of their third-generation System/360 machines in less than the anticipated 10 years. Second-generation computers were manufactured and marketed for six full years from 1959 to 1965. Machines of this vintage dropped in used value from over 70% of the original purchase price to around 40% of the purchase price within a year after System/360 was introduced. With sales prices so sharply reduced, rental rates of the second generation machines were under considerable pressure. Whether this price pattern will be repeated with third-generation equipment remains a question for the future.

COMPULEASE CORPORATION (A)

ᴧᴧᴧ

Late in the evening of December 10, 1965, James A. Kralik, president of the newly formed Compulease Corporation, was in the process of deciding where his company should concentrate its lease-writing efforts.

Meeting with investment banker

Two hours previously Mr. Kralik had returned home after a successful meeting with the partner in charge of corporate finance at the investment banking firm of Bachman, Dillard and Hanover (BD&H). After a number of previous visits, Mr. Kralik felt that he had, at last, convinced the BD&H partner that an investment in a firm involved in computer leasing (see Note: Computer Leasing Industry, pp. 265–78) would offer a rewarding profit opportunity to a small syndicate of private investors. BD&H could quickly put together a financially sophisticated group of individuals willing to provide venture capital from among its partners and wealthy clients, and Compulease could represent a vehicle for the investor group to participate in the rapidly growing area of computer leasing.

While a specific financing proposal for Compulease was not made final during the meeting, the investment banker indicated that the BD&H group might be expected to put up $960,000 in return for a 78% interest in Compulease. Mr. Kralik and the other co-founders, John Bailey and Philip Jameson, would then receive a 22% interest in the company for $40,000 plus their efforts in organizing the new venture.

The investor group would be seeking capital gains. Their goal would also be to offer additional Compulease common stock to the public. The investment banker felt that a year of operating history would be sufficient to give Compulease the earnings base necessary to guarantee a successful public offering.

At the conclusion of the December 10 meeting the investment banker asked Mr. Kralik to meet with him again on December 22. The proposed meeting would be attended by a number of BD&H partners and the clients of BD&H who might be interested in participating in the Compulease financing. Prior to this meeting, BD&H would make sure that each member of the potential investor group was familiarized with the computer leasing industry. Instead of providing background information then, the main purpose of the December

22 meeting, aside from ascertaining investor interest, would be to discuss how Compulease ought to enter the field of computer leasing. The discussion would revolve around the pros and cons of writing long-term versus short-term computer leases. Mr. Kralik would be expected to present a convincing case for concentrating his company's efforts in one area or the other.

Mr. Kralik felt certain that the long-term versus short-term leasing decision he had to make in his proposal to the investors would be extremely important in the future development of his company. With this thought in mind, he set out to review the two types of leases.

The factors to be considered

Mr. Kralik knew that existing publicly owned firms specializing in the two types of leases differed markedly in at least four key areas: (1) the accounting principles adopted for reporting earnings to shareholders; (2) the amount of risk assumed in the course of normal business activity; (3) the potential return on investments in computer equipment; and (4) the type of technical expertise needed by management in order to assure long-run corporate success.

Reporting the earnings

Mr. Kralik was aware that for tax purposes, the accounting policies adopted by most computer leasing companies were the same, regardless of whether they specialized in long-term or short-term leases. In their tax accounts, both types of companies assumed a 15% salvage value and depreciated their machines over eight years by the sum-of-the-years-digits method.

While their tax accounting conventions were similar, the accounting principles used by the two types of firms in reporting income to shareholders differed dramatically. Exhibits 1 and 2 show how a computer system costing $1,000,000 would appear for tax and shareholder reports under the two leasing strategies.

As shown in line 23 of Exhibit 2, companies specializing in short-term leases generally assumed a 15% salvage value and depreciated their equipment over *10* years using the *straight-line* method in the determination of earnings for shareholder reporting. For companies concentrating on long-term full payout leases, depreciation never entered shareholder financial statements at all. These companies recorded the total amount of future lease payments as an asset, effectively transforming a piece of equipment into an account receivable. Under this accounting convention, annual income was not determined by simply adding up the total monthly rental payments received during the year. Instead, as shown in line 20 of Exhibit 1, the total value of lease payments due during the six and one-half years that the lease remained in force was calculated, and from this amount the original cost of the machine (less a 10% estimated salvage value) was deducted. The remaining amount, called unearned income, was "earned" over the life of the lease. A sum-of-the-years-digits technique, line 27 of Exhibit 1, was used to allocate "unearned income" in the annual profit and loss statements. The effect of this treatment was to throw the bulk of the income into the early years of the lease when the major cost item, interest expense, was highest.

In shareholder reports, both the long-term and short-term leases generated a profit in the first year. The initial profit in each case amounted to about 10% of the equity originally invested. ($19,800/$200,000 = 9.9% Exhibit 1; $32,799/$334,000 = 9.8% Exhibit 2.) Over the longer term a company writing short-term leases would report to shareholders (from this particular lease) steadily rising annual earnings for a period of four years, as shown in line 30 of Exhibit 2; whereas a company writing long-term leases would report steadily *declining* earnings over the entire period of the lease as shown in line 34 of Exhibit 1.

Risk

A wide gap separated the amount of risk that would be assumed by Compulease under the two leasing alternatives being considered by Mr. Kralik. If his decision took the company into the area of full payout leases, Mr. Kralik knew that the risk to Compulease from the standpoint of technological obsolescence would be greatly diminished. The only real threat from obsolescence would come in the options he would have to grant to lessees allowing them to "trade up" into larger computer systems (if they paid Compulease a small penalty fee) after three to four years of a six and one-half year lease. Mr. Kralik felt that computer manufacturers would probably retain their policy of allowing at least 40% of the original purchase price of four-year-old equipment on trade-ins for more expensive systems, so he was confident that losses could be avoided even if most options were exercised.

Companies writing short-term leases accepted almost all the risks of shortened machine life due to technological obsolescence. It was Mr. Kralik's opinion, however, that third-generation computers would not become technologically obsolete before 1974. A machine purchased in 1966 would thus have at minimum an eight-year life.

Borrowing capacity

Since the risk arising from technological obsolescence was small with full payout leases, the Manufacturers Chemical Bank of New York had given Mr. Kralik assurances that it would advance up to 80% of the cost of third-generation computer equipment placed under this type of lease. The effective interest rate on such a loan would be about 9%.

In contrast, the same bank would be willing to advance only two thirds of the cost of computer equipment placed on short-term leases, a figure Mr. Kralik understood to be practically standard for all companies writing similar leases in the industry.

Although commercial banks were willing to lend leasing companies a large fraction of the cost of acquiring computer systems, they also desired to have the loan on each system repaid as rapidly as possible. For this reason, leasing companies were generally required to amortize loan principal with the full after-tax cash flow resulting from lease payments (line 14 of Exhibit 1 and line 15 of Exhibit 2). For a computer system out on a short-term lease, the bank would be paid in 4 years and 7 months. For a system on a long-term lease, the banks were willing to wait 5½ years to recover their full loans.

Expertise required to compete successfully

Before committing Compulease to a particular leasing strategy, Mr. Kralik had to consider the differences in operating and technical expertise required for long-run corporate success under the two leasing alternatives. Exhibit 3 describes the management as it existed in December, 1965.

If Compulease concentrated on short-term leases, the ability to quickly remarket returned computer equipment to second users would be of key importance to the company's ultimate success. In that case, Compulease would require a staff of specialists to provide programming assistance to second users, and some systems experts to assist in installing used computers in situations where compatibility problems might reasonably be anticipated.

Most of the need for technical expertise in the computer field could be avoided if Mr. Kralik limited his company to full payout leases. The second-user problem would all but disappear with this strategy, and Compulease's problems would probably be more narrowly limited to those of a financial nature.

Returns

Mr. Kralik saw obvious advantages in terms of limited risk and greater debt leverage accruing to companies writing full payout leases, and this same fact had not escaped the notice of potential lessees. Indeed, the concessions demanded by potential lessees grew larger as the fixed term of a proposed computer lease grew longer. In order to get a 6½-year full payout lease, companies writing these leases were usually forced to forgo any overtime premium for machine usage over 176 hours per month, and to give the lessee an option allowing him to buy the machine at 40% of the original purchase price when the initial lease term expired. Leasing companies writing only short-term leases gave no such purchase options to their lessees, and if Mr. Kralik chose this strategy, he expected to be still collecting around 74% of the manufacturers' presently published standard rental rate some 10 years after the equipment was originally placed in service.

Those companies writing short-term leases accepted almost all the risk of shortened machine life due to technological obsolescence. In return they would enjoy any benefits that might result if (1) their machines could be profitably rented beyond the 10-year anticipated life, or (2) the computers could be sold at the end of 10 years for more than 40% of their original cost, or (3) the discount (below manufacturers' rental rates) needed to keep the machines in the field did not increase two percentage points per year, as assumed in Exhibit 2.

Working with the tax accounting reports in Exhibits 1 and 2, Mr. Kralik had done a discounted cash flow analysis of the return on equity after all debt had been repaid under the two leasing alternatives (Exhibit 4). The returns to investors in Compulease appeared to be comparable under both leasing strategies.

Mr. Kralik then decided to calculate how sensitive the return under the short-term leasing alternative might be to changes in anticipated life, resale value, and rental rates. Exhibit 5 shows the results of his analysis. Mr. Kralik based the study on his opinion that third-generation computers would not become technologically obsolete before 1974, giving a machine purchased in 1966 a minimum life of eight years. In a similar vein, he felt that lease discounts necessary to keep third-generation computers fully utilized would not increase faster than four percentage points per year before the machines became technologically obsolete. Once third-generation computers were finally superseded by fourth-generation computers, Mr. Kralik felt that he would still be able to sell his obsolete equipment for at least 40% of its original cost. The conclusion Mr. Kralik drew from Exhibit 5 was that under the most unfavorable circumstances, Compulease's return on equity would be about 10%. Under circumstances of long life, no deterioration in rental rates, and high resale values, the return might rise as high as 16%.

Exhibit 1

COMPULEASE CORPORATION (A)

FINANCIAL STATEMENTS RELATING TO A $1,000,000 COMPUTER ON A 6½-YEAR LEASE CONTRACT (FULL PAYOUT)

BOOK VERSUS TAX ACCOUNTING FOR COMPULEASE CORPORATION

Rows 1–17 — *Leasing Company Tax Reports*

#		1966	1967	1968	1969	1970	1971	Mid-1972
1	IBM rental rate	$256,000	$256,000	$256,000	$256,000	$256,000	$256,000	$128,000
2	(1) Discount allowed	51,200	51,200	51,200	51,200	51,200	51,200	25,600
3	Gross lease payments	204,800	204,800	204,800	204,800	204,800	204,800	102,400
4	(2) Depreciation	189,000	165,000	142,000	118,000	94,500	70,500	23,700
5	(3) Interest (9% of line 14)	72,000	64,300	52,500	39,800	25,800	10,600	0
6	Selling, general and administrative	37,600	3,000	3,000	3,000	3,000	3,000	1,500
7	Pretax profit (loss)	(93,800)	(27,500)	7,300	44,000	81,500	120,700	77,200
8	Taxes (before investment credit)	0	0	0	0	5,700	60,300	38,600
9	(4) Investment credit used	0	0	0	0	2,800	30,100	37,100
10	Net profit	(93,800)	(27,500)	7,300	44,000	78,600	90,500	75,700
11	Add depreciation	189,000	165,000	142,000	118,000	94,500	70,500	23,700
12	Total cash inflow	95,200	137,500	149,300	162,000	173,100	161,000	99,400
13	(5) Sale for residual value	0	0	0	0	0	0	298,700
14	Debt outstanding (start of year)	800,000	704,800	567,300	418,000	256,000	82,900	121,900
15	Equity invested (start of year)	200,000	200,000	200,000	200,000	200,000	200,000	0
16	Remaining investment credit	70,000	70,000	70,000	70,000	67,200	37,100	0
17	Tax loss carry-forward	93,800	121,300	114,000	70,000	0	0	0

(Mid-1972 liquidation figures also shown in this block: 0 / (276,200) / 0)

Rows 18–36 — *Leasing Company Shareholder Reports*

#		1966	1967	1968	1969	1970	1971	Mid-1972
18	Gross rental payment	204,800						
19	Lease term 6½ years							
20	Total lease payments over term	1,331,200						
21	Cost of machine	1,000,000						
22	Less residual	100,000						
23	Net cost	900,000						
24	Unearned income available	431,200						
25	Less lease acquisition cost	37,600						
26	Remaining unearned income	393,600						
27	% taken of total above	.250	.214	.179	.143	.107	.071	.036
28	Income	98,400	84,100	70,500	56,300	42,200	27,900	14,200
29	Selling, general, and administrative	0	3,000	3,000	3,000	3,000	3,000	1,500
30	Interest	72,000	64,300	52,500	39,800	25,800	10,600	0
31	Pretax profit	26,400	16,800	15,000	13,500	13,400	14,300	12,700
32	Taxes (before investment credit)	13,200	8,400	7,500	6,700	6,700	7,100	6,300
33	Investment credit used	6,600	4,200	3,700	3,300	3,300	3,500	3,200
34	After-tax profit	19,800	12,600	11,200	10,100	10,000	10,700	9,600
35	Carry-forward investment credit	63,400	59,200	55,500	52,200	48,900	45,400	42,200
36	Sale for residual value							292,200

Assumptions:

(1) Discount: 20% of IBM rental rate.

(2) Depreciation: eight years sum-of-the-years' digits, 15% residual for tax purposes.

(3) Interest: 9% rate on outstanding balance, which is reduced each year by the full cash flow.

(4) Investment credit: 7% investment credit deducted from tax liability as fast as possible, rather than evenly amortized over the life of the asset.

(6) Cash flow from liquidation: the computer is sold for 40% of original cost at mid-1972; taxes paid at the corporate rate (0.5).

Exhibit 2

COMPULEASE CORPORATION (A)

FINANCIAL STATEMENTS RELATING TO A $1,000,000 COMPUTER PLACED UNDER A TWO-YEAR LEASE CONTRACT

BOOK VERSUS TAX ACCOUNTING FOR COMPULEASE CORPORATION

		1966	1967	1968	1969	1970	1971	1972	1973	1974	1975	
1	IBM rental rate	$256,000	$256,000	$256,000	$256,000	$256,000	$256,000	$256,000	$256,000	$256,000	$256,000	
2	(1)Discount allowed	25,600	25,600	30,720	35,840	40,960	46,080	51,200	56,320	61,440	66,560	
3	Overtime premium	7,680	7,680	7,680	7,680	7,680	7,680	7,680	7,680	7,680	7,680	
4	Gross rentals	238,080	238,080	232,960	227,840	222,720	217,600	212,480	207,360	202,240	197,120	
5	Maintenance expense (10% of line 1)	25,600	25,600	25,600	25,600	25,600	25,600	25,600	25,600	25,600	25,600	Leasing Company Tax Reports
6	(2)Depreciation expense	188,889	165,278	141,667	118,056	94,444	70,833	47,222	23,611	.....	.....	
7	(3)Interest (9% of line 18)	59,940	48,354	35,726	22,375	8,238	.....	.....	.....	.....	.....	
8	Selling, general, and administrative	23,808	23,808	23,296	22,784	22,272	21,760	21,248	20,736	20,224	19,712	
9	Pretax profit (loss)	(60,157)	(24,960)	6,672	39,025	72,166	99,407	118,410	137,413	156,416	151,808	
10	Taxes (before investment credit)	.....	.....	.....	.....	16,373	49,703	59,204	68,706	78,208	75,904	
11	(4)Investment credit used	.....	.....	.....	.....	8,186	24,851	29,602	7,359	.....	.....	
12	Net profit	(60,157)	(24,960)	6,672	39,025	63,979	74,555	88,807	76,066	78,208	75,904	
13	Add depreciation	188,889	165,278	141,667	118,056	94,444	70,833	47,222	23,611	.....	.....	
14	Total cash inflow	128,732	140,318	148,338	157,081	158,424	145,388	136,030	99,677	78,208	75,904	
15	Debt repayment	128,732	140,318	148,338	157,081	91,531	.....	.....	.....	.....	.....	
16	Available for equity holders	.....	.....	.....	.....	66,893	145,388	136,030	99,677	78,208	75,904	
17	(5)After tax cash flow from liquidation	.....	.....	.....	.....	.....	.....	.....	.....	.....	.....	
18	Debt outstanding (start of yr.)	666,000	537,268	396,950	248,612	91,531	.....	.....	.....	.....	.....	
19	Equity invested (start of yr.)	334,000	334,000	334,000	334,000	334,000	267,107	121,719	(14,311)	(113,988)	(192,196)	
20	Remaining investment credit	70,000	70,000	70,000	70,000	61,813	36,962	7,359	.....	.....	.....	
21	Tax loss carry-forward	60,157	85,117	78,445	39,420	.....	.....	.....	.....	.....	.....	
22	Gross rentals	238,080	238,080	232,960	227,840	222,720	217,600	212,480	207,360	202,240	197,120	
23	(2)Depreciation	85,000	85,000	85,000	85,000	85,000	85,000	85,000	85,000	85,000	85,000	
24	Maintenance	25,600	25,600	25,600	25,600	25,600	25,600	25,600	25,600	25,600	25,600	
25	(3)Interest	59,940	48,354	35,726	22,375	8,238	.....	.....	.....	.....	.....	Leasing Company Shareholder Reports
26	Selling, general, and administrative	23,808	23,808	23,296	22,784	22,272	21,760	21,248	20,736	20,224	19,712	
27	Pretax profit	43,732	55,318	63,338	72,081	81,610	85,240	80,632	76,024	71,416	66,808	
28	Taxes (before investment credit)	21,866	27,659	31,669	36,040	40,805	42,620	40,316	38,012	35,708	33,404	
29	(4)Investment credit used	10,933	13,829	15,834	18,020	11,384	.....	.....	.....	.....	.....	
30	Net profit	32,799	41,488	47,503	54,061	52,189	42,620	40,316	38,012	35,708	33,404	
31	(5)After-tax cash flow from liquidation	.....	.....	.....	.....	.....	.....	.....	.....	.....	.....	
32	Remaining investment credit	59,067	45,238	29,404	11,384	.....	.....	.....	.....	.....	.....	

Assumptions:
(1) Discount: 10% of the IBM rate, through 1967; increasing by 2 percentage points per year thereafter to 26% in 1975.
(2) Depreciation: 8 yrs. sum-of-the-years' digits, 15% residual value for tax purposes; 10 yrs. straight line, 15% residual for shareholders.
(3) Interest: 9% rate on outstanding balance which is reduced each year by the full cash flow.
(4) Investment Credit: 7% investment credit deducted from tax liability as fast as possible rather than evenly amortized over the life of the asset.
(5) Cash flow from liquidation: The computer is sold for 40% of original cost at the end of 1975; taxes paid at the corporate rate (50%).

Exhibit 3

COMPULEASE CORPORATION (A)

MANAGEMENT

Name	*Positions and Offices Held*
James A. Kralik	Chairman of the Board of Directors, and President
Philip R. Jameson	Executive Vice President and Director
John M. Bailey	Vice President of Marketing and Director
Sherman L. Gerard	Director

James A. Kralik was Vice President—Systems Analysis for The Data Control Corporation from 1963 to 1965. Prior to 1963 he was a consultant to various companies specializing in computer programming assistance.

Philip R. Jameson became treasurer of the Industrial Leasing Corporation in 1960 and still held that positio nin December, 1965.

John M. Bailey became a sales manager for the Digital Data Corporation in 1959 and still held that position in December, 1965.

Sherman L. Gerard was a partner in the investment banking firm of Bachman, Dillard and Hanover.

The company planned to hire two salesmen and one office secretary in the near future.

Exhibit 4

COMPULEASE CORPORATION (A)

CASH RETURN AFTER DEBT REPAYMENT ON $1,000,000 LEASE

Year	Short-Term Lease Outflow	Short-Term Lease Inflow	Full-Payout Lease Outflow	Full-Payout Lease Inflow
1	$334,000	$ 0	$200,000	$ 0
2		0		0
3		0		0
4		0		0
5		66,893		0
6		145,388		78,100
7		136,029		398,100
8		99,676		
9		78,208		
10		350,904		
	Internal rate of return = 12.9%		Internal rate of return = 13.3%	

Exhibit 5

COMPULEASE CORPORATION (A)

SENSITIVITY ANALYSIS–DISCOUNTED CASH FLOW RATE OF RETURN ON EQUITY
INVESTED IN COMPUTERS PLACED ON SHORT-TERM LEASES

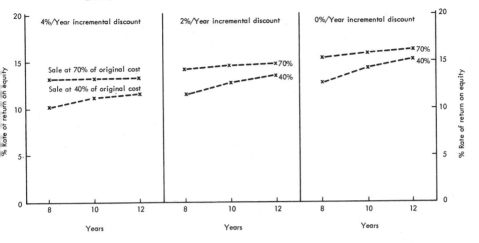

COMPULEASE CORPORATION (B)

∧∧

Late in December, 1967, Mr. James A. Kralik, president of Compulease Corporation, was considering whether his company should continue to purchase third-generation computer equipment.

Corporate history

Compulease Corporation had shown dramatic growth in the area of short-term leasing since its inception in 1965. The company had remained closely held during its first year. During this period the original investor group put together by BD&H had participated in three rounds of private financing. In the first round, which occurred in January, 1966, the BD&H group had purchased 77,777 shares of Compulease common stock at $12.34 for a total commitment of $960,000. The Compulease co-founders, James Kralik, Philip Jameson, and John Bailey, had received 22,223 shares for a total consideration of $40,000. In two later rounds of private financing during 1966, the BD&H group had purchased, for $10 a share, an additional 233,333 shares of the company's common stock. Since the Compulease co-founders had exhausted their personal resources in the first round of financing, they were not able to purchase additional shares in later financing.

As originally planned, Compulease went public early in January, 1967, by offering 317,144 shares at a price of $20 a share. By the end of 1967, the company's common stock price had risen to $46, giving handsome paper profits to the original investors in Compulease and the purchasers of shares in the initial public offering.

Compulease expected to report earnings per share of $1.63 for 1967, a figure up nearly 70% from the $0.97 earned in 1966. Based on the 1967 earnings estimate, the company's common stock was selling at over 28 times earnings, a conservative figure by industry standards, as Exhibit 1 indicates.

The company's return on equity

When his company had started purchasing third-generation computer equipment two years earlier, Mr. Kralik had been well aware that the useful life of these machines would *not* be determined by any physical deterioration. Since the obsolescence would be technological rather than physical, the remaining life of a third-generation computer purchased in 1965 would be the same as the remaining life of a similar machine purchased two years later, in December, 1967. The fact that similar equipment became obsolete at a specific *point* in time (shortly after the introduction of a new computer generation) rather than after an elapsed *period* of time made the continued purchase of third-generation machines a somewhat hazardous undertaking. This was true because those machines purchased earliest in the life cycle of the third generation were all but certain to earn the highest returns. Were Mr. Kralik to continue purchasing third-generation equipment for many more years, he could be certain of sustaining losses on those computers purchased too late in the product's life cycle to allow an economic return.

In his original 1965 projections (see Compulease Corporation [A]) Mr. Kralik estimated that the life cycle of third-generation computer equipment would extend through 1975. The passage of two years had not caused him to significantly revise these estimates. Thus, in calculating the return on equity invested in third-generation equipment purchased during 1968, he felt safe in assuming a remaining life of only eight years. Exhibit 2 shows that a two-year decline in life would cause the expected return on equity invested in third-generation equipment to drop from 12.9% to 11.7%.

Mr. Kralik was a little perturbed at the prospect of investing greater and greater sums of money at successively lower returns, and he wondered how the shareholders of Compulease would fare if the company continued its buying activity for at least another year. He was somewhat puzzled as to how he should go about evaluating the financial impact on shareholders of an additional year of purchasing third-generation equipment, but he decided to approach the problem from two different viewpoints, with an eye toward finally comparing the results of the two approaches.

First approach to shareholders' return on investment

Mr. Kralik's first attempt at estimating the impact of continuing computer purchases was based on valuing the cash flows generated through operations. Exhibit 3 shows Compulease's actual earnings reports through 1967 and estimated financial statements through 1975, assuming a halt in computer purchasing activity by the end of 1967. All future cash flows would be used first to retire outstanding debt, as was required in the company's agreement with its bank lenders. The cash flow remaining after debt amortization could then be returned to the shareholders, along with the cash realized from ultimately selling the computer equipment at the end of 1975.

At lines 25 and 26 of Exhibit 3, the company's cash flow is expressed on a per share basis to make possible a calculation of the rate of return to shareholders who bought the company's common stock at different prices.

According to Mr. Kralik's calculations (assuming all computer purchases were halted at the end of 1967), the original investors, who purchased their shares at an average cost of $10, would realize a rate of return equal to 17% on their investment if (1) they ignored all price gyrations in the stock market and held their shares through 1975, and (2) the company paid out its entire cash flow after debt amortization. Those investors who purchased their stock a year later at the initial public offering price of $20 a share would receive a return of only 8.8% under similar assumptions (line 28, Exhibit 3).

Mr. Kralik was a little unhappy about the return to the second group of investors. He wondered how a third group would fare under the same type of analysis if Compulease sold a new issue of common stock in 1968, thus allowing the company to continue purchasing third-generation computers for at least another year.

Mr. Kralik was advised by his investment banker that Compulease could easily raise enough equity through a common stock offering at $40 a share to enable the company to purchase some $40 million worth of third-generation computers in 1968. The sale of 306,000 shares of common stock would raise approximately $12,250,000. This amount, added to the earnings of $1,050,000 retained in 1967, would enlarge the company's equity base by $13,300,000. Compulease could borrow $26,700,000 (at a 2 to 1 debt-equity ratio) on this base, achieving a total potential cash infusion of nearly $40 million in 1968.

Exhibit 4 is Mr. Kralik's revision of the pro forma financial statements for Compulease Corporation for 1968–75, assuming a third round of external financing in 1968 and the purchase in that year of some $40 million worth of third-generation computer equipment. Mr. Kralik noted that under the continued buying assumption, the rate of return to the first two sets of investors rose from 17% to 21% and from 8.8% to 13.5% respectively (lines 27 and 28, Exhibits 3 and 4). Continued equipment purchases for at least another year would clearly be advantageous to these investors.

While the first two groups of investors profited substantially from a third year of purchasing activity, Mr. Kralik was startled to see that the last group of investors, who would purchase their shares at $40, could expect a return of only 4.4% (line 29, Exhibit 4) if they held their shares through 1975.

Second approach to shareholders' return on investment

Since no investor would knowingly place his capital at 4.4% in a situation as risky as computer leasing, Mr. Kralik felt that his valuation model based on discounting the cash flows from operations might be inappropriate. Investors were probably not looking to Compulease's future operating cash flows in making their stock purchase decisions. They were far more likely to count on getting their return through selling their shares in the open market at higher future prices. Their return might thus be entirely independent of Compulease's estimated future operating cash flows. The fact that the trading volume in Compulease's common stock was averaging 6% of the outstanding shares per week tended to give support to the idea that many investors were looking for profits from this security in the short run rather than through 1975. If investors were looking to a higher future stock price for their return on investment, Mr. Kralik felt they probably paid close attention to two factors contributing to future stock prices: (1) estimates of future earnings per share and (2) computer leasing industry price-earnings ratios.

Since Mr. Kralik was fairly confident of the earnings projections in Exhibits 3 and 4 (lines 38 and 39), he computed the price-earnings ratios necessary to keep the price of Compulease stock high enough to assure a 15% compound annual rate of return on his investment to an investor who purchased stock near the current price and held the stock over the next one to three years.

This analysis, presented in Exhibit 5, indicated clearly that investors in Compulease would be far less vulnerable to a downward reevaluation of price-earnings ratios in the computer leasing industry if equipment purchases were continued another year. Indeed, Mr. Kralik feared that the high price-earnings ratios characteristic of this industry might be a direct result of investors' expectations that the high rate of earnings growth from 1966 to 1967 would be repeated in the future. If Compulease failed to purchase computers through 1968, the projected growth in its per share earnings in the period 1967–68 promised to drop from 52% to 15%. A decline of this magnitude in the growth rate might be the very factor to precipitate the drop that Mr. Kralik feared in the company's price-earnings ratio.

Comparing the models

From the analysis of both valuation models, Mr. Kralik saw strong arguments for continuing computer purchases through 1968 in spite of the increased hazards inherent in pursuing such a policy. On the other hand, he felt that similar arguments might lead him to continue equipment purchases right into the 1970's.

Looking to the future

Although the decision regarding a cutoff date for purchases of third-generation computer equipment was the most immediate corporate problem, Mr. Kralik recognized a second problem of equal significance looming in the future. When Compulease did finally stop purchasing third-generation computers, Mr. Kralik was counting on the lapse of a number of years before the company could begin buying fourth-generation machines. Similarly, because of debt repayment terms, it would be four years before the company could use any significant portion of its cash flow for reinvestment or return to the shareholders. During this "dead" period between the third and fourth generation, Compulease would have no growth in its existing business and no cash to get into a new business. Fortunately, reported earnings would still rise about 15% a year for three years after new purchases ceased (Exhibits 3 and 4, lines 38 and 39), but even so Mr. Kralik thought that investors would probably take an unfavorable view of any company that remained inactive for a long period of time and drastically reduced its price-earnings multiple.

Mr. Kralik currently felt boxed into a situation where to maintain the price of his company's stock, he might have to commit increasing sums of money in situations offering decreasing expected returns. To avoid this problem, he felt that Compulease would have to diversify into some new business area in the near future. He wondered whether this diversification move should be into the area of commercial finance or some area outside of finance within the computer industry. Exhibit 1 provides financial data on possible fields within the computer industry, and Exhibit 6 contains data on two commercial finance companies.

Exhibit 1

COMPULEASE CORPORATION (B)

Financial Facts on Companies Operating in the Data Processing Industry

Company	Sales (Thousands) Latest 12 Months	Principal Activity	Five-Year Earnings per Share 1963	1964	1965	1966	1967E	Recent Price	P-E Ratio ('67 Earns)
Applied Data Research	$ 1,386	Software	$ 0.35D	$0.30	$ 0.21	$0.04	$0.30	17	57
ARIES Corp.	3,198	Software	0.09	0.25	0.13	0.50	0.50	23½	47
Automatic Data Proc.	8,900E	Svc. Bur.	0.03	0.09	0.19	0.50	c.80	43⅜	54
C-E-I-R	21,862	Svc. Bur.	(a—0.45D	0.65	0.79	0.13)	0.25	17⅜	69
			(b—1.20D	0.98	1.12	0.88)			
Calif. Computer Prod.	11,318	Hardware	0.18	0.58	0.55	0.67	c1.22	85¾	70
Computer Applications	24,542	Software	0.31	0.58	0.18	0.46	0.55	21¼	39
Computer Sciences	38,860	Software	0.12	0.07	(a—0.04D	0.17)	c.40	26⅛	65
					(b—0.07	0.66)			
Computer Usage	12,000E	Software	0.20	0.37	0.53	0.64	0.90	43½	48
Comp. & Software(f)	12,045	Svc. Bur.	0.09	0.19	0.33	0.44	0.75	33½	45
Data Proc. Fin. & Gen.	3,500	Leasing	0.02	0.04	0.17	0.60	1.50	71⅜	48
Data Products Corp.	12,500E	Hardware	0.40D	0.22	0.05D	0.04	c.21	14⅜	68
Decision Systems(g)	780	Software	0.35	0.41	0.03	0.79D	0.82D	2½	..
Digitek Corp.	825E	Software	0.03	0.07	0.15	0.28	1.35D	5¾	..
Elec. Comp. Prog. Inst.	2,406	Schools	0.13	0.18	0.34	0.54	0.85	42¼	50
Gerber Scientific Inst.	6,751	Hardware	0.24	0.14	0.56	0.62	0.95	39½	42
Informatics Inc.(h)	6,428	Software	0.14D	0.15	0.19	0.37	c.51	31¾	62
Leasco Data Proc.	3,250	Leasing	0.24	0.35	0.54	0.88	1.40	76⅞	55
Levin-Townsend Comp.	3,938	Leasing	0.01	0.27	0.32	0.41	c1.14	41⅝	37
Planning Research	16,021	Software	0.49	0.56	1.10	0.96	c1.29	47⅜	37
Programming & Syst.	1,283	Schools	0.01D	0.05D	0.11	0.12	c.30	16½	55
Randolph Computer	2,958	Leasing	n.a.	n.a.	0.12D	0.77	1.25	36⅞	30
Scientific Comp.(i)	2,000E	Svc. Bur.	0.42D	0.17D	0.12	(i)	0.25	6½	26
TBS Comp. Centers (j)	2,509	Svc. Bur.	0.15	0.35	0.37	0.43	c.33	11½	35
University Computing	9,000E	Svc. Bur.	0.04	0.21	0.40	0.93	2.00	113	57

D—Deficit. E—Estimated. n.a.—Not applicable.

a—Actual, from operations. b—As reported, after special credits and/or charges (later restated). c—Actual, as reported, for FY 1967. f—Formerly Telecomputing Corp.; now 61%—held by Whittaker Corp. g—Formerly Computronics, Inc. h—70%—held by Data Products Corp. i—23%—held by Control Data Corp.; changed to fiscal year basis in 1966; earnings for six months ended 6/30/66 reported as $0.09 per share. j—Formerly Tabulating & Business Services Inc.

Source: "THINKing Big," *Barron's*, September 18, 1967.

Exhibit 2

COMPULEASE CORPORATION (B)

DISCOUNTED CASH FLOW RATE OF RETURN ON THE
CORPORATION'S INVESTMENT IN THIRD-GENERATION
COMPUTER EQUIPMENT

Life of Equipment (Years)	*Rate of Return*
4	Loss
5	7.0%
6	10.3
7	11.3
8.	11.7
10	12.9

Source: Calculated from Exhibit 2, Compulease Corporation (A).

Exhibit 3

COMPULEASE CORPORATION (B)

Actual Financial Statements, 1966–67, and Pro Forma Statements, 1968–75 Assuming Purchasing Activity Ceases by the Close of 1967

	1 Year	1966	1967	1968	1969	1970	1971	1972	1973	1974	1975	
2	Gross equipment purchases	10,000,000	20,000,000	0	0	0	0	0	0	0	0	
3	Gross equipment owned	10,000,000	30,000,000	30,000,000	30,000,000	30,000,000	30,000,000	30,000,000	30,000,000	30,000,000	30,000,000	
4	IBM rental rate	2,553,191	7,659,574	7,659,574	7,659,574	7,659,574	7,659,574	7,659,574	7,659,574	7,659,574	7,659,574	
5	Discount allowed	255,319	765,957	919,149	1,072,340	1,225,532	1,378,723	1,531,915	1,685,106	1,838,298	1,991,489	
6	Overtime premium	76,596	229,787	229,787	229,787	229,787	229,787	229,787	229,787	229,787	229,787	
7	Net rent received	2,374,468	7,123,404	6,970,213	6,817,021	6,663,830	6,510,638	6,357,447	6,204,255	6,051,064	5,897,872	
8	Maintenance expense	255,319	765,957	765,957	765,957	765,957	765,957	765,957	765,957	765,957	765,957	
9	Depreciation expense	1,888,889	5,430,555	4,722,222	4,013,889	3,305,555	2,597,222	1,888,889	1,180,556	472,222	0	
10	Interest expense	600,000	1,684,647	1,328,205	952,093	554,539	133,613	0	0	0	0	
11	General, selling, and administrative	237,447	712,340	697,021	681,702	666,383	651,064	635,745	620,426	605,106	589,787	
12	Pretax profit	−607,187	−1,470,096	−543,194	403,380	1,371,395	2,362,782	3,066,856	3,637,317	4,207,778	4,542,128	Tax
13	Taxes	0	0	0	0	0	758,540	1,533,428	1,818,658	2,103,889	2,271,064	Reports
14	After-tax profit	−607,187	−1,470,096	−543,194	403,380	1,371,395	1,983,511	2,300,142	2,727,987	2,148,576	2,271,064	
15	Depreciation expense	1,888,889	5,430,555	4,722,222	4,013,889	3,305,555	2,597,222	1,888,889	1,180,556	472,222	0	
16	Investment credit used	0	0	0	0	0	379,270	766,714	909,329	44,687	0	
17	Total cash inflow	1,281,702	3,960,460	4,179,028	4,417,269	4,676,951	4,580,734	4,189,031	3,908,543	2,620,798	2,271,064	
18	Liquidation inflow in 1976	8,250,000										
19	Debt outstanding	6,666,667	18,718,298	14,757,838	10,578,810	6,161,541	1,484,591	0	0	0	0	
20	Capital from investors	3,333,333	10,000,000	10,000,000	10,000,000	10,000,000	10,000,000	6,903,857	2,714,826	−1,193,717	−3,814,515	
21	Unused investment credit	700,000	2,100,000	2,100,000	2,100,000	2,100,000	1,720,730	954,016	44,687	0	0	
22	Tax loss carryover	607,187	2,077,283	2,620,476	2,217,096	845,701	0	0	0	0	0	
23	Shares sold in year	333,333	317,144	0	0	0	0	0	0	0	0	
24	Total shares outstanding	333,333	650,478	650,478	650,478	650,478	650,478	650,478	650,478	650,478	650,478	
25	Cash return per share	0	0	0	0	0	4.76	6.44	6.01	4.03	3.49	
26	Liquidation return per share in 1976	12.68										
27	ROR 1st investor	0.171										
28	ROR 2nd investor	0.088										
29	Net rent received	2,374,468	7,123,404	6,970,213	6,817,021	6,663,830	6,510,638	6,357,447	6,204,255	6,051,064	5,897,872	
30	Depreciation expense	850,000	2,550,000	2,550,000	2,550,000	2,550,000	2,550,000	2,550,000	2,550,000	2,550,000	2,550,000	
31	Maintenance expense	255,319	765,957	765,957	765,957	765,957	765,957	765,957	765,957	765,957	765,957	
32	Interest expense	600,000	1,684,647	1,328,205	952,093	554,539	133,613	0	0	0	0	
33	General, selling, and administrative	237,447	712,340	697,021	681,702	666,383	651,064	635,745	620,426	605,106	589,787	
34	Pretax profit	431,702	1,410,460	1,629,029	1,867,269	2,126,951	2,410,004	2,405,745	2,267,872	2,130,000	1,992,128	Shareholder
35	Taxes	215,851	705,230	814,514	933,634	1,063,475	1,205,002	1,202,872	1,133,936	1,065,000	996,064	Reports
36	Investment credit used	107,926	352,615	407,257	466,817	531,738	233,648	0	0	0	0	
37	After-tax profit	323,777	1,057,845	1,221,771	1,400,452	1,595,213	1,438,649	1,202,872	1,133,936	1,065,000	996,064	
38	Earnings per share	0.97	1.63	1.88	2.15	2.45	2.21	1.85	1.74	1.64	1.53	
39	Unused investment credit	592,074	1,639,460	1,232,202	765,385	233,648	0	0	0	0	0	

Assumptions: Investor No. 1 purchases @ $10 per share in January, 1966; Investor No. 2 purchases @ $20 per share in January, 1967.

Exhibit 4

COMPULEASE CORPORATION (B)

ACTUAL FINANCIAL STATEMENTS, 1966–67, AND PRO FORMA STATEMENTS, 1968–75 ASSUMING PURCHASING ACTIVITY CEASES BY THE CLOSE OF 1968

		1966	1967	1968	1969	1970	1971	1972	1973	1974	1975
1	Year										
2	Gross equipment purchases	10,000,000	20,000,000	40,000,000	0	0	0	0	0	0	0
3	Gross equipment owned	10,000,000	30,000,000	70,000,000	70,000,000	70,000,000	70,000,000	70,000,000	70,000,000	70,000,000	70,000,000
4	IBM rental rate	2,553,191	7,659,574	17,872,340	17,872,340	17,872,340	17,872,340	17,872,340	17,872,340	17,872,340	17,872,340
5	Discount allowed	255,319	765,957	2,144,681	2,502,128	2,859,574	3,217,021	3,574,468	3,931,915	4,289,362	4,646,808
6	Overtime premium	76,596	229,787	536,170	536,170	536,170	536,170	536,170	536,170	536,170	536,170
7	Net rent received	2,374,468	7,123,404	16,263,830	15,906,383	15,548,936	15,191,489	14,834,042	14,476,596	14,119,149	13,761,702
8	Maintenance expense	255,319	765,957	1,787,234	1,787,234	1,787,234	1,787,234	1,787,234	1,787,234	1,787,234	1,787,234
9	Depreciation expense	1,888,889	5,430,555	12,277,777	10,625,000	8,972,222	7,319,444	5,666,667	4,013,889	2,361,111	944,444
10	Interest expense	600,000	1,684,647	3,728,205	2,907,225	2,041,309	1,126,414	158,132	0	0	0
11	General, selling, and administrative	237,447	712,340	1,626,383	1,590,638	1,554,894	1,519,149	1,483,404	1,447,660	1,411,915	1,376,170
12	Pretax profit	−607,187	−1,470,096	−3,155,770	−1,003,714	1,193,277	3,439,248	5,738,606	7,227,813	8,558,889	9,653,853
13	Taxes	0	0	0	0	0	0	2,067,182	3,613,907	4,279,444	4,826,927
14	After-tax profit	−607,187	−1,470,096	−3,155,770	−1,003,714	1,193,277	3,439,248	4,705,015	5,420,860	6,338,900	4,826,927
15	Depreciation expense	1,888,889	5,430,555	12,277,777	10,625,000	8,972,222	7,319,444	5,666,667	4,013,889	2,361,111	944,444
16	Investment credit used	0	0	0	0	0	0	1,033,591	1,806,953	2,059,456	0
17	Total cash inflow	1,281,702	3,960,460	9,122,007	9,621,286	10,165,499	10,758,692	10,371,681	9,434,749	8,700,011	5,771,371
18	Liquidation inflow in 1976	19,250,000									
19	Debt outstanding	6,666,667	18,718,298	41,424,505	32,302,498	22,681,212	12,515,713	1,757,021	0	0	0
20	Capital from investors	3,333,333	10,000,000	10,000,000	23,333,333	23,333,333	23,333,333	23,333,333	14,718,673	5,283,925	−3,416,087
21	Unused investment credit	700,000	2,100,000	4,900,000	4,900,000	4,900,000	4,900,000	3,866,409	2,059,456	0	0
22	Tax loss carryover	607,187	2,077,283	5,233,053	6,236,767	5,043,490	1,604,242	0	0	0	0
23	Shares sold in year	333,333	317,144	306,887	0	0	0	0	0	0	0
24	Total shares outstanding	333,333	650,478	957,365	957,365	957,365	957,365	957,365	957,365	957,365	957,365
25	Cash return per share	0	0	0	0	0	0	9.00	9.85	9.09	6.03
26	Liquidation return per share in 1976	20.10									
27	ROR 1st investor	0.211									
28	ROR 2nd investor	0.135									
29	ROR 3rd investor	0.044									
30	Net rent received	2,374,468	7,123,404	16,263,830	15,906,383	15,548,936	15,191,489	14,834,042	14,476,596	14,119,149	13,761,702
31	Depreciation expense	850,000	2,550,000	5,950,000	5,950,000	5,950,000	5,950,000	5,950,000	5,950,000	5,950,000	5,950,000
32	Maintenance expense	255,319	765,957	1,787,234	1,787,234	1,787,234	1,787,234	1,787,234	1,787,234	1,787,234	1,787,234
33	Interest expense	600,000	1,684,647	3,728,205	2,907,225	2,041,309	1,126,414	158,132	0	0	0
34	General, selling, and administrative	237,447	712,340	1,626,383	1,590,638	1,554,894	1,519,149	1,483,404	1,447,660	1,411,915	1,376,170
35	Pretax profit	431,702	1,410,460	3,172,007	3,671,286	4,215,499	4,808,692	5,455,272	5,291,702	4,970,000	4,648,298
36	Taxes	215,851	705,230	1,586,004	1,835,643	2,107,750	2,404,346	2,727,636	2,645,851	2,485,000	2,324,149
37	Investment credit used	107,926	352,615	793,002	917,821	1,053,875	1,202,173	472,588	0	0	0
38	After-tax profit	323,777	1,057,845	2,379,005	2,753,464	3,161,624	3,606,519	3,200,225	2,645,851	2,485,000	2,324,149
39	Earnings per share	0.97	1.63	2.48	2.88	3.30	3.77	3.34	2.76	2.60	2.43
40	Unused investment credit	592,074	1,639,460	3,646,458	2,728,636	1,674,761	472,588	0	0	0	0

Rows 12–17 are bracketed as **Tax Reports**; rows 30–39 are bracketed as **Shareholder Reports**.

Assumptions: Investor No. 1 purchases @ $10 per share in January, 1966; investor No. 2 purchases @ $20 per share in January, 1967; investor No. 3 purchases @ $40 per share in January, 1968.

Exhibit 5

COMPULEASE CORPORATION (B)

MARKET PRICES OF COMPULEASE CORPORATION COMMON STOCK NECESSARY TO SUSTAIN VARIOUS RATES OF RETURN TO INVESTORS

	Year	Projected Earnings per Share*	Market Price† Necessary for Compound Annual Rate of Return of			Price-Earnings Ratio Required for Compound Annual Rate of Return of		
			5%	15%	25%	5%	15%	25%
Assumes computer purchases cease after 1967	1968	$1.88	$42.00	$46.00	$50.00	22.3	24.5	26.6
	1969	2.15	44.20	53.00	62.50	20.6	24.7	29.0
	1970	2.45	46.40	61.00	78.30	18.9	24.9	32.0
Assumes computer purchases cease after 1968	1968	2.48	42.00	46.00	50.00	16.9	18.5	20.2
	1969	2.88	44.20	53.00	62.50	15.3	18.4	21.7
	1970	3.30	46.40	61.00	78.30	14.1	18.5	23.7

* Lines 38 and 39, Exhibits 3 and 4.
† Assumes initial purchase at $40 a share.

Exhibit 6

COMPULEASE CORPORATION (B)

FINANCIAL DATA—COMMERCIAL FINANCE COMPANIES

Year	Earnings per share	Average P-E Ratio	Return on Equity*
Commercial Credit Corporation			
1966	$2.24	12.5	7.6%
1965	2.26	16.5	7.8
1964	3.07	13	11.2
1963	2.98	14.5	11.4
1962	2.97	15	11.9
C.I.T. Financial Corporation			
1966	2.74	10.5	12.5
1965	2.63	12.5	12.7
1964	2.54	14.5	12.7
1963	2.47	17.0	12.8
1962	2.43	16.5	13.0

* Defined as net profit/net worth.

ECONOMY SHIPPING COMPANY

In the spring of 1950 the controller of the Economy Shipping Company, located near Pittsburgh, was preparing a report for the executive committee regarding the feasibility of repairing one of the company's steam riverboats or of replacing the steamboat with a new diesel-powered boat.

The Economy Shipping Company was engaged mainly in the transportation of coal from the nearby mines to the steel mills, public utilities, and other industries in the Pittsburgh area. The company's several steamboats also on occasion carried cargoes to places as far away as New Orleans. All the boats owned by Economy were steam powered. All were at least 10 years old, and the majority were between 15 and 30 years old.

The steamboat the controller was concerned about, the *Cynthia*, was 23 years old and required immediate rehabilitation or replacement. It was estimated that the *Cynthia* had a useful life of another 20 years provided that adequate repairs and maintenance were made. Whereas the book value of the *Cynthia* was $39,500, it was believed that she would bring somewhat less than this amount, possibly around $25,000, if she was sold in 1950. The total of immediate rehabilitation costs for the *Cynthia* was estimated to be $115,000. It was estimated that these general rehabilitation expenditures would extend the useful life of the *Cynthia* for about 20 years.

New spare parts from another boat, which had been retired in 1948, were available for use in the rehabilitation of the *Cynthia*. If these parts were used on the *Cynthia*, an estimate of their fair value was $43,500, which was their book value. Use of these parts would in effect decrease the immediate rehabilitation costs from $115,000 to $71,500. It was believed that if these parts were sold on the market they would bring only around $30,000. They could not be used on any of the other Economy steamboats.

Currently, the *Cynthia* was operated by a 20-man crew. Annual operating costs for the 20-man crew would be approximately as follows:

Wages..............................$110,200
Vacation and sickness benefits............ 1,880
Social security payments................ 2,400
Life insurance........................ 1,800
Commissary supplies.................... 15,420
Repairs and maintenance................ 24,400
Fuel................................ 34,500
Lubricants........................... 550
Miscellaneous service and supplies........ 12,000
        Total..........................$203,150

It was estimated that the cost of dismantling and scrapping the *Cynthia* at the end of her useful life after the overhaul would be offset by the value of the scrap and used parts taken off the boat.

II

An alternative to rehabilitating the steamboat was the purchase of a diesel-powered boat. The Quapelle Company, a local boat manufacturer, quoted the price of $325,000 for a diesel boat. An additional $75,000 for a basic parts inventory would be necessary to service a diesel boat, and such an inventory would be sufficient to service up to three diesel boats. If four or more diesels were purchased, however, it was estimated that additional spare parts inventory would be necessary.

The useful life of a diesel-powered boat was estimated to be 25 years; at the end of that time the boat would be scrapped or completely rehabilitated at a cost approximating that of a new boat. The possibility of diesel engine replacement during the 25-year life was not contemplated by the controller, since information from other companies having limited experience with diesel-powered riverboats did not indicate that such costs needed to be anticipated; but a general overhaul of the engines, costing at current prices $60,000, would be expected every 10 years.

One of the features the Quapelle Company pointed out was the 12% increase in average speed of diesel-powered boats over the steamboats. The controller discounted this feature, however. The short runs and lock-to-lock operations involved in local river shipping would prohibit the diesel boats from taking advantage of their greater speed, since there was little opportunity for passing and they would have to wait in turn at each lock for the slower steamboats. In 1950, out of about 40 boats only two diesel boats were operating on the river. The controller felt it would be many years, if at all, before diesel boats displaced the slower steamboats.

After consulting the Quapelle Company and other companies operating diesel-powered boats, the controller estimated that the annual operating costs of such a boat would total $156,640, broken down as follows:

```
Wages for a 13-man crew................$ 77,300
Vacation and sickness benefits............   1,320
Social security payments.................   1,680
Life insurance...........................   1,170
Commissary supplies....................  10,020
Repairs and maintenance*...............  21,700
Fuel..................................  28,800
Extra stern repairs.....................   2,000
Miscellaneous service and supplies........  12,650
         Total..........................$156,640
```
* Excluding possible major overhaul of diesel engines.

Although the Economy controller had not considered the matter, the user of this case may assume that at the end of the 20th year the diesel boat would have a realizable value of $32,500 and the inventory of parts of $37,500.

III

The controller was also concerned at this time with a city smoke ordinance, which had been signed in 1948 to take effect in 1952. To comply with the regulations of the ordinance, all hand-fired steamboats had to be converted to stoker firing. Several of the Economy steamboats were already stoker fired; the *Cynthia*, however, was hand fired. The additional cost of converting the *Cynthia* to stoker firing was estimated to be $40,000, provided it was done at the same time as the general rehabilitation. This $40,000 included the cost of stokers and extra hull conversion and was not included in the $115,000 rehabilitation figure. The controller also knew that if $115,000 were spent presently in rehabilitating the *Cynthia* and it was found later that no relief or only temporary relief for one or two years was to be granted under the smoke ordinance, the cost of converting to stoker firing would no longer be $40,000 but around $70,000. The higher cost would be due to rebuilding, which would not be necessary if the *Cynthia* was converted to stoker firing at the time of her general rehabilitation.

Conversion would reduce the crew from 20 to 18, with the following details:

```
Wages...............................$100,650
Vacation and sickness benefits............   1,650
Social security payments.................   2,200
Life insurance..........................   1,620
Commissary supplies....................  13,880
Repairs and maintenance*...............  24,400
Fuel*.................................  34,500
Lubricants*............................     550
Miscellaneous service and supplies*.......  12,000
         Total..........................$191,450
```
* These costs would remain the same, whether the crew was 20 or 18 men.

IV

All operating data the controller had collected pertaining to crew expenses were based on a 2-shift, 12-hour working day, which was standard on local riverboats. He had been informed, however, that the union representing crew members wanted a change to a three-shift, eight-hour day. If the union insisted on an eight-hour day, accommodations on board the steamers or the diesels would have to be enlarged. The controller was perturbed by this, because he knew the diesels could readily be converted to accommodate three crews whereas steamers could not. How strongly the union would insist on the change and when it would be put into effect, if ever, were questions for which the controller could get no satisfactory answers. He believed that the union might have a difficult time in getting acceptance of its demands for three eight-hour shifts on steamers, since because of space limitations it would be very difficult, if not impossible, to convert the steamers to hold a larger crew. The controller thought that the union might succeed in getting its demands accepted, however, in the case of diesel-powered boats. One of the diesel boats currently operating in the Pittsburgh area had accommodations for three crews, although it was still operating on a two-shift basis. The diesel boats that the Quapelle Company offered to build for Economy could be fitted to accommodate three crews at no additional cost.

V

Another factor the controller was considering at this time was alternative uses of funds. In the spring of 1950, Economy had sufficient funds to buy four diesel-powered boats; however, there were alternative uses for these funds. The other projects the management was considering at this time had an estimated return of at least 10% after taxes. The income tax rate at the time was 48%.

THE SUPER PROJECT

In March, 1967, Mr. Crosby Sanberg, manager, financial analysis at General Foods Corporation, told a casewriter, "What I learned about incremental analysis at the Business School doesn't always work." He was convinced that under some circumstances "sunk costs" were relevant to capital project evaluations. He was also concerned that financial and accounting systems did not provide an accurate estimate of "incremental costs and revenues" and that this was one of the most difficult problems in measuring the value of capital investment proposals. Mr. Sanberg used the Super project[1] as an example.

Super was a new instant dessert, based on a flavored, water soluble, agglomerated powder. Although a four-flavor line would be introduced, it was estimated that chocolate would account for 80% of total sales.

General Foods was organized along product lines in the United States. Foreign operations were under a separate division. Major U.S. product divisions included Post, Kool-Aid, Maxwell House, Jell-O, and Birds Eye. Financial data for General Foods are given in Exhibits 1, 2, and 3.

The capital investment project request for Super involved $200,000 as follows:

Building modifications..................	$ 80,000 *rev.*
Machinery and equipment..............	120,000
	$200,000

Part of the expenditure was required for modifying an existing building, where Jell-O was manufactured. Available capacity of a Jell-O agglomerator[2] would be used in the manufacture of Super, so that no cost for the key machine was included in the project. The $120,000 machinery and equipment item represented packaging machinery.

The market

The total dessert market was defined as including powdered desserts, ice creams, pie fillings, and cake mixes. According to a Nielsen survey, powdered

---

[1] The name and nature of this new product have been disguised to avoid the disclosure of confidential information.

[2] Agglomeration is a process by which the processed powder is passed through a steam bath and then dried. This "fluffs up" the powder particles and increases solubility.

desserts constituted a significant and growing segment of the market; their 1966 market share had increased over the preceding year. Results of the Nielsen survey follow:

DESSERT MARKET
AUGUST–SEPTEMBER, 1966, COMPARED WITH AUGUST–SEPTEMBER, 1965

	Market Share August–September, 1966	% Change from August–September, 1965 Share	Volume
Jell-O	19.0%	+3.6	+40.0
Tasty	4.0	+4.0	(New)
Total powders	25.3	+7.6	+62.0
Pie fillings and cake mixes	32.0	−3.9	(No change)
Ice cream	42.7	−3.4	+ 5.0
Total market	100.0%		+13.0

On the basis of test market experience, General Foods expected Super to capture a 10% share of the total dessert market. Eighty percent of the expected volume of Super would come from a growth in total market share or growth in the total powdered segment, and 20% would come from erosion of Jell-O sales.

Production facilities

Test market volume was packaged on an existing line, inadequate to handle long-run requirements. Filling and packaging equipment to be purchased had a capacity of 1.9 million units on a two-shift, five-day workweek basis. This represented considerable excess capacity, since 1968 requirements were expected to reach 1.1 million units and the national potential was regarded as 1.6 million units. However, the extra capacity resulted from purchasing standard equipment, and a more economical alternative did not exist.

Capital budgeting procedure

Capital investment project proposals submitted under procedures covered in the General Foods Accounting and Financial Manual were identified as falling into one of the following classifications:

1. Safety and Convenience
2. Quality
3. Increase Profit
4. Other

These classifications served as a basis for establishing different procedures and criteria for accepting projects. For example, the Super project fell in the third classification, "increase profit." Criteria for evaluating projects are given in Exhibit 4. In discussing these criteria, Mr. Sanberg noted that the payback and return guidelines were not used as "cutoff" measures. Mr. Sanberg added: "Payback and return on investment are rarely the only measure of acceptability. Criteria vary significantly by type of project. A relatively high return might be required for a new product in a new business category. On the other hand, a much lower return might be acceptable for a new product entry which represented a continuing effort to maintain leadership in an existing business by, for example, filling out the product line."

Estimates of payback and return on funds employed were required for each profit-increasing project requiring a total of $50,000 or more of new capital funds and expense before taxes. The payback period was the length of time required for the project to repay the investment from the date the project became operational. In calculating the repayment period, only incremental income and expenses related to the project were used.

Return on funds employed (ROFE) was calculated by dividing 10-year average profit before taxes by the 10-year average funds employed. Funds employed included incremental net fixed assets plus or minus related working capital. Start-up costs and any profits or losses incurred prior to the time when the project became operational were included in the first profit and loss period in the financial evaluation calculation.

Capital budgeting atmosphere

A General Foods accounting executive commented on the atmosphere within which capital projects were reviewed, as follows: "Our problem is not one of capital rationing. Our problem is to find enough good solid projects to employ capital at an attractive return on investment. Of course, the rate of capital inputs must be balanced against a steady growth in earnings per share. The short-term impact of capital investments is usually an increase in the capital base without an immediate realization of profit potential. This is particularly true in the case of new products.

"The food industry should show a continuous growth. A cyclical industry can afford to let its profits vary. We want to expand faster than the gross national product. The key to our capital budgeting is to integrate the plans of our eight divisions into a balanced company plan which meets our overall growth objectives. Most new products show a loss in the first two or three years, but our divisions are big enough to introduce new products without showing a loss."

Documentation for the Super project

Exhibits 5 and 6 document the financial evaluation of the Super project. Exhibit 5 is the summary appropriation request prepared to justify the project to management and to secure management's authorization to expend funds on a capital project. Exhibit 6 presents the backup detail. Cost of the market test was included as "Other" expense in the first period because a new product had to pay for its test market expense, even though this might be a sunk cost at the time capital funds were requested. The "Adjustments" item represented erosion of the Jell-O market and was calculated by multiplying the volume of erosion times a variable profit contribution. In the preparation of Exhibit 6 costs of acquiring packaging machinery were included, but no cost was attributed to the 50% of the capacity of a Jell-O agglomerator to be used for the Super project because the General Foods Accounting and Financial Manual requested that capital projects be prepared on an incremental basis as follows:

"The incremental concept requires that project requests, profit projections, and funds-employed statements include only items of income and expense and investment in assets which will be realized, incurred, or made directly as a result of, or are attributed to, the new project."

Exchange of memos on the Super project

After receiving the paper work on the Super project, Mr. Sanberg studied the situation and wrote a memorandum arguing that the principle of the preceding quotation should not be applied to the Super project. His superior agreed with the memorandum and forwarded it to the corporate controller with the covering note contained in Appendix I. The controller's reply is given in Appendix II.

APPENDIX I

March 2, 1967

TO: J. C. Kresslin, Corporate Controller
FROM: J. E. Hooting, Director, Corporate Budgets and Analysis

Super Project

At the time we reviewed the Super project, I indicated to you that the return on investment looked significantly different if an allocation of the agglomerator and building, originally justified as a Jell-O project, were included in the Super investment. The pro rata allocation of these facilities, based on the share of capacity used, triples the initial gross investment in Super facilities from $200,000 to about $672,000.

I am forwarding a memorandum from Crosby Sanberg summarizing the results of three analyses evaluating the project on an:

    I.   Incremental basis
    II. Facilities-used basis
    III. Fully allocated facilities and costs basis

Crosby has calculated a 10-year average ROFE using these techniques.

Please read Crosby's memo before continuing with my note.

*   *   *   *   *

Crosby concludes that the fully allocated basis, or some variation of it, is necessary to understand the long-range potential of the project.

I agree. We launch a new project because of its potential to increase our sales and earning power for many years into the future. We must be mindful of short-term consequences, as indicated by an incremental analysis, but we must also have a long-range frame of reference if we are to really understand what we are committing ourselves to. This long-range frame of reference is best approximated by looking at fully allocated investment and "accounted" profits, which recognize fully allocated costs because, in fact, over the long run all costs are variable unless some major change occurs in the structure of the business.

Our current GF preoccupation with only the incremental costs and investment causes some real anomalies that confuse our decision making. Super is a good example. On an incremental basis the project looks particularly attractive because by using a share of the excess capacity built on the coat tails of the lucrative Jell-O project, the incremental investment in Super is low. If the excess Jell-O capacity did not exist, would the project be any less attractive? In the short term, perhaps yes because it would entail higher initial risk, but in the long term it is not a better project just because it fits a facility that is temporarily unused.

Looking at this point from a different angle, if the project exceeded our investment hurdle rate on a short-term basis but fell below it on a long-term basis (and Super comes close to doing this), should we reject the project? I say yes because over the long run as "fixed" costs become variable and as we have to commit new capital to support the business, the continuing ROFE will go under water.

In sum, we have to look at new project proposals from both the long-range and the short-term point of view. We plan to refine our techniques of using a fully allocated basis as a long-term point of reference and will hammer out a policy recommendation for your consideration. We would appreciate your comments.

February 17, 1967

TO: J. E. Hooting, Director, Corporate Budgets and Analysis
FROM: C. Sanberg, Manager, Financial Analysis

Super Project: A Case Example of Investment Evaluation Techniques

This will review the merits of alternative techniques of evaluating capital investment decisions using the Super project as an example. The purpose of the review is to provide an illustration of the problems and limitations inherent in using incremental ROFE and payback and thereby provide a rationale for adopting new techniques.

ALTERNATIVE TECHNIQUES

The alternative techniques to be reviewed are differentiated by the level of revenue and investment charged to the Super project in figuring a payback and ROFE, starting with incremental revenues and investment. Data related to the alternative techniques outlined below are summarized [at the end of this appendix].

Alternative I Incremental Basis

Method. The Super project as originally evaluated considered only incremental revenue and investment, which could be directly identified with the decision to produce Super. Incremental fixed capital ($200M) basically included packaging equipment.

Result. On this basis the project paid back in seven years with a ROFE of 63%.

Discussion. Although it is General Foods' current policy to evaluate capital projects on an incremental basis, this technique does not apply to the Super project. The reason is that Super extensively utilizes existing facilities, which are readily adaptable to known future alternative uses.

Super should be charged with the "opportunity loss" of agglomerating capacity and building space. Because of Super the opportunity is lost to use a portion of agglomerating capacity for Jell-O and other products that could potentially be agglomerated. In addition, the opportunity is lost to use the building space for existing or new product volume expansion. To the extent there is an opportunity loss of existing facilities, new facilities must be built to accommodate future expansion. In other words, because the business is expanding Super utilizes facilities that are adaptable to predictable alternative uses.

Alternative II Facilities-Used Basis

Method. Recognizing that Super will use half of an existing agglomerator and two thirds of an existing building, which were justified earlier in the Jell-O project, we added Super's pro rata share of these facilities ($453M) to the incremental capital. Overhead costs directly related to these existing facilities were also subtracted from incremental revenue on a shared basis.

Result. ROFE, 34%.

Discussion. Although the existing facilities utilized by Super are not incremental to this project, they are relevant to the evaluation of the project because potentially they can be put to alternative uses. Despite a high return on an incremental basis, if the ROFE on a project was unattractive after consideration of the shared use of existing facilities, the project would be questionable. Under these circumstances, we might look for a more profitable product for the facilities.

In summary, the facilities-used basis is a useful way of putting various projects on a common ground for purposes of *relative* evaluation. One product using existing capacity should not necessarily be judged to be more attractive than another practically identical product which necessitates an investment in additional facilities.

Alternative III Fully Allocated Basis

Method. Further recognizing that individual decisions to expand inevitably add to a higher overhead base, we increased the costs and investment base developed in Alternative II by a provision for overhead expenses and overhead capital. These increases were made in year 5 of the 10-year evaluation period, on the theory that at this point a number of decisions would result in more fixed costs and facilities. Overhead expenses included manufacturing costs, plus selling and general and administrative costs on a per unit basis equivalent to Jell-O. Overhead capital included a share of the distribution system assets ($40M).

Result. ROFE, 25%.

Discussion. Charging Super with an overhead burden recognizes that overhead costs in the long-run increase in proportion to the level of business activity, even though decisions to spend more overhead dollars are made separately from decisions to increase volume and provide the incremental facilities to support the higher volume level. To illustrate, the Division-F1968 Financial Plan budgets about a 75% increase in headquarters' overhead spending in F1968 over F1964. A contributing factor was the decision to increase the sales force by 50% to meet the demands of a growing and increasingly complex business. To further illustrate, about half the capital projects in the F1968 three-year Financial Plan are in the "nonpayback" category. This group of projects comprises largely "overhead facilities" (warehouses, utilities, etc.), which are not directly related to the manufacture of products but are necessary components of the total business. These facilities are made necessary by an increase in total business activity as a result of the cumulative effect of many decisions taken in the past.

The Super project is a significant decision which will most likely add to more overhead dollars as illustrated above. Super volume doubles the powdered dessert business category; it increases the Division businesses by 10%. Furthermore, Super requires a new production technology: agglomeration and packaging on a high-speed line.

CONCLUSIONS

1. The incremental basis for evaluating a project is an inadequate measure of a project's worth when existing facilities with a known future use will be utilized extensively.

2. A fully allocated basis of reviewing major new product proposals recognizes that overheads increase in proportion to the size and complexity of the business, and provides the best long-range projection of the financial consequences.

ALTERNATIVE EVALUATIONS OF SUPER PROJECT
(FIGURES BASED ON 10-YEAR AVERAGES;
IN THOUSANDS OF DOLLARS)

	I Incremental Basis	II Facilities- Used Basis	III Fully Allocated Basis
Investment:			
Working capital............	267	267	267
Fixed capital:			
Gross...................	200	653	672
Net.....................	113	358	367
Total net investment.......	380	625	634
Profit before taxes*.............	239	211	157
ROFE......................	63%	34%	25%

Jell-O Project:
Building................. $200 × ⅔ = $133
Agglomerator............ 640 × ½ = 320
                                    $453

* Note: Assumes 20% of Super volume will replace existing Jell-O business.

APPENDIX II

TO: Mr. J. E. Hooting, Director, Corporate Budgets and Analysis
FROM: Mr. J. C. Kresslin, Corporate Controller
SUBJECT: SUPER PROJECT

March 7, 1967

On March 2 you sent me a note describing Crosby Sanberg's and your thoughts about evaluating the Super project. In this memo you suggest that the project should be appraised on the basis of fully allocated facilities and production costs.

In order to continue the dialogue, I am raising a couple of questions below.

It seems to me that in a situation such as you describe for Super, the real question is a *management decision* as to whether to go ahead with the Super project or not go ahead. Or to put it another way, are we better off in the aggregate if we use half the agglomerator and two thirds of an existing building for Super, or are we not, on the basis of our current knowledge?

It might be assumed that, for example, half of the agglomerator is being used and half is not and that a minimum economical size agglomerator was necessary for Jell-O and, consequently, should be justified by the Jell-O project itself. If we find a way to utilize it sooner by producing Super on it, aren't we better off in the aggregate, and the different ROFE figure for the Super project by itself becomes somewhat irrelevant? A similar point of view might be applied to the portion of the building. Or if we charge the Super project with half an agglomerator and two thirds of an existing building, should we then go back and relieve the Jell-O projects of these costs in evaluating the management's original proposal?

To put it another way, since we are faced with making decisions at a certain time on the basis of what we then know, I see very little value in looking at the Super project all by itself. Better we should look at the total situation before and after to see how we fare.

As to allocated production costs, the point is not so clear. Undoubtedly, over the long haul, the selling prices will need to be determined on the basis of a satisfactory margin over fully allocated costs. Perhaps this should be an additional requirement in the course of evaluating capital projects, since we seem to have been surprised at the low margins for "Tasty" after allocating all costs to the product.

I look forward to discussing this subject with you and with Crosby at some length.

Exhibit 1

THE SUPER PROJECT
CONSOLIDATED BALANCE SHEET OF GENERAL FOODS CORPORATION
FISCAL YEAR ENDED APRIL 1, 1967
(Dollar figures in millions)

ASSETS

Cash...	$ 20
Marketable securities..	89
Receivables...	180
Inventories...	261
Prepaid expenses..	14
Total current assets....................................	$564
Land, buildings, equipment (at cost, less depreciation)...........	332
Long-term receivables and sundry assets.......................	7
Goodwill..	26
Total assets...	$929

LIABILITIES AND STOCKHOLDERS' EQUITY

Notes payable..	$ 22
Accounts payable...	86
Accrued liabilities..	73
Accrued income taxes.......................................	57
Total current liabilities...............................	$238
Long-term notes..	39
3⅜% debentures..	22
Other noncurrent liabilities..................................	10
Deferred investment tax credit...............................	9
Stockholders' equity:	
Common stock issued....................................	164
Retained earnings......................................	449
Common stock held in treasury, at cost.....................	(2)
Total stockholders' equity..............................	$611
Total liabilities and stockholders' equity...................	$929
Common stock—shares outstanding at year-end.................	25,127,007

Exhibit 2
THE SUPER PROJECT

COMMON STOCK PRICES OF GENERAL
FOODS CORPORATION
1958–67

Year	*Price Range*
1958	$24 –$ 39¾
1959	37⅛– 53⅞
1960	49⅛– 75½
1961	68⅝– 107¾
1962	57¾– 96
1963	77⅝– 90½
1964	78¼– 93¼
1965	77½– 89⅞
1966	62¾– 83
1967	65¼– 81¾

Exhibit 3

THE SUPER PROJECT

TEN-YEAR SUMMARY OF STATISTICAL DATA OF GENERAL FOODS CORPORATION, 1958–67

(All dollar amounts in millions, except assets per employee and figures on a share basis)

Fiscal years	1958	1959	1960	1961	1962	1963	1964	1965	1966	1967
EARNINGS										
Sales to customers (net)	$1,009	$1,053	$1,087	$1,160	$1,189	$1,216	$1,338	$1,478	$1,555	$1,652
Cost of sales	724	734	725	764	769	769	838	937	965	1,012
Marketing, administrative, and general expenses	181	205	236	261	267	274	322	362	406	449
Earnings before income taxes	$ 105	$ 115	$ 130	$ 138	$ 156	$ 170	$ 179	$ 177	$ 185	$ 193
Taxes on income	57	61	69	71	84	91	95	91	91	94
Net earnings	$ 48	$ 54	$ 61	$ 67	$ 72	$ 79	$ 84	$ 86	$ 94	$ 99
Dividends on common shares	24	28	32	35	40	45	50	50	53	55
Retained earnings—current year	24	26	29	32	32	34	34	36	41	44
Net earnings per common share	$ 1.99	$ 2.21	$ 2.48	$ 2.69	$ 2.90	$ 3.14	$ 3.33	$ 3.44	$ 3.73	$ 3.93
Dividends per common share	$ 1.00	$ 1.15	$ 1.30	$ 1.40	$ 1.60	$ 1.80	$ 2.00	$ 2.00	$ 2.10	$ 2.20
ASSETS, LIABILITIES, AND STOCKHOLDERS' EQUITY										
Inventories	$ 169	$ 149	$ 157	$ 189	$ 183	$ 205	$ 256	$ 214	$ 261	$ 261
Other current assets	144	180	200	171	204	206	180	230	266	303
Current liabilities	107	107	126	123	142	162	202	173	219	238
Working capital	$ 206	$ 222	$ 230	$ 237	$ 245	$ 249	$ 234	$ 271	$ 308	$ 326
Land, buildings, equipment, gross	$ 203	$ 221	$ 247	$ 289	$ 328	$ 375	$ 436	$ 477	$ 517	$ 569
Land, buildings, equipment, net	125	132	148	173	193	233	264	283	308	332
Long-term debt	49	44	40	37	35	34	23	37	54	61
Stockholders' equity	$ 287	$ 315	$ 347	$ 384	$ 419	$ 454	$ 490	$ 527	$ 569	$ 611
Stockholders' equity per common share	$11.78	$12.87	$14.07	$15.46	$16.80	$18.17	$19.53	$20.99	$22.64	$24.32
CAPITAL PROGRAM										
Capital additions	$ 28	$ 24	$ 35	$ 40	$ 42	$ 57	$ 70	$ 54	$ 65	$ 59
Depreciation	11	14	15	18	21	24	26	29	32	34
EMPLOYMENT DATA										
Wages, salaries, and benefits	$ 128	$ 138	$ 147	$ 162	$ 171	$ 180	$ 195	$ 204	$ 218	$ 237
Number of employees (in thousands)	21	22	22	25	28	28	30	30	30	32
Assets per employee (in thousands)	$ 21	$ 22	$ 23	$ 22	$ 22	$ 23	$ 24	$ 25	$ 29	$ 29

Per share figures calculated on shares outstanding at year-end and adjusted for 2 for 1 stock split in August, 1960.

Exhibit 4

THE SUPER PROJECT

CRITERIA FOR EVALUATING PROJECTS BY GENERAL FOODS CORPORATION

The basic criteria to be applied in evaluating projects within each of the classifications are set forth in the following schedule:

Purpose of Project	*Payback and ROFE Criteria*

a) SAFETY AND CONVENIENCE:

1. Projects required for reasons of safety, sanitation, health, public convenience, or other overriding reason with no reasonable alternatives. Examples: sprinkler systems, elevators, fire escapes, smoke control, waste disposal, treatment of water pollution, etc.

2. Additional nonproductive space requirements for which there are no financial criteria. Examples: office space, laboratories, service areas (kitchens, restrooms, etc.).

Payback—return on funds projections not required but the request must clearly demonstrate the *immediate* need for the project and the lack or inadequacy of alternative solutions.

Requests for nonproductive facilities, such as warehouses, laboratories, and offices should indicate the advantages of owning rather than leasing, unless no possibility to lease exists. In those cases where the company owns a group of integrated facilities and wherein the introduction of rented or leased properties might complicate the long-range planning or development of the area, owning rather than leasing is recommended. If the project is designed to improve customer service (such as market centered warehouses) this factor is to be noted on the project request.

If payback and ROFE cannot be computed, it must be clearly demonstrated that the improvement is identifiable and desirable.

b) QUALITY:

Projects designed primarily to improve quality.

c) INCREASE PROFIT:

1. Projects that are justified primarily by reduced costs.

Projects with a payback period *up to 10 years* and a 10-year return *on* funds *as low as 20%* PBT are considered worthy of consideration, provided (1) the end product involved is believed to be a reasonably permanent part of our line or (2) the facilities involved are so flexible that they may be usable for successor products.

2. Projects that are designed primarily to increase production capacity for an existing product.

Projects for a proven product where the risk of mortality is small, such as coffee, Jell-O Gelatin, and cereals, should assure a payback in *no more than 10 years* and a 10-year PBT return on funds of *no less* than 20%.

3. Projects designed to provide facilities to manufacture and distribute a new product or product line.

Because of the greater risk involved such projects should show a high potential return *on* funds (not less than a 10-year PBT return of 40%). Payback period, however, might be as much as *10 years* because of losses incurred during the market development period.*

d) OTHER:

This category includes projects which by definition are excluded from the three preceding categories. Examples: standby facilities intended to insure uninterrupted production, additional equipment not expected to improve profits or product quality and not required for reasons of safety and convenience, equipment to satisfy marketing requirements, etc.

While standards of return may be difficult to set, some calculation of financial benefits should be made where possible.

* These criteria apply to the United States and Canada only. Profit-increasing capital projects in other areas in categories c1 and c2 should offer at least a 10-year PBT return of 24% to compensate for the greater risk involved. Likewise, foreign operation projects in the c3 category should offer a 10-year PBT return of at least 48%.

Exhibit 5

THE SUPER PROJECT
CAPITAL PROJECT REQUEST FORM OF GENERAL FOODS CORPORATION

NY 1292-A 12-63
PTD. IN U.S.A.

December 23, 1966
Date

"Super" Facilities _____ 66-42
Project Title & Number

New Request [X]   Supplement [ ]

Expansion-New Product [X] A

Jell-O Division - St. Louis
Division & Location

Purpose [ ] R

PROJECT DESCRIPTION

To provide facilities for production of Super, chocolate dessert. This project included finishing a packing room in addition to filling and packaging equipment.

· SUMMARY OF INVESTMENT	
NEW CAPITAL FUNDS REQUIRED	$ 200M
EXPENSE BEFORE TAXES	--
LESS: TRADE-IN OR SALVAGE, IF ANY	--
Total This Request	$ 200M
PREVIOUSLY APPROPRIATED	--
Total Project Cost	$ 200M

FINANCIAL JUSTIFICATION*		
ROFE (PBT BASIS) - 10 YR. AVERAGE	62.9	%
PAYBACK PERIOD April, F'68 Feb.F'75 FROM TO	6.83	YRS.
NOT REQUIRED ·		[ ]
* BASED ON TOTAL PROJECT COST AND WORKING FUNDS OF	$ 510M	

ESTIMATED EXPENDITURE RATE		
QUARTER ENDING Mar. F19 67	$ 160M	
QUARTER ENDING June F19 68	40M	
QUARTER ENDING F19		
QUARTER ENDING F19		
REMAINDER		

OTHER INFORMATION		
MAJOR [ ] SPECIFIC ORDINARY [ ] BLANKET [ ]		
INCLUDED IN ANNUAL PROGRAM YES [ ] NO [ ]		
PER CENT OF ENGINEERING COMPLETED	80	%
ESTIMATED START-UP COSTS	$ 15M	
ESTIMATED START-UP DATE	April	

LEVEL OF APPROVAL REQUIRED
[ ] BOARD [ ] CHAIRMAN [ ] EXEC. V.P. [ ] GEN. MGR.

SIGNATURES		DATE
DIRECTOR CORP. ENG.		
DIRECTOR B & A		
GENERAL MANAGER		
VICE PRESIDENT		
EXEC. VICE PRESIDENT		
PRESIDENT		
CHAIRMAN		

For Division Use - Signatures	
NAME AND TITLE	DATE

Exhibit 5—Continued

INSTRUCTIONS FOR CAPITAL PROJECT REQUEST FORM NY 1292-A

The purpose of this form is to secure management's authorization to commit or expend funds on a capital project. Refer to Accounting and Financial Manual Statement No. 19 for information regarding projects to which this form applies.

NEW REQUEST—SUPPLEMENT: Check the appropriate box.

PURPOSE: Identify the primary purpose of the project in accordance with the classifications established in Accounting and Financial Statement No. 19, i.e., Sanitation, Health and Public Convenience, Non-Productive Space, Safety, Quality, Reduce Cost, Expansion— Existing Products, Expansion—New Products, Other (specify). Also indicate in the appropriate box whether the equipment represents an addition or a replacement.

PROJECT DESCRIPTION: Comments should be in sufficient detail to enable Corporate Management to appraise the benefits of the project. Where necessary, supplemental data should be attached to provide complete background for project evaluation.

SUMMARY OF INVESTMENT:

New Capital Funds Required: Show gross cost of assets to be acquired.

Expense before Taxes: Show incremental expense resulting from project.

Trade-in or Salvage: Show the amount expected to be realized on trade-in or sale of a replaced asset.

Previously Appropriated: When requesting a supplement to an approved project, show the amount previously appropriated even though authorization was given in a prior year.

FINANCIAL JUSTIFICATION:

ROFE: Show the return on funds employed (PBT basis) as calculated on Financial Evaluation Form NY 1292-C or 1292-F. The appropriate Financial Evaluation Form is to be attached to this form.

Not Required: Where financial benefits are not applicable or required or are not expected, check the box provided. The non-financial benefits should be explained in the comments.

In the space provided, show the sum of The Total Project Cost plus Total Working Funds (line 20, Form NY 1292-C or line 5, Form NY 1292-F) in either of the first three periods, whichever is higher.

ESTIMATED EXPENDITURE RATE: Expenditures are to be reported in accordance with accounting treatment of the asset and related expense portion of the project. Insert estimated quarterly expenditures beginning with the quarter in which the first expenditure will be made. The balance of authorized funds unspent after the fourth quarter should be reported in total.

OTHER INFORMATION: Check whether the project is a major, specific ordinary, or blanket, and whether or not the project was included in the Annual Program. Show estimated percentage of engineering completed; this is intended to give management an indication of the degree of reliability of the funds requested. Indicate the estimated start-up costs as shown on line 32 of Financial Evaluation Form NY 1292-C. Insert anticipated start-up date for the project; if start-up is to be staggered, explain in comments.

LEVEL OF APPROVAL REQUIRED: Check the appropriate box.

Exhibit 6

THE SUPER PROJECT

FINANCIAL EVALUATION FORM OF GENERAL FOODS CORPORATION
(Dollar figures in thousands)

MY 1292-C 30-64
PTR. IN U.S.A.

Division: Jell-O	Location: St. Louis	Project Title: The Super Project	Project No.: 67-89	Date / Supplement Se.

PROJECT REQUEST DETAIL	1ST PER.	2ND PER.	PER.	PER.	PER.	RETURN ON NEW FUNDS EMPLOYED – 10-YR. AVG.		
							PAT (C ÷ A)	PBT (B ÷ A)
1. LAND	$					A = NEW FUNDS EMPLOYED (LINE 21)	$ 380	$ 380
2. BUILDINGS	80					B = PROFIT BEFORE TAXES (LINE 35)	///	$ 239
3. MACHINERY & EQUIPMENT	120					C = NET PROFIT (LINE 37)	$ 115	///
4. ENGINEERING						D = CALCULATED RETURN	30.2 %	62.9 %
5. OTHER (EXPLAIN)								
6. EXPENSE PORTION (BEFORE TAX)						PAYBACK YEARS FROM OPERATIONAL DATE		
7. SUB-TOTAL	$ 200					PART YEAR CALCULATION FOR FIRST PERIOD		— YRS.
8. LESS: SALVAGE VALUE (OLD ASSET)						NUMBER OF FULL YEARS TO PAY BACK		6.00 YRS.
9. TOTAL PROJECT COST*	$ 200					PART YEAR CALCULATION FOR LAST PERIOD		0.83 YRS.
10. LESS: TAXES ON EXP. PORTION						TOTAL YEARS TO PAY BACK		6.83 YRS.
11. NET PROJECT COST	$ 200							

* Same as Project Request	1ST PER.	2ND PER.	3RD PER.	4TH PER.	5TH PER.	6TH PER.	7TH PER.	8TH PER.	9TH PER.	10TH PER.	11TH PFR.	10-YR.
FUNDS EMPLOYED	F 68	F 69	F 70	F 71	F 72	F 73	F 74	F 75	F 76	F 77	—	AVG.
12. NET PROJECT COST (LINE 11)	$ 200	200	200	200	200	200	200	200	200	200	///	
13. DEDUCT DEPRECIATION (CUM.)	19	37	54	70	85	98	110	121	131	140	///	
14. CAPITAL FUNDS EMPLOYED	$ 181	163	146	130	115	102	90	79	69	60	///	113
15. CASH	124	134	142	151	160	160	169	169	178	173		157
16. RECEIVABLES												
17. INVENTORIES	207	223	237	251	266	266	281	281	296	296		260
18. PREPAID & DEFERRED EXP.												
19. LESS CURRENT LIABILITIES	(2)	(82)	(108)	(138)	(185)	(185)	(184)	(195)	(195)	(207)	(207)	(150)
20. TOTAL WORKING FUNDS (15 THRU 19)	329	274	271	264	241	242	255	255	267	267		267
21. TOTAL NEW FUNDS EMPLOYED (14 + 20)	$ 510	437	417	394	356	344	345	334	336	327	///	380

PROFIT AND LOSS												
22. UNIT VOLUME (in thousands)	1100	1200	1300	1400	1500	1500	1600	1600	1700	1700		1460
23. GROSS SALES	$2200	2400	2600	2800	3000	3000	3200	3200	3400	3400		2920
24. DEDUCTIONS	88	96	104	112	120	120	128	128	136	136		117
25. NET SALES	2112	2304	2496	2688	2880	2880	3072	3072	3264	3264		2803
26. COST OF GOODS SOLD	1100	1200	1300	1400	1500	1500	1600	1600	1700	1700		1460
27. GROSS PROFIT	1012	1104	1196	1288	1380	1380	1472	1472	1564	1564		1343
GROSS PROFIT % NET SALES	%											
28. ADVERTISING EXPENSE												
29. SELLING EXPENSE	1100	1050	1000	900	700	700	730	730	750	750		841
30. GEN. AND ADMIN. COSTS												
31. RESEARCH EXPENSE												
32. START-UP COSTS	15											2
33. OTHER (EXPLAIN) Test Mkt.	360											36
34. ADJUSTMENTS (EXPLAIN) Erosion	180	200	210	220	230	230	240	240	250	250		225
35. PROFIT BEFORE TAXES	$(643)	(146)	(14)	168	450	450	502	502	564	564		239
36. TAXES	(334)	(76)	(7)	87	234	234	261	261	293	293		125
36A. ADD: INVESTMENT CREDIT	(1)	(1)	(1)	(1)	(1)	(1)	(1)	(1)	–	–		(1)
37. NET PROFIT	(308)	(69)	(6)	82	217	217	242	242	271	271		115
38. CUMULATIVE NET PROFIT	$(308)	(377)	(383)	(301)	(84)	133	375	617	888	1159		
39. NEW FUNDS TO REPAY (21 LESS 38)	$ 818	814	800	695	440	211	(30)	(283)	(552)	(832)		

Exhibit 6—Continued

INSTRUCTIONS FOR PREPARATION OF FORM NY 1292-C FINANCIAL EVALUATION

This form is to be submitted to Corporate Budget and Analysis with each profit-increasing capital project request requiring $50,000 or more of capital funds and expense before taxes.

Note that the ten-year term has been divided into eleven periods. The first period is to end on the 31 March 31st following the operational date of the project, and the P & L projection may thereby encompass any number of months from one to twelve, e.g., if the project becomes operational on November 1, 1964, the first period for P & L purposes would be 5 months (November 1, 1964 through March 31, 1965). The next nine periods would be fiscal years (F'66, F'67, etc.) and the eleventh period would be 7 months (April 1, 1974 through October 30, 1974). This has been done primarily to facilitate reporting of projected and actual P & L data by providing for fiscal years. See categorized instructions below for more specific details.

Project Request Detail: Lines 1 through 11 show the breakdown of the Net Project Cost to be used in the financial evaluation. Line 8 is to show the amount expected to be realized on trade-in or sale of a replaced asset. Line 9 should be the same as the "Total Project Cost" shown on Form NY 1292-A, Capital Project Request. Space has been provided for capital expenditures related to this project which are projected to take place subsequent to the first period. Indicate in such space the additional costs only; do not accumulate them.

Funds Employed:

Capital Funds Employed: *Line 12* will show the net project cost appearing on line 11 as a constant for the first ten periods except in any period in which additional expenditures are incurred; in that event show the accumulated amounts of line 11 in such period and in all future periods.

Deduct cumulative depreciation on *line 13*. Depreciation is to be computed on an incremental basis i.e., the net increase in depreciation over present depreciation on assets being replaced. In the first period depreciation will be computed at one half of the first year's annual rate; no depreciation is to be taken in the eleventh period. Depreciation rates are to be the same as those used for accounting purposes. *Exception:* When the depreciation rate used for accounting purposes differs materially from the rate for tax purposes, the higher rate should be used. A variation will be considered material when the first full year's depreciation on a book basis varies 20% or more from the first full year's depreciation on a tax basis.

The ten-year average of Capital Funds Employed shall be computed by adding line 14 in each of the first ten periods and dividing the total by ten.

Total Working Funds: Refer to Financial Policy No. 21 as a guide in computing new working fund requirements. Items which are not on a formula basis and which are normally computed on a five-quarter average shall be handled proportionately in the first period. For example, since the period involved may be less than 12 months, the average would be computed on the number of quarters involved. Generally, the balances should be approximately the same as they would be if the first period were a full year.

Cash, based on a formula which theorizes a two weeks' supply (2/52nds), should follow the same theory. If the first period is for three months, two-thirteenths (2/13ths) should be used; if it is for 5 months, two-twenty-firsts (2/21sts) should be used, and so forth. Current liabilities are to include one half of the tax expense as the tax liability. The ten-year averages of Working Funds shall be computed by adding each line across for the first ten periods and dividing each total by ten.

Profit and Loss Projection

P & L Categories (Lines 22 through 37): Reflect only the incremental amounts which will result from the proposed project; exclude all allocated charges. Include the P & L results expected in the individual periods comprising the first ten years of the life of the project. Refer to the second paragraph of these instructions regarding the fractional years' calculations during the first and eleventh periods.

Any loss or gain on the sale of a replaced asset (see line 8) shall be included in line 33.

As indicated in the caption Capital Funds Employed, no depreciation is to be taken in the eleventh period.

The ten-year averages of the P & L items shall be computed by adding each line across for the eleven periods (10 full years from the operational date) and dividing the total by ten.

Adjustments (Line 34): Show the adjustment necessary, on a before-tax basis, to indicate any adverse or favorable incremental effect the proposed project will have on any other products currently being produced by the corporation.

Investment Credit is to be included on Line 36-A. The Investment Credit will be spread over 8 years, or fractions thereof, as an addition to PAT.

Return on New Funds Employed: Ten-year average returns are to be calculated for PAT (projects requiring Board approval only) and PBT. The PAT return is calculated by dividing average PAT (line 37) by average new funds employed (line 21); the PBT return is derived by dividing average PBT (line 35) by average new funds employed (line 21).

Payback Years from Operational Date:

Part Year Calculation for First Period: Divide number of months in the first period by twelve. If five months are involved, the calculation is 5/12 = .4 years.

Number of Full Years to Pay Back: Determined by the last period, excluding the first period, in which an amount is shown on line 39.

Part Year Calculation for Last Period: Divide amount still to be repaid at the end of the last full period (line 39) by net profit plus the *annual* depreciation in the following year when payback is completed.

Total Years to Pay Back: Sum of full and part years.

P. T. PERTAMINA—GULF INDUSTRIAL PROCESSING

In 1969 Gulf Oil Corporation signed an agreement with the government of Indonesia permitting Gulf to construct and operate in Indonesia a plant for the purpose of bagging imported fertilizer.

The operation would be a joint venture between Gulf and Pertamina, Indonesia's state-owned petroleum company. Gulf was to hold 51% of the shares and would be generally responsible for the management of the operation. The joint enterprise was to be named P.T. Pertamina—Gulf Industrial Processing.

Gulf had long been active in Asia. However, the company did not have other major holdings in Indonesia, although that country had been an important source of oil for the world for many years. In fact, Royal Dutch Shell had its beginning in Indonesia when the area was under Dutch control. Shell began to extract oil from Sumatra before 1900; Stanvac entered Indonesia in 1912; and Caltex began local operations in 1935. After independence, the Sukarno regime (1949 to 1967) took over the Shell properties and required the other oil companies to operate under production sharing agreements with the newly created national oil company.

After the fall of the Sukarno regime in 1967, interest by foreign investors in the opportunities provided by this chain of islands, with a population of 113 million (1968), grew dramatically. Oil firms, mining enterprises, and manufacturing firms made application to the Indonesian Government for permission to invest in the country. Gulf was among these firms.

Gulf was interested in establishing a listening post in this potentially important country, the fifth most populous in the world. The bagging of fertilizer presented a particularly attractive opportunity for Gulf to establish an operation that could fulfill this role. Gulf had conducted similar bagging operations in the United States and the required investment, the size of which would depend partly on the technology chosen, would in any case not be overwhelmingly large. Pertamina would, it was thought, make an ideal partner in this venture. Pertamina had handled most of the fertilizer importing in Indonesia, and would be a likely partner for future operations that Gulf might undertake in the country.

The plant design was handed to an American engineer who had designed plants for similar processes in the United States. The engineer, Don Myers, was fascinated with his assignment. He realized quickly that conditions in Indonesia were very different from those that he had faced in his previous assignments in the United States. Labor costs were extremely low, for example. An unskilled worker could be hired for Rp.30 per hour.[1] Once hired a worker could not be easily laid off or dismissed. Locally borrowed capital was, on the other hand, very expensive. Five-year loans for equipment could sometimes be arranged from state-owned banks for 12% per year, a preferential rate that was generally available only to domestic firms. The normal rate, if funds could be obtained at all, would be at least double this. Working capital from a state bank cost 24% per year. Other sources were even more expensive.

Indonesia had gone through a period of rapid inflation. For example, annual price increases had reached a rate of 650% in 1966. Over the past two years, however, prices had been rather stable, increasing by not more than 10% per year. The history of unstable currency seemed to be changing. The exchange rate had remained stable at about Rp.378/$1.00 for a number of months, and restrictions on currency transactions had been relaxed considerably.

Mr. Myers set out to learn the rudiments of the Indonesian language and quickly found himself picking up an understanding of local customs. For example, he discovered that the ceremonial burial of five water buffalo heads on the building site had to be accomplished before a building was started and that a selamatan (ceremonial feast) was always to be held if a workman was killed or injured during the construction of the facilities.

Adjustments of American ways of doing things began early. A likely site was an old coal dump, which had been used previously as a storage area for the port bunkering facility. The excess coal and dust would have to be cleared from the site by hand, without the use of bulldozers, and loaded on to trucks. The building site would then be prepared by packing the residual earth and coal dust using ancient hand-powered rollers.

Mr. Myers was certain that the plant design would have to reflect local conditions and take into account such local customs and methods.

The role of fertilizer bagging

In Indonesia, agriculture engages 70% of the adult male population. Big, estate-organized agriculture on Sumatra and Java is devoted mainly to export; much of the rest is subsistence agriculture. Rice is the staple food and chief crop. Major plantation crops are rubber, tea, coffee, cinchona bark, palm kernels, and sugar. Others are copra, cacao, spices, agava fiber, and kapok. In addition to rice, the chief food crops are maize, cassava, sweet potatoes, peanuts, and soybeans.

Like many other developing countries, Indonesia faces a struggle to increase agricultural productivity in order to feed its large and rapidly growing

---

[1] For ease of calculation an exchange rate of 400 Rupiah equal to 1 U.S. Dollar is used in this case.

population. The problem is exacerbated by a tendency for rapid urbanization of the population, which is lowering the agricultural labor force relative to the total population, and creating growing urban unemployment.

One of the methods employed to increase productivity among subsistence farmers is to encourage them to use nitrogenous fertilizers in place of the more traditional methods. The most concentrated solid form of nitrogen available is a white, crystalline, water-soluble compound called urea. For use as a fertilizer, urea is manufactured in pellet form.

Indonesian imports of urea have grown rapidly in recent years. Vessels loaded with bagged urea were berthed at Indonesian ports. The cargo was discharged using ship's gear or shore cranes. Initially, the cargo was warehoused at or near the wharf. Subsequently the bags were dispatched to their field storage location.

In an effort to reduce the costs of importing fertilizer, it was decided to consider importing bulk fertilizer and bagging the product in Indonesia. An estimate of the potential savings from undertaking bagging in Indonesia is shown in Exhibit 1. As shown in the exhibit, the landed cost differential between the bulk and the bagged product (that is, the difference between the cost of a ton of urea, packaged in 20 bags, landed on the wharf at Djakarta, and the cost of a ton of urea still in the bulk-carrier, alongside the wharf at Djakarta) was about $23 per metric ton. The cost of moving bulk urea through an Indonesian port appeared likely to be about one half the U.S. port cost. Most of this difference resulted from the higher labor costs for stevedoring at the U.S. ports. A further advantage of bagging the urea in Indonesia was that a large portion of the cost of bagging would become a local currency item rather than a foreign exchange cost. Moreover, employment, income and services would be generated at the Indonesian port.

Meeting the fertilizer need

Gulf management thought that certain criteria would have to be met in the design of the plant. Assuming that good, clean, dry urea was delivered on ship alongside the bagging operation, Gulf had to assure that the handling and bagging facilities met high standards. Discharging bulk urea from ocean-going vessels with open holds requires close supervision; synchronization of equipment discharge capacity with receiving, bagging, and storage capacity; precautionary measures against inclement weather; and properly designed equipment, including discharge, bagging, and storage facilities.

It was also considered important to avoid much division of responsibility among various port authority groups. It was considered that excessive work stoppages, loss of material, misunderstandings, lower rates of discharge and bagging, and general operating problems would be minimized if the entire unloading and bagging operation was run as a single entity. In view of these several considerations, Gulf approached the project not as merely a bagging plant but as a complete process aimed at performing all operations necessary to transform bulk urea in the hold of a ship into bagged urea ready for dispatch to the farmer. In addition, Indonesian farmers had become accustomed to an imported product. Gulf management thought that it was necessary that the bagging of urea in Indonesia produce a comparable product, with uniform, well sealed, clearly marked, and accurately weighed bags.

The logical location for the bagging operation appeared to be Tandjung Priok, the principal port of Djakarta. Land was acquired, including the old coal dump which already had a wharf, and a railroad siding. The plant was to be designed to have an average throughput of 300,000 metric tons per year. Demand was expected to be seasonal, however, with 75% of the consumption of fertilizer taking place before or during the wet season (i.e., December through March). Absolute maximum capacity of the contemplated plant would be, it was thought, 400,000 metric tons per year. Mr. Myers estimated that total investment in the bagging operation might amount to $2.5 million, depending on the method of production used.

The approach considered by Gulf was to operate the joint venture (hereafter referred to as PGIP) on a tolling basis; that is, customers would pay a service charge (excluding taxes, but including bags, bulk unloading, bagging, and loading out of bagged product via truck or rail) of $10.00 per metric ton. The venture would be entirely a service operation, with the fertilizer owned by either the fertilizer manufacturer or the customer.

Alternative production and handling methods

Bagging could be accomplished in a number of different ways. Plants had been built in Singapore, for example, using very little machinery. They depended primarily on large numbers of workers who would fill bags with shovels and weigh them on simple scales. In the United States, on the other hand, bagging operations were usually highly automated.

PGIP could choose methods at one of these extremes or it could take some middle route.

The general steps in the process

The activities to be considered could be broken down into five simple sequential steps:

1. Unloading the carrier vessel and movement of product to bulk storage.
2. Removal from bulk storage to the bagging operation.
3. Bagging.
4. Removal from the bagging operation to bagged storage.
5. Dispatch to the customer.

Within the first four steps there was a basic choice of using more labor-intensive or more capital-intensive methods. The process alternatives are described below and are also shown diagramatically in Exhibit 2.

The alternatives

1. Unloading. Bulk carrier vessels would be berthed at the wharf adjoining the plant site. The first step involved removing the fertilizer from the hold of the ship and placing it in a bulk storage area on the plant site. The fertilizer had to be protected from moisture and the important factors determining the choice of unloading method were: the speed of unloading; the relative cost of the alternative methods; the likely waste due to spillage; and the degree of protection from inclement weather. In order to avoid demurrage charges,[2] which ranged from $2,000 to $5,000 per day depending on the size of the vessel delayed, it was necessary to ensure that any method of unloading was capable of removing 3,000 metric tons per day from the ship to the bulk-storage area while the ship was alongside the wharf.

The basic choice faced by PGIP was between emptying the ship by an automatic device attached to a "marine leg," or by means of large buckets attached to the ship's gear. A marine leg is a device that permits the introduction of a probe or leg into each hold of a ship in turn. The leg may carry a bucket conveyor or a sucking head. The leg is mounted on a tower which, in turn, is mounted on tracks and can traverse up and down the wharf to provide access to each hold without moving the ship. It was estimated that a marine leg could be constructed at the PGIP wharf, complete with a suitable extraction device, associated conveyor and weigher system to move the fertilizer into the plant, for $150,000. It was planned to store the bulk fertilizer in heaps on the floor of the plant. Storage capacity would be 40,000 metric tons.

Round-the-clock operation of the marine leg conveyor would require four operators at a rate of Rp.100 per hour, one operator for each of the four shift groups necessary to maintain continuous, three-shift availability of labor, seven days per week. In addition, one hatch man on each shift would be required to supervise and guide the unloading head aboard the ship at a rate of Rp.75 per hour. As the marine leg emptied each hold, a crew of eight laborers on each shift would be required to clean out the hold, using shovels, brooms and a bucket attached to the ship's gear. The rate of pay for these laborers would be Rp.30 per hour. Mr. Myers estimated that maintenance and replacement costs for the marine leg would amount to $30,000 per year.

To achieve the required unloading rate, using the alternative method with the ship's gear, would require three automatic grabs at a total purchase and installation cost of $20,000. Each shift would use four winch drivers to operate the ship's gear at an hourly rate of Rp.75. In addition, a gang of 30 laborers at Rp.30 per hour would be needed to service each grab by trimming (i.e., shoveling the product to a position accessible to the grab) in the hold as the unloading operation proceeded. It was estimated that maintenance and replacement parts for the grabs would cost $10,000 per year.

2. Bulk storage and removal to bagging. The second step in the process was to move the fertilizer from the bulk storage area prior to bagging. Each bag had to be filled and sealed. If automatic methods of filling the bags were to be chosen, it would be necessary to provide a system of moving the bulk product from the storage area to some form of elevated hopper. If the

---

[2] Charges for having a vessel in port beyond a prearranged period of time.

bags were to be hand filled, there would be no necessity to elevate the bulk product. If automatic, or semiautomatic bagging methods were to be used, however, and the product had to be elevated, there was a choice among alternative methods of moving the fertilizer from bulk storage to hopper. First, a suitable conveyor would be required so that the product could be raised to the level of the hopper. The alternatives lay in the method of feeding the conveyor. Either the product was to be shoveled onto the conveyor by hand, or it was to be moved to the conveyor by mechanical means. It was estimated that the purchase and installation cost of a conveyor and hoppers would be $50,000 and that maintenance and other costs of operation would be $10,000 per year. If the conveyor was to be hand loaded a crew of 70 laborers would be required for each shift, at an hourly rate of Rp.30. If the product was to be moved by mechanical means, the most suitable machine appeared to be a front-end loader. Two front-end loaders could provide the necessary capacity. Each machine was estimated to cost about $12,000 delivered. A crew of two drivers per shift at an hourly rate of Rp.75 would operate the machines. It was estimated that the two loaders would cost about $12,000 per year in operating, maintenance, and replacement costs.

3. Bagging. Three basic alternatives could be considered: (*a*) a completely automatic bagging operation, (*b*) a completely hand-bagging operation, or (*c*) a partially automated method.

(*a*) *Fully automatic bagging.* In a fully automatic bagging unit, a polypropylene bag, complete with polyethylene liner would be attached by an operator to a conveyor. The bags would be attached by four small clips, the conveyor holding the bag and liner open sufficiently for the penetration of a filler head. The bags would move, suspended from the conveyor, under the filler head which would automatically meter 50 kgs. of product on the arrival of each bag. The bags would then move to a heat-sealing head which would fasten both liner and outer bag. The bag would be dropped onto a belt conveyor and would pass through a metallic detection device (to check for foreign matter in the fertilizer) and over an automatic weigher. Bags containing foreign matter or over/under weight would be automatically pushed off the conveyor for rebagging. Passed bags would be piled on pallets and left for removal. Two automatic lines operating continuously would be needed to maintain the required PGIP capacity of around 40 tons per hour. Two men at a rate of Rp.75 per hour would be required to operate each line for a shift. The cost of equipment for each line would be $150,000, installed. Operating, maintenance and replacement expenses were estimated at $60,000 per year for the two lines.

(*b*) *Hand bagging.* Gangs of laborers would transfer fertilizer from the storage heaps into hand-held bags, using shovels or small buckets. When the bag was approximately filled, it would be passed to a platform weigher and topped off to the correct weight by the addition of fertilizer; a small trowel or a shovel would be used. The liner would then be tied and the outer bag would be sewn by hand. A crew of 140 laborers on each shift would be required to provide the same bagging rate as the two automatic lines. The rate of pay would be Rp.30 per hour per worker.

(c) *Semiautomatic bagging.* As in the case of the automatic lines, the bagging line would be fed from hoppers. A polypropylene bag would be removed from a stack of new bags and snapped open. The opened bag and liner would be held to the filling spout of a semiautomatic weigher. The weigher would be activated by pulling a lever, upon which 50 kg. of product would drop into the held bag. The inner lining of the bag would be tied, using nylon twine. The bag would be visually inspected for damage and faulty tying of the liner. The outer bag would then be sewn, using an industrial sewing machine. The sewn bag would be dropped onto a pallet to await removal. The several positions in the bagging line would be connected by a roller conveyor.

Eight semiautomatic bagging lines would be required to provide the necessary capacity. Each line would be operated by a crew of six men on each shift, at a rate of Rp.30 per hour. The installed cost of equipment for each line would be $4,000. Operating and maintenance costs for the eight lines were estimated at $6,000 per year.

4. Bag storage. After removal from the bagging operation the bags would be stacked. Alternative methods of transporting the bags to the stacks could be considered. If the job was done by hand, a crew of 50 laborers per shift would be required, at Rp.30 per man-hour, to carry and stack the bags. Alternatively, five small fork-lift trucks, each requiring one driver, and a team of eight laborers could perform the same task. Each truck would cost $5,000 and would require about $2,500 in operating and maintenance costs. The driver's rate would be Rp.75 per hour. In order to use the fork-lift method it would be necessary to place the bags onto pallets. Storage space for the bagged product was limited to 12,000 metric tons.

5. Dispatch. No alternatives were considered in this area. The bags, it was decided, would be loaded to rail or road trucks by contract labor at a cost of approximately $0.10 per ton. This labor would be made available, on demand, by contractors in the port area.

Description of a "middle" technology

Exhibit 3 depicts a possible layout of the PGIP bagging plant using a middle form of technology, between the very labor-intensive and the fully automated extremes. The choices made in adopting this particular solution are indicated by the heavy line path through the decision diagram in Exhibit 2. A summary of the required labor force for this alternative is given in Exhibit 4.

1. Unloading. Ships, loaded with 8,000 to 15,000 tons of bulk urea, are berthed alongside the wharf. Fertilizer is extracted from the holds by means of the marine leg bucket conveyor. The marine leg traverses up and down the wharf, giving access to each hold. Removal of the residual fertilizer left by the conveyor, and cleaning of each hold of the vessel is carried out by laborers loading one-ton containers, which are hoisted to the conveyor by the ship's gear. While the cleaning of the hold is taking place, the marine leg is moved to a full hold to ensure maximum unloading rate.

The marine leg bucket conveyor transports the product to a roof-level conveyor system running to four bulk storage areas and to the bagging hopper.

PGIP is required to unload ships at the rate of at least 3,000 metric tons per 24-hour period. The normal operating speed of the marine leg is 200 tons per hour. For purposes of determining the accountability of product, shrinkage allowance, and processing charges, the shippers' weight of product is used as input tonnage. Intake weight is checked by an electronic Beltvayer automatic scale, incorporated in the conveyor.

2. Bulk storage. Four areas in the main building are used for the storage of bulk fertilizer. The total bulk storage capacity is 40,000 metric tons. PGIP must ensure that every shipment is stored separately. There is to be no co-mingling of products or shipments in the bulk storage areas. The fertilizer is simply dumped on the floor in separate piles by the conveyor system.

The fertilizer is transported from the bulk storage areas to the centrally located conveyor pit by front-end loaders. Two front-end loaders, each with one operator, work round the clock. The two machines would be capable of handling 100 tons per hour, and would provide sufficient excess capacity to cover the expected level of breakdowns. From the pit the fertilizer is carried by the conveyor to the bagging hoppers.

3. Bagging. The bagging weighers are fed from the hoppers. Fertilizer may be fed directly from the marine leg to the hoppers; however, the disparity between the unloading rate necessary to avoid demurrage and the bagging rate of 40 tons per hour means that most of the product must be stored in bulk form before bagging.

The bagging operation is carried out at eight "bagging lines." Each bagging line is a simple flow operation consisting of five operator positions. All positions are connected by dead roller conveyor sections. The activities at each bagging line, in order of their occurrence for each bag produced are:

(1) One man removes a polypropylene bag from a stack of new bags and tubes the bag by snapping it full of air. The bags have a polyethylene inner lining. He then takes the open bag and holds it to the filling spout of a semi-automatic weigher which deposits a predetermined amount (either 50 kg. or 25 kg.) of fertilizer into the bag. The automatic weigher is fed from the bagging hoppers.

(2) One man takes the filled bag and ties the top of the inner liner with nylon twine.

(3) One man inspects the filled bag and checks for apparent damage or faulty tying of the liner.

(4) One man sews the top of the outer bag with nylon twine using an industrial sewing machine.

(5) Two men remove the sewn bag from the roller conveyor and place it on a pallet.

4. Bag storage. The filled pallets containing 20 x 50 kg. or 40 x 25 kg. bags are transported to the bag storage area by fork-lift truck. Up to five fork-lift trucks, each operated by one driver, may be in use at any time.

Bags are removed from pallets in the storage area. Shortage of pallets prevents stacking of palletized bags. The bags are stacked 25 high in 8' x 8' stacks allowing 4 feet around the stack for access. The weight in each stack would be thus 20 metric tons. There is a total capacity for storing 12,000 metric tons of fertilizer in bagged form. Eight laborers per shift are occupied in removing bags from pallets to stacks.

5. Dispatch. Bags are loaded to rail cars or trucks by hand, using contract labor.

Exhibit 1

P. T. PERTAMINA—GULF INDUSTRIAL PROCESSING

ESTIMATED COMPARATIVE COSTS PER METRIC TON OF SHIPPING BULK AND BAGGED UREA FROM U.S. PORTS TO DJAKARTA*

	Vessel	
Gulf Ports	U.S. Flag ($/ton m.)	Foreign ($/ton m.)
Bagged		
1. Urea cost FAS (Free Alongside Ship)	$ 45.00	$45.00
2. Stevedoring and bagging, U.S. port	19.50	19.50
3. Freight cost	47.00	20.00
4. Stevedoring and handling, Djakarta	1.75	1.75
5. Landed cost	$113.25	$86.25
Bulk		
1. Urea cost FAS	$ 45.00	$45.00
2. Stevedoring and handling, U.S. port	2.00	2.00
3. Freight cost	44.00	17.00
4. Cost alongside wharf, Djakarta	$ 91.00	$64.00
Cost differential†	$ 22.25	$22.25
U.S. West Coast		
Bagged		
1. Urea cost FAS	$ 45.00	$45.00
2. Stevedoring and bagging, U.S. port	22.50	22.50
3. Freight cost	34.00	15.00
4. Stevedoring and handling, Djakarta	1.75	1.75
5. Landed cost	$103.25	$84.25
Bulk		
1. Urea cost FAS	$ 45.00	$45.00
2. Stevedoring and handling, U.S. port	3.00	3.00
3. Freight cost	32.00	13.00
4. Cost alongside wharf, Djakarta	$ 80.00	$61.00
Cost differential†	$ 23.25	$23.25

* Abstracted from "A Case Study of the Feasibility of Shipping Bulk Urea Fertilizer under Tropical Conditions," Tennessee Valley Authority.

† Cost differential represents the gross import substitution potential for local bagging. If the bulk urea can be landed, bagged, and prepared for dispatch for less than the cost differential, there is a potential saving in local bagging.

Exhibit 2

P. T. PERTAMINA—GULF INDUSTRIAL PROCESSING

DIAGRAM OF PRODUCTION PROCESS ALTERNATIVES

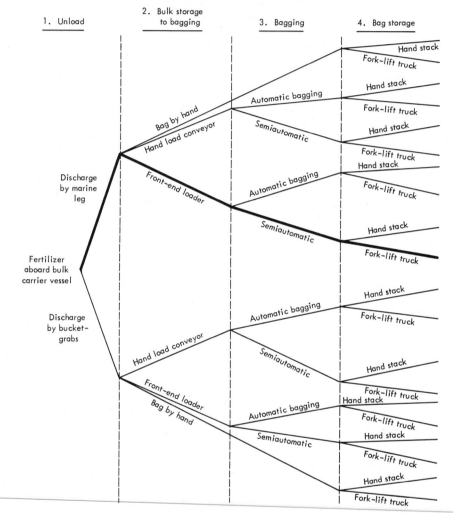

Exhibit 3

P. T. PERTAMINA—GULF INDUSTRIAL PROCESSING

DIAGRAM OF PGIP PLANT LAYOUT
FOR "MIDDLE" METHOD

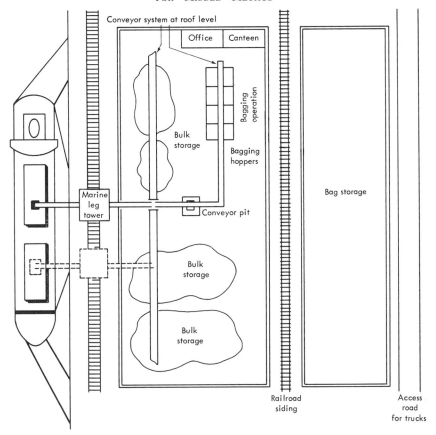

Exhibit 4

P. T. PERTAMINA—GULF INDUSTRIAL PROCESSING

SUMMARY OF PGIP WORKERS FOR 4-GROUP, 3-SHIFT OPERATION
(Middle technology alternative)

Task	Per Shift	Total
Maintenance mechanic*	1	4
Maintenance supervisor*	—	1
Marine leg operator	1	4
Hatch man	1	4
FE loader and FL truck operators	7	28
Bag filling	8	32
Liner fastening	8	32
Checkers on bag line	8	32
Sewing machine operator	8	32
Pallet loading	16	64
Pallet unloading	8	32
Sweepers	8	32
Tally clerks*	5	20
Security guards (1 chief)*	4	17
Works manager*		1
Plant operator (expert)*		1
		329

Direct workers = 285

* Overhead Personnel

MRC, INC. (A)

^^

In late March, 1961, Archibald Brinton, president of MRC, Inc., was grappling with the question of whether to acquire American Rayon, Inc. (ARI). Mr. Brinton was troubled by ARI's erratic earnings record and mediocre long-run outlook. However, he recognized that MRC could benefit greatly from ARI's liquidity and borrowing capacity. He was therefore inclined to go through with the acquisition, provided ARI could be purchased at a price that promised to yield MRC an adequate return on its money.

BACKGROUND INFORMATION ON MRC

MRC was a Cleveland based manufacturing concern with 1960 earnings of $3.9 million on sales of over $118 million. The most important product lines were power brake systems for trucks, buses, and automobiles; industrial furnaces and heat treating equipment; and automobile, truck, and bus frames. Exhibit 1 presents data on the operating results and financial position of MRC.

Diversification program

Upon becoming chief executive officer in 1957, Mr. Brinton had initiated an active program of diversification by acquisition. The need for rapid diversification seemed compelling. Until 1957, virtually all sales were made to less than a dozen large companies in the automotive industry, with car and truck frames accounting for 85% of the $70 million sales total. As a result, earnings, cash flow, and growth were constantly exposed to the risks inherent in selling to a few customers, all of which operated in a highly cyclical and competitive market. Previous attempts at internal diversification had floundered on management's lack of expertise in markets and technologies outside the automotive area. Mr. Brinton had therefore turned to acquisitions as a means of buying up established sales and earnings as well as managerial and technical knowhow. In Mr. Brinton's words, the acquisition strategy was "intended (1) to achieve related diversification and thus lessen vulnerability to technological change in a single industry; (2) to stabilize earnings and cash flow; (3) to uncouple growth prospects from the cyclical and unexciting automotive industry; and (4) to escape the constant threat of backward integration by one or more major customers." The drive for diversification had been intensified in 1959 when Chrysler announced a move toward unitized, i.e., "frameless" body construction.

By the end of 1960, the diversification campaign had resulted in the completion of five acquisitions, two of which were major transactions. Acquisition of Ross Engineering Corporation increased MRC sales by $27 million in 1957, and the purchase of Surface Combustion Corporation in 1959 added about $38 million to annual sales. The acquisition history of MRC is shown in Exhibit 2. Significantly, total sales increased almost $50 million between 1956 and 1960, despite a $30 million decline in automotive sales over that period.

Management structure

While the diversification program had reduced MRC's dependence on any one industry, it had also created significant strains on the company's organization structure and financial position.

As the acquisition program carried MRC into a widening variety of markets and technologies, it had become increasingly apparent that the company's highly centralized decision making processes were ill suited to the needs of a diversified corporation. By the end of 1959, it was clear the headquarters management group could not acquire or maintain detailed knowledge of all the products, markets and technologies embraced by MRC. Since continued rapid diversification was considered imperative, the company had shifted to a highly decentralized management structure, which transferred substantial decision making power to division managers.

In 1961, there were seven divisions. All marketing, purchasing, manufacturing, research and development, personnel matters, and accounting were handled at the division level. Each division had its own general manager (usually a vice president), who reported directly to Mr. Brinton and had the primary responsibility for the growth and profitability of his division. A division manager could get stock options and earn an annual bonus of up to 60% of his base salary, depending on the earnings and growth of his division. Divisional sales and earnings goals were formalized in an annual budget and in a rolling five-year plan, which were formulated by each general manager and submitted each November to the head office for review by Mr. Brinton and the corporate staff.

The corporate staff provided legal, administrative, and financial support to the divisions and handled external affairs, financing, and acquisitions as well. The staff, including corporate officers, numbered less than 60 people about half of whom would be classified as secretarial and clerical.

Mr. Brinton felt that he could exercise adequate control over the decentralized organization through his power to hire and fire at the division manager level and, more importantly, through control of the elaborate capital budgeting system. Appendix A discusses MRC's capital budgeting procedures.

No acquisitions were made in 1960. But by 1961, Mr. Brinton was confident that the organization was capable of smoothly assimilating new operations, and his staff had identified and opened preliminary discussions with a number of attractive acquisition prospects. However, the financial problems brought on by the strain of financing past acquisitions had become pressing.

Finances

The acquisition campaign had been hampered from the outset by MRC's low price-earnings (P/E) multiple. Although growth was an explicit objective of the acquisition program, MRC could not exchange its shares for those of high P/E, growth companies without absorbing a stiff dilution in per share earnings. It was feared that such dilution of earnings per share would further depress the P/E ratio and thus make it still more difficult to swap stock with growth companies. Consequently, MRC had been forced to rely heavily on debt financing for most of its acquisitions.

By early 1961, MRC had largely exhausted its borrowing capacity. Between 1956 and 1960, long-term debt had risen from less than $4 million to more than $22 million. Although it appeared that capital expenditures planned for 1961 could be funded with internally generated funds, the near exhaustion of debt capacity posed a serious threat to the acquisition strategy. Discussions with commercial banks, life insurance companies, and investment bankers had made it clear that any further increases in long-term debt, without a substantial infusion of new equity, would be extremely difficult, and probably impossible. Investment bankers had further pointed out that long-term lenders would probably insist on severely restricting the company's flexibility to make cash acquisitions, even if it should prove feasible to raise new debt. With MRC near its debt limit and the P/E ratio around 10 times, the entire diversification campaign was in danger of collapsing.

ARI, with its $20 million of marketable securities, appeared to provide a convenient new source of funds with which to fuel the acquisition program.

BACKGROUND INFORMATION ON ARI

American Rayon, Inc., a Philadelphia based corporation, was the third largest producer of rayon in the United States.[1] In 1960, ARI had recorded sales of $55 million and a pretax profit of $5 million, after three years of severe profit problems (see Exhibits 3 and 4). By early 1961 the company's stock was trading at less than half of book value on the New York Stock Exchange and top management feared that the company's new-found profitability, along with its great liquidity and a disenchanted shareholder group, would make ARI attractive to raiders. Consequently, management was seeking to arrange a marriage with a congenial partner. ARI's investment banker had brought the company to the attention of Mr. Brinton, who had expressed tentative interest in a deal.

---

[1] Rayon is a glossy fiber made by forcing a viscous solution of modified cellulose (wood pulp) through minute holes and drying the resulting filaments.

Acquisition investigation

The results of MRC's investigation were mixed. On the plus side, ARI had over $20 million in liquid assets that were not needed for operations, no short or long-term debt, and a modern central manufacturing facility. It appeared that the company could be purchased for about $40 million worth of MRC common stock. Moreover, although ARI top management was elderly, James Clinton, the 64-year-old president, was willing to stay on for two years after the acquisition to give MRC personnel a chance to learn the business before his retirement.

On the other hand, the longer-term outlook for the rayon industry was grim. The rayon industry had enjoyed one of the most spectacular successes in the history of American enterprise. For example, the American Viscose Corporation, which founded the industry in 1910, achieved in its first 24 years aggregate net earnings of $354,000,000 or 38,000% of original investment, while financing rapid expansion entirely out of earnings.[2] But rayon began to falter in the early 1950's as competing synthetics such as nylon and acrylic became popular. Style and fashion shifts also made cotton more attractive. The net effect was to force production cutbacks in rayon, and by the end of the 1950's many companies, including Du Pont, had withdrawn from the rayon industry altogether.

With shrinking industry volume, ARI had experienced increasing earnings difficulties. These difficulties could be traced directly to the declining use of rayon in automobile tire cord, the market accounting for upwards of 60% of ARI's output. First tried in tire construction in 1940, the use of rayon in tire manufacture reached an annual peak around 1955.[3] With the advent of nylon cord, however, rayon's market share in tire cord began to decline. Between 1955 and 1960, rayon's share of the total tire cord market dropped from 86% to 64%, and the total poundage of rayon so used dropped 38% (see Exhibit 5).

Prospects for ARI

It was clear to MRC management that the medium to long-run future must hold continuing decline and eventual liquidation for ARI. If purchased, ARI could not be expected to contribute to the MRC growth objectives, and in time it might well become a serious drag on earnings. Consequently, Mr. Brinton was somewhat leery of pushing through to an acquisition. He was not at all sure that ARI, trapped in a decaying industry, would contribute to the strategic objectives of the diversification program. He was afraid that MRC would get entangled in a dying business, and he knew that MRC management lacked the technical know-how to contribute to the profitability of ARI, should Mr.

---

[2] Jesse W. Markham, *Competition in the Rayon Industry* (Cambridge, Mass.: Harvard University Press, 1952), p. 16.

[3] C. A. Litzler, "The Fluid Tire Cord Situation," *Modern Textiles Magazine*, September 1966, p. 20.

Victor's forecasts prove optimistic. Moreover, he was not at all sure that the recently overhauled organization structure could easily assimilate a company as large as ARI. In the face of these concerns, he was reluctant to move quickly, whatever the DCF-ROI (discounted cash flow-return on investment) numbers might show.

However, the near-term picture, as presented by Richard Victor, vice president for mergers and acquisitions, was not entirely unappealing. Although losses were sustained in 1957 and 1958 the company had subsequently returned to profitability as a result of substantial reductions in overhead, sale or liquidation of marginal and unprofitable operations, streamlining the marketing and R&D organizations, and consolidating production in a new manufacturing facility. Based on the investigation and analysis of his staff, he estimated that ARI would be able to maintain current volume, prices and margins through 1964, followed thereafter by annual sales declines of 10% to 15%. He also estimated that assumption of numerous staff responsibilities by the MRC corporate staff would add about one percentage point to ARI's before tax profit margin. Exhibit 6 shows pro forma income statements for ARI prepared by the MRC acquisition team.

From a financing point of view, it was thought that capital spending needs over the next six to eight years would average no more than $300,000 annually. Mr. Victor felt that, if anything, his estimates understated future profits, since he expected ARI to pick up market share as smaller companies continued to withdraw from the rayon industry.

VALUATION

At a price of $40 million, ARI looked cheap. But Mr. Brinton insisted that any acquisition undertaken by MRC must promise to yield an adequate return, as measured by its discounted cash flow rate of return (DCF-ROI).[4] Mr. Brinton regarded an acquisition decision as a special case of the capital budgeting decision. Like a capital budgeting project, an acquisition required the commitment of economic resources, cash or common stock or debt capacity, in the expectation of realizing a future income stream. Consequently, the primary valuation procedure used in acquisitions was conceptually identical to the capital budgeting procedure (see Appendix A). All outlays and all cash inflows that were expected to result from undertaking a particular transaction were projected, and the DCF-ROI was found. In terms of required rates of return, acquisitions were considered to be very similar to new product introductions.

Exhibit 7 shows management's forecast of MRC's per share income for the next three years.

MRC's common stock had closed the day before at 14½. ARI had closed at 15.

---

[4] This measure of effectiveness is also commonly known as the internal rate of return, the time adjusted rate of return, and the yield.

Exhibit 1

MRC, INC. (A)

FOUR-YEAR SUMMARY OF FINANCIAL DATA

(Dollar figures in millions except per share data)

	1957	1958	1959	1960
Results of Operations				
Sales:				
Automotive and transportation	$ 76.4	$49.7	$56.8	$ 41.3
Capital goods	30.0	26.0	27.5	54.3
Building and construction	—	—	2.7	14.2
Aerospace and defense	0.9	0.7	1.8	8.3
Total	$107.3	$76.4	$88.8	$118.1
Net earnings	5.5	3.0	4.0	3.9
Depreciation and amortization	1.4	1.5	1.7	2.3
Cash funds from operations*	6.2	3.8	4.9	5.5
Return on total capital	12.6%	8.1%	7.8%	9.3%
Return on common equity	18.4%	8.9%	14.3%	13.2%
Common Stock				
Net earnings per share†	$ 1.73	$ 0.82	$ 1.18	$ 1.16
Common dividends per share	0.94	0.79	0.75	0.75
Market price	13–8	10–8	15–9	13–9
Average price-earnings ratio	6.5	12.1	10.3	9.5
Average dividend yield	8.4%	7.9%	6.2%	6.8%
Financial Position				
Working capital	$ 26.9	$22.5	$28.7	$ 31.3
Net property, plant, and equipment	15.6	16.0	23.1	28.4
Long-term debt	4.3	9.6	16.5	22.7
Preferred and common shareholders' equity	39.6	39.5	40.5	41.6

* Net earnings plus depreciation, amortization, and deferred taxes, less preferred dividends.
† Calculated on average number of shares outstanding during the year.

Exhibit 2

MRC, INC. (A)

ACQUISITION HISTORY OF MRC, INC.

December, 1957........ Acquired J. O. Ross Engineering Corporation in exchange for 281,000 shares.

March, 1958......... Acquired Hartig Engine and Machine Company, Mountainside, New Jersey, for cash and notes.

October, 1958........ Acquired Transportation Division of Consolidated Metal Products Corporation, Albany, New York, and moved operations to Owosso, Michigan, Division.

April, 1959.......... Acquired Nelson Metal Products Company, Grand Rapids, Michigan, for cash.

November, 1959....... Acquired Surface Combustion Corporation, Toledo, Ohio, for $23 million cash.

Exhibit 3

MRC, INC. (A)

FIVE-YEAR SUMMARY OF FINANCIAL DATA ON AMERICAN RAYON, INC.

(Dollar figures in millions except per share data)

	1956	1957	1958	1959	1960
Results of Operations					
Net sales............................	$59.3	$58.1	$47.9	$62.1	$54.5
Earnings before taxes.................	9.4	(2.3)	(6.2)	1.7	4.8
Pretax profit margin..................	15.9%	—	—	2.7%	8.8%
Net earnings........................	$ 4.5	$(1.2)	$(3.2)	$ 0.8	$ 2.5
Depreciation and amortization.........	3.9	4.0	4.1	4.3	3.3
Cash funds from operations............	8.4	2.8	0.9	5.1	5.8
Return on total capital...............	5.3%	—	—	1.0%	3.4%
Return on common equity.............	5.9%	—	—	1.1%	3.8%
Common Stock					
Net earnings per share*...............	$ 2.45	$(0.65)	$(1.69)	$ 0.44	$ 1.34
Common dividend per share*..........	3.00	1.75	—	—	—
Book value per share*................	39.68	39.05	37.37	37.79	36.42
Market price........................	48–37	24–11	14–6	13–8	19–9
Average price-earnings ratio...........	17	—	—	23.9	10.4
Financial Position					
Working capital.....................	$39.1	$38.8	$36.6	$37.9	$41.2
Net property, plant, and equipment. ..	36.6	34.1	34.2	33.8	23.9
Long-term debt......................	—	—	—	—	—
Common shareholders' equity.........	75.4	74.2	71.0	71.8	65.2

* Based on 1,851,255 common shares outstanding.

Exhibit 4

MRC, INC. (A)

BALANCE SHEET OF AMERICAN RAYON, INC.
AS OF DECEMBER 31, 1960

(In thousands)

ASSETS

Cash.	$ 2,564
U.S. Government securities*.	20,024
Accounts receivable, net.	11,863
Inventories:	
Finished goods.	4,376
In process.	2,161
Raw materials and supplies.	3,919
	$10,456
Prepaid expenses.	283
Current assets.	$45,190
Property, plant, and equipment, net.	23,912
Other.	125
Total assets.	$69,227

LIABILITIES AND SHAREHOLDERS' EQUITY

Accounts payable.	$ 2,863
Accrued items.	1,145
Current liabilities	$ 4,008
Common stock.	26,959
Retained earnings.	38,260
Shareholders' equity.	$65,219
Total liabilities and shareholders' equity.	$69,227

* Carried at cost plus accrued interest which approximates market.

Exhibit 5

MRC, INC. (A)

CONSUMPTION OF TIRE CORD

(In millions)

	Rayon		Nylon		Cotton		Total
Year	Pounds	Market Share	Pounds	Market Share	Pounds	Market Share	Pounds
1947.	214.6	43%	n.a.	—	285.1	57%	499.7
1950.	297.0	64	n.a.	—	165.4	36	462.4
1955.	406.9	86	49.2	10%	16.7	4	472.8
1956.	343.0	83	58.6	14	10.6	3	412.2
1957.	318.5	77	83.2	20	10.3	3	412.0
1958.	253.0	71	97.9	27	7.1	2	358.0
1959.	287.1	70	120.3	29	3.9	1	411.2
1960.	251.3	64	138.1	35	3.1	1	392.5

Sources: 1947–55: U.S. Bureau of the Census, *Statistical Abstract of the United States–1967* (Washington, D.C.: U.S. Government Printing Office), p. 761; 1956–60: American Rayon, Inc., Proxy Statement, March 28, 1961, p. 6.

Exhibit 6

MRC, INC. (A)

PRO FORMA INCOME STATEMENTS OF AMERICAN RAYON, INC.

(In thousands)

Year Ended	1961	1962	1963	1964	1965	1966	1967
Net sales..................	$55,000	$55,000	$55,000	$52,000	$48,000	$42,600	$40,070
Earnings before taxes........	4,840	5,390	5,390	3,640	2,724	1,917	841
Federal income taxes........	2,323	2,587	2,587	1,747	1,308	920	404
Net earnings...............	2,517	2,803	2,803	1,893	1,416	997	437
Depreciation...............	3,000	3,000	3,000	3,000	3,000	3,000	3,000
Cash funds from operations...	5,517	5,803	5,803	4,893	4,416	3,997	3,437

Exhibit 7

MRC, INC. (A)

THREE-YEAR FORECAST OF MRC EARNINGS

Year Ended	1961	1962	1963
Net earnings*..............	$4,723,000	$5,054,000	$5,458,000
Earnings per share†.........	$ 1.46	$ 1.59	$ 1.74

* Assumes funding for all projects tentatively approved in 1961 capital budget, but no new acquisitions.
† Based on 2,706,896 common shares outstanding and preferred dividends of $760,000.

APPENDIX A

MRC, INC. (A)

CAPITAL BUDGETING PROCEDURES OF MRC, INC.

The formal capital budgeting procedures of MRC were outlined in a 49-page manual written for use at the divisional level and entitled "Expenditure Control Procedures." This document outlined (1) the classification scheme for types of funds requests, (2) the minimum levels of expenditure for which formal requests were required, (3) the maximum expenditure which could be authorized on the signature of corporate officers at various levels, (4) the format of the financial analysis required in a request for funds to carry out a project, and finally (5) the format of the report which followed the completion of the project and evaluated its success in terms of the original financial analysis outlined in (4).

Classification scheme for funds requests

The manual defined two basic classes of projects: profit improvement and necessity. Profit improvement projects included:

a) Cost reduction projects.
b) Capacity expansion projects in existing product lines.
c) New product line introductions.

Necessity projects included:

All projects where profit improvement was not the basic purpose of the project, such as those for service facilities, plant security, improved working conditions, employee relations and welfare, pollution and contamination prevention, extensive repairs and replacements, profit maintenance, and services of outside research and consultant agencies. Expense projects of an unusual or extraordinary character included in this class were those expenses which did not lend themselves to inclusion in the operating budget and could normally be expected to occur less than once per year.

Minimum amounts subject to formal request

Not all divisional requests for funds required formal and specific economic justification. Obviously, normal operating expenditures for items such as raw materials and wages were managed completely at the level of the divisions. Capital expenditures and certain nonrecurring operating expenditures were subject to formal requests and specific economic justification if they exceeded certain minimum amount levels specified below.

Project Appropriation Requests were to be issued as follows:

1. Capital:

Projects with a unit cost equal to or more than the unit cost in the following schedule shall be covered by a Project Appropriation Request; items with lesser unit costs shall be expensed.

Land improvements and buildings	$1,000
Machinery and equipment	500
Tools, patterns, dies, and jigs	250
Office furniture and office machines	100

2. Expense:

Expenses of an unusual or extraordinary character which do not lend themselves to inclusion in the operating budget and could normally be expected to occur less than once per year shall be covered by a Project Appropriation Request.

The minimum amount at which a Project Appropriation Request for expense is required is $10,000.

Approval limits of corporate officers

Officers at various management levels within MRC had the authority to approve a division's formal request for funds to carry out a project subject to the maximum limitations shown below.

Approvals. Requests shall be processed from a lower approval level to a higher approval level in accordance with the chart below to secure the approving authorities' initials (and date approved) signifying approval. Lower approvals shall be completed in advance of submission to a higher level.

Expense projects:
Minimum up to $10,000................... Division manager
$10,000 up to $50,000..................... Corporate president
$50,000 and over......................... Board of directors

Capital projects:
Minimum up to $5,000................... Division manager
$5,000 up to $50,000..................... Corporate president
$50,000 and over......................... Board of directors

Expense and capital combinations:
    Required approvals shall be the higher approval level required for
either the capital or expense section in accordance with the above
limits.

Project Appropriation Request

The formal financial analysis required in a request for funds was called a
Project Appropriation Request (PAR). The format of a PAR is shown in
Exhibit A–1. The key output factors in the analysis (which included the
amount of the total appropriation, the discounted cash flow rate of return on
the investment, and the payback period) were summarized on the opening
page under "Financial Summary" for easy reference.

The PAR originated at the divisional level and circulated to the officers
whose signatures were necessary to authorize the expenditure. If the project
was large enough to require the approval of an officer higher than the division
manager, then five other men in the corporate financial group also reviewed
the proposal. This group included the controller, the tax manager, the director
of financial planning, the treasurer, and the vice president of finance. These
men did not review very small projects, however, since capital items under
$5000 never reached the corporate office. Division managers could authorize
these small projects on their own signature.

Project Evaluation Report

On each PAR, the corporate controller had the option of indicating whether
or not he desired a Project Evaluation Report (PER). When requested, the
division manager submitted this report one year after the approved project
was completed. The report indicated how well the project was performing in
relation to its original cost, return on investment (ROI), and payback
estimates.

The stream of PARs reaching the corporate office

During 1960, MRC approved 70 PARs calling for the expenditure of more
than $17 million.

A sample evaluation made in 1961 of some of the projects which the board
of directors had approved in earlier years is reproduced as Exhibit A–2.

Scrutinizing a PAR at the presidential level

In discussing capital budgeting at MRC, Mr. Brinton stated that the largest projects, involving more than a million dollars, were almost always discussed informally between the president and the division manager at least a year before a formal PAR was submitted. He said:

Let's look at a project involving a facilities expansion. The need for a new plant addition in most of our business areas doesn't sneak up on you. It can be foreseen at least a couple of years in advance. An enormous amount of work is involved in submitting a detailed economic proposal for something like a new plant. Architects have to draft plans, proposed sites have to be outlined, and construction lead times need to be established. No division manager would submit a complete request for a new facilities addition without first getting an informal green light that such a proposal could receive favorable attention. By the time a formal PAR is completed on a large plant addition, most of us are pretty well sold on the project.

In response to the question, "What are the most significant items that you look at when a new PAR lands on your desk?" Mr. Brinton responded as follows:

The size of the project is probably the first thing that I look at. Obviously, I won't spend much time on a $15,000 request for a new fork-lift truck from a division manager with an annual sales volume of $50 million.

I'd next look at the type of project we're dealing with to get a feel for the degree of certainty in the rate of return calculation. I feel a whole lot more comfortable with a cost reduction project promising a 20% return than I would with a volume expansion project which promises the same rate of return. Cost reduction is usually an engineering problem. You know exactly how much a new machine will cost and you can be fairly certain about how many man-hours will be saved. On a volume expansion you're betting on a marketing estimate and maybe the date for getting a plant on stream. These are fairly uncertain variables.

On a new product appropriation, things get even worse. Here you're betting on both price and volume estimates, and supporting data can get awfully thin. Over all, I think our cost reduction projects have probably yielded higher returns and have been less risky than either plant expansion or new product proposals. They don't, of course, eat up anything like the amount of capital that the other two types of projects can require.

The third and perhaps most important item that I look for is the name of the division manager who sent the project up. We've got men at the top and at the bottom of the class just like any organization. If I get a project from a man who has been with the company for a few years, who has turned a division around, or shown that he has a better command of his business than anyone else in his industry, then I'll usually go with his judgment. If his business is going to pot, however, I may take a long hard look, challenge a lot of the assumptions, and ask for more justification.

Fourth, I look at the ROI figure. If the project is a large one, I have the finance people massage the numbers to see what happens to the ROI if some of the critical variables like volume, prices, and costs are varied. This is an area where knowing your division manager is enormously important. Some men, particularly those with a sales background, may be very optimistic on volume projections. In this kind of situation you feel more comfortable if you can knock the volume down 25% and still see a reasonable return.

I haven't established formal and inviolable hurdle rates which each and every project must clear. I want to avoid giving the division people an incentive to stretch their estimates on marginal projects or, alternatively, to build in fat cushions—insurance policies—on great projects. Still, I generally look for a minimum DCF-ROI of about 12% on cost reduction proposals, 15% to 16% on large volume expansion projects and 18% to 20% or even more on new product introductions. But these aren't magic numbers. Projects showing lower yields are sometimes accepted.

Strategic capital investments

Mr. Brinton later commented on a question regarding the role of capital budgeting in overall corporate strategy.

In general we'll invest our capital in those business areas that promise the highest return. Usually you can't afford to establish a position in a market on just the hope that a return will materialize in the future. Du Pont can afford to invest $75 million in a new fiber, but MRC can't. We can afford to invest a few million dollars in projects of this nature—and we have in areas like continuous casting and iron ore pelletizing—but most of our projects have to promise a prompt return.

Exhibit A–1

MRC, INC. (A)

PROJECT APPROPRIATION REQUEST

NUMBER–SUPPLEMENT

Division Power Controls			Department		Location	

Title Disc Brake Manufacturing Facility							

Profit Improvement X	Necessity	Predicted Life 15 Years	Underrun	Overrun	Starting Date July 1961	Completion Date April 1963

1. DESCRIPTION AND JUSTIFICATION

The U.S. automotive industry is experiencing a trend to the use of disc braking systems for passenger cars and light trucks. Our market research indicates this type of braking system will be widespread within 5 years and the Power Controls Division can be a major supplier of these systems if we act now to provide the required manufacturing facilities.

2. FINANCIAL SUMMARY

	This Request	Previous Approved Requests	Total Project	Approval and Distribution of Copies					
				Division	Date	No.	Corporate	Date	No.
Capital	4,875,000	_____	4,875,000	Issued By			Group V.P.		
Working Capital	1,950,000		1,950,000				Group V.P.		
Expense	975,000		975,000						
Total	7,800,000		7,800,000				Controller		
Less Salvage Value of Disposals							Tax Manager		
Net							Mgr. Fin. Planning		
Book Value of Disposals							Treasurer		
Project Budgeted Amount			7,800,000				Financial V.P.		
Return on Investment (after Tax)			16%	Division Controller			President		
Period to Amortize (after Tax)			3.6 Years	Division Manager			For the Board		
Accounting Distribution				Project Evaluation Report Required	Yes	No			

Estimated Timing of Expenditures – By Quarter and Year							
3/61	4/61	1/62	2/62	3/62	4/62	1/63	2/63
$ 75,000	$125,000	$1,125,000	$1,500,000	$1,500,000	$1,875,000	$ 900,000	$ 700,000

Exhibit A-1—Continued

PRESENT VALUE OF CASH FLOWS

YEAR	YEAR OF OPER-ATION	DISBURSEMENTS	CASH RETURNS	15% TRIAL INTEREST RATE Factor	PRESENT WORTH Disbursements	Cash Returns	16% TRIAL INTEREST RATE Factor	PRESENT WORTH Disbursements	Cash Returns	% TRIAL INTEREST RATE Factor	PRESENT WORTH Disbursements	Cash Returns
1961	2 Prior	200					1.346	269				
1962	1 Prior	6,000	218				1.160	6,960	253			
						Beginning of Operations						
1963	At 1	1,600	468	1.000	xxxxxxxxxxx	xxxxxxxxxxx	1.000	1,132	xxxxxxxxxxx	1.000		xxxxxxxxxxx
1963	1		641		xxxxxxxxxxx		.862	xxxxxxxxxxx	553		xxxxxxxxxxx	
	2		1,792				.743		1,331			
	3		1,686				.641		1,081			
	4		1,601				.552		884			
	5		1,523				.476		725			
	6		1,473				.410		604			
	7		1,443				.354		511			
	8		1,439				.305		439			
	9		1,434				.263		377			
	10		1,337				.227		325			
	11		1,241				.195		261			
	12		1,241				.168		208			
	13		1,241				.145		180			
	14		1,400				.125		155			
	15		1,950				.108		151			
	15 Return Work Cap.						.108		210			
	15 Residual Plant	885					.108		96			
	18											
	19											
	20											
	21											
	22											
	23											
	24											
	25											
	26											
	27											
	28											
	29											
	30											
TOTALS		7,800	24,445					8,361	8,344			
CASH RETURNS LESS DISBURSEMENTS		xxxxxxxxxxx	xxxxxxxxxxx		xxxxxxxxxxx			xxxxxxxxxxx	(17)		xxxxxxxxxxx	
DISBURSEMENTS CASH RETURNS		xxxxxxxxxxx			xxxxxxxxxxx			xxxxxxxxxxx	1.0		xxxxxxxxxxx	

Exhibit A–2

MRC, INC. (A)

SUMMARY OF SELECTED PROJECT EVALUATION REPORTS, AUGUST, 1960

(Dollar figures in thousands)

Project Number	Description	Date Approved	Project Amount		Rate of Return		Payback Period (Years)	
			Forecast	Actual	Forecast	Actual	Forecast	Actual
FA-157	Roll Forming Mill	1/58	$193	$193	37%	42%	2.5	2.3
FA-151	Univ. Paint Mach. Unloader	7/59	98	43	>30	>30	2.6	1.6
FA-147	Loading Equip. '65 Buick	7/57	80	79	29	29	3.1	3.3
P 352–51	"V" Band Couplings Program	8/59	58	90	>30	Loss	0.7	Loss
P 328–29	New Gas Furnace Line	6/56	495	491	>50	43 est.	1.0	1.7 est.
P-532	Aluminum Die Cast Equipment	5/59	86	86	>30	>30	2.2	2.0
P-547	(2) W-S #1 AC Chuckers	7/59	66	66	>30	>30	2.0	1.4
64-129C	(2) W-S Chuckers	12/58	116	114	12	Loss	5.5	Loss

MRC, INC. (B)

∧∧∧

In mid-1966, top management of MRC, Inc. was considering a $30,500,000 capital budget proposal which would carry one of the company's divisions into the production of polyester fiber. Through its ARI division, the company was already heavily involved in the production of rayon fiber for tire cord, but this market was rapidly shrinking because of competitive inroads made by both nylon and polyester. An entry into polyester fiber, then, might allow MRC to preserve its market position in tire cord, and also move the company into the production of polyester fiber for other end uses.

BACKGROUND INFORMATION ON MRC, INC.

In 1966, sales of the 13 divisions of MRC were running at an annual rate of $340 million. No single division accounted for as much as 20% of total sales, but the largest five divisions contributed 70% of the total. The product lines of the various MRC divisions are shown in Exhibit 1.

The most important product lines in terms of sales were: (1) industrial furnaces and heat treating equipment; (2) parts used in the manufacture of railroad rolling stock and other foundry products; (3) rayon fiber for automobile tire cord and apparel fabrics; (4) auto, truck, and bus frames; and (5) power brake systems for autos, trucks, and buses.

Diversification through acquisition

Between 1961 and 1965, MRC had nearly tripled sales and earnings. (See Exhibit 2 for financial data for 1961–66.) During this period the company had an active program of diversification by acquisition and concluded acquisitions at an average rate of one new company per year. Exhibit 3 shows the acquisition history of MRC. Five of these transactions were major. Ross Engineering increased MRC sales in 1957 by $27 million. The purchase of Surface Combustion in 1959 added about $38 million to annual sales. In 1961, American Rayon boosted the company's growing sales volume by about $55 million. And the acquisition of Steel City Electric and National Castings in 1963 and 1965 added about $16 million and $73 million, respectively, to annual sales.

347

For background information on the diversification program and the resultant decentralization of the management structure see MRC, Inc. (A).

BACKGROUND INFORMATION ON AMERICAN RAYON, INC.

In the spring of 1961, MRC had merged with American Rayon, Inc. (ARI) by an exchange of common stock. Almost all of ARI's sales consisted of rayon fiber, and more than 60% of these sales consisted of rayon tire cord for use in the production of automobile tires. At the time of the merger, ARI was the third largest U.S. producer of rayon and the future of this fiber was extremely uncertain. See the (A) case for background on this transaction and on the outlook for the rayon industry.

Efforts to diversify ARI

Over the period 1961–66, ARI performed profitably, although not satisfactorily in the later years, as shown below:

Year	Sales Index of ARI Fibers Division	Pretax Profit as a % of Sales
1961	100	6%
1962	100	8
1963	112	10
1964	115	9
1965	118	7
1966	124	4

The aggregate use of rayon in tire cord continued to decline during this period, and efforts were undertaken to reduce the division's dependence on the tire cord market. In 1964, after retirement of the original division manager, MRC invested $8 million in a facility to produce high-wet modulus rayon staple fiber, which was used principally in wearing apparel.[1] At the time this project was proposed by the new division manager, the selling price of the fiber was between 44 and 45 cents a pound. ARI management had felt that the price would decline to about 36 cents a pound within five years and stabilize there. At this reduced price level, the plant addition promised a five-year payback and a healthy DCF–ROI.

According to Archibald Brinton, president of MRC:

ARI had process problems during the first year after the facility opened. These problems cut heavily into the division's profits. We also had some problem in getting the textile manufacturers to switch to our fiber. The textile people won't switch to the fiber of a new manufacturer until it's been thoroughly tested and evaluated. This testing is a costly and time-consuming process.

By the beginning of the second year after the plant was completed, the selling price of high-wet modulus rayon was down to 26 cents a pound.

---

[1] Staple fiber is "short length" fiber (approximately 1 to 1½ inches) such as is found in cotton bolls.

Man-made fiber manufacture is a continuous process production operation. You run the plants 24 hours a day, 7 days a week. The production costs are such that you have to run at close to capacity to make any profit. If you cut back production very far, you might as well shut down entirely. We had a choice. If you cut production, your unit costs skyrocket; if you keep producing, your inventories skyrocket. With us it was a question of whether we might be better off shutting the plant down completely until prices firmed. We finally decided to keep it running, and made staple fiber until it was coming out of our ears. Prices are firming now, but although we've had three price rises in the last nine months, they are still not up to 36 cents a pound.

In 1966, ARI was still heavily dependent on rayon tire cord as the principal source of its business. During 1965, total industry production of rayon tire cord amounted to 210 million pounds. This production was split about equally by ARI—25%; American Viscose Corporation Division of FMC—30%; Beaunit Corporation—23%; and American Enka Corporation—23%.

Threats to the tire cord market

By 1966, the only real market remaining for rayon tire cord was the original equipment tire market.[2] Of the 210 million pounds of rayon tire cord used for all classes of tires in 1965, about 150 million pounds went into the 50 million passenger car tires required by the original equipment manufacturers (OEMs). The OEMs had purchased rayon cord tires almost exclusively through 1965, but nylon started to break into this market when Chevrolet Division of General Motors Corporation indicated in 1966 that it would provide tires with nylon cord on the 1968 models. "The use of . . . nylon for Chevrolet production for this first year could mean a market of approximately 10,000,000 tires. . . ."[3]

If rayon cord were ultimately displaced from OEM passenger car tires, the rayon industry stood to lose approximately 150 million pounds of its market. As this last market started to switch, rayon producers would find it increasingly difficult to remain price competitive with nylon.

The nylon producers may be in a position . . . to further reduce the price of their material. However, the rayon producers most probably will not be in a position to do the same because of the decrease . . . in usage of their materials.[4]

Du Pont recently pointed to acetate yarn as an example of a fiber having passed the low point in raw material price and already having capitalized fully on the lower cost attainable through very large scale of production. . . . This may also be the case for rayon staple fiber.[5]

---

[2] Original equipment tires are purchased from tire manufacturers and placed on new cars by auto manufacturers.

[3] C. A. Litzler, "The Fluid Tire Cord Situation," *Modern Textiles Magazine*, September, 1966, p. 22.

[4] Ibid.

[5] National Advisory Commission on Food and Fiber, *Cotton and Other Fiber Problems and Policies in the United States*, Technical Papers, Vol. 2 (Washington, D.C., 1967), p. 43.

The rise of polyester

While nylon was rapidly replacing rayon as the principal fiber in tire cord, a new fiber, polyester, was becoming important.[6] Five million pounds of this fiber were used in 1963 by tire manufacturers, 19 million pounds was the estimated use in 1966, and a Goodyear spokesman predicted that over 100 million pounds would be used in tire cord by 1970.[7]

Polyester was considered by some to be the "third generation" man-made fiber after rayon and nylon. The fiber had shown very rapid growth in recent years (Exhibit 4). After Du Pont's polyester patent expired in July, 1961, competition rapidly appeared, prices declined, and new markets opened up to the fiber. Much of polyester's success up to 1966 was due to the enthusiasm that greeted the introduction of stay-press fabric in wearing apparel. In 1956, the total production of polyester fiber for all uses was about 20 million pounds. By 1965, polyester output reached over 400 million pounds. Du Pont was the major producer of polyester fiber, accounting for well over one half of total U.S. production.

ALTERNATIVE COURSES OF ACTION IN THE FACE OF CHANGE

In mid-1966, the management of MRC was considering alternative courses of action with regard to the ARI division. The profits of this division were unsatisfactory when viewed in relation to the amount of capital required to support its operations. With the market for ARI's major product line facing even greater near-term difficulty than in the past (owing to the Chevrolet decision), the company had to (1) continue realizing progressively less satisfactory returns on the assets employed by ARI, or (2) commit a substantial amount of new capital to production facilities for new fibers, or (3) get out of certain areas of the rayon business.

Leaving the market

The alternative of getting out of the rayon business entirely or in part presented a problem since the physical plant of ARI was on the books of the company at a net book value of about $20 million. If this was sold substantially below book value, MRC would have to absorb a substantial nonrecurring loss on the sale, which would probably reduce the company's 1966 earnings per share below the level achieved in 1965. Although this loss would be nonrecurring, MRC management felt that investors might confuse it with a downturn in earnings from normal operations. The company was in the middle of its fifth consecutive year of earnings progress in 1966. Its stock prices had

---

[6] Polyester (polyethylene terephthalate) is a long chain polymer formed in the condensation reaction between ethylene glycol (permanent antifreeze) and dimethyl terephthalate. Du Pont's dacron is the best-known brand of polyester fiber.

[7] *Oil, Paint and Drug Reporter*, November 21, 1966, pp. 4 and 52.

been moving up steadily since 1961 in response to these earnings gains, and management was reluctant to risk this share-price progress to investor misunderstanding.

Investing in new fibers

While selling the ARI division was not a particularly attractive alternative, investing in facilities for producing newer fibers also raised some difficult problems. First, since nylon seemed to have already neared a peak in tire cord use, an investment in a facility to produce this fiber would be practically obsolete by the time it was completed. On the other hand, polyester had not reached the point of acceptance in tire production to justify the construction of a large new plant just to serve this segment of the polyester market. New fiber plants had to be large to be economically competitive. As a representative example, Exhibit 5 shows the variation in production costs of rayon fiber as the size of the producing plant increases. Economies of scale are clearly evident here, as they are in most chemical production processes.[8] Similar production economies could be expected in polyester fiber production. For this reason, if MRC went into the production of polyester tire cord, it would be necessary to produce polyester fiber for other uses as well. This would put the company into the textile fiber business against firms such as Du Pont. Except for the venture into high-wet modulus rayon staple fiber in 1964, the company had had little contact with textile mills, and had competed directly with large apparel fiber manufacturers such as Du Pont only to a limited extent.

THE POLYESTER PROPOSAL

In mid-1966, top management of MRC was considering a specific proposal that would carry the corporation heavily into the production of polyester fiber for tire cord and apparel fabrics. This proposal had been initiated by the ARI division general manager, John Wentworth, an experienced and extremely well-regarded young executive who had been lured away from Monsanto Company after MRC's experience with high-wet modulus rayon staple fiber.

During the period 1966–71, the project would call for an investment of $30.5 million (Exhibit 6). About $20.2 million of this amount would be used to construct a new plant for the production of polyester fiber, $5.3 million would be used for plant additions to reduce the production costs of high-wet modulus rayon fiber and expand production capacity, and $5.0 million would be added to working capital in support of the increased level of sales.

Over a period of three years, the new facility would give ARI the capacity to produce up to 50 million pounds a year of polyester fiber and resin. Ten million pounds would go into tire cord, 30 million pounds would be marketed as staple fiber in competition with firms such as Du Pont, and 10 million pounds of resin chips would be sold to other polyester fabricators.

---

[8] S. C. Schuman, "How Plant Size Affects Unit Costs," *Chemical Engineering*, May, 1965, pp. 173–76.

Economics of the polyester venture

Exhibit 7 shows the profit and cash flow projections for the first five years of the project's life. The volume and price assumptions underlying these calculations are shown at the bottom of the exhibit. Although polyester staple fiber was selling for 84 cents a pound in mid-1966, the analysis assumes that this price will have declined to 70.5 cents a pound by 1969. Exhibit 8 shows the profit, cash flow, and DCF-ROI projections over the 15-year life of the facility assuming that the volume and price projections of 1971 continue through 1981. The second ROI calculation assumes that all polyester selling prices decline 10% in 1972 and remain at those levels for the final 10 years of the project's life.

The competitive environment

During the months that the MRC management was mulling over the new fiber project, the competitive situation in polyester was in considerable turmoil. In late March, 1966, Du Pont announced that it would build a new polyester facility capable of producing 200 million pounds a year by the end of 1968. The plant was to be twice the size of Du Pont's two other polyester plants and was to be called the Cape Fear plant. This facility, plus other announced additions at Du Pont's other polyester plants, would raise the company's capacity in polyester fiber from 240 million pounds a year in February, 1966 (versus 456 million pounds for the industry at that date), to over 600 million pounds a year by the end of 1968. Exhibit 9 shows the production capacity of the U.S. companies producing polyester resins at February, 1966, plus the announced capacity additions due to come on-stream at least by the end of 1968. The exhibit also shows the 1965 total sales volume of these companies, the other fibers they manufactured, and their average return on total capital during the period 1961–65.

In April, 1966, an article in *Chemical Week* mentioned a number of other important competitive factors in the polyester situation:[9]

Polyester sales in '65 increased 50% over '64 and '66 growth is projected for at least 35% to 500 million lbs. Demand got out of hand last year because a 14¢/lb. price decrease was coupled with an unexpectedly enthusiastic acceptance of polyester blends in durable-press apparel. . . .

If all announced new capacity is built as scheduled, by the end of '68 U.S. production capability would be nearly 1.25 billion lbs./year. . . .

With the Du Pont capacity disclosure, other polyester fiber producers theorize that marginal producers may scale down expansion plans and potential producers may think twice before entering the market. Intense competition in other fibers is in store as well.

THE POINT OF DECISION

It was in this environment that the management of MRC had to make its decision on the polyester fiber proposal.

---

[9] *Chemical Week*, April 2, 1966, p. 21.

Exhibit 1

MRC, INC. (B)

DIVISIONS OF MRC

Capitol Foundry

Cast alloy steel grinding balls; volume or job-lot production of gray, white, and nickel-chrome iron; chrome-molybdenum and austenitic-manganese steel castings.

ARI Fibers

Tyrex rayon tire yarns, cords, and fabrics; high tenacity rayon yarns, plied yarns, cords (adhesive-treated and untreated) for mechanical rubber goods; rayon textile yarns; rayon staple fiber; polyester tire yarn, cord, and fabric.

Janitrol Aero

Heat transfer equipment for aircraft and missiles; electronic cooling equipment; pneumatic, hydraulic, and cryogenic controls; high pressure couplings and duct supports; liquid heaters for ground support; aircraft and portable heaters; gas turbine combustion systems; gas turbine accessories; hot fuel priming units.

Janitrol

Heating and air conditioning equipment for residential, commercial, and industrial applications, including gas and oil-fired furnaces, unit heaters, gas conversion burners, gas and oil-fired boilers, central air conditioning systems, electric/gas year-round heat/cool packages, rooftop heating and cooling units, electric heat pumps, makeup air heaters.

Midland Frame

Passenger car, truck, and bus chassis frames; miscellaneous stampings and weldments.

National Castings

Couplers, draft gears, car trucks, cushioned underframes for railroad, mine, and industrial haulage systems; malleable, pearlitic malleable steel castings for metalworking industries.

Power Controls

Air-brake systems; vacuum power brake systems; power controls; electro-pneumatic door controls; air compressors; air actuating cylinders; emergency relay valves; zinc and aluminum die castings.

Ross Engineering

"Engineered Atmospheres" for processing, drying or curing pulp, paper, rubber, chemicals, food, textiles, wood and wood products, et al.; coil processing and metal decorating lines; textile dryers and curing machinery; air heaters; fume incinerators; web conditioners; dryer drainage systems; SUPERTHERM high temperature hot fluid heating systems.

Steel City

Switch, outlet, and floor boxes; conduit and cable fittings; hangers and supports; metal framing systems for conduit lighting and electrical equipment; slotted angle.

Surface Combustion

Industrial burners; heat-treat furnaces; heat-processing equipment for glass and ceramics; steel mill equipment; process and comfort air dehumidification and bacterial removal systems; continuous dryers; iron pelletizing and reducing equipment and plants; gas generators for metallurgical, food, and chemical applications.

Waldron-Hartig

Machinery for paper, film, foil, and textile coating, converting, laminating, embossing, and treating; metal coil coating and processing lines; plastics extruders, blow molding machinery, and film and sheeting lines; power transmission couplings.

Webster Engineering

Gas and oil burners for boilers in large buildings and industry; FANDAIRE air-cooled condensers, condensing units, and chillers.

MRC of Canada, Ltd.
Power Controls
Surface Combustion

Products similar to those of the Power Controls, Ross Engineering, and Surface Combustion Divisions in the United States.

Exhibit 2

MRC, INC. (B)

SIX-YEAR SUMMARY OF FINANCIAL DATA

(Dollar figures in millions except for per share data)

	1961	1962	1963	1964	1965	1966
OPERATIONS						
Sales:						
Automotive and transportation.........	$ 57.8	$ 73.2	$ 80.9	$ 82.5	$ 94.2	$102.6
Capital goods.........................	42.7	48.2	47.3	65.1	94.8	125.7
Building and construction..............	12.4	18.3	31.2	33.4	34.5	33.5
Railroad..............................	—	—	—	—	39.6	42.7
Consumer goods......................	16.5	15.0	14.9	16.2	18.7	18.0
Aerospace and defense.................	8.3	11.6	15.7	13.9	14.3	21.6
Total..........................	$137.6	$166.3	$190.1	$211.1	$296.1	$344.1
Net income...........................	5.5	5.9	7.6	8.7	14.1	17.6
Depreciation and amortization of intangibles........................	4.3	4.6	5.2	5.1	6.9	7.4
Cash funds generated*...................	9.0	9.8	12.0	14.0	19.8	24.1
Federal income taxes....................	3.2	6.1	8.2	8.5	12.5	16.6
Profit margin...........................	7.4%	9.1%	10.5%	9.8%	10.7%	11.4%
Depreciation rate.......................	4.5	4.7	4.8	4.5	4.7	4.7
Earned on total capital..................	5.3	6.3	7.8	9.1	10.4	12.1
Earned on common equity...............	5.3	6.5	8.2	9.7	12.6	13.7
COMMON STOCK						
Net income per share†‡...................	$ 0.84	$ 0.97	$ 1.47	$ 1.82	$ 2.66	$ 3.33
Dividends per share†....................	0.75	0.75	0.75	0.85	0.95	1.22
Cash funds generated per share*†‡.........	1.60	1.85	2.57	2.96	4.15	4.90
Net tangible book value—per share†.......	15.86	17.00	17.64	18.63	20.70	22.52
Market price†..........................	13–11	14–10	16–12	19–15	26–18	30–22
Dividend payout ratio...................	49%	45%	33%	31%	28%	31%
Average annual price-earnings ratio........	15.1	11.3	10.5	10.3	8.2	7.9
Average annual dividend yield............	5.8%	6.0%	4.9%	4.6%	4.4%	4.7%
Number of shareholders.................	13,125	12,165	11,750	12,725	12,750	15,150
FINANCIAL POSITION						
Working capital.........................	$ 58.6	$ 47.4	$ 50.1	$ 49.3	$ 69.4	$ 70.2
Net property, plant, and equipment........	42.4	43.8	44.6	49.3	66.6	72.4
Long-term debt.........................	—	—	—	13.5	9.0	7.9
Preferred and common shareholders' equity.	105.6	96.5	100.6	91.9	134.2	142.3
Additions to property, plant, and equipment........................	1.4	2.5	3.2	9.9	9.1	14.4
Number of employees...................	8,000	8,500	9,000	9,300	14,000	14,600

* Net income and provisions for depreciation, amortization of intangibles, and deferred income taxes, less preferred dividends.
† Adjusted for 2 for 1 splits in 1964 and 1966.
‡ Calculated on average number of shares outstanding during the year.

Exhibit 3

MRC, INC. (B)

ACQUISITION HISTORY OF MRC

December, 1957:	Acquired J. O. Ross Engineering Corporation in exchange for 281,000 shares.
March, 1958:	Acquired Hartig Engine and Machine Company, Mountainside, New Jersey, for cash and notes.
October, 1958:	Acquired Transportation Division of Consolidated Metal Products Corporation, Albany, New York, and moved operations to Owosso, Michigan Division.
April, 1959:	Acquired Nelson Metal Products Company, Grand Rapids, Michigan, for cash.
November, 1959:	Acquired Surface Combustion Corporation, Toledo, Ohio, for $23 million cash.
May, 1961:	Merged American Rayon, Inc. by exchange of common stock.
January, 1962:	Acquired Wright Manufacturing Company, Phoenix, producer of air conditioning equipment.
March, 1962:	Acquired Fandaire Division, a producer of commercial air conditioning systems, from Yuba Consolidated Industries, Inc.
December 31, 1962:	Acquired the precision machine business of J. Leukart Machine Company, Columbus, Ohio.
April 1, 1963:	Purchased Steel City Electric Company from Martin Marietta Corporation.
April 22, 1965:	Merged National Castings Company, by exchange of 299,787 shares of $4.75 cumulative convertible preferred stock on basis of 45/100 share of preferred stock for each share of National Castings common stock. National Castings operated as two divisions.
Fall, 1965:	Acquired Grand Rapids Bright Metal Company.

Exhibit 4

MRC, INC. (B)
U.S. FIBER CONSUMPTION (IN MILLIONS OF POUNDS) AND PRICES
(IN DOLLARS PER POUND)

Year	Natural Fibers — Cotton Pounds	Cotton Staple Price $	Natural Fibers — Wool Pounds	Wool Staple Price $	Man-Made Fibers — Rayon Pounds	Rayon Staple Price $	Nylon Pounds	Nylon Staple Price $	Polyester Pounds	Polyester Staple Price $
1910	n.a.		n.a.		*					
1930	2,617		263		119	0.40				
1935	2,755		418		200	0.31				
1940	3,959		408		300	0.25	*			
1945	4,516	0.39	645		420	0.25	25			
1950	4,683	0.57	635	1.41	650	0.36	75	1.65	*	
1955	4,382	0.39	414	1.08	966	0.34	231	1.48	13	1.60
1956		0.33		1.08	870	0.32	246	1.30	20	1.35
1957		0.36		1.22	836	0.31	293	1.30	38	1.41
1958		0.33		0.90	750	0.31	293	1.20	44	1.41
1959		0.30		1.02	848	0.33	356	1.06	79	1.36
1960	4,191	0.31	411	1.07	716	0.28	376	0.92	110	1.36
1961		0.31		1.03	797	0.28	455	0.92	112	1.24
1962	4,188	0.30	429	1.09	884	0.28	551	0.92	162	1.14
1963	4,040	0.29	412	1.18	960	0.28	625	0.92	223	1.14
1964	4,244	0.29	357	1.28	975	0.28	754	0.92	274	0.98
1965	4,477	0.29	387	1.19	1,046	0.28	861	0.82	416	0.84
1966	4,633 est.		370 est.		1,026 est.		978 est.		545 est.	

Fibers compete for shares of the total fiber market principally on the basis of relative prices and relative quality characteristics. Relative prices appear to have been an important consideration in the substitution of rayon for cotton in certain uses. The noncellulose fibers offer serious price competition for apparel wool. However, price advantage has not accounted for the rapid increase in share of the fiber market gain by noncellulose fibers, although sharply reduced prices in recent years have undoubtedly expanded their use.

Synthetic fibers yield a greater amount of fabric from a pound of fiber than does cotton, thus reducing the price of synthetic fiber per unit of product output. The equivalent net weight pounds of cotton staple for each pound of man-made fiber is (a) rayon staple fiber, 1.10; and (b) nylon and polyester staple fiber, 1.37.

* Date of fiber introduction.

Sources: Statistical Abstract of the United States—1967, pp. 642, 760, 761. Textile Organon: December, 1966, p. 199; February, 1967, pp. 28, 29. Modern Textiles Magazine, December, 1965. National Advisory Commission on Food and Fiber, Cotton and Other Fiber Problems and Policies in the United States, Technical Papers, Vol. 2 (Washington, D.C., 1967), pp. 24, 33, 36, 39.

Exhibit 5

MRC, INC. (B)

VARIATION IN UNIT COST OF PRODUCTION WITH SIZE OF PLANT

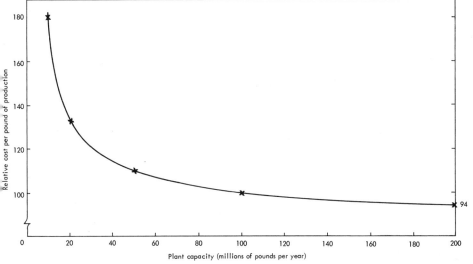

Based on a chart in Jesse W. Markham, *Competition in the Rayon Industry* (Cambridge, Mass.: Harvard University Press, 1952), p. 150.

Exhibit 6

MRC, INC. (B)

CAPITAL INVESTMENT IN POLYESTER

(In millions)

	ARI Division
Working capital	$ 6.5
Production facilities	20.3
Total existing investment	$26.8
Between 1/1/67 and 12/31/71, additional investments were to be made as follows:	
Polyester resin and fiber plant	$17.4
Polyester tire cord spinning facility	1.8
Other polyester facilities	1.0
Polyester plants	$20.2
Various rayon additions	5.3
Total plant additions	$25.5
Additional accounts receivable and inventories	5.0
Total additional investment	$30.5
Grand total	$57.3

The timing and size of the cash expenditure for the project would be as follows:

	1967	1968	1969	1970	1971	Five-Year Totals
Additions to plant	$16.9	$5.7	$0.9	$1.0	$1.0	$25.5
Additions to working capital	1.1	3.3	0.6	0	0	5.0
	$18.0	$9.0	$1.5	$1.0	$1.0	$30.5

Exhibit 7

MRC, INC. (B)

FIVE-YEAR SALES, PROFIT, CASH FLOW, AND PRICE FORECASTS OF PROJECT
(Dollar figures in millions)

		1967				1968		
	Total	Poly-ester	Hi-Wet Modulus Rayon Staple	Rayon Tire Cord	Total	Poly-ester	Hi-Wet Modulus Rayon Staple	Rayon Tire Cord
Net sales	$50.0	$ 6.4	$4.9	$38.7	$68.3	$21.5	$7.7	$39.1
Cost of sales:								
Normal	40.5							
Extraordinary start-up	0.5							
Depreciation	2.1	0.1		2.0	2.9	1.0		1.9
Total cost of sales	$43.1				$56.2			
Gross income	$ 6.9				$12.1			
Nonmanufacturing expense	4.0				6.3			
Income before interest and income taxes	$ 2.9	$(1.2)		$4.1	$ 5.8	$ 0.9		$4.9
Interest	0.0				0.0			
Income before taxes	$ 2.9				$ 5.8			
Income taxes @ approx. 50%:								
Current	1.4				2.5			
Deferred	—				0.4			
Total	$ 1.4				$ 2.9			
Less investment credit	0.2				$ 0.5			
Net provision	$ 1.2				$ 2.4			
Net income	$ 1.7				$ 3.4			
Depreciation and deferred taxes	2.1				3.3			
Cash flow	$ 3.8				$ 6.7			

	Product Sold (Millions of Lbs.)	Price ($ per Lb.)		Product Sold (Millions of Lbs.)	Price ($ per Lb.)
Rayon staple (hi-wet modulus)	16	$0.310	*Consumer*	25	$0.310
Rayon tire cord	67	0.578	*Auto*	67.5	0.578
Polyester:					
Tire cord	7.5	0.850	*Auto*	10	0.809
Staple fiber	0.0	0.785	*Consumer*	18.8	0.725
Resin (or polymer)	0.0	0.380		0.0	0.380
Total polyester	7.5	$0.850		28.8	$0.754

	1969				1970				1971		
Total	Poly-ester	Hi-Wet Modulus Rayon Staple	Rayon Tire Cord	Total	Poly-ester	Hi-Wet Modulus Rayon Staple	Rayon Tire Cord	Total	Poly-ester	Hi-Wet Modulus Rayon Staple	Rayon Tire Cord
$79.8	$32.9	$7.7	$39.2	$79.7	$32.8	$7.7	$39.2	$79.5	$32.6	$7.7	$39.2
3.3	1.7	1.6		3.3	—	—		3.4	—	—	
$57.8				$57.8				$57.8			
$22.0				$21.9				$21.7			
6.5				6.6				6.6			
$15.5	$10.5		$5.0	$15.3	$10.3		$5.0	$15.1	$10.1		$5.0
0.0				1.5				1.1			
$15.5				$13.8				$14.0			
6.9				5.7				6.2			
0.9				0.5				0.3			
$ 7.8				$ 6.2				$ 6.5			
0.7				0.1				0.1			
$ 7.1				$ 6.1				$ 6.4			
$ 8.4				$ 7.7				$ 7.6			
4.1				3.8				3.7			
$12.5				$11.5				$11.3			

Product Sold (Millions of Lbs.)	Price ($ per Lb.)	Product Sold (Millions of Lbs.)	Price ($ per Lb.)	Product Sold (Millions of Lbs.)	Price ($ per Lb.)
25	$0.310	25	$0.310	25	$0.310
67.8	0.578	67.8	0.578	67.8	0.578
10	0.795	10	0.795	10	0.795
30	0.705	30	0.705	30	0.705
10	0.380	10	0.372	10	0.350
50	$0.658	50	$0.656	50	$0.652

Exhibit 8

MRC, INC. (B)
CASH FLOWS FROM POLYESTER PROJECT, 1967–81
(In thousands)

Year	Existing	New	Income after Tax	Cash Flow from Operations
	—Investment—		*Income*	*Cash Flow from*
Year	*Existing*	*New*	*after Tax*	*Operations*
1967.........	$26,800	$18,029	$1,663	$ 3,788
1968.........		8,995	3,416	6,740
1969.........		1,480	8,397	12,543
1970.........		1,000	7,710	11,477
1971.........		1,000	7,597	11,286
1972.........			7,427	10,869
1973.........			7,659	10,611
1974.........			7,861	10,385
1975.........			8,034	10,184
1976.........			8,186	10,009
1977.........			8,317	9,853
1978.........			8,431	9,714
1979.........			8,529	9,590
1980.........			8,574	9,521
1981.........			8,574	{ 9,496 { 14,338 ← return of working capital and plant write-off

Discounted cash flow return on investment = 15.2%
DCF–ROI   assuming 10% decline in selling
prices of polyester, 1972–81   = 13.6%

Exhibit 9

MRC, INC. (B)

CURRENT AND PLANNED CAPACITY OF POLYESTER FIBER COMPETITORS

	Polyester Capacity Feb., 1966 (In Millions of Pounds)	Announced Expansion by End of 1968 (In Millions of Pounds)	Number of Plants End of 1968	Other‡ Fibers Manufactured	Total Sales Volume of Company in 1965 (In Millions)	Average Return on Total Capital (1961–65)
Allied Chemical	0	?	?	N	$1,121	10%
American Enka	0	?	?	N, R	193	11
American Viscose (Div. FMC)	0	?	?	A, R		
Beaunit Fibers (Div. Beaunit Corp.)	0	?	?	R		
Chemstrand (Div. Monsanto)	20	40	1	N	1,468	9
Du Pont	240	360	3	A, N	3,020	19
Fiber Industries*	95	155	2	A, N, R	862	8
Firestone Tire & Rubber	0	?	?	N	1,610	9
Goodyear Tire & Rubber	60	40	1		2,226	10
Hercules	0	30	1		532	13
ARI Fibers (Div. MRC)	0	?	?	R		
Phoenix Works, Inc. (Sub. Bates Mfg. Co.)	0	25	1			
Tennessee Eastman Co. (Div. Eastman Kodak)	50	100	2	A		
U.S. Rubber Company	0	?	?			
Vectra Co.† (Div. Nat. Plastic Products)	0	?	?	N		
	465	750	11			

* Owned 62.5% by Celanese Corp. of America.
† Jointly owned by Enjay Chemical Co. & J. P. Stevens & Co.
‡ A = Acetate; N = Nylon; R = Rayon.

GENERAL HOLDINGS CORPORATION

One of the critical problems confronting management and the board of General Holdings Corporation in the early 1960's was the determination of a minimum acceptable rate of return on new capital investments. While this question had been under discussion within the company for several years, so far the people involved had been unable to agree even on what general concept of a minimum acceptable rate they should adopt. They were about evenly divided between using a single cutoff rate based on the company's overall weighted average cost of capital and a system of multiple cutoff rates said to reflect the risk–profit characteristics of the several businesses or economic sectors in which the company's subsidiaries operated. In late 1963, management was asked by the board to restudy the issue of single versus multiple cutoff rates and to recommend which approach the company should follow in the future.

General Holdings Corporation was formed in 1923 with the merger of several formerly independent firms operating in the oil refining, pipeline transportation, and industrial chemical fields. Over the following 40 years, the company integrated vertically into exploration and production of crude oil and marketing refined petroleum products, and horizontally into plastics, agricultural chemicals, and real estate development. The company was organized as a holding company with semiautonomous operating subsidiaries working in each of the above areas of activity. Its total assets exceeded $2 billion in 1963, and its capital expenditures averaged about $150 million a year in recent years.

Although management was unable to decide whether the company should use single or multiple cutoff rates, it had worked tentatively with a single corporationwide rate for about five years. The company's basic capital budgeting approach during this period had been to accept all proposed investments with a positive net present value when discounted at the company's estimated weighted average cost of capital. As cost of capital was defined and used in this process, the company, in effect, accepted projects down to the point where there would be no dilution in expected earnings per share of common stock.

The cost of capital discount rate used in the net present value discounting procedure was 10%, estimated as follows: First, an estimate was made of the expected proportions of future funds sources. Second, costs were assigned to each of these sources. Third, a weighted average cost of capital was calculated on the basis of these proportions and costs. Finally, this weighted average was adjusted upward to reflect the fact that no return at all was earned on a substantial proportion of the company's investments.

On the basis of the company's financing experience during the 1950's, company officials estimated that future capital investments would be financed about one third from debt and two thirds from depreciation and retained earnings combined. The company had not sold common stock for many years and had no plans to do so in the foreseeable future.

The primary consideration behind the costs assigned to the above funds sources was to avoid accepting projects with expected returns so low that the stockholders' expected earnings per share would be diluted. If the stockholders could reinvest their funds at a higher rate of return outside the company than management could inside, so the argument ran, the funds involved should be distributed to the stockholders rather than invested or reinvested internally. With this objective in mind, the company's future cost of debt was estimated at 2.5% after taxes, assuming a one third proportion of debt to total fund sources. Depreciation and retained earnings were thought to be exactly the same as common stock from the stockholders' point of view. In costing depreciation and retained earnings, therefore, the management started with the reciprocal of the company's probable long-term price–earnings ratio. This ratio was thought to be about 15 times. In addition, however, because this 15-times ratio was thought to reflect an assumed continuation of past growth in earnings per share, an adjustment was made, reducing the assumed price–earnings ratio to 10 times. The lower ratio was thought to reflect more accurately the long-term relationship between current market prices and expected earnings per share.

Combining these proportions and costs, the company's weighted average cost of capital came out at 7.5%.

Source	Estimated Proportions of Future Funds Sources	Estimated Future Cost, after Taxes
Debt	33%	2.5%
Depreciation and retained earnings	67	10.0
Weighted average cost		7.5%

This 7.5% assumed that at least 7.5% would be earned on the total capital employed by the company. In fact, however, total capital employed included not only successful projects but also unsuccessful projects and certain necessary investments that resulted in little, if any, return. About 25% of the company's investments typically fell into the second and third categories. Thus, to earn 7.5% on an overall basis it was necessary to earn at least 10%

after taxes on the 75% of the company's projects where an actual return was expected. This is the 10% discount rate that was used by the company in determining the net present value of proposed capital expenditures.

The idea of using the single 10% discount rate on a corporationwide basis had been strongly opposed from the beginning by several of the operating subsidiaries of General Holdings. These subsidiaries argued that the internal allocation of funds by the parent company among its principal operating subsidiaries should be based upon a system of multiple target rates of return reflecting the unique risk–profit characteristics of the industry or economic sector in which each subsidiary operated.

Those arguing in favor of multiple target rates of return usually began by pointing out that General Holdings Corporation was really just a holding company with a number of operating subsidiaries in several related and unrelated industries. Each of these operating affiliates faced numerous competitors and a unique risk–profit environment. Some of these competitors operated in only one industry or economic sector; others were parts of more complex groupings, such as General Holdings. However this might be, those arguing in favor of multiple cutoff rates did so on the grounds that given the underlying strategic decision to be in, say, pipelines or refining or plastics, the parent company had then to adopt minimum acceptable rates of return related to the competitive risk–profit characteristics inherent in each area.

To do otherwise was alleged to have two important undesirable outcomes. The first of these was that a high companywide rate, such as the company's present 10% discount rate, resulted in the company or its affiliates not going into some highly profitable ventures. Gas transmission pipelines were an often-cited example of this. Gas pipelines had been ruled out by General Holdings in the past because the regulated 6% return on invested capital was well below the company's 10% minimum. In spite of this low regulated return, however, gas transmission companies were typically highly leveraged because of the limited economic risk involved in their operation, and their common stocks often sold in the 30 times price–earnings range. Since this was double General Holdings' normal price–earnings ratio, it was argued that the company's stockholders would have benefited had the parent company allowed its pipeline affiliate to expand along with the gas transmission industry.

The second undesirable outcome of using a high single cutoff rate was that it was said to favor investment projects or alternatives with low initial funds commitments almost without regard to the subsequent operating cost streams that could be expected to follow. In part, this was simply reiterating the point that the company had been underinvesting in the low risk parts of its business or businesses. But more was involved. Where operating economies of scale were concerned, particularly in capital intensive areas, a higher than justified rate penalized high initial investment–low operating cost alternatives in favor of low initial investment–high operating cost alternatives or projects. In short, the company tended to underinvest initially at the expense of higher future operating costs, and deferred related investments whose importance was underrated as a result of using an inappropriately high discount rate in low risk situations.

The specific alternative proposed by the supporters of multiple cutoff rates in lieu of a single companywide rate involved determining several rates, based on the estimated cost of capital inherent in each of the economic sectors or industries in which the company's principal operating subsidiaries worked. Weighted average cost of capital cutoff rates reflecting their specific risk–profit environments would be determined for the company's production-exploration, pipeline transportation, refining, and marketing affiliates in the oil industry, as well as for its plastics, industrial chemicals, agricultural chemicals, and real estate subsidiaries operating outside the oil industry. For example, cutoff rates of 16%, 11%, 8%, and 6%, respectively, were proposed for the production-exploration, chemicals, real estate, and pipeline parts of the business. All the other rates proposed fell within this range. The suggestion was that these multiple cutoff rates determine the minimum acceptable rate of return on proposed capital investments in each of the main operating areas of the company.

It was proposed that the weighted average cost of capital in each operating sector be developed as follows. First, an estimate would be made of the usual debt and equity proportions of independently financed firms operating in each sector. Several such independents competed against each of the company's affiliates. Second, the costs of debt and equity given these proportions and sectors would be estimated in accordance with the concepts followed by the company in estimating its own costs of capital in the past. Third, these costs and proportions would be combined to determine the weighted average cost of capital, or minimum acceptable rate of return, for discounting purposes in each sector.

These multiple hurdle or discount rates had been calculated for several periods in the past, and invariably when their weighted average was weighted according to the company's relative investment in each sector, it exceeded the company's actual overall average cost of capital. This differential was attributed to the fact that the sector hurdle rates calculated as described above tended to overlook the risk diversification benefits of many investments undertaken by General Holdings. As compared with a nonintegrated enterprise operating in any given branch, a vertically and horizontally integrated firm such as General Holdings enjoyed some built-in asset diversification as well as important captive markets between certain of its vertically integrated parts. For example, the risks associated with a refinery investment by an integrated company like General Holdings were said to be much less than for an identical investment made by an independent. It was proposed that this diversification premium be allocated back and deducted from the multiple subsidiary discount rates in proportion to the relationship of the investment in each subsidiary to the company's total assets.

While it had been impossible to accurately appraise the overall impact of changing from a single rate to multiple target rates, it could be foreseen that both the company's asset structure and the probable size of its future capital expenditures would be affected. It was anticipated, for example, that up to one third of future capital expenditures might be shifted from one to another operating sector or affiliate with the adoption of multiple hurdle rates. In addition, the company's expected average annual capital budget could easily increase from $150 million to $175 million or more. An annual budget of this magnitude would force reconsideration of the company's traditional debt, common stock, and dividend policies.

As management and the board of General Holdings began their latest review of the controversy between using single or multiple minimum acceptable cutoff rates, the officers of the operating subsidiaries were asked to restate their positions. Those behind the present single target rate contended that the stockholders of General Holdings would expect the company to invest their funds in the highest return projects available. They suggested that without exception the affiliates backing multiple rates were those that were unable to compete effectively for new funds when measured against the corporate group's actual cost of capital. Against this, the multiple hurdle rate proponents pointed out again that if the parent company was serious about competing over the long run in industries with such disparate risk–profit characteristics as they faced, it was absolutely essential to relate internal target rates of return to these circumstances. They felt that division of the overall corporate investment pot should be based primarily on the company's long-term strategic plans. It was against this background that the final choice between single versus multiple cutoff rates had to be decided.

AMALGAMATED MANUFACTURING
CORPORATION (A)

∧∧

The Amalgamated Manufacturing Corporation was a large manufacturer of heavy industrial equipment with its main headquarters and production facilities located in the metropolitan Chicago area. The company had grown over a long period of years. Its principal sales volume was in a specialized line of industrial equipment, which accounted for more than half of its 1964 sales volume. Technological developments had limited sales of new equipment in this major line of the company's production in recent years, and it seemed unlikely that original equipment sales would expand beyond their 1965 volume. Although the demand for replacement parts would remain high for several years to come, it would eventually be limited by the cessation of growth and possible decline in the sale of new equipment.

The management of Amalgamated was thus confronted with the difficult task of maintaining a satisfactory rate of growth in the overall volume of the company's sales and earnings. Two main strategies were adopted. One was to intensify the company's research and development efforts in product lines that had previously accounted for a relatively small portion of Amalgamated's total volume but seemed to offer more promising opportunities for long-term growth than its main line of industrial equipment. The second was to inaugurate a vigorous search for companies Amalgamated might acquire in industries other than its main product line. The successful implementation of these strategies explains in part the growth of Amalgamated in recent years (Exhibit 1) and its sound financial position at the end of 1964 (Exhibit 2).

Amalgamated was particularly interested in acquiring small companies with promising products and management personnel but without established growth records. The management of Amalgamated hoped to be able to acquire several such companies each year, preferably before their earning capacity had been sufficiently well established to command a premium price. In this way it hoped over a period of years to build a broad base for expansion and diversification.

The management of Amalgamated was aware that the potential rate of growth of many small companies was limited by inadequate capital resources and distribution systems. It was convinced that Amalgamated's abundant

367

capital resources and nationwide distribution system could greatly facilitate the growth of many such companies. Consequently, it hoped that Amalgamated would be able to acquire promising small companies on terms that would be mutually attractive because of the complementary character of the contributions that Amalgamated and any small companies it might acquire could make to the combined enterprise.

In following the strategy of expanding in part through acquisitions, the management of Amalgamated recognized that a variety of problems would be encountered. One was that such a policy would have to be in accord with the rather strict interpretation by the Supreme Court and the Justice Department of allowable mergers or acquisitions under the antitrust laws. Among other things, this would mean that most of the companies to be acquired by Amalgamated would have to be small in size. Even so, only a few companies could be acquired in any one year. Consequently, if these acquisitions were to have a significant impact on the growth rate of Amalgamated, it was important that wise decisions be made in selecting the companies to be purchased from the many potentially available for acquisition. The management of Amalgamated anticipated that for each company it should attempt to acquire, many companies might have to be screened.

(There are, of course, many facets to any decision concerning a potential acquisition. Among the most important is the caliber of the management of the company to be acquired, provided that the old management is expected to remain. Likewise, the quality of the company's product line, research capabilities, and patent position, if any, are prime considerations. Others are the degree to which the products of the two companies would mesh and the extent to which the value of the acquired company would be enhanced by an association with an established company. The acceptability of the acquisition under the antitrust laws would also have to be evaluated.)

Even after a prospective acquisition had passed the preliminary screening tests established by the management of Amalgamated, there still remained the difficult task of determining the maximum offering price that would be placed on the stock or assets of the company to be acquired. Until such an evaluation was made, serious negotiations with the potential sellers could not commence.

In order to apply consistent standards and to minimize the work load, the financial staff of Amalgamated had been requested by its top management to work out a standardized procedure to be used in evaluating potential acquisitions. The method used in evaluating the Norwood Screw Machinery Company, discussed below, is typical of that ordinarily used by Amalgamated.

The remainder of the case will describe very briefly the Norwood Screw Machinery Company and then discuss in more detail the method by which the financial staff arrived at a figure to recommend to management as a possible maximum purchase price. Not all the members of the management were convinced of the validity of the method of evaluation currently being used by Amalgamated. The final section of the case outlines briefly the doubts expressed by these members.

NORWOOD SCREW MACHINERY COMPANY

The Norwood Screw Machinery Company was a relatively small company with a diversified line of screw machinery products. It had a plant with approximately 75,000 square feet and employed about 75 persons. Its sales organization was rudimentary. In the opinion of both the Norwood and Amalgamated managements, this was one explanation for Norwood's relatively low volume of sales and profits.

Amalgamated had an interest in acquiring Norwood, if a satisfactory price could be agreed on, because Amalgamated was favorably impressed by the quality of Norwood's management and by its product lines. Norwood manufactured various standard screw machine products for which competition was severe and growth prospects were limited. It also had several proprietary products on which it earned a much higher rate of profit and from which it expected to achieve substantial growth. In addition, Norwood had several promising products scheduled to be put on the market in the near future. These items, several of which were revolutionary by industry standards, were expected to make a major contribution to Norwood's future growth. The management of Norwood also anticipated improvements in its production processes, which would increase its gross margin on sales above the relatively high level already prevailing.

Preliminary negotiations toward an acquisition of Norwood by Amalgamated were begun in mid-1965. The management of Amalgamated had considerable confidence in the quality of Norwood's management and shared its hopes that Norwood would be successful in developing new and improved products. Both managements believed that Norwood's products could be marketed much more successfully by the combined organization than by Norwood acting alone.

Amalgamated's information as to other aspects of Norwood's operations was much more scanty. Norwood had furnished Amalgamated with audited financial statements only for the year ending December 31, 1964 (Exhibits 3 and 4). The financial staff of Amalgamated was informed that the deficit in the retained earnings account (Exhibit 4) and the negligible charge against net income for income tax accruals (Exhibit 3) resulted from operating losses incurred in 1962 and 1963. These losses, however, were attributed to temporary conditions and were not regarded by the management of either company as indicative of Norwood's potential earning capacity. Preliminary unaudited statements for the first seven months of 1965 showed sales of approximately $550,000 and profits before taxes of about $100,000.

The management of Amalgamated recognized that a much more thorough examination would be necessary before a firm offer could be made to Norwood for the acquisition of its stock or assets. Among other things, much more detailed financial information would be needed for the years preceding 1964 and for the first part of 1965. Other aspects of Norwood's operations, such as the strength of its patent position, would also have to be subjected to detailed scrutiny by Amalgamated. In the meanwhile, however, preliminary negotiations were instituted. In connection with these negotiations, the financial staff of Amalgamated was requested by its top management to prepare an estimate of the maximum price at which Amalgamated might consider acquiring Norwood based on the limited information then available. Such an estimate might help to determine whether the probability that a deal could be worked out was high enough to justify the detailed examination of Norwood that would have to be undertaken before Amalgamated could make a firm offer.

AMALGAMATED'S METHOD OF EVALUATING ACQUISITIONS

Basic approach

As previously noted, Amalgamated's financial staff had worked out a fairly standardized method of evaluating potential acquisitions. This value was calculated by discounting at Amalgamated's cost of capital the future cash flow to be derived from the acquisition. The present worth of this future cash flow was the maximum price that Amalgamated would be willing to pay for an acquisition.

The future cash flow of a potential acquisition was obtained by forecasting the future profits, working capital, capital expenditures, depreciation, and other items affecting the cash flow to be derived from the acquisition. These forecasts were reviewed by the financial staff with other Amalgamated personnel who were familiar with the products and with the industry of the company under consideration.

Forecast of future cash flows

Typically three forecasts were considered in evaluating a company: an optimistic forecast (quite often the forecast submitted by the company to be purchased); a "most likely" forecast (the one that qualified Amalgamated personnel believed most likely to be realized); and, finally, a minimum forecast (reflecting the minimum growth reasonably to be expected from the potential acquisition). The cash flows resulting from each of these forecasts were then discounted at Amalgamated's cost of capital to arrive at a range of values for the company.

Although these three sets of forecasts were normally prepared, the management usually decided on the terms to be offered for a potential acquisition on the basis of the minimum forecast. This procedure was used because management had found that very frequently the *actual* growth rate of its acquisitions had not been as rapid as the minimum forecast.

As an illustration of the divergence often reflected in these forecasts, the president of Norwood estimated that the annual increase in sales would be about $400,000 a year for the next three years under *Norwood's* management, but the annual rate of growth could be as large as $2,000,000 if *Amalgamated* were to acquire Norwood. In contrast, on the assumption that Amalgamated acquired Norwood, the minumum forecast made by Amalgamated's staff for the same three years projected a growth in sales averaging about one third as large as that estimated by Norwood's management. This staff forecast, shown in Exhibit 5, assumes that Amalgamated would acquire Norwood at the beginning of 1966.

Amalgamated's normal procedure was to forecast for a five-year period the cash flows to be used in its evaluation. It then held constant the cash flow predicted for years 6 to 10. The staff preparing the forecasts recognized that this procedure introduced a conservative factor in its evaluation, but this element of conservatism was thought desirable as a means of counterbalancing the tendency cited above to overestimate the growth rate for the first five years. Finally, in year 10 a terminal value was placed on the company to be acquired. In effect, then, Amalgamated's procedure valued a potential acquisition as the sum of the present worth of the cash flow to be realized over the next 10 years plus the present worth of the terminal value at the end of the 10th year.

Assignment of terminal value

The decision to use a terminal value at the end of the 10th year was prompted by two factors. First, it was recognized that in the normal case Amalgamated would still own a company from which cash flows would be derived and which would, therefore, be of value to Amalgamated at the end of the 10-year period. Second, it seemed impractical to Amalgamated to attempt to forecast cash flows for longer than 10 years.

In the past Amalgamated had used several different approaches to set a terminal value on a potential acquisition at the end of the 10th year. These approaches included (1) the book value of the acquired company at this date; (2) its liquidating value at this date, that is, an estimate of the value of its assets but not as a going concern; and (3) a value based on an estimated sale of the acquired company at a specified multiple of earnings at the end of the 10th year.

However, Amalgamated's staff recognized that each of these procedures had serious limitations. Book value and liquidating value often would not reflect the worth of a company based on its present and potential earnings. The sale of a company at a specified multiple of 10-year earnings was regarded as a more adequate reflection of the value of the company in that year. The possible tax adjustments resulting from capital gains or losses arising from the sale, as well as the appropriate price-earnings multiplier for each company, were recognized as presenting additional complications for this method of determining a terminal value. Furthermore, Amalgamated's staff was concerned about a possible internal contradiction in this approach to the problem. It reasoned that to value the company in the 10th year at a specified price-earnings multiplier would be somewhat unrealistic: if the company's performance were satisfactory, Amalgamated probably would not be willing to sell; and if its performance were poor, Amalgamated probably would not be able to obtain the value indicated by the price-earnings multiplier.

At the time of the Norwood evaluation Amalgamated's staff was using a somewhat different approach. The terminal value of the company in year 10 was assumed to be the present worth of 20 years of additional cash flow. The annual rate of cash flow for years 11 through 30 was normally assumed to be equal to that for years 6 to 10, with the possible exception of adjustments for certain noncash expenses such as are shown in Exhibit 5. This procedure was believed to reflect more satisfactorily Amalgamated's intention in making an acquisition, that is, to realize a satisfactory cash flow over the long run.

Obviously, an assignment of a terminal value based on a discounting of the estimated cash flows (or earnings) from years 11 through 30 would not necessarily require Amalgamated to retain the company for 30 years in order for the acquisition to be profitable. For example, if Amalgamated could sell an acquisition at the end of the 10th year for the calculated terminal value, then, disregarding possible capital gains taxes, the investment would be just as profitable as if the assumed 20 years of additional earnings were realized in years 11–30. The Amalgamated procedure ignored years beyond year 30 because their contribution to the present worth of the terminal value with a discount rate as high as 10%, or thereabouts, would be negligible.

Working capital and capital expenditures

In determining the cash flows that would be caused by an acquisition, estimates also had to be made of changes in working capital requirements and of prospective capital outlays. If no better evidence was available, working capital requirements for a proposed acquisition were based on an historical analysis of relevant financial ratios of the company or industry for previous years. Expenditures on fixed assets were estimated at a level designed to maintain physical facilities in good working order and to handle the projected increases in sales volume.

Since sales volume was estimated to increase only for the first five years, as noted above, working capital requirements were generally considered to remain constant after year five. A typical assumption with respect to capital expenditures was that they would be equal to depreciation outlays after year five. The Norwood evaluation was made in this manner (Exhibit 5).

Treatment of debt

The financial staff of Amalgamated eliminated debt from the capital structure of potential acquisitions by assuming in its cash flow estimates that this debt would be paid off in full in year zero. As a corollary, interest charges associated with this debt were also eliminated from the estimates of cash outflows for subsequent years. The rationale for this treatment of debt and associated interest charges was that the future earnings of an acquisition should not be benefited by the use of leverage in the capital structure. This treatment was designed to permit all potential acquisitions to be evaluated on a comparable basis.

Estimate of cost of capital

Amalgamated's practice at the time of the Norwood acquisition was to discount its cash-flow estimates for future years at a rate of 10%. This figure was assumed to be an approximation of Amalgamated's cost of equity capital. As Exhibit 2 indicates, Amalgamated's capital structure consisted almost entirely of common equity. Management, however, was not committed to such a capital structure as a matter of company policy; it was, in fact, actively considering the possible benefits to be derived from a larger proportion of senior capital in its capital structure.

Application of procedure to Norwood

Exhibit 5 shows in detail how Amalgamated's procedure was applied in the evaluation of Norwood. The cash flow from Norwood was calculated first by estimating after-tax profits in years 1 to 10 and then adding back noncash expenses such as depreciation and amortization. From this sum the cash required for additions to working capital and new capital expenditures was subtracted. In addition, all long-term debt was assumed to be retired at the beginning of 1966 and was shown as an initial outlay. The resulting total represents the estimated cash contribution to be derived from Norwood over the 10-year period beginning January 1, 1966. The cash contribution of each year was then discounted at 10% to obtain an estimate of the present worth of contributions from operations over the next 10 years. The estimated terminal value of Norwood at the end of year 10 was then computed as the present worth of 20 additional years of earnings, that is, the earnings of years 11–30 discounted to year zero at 10%. The sum of the estimated present worth of the contribution from operations for the first 10 years and of the present worth of the terminal value assigned to Norwood represents Amalgamated's estimate of the purchase price that it would be justified in paying for all the outstanding stock of Norwood. This sum amounted to $4,465,000 for Norwood (Exhibit 5).

VIEWS OF OTHER MEMBERS OF AMALGAMATED'S MANAGEMENT

Although the evaluation procedure described in the preceding section was that currently used by Amalgamated, its merits were still under active debate within the company. Some members of management, for example, thought that in evaluating a potential acquisition more emphasis should be placed on the effect on Amalgamated's earnings per share. Mr. Simpson, a company director who was especially interested in Amalgamated's acquisition program, shared this view and contended vigorously that the $4,465,000 price for Norwood, as calculated in Exhibit 5, was far too high. He prepared the following illustrative data to support his position.

Hypothetical levels of profits after taxes to be derived from Norwood	$100,000	$200,000	$300,000	$400,000
Approximate earnings per share of Amalgamated without acquisition of Norwood	$5	$5	$5	$5
Number of shares of Amalgamated's stock that could be exchanged for all outstanding shares of Norwood without diluting Amalgamated's earnings per share	20,000	40,000	60,000	80,000
Approximate market value of Amalgamated's common stock at time of contemplated acquisition	$50	$50	$50	$50
Implicit value placed on Norwood by earnings-per-share criterion	$1,000,000	$2,000,000	$3,000,000	$4,000,000

Mr. Simpson pointed out that even if Norwood's profits after taxes were assumed to expand to $400,000, far in excess of its 1964 or probable 1965 level, the acquisition would result in a dilution of Amalgamated's earnings per share. In no circumstances, he contended, could Norwood's earnings expand sufficiently to overcome this dilution in earnings per share for at least several years. While Mr. Simpson did not deny that Norwood was a promising young company, he argued that no one could foresee the future well enough to predict with confidence that Norwood's profits after taxes would soon reach or exceed a level of $400,000 or $500,000, the minimum range needed to prevent a dilution in Amalgamated's earnings per share.

In this connection Mr. Simpson urged that his numerical illustration was highly conservative in that it assumed no growth in Amalgamated's future earnings per share. In fact, the $5 figure understated reported earnings in 1964 and even more so the projected earnings for 1965. A reasonable allowance for the growth in Amalgamated's earnings per share over the next several years, he pointed out, would require that Norwood's profits after taxes be substantially larger than the top figure of $400,000 shown in his numerical illustration to prevent a dilution in Amalgamated's earnings per share for an indefinite and possibly permanent period.

The proponents of the discounted cash flow method of evaluating acquisitions such as Norwood conceded to Mr. Simpson that it would be preferable for Amalgamated to acquire Norwood for cash rather than by an exchange of stock. But they pointed out to him that since Amalgamated was in a highly liquid position an outright purchase for cash was feasible. Thus Amalgamated's earnings per share would increase provided that the return on Amalgamated's investment in Norwood exceeded that available from money market securities.

Mr. Simpson responded that he recognized the validity of this argument if the Norwood acquisition were viewed in isolation. As a general principle, however, he stated that Norwood should be considered as one of a series of companies that Amalgamated hoped to acquire each year. Mr. Simpson pointed out that, although Amalgamated could probably acquire Norwood without resorting to outside financing, such financing would be required if

Amalgamated pressed its planned program of acquisitions vigorously. He concluded, therefore, that the Norwood acquisition should be required to pass the same earnings-per-share hurdle that he felt would have to be applied to subsequent acquisitions. In summary, then, Mr. Simpson continued to press his original contention, namely, that Norwood should be acquired only if the price were such that no dilution in earnings per share would result if the acquisition were made by an exchange of stock. The most he would concede was that a reasonable time should be allowed so that Norwood's profits would reflect the anticipated benefits from the combined operation before calculating the effect on Amalgamated's earnings per share of acquiring or not acquiring Norwood.

Other influential members of Amalgamated's management were concerned about the impact of the Norwood acquisition on Amalgamated's return on its book investment. They pointed out that Amalgamated was currently earning approximately 8% on the book value of its equity capital. If Norwood were to be acquired for $4,500,000, it would have to earn about $360,000 after taxes to match this rate of return. At best, they contended, several years would pass before earnings of this amount could be reasonably anticipated. Meanwhile the acquisition of Norwood would dilute Amalgamated's return on its book investment.

With these widely conflicting views regarding the appropriate means of evaluating potential acquisitions, all parties concerned were anxious to arrive at a consensus as to the best procedure as soon as possible. Without such a consensus, continuing differences of judgment were bound to occur. These differences would inevitably slow down the company's acquisition program. In addition, favorable opportunities might be rejected and poor ones accepted unless a consistent and defensible method of valuing potential acquisitions could be agreed upon as company policy.

Exhibit 1

AMALGAMATED MANUFACTURING CORPORATION (A)

SELECTED OPERATING DATA, 1960–64

Year	Net Sales*	Income after Taxes*	Earnings per Common Share	Dividends per Common Share	Market Price of Common Stock
1960	$157.8	$ 9.0	$3.87	$2.20	$33–57
1961	158.4	8.6	3.62	2.00	38–45
1962	167.0	8.2	3.41	2.00	38–54
1963	183.3	10.4	4.50	2.00	45–55
1964	200.6	11.8	5.11	2.00	45–55

* In millions of dollars.

Exhibit 2

AMALGAMATED MANUFACTURING CORPORATION (A)

BALANCE SHEET AS OF DECEMBER 31, 1964

(In thousands of dollars)

ASSETS

Current assets:

Cash	$ 5,344
Marketable securities	8,752
Accounts and notes receivable	32,304
Inventories	48,674
Total current assets	$ 95,074
Net fixed assets	103,537
Patent rights and other intangibles	3,086
Other assets	2,304
Total assets	$204,001

LIABILITIES AND STOCKHOLDERS' EQUITY

Current liabilities:

Accounts and notes payable	$ 13,458
Income taxes payable	9,649
Accrued expenses and other liabilities	4,529
Total current liabilities	$ 27,636
Other liabilities (provision for pensions; various reserve accounts; and minority interest)	20,258
Mortgage notes and other noncurrent liabilities	2,927
Total liabilities	$ 50,821
Capital stock:	
Preferred stock	$ 8,478
Common stock	47,319
Retained earnings	97,383
Total stockholders' equity	$153,180
Total liabilities and stockholders' equity	$204,001

Exhibit 3

AMALGAMATED MANUFACTURING CORPORATION (A)

NORWOOD SCREW MACHINERY COMPANY

INCOME STATEMENT FOR YEAR ENDING DECEMBER 31, 1964

(In thousands of dollars)

Net sales	$729.4
Deduct: Cost of goods sold	334.8
Gross profit on sales	$394.6
Deduct: Selling and administrative expenses	252.6
Net operating income	$142.0
Other income less other deductions	14.2
Net profit before income taxes	$156.2
Provision for income taxes	7.8
Net income	$148.4

Exhibit 4

AMALGAMATED MANUFACTURING CORPORATION (A)
NORWOOD SCREW MACHINERY COMPANY

BALANCE SHEET AS OF DECEMBER 31, 1964

(In thousands of dollars)

ASSETS

Current assets:

Cash	$ 109
Accounts receivable	130
Inventories	484
Prepaid expenses	37
Total current assets	$ 760
Net plant and equipment	456
Patents and other intangibles	230
Miscellaneous other assets (including large fire loss claim)	218
Total assets	$1,664

LIABILITIES AND STOCKHOLDERS' EQUITY

Current liabilities:

Accounts payable	$ 88
Advances from officers	84
Notes payable	116
Accrued expenses	19
Accrued taxes	26
Total current liabilities	$ 333
Debentures payable	273
Total liabilities	$ 606

Stockholders' equity:

Common stock	$ 154
Paid-in capital	1,260
Retained earnings (deficit)	(356)
Total equity	$1,058
Total liabilities and equity	$1,664

Exhibit 5

AMALGAMATED MANUFACTURING CORPORATION (A)

Norwood Acquisition Study, Evaluation of Company

(In thousands of dollars)

	Initial Outlay	1966	1967	1968	1969	1970	1971	1972	1973	1974	1975	Total
I. OPERATING STATEMENT												
Net sales		$1,866	$2,500	$3,200	$3,800	$4,400	$4,400	$4,400	$4,400	$4,400	$4,400	$37,766
Cost of sales		840	1,050	1,280	1,444	1,672	1,672	1,672	1,672	1,672	1,672	14,646
Gross profit		$1,026	$1,450	$1,920	$2,356	$2,728	$2,728	$2,728	$2,728	$2,728	$2,728	$23,120
Deduct:												
Selling, general, and administrative		560	750	960	1,140	1,320	1,320	1,320	1,320	1,320	1,320	11,330
Research and development		94	126	160	190	220	220	220	220	220	220	1,890
Net profit before tax		$ 372	$ 574	$ 800	$1,026	$1,188	$1,188	$1,188	$1,188	$1,188	$1,188	$ 9,900
Tax at 50%		186	286	400	514	594	594	594	594	594	594	4,950
Net profit after tax		$ 186	$ 288	$ 400	$ 512	$ 594	$ 594	$ 594	$ 594	$ 594	$ 594	$ 4,950
Cash flow:												
Add:												
Depreciation		88	96	96	96	120						496
Other noncash charges against income		28	28	28	28	28	28	28	28	28	20	272
Deduct:												
Increase in working capital		...	...	160	180	180						520
Capital expenditures		84	...	...	260	...						344
Long-term debt	$ 218*											218
Mortgages	22*											22
Cash contribution from 10 years' operations	$(240)	$ 218	$ 412	$ 364	$ 196	$ 562	$ 622	$ 622	$ 622	$ 622	$ 614	$ 4,614
Present worth contribution at 10%	(240)	198	340	273	134	349	351	319	290	264	237	2,515

II. TOTAL PRESENT WORTH VALUE OF COMPANY AT A 10% DISCOUNT FACTOR

Present worth contribution from operations.................$2,515

Terminal value—present worth of 20 added years of earnings.............1,950

Total present worth value of company...............$4,465

* These outlays are assumed to be made on January 1, 1966.

AMALGAMATED MANUFACTURING
CORPORATION (B)

∧∧

As the case of Amalgamated Manufacturing Corporation (A) indicates (pp. 367–78), there was resistance within the Amalgamated top-management group to acquisitions that would dilute earnings per share even though such acquisitions could be justified by the use of Amalgamated's discounted-cash-flow method of evaluating acquisitions. Consequently, acquisitions that could be financed by cash rather than by an exchange of stock were favored by the management of Amalgamated. This preference was shared by the advocates of both the discounted-cash-flow method and the earnings-per-share method.

One reason for this preference was the low price-earnings multiple at which Amalgamated stock was selling. As Exhibit 1 of the (A) case (p. 375) shows, the average market price of Amalgamated stock was only about 10 times its earnings per share in 1964, and it had not greatly exceeded this figure during most of the 1960–64 period. In 1965 the market price of Amalgamated stock did not rise sufficiently to match the increase in earnings during the first half of 1965. Consequently, at the time of the Norwood negotiations the stock was selling at considerably less than 10 times current earnings per share.

The management of Amalgamated believed that for several years the stock market had valued its shares mainly in terms of the limited outlook for expansion in its main line of equipment rather than in terms of the growth that management believed would result from its aggressive research and development efforts in expanding product areas and from its acquisition program. Until the market placed more weight on these phases of Amalgamated's activities, management preferred to make acquisitions for cash rather than through an exchange of stock.

This preference posed a dilemma. If Amalgamated had to rely on internally generated cash, the pace of its acquisition program would be severely constrained. On the other hand, more acquisitions could be made if they were "paid for" by an exchange of stock, but the price of those acquired for stock would be likely to be excessive in the judgment of the management of Amalgamated.

As a means of resolving this dilemma and of accomplishing other company objectives, Amalgamated had developed a "buy-out" plan for financing acquisitions. Under this plan Amalgamated paid part of the purchase price when the purchase agreement was signed and agreed to make further payments conditional in amount on the future profits of the company being acquired.

From Amalgamated's viewpoint management thought that this method of purchase had several advantages. (1) It reduced Amalgamated's original investment and consequently the risk involved in a new acquisition. (2) It enabled the acquisition to pay for itself partially out of its future profits, thereby deferring and possibly reducing the cash drain on Amalgamated. (3) If the key executives of the company being acquired were also major stockholders, it provided them with a powerful incentive to remain with Amalgamated and to perform well since part of their payment depended on the profits generated by the acquired company. (4) It sometimes offered a tax advantage to selling stockholders, thereby enabling Amalgamated to negotiate more favorable terms for the acquisition than would otherwise have been possible. (5) Finally, it often served as a means of reconciling the divergent views of Amalgamated's management and the owners of the selling company concerning the profit potentialities of the selling company. If the future profits of the selling company proved to be relatively low, the total price that Amalgamated would be obligated to pay would be correspondingly reduced. On the other hand, if the normally optimistic profit estimates of the owners of the selling company proved to be correct, they would benefit by the profit sharing contingency in the buy-out plan. Moreover, in those instances in which the optimistic estimates of the sellers were correct Amalgamated could well afford to pay a premium price.

In reviewing the possible acquisition of the Norwood Screw Machinery Company the financial staff of Amalgamated had prepared a tentative buy-out proposal for the consideration of its top management. This plan was typical of others that had been employed by Amalgamated in previous acquisitions. The Norwood plan was based on the same profit projections and other financial data shown in Exhibit 5 of the (A) case (p. 378). This plan, as summarized in Exhibit 1, contained the following provisions:

1. On the closing of the purchase agreement (assumed to occur on December 31, 1965) Amalgamated would pay $2,000,000 to the stockholders of Norwood for all its outstanding stock. Amalgamated would also pay off Norwood's long-term debt of $240,000 as of this date.

2. The Norwood stockholders would be given 695,000 "certificates of participation" in the combined companies. Amalgamated would guarantee a payment of $3 for each certificate. The holders of the certificates would share in the profits of the Norwood division of Amalgamated over the next 10 years. The certificates could be redeemed at the option of the holders at the end of any year within the 10-year period. On redemption the certificate holder would receive his guaranteed $3 per certificate plus his share of the profits that had accrued at the time of redemption. All certificates had to be presented for redemption by the end of the 10th year.

This buy-out plan committed Amalgamated to a minimum payment of $4,325,000 for the acquisition of Norwood, nearly half of which would be deferred from 1 to 10 years. This guaranteed payment was significantly lower than the maximum cash outlay of $4,465,000—as estimated in Exhibit 5 of the (A) case—which Amalgamated could afford to make in an outright purchase of Norwood. The smaller guaranteed payment, however, was offset by the right of the former Norwood stockholders to share in part of the profits of the Norwood division under Amalgamated's ownership for the next 10 years.

3. For each of the 10 years after the acquisition, Amalgamated would subtract from the profits of the Norwood division 10% of its initial investment in Norwood, or $224,000. The remaining profits of each year would be split between Amalgamated and the holders of the certificates of participation, with 25% going to Amalgamated and 75% *accruing* to the certificate holders.

4. All the cash realized from the Norwood division would go to Amalgamated. Cash would be paid out to the holders of certificates of participation *only* when these certificates were turned in for redemption. When certificates were turned in for redemption, Amalgamated would be considered to be the holder of these certificates and would participate on a pro rata basis with the other certificate holders in the share of the profits accruing to the certificate holders. In effect, the 75% share of the annual profits in excess of $224,000 would be reduced in order to reflect the proportion of the certificates redeemed to date.

Outstanding certificates could be redeemed in any amount at the end of any year from 1 to 10. The timing of the redemption of the certificates would affect Amalgamated's profitability index. (The profitability index was defined by Amalgamated as the discount rate required to equate the present worth of all cash outlays with that of all cash inflows. The terminal value at the end of year 10, as described in the (A) case, was treated as a cash inflow. In other words, the profitability index was substantially equivalent to the estimated "internal rate of return" as this concept is commonly defined.)

*   *   *   *   *

Exhibit 1 illustrates the buy-out plan suggested by the Amalgamated staff for the Norwood acquisition. The data are taken from the preceding description and from the profit projections recorded in Exhibit 5 of the (A) case. Calculations are presented in Exhibit 1 for three possible patterns of redemption: (1) all certificates are assumed to be redeemed at the end of year 1; (2) the same assumption is made for year 5; and (3) for year 10. The profitability index for all combinations of redemptions of certificates in various years will be between those calculated for total redemption in years 1 and 10.

In computing the profitability indices shown in Exhibit 1 the cash outflows consist of the initial outlay of $2,240,000 at the beginning of the first year, and, as the case may be, the outlays required to redeem the outstanding certificates at the end of the 1st, 5th, or 10th years, respectively. The cash inflows are the same as those shown in the next to last line of the cash inflows recorded in Exhibit 5 of the (A) case. The terminal value is calculated as the present worth of an estimated level stream of annual cash inflows of $594,000 for years 11 through 30. Profits after taxes and cash flows are assumed to be equal for years 11 through 30: more explicitly, all noncash expenses except depreciation are assumed to have been exhausted by year 10; capital expenditures are assumed to be equal to depreciation; and net working capital is assumed to remain unchanged after year 10. Under the assumptions of Exhibit 1 the profitability indices range from 11.5% to 13.9% depending on the timing of the redemption of the certificates of participation.

*   *   *   *   *

The specific buy-out plan outlined for the Norwood acquisition was only one of several used by Amalgamated. In some cases, for example, the profits of the acquired company were split directly with the former shareholders without first allocating to Amalgamated all the profits up to 10% on its initial investment. However, the basic procedure and objective of Amalgamated remained the same—to set payment terms that would be consistent with the maximum purchase price as calculated in the (A) case and would give Amalgamated a satisfactory return (computed on a discounted-cash-flow basis) on its actual cash commitments.

Exhibit 1

AMALGAMATED MANUFACTURING CORPORATION (B)

NORWOOD ACQUISITION STUDY: BUY-OUT PLAN

(In thousands of dollars)

I. BUY-OUT PLAN

	Initial Outlay	1966	1967	1968	1969	1970	1971	1972	1973	1974	1975
Original cash payment	$2,000										
Long-term debt repayment	240										
Net profit after taxes		$186	$288	$400	$512	$594	$594	$594	$594	$594	$594
Amalgamated's share at 10%		224	224	224	224	224	224	224	224	224	224
Balance available for accrual		0	26*	176	288	370	370	370	370	370	370
Amalgamated's share of profits (25%)		0	6	44	72	92	92	92	92	92	92
Accrue 75% to Norwood		0	20	132	216	278	278	278	278	278	278
Cumulative amount accrued to Norwood		$ 0	$ 20	$ 152	$ 368	$ 646	$ 924	$1,202	$1,480	$1,758	$2,036
Add: Guaranteed amount ($3 a share)		2,085	2,085	2,085	2,085	2,085	2,085	2,085	2,085	2,085	2,085
Total delayed payment to Norwood		$2,085	$2,105	$2,237	$2,453	$2,731	$3,009	$3,287	$3,565	$3,843	$4,121
Profitability index to Amalgamated		11.5%				12.5%					13.9%
		(If all certificates redeemed in 1966)				*(If all certificates redeemed in 1970)*					*(If all certificates redeemed in 1975)*

II. CALCULATION OF PROFITABILITY INDEXES

	Initial Outlay	1966	End of 1966	1967	1968	1969	1970	End of 1970	1971	1972	1973	1974	1975	End of 1975	Ter. Val. Yrs. 1976–95†	Profitability Index†
1. All certificates redeemed at end of 1966	-2,240	218	-2,085													11.5%
2. All certificates redeemed at end of 1970	-2,240	218		412	364	196	562	-2,731							594/yr.	12.5%
3. All certificates redeemed at end of 1975	-2,240	218		412	364	196	562		622	622	622	622	614	-4,121	594/yr.	13.9%

* Balance after adjustment for 1966 profit deficiency.

† The profitability index is the annual rate of discount at which the present worth of expected cash outlays is just equal to the present worth of expected cash inflows. Included in the cash inflows is an annuity of $594,000 annually received at the end of each year from 1976–95, inclusive.

COOPER INDUSTRIES, INC.

^^

In May, 1972, Robert Cizik, executive vice president of Cooper Industries, Inc., was reviewing acquisition candidates for his company's diversification program. One of the companies, Nicholson File Company, had been approached by Cooper Industries three years earlier but had rejected all overtures. Now, however, Nicholson was in the middle of a takeover fight that might provide Cooper with a chance to gain control.

Cooper Industries

Cooper Industries was organized in 1919 as a manufacturer of heavy machinery and equipment. By the mid-1950's, the company was a leading producer of engines and massive compressors used to force natural gas through pipelines and oil out of wells. Management was concerned, however, over its heavy dependence on sales to the oil and gas industries and the violent fluctuation of earnings caused by the cyclical nature of heavy machinery and equipment sales. Although the company's long-term sales and earnings growth had been above average, its cyclicality had dampened Wall Street's interest in the stock substantially. (Cooper's historical operating results and financial condition are summarized in Exhibits 1 and 2.)

Initial efforts to lessen the earnings volatility were not successful. Between 1959 and 1966, Cooper acquired (1) a supplier of portable industrial power tools, (2) a manufacturer of small industrial air and process compressors, (3) a maker of small pumps and compressors for oil field applications, and (4) a producer of tire changing tools for the automotive market. The acquisitions broadened Cooper's markets but left it still highly sensitive to general economic conditions.

A full review of Cooper's acquisition strategy was initiated in 1966 by the company. After several months of study, three criteria were established for all acquisitions. First, the industry should be one in which Cooper could become a major factor. This requirement was in line with management's goal of leadership within a few distinct areas of business. Second, the industry should be fairly stable with a broad market for the products and a product line of largely "small ticket" items. This product definition was intended to eliminate any company that had undue profit dependence upon a single customer or

384

several large sales per year. Finally, it was decided to acquire only leading companies in their respective market segments.

The new strategy was initially implemented with the acquisition in 1967 of the Lufkin Rule Company, the world's largest manufacturer of measuring rules and tapes. Cooper acquired a quality product line, an established distribution system of 35,000 retail hardware stores throughout the United States, and plants in the United States, Canada, and Mexico. It also gained the services of William Rector, president of Lufkin, and Hal Stevens, vice president of sales. Both were extremely knowledgeable in the hand tool business and had worked together effectively for years. Their goal was to build through acquisition a hand tool company with a full product line that would use a common sales and distribution system and joint advertising. To do this they needed Cooper's financial strength.

Lufkin provided a solid base to which two other companies were added. In 1969, the Crescent Niagara Corporation was acquired. The company had been highly profitable in the early 1960's, but had suffered in recent years under the mismanagement of some investor–entrepreneurs who gained control in 1963. A series of acquisitions of weak companies with poor product lines eroded the company's overall profitability until, in 1967, a small loss was reported. Discouraged, the investors wanted to get out and Cooper—eager to add Crescent's well-known and high-quality wrenches, pliers, and screwdrivers to its line—was interested. It was clear that some of Crescent's lines would have to be dropped and inefficient plants would have to be closed, but the wrenches, pliers, and screwdrivers were an important part of Cooper's product policy.

In 1970, Cooper further expanded into hand tools with the acquisition of the Weller Electric Corporation. Weller was the world's leading supplier of soldering tools to the industrial, electronic, and consumer markets. It provided Cooper with a new, high-quality product line and production capacity in England, West Germany, and Mexico. (Information on the three acquisitions is provided in Exhibit 3.)

Cooper was less successful in its approach to a fourth company in the hand tool business, the Nicholson File Company. Nicholson was on the original "shopping list" of acceptable acquisition candidates which Mr. Cizik and Mr. Rector had developed, but several attempts to interest Nicholson in exploring merger possibilities had failed. The Nicholson family had controlled and managed the company since its founding in 1864 and Paul Nicholson, chairman of the board, had no interest in joining forces with anyone.

Nicholson File Company

But Nicholson was too inviting a takeover target to be overlooked or ignored for long. A relatively poor sales and profit performance in recent years, conservative accounting and financial policies, and a low percentage of outstanding stock held by the Nicholson family and management all contributed to its vulnerability. Annual sales growth of 2% was far behind the industry growth rate of 6% per year, and profit margins had slipped to only one third those of other hand tool manufacturers. In 1971, the Nicholson common stock was trading near its lowest point in many years and well below its book value of $51.25. Lack of investor interest in the stock was reflected in its low price–earnings ratio of 10–14, which compared with 14–17 times earnings for other leading hand tool companies. The stock was clearly selling on the basis of its dividend yield, with only limited hopes for capital appreciation. (Exhibits 4 and 5 show Nicholson's operating results and balance sheets.)

What made Nicholson so attractive was its basic competitive strength— strengths that the family-dominated management had not translated into earnings. The company was one of the largest domestic manufacturers of hand tools and was a leader in its two main product areas. Nicholson held a 50% share of the $50 million market for files and rasps, where it offered a broad, high-quality line with a very strong brand name. Its second product line, hand saws and saw blades, also had an excellent reputation for quality and held a 9% share of this $200 million market. Only Sears, Roebuck and Company and Disston, Inc. had larger market shares.

Nicholson's greatest asset, however, was its distribution system. Forty-eight direct salesmen and 28 file and saw engineers marketed its file, rasp, and saw products to 2,100 hardware wholesalers in the United States and Canada. These wholesalers in turn sold to 53,000 retail outlets. Their efforts were supported by heavy advertising and promotional programs. Overseas the company's products were sold in 137 countries through 140 local sales representatives. The company seemed to have all the necessary strengths to share fully in the 6–7% annual sales growth forecast for the industry.

The raid by H. K. Porter Company

Cooper was not alone in its interest in Nicholson. H. K. Porter Company, a conglomerate with wide ranging interests in electrical equipment, tools, non-ferrous metals, and rubber products, had acquired 44,000 shares of Nicholson stock in 1967 and had been an attentive stockholder ever since. On March 3, 1972, Porter informed Nicholson management of its plan to tender immediately for 437,000 of Nicholson's 584,000 outstanding shares at $42 per share in cash. The offer would terminate on April 4, unless extended by Porter; and the company was unwilling to acquire less than enough shares to constitute a majority.

Nicholson management was alarmed by both the proposal and the proposer. The company would contribute less than one sixth of the combined sales and would clearly be just another operating division of Porter. It was feared that Porter's quest for higher profits might lead to aggressive cost cutting and the elimination of marginal product lines. Nicholson's Atkins Saw Division seemed especially vulnerable in view of its low profitability.

Loss of control seemed both painful and likely. The $42 cash offer represented a $12 premium over the most recent price of the stock and threatened to create considerable stockholder interest. The disappointing performance of the stock in recent years would undoubtedly increase the attractiveness of the $42 offer to Nicholson's 4,000 stockholders. And the Nicholson family and management owned only 20% of the outstanding shares—too little to assure continued control.

Immediately after learning of the Porter tender offer, Mr. Cizik and Mr. Rector approached the Nicholson management with an offer of help. It was clear that Nicholson had to move immediately and forcefully; the first ten days of a tender offer are critical. Cizik and Rector stressed that Nicholson must find a better offer and find it fast. Indeed, Cooper would be willing to make such an offer if Nicholson's management and directors would commit themselves to it—now.

Nicholson was not ready for such decisive action, however, and three days passed without any decision. With each day the odds of a successful counteroffer diminished. Finally, the Cooper officers decided the risks were too great and that Porter would learn of Cooper's offer of help and might retaliate. Cooper's stock was depressed and it was possible that an angry Porter management might strike for control of Cooper. The offer was withdrawn.

By late March, the situation was increasing in seriousness. Management of Nicholson moved to block the raid. It personally talked with the large shareholders and it made a strong public statement recommending against the offer. But announcements by Porter indicated that a substantial number of Nicholson shares were being tendered. It was no longer a matter of whether or not to be acquired. The issue was, By whom!

Management sought to find an alternative merger that would ensure continuity of Nicholson management and operating independence. Several companies had communicated with Nicholson in the wake of the Porter announcement, but no one other than Cooper had made a specific proposal. This was largely due to their reluctance to compete at the price levels being discussed or to enter into a fight with Porter.

Finally, on April 3, agreement was reached with VLN Corporation on the terms of a merger with VLN. VLN was a broadly diversified company with major interests in original and replacement automotive equipment and in publishing. Under the VLN merger terms, one share of new VLN cumulative convertible preferred stock would be exchanged for each share of Nicholson common stock. The VLN preferred stock would pay an annual dividend of $1.60 and would be convertible into five shares of VLN common stock during the first year following the merger, scaling down to four shares after the fourth year. The preferred stock would be callable at $50 a share after the fifth year and would have liquidating rights of $50 per share. (See Exhibit 6 for a financial summary of VLN.)

Nicholson management, assured of continued operating independence, supported the VLN offer actively. In a letter to the stockholders, Paul Nicholson pointed out that (1) the exchange would be a tax-free transaction, (2) the $1.60 preferred dividend equalled the current rate on the Nicholson common stock, and (3) a preferred share was worth a minimum of $53.10 (VLN common stock had closed at $10.62 on the day prior to the offer). He felt confident that the necessary majority of the outstanding common stock would be voted in favor of the proposed merger when it was brought to a vote in the fall. (Under Rhode Island law, a simple majority was sufficient to author- ize the merger.)

Porter quickly counterattacked by pointing out to Nicholson stockholders that VLN common stock had recently sold for as low as $4⅝, which would put a value in the first year of only $23.12 on the VLN preferred stock. Fur- thermore, anyone who converted into VLN common stock would suffer a sharp income loss since VLN had paid no common dividends since 1970.

Nicholson's stockholders were thus presented with two very contradictory appraisals of the VLN offer. Each company based its argument on some stock price, either the highest or the lowest, that would make the converted pre- ferred stock compare favorably or not with the $42 cash offer.

Opportunity for Cooper?

Mr. Cizik and his staff were still attracted by the potential profits to be realized from Nicholson. It was felt that Nicholson's efforts to sell to every market segment resulted in an excessive number of products, which held down manufacturing efficiency and ballooned inventories. Cooper estimated that Nicholson's cost of goods sold could be reduced from 69% of sales to 65%.

The other major area of cost reduction was Nicholson's selling expenses. There was a substantial overlap of Nicholson's sales force and that established by Cooper for its Lufkin-Weller-Crescent hand tool lines. Elimination of the sales and advertising duplications would lower selling, general and adminis- trative expenses from 22% of sales to 19%.

There were other possible sources of earnings, but they were more diffi- cult to quantify. For instance, 75% of Nicholson's sales were to the industrial market and only 25% to the consumer market. In contrast, sales by Cooper's hand tool group were distributed between the two markets in virtually the exact opposite proportions. Thus, sales increases could be expected from Nicholson's "pulling" more Cooper products into the industrial markets and vice versa for the consumer market. Also, Cooper was eager to use Nichol- son's strong European distribution system to sell its other hand tool lines.

The battle between Porter and VLN seemed to provide Cooper with an unexpected, second opportunity to gain control of Nicholson. Porter had ended up with just 133,000 shares tendered in response to its offer—far short of the 249,000 shares needed to give it majority control.[1] Its slate of directors had been defeated by Nicholson management at the Nicholson annual meeting on April 21. T. M. Evans, president of Porter, now feared that Nicholson might consummate the merger with VLN and that Porter would be faced with the unhappy prospect of receiving VLN preferred stock for its 177,000 shares of Nicholson stock. Mr. Evans knew that the VLN stock had been a lackluster

---

[1] Porter needed 292,584 shares to hold 50.1% majority control. It already owned 43,806 shares and needed, therefore, an additional 248,778 shares.

performer and might not show any significant growth in the near term. Furthermore, the $1.60 dividend rate seemed low in relation to current market yields on straight preferred stocks of 7%. Finally, he feared that it would be difficult to sell a large holding of VLN stock, which traded in small volume on the American Stock Exchange.

On the other hand, a merger of Cooper and Nicholson would allow Mr. Evans to convert his Nicholson shares into either common stock or convertible preferred stock of Cooper. This was a much more attractive alternative, assuming that an acceptable exchange rate could be set. Mr. Evans anticipated that earnings should rebound sharply from the cyclical downturn in 1971, and felt that Cooper stock would show significant price appreciation. Furthermore, Cooper stock was traded on the New York Exchange, which provided substantial liquidity. At a private meeting in late April, Mr. Evans tentatively agreed to support a Cooper-Nicholson merger on the condition that he receive Cooper common or convertible securities in a tax-free exchange worth at least $50 for each Nicholson share he held.

Mr. Cizik was now faced with the critical decision of whether or not to move for control. Cooper had acquired 29,000 shares of Nicholson stock during the preceding month in the open market—in part to build some bargaining power but largely to keep the loose shares out of the hands of Porter. Still uncommitted, however, were an estimated 50,000–100,000 shares that had been bought by speculators in the hope of an escalation of acquisition offers. Another 150,000–200,000 shares were unaccounted for, although Mr. Cizik suspected that a considerable number would go with the recommendation of Nicholson management. (Exhibit 7 shows Mr. Cizik's best estimate of the distribution of Nicholson stock in early May.) His hopes for gaining 50.1% of the Nicholson shares outstanding[2] depended upon his gaining support of at least 86,000 of the shares still either uncommitted or unaccounted for.

If he decided to seek control, it would be necessary to establish both the price and the form of the offer. Clearly, the terms would have to be sufficiently attractive to secure the shares needed to gain majority control.

Mr. Cizik also felt that the terms should be acceptable to the Nicholson management. Once the merger was complete, Cooper would need to work with the Nicholson family and management. He did not want them to feel that they and other Nicholson stockholders were cheated by the merger. As a matter of policy Cooper had never made an "unfriendly" acquisition and this one was to be no exception. The offer should be one that would be supported by the great majority of the stockholders.

However, the price and the form of the payment had to be consistent with

---

[2] Nicholson File was incorporated in Rhode Island. Under Rhode Island corporation law, a merger can be voted by shareholders holding a majority of the common stock outstanding. For reasons specific both to the laws of Rhode Island and to the Nicholson situation, dissenting stockholders of Nicholson would not be entitled to exercise the rights of dissent and would be forced to accept the exchange offer.

Cooper's concern that the acquisition earn a satisfactory long-term return and improve the trend of Cooper's earnings per share over the next five years. (A forecast of Cooper's earnings per share is shown in Exhibit 8.) The company anticipated making additional acquisitions, possibly on an exchange of stock basis, and maintenance of a strong earnings pattern and stock price was therefore important. On May 3, the common stock of Cooper and Nicholson closed at $24 and $44 respectively.

Exhibit 1

COOPER INDUSTRIES, INC.

CONDENSED OPERATING AND STOCKHOLDER INFORMATION

	1967	1968	1969	1970	1971
Operations (In millions):					
Net sales	$ 198	$ 206	$ 212	$ 226	$ 208
Cost of goods sold	141	145	154	164	161
Depreciation	4	5	4	4	4
Selling and administrative expenses	23	25	29	29	29
Interest expense	1	2	3	4	3
Income before taxes and extraordinary items	$ 29	$ 29	$ 22	$24	$ 11
Income taxes	14	15	11	12	5
Income before extraordinary items	$ 15.2	$ 13.9	$ 10.6	$ 12.4	$ 5.6
Preferred dividend	1.0	.9	.9	.9	.9
Net income applicable to common stock	$ 14.2	$ 13.0	$ 9.7	$ 11.5	$ 4.7
Per Share of Common Stock:					
Earnings before extraordinary items	$ 3.34	$ 3.07	$ 2.33	$ 2.75	$ 1.12
Dividends	1.20	1.25	1.40	1.40	1.40
Book value	16.43	17.26	18.28	19.68	18.72
Market price	23–59	36–57	22–50	22–35	18–38
Price-earnings ratio	7–18	12–19	9–22	8–13	16–34

Exhibit 2

COOPER INDUSTRIES, INC.

BALANCE SHEET AS OF DECEMBER 31, 1971

(In millions)

ASSETS		LIABILITIES AND NET WORTH	
Cash	$ 9	Accounts payable	$ 30
Accounts receivable	49	Accrued taxes	3
Inventories	57	Long-term debt due	5
Other	2	Total current liabilities	$ 38
Total current assets	$117	Long-term debt*	34
Net plant and equipment	47	Deferred taxes	4
Other	8	Preferred stock	11
Total assets	$172	Common equity (4,218,691 shares outstanding)	85
		Total liabilities and net worth	$172

* Maturities of long-term debt are $5.5 million, $6.0 million, $4.0 million, $2.0 million, and $2.0 million in the years 1972 through 1976 respectively.

Exhibit 3

COOPER INDUSTRIES, INC.

SUMMARY OF RECENT ACQUISITIONS

(In millions)

	Year Preceding Acquisition by Cooper				
	Sales	Net Income	Book Value	Acquisition Price Paid	Form of Transaction
Lufkin Rule Company...............	$22	$1.4	$15	$20.6	Convertible preferred
Crescent Niagara Corporation..........	16	0.04	4.9	12.5	Cash
Weller Electric Corporation...........	10	0.9	4.4	14.6	Common stock

Exhibit 4

COOPER INDUSTRIES, INC.

CONDENSED OPERATING AND STOCKHOLDER INFORMATION FOR NICHOLSON FILE COMPANY

	1967	1968	1969	1970	1971
Operations (In millions):					
Net sales..........................	$48.5	$49.1	$53.7	$54.8	$55.3
Cost of goods sold..................	32.6	33.1	35.9	37.2	37.9
Selling, general, and administrative expenses.........................	10.7	11.1	11.5	11.9	12.3
Depreciation expense...............	2.0	2.3	2.4	2.3	2.1
Interest expense....................	0.4	0.7	0.8	0.8	0.8
Other deductions...................	0.3	0.1	0.2	0.2	0.2
Income before taxes................	$ 2.53	$ 1.85	$ 2.97	$ 2.42	$ 2.02
Taxes*............................	0.60	0.84	1.31	0.88	0.67
Net income........................	$ 1.93	$ 1.01	$ 1.66	$ 1.54	$ 1.35
Percentage of Sales:					
Cost of goods sold..................	67%	67%	67%	68%	69%
Selling, general, and administrative expenses.........................	22%	23%	21%	22%	22%
Income before taxes................	5.2%	3.8%	5.5%	4.4%	3.7%
Stockholder Information:					
Earnings per share..................	$ 3.19	$ 1.65	$ 2.88	$ 2.64	$ 2.32
Dividends per share.................	1.60	1.60	1.60	1.60	1.60
Book value per share...............	45.66	48.03	49.31	50.20	51.25
Market price.......................	33-46	35-48	29-41	25-33	23-32
Price-earnings ratio................	10-14	21-30	10-14	9-13	10-14

* The ratio of income taxes to income before taxes has been reduced primarily by the investment tax credit and by the inclusion in income of equity in net income of partially-owned foreign companies, the taxes for which are provided for in the accounts of such companies and not in the tax provision of Nicholson. It was estimated that the average tax rate would be 40% in future years.

Exhibit 5

COOPER INDUSTRIES, INC.

BALANCE SHEET OF NICHOLSON FILE COMPANY AS OF DECEMBER 31, 1971

(In millions)

ASSETS		LIABILITIES AND NET WORTH	
Cash	$ 1	Accounts payable	$ 2
Accounts receivable	8	Other	2
Inventories*	18	*Total current liabilities*	$ 4
Other	1	Long-term debt	12
Total current assets	$28	Common stock	31
Investment in subsidiaries	3	*Total liabilities and net worth*	$47
Net plant and equipment	16		
Total assets	$47		

* Inventories in the amount of $11.8 million are priced at cost on the last-in, first-out method. The estimated replacement cost exceeds the carrying amounts by $9.2 million. The remaining inventories are priced at the lower of cost on the first-in, first-out method or market.

Exhibit 6

COOPER INDUSTRIES, INC.

CONDENSED OPERATING AND STOCKHOLDER
INFORMATION FOR VLN CORPORATION

	1967	1968	1969	1970	1971
Operations (In millions):					
Net sales	$45	$97	$99	$98	$100
Net income	1.97	3.20	3.20	1.13	2.98
Financial Position (In millions):					
Current assets	$25	$46	$49	$41	$ 46
Current liabilities	6	11	15	10	13
Net working capital	19	35	34	31	33
Long-term debt	10	18	16	15	17
Shareholders' equity	21	36	40	39	41
Stockholder Information:					
Earnings per share	$ 0.78	$ 0.61	$ 0.53	$ 0.27	$ 0.54
Dividends per share	—	—	—	.20	—
Shareholders' equity per share	8.23	9.64	10.00	9.24	9.69
Market price range	6–17	10–18	7–18	4–10	5–8
Price-earnings ratio	8–22	16–30	13–34	15–37	9–15

Exhibit 7

COOPER INDUSTRIES, INC.

ESTIMATED DISTRIBUTION OF NICHOLSON FILE COMPANY STOCK

Shares supporting Cooper:
H. K. Porter	177,000	
Cooper Industries	29,000	206,000

Shares supporting VLN:
Nicholson family and management	117,000	
Owned by VLN	14,000	131,000

Shares owned by speculators	50–100,000
Shares unaccounted for	197–147,000
Total Nicholson shares outstanding	584,000

Exhibit 8

COOPER INDUSTRIES, INC.

FIVE-YEAR FORECAST OF EARNINGS, EXCLUDING
NICHOLSON FILE COMPANY*

	1972	1973	1974	1975	1976
Net income available to common stockholders (in millions)	$11.0	$11.9	$12.8	$13.8	$15.0
Number of shares outstanding (in millions)	4.21	4.21	4.21	4.21	4.21
Primary earnings per share	$ 2.61	$ 2.83	$ 3.04	$ 3.27	$ 3.56

* Casewriter's estimates

ASSOCIATED TECHNOLOGY
LABORATORIES, INC.

∧∧∧

By late April, 1958, negotiations concerning the statutory merger of Magnus Controls, Inc., and Associated Technology Laboratories, Inc., (ATL) had reached their final stages. The primary problem remaining was to determine a basis on which shares of ATL common stock would be exchanged for those of Magnus Controls. Once the directors of each firm had agreed on this point, the proposed merger could be set before the stockholders of the two companies for their approval; and if two thirds of each organization's stockholders voted in favor of the move, the merger would be effected.

The price determination problem had been delayed until the end of the negotiations for several reasons. First, interest in the possibilities of a merger had been developed over more than a year's time, during which the stock market appraisal of each company's worth had been subject to considerable variation. Second, the management of each firm realized that there were significant difficulties involved in assessing the relative values of organizations as basically dissimilar as Magnus Controls and ATL. Finally, neither firm had at any time been fully committed to the merger from an operational standpoint; each had at its disposal alternative means of accomplishing the hoped-for objective of the merger. All of these considerations posed difficulties for the managements of the two firms in arriving at an exchange basis that they felt could be presented as reasonable to their respective shareholders.

Interest in the possibility of merger with Magnus Controls was a fairly recent development at ATL. Throughout most of its corporate history the company had received offers to merge or sell out on the average of twice per month, and invariably these offers had been discouraged. For more than a year, however, ATL had been engaged in contract negotiations with Magnus Controls aimed at the joint development and marketing of certain specialized industrial products. While no contract had ever actually been agreed upon, the management and various other employees of the two companies had developed a cordial relationship with each other. This factor, together with a number of other considerations noted below, had caused ATL management to reevaluate its position with respect to merger.

394

ATL was located in southern New England. The company was incorporated in 1945 to take over a laboratory that had been organized by Columbia University during World War II for work on electronic antisubmarine devices. The Columbia group was joined by personnel with similar skills from the Radiation Laboratory of Massachusetts Institute of Technology and the Radio Research Laboratory of Harvard University, both of which had also been established during the war for the development of electronic countermeasures. By April, 1958, the engineering staff had grown to about 400.

ATL was primarily occupied with the development of electronic systems ordered under government contracts or subcontracts, generally in the technical fields of radar moving target indicators, radar performance monitors, microwave components, and communications equipment. The company also produced analog and specialized digital computer devices for military applications, and electronic gauging and automatic control devices for industrial application. Historically these industrial products had accounted for less than 10% of annual sales volume, while approximately 90% of the company's sales had been to the government or to government agencies. In contrast, sales of the Magnus Controls organization were in almost the inverse ratio of industrial to government business.

A preponderant dependence on government business was not the ideal situation in which ATL management wished to be. For several years the company's top executives had advocated the development of products and a marketing force aimed at industrial customers. In part they were motivated by the potentially greater profitability of industrial sales; additionally, they viewed industrial sales as being inherently more stable than government work. For example, ATL's sales had leveled off in the 1954–56 period as a result of (a) the post-Korean decline in annual defense expenditures from $54 billion to $41 billion; (b) the completion of a $9 million government contract for a weapons control system; and (c) the shift in emphasis in defense spending from production to research and development work.

The possibilities for commercial products that were uncovered by ATL engineering and scientific personnel in the course of contract research and development work often stimulated the interest of company executives. Over a period of time a number of commercial products had actually been brought to the production stage by ATL's engineering staff. Since the firm specialized in electronics technology, most of these products were in the field of "automation controls," the process whereby industrial machining processes could be performed using an electronically programmed and controlled set of operations. A typical device which ATL had developed for this purpose, and which might ultimately be an important component of an automated process, was the Inchworm motor. The Inchworm permitted and controlled microscopic tool or workpiece movements under heavy loads in automated centerless grinder operations. As a single product the Inchworm had limited value, although as part of a fully automated system the device might often be invaluable.

The Inchworm had been developed not in response to a particular industrial customer's requirements but rather in the hope that once it had proved successful it could be marketed to a wide number of firms. Unfortunately, marketing efforts had developed into a greater problem than was originally anticipated. ATL's small industrial marketing staff discovered that unless the customer could be shown specific applications in his operations where the Inchworm could be utilized, he was generally not interested. Furthermore, even when an application was found, the customer normally resisted making major changes in his existing process.

The Inchworm experience served to point up several characteristics of industrial marketing that had not previously been fully appreciated by ATL management. In the first place they found that many potential industrial customers were skeptical of products emanating from small electronics firms. Purchasing agents and engineering personnel of many large firms were approached almost daily by salesmen who were totally unfamiliar to them, representing various electronics organizations and attempting to sell some new device or process. The customer personnel often did not have sufficient time to review all the new ideas and products presented to them and so tended to rely on their established buying relationships to fulfill their needs.

In the second place, ATL's marketing personnel found that even when potential customers did express interest in the firm's product, they wanted to see a completely automated system rather than a single component part with limited applications. The cost of developing such a system was typically far greater than ATL could afford, or than the customer was willing to pay.

Finally, the ATL executives discovered that they had no really effective way of following the industrial markets sufficiently closely to be able to forecast future customer requirements. Knowing what the customer would want a year or more in advance of the actual need was critical to successful product development, but to be able to forecast these needs a firm had to maintain constant contact with the customer. Without adequate personnel ATL executives could not hope to achieve this sort of relationship; and unless they did they would not know which of the many available possibilities to pursue. This was viewed as a most critical problem.

A second major problem connected with dependence on government markets and of concern to ATL management was a disturbing trend evident in government purchasing procedures. Essentially, the trend was toward research and development contracts covering entire systems—in the case of communications, for example, "communications systems," which included not only the radio and electronic equipment involved but also antennae, power generators, and the like. Under this practice smaller firms were at a disadvantage in bidding for large contracts, since they were often unable to establish the degree of financial strength required by the contracting agent or officer. In such cases the small firms would be relegated to the position of subcontractor, which was even more risky than accepting government business at the prime contractor level.

The impact of this aspect of government purchasing policy had been driven home to ATL during early 1957, when an important project for which the firm had performed all preliminary research was contracted to a large airframe company for development. The amount involved in the development contract was approximately $20 million, and it promised to yield considerably greater profits than the preliminary research. In the eyes of the contracting officer, ATL—with peak annual sales up to that point of only $12.3 million—was not nearly strong enough financially to justify a contract of the size indicated. The fact that independent sources outside of ATL were willing to guarantee that the work would be adequately financed did not alter the contracting officer's stand. His position was that he would have to justify his decision to superiors on the basis of actual financial data and operating experience; the fact that bank credit or some other source of funds was available, if necessary, for the performance of the contract would not constitute the type of justification required.

In the period following the failure to get the $20 million contract and up to the time of negotiations with Magnus Controls, the trend toward fewer and larger contracts continued and ATL management encountered other instances where the company's relatively small size prohibited it from getting attractive prime contract business. By late 1957 ATL management was convinced that some method of increasing the organization's financial strength would have to be evolved if the company was to continue to operate effectively in the government market. Aside from joining with a larger organization two alternatives seemed feasible: a public sale of stock, or combination with a smaller firm. Both of these alternatives, however, had disadvantages.

A public sale of common stock in an amount sufficiently large to materially improve the company's financial position, according to ATL management's reasoning, might tend to restrict the freedom currently enjoyed by the company to pursue various basic research objectives. While not a particular threat to control, large numbers of public stockholders might obligate the firm to concentrate more on immediate profits than had historically been necessary, perhaps to the detriment of long-term growth and stability. As of early 1958, 35% of ATL stock was owned by employees, 55% by two large and highly regarded venture capital organizations, and only 10% by the public. The venture capital interests had consistently been willing to respect the judgment of management, although there had at times been minor disagreements. These organizations were primarily occupied with supplying capital for small, scientifically oriented firms to which other sources of funds were not available. Their influence was normally limited to financial affairs and was exerted only sparingly. By design, however, they attempted to keep their investments in young enterprises, and when a particular investment had "matured"—i.e., was no longer dependent on their support—they generally sought to withdraw from their position.

The large employee stockholdings and the small amount of publicly owned stock, combined with the traditionally agreeable attitude of the venture capital interests, had led to a high degree of flexibility for ATL in the past. Management believed that this situation might change if investment banking interests and new stockholder groups were to exercise influence in the future.

With respect to combining with smaller firms ATL management had initiated action on several occasions, but without success. Many smaller firms evidenced the same attitude toward ATL as ATL had historically shown toward larger firms interested in merger. By early 1958 ATL management conceded that while not impossible, it was unlikely that a smaller firm with the desired characteristics could be acquired, at least within the next few years. Moreover, a combination with a smaller firm would not really add the kind of financial strength that would be necessary. Consideration of the above factors by ATL coincided with the contract negotiations with Magnus Controls, and in early 1958 ATL management decided to reevaluate its position in relation to the larger organization.

ATL's original introduction to Magnus Controls had come in the fall of 1956 when Mr. Brown, an independent consultant, had inquired whether ATL management would be interested in discussing the possibility of merger with the larger firm. Magnus Controls, with central offices in the Midwest, was one of the largest manufacturers of electrical control devices in the United States. The firm produced a wide variety of switches and regulators for electrical motors and related equipment, ranging from refrigerator controls selling for less than one dollar apiece to electric machine tool control systems costing in excess of $500,000, for use in steel, paper, and textile mills. A detailed description of the firm's most important products in early 1958 was as follows:

General purpose motor control and accessories for both A.C. and D.C. applications; machine tool control; mill and crane control; textile control; rubber mill control; marine and navy control; control centers; small motor switches for appliances and power tools; refrigeration control for refrigerators, freezers, and air conditioners; unit breakers for distribution of power and protection of electrical circuits; power relays and switches for commercial aircraft; and industrial safety switches.

Engineered electrical regulation systems included standard items of Magnus Controls equipment as components, as well as specially manufactured equipment. Such systems were designed for continuous process lines in steel mills, automotive plants, paper mills, aluminum mills, refineries, and rubber plants, as well as many other industries requiring synchronized operations.

The company operated eight manufacturing plants, of which five were located in the Midwest. Of the remaining three, which together accounted for only about 20% of Magnus Controls' productive capacity, one was located in New York City and two were on the West Coast. In addition to manufacturing facilities, the firm maintained 17 warehouses located in major market areas and 58 sales offices in principal cities throughout the United States. The latter were staffed by more than 300 sales engineers and had been instrumental in maintaining the company's position of strength in the industry.

ATL's initial response to Mr. Brown's inquiry was distinctly negative; nevertheless, a few weeks later ATL was again approached by a Magnus Controls representative, this time from Magnus Controls' product engineering department. He explained that Magnus Controls was very much interested in developing a line of "automation controls" to supplement and eventually supersede, in all likelihood, several of the company's existing product lines. To this end he suggested that the two concerns might collaborate in a joint research and development venture, and it was for this purpose that the two firms had been engaged in the contract negotiations mentioned above.

Specifically, the two firms would attempt to develop a continuous process system that would permit metal fabricators to use rolls of raw material in place of sheet metal. The system would probably incorporate a data accumulation center with such devices as Beta-Ray thickness gauges (on which ATL had done research work), photoelectric pinhole detectors, and other similar products. The heavy driving and regulation machinery would be developed by Magnus Controls and would be designed to use the electronic gear that ATL would develop. Work on the project had never commenced, owing to difficulties in determining the value of contributions made by each firm. The negotiations, however, ultimately led to the reconsideration of a potential merger.

The acceptance of merger as a possibility by ATL management had been a slow process. One very important favorable factor was the recognition that Magnus Controls was an "engineering" oriented organization rather than one primarily motivated by financial objectives. ATL personnel were consistently impressed by the relatively greater importance placed by Magnus Controls representatives on the technical aspects of the system as opposed to the cost considerations. In their opinion, this view contrasted with the attitudes evidenced by companies and financial organizations with whom they had previously had contact.

In addition, ATL personnel discovered that the more mechanical aspects of industrial product development deserved far greater consideration than had originally been assigned them. For this reason a skilled and experienced manufacturing staff was of great value.

Against this background actual merger negotiations were commenced with Magnus Controls in February, 1958. The chief responsibility for conducting negotiations on behalf of ATL was given to Mr. Henry Morse, treasurer of the firm. His counterpart for Magnus Controls was Mr. J. C. Walter, financial vice president.

Mr. Morse's position

In Mr. Morse's opinion the chief objective of Magnus Controls in negotiating the merger was to gain access to ATL's highly regarded electronics research staff. The use of electronic controls in industrial processes appeared to have a bright future; already many of Magnus Controls' competitors in the motor control field (among which were General Electric, Westinghouse,

Square D, Allen-Bradley, and some 30 others) had undertaken to apply electronics to their products. Magnus Controls, with an outstanding engineering staff but lacking an electronics research group, was certainly aware of this situation.

Mr. Morse recognized that if it wished, Magnus Controls could build up its own electronics research group. Such a move, however, would certainly involve a considerable amount of time—perhaps several years. Alternatively, there were a number of other small, research-oriented firms that Magnus Controls might seek to acquire or consolidate, although at present he was quite sure that none of these firms had been directly approached.

Mr. Morse and most others in ATL management, as well as Mr. Walter and his associates, were eager to conclude their negotiations as soon as possible. For this purpose a "final" meeting had been scheduled during the last week in April to determine a basis whereby the outstanding shares of ATL common stock, together with 20,833 shares reserved for conversion of ATL's 5¾% subordinated convertible notes due July 1, 1972 (see note 1 to Exhibit 3) and 21,025 shares reserved against the stock options outstanding, would be exchanged for stock in Magnus Controls. In preparation for this meeting Mr. Morse had set down the most important provisions to which the respective managements had tentatively agreed—contingent, of course, on an exchange price agreement:

1. ATL would operate as an autonomous division of Magnus Controls.
2. ATL would have one representative on Magnus Controls' Board of Directors, as soon as an opening occurred.
3. Merger would be effected by a tax-free exchange of stock.
4. No personnel changes would be involved in the merger. There would be, however, an exchange of personnel between Magnus Controls and the ATL division from time to time.

In addition to the provisions above, Mr. Morse wrote down a number of his own observations, based in part on his discussions with others in or connected with the ATL organization, which he wished to keep in mind during the price negotiation.

1. There should not be any difficulty with ———— and ———— (the 55% venture capital owners of ATL) if the price is in line with the market of the past few months. Those organizations have carried their investments in ATL at "market" value for their own reporting purposes. They might object if they were to end up with stock worth less than when last they reported to owners, which was on December 31, 1957. Otherwise, they would probably be happy with the move (and have so stated) since they feel that their money has had its maximum effect by now and they are eager to put it to work in a less mature investment situation. I doubt that they will object seriously to any reasonable price over 30, but this is a good arguing point. To the best of my knowledge they have not been in touch with Magnus and would not sell out without consulting us first.
2. Some of our [ATL] people have noted that the stock market has turned

up from last fall's lows. With the increasing interest in electronics companies they have mentioned that our stock "ought to hit $100 before very long." While I personally suspect that this is unlikely (based on our present earnings), we shall nevertheless have to keep these people happy.

3. Magnus Controls' sales organization would certainly be a great help to our existing industrial products as well as a guide to future developments.

4. We ought not to underestimate the value of their established manufacturing operations.

5. With Magnus Controls' backing we can probably win government prime contracts up to $40 or $50 million, versus our apparent limit of $6–8 million at present. This would increase our profitability enormously.

Pertinent data on earnings and balance sheets of the two companies appear in Exhibits 1–3. Exhibit 4 presents price ranges, earnings, and book values per common share.

Mr. Morse realized that both his observations and the provisions already agreed to were subject to change in the process of bargaining. He would, of course, discuss bargaining limits and strategy, as well as an initial bid and other relevant factors, with other ATL executives before the meeting with Mr. Walter; but in the end, he realized, he would be the one responsible for the success or failure of the negotiations from ATL's standpoint.

Exhibit 1

ASSOCIATED TECHNOLOGY LABORATORIES, INC.

SUMMARIES OF EARNINGS

(Dollar amounts in thousands, except for per share figures)

| | Year Ended December 31 | | | | | | | | | | Two Months Ended | | | |
| | | | | | | | | | | | Feb. 28, 1957 (Unaudited) | | Feb. 28, 1958 (Unaudited) | |
	1953	%	1954	%	1955	%	1956	%	1957	%		%		%
Magnus Controls, Inc.														
Net sales	$62,482	100	$54,188	100	$61,575	100	$79,367	100	$74,870	100	$12,941	100	$11,632	100
Operating profit	12,060	19	8,431	16	12,103	20	15,380	19	13,234	18	2,518	19	1,729	15
Income before federal income tax	12,204	20	8,673	16	12,241	20	15,582	20	13,433	18	2,561	20	1,731	15
Provision for federal income tax	8,451	14	4,580	8	6,611	11	8,680	11	7,484	10	1,403	11	985	8
Net income	3,753	6	4,093	8	5,630	9	6,902	9	5,949	8	1,158	9	746	6
Earnings per common share*	2.84	...	3.10	...	4.26	...	5.23	...	4.51	...	0.88	...	0.57	...
Dividends per common share*	1.25	...	1.50	...	1.80	...	2.30	...	2.50	...	0.50	...	0.50	...
ATL, Inc.														
Net sales†	$ 6,563	100	$10,515	100	$ 9,178	100	$10,478	100	$12,272	100	$ 1,614	100	$ 1,659	100
Operating profit	388	6	884	8	731	8	655	6	844	7	109	7	112	7
Interest expense	122	2	97	1	34	1	31	1	120	1	9	1	33	2
Income before federal income tax	273	4	806	8	717	8	619	6	725	6	101	6	78	5
Provision for federal income tax	137	2	433	4	354	4	313	4	381	3	49	3	40	2
Net income	136	2	373	4	363	4	306	3	344	3	52	3	38	2
Special credit‡			39	...					98	1				
Net income and special credit	136	2	412	4	363	4	306	3	442	4	52	3	38	2
Earnings per common share‡	0.72	...	1.92	...	1.84	...	1.55	...	1.73	...	0.26	...	0.19	...
Dividends per common share	...	...	...	...	...	...	...	...	...	...	...	...	...	...

* Adjusted for 2 for 1 stock split in 1956.
† Substantially all of the sales during the period were under U.S. government contracts or subcontracts, which are subject to termination.
‡ The special credits in 1954 and 1957 represent profit on sale of land (net of federal income tax of $13,833 in 1954 and $32,566 in 1957). The special credits are equivalent to $0.20 per share in 1954 and $0.49 in 1957. Net income and special credits for 1954 and 1957 amount to $2.12 and $2.22 per share, respectively.

Exhibit 2

ASSOCIATED TECHNOLOGY LABORATORIES, INC.

MAGNUS CONTROLS, INC., BALANCE SHEETS
DECEMBER 31, 1957 (AUDITED) AND FEBRUARY 28, 1958 (UNAUDITED)

(Dollar amounts in thousands)

ASSETS		December 31, 1957	February 28, 1958 (Unaudited)
Cash and U.S. government securities...............		$ 2,939	$ 3,293
Accounts receivable (net of reserve)................		7,472	7,469
Inventories:			
Raw materials and supplies.....................	$ 1,785		$ 1,724
Purchased parts...............................	1,564		1,404
Work in process..............................	4,829		4,135
Manufactured parts and finished apparatus........	6,742		6,714
Total inventories...........................		$14,920	$13,977
Total current assets.........................		$25,331	$24,739
Property, plant, and equipment (at cost):			
Land..	$ 1,751		$ 1,751
Buildings......................................	11,751		11,755
Machinery, equipment, tools, etc................	9,110		9,230
Furniture, fixtures, etc.........................	2,279		2,341
Construction in process........................	3,305		5,344
	$28,196		$30,421
Less: reserve for depreciation....................	7,813		8,097
Property, plant and equipment (net)..............		$20,383	$22,324
Other assets....................................		439	475
Total assets...............................		$46,153	$47,538
LIABILITIES			
Accounts payable...............................		$ 1,115	$ 1,080
Dividend payable...............................			660
Accrued expenses...............................		2,217	2,249
Accrued taxes..................................		1,585	2,233
Total current liabilities.......................		$ 4,917	$ 6,222
Reserve for deferred federal taxes on income*........		2,861	2,854
Capital stock, surplus, and reserves:			
Common stock, par value $10.00 per share, authorized, 2,000,000 shares, issued and outstanding 1,319,996 shares..........................	$13,200		$13,200
Earned surplus................................	23,675		23,761
Reserve for possible inventory losses and other contingencies...............................	1,500		1,500
Total capital stock, surplus, and reserves.........		$38,375	$38,461
Total liabilities and net worth.................		$46,153	$47,538

* Reserve for Deferred Federal Taxes on Income: This represents the balance of the temporary tax saving resulting from the company's election to claim depreciation for federal income taxes in excess of the normal provision included in operations on facilities covered by a necessity certificate. The reserve is now being used to offset federal income taxes on the normal depreciation not presently allowable.

Exhibit 3

ASSOCIATED TECHNOLOGY LABORATORIES, INC.

ATL, INC., BALANCE SHEETS
DECEMBER 31, 1957, AND FEBRUARY 28, 1958
(Dollar amounts in thousands)

ASSETS		Dec. 31, 1957		Feb. 28, 1958 (Unaudited)
Cash...		$ 327		$ 278
Accounts receivable............................		2,632		2,289
Inventories (at the lower of cost or market):				
Finished goods................................$	286		$ 344	
Work in process (less progress payments received: 1957—$683,495; 1958—$972,384).............	2,689		3,047	
Materials and supplies.........................	146		141	
Total inventories............................		$ 3,121		$ 3,532
Total current assets..........................		$ 6,080		$ 6,099
Investments and notes receivable....................		124		150
Property, plant, and equipment (at cost)............$	2,233		$ 2,247	
Less: accumulated depreciation and amortization...	939		968	
Property, plant, and equipment (net).............		$ 1,294		$ 1,279
Prepaid expenses and deferred charges...............		71		71
Other assets......................................		41		39
Total assets...............................		$ 7,610		$ 7,638

LIABILITIES				
Notes payable to bank............................		$ 2,200		$ 2,500
Accounts payable................................		701		328
Accrued expenses................................		543		566
Accrued taxes...................................		367		406
Total current liabilities......................		$ 3,811		$ 3,800
Long-term debt:				
5% mortgage note due 1959 to 1965...............$	300		$ 300	
5% mortgage note due May 14, 1960..............	50		50	
5¾% subordinated convertible notes, due July 1, 1972*..	1,000		1,000	
Total long-term debt.........................		$ 1,350		$ 1,350
Stockholders' equity:				
Capital stock, par value $1 per share,† authorized—500,000 shares, issued and outstanding: 1957—199,605 shares; 1958—199,699 shares; at stated value..................................$	893		$ 894	
Earned surplus................................	1,556		1,594	
Total stockholders' equity....................		$ 2,449		$ 2,488
Total liabilities and stockholders' equity........		$ 7,610		$ 7,638

* Convertible at $48/share; 20,833 shares of capital stock are reserved for the purpose of conversion.
† Options are outstanding for 21,025 shares at prices from $18.50 to $43.00 per share; also, see note *.

Exhibit 4

ASSOCIATED TECHNOLOGY LABORATORIES, INC.

Common Stock Price Ranges, Earnings, and Book Value

I. COMMON STOCK PRICE RANGES*

	Magnus Controls, Inc.		*ATL, Inc.*			
			Bid		*Asked*	
	High	*Low*	*High*	*Low*	*High*	*Low*
1954†	$32\frac{3}{8}$	$19\frac{1}{2}$	$18\frac{1}{8}$	10	$18\frac{5}{8}$	$10\frac{1}{2}$
1955	43	$28\frac{1}{4}$	$36\frac{1}{4}$	$17\frac{1}{8}$	$38\frac{1}{8}$	$23\frac{3}{4}$
1956:						
1st quarter	52	$36\frac{1}{2}$	44	29	46	$30\frac{1}{2}$
2nd quarter	$55\frac{7}{8}$	$49\frac{1}{8}$	51	$38\frac{1}{2}$	54	40
3rd quarter	$61\frac{1}{4}$	$53\frac{1}{2}$	$39\frac{1}{2}$	37	$41\frac{1}{2}$	$38\frac{1}{2}$
4th quarter	65	53	$37\frac{1}{2}$	34	$39\frac{1}{2}$	36
1957:						
1st quarter	$64\frac{3}{4}$	$51\frac{1}{2}$	37	29	39	31
2nd quarter	$61\frac{3}{4}$	$51\frac{1}{2}$	52	$34\frac{1}{4}$	54	$36\frac{1}{2}$
3rd quarter	$63\frac{1}{4}$	45	$51\frac{1}{2}$	33	$53\frac{1}{2}$	36
4th quarter	46	$38\frac{1}{2}$	38	27	42	30
1958:						
1st quarter	46	$40\frac{1}{2}$	47	33	52	36
	April 28, 1958, close: 45		April 30, 1958, bid: $43\frac{1}{2}$–44			

* The price ranges of the sales prices of Magnus Controls' common stock on the New York Stock Exchange and the bid and asked prices of ATL's capital stock in the over-the-counter market as reported by National Quotation Bureau, Inc., for the years 1954 and 1955 and the nine quarterly periods ended March 31, 1958.

† 1954 bid and asked prices for ATL capital stock are for the month of December only. Over-the-counter trading in ATL capital stock began in November 1954.

II. EARNINGS PER COMMON SHARE

	Magnus Controls, Inc.	*ATL, Inc.*
Year: 1953	$2.84	$0.72
1954	3.10	1.92
1955	4.26	1.84
1956	5.23	1.55
1957	4.51	1.73
Two months ended:		
February 28, 1958	0.57	0.19

Note: The foregoing tabulation has been prepared from information set forth in the summaries of earnings in Exhibit 1.

III. BOOK VALUES PER COMMON SHARE

	Magnus Controls, Inc.	*ATL, Inc.*
Book value, February 28, 1958	$29.14	$12.46

UNITED TERMINAL CORPORATION

In January, 1971, Jack Mason, vice president of San Francisco Capital Corporation, was reviewing the situation of United Terminal Corporation of Sunnyvale, California. United Terminal Corporation (UTC) was one of 49 companies in San Francisco Capital's portfolio of venture capital investments. (See Exhibit 1 for a summary of the portfolio.) Since San Francisco Capital's initial investment of $250,000 in UTC in December, 1969, UTC's sales and profit projections had not been met. In fact, UTC had posted a loss of over $1 million in its first nine months of operations. The company now needed an additional $600,000 to provide working capital to support the anticipated sales growth. The investment banker who had arranged the first-round financing was unprepared and unwilling, however, to help raise additional capital. Mr. Mason knew that he would have to take a leading role in structuring any second round of financing and in maintaining the interest and financial support of the other first-round investors in UTC.

THE COMPANY

UTC was a manufacturer of cathode ray tube[1] computer terminals for use principally in the newspaper industry. In the past, newspaper editors and reporters typed a story, corrected the story on the typed original, and then gave the corrected version to a typesetter operator who retyped the story on a typesetting machine. The UTC equipment eliminated the need to retype the story and saved time in transferring the news from the reporter to the "set type" form. With the UTC terminals, an editor or reporter typed a story, which was then displayed on the screen. The news copy could then be revised without retyping the entire article. The corrected copy was stored in the computer's memory bank until it was sent directly by wire to a typesetter machine, which set the story in type, ready to be printed. A single terminal sold for $13,000. UTC's more complete system sold for $130,000 to $200,000 and included a powerful memory capacity, several terminals, and a sophisticated minicomputer to coordinate the various terminals. (See Exhibit 2 for an illustration of the company's product.)

---

[1] A cathode ray tube (CRT) consists of an electron beam passing over a phosphor-coated glass surface. The most commonly known CRT is a television screen.

History of UTC

UTC began as a division of United Cable Co. of San Leandro, California. During the 1960's United Cable, a closely held manufacturer of electrical cable and hardware for electric power companies, had accumulated close to $1 million in excess working capital. The management decided to invest the excess working capital in the rapidly growing area of computer peripheral equipment. Lacking experience in the electronics field, the managers of United Cable sought a qualified person to develop the new division. In 1963, Charles Sill joined United Cable in that capacity.

Mr. Sill was well qualified for the job. He had graduated from the Massachusetts Institute of Technology with a B.A. in electrical engineering in 1955. After working with two large electric companies on government contracts, he formed Consulectric, Inc., in 1959 to do electronic consulting work for the government. In spite of Consulectric's growth to $5 million in revenue, several major investors became dissatisfied with Mr. Sill's handling of administrative and accounting details and finally were able to move for his replacement as president in 1963. Consulectric went bankrupt shortly thereafter. When Mr. Sill joined United Cable, he took with him many of the designs and ideas he had developed at Consulectric.

At United Cable Mr. Sill continued to work on his ideas for an improved cathode ray tube display terminal. After several important engineering accomplishments, some of which were later patented, he succeeded in producing a high-quality terminal with a display capacity significantly exceeding that of competitive equipment manufactured by such well-known names as Raytheon, RCA, General Electric, Bunker-Ramo, and IBM. This improved terminal was well received and within a short while several thousand requests for additional information and demonstrations were received. In terms of potential volume of business, the two most important inquiries came from American Telephone and Telegraph Company and Associated Press. Both leads were explored and subsequently resulted in some equipment installations.

By early 1969 it became apparent to the owners of United Cable that the management and financial commitment necessary to capitalize fully on the potential of their display equipment was beyond their capacity or interest. During the previous six years over $1 million had been spent on research and development in the electronics division to bring the terminal to market. The division had yet to show a profit. In addition to the division's losses, United Cable had experienced an overall decline in profitability which limited its ability to invest further in the division. The management of United Cable decided, therefore, to sell the designs, patents, inventory, current backlog, and all facilities of the electronics division as a package in order to recover the major part of its investment.

While United Cable management approached possible corporate customers about buying the electronics division, Mr. Sill began to assess his position in the proposed spin-off. The technical advances which had brought the CRT to its current stage had been the direct result of his technical leadership. A major part of the future value of the electronics division would depend on his innovative ability. Mr. Sill was uncomfortable with the thought that he—or at least his ideas—would be sold with the division. He mentioned the proposed sale of the division to Bill Hansen, whom he knew from joint work on various church committees. After discussing the situation, Mr. Hansen suggested that Mr. Sill should try to raise money from a venture capital source and buy the division himself.

The idea of again heading his own company appealed to Mr. Sill. He was eager to continue his research on cathode ray tube display terminals and to build a strong, healthy company on the basis of products of superior quality, partially to make up for the failure of Consulectric. He approached Ben Taylor, a partner in the San Francisco investment banking firm of Brown and Taylor, Inc., about venture capital financing. The firm was not very active in venture placements, but it had put together five deals previously and prided itself on never losing money for its investors. After reviewing the tentative structure for the proposed spin-off company and its financial needs, Mr. Taylor met with Mr. Sill to discuss the management of the proposed company. Mr. Sill admitted his dislike for housekeeping details of management. These details, he explained, took time that could be better spent designing new equipment. It was finally agreed that a man with a strong record of administrative competence should be sought to become president of the company. Clearly, an institutional investor would look critically at the management structure of the firm before investing money.

In June, 1969, Mr. Sill talked with Mr. Hansen and suggested that Mr. Hansen become president of the proposed company. Mr. Hansen had an excellent record of achievement with Mobil Oil Corporation. After graduating from Brigham Young University with a B.S. in marketing and a minor in accounting in 1952, he had joined Mobil Oil as a marketing representative in Los Angeles. He had progressed rapidly to Area Sales Manager; District Manager, Denver; Manager, Corporate National Sales, New York City; and in 1967, to Division General Manager for the Western States. He was respected as being a "straight shooter" and an excellent manager.

Mr. Hansen decided to accept the offer to become the president of the company, provided adequate financing could be arranged to buy the division from United Cable. The decision insured that he and his family would remain comfortably settled in northern California. He also respected Mr. Sill's technical competence and felt that Mr. Sill's ideas could be the basis for a very successful company.

Brown and Taylor was encouraged by the addition of Mr. Hansen to UTC's management team and was confident that it could raise the necessary money. A prospectus was drawn up in August, 1969, and a number of prospective investors were approached. Mr. Hansen had estimated that the company would need $2.3 million—$1.0 million to buy the division from United Cable and $1.3 million to provide working capital for at least the first 18 months of operation. The company was valued at $5.0 million and investors were offered 45% of the company for $2.25 million. The remainder of the ownership would be held by management and by Brown and Taylor in return for past and future services. Brown and Taylor began by approaching several insurance companies and small business investment companies (SBICs[2]). The prospective investors viewed the proposal with little interest. The most often cited reasons for investor reluctance were (1) Mr. Sill's previous association with Consulectric, (2) uncertainties about widespread acceptance of the product in the face of larger competitors, and (3) the high valuation of the company.

INITIAL INVESTMENT IN UTC

Jack Mason, vice president of San Francisco Bay National Bank's SBIC, agreed that the UTC deal was overpriced. He also believed that the venture had the potential for large profits. The market for UTC's systems seemed potentially enormous. Several personal checkings convinced Mr. Mason that Mr. Sill's technical ability in computer hardware and software was "near genius." While working with the electronics division, he had accomplished several engineering "firsts" which had substantially advanced the state of CRT technology. Mr. Sill and several of his customers felt that UTC's systems as applied to the newspaper field were 18 months ahead of any competitors. Mr. Mason believed that Mr. Sill had the capacity to maintain a technological superiority over such large manufacturers as IBM and Raytheon.

Mr. Mason called Mr. Taylor to inquire whether a more favorable price could be arranged. It was proposed that the company be valued at $3.8 million. The investors would receive 47% of the company for $1.8 million, with management and Brown and Taylor receiving the remaining 53%. Of the $1.8 million offering, $1.45 million was to be used primarily for working capital needs and for purchase of some capital equipment. The remaining $350,000 was allotted for the down payment to United Cable for the electronics division package. UTC would then owe United Cable an additional $650,000 to be secured by three noninterest-bearing notes of $100,000 due after the third year, $250,000 due after the fourth year, and $300,000 due after the fifth year, thus constituting the purchase price of $1 million. Exhibit 3 shows a pro forma balance sheet for the division as of August, 1969.

With the lower company valuation and with support from San Francisco

---

[2] Small business investment companies were authorized under the Small Business Investment Act of 1958. In order to encourage investors to invest in small companies the Act offers tax advantages to owners of SBICs and liberal borrowing terms to the SBICs. Prior to 1968 banks were allowed to establish wholly owned SBICs, and many banks took advantage of the SBIC opportunity. San Francisco Capital was a wholly owned subsidiary of the San Francisco Bay National Bank, which was one of the leading commercial banks in California with total assets in excess of $3.5 billion. Approximately 80% of San Francisco Capital's portfolio companies were also customers of the bank.

Capital, Brown and Taylor was able to obtain commitments for the rest of the issue. The deal was closed on December 5, 1969. Stock ownership of the company is listed in Exhibit 4.

In exchange for the $1.8 million financing, UTC issued 18,000 shares of 6¼% convertible preferred stock with $100 par value. Dividends would be payable after September 1, 1972 and each share of preferred stock was convertible into three common shares. The 18,000 preferred shares would thus convert into 54,000 common shares, which would represent 47.4% of the company's 114,000 common shares to be then outstanding. The preferred investors were allowed voting rights equal to their percentage of the common stock on a fully diluted basis. In order to protect the interests of the preferred shareholders, the shares held by Brown and Taylor could not be voted with management on close votes. In addition, the preferred investors were each allowed a seat on the board of directors.

UTC'S FIRST YEAR

The initial marketing efforts by UTC consisted of grading the hundreds of inquiries received and following up the most promising ones. Detailed discussions were held with a cable television group interested in providing a "newspaper of the air" and a British airline interested in engineering a cathode ray tube terminal reservation system. Mr. Sill and Mr. Hansen found the CATV and the airline discussions challenging but finally decided that financial and engineering limitations required concentration by the company on the already established newspaper and newswire market. Mr. Hansen felt that UTC's success depended on selecting one industry and serving it well.

The Associated Press newswire service represented a substantial opportunity for UTC. AP was counting on the UTC equipment to eliminate retyping in the editing process and to increase the speed of newswire transmission. This would reduce news backups, which plagued all the wire service companies, and would give AP an important competitive advantage over UPI. The Associated Press planned to install one memory unit with three or four display terminals in each of its 40 regional offices. This represented in excess of $4 million of sales. Although no contracts had been signed for any future deliveries, Mr. Hansen believed that Mr. Sill's excellent working relationship with the AP director of research and the excellent performance of the UTC system put UTC in an extremely strong position.

In April, 1970, UTC's competitive position was threatened unexpectedly by the development by Industrial Graphics Corporation of a text-editing terminal of superior quality. When the Industrial Graphics machine was shown at the American Newspaper Publishers Association Show in New Orleans in June, 1970, the machine appeared to be technically superior to UTC gear and it drew great interest. After recognizing that the performance of Industrial Graphics gear was better than that of UTC, Mr. Sill and Mr. Hansen decided that it would be necessary to entirely redesign the UTC terminal. Although the Industrial Graphics terminal was less flexible than the UTC system, it was easier to read and the equipment itself looked more professional. The redesign was necessary to change the terminal from a straight stroke generator system to a dot raster system of character delineation utilizing medium- and large-scale integrated circuits. This change had recently become economically feasible because the price of medium- and large-scale integrated circuits (upon which the dot raster system depends) had declined drastically. The dot raster system also generated more readable characters than the straight stroke.

After seeing the Industrial Graphics terminal Mr. Sill felt that all production of the UTC system should stop until a new terminal could be designed. "There's no use riding a dead horse," he commented. On the other hand, Mr. Hansen argued that the two systems then underway should be completed to meet customer commitments before redesign was begun. Mr. Sill was unhappy about finishing the systems and postponing redesign one and a half to two months. He felt the customers would be better off waiting six months for a better terminal. Mr. Hansen's argument—that developing a reputation for delivery of equipment on schedule would be more important in the long run than the extra 6–8 weeks of redesign time—finally prevailed and Mr. Sill reluctantly completed the two systems.

Once the two unfinished terminal systems were completed, all production and marketing efforts of the company were curtailed. The situation was desperate. Between December, 1969, and September, 1970, over $1 million had been lost on sales of only $121,000 and the company still did not have a superior product or a well-developed production process. (See Exhibits 5 and 6 for financial statements.) Mr. Sill and four other engineers went to work designing the new terminal. From September through December, 1970, no new systems were produced nor were any new sales commitments made. Basically, the company marked time while the engineers designed and redesigned the terminal. Finally in December Mr. Sill was satisfied that the company had produced a terminal superior to that of Industrial Graphics. In fact, he was confident that the UTC systems were now far superior because of their greater capacity, flexibility, speed, and lower cost. UTC's basic terminal would sell for $13,000 whereas the Industrial Graphics terminal sold for $16,000. In January, 1971, UTC had an order backlog of almost $400,000.

OUTLOOK FOR SECOND YEAR

Product

After the redesign was completed the UTC line consisted of three products: the 3400 Rotating Magnetic Storage Memory System, the smaller 3101 Disk Storage Memory System, and the 5200 Display Terminal which could be operated either as a stand-alone unit or in conjunction with either the

3400 or the 3101 data base. Basically the 3400 and 3101 systems served as memories for the large-scale storing of text, allowed text editing with the use of the 5200 CRT terminals, and accepted data from newswire service lines. They were also communications centers for originating and directing data to a variety of output devices.

A major selling point of the UTC equipment was its "systems" nature. The Industrial Graphics product consisted essentially of a terminal that had to be programmed to operate with a large central computer. In contrast, the 3400 and 3101 systems could be built up to meet customer specifications as an integrated system. For example, a small paper could start with a single 5200 terminal with its own data base to be used as a stand-alone copy editor, and then could gradually build up a system consisting of several 5200 terminals and a 3400 data base. Along with the equipment, UTC also provided all programming necessary to make it compatible with the customer's existing computer-controlled equipment.

UTC management believed that production of the redesigned terminals would be no problem. Approximately one third of UTC's production space would be used for making prototype integrated circuits. Once these circuits were checked out as having the characteristics needed in their particular application, production of additional printed circuits would be contracted out. Production of the various systems would consist mainly of assembling the 5200 terminal and the two data base systems to customer specifications. During the production assembly stages, each circuit would be thoroughly checked by a computer programmed to simulate the circuit's various functions. A failure to function properly would be immediately picked up by the simulation program and corrected. All of UTC's systems were built in modular configuration and each integrated circuit was a plug-in unit in itself. This made service easier and faster.

Market potential

The newspaper industry dwarfed Associated Press in terms of sales potential for UTC and offered a substantial base for long-term growth. In recent years, American newspapers had aggressively begun to modernize plant and automate office procedures. For example, a newsletter published in the fall of 1970 by Composition Information Services, Inc., stated that photocomposition processes had been adopted by 61% of all American newspapers in the last decade, creating a $35 to $40 million annual market for the several companies that manufactured photocomposition equipment. The management of UTC believed that automation of the flow of information was the next priority for the newspaper industry and that the market for the display terminals and memory devices was potentially greater than the market for photocomposition equipment. The size of the market for text editing terminals alone, for example, was projected in articles in 1970 in both *Electronic News* and *Editor & Publisher* to be $15 to $20 million annually; and sales of terminals for use in display and classified advertising would significantly increase the annual dollar volume of the terminal market as a whole. The magnitude of the industry's need for terminals was illustrated by the fact that a Midwest newspaper which was then evaluating the use of text editing terminals for editorial use would require 90 terminals to accommodate its editors; a West Coast newspaper would require 50 terminals for the classified advertising application alone.

The Associated Press was recommending UTC's equipment to subscribers in order to have a fully compatible and integrated system. From a competitive standpoint, a fully integrated system would "tie-up" subscribers and reduce the risk of losing them to UPI. In AP's roster of 1,200 subscribers, there were about 200 newspapers which could each use $1 million worth of equipment, another 300 each of which could use $500,000 worth, and yet another 400 each of which could use roughly $100,000 thus creating a potentially enormous market. (See Exhibit 7.)

There was the risk, however, that newspapers might be slow to adopt the equipment because of union problems. Photon, Inc., a manufacturer of automated typesetting equipment designed to eliminate several manual steps in the preparation of set type, had approached several newspapers that had had labor problems and had sold the equipment on the basis of reduced dependence on labor. The American Newspaper Guild and the typographical setters unions were incensed over the actions of Photon, and the word got out that any paper which did business with that company could expect labor troubles. As a result, Photon suffered considerable resistance on the part of large newspapers. In contrast, UTC designed its equipment to increase the productivity and speed of newspaper editors and typesetters, and by stressing these advantages—not the elimination of jobs—UTC had met a favorable response by most newspaper owners. Currently a jurisdictional dispute between the Associated Press and the Newspaper Guild concerning who would have control over UTC equipment was in court for settlement. AP was optimistic that the court would decide in its favor, thus allowing more freedom in future installation.

Competition

Competition came from other manufacturers of cathode ray tube display systems and from optical scanning producers. There were over 100 manufacturers of cathode ray tube terminals for various uses. To date, only Industrial Graphics and UTC had developed systems for the newspaper industry. Since there were many conventions peculiar to the newspaper uses, UTC management felt that it and Industrial Graphics were 18 months ahead of any other possible competitors. Mr. Sill recognized that other manufacturers could do what he had done from an engineering standpoint, but the money and time would be almost prohibitive. The only computer manufacturer with equipment capable of equaling the performance of the UTC system 3400 was IBM, and the IBM 360 would require significant modifications and sophisticated programming to meet the newspaper needs.

Somewhat indirect competition to UTC came from optical scanning manufacturers and from IBM. Optical scanning systems were used in book publishing to transfer printed material into machine language which could be fed into a typesetter. The systems eliminated the step of retyping once an original typed copy was available, but were very limited by the unavailability of editing features. The American Newspaper Publishers Association was supporting optical character recognition equipment as a significant innovation, but Mr. Sill felt that CRT systems would be much more important.

Management and staff

The company employed approximately 30 people, most of whom were in engineering, production, prototype printed circuit manufacturing, and drafting. The engineering staff included Mr. Sill and four other engineers. Recently the company had hired three computer programmers and was planning to add gradually to its technical staff as the company grew. The company was presently negotiating a sales and service agreement whereby a company in the graphic arts industry would distribute and service UTC's 5200 text-editing display terminal and 3101 memory system throughout the country. UTC intended to market directly its 3400 magnetic memory system and terminals to the Associated Press and other large systems users. AP men had been trained to maintain old equipment installations, although Mr. Sill had done special servicing by flying to several locations up to now.

Mr. Sill was looking forward to the time when Mr. Hansen and the marketing staff would know enough about the UTC system to be able to sell it effectively without his active assistance. He also hoped to give up some of the responsibility for production, programming, installation, and servicing and to concentrate on new product development.

Additional financing needs

Mr. Mason of San Francisco Capital still had confidence in Mr. Sill and Mr. Hansen and in their ability to make UTC profitable if given proper backing. He had spent a considerable amount of time at the company's plant during the past year and had participated in a number of the critical pricing and product-market decisions. He felt that Mr. Hansen had proved himself to be an able small business manager. Several things had changed since December, 1969, and most of the changes seemed for the better. The redesigned system was now technically better than the Industrial Graphics equipment. And the conservative sales and earnings forecasts, based largely on sales to the Associated Press, were encouraging. (See Exhibit 8 for projected statements.)

Mr. Mason could not detach himself totally, however, from the disastrous year that UTC had just completed. The company's product position and sales potential had appeared equally bright at the time of the initial financing in December, 1969. There certainly seemed to be justification for the concern among some of the other investors that UTC might be forced without warning into another major product redesign. The potential payoff from investing the additional $600,000 was large, but Mr. Mason wondered if it was sufficient to justify further investment in such a high-risk venture.

He was also considering what form the investment should take and the price at which the securities should be sold. Mr. Sill and Mr. Hansen wished to avoid the fixed financial charges of a debenture and were pressing for a common stock issue priced at $30 a share. They felt that the company was stronger than at the time of the initial financing when stock was sold, on a converted basis, for $33⅓ a share (the $100 preferred stock was convertible into three shares of common stock). A low issue price would result in substantial dilution of their ownership in UTC—a prospect which troubled each of them.

Mr. Mason did not believe that the other investors would accept a common stock issue for the second-round financing. For the majority of the venture capital industry, 1970 had been an extremely difficult period. Many portfolio companies had been forced into bankruptcy by the downturn in capital equipment purchasing and the slowdown in industrial sales and collections. As a result, many venture capitalists were working around the clock trying to keep their holdings in order. All had a few companies in trouble, and many had allocated personnel for direct management of such companies to keep them in business and under control while longer term solutions could be found. Most venture capitalists were still quite concerned about the state of the economy, the health of their portfolio companies, and the deterioration of their firms' stock prices. (See Exhibit 9.) In this mood of pessimism, venture capitalists seemed to want the greater security of a debt issue.

If it was decided to use a debt instrument, a decision would have to be made on the form of the debt. It seemed clear that a straight interest debenture could not provide adequate return, given the amount of risk, without imposing severe financial charges on the company. The choice was between a convertible debenture and a debenture with detachable warrants[3] to buy common stock at a price fixed at the time of closing the deal. Some of the investors favored debt with detachable warrants. This financing instrument would permit them to maintain the liquidity of their venture capital firms through annual receipt of principal repayments without forcing them to forgo the equity option. The investors would be able to get the "seed money" out of the investment while retaining the right to buy stock at a favorable price.

Mr. Mason appreciated the arguments for a warrant issue, but he felt that the alternative to a common stock issue should be a convertible debenture. He proposed issuance of $600,000 principal amount of a 7½% convertible, subordinated note due February 13, 1978, and convertible into 52,531 shares of the common stock of UTC. Interest would not accrue for 18 months from

---

[3] The debenture would provide for fixed interest and sinking fund payments and would not be convertible into common stock. However, investors would receive warrants that could be detached from the debenture and exercised independently of the debenture.

the date of the notes. The notes would be prepayable without penalty at UTC's option after five years or from the proceeds of a public offering of UTC's securities. Otherwise, the notes would not be callable.

The low conversion price reflected Mr. Mason's strong belief that all the initial investors in this syndicate should have the responsibility as well as the opportunity to increase their ownership of UTC. Therefore he felt that if one or more of the initial investors did not "step up" for their share of the second round, they should be willing to suffer substantial resultant dilution.

Mr. Mason was concerned, however, that the low conversion price would result in such severe ownership dilution for Mr. Sill and Mr. Hansen, who could not purchase any of the planned $600,000 issue, that their motivation would be adversely affected. Although UTC had not performed according to projections to date, he proposed that Mr. Sill and Mr. Hansen receive 10-year warrants to purchase an aggregate of 28,860 shares of common stock at a price of $11.42 a share. The exercise of the warrants would be subject to the attainment by UTC of certain performance standards. Specifically, 20% of the warrants could be exercised each year from 1971 through 1975 if the following pretax earnings levels were met or exceeded by the company:

	1971	1972	1973	1974	1975
Pretax earnings	0	$375,000	$650,000	$875,000	$1,100,000

At the board meeting in December, 1970, Mr. Hansen had said that he was anxious to have the additional financing soon. Therefore, Mr. Mason wanted to reach a decision within a week on whether to increase San Francisco Capital's investment in United Terminal by participating in the second-round financing and, if he decided to do so, on what terms he should recommend that the financing be structured.

Exhibit 1

UNITED TERMINAL CORPORATION
SUMMARY OF THE PORTFOLIO OF SAN FRANCISCO CAPITAL CORPORATION

Jack Mason and Ben Brooks, the two officers of San Francisco Capital, were responsible for making new investments and for monitoring the 49 companies already in the portfolio. San Francisco Capital had a total of $5.4 million invested in the 49 companies. The smallest investment was $2,000 in a wholesale distributor of electronic components. The largest investment was $345,000 in a manufacturer of industrial processing equipment using state-of-the-art high-energy electron and ion beams with pulsed power sources. Median investment size was $100,000.

The portfolio companies operated in the following areas: (1) Manufacture of data processing equipment; (2) manufacture of electronic transmitting and receiving equipment; (3) research and manufacturing in electronics; (4) manufacture of components for the electronics industry; (5) manufacture of microwave components; (6) cable television; (7) research and development of a computer system for block trading of securities; (8) manufacture of electronics equipment; (9) research in digital data communications; (10) production and design of automation devices; (11) manufacture of electronic connectors and connector modules; (12) wholesaling of electronic components; (13) manufacture of communications products for use in the loss-prevention market; (14) medical diagnostic services; (15) electronic assembly and manufacturing under contract or subcontract; (16) offshore lobster fishing; (17) maintenance of aviation, electronic, and heavy-duty equipment at U.S. government facilities; (18) AM radio stations; (19) manufacture of live magnetic tape cleaner for use in data processing centers; (20) manufacture of cookware, leisure and casual furniture, and giftware; (21) manufacture of a wide line of machinery for plastic packaging industry; (22) production of architectural precast concrete building wall panels; (23) design and manufacture of precision castings for wide industrial use; (24) design of automatic wave soldering systems for use in soldering printed circuits; (25) manufacture of electron volt parts which incorporate the concept of modular components to ion and electron beam technology with broad application for use in industrial, scientific, and educational laboratories; (26) operation of 17 self-service drive-in restaurants; (27) manufacture of rigid thermoplastic sheeting by the extrusion process; (28) development of a nonintervention heart assist device; (29) manufacture of a solid-state programmable digital controller; (30) development of an electro-optical mark reading system for direct conversion into computer language; (31) publication of mathematics textbooks; (32) production of wigs; (33) development of a steam engine for use in various on- and off-road motive power applications; (34) merchandising of men's and boys' clothing through leased departments in discount stores; (35) manufacture of plasma arc welding and cutting torches and systems; (36) research in thermionics; (37) manufacture of semiconductor components; (38) manufacture of information storage devices for the data processing industry; (39) distribution of gases, supplies and equipment for welding, industrial, and medical uses.

Exhibit 2

UNITED TERMINAL CORPORATION
ILLUSTRATION OF EDITING DISPLAY TERMINAL EDS/5200

Exhibit 3

UNITED TERMINAL CORPORATION
STATEMENT OF FINANCIAL POSITION AT AUGUST 1, 1969, PRO FORMA
TO INCLUDE PROPOSED FINANCING
(Dollar figures in thousands)

ASSETS		LIABILITIES AND EQUITY	
Current assets:		*Current liabilities:*	
Cash	$1,337	n.a.	
Accounts receivable	20		
Inventory	154		
Work in process	377	*Long-term debt:*	
Value of leased equipment	96	Notes payable*	$ 650
Total current assets	$1,984		
		Owners' equity:	
		6¼% convertible preferred	
		stock†	$1,800
Fixed assets:		Retained earnings	(350)
Capital equipment and tools	121	Common stock	5
		Total equity	$1,455
Total assets	$2,105	Total liabilities and equity	$2,105

Common stock outstanding: 54,696 shares

* Noninterest-bearing notes due to United Cable Co., subordinated to ordinary bank debt and without claim on assets. Retirement schedule: $100,000 after three years, $250,000 after four years, and $300,000 after five years.
† Convertible into 54,000 common shares. Dividend payments to commence after September 1, 1972.

Exhibit 4

UNITED TERMINAL CORPORATION
LIST OF STOCKHOLDERS AS OF JANUARY, 1971

	Cost	Shares of Preferred Stock	Shares of Common Stock Assuming Conversion	% of Pro Forma Common Stock
Preferred stockholders:				
California Life and Casualty	$ 500,000	5,000	15,000	13.2%
San Francisco Capital	250,000	2,500	7,500	6.6
Oakland Merchant Capital	250,000	2,500	7,500	6.6
San Francisco Bay National Bank Employees Trust Fund	250,000	2,500	7,500	6.6
Various Blacksmith Family Trusts	300,000	3,000	9,000	7.8
Two private investors	250,000	2,500	7,500	6.6
	$1,800,000	18,000	54,000	47.4%
Common stockholders:				
Bill Hansen	$ 0		23,940	21 %
Charles Sill	0		23,940	21
John Barron (production mgr.)	0		2,280	2
United Cable Co.	0		5,700	5
Brown and Taylor	0		4,140	3.6
			60,000	52.6%
Total			114,000	100.0%

Exhibit 5

UNITED TERMINAL CORPORATION
BALANCE SHEET AT SEPTEMBER 30, 1970
(In thousands)

ASSETS

Cash	$ 54
Short-term securities, at cost which approximates market	323
Accounts receivable, trade, less allowance of $1,150 for doubtful accounts	97

Inventories:

Raw materials	$ 126
Discs, drums, and computers	166
Work in process	122
	$ 414
Prepaid expenses	7

Fixed assets:

Used in operations, at cost	$ 221
Leased to others, at cost	60
	$ 281
Less accumulated depreciation	56
	$ 225

Deferred charges, patents, and other assets:

Deferred interest expense	$ 172
Patents and other assets	33
	$ 205
	$1,325

LIABILITIES

Accounts payable, trade	$ 76
Accrued expenses	26
Long-term note payable	650

STOCKHOLDERS' EQUITY

$6\frac{1}{4}\%$ cumulative convertible preferred stock, $100 par value, authorized, issued and outstanding 18,000 shares	1,800
Common stock, $0.10 par value, authorized 150,000 shares, issued and outstanding 60,000 shares	6
Accumulated deficit	(1,233)
	$1,325

Exhibit 6

UNITED TERMINAL CORPORATION
Statement of Operations from Inception (December 5, 1969) to
September 30, 1970
(In thousands except per share data)

Revenues:

Sales...		$ 121
Rental income..		30
Interest income......................................		56
		$ 207

Expenses:
Engineering, production, and related costs:

Research and development..........................	$318	
Production costs...................................	181	
Inventory losses...................................	216	$ 715
Depreciation..		70
Selling, general, and administrative expenses...........		183
Interest expense......................................		35
Loss before extraordinary item..........................		$ 796

Extraordinary item:
Reduction of values assigned to assets acquired from

United Cable Co. (Note A).........................		304
Net loss..		$1,100

Losses per common share:

Loss before extraordinary item........................		$ 13.19
Extraordinary item...............................		5.03
Net loss..		$ 18.22

Note A: As of September 30, 1970, United Terminal reduced the amounts at which certain assets acquired from United Cable Co. were originally stated to amounts which in its opinion are representative of the minimum value of such assets in the company's future business activities. Such reduction appears as an extraordinary item in the statement of operations.

Exhibit 7

UNITED TERMINAL CORPORATION
MARKET POTENTIAL ANALYSIS
(Dollar figures in thousands)

Circulation	Number of Papers	Product Line 3400 High	3400 Low	3101 High	3101 Low	5200 High	5200 Low
500,000–over	11						
Single paper requirements		$ 1,400	$ 700			$ 4,000	$ 1,300
Group dollar total		15,400	7,700			39,000	13,000
250,000–500,000	28						
Single paper requirements		700	350			2,000	650
Group dollar total		19,600	9,800			56,000	18,000
100,000–250,000	91						
Single paper requirements		350	175			1,000	325
Group dollar total		32,000	16,000			91,000	27,000
50,000–100,000	119						
Single paper requirements		140	70			160	100
Group dollar total		17,000	8,000			19,000	12,000
25,000–50,000	249						
Single paper requirements				$ 39	$ 13	104	52
Group dollar total				9,700	3,200	25,700	12,800
10,000–25,000	472						
Single paper requirements				13	—	52	13
Group dollar total				6,100	—	24,500	6,100
00,000–10,000	468						
Single paper requirements						13	—
Group dollar total						6,000	—
Total		$84,000	$41,500	$15,800	$3,200	$261,200	$88,900

Note: The value of each product was extended for a sample paper in the group and brought to a total for the group. A wide range exists between the high and the low assumptions. However, using the low for all products, a very large market exists within the newspaper industry. This approach is for newspapers only and looks at the total market size if the newspapers ordered all of their equipment needs. The market potential analysis excludes commercial printing and all foreign newspapers, commercial printers, and newswire services, domestic and foreign.

Exhibit 8

UNITED TERMINAL CORPORATION

PROJECTED INCOME AND CASH FLOW STATEMENTS FOR 1971, TOGETHER WITH ANNUAL FORECAST FOR 1972

(In thousands)

	Jan.	Feb.	Mar.	Apr.	May	June	July	Aug.	Sept.	Oct.	Nov.	Dec.	Totals	1972 Forecast
							Projected Monthly Income Statements, 1971							
Sales and lease income	$ 5	$ 35	$ 100	$175	$200	$230	$250	$270	$300	$320	$350	$380	$2,615	$4,950
Cost of sales	—	$ 14	$ 43	$ 75	$ 86	$ 99	$101	$116	$129	$138	$150	$163	$1,114	$2,138
Depreciation	$ 6	6	6	6	6	6	6	6	6	6	6	6	72	145
Salaries	20	20	30	35	35	45	45	50	55	55	60	65	515	1,150
Outside services	5	7	1	—	—	1	—	—	1	—	—	4	19	34
Total cost of sales	$ 31	$ 47	$ 80	$116	$127	$151	$152	$172	$191	$199	$216	$238	$1,720	$3,467
Gross margin	$(26)	$(12)	$ 20	$ 59	$ 73	$ 79	$ 98	$ 98	$109	$121	$134	$142	$ 895	$1,483
Operating expenses	18	18	20	22	23	25	25	25	25	27	30	30	288	475
Operating income	$(44)	$(30)	$ 0	$ 37	$ 50	$ 54	$ 73	$ 73	$ 84	$ 94	$104	$112	$ 607	$1,008
Other charges*	1	—	1	1	1	1	2	3	3	3	3	4	23	78
Net income before research and development	$(45)	$(30)	$ (1)	$ 36	$ 49	$ 53	$ 71	$ 70	$ 81	$ 91	$101	$108	$ 584	$ 930
Research and development	20	20	20	20	20	25	35	35	30	30	30	30	315	475
Net income before taxes	$(65)	$(50)	$(21)	$ 16	$ 29	$ 28	$ 36	$ 35	$ 51	$ 61	$ 71	$ 78	$ 269	$ 455

* Includes interest.

Exhibit 8—Continued

PROJECTED MONTHLY CASH FLOWS, 1971

	Jan.	Feb.	Mar.	Apr.	May	June	July	Aug.	Sept.	Oct.	Nov.	Dec.	Totals
Raw material and component purchases	—	$132	$ 86	$ 98	$100	$116	$129	$137	$150	$163	$160	$160	$1,431
Monthly cash expenses	$63	65	72	78	79	87	106	111	112	113	120	130	1,136
Collections	—	—	—	35	100	175	200	230	250	270	300	320	1,880
Monthly cash need	$63	$197	$158	$141	$ 79	$ 28	$ 35	$ 18	$ 12	$ 6	$(20)	$(30)	$ 687
Cumulative cash need	63	260	418	559	638	666	701	719	731	737	717	687	

1971 WORKING CAPITAL REQUIREMENTS

Requirements

1. Peak cash need (October)............ $737
2. Manufacturing equipment............ 50
3. Retained leases.................... 100
4. Short-term demonstration models...... 100

    Total............................ $987

Sources

1. January cash position............ $100
2. New financing.................... 600
3. Accounts receivable financing.... 287

    Total........................ $987

Exhibit 9

UNITED TERMINAL CORPORATION
STOCK PRICES OF SBICS AND VENTURE CAPITAL COMPANIES

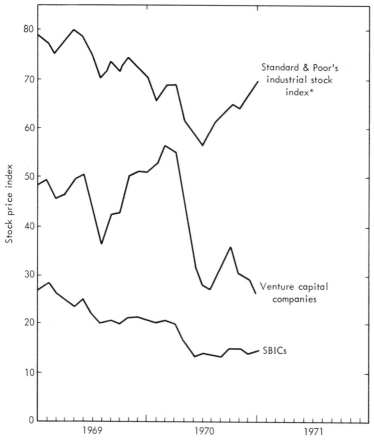

* Scaled to 1941–43 = 7.
Source: *SBIC/Venture Capital*, published by S. M. Rubel & Company, various monthly issues.

HARRINGTON CORPORATION

In March, 1971, Paul Brooks was working on a proposal to purchase his employer, the Harrington Corporation. The Harrington Corporation, with corporate headquarters in Boston, Massachusetts, was a leading manufacturer of commercial desk calendars. Mr. Brooks, vice president of finance and administration, considered the company an excellent acquisition opportunity, provided he should conclude that the owner's asking price was acceptable, and provided he could arrange satisfactory financing for the transaction.

BACKGROUND

A few weeks earlier, Thaddeus Baring, board chairman, president, and sole owner of Harrington Corporation, had informed his senior management group that he intended to retire from business and was about to initiate a campaign to sell the company. For several years, his physician had been urging him to avoid all stress and strain; now Mr. Baring had decided to sever his business connections and devote his time to travel and a developing interest in art history and collection.

On the basis of previous offers for the company, Mr. Baring had decided to ask for $10 million, with a minimum of $8 million immediately payable in cash. He thought acquisitive corporations should find this price attractive, and he believed it would be easy to dispose of the corporation.

Mr. Baring had assured the management group that their jobs and benefits would be well protected by the terms of any sale contract that he might negotiate. Despite his faith in Mr. Baring's good intentions, Mr. Brooks had been quite apprehensive about the prospect of having his career placed in the hands of an unknown outsider. However, after some reflection, Mr. Brooks had concluded that the sale decision should be viewed as an opportunity to acquire control of a highly profitable enterprise. Purchase of Harrington would not only assure career continuity but also provide a chance to turn a profit in the company's equity. Mr. Brooks had realized that his personal financial resources were far too limited to allow him to bid alone for control of Harrington. Consequently, he had persuaded Kim Darby, vice president–marketing, Keith Jackson, vice president–manufacturing, and Waldo Sloane, the controller, to join him in trying to buy the corporation, rather than standing by while control passed to an outsider. In response to Mr. Brooks' request,

Mr. Baring had agreed to defer all steps to merchandise the company until he should have accepted or rejected a purchase proposal from the management group, provided this proposal was submitted within six weeks.

Because of his background in finance and his role in initiating the project, Mr. Brooks had assumed primary responsibility for assessing the profit potential of the opportunity and for structuring a workable financial plan for the acquisition. Since Mr. Baring had not yet solicited bids from other potential purchasers, Mr. Brooks believed that it would be most realistic to regard Mr. Baring's stated sale terms as fixed and nonnegotiable.

Mr. Brooks, then, needed to determine whether he could meet the asking price and still realize a profit commensurate with the risk in this purchase. Moreover, he needed to figure out how the management group, with roughly a quarter of a million dollars between them, could finance the purchase and at the same time obtain voting control of the corporation.

Thus far Mr. Brooks had managed to obtain a tentative commitment for a $3,000,000 unsecured bank term loan, and he had persuaded Mr. Baring to accept unsecured notes for the noncash portion of the purchase price. He was still faced with the problem of raising close to $5,000,000 on an equity base of $250,000 without giving up control to outsiders.

Mr. Brooks now had three weeks in which to come up with a workable financial plan or lose the deal. He was acutely aware that the life savings of his associates and himself would ride on his judgment and ingenuity.

THE COMPANY

The Harrington Corporation was the leading producer of business calendars in the United States. The company was established in 1920 by Joshua Harrington (Mr. Baring's maternal grandfather) to do contract printing of commercial calendars. Mr. Baring had joined the organization in 1932 upon graduation from college, and in 1937, he had inherited the company.

Under Mr. Baring's leadership primary emphasis was placed on controlled expansion in the established line of business. By 1971, Harrington, with an estimated 60–65% share of its market, had been for over a decade the largest company in a small but lucrative industry. Operations had been profitable in every year since 1932, and sales had increased in every year since 1955. In 1970, the most recently completed fiscal year, earnings had amounted to $983,000 on sales of approximately $7.6 million. The return on average invested capital in 1970 was over 20%. Over the past five years, sales had increased at a 7% compound rate, while earnings, benefiting from substantial cost reductions, had more than doubled. Exhibits 1 through 3 present recent financial figures for the company.

Products

As noted above, Harrington's principal products were commercial desk calendars. The company designed and manufactured disposable page and flipover page desk calendar pads in a variety of sizes. The company also sold desk calendar bases which were purchased from outside suppliers who manufactured to Harrington's specifications. In 1970, standard desk calendar pads had contributed approximately 80% of net sales and 90% of earnings before taxes. Bases accounted for 10% of sales, and miscellaneous merchandise, chiefly wall calendars, accounted for the rest.

Sales were highly seasonal. Most final consumers did not start using calendars for the forthcoming year until November or December of the current year. In consequence about 90% of Harrington's total shipments typically took place between June and December, with about 60% of shipments concentrated in the third quarter and 25% in the fourth quarter. Since calendar pads were dated, any merchandise remaining in stock at the end of the selling season was subject to rapid obsolescence.

Manufacturing

The production process was relatively simple, employing widely available skills and technology. Highspeed offset presses were used to print appropriate dates on paper purchased in bulk from outside suppliers; the printed sheets were then trimmed to the required sizes and stored for shipment. The entire process was highly automated and was characterized by high fixed costs, high set-up costs, and low variable costs.

In spite of highly seasonal sales, Harrington operated on level production schedules. Since the product lines were for all practical purposes undifferentiated from competing lines and the relevant production technology was well known, the capacity to sell on the basis of price, while achieving a good return on invested capital, was regarded by management as a critical success factor in the industry. Minimum production costs were therefore imperative.

Level production enabled the company to take advantage of extremely long production runs and thus to minimize down time, the investment in equipment, expensive set ups, and the use of transient labor. Level production in conjunction with the company's dominant market share provided scale economies well beyond the reach of any competitor.

The combination of seasonal sales and level production resulted in the accumulation of large seasonal stocks. However, by concentrating the sales effort in the middle six months of the year, Harrington was able to circumvent most of the risk usually connected with level production in a seasonal company in return for modest purchase discounts. Since they could easily predict their needs for Harrington products as their budgets for the forthcoming year took shape, customers were willing to place their orders well in advance of shipment. As a result, Harrington could manufacture against a firm backlog in the last few months of the year and thus circumvent the risk of overproducing and ending the year with large stocks of outdated finished goods.

Harrington maintained production facilities in western Massachusetts and, through a wholly owned subsidiary, in Puerto Rico. Earnings of the Puerto Rican subsidiary, which sold all its output to the U.S. parent, were entirely exempt from U.S. taxes and until 1982 would be exempt from all Puerto Rican taxes. The tax exemption on Puerto Rican production accounted for Harrington's unusually low income tax rate. All Harrington plants and equipment were modern and excellently maintained. A major capital expenditures program, completed in 1966, had resulted in Harrington's having the most modern facilities in the industry. At the predicted rate of future sales growth, Mr. Jackson, the chief production officer, did not anticipate any need for substantial capital expenditures for at least 5 or 6 years.

None of the company's work force was represented by labor unions.

Marketing

As its products were nondifferentiable, Harrington's marketing program concentrated on providing high quality customer service and a uniformly high quality product. Harrington products were sold nationwide to about 1,800 accounts. Geographically the company was strongest in the Northeast, the Southwest, and the far West. Large accounts were handled by the company's five-man sales force, and smaller accounts were serviced by office supply wholesalers. Roughly 10% of sales had gone to the federal government in 1970. The company's six largest customers generally accounted for about 20% of sales.

Even though the product was undifferentiated, Mr. Darby, the marketing vice president, believed that it did have some significant advantages from a marketing viewpoint. Selling costs were extremely low, as consumption of the product over the course of a year automatically generated a large replacement demand without any effort on the part of Harrington. About 95% of total sales generally consisted of reorders from the existing customer base, with only 5% of sales going to new customers. Historically over 98% of the customer base annually reordered Harrington pads and, as needed, additional Harrington bases. By dealing with only one source of supply, the customer was able to take maximum advantage of discounts for volume purchases. As the product was virtually immune to malfunction and the resultant customer dissatisfaction, once Harrington bases had been installed the typical buyer never received any incentive to spend time and money on a search for alternative sources. Consumption of Harrington products was, in addition, extremely insensitive to budget cuts, economy drives, consumer whims, and the like. The desk calendar was a small ticket but high priority item. It was an essential in the work routines of most of its end users, and it was not expensive enough to yield a meaningful reward in savings to would-be cutters. As a dated product, the desk calendar, unlike many other office products, represented a nondeferrable purchase.

Finances

The dominant influence on Harrington's financial policy was Mr. Baring's still vivid memory of the Great Depression. Mr. Baring steadfastly refused to consider levering his equity in the company. Accordingly, Harrington operated with an all equity capitalization. The size of the capital budget was determined by the volume of internally generated funds in conjunction with Mr.

Baring's decision on how much to withdraw in the form of dividends. Dividend payments had sometimes been sharply contracted to accommodate capital investment opportunities. Over the past three years, however, internally generated funds had been plentiful, and dividends had averaged 70% of net earnings.

Like the capital budget, the seasonal accumulation of inventories and receivables was financed from internal sources. To minimize warehousing expenses for finished goods, Harrington provided generous credit terms to customers who accepted early shipments. Payments for June through October shipments were not due until the end of November, although substantial discounts were offered for earlier payment. The collection period averaged 60 days. Credit experience was excellent, and generous credit terms were considered a key factor in the company's competitive success.

Although the company had not resorted to seasonal borrowing in close on ten years, it maintained for emergency purposes two $1 million lines of credit at Boston banks. Exhibit 4 shows 1970 working capital balances by month.

Harrington's credit with suppliers was excellent. All trade obligations were promptly paid when due.

Management

The senior management team consisted of Mr. Baring plus the four individuals interested in buying the corporation. Transfer of ownership to the latter would not occasion much change in the *de facto* management of the organization. Although Mr. Baring continued to exercise the final authority on all major issues of policy and strategy, over the past few years he had gradually withdrawn from day-to-day affairs and now spent much of his time in Europe and Puerto Rico. As Mr. Baring had relaxed his grip on Harrington's affairs, he had increasingly delegated the general management of the firm to Mr. Brooks.

Compensation was extremely lush at the senior executive level. Mr. Baring drew an annual salary of $200,000; his four key subordinates received an average salary of $45,000. In addition, the four senior executives received annual bonuses which aggregated 10% of earnings before taxes and bonuses.

Apart from Mr. Brooks, the members of the purchasing group were all in their early 50's and between them represented close to 90 years experience in the business. After being graduated from a leading graduate school of business administration, Mr. Brooks, age 40, had worked for five years in the venture capital department of a large Boston bank and for two years in his own management consulting firm before joining Harrington.

COMPANY PROSPECTS

The overall prospect was for continued growth at a steady, though unspectacular, pace. The rate of Harrington sales growth, management believed, was closely correlated with the rate of growth in the size of the domestic white collar work force. Given expectations of a continuing shift of labor out of agricultural and blue collar occupations and into white collar positions, this suggested that the company should grow somewhat faster than the economy as a whole. Assuming no material changes in product lines or market share, management thought sales growth would average about 5–6% per annum in the foreseeable future. Profit margins were expected to improve somewhat over the next few years, as volume expanded and an increasing proportion of new production was directed to the tax-exempt Puerto Rican facility.

Competition

Although the commercial desk calendar industry was profitable indeed for its leading participant, it was not, in the opinion of Harrington management, an attractive area for potential new competitors. At present the industry was divided between Harrington with roughly a 60–65% share of market and Algonquin Industries, a privately held company, with an estimated 20–25% share. Algonquin's strength was concentrated in the Midwest and Southeast. The remainder of industry sales was fragmented among a host of small, financially weak printing shops. Harrington management found it difficult to imagine how a potential competitor could arrive at an economically justifiable decision to enter their market. Price was the only conceivable basis on which a new entrant could compete, but, lacking the scale economies available to Harrington, a new entrant would necessarily be a high cost competitor. Mr. Darby estimated that it would take a new entrant at least 3–5 years to reach breakeven, assuming no retaliatory price cuts by Harrington. Furthermore, entering this market would necessitate a minimum capital investment of $1.5–2 million plus the working capital needed to support seasonal sales. On balance, it seemed unlikely that a potential competitor would brave these obstacles in the hope of grabbing a share of a $13–14 million industry with mediocre growth prospects.

Mr. Baring judged that Harrington's financial strength, relative cost advantages, and entrenched distribution system had served to deter Algonquin from trying to invade any of Harrington's prime market areas. Likewise, he thought Harrington could not take away a substantial market share from Algonquin without risking a price war that might seriously impair margins for a protracted period.

Unexploited opportunities

The business plan finally approved by Mr. Baring had not incorporated a diversification scheme vigorously advanced by the other members of senior management. The vice presidents had contended that Harrington could significantly boost both the rate of growth and level of earnings by using its cash flow and its production and distribution strengths to expand into related product lines. The proposal had called for expansion into other dated products, such as appointment books, planning books, and the like, imprinted with the name, logo, or other message of the customer, and into desk calendars similarly imprinted. Mr. Brooks had estimated that this project would require an initial capital investment of $100,000 and special product development and merchandising expenses of $450,000 spread over the first two years of the undertaking. It had been estimated that the new line should yield sales of approximately $500,000 in the first full year of operation with a growth rate of about 40% per annum in years 2 through 4, as the line achieved nationwide distribution and recognition. A 12–15% growth rate was anticipated in subsequent years. It was thought that this type of product line would have a profit margin before taxes of about 6%. The management group believed that the proposed line could serve as a profitable first step toward developing a full line of desk top products for commercial, industrial, and government markets.

Mr. Baring had rejected the proposal on several grounds. He had observed that the proposal advocated entering a riskier line of business in which none of the management group had experience. In the proposed line of business the customer could choose among a variety of competing designs, and manufacturers had to actively generate repeat sales. He had also pointed out that the project would require a substantial investment in working capital for seasonal sales, if the new line grew as predicted. Finally he had stated that he was quite content with his present income and, at his age, unwilling to reinvest earnings in the hope of achieving a strong position in a more competitive and less profitable business than the present one.

With Mr. Baring out of the picture, the management group would have the freedom to pursue its growth program. Mr. Brooks believed that over a period of years Harrington's growth rate could be improved significantly if earnings were reinvested in related businesses rather than disbursed as dividends. The higher growth rate would be translated into profits for management, if the faster growth allowed them to take the company public at a higher price-earnings ratio.

THE PURCHASE PROPOSAL

Mr. Brooks recognized that a successful proposal would have to blend and reconcile the interests and goals of all parties to the transaction: the seller, the buyers, and external suppliers of finance.

The management group had determined that between them they could raise at most about $250,000 for investment in Harrington. Raising this amount would necessitate drawing down savings accounts, refinancing home mortgages, and liquidating positions in the stock market. Mr. Brooks was prepared to commit $80,000, Mr. Jackson $70,000, and Messrs. Darby and Sloane $50,000 apiece. It had been tentatively agreed that all members of the management group would buy stock at the same price. It had also been tentatively concluded that the group would not accept a proposal that left them with less than 51% of the shares. With less than 51% of the stock the management group might not achieve the autonomy to establish corporate policy or to dispose of the company where and as they chose.

Valuation

As pointed out above, Mr. Brooks believed that Mr. Baring's asking terms of $10 million with a minimum of $8 million in cash would remain fixed, at least until the company had been shown to a number of prospective buyers. In the past year, Mr. Baring had held discussions with two companies that had made unsolicited bids to purchase Harrington. The first offer, $7.5 million in cash, had come from a medium-sized firm with a diversified line of office products. It had been rejected by Mr. Baring on the basis of price. The second offer had come from a highly diversified medium-sized company sporting a price–earnings ratio of 40 and seeking to establish a position in office products through a series of acquisitions. The final offer had come to $18 million in letter stock[1] of the acquirer. Mr. Baring had found this bid extremely tempting, but had been unwilling to tie up his wealth in unmarketable shares of a company with which he was not intimately familiar. The acquirer, lacking excess debt capacity and unwilling to float new stock, had backed out of the discussions.

Mr. Brooks had, in addition, assembled financial figures on the publicly traded companies he thought most comparable to Harrington. These data are presented in Exhibit 5.

Financing

In terms of the mechanics of the transaction, Mr. Brooks planned to effect the purchase through a new corporation in which the management group would buy 250,000 common shares at $1.00 a share. Given the management group's $250,000 versus the $10 million asking price, the biggest problem facing Mr. Brooks was how to fund the new company at all, not to mention the objective of keeping control in the management group. Mr. Brooks had managed to obtain tentative commitments for $5.25 million, including the management group's $250,000. Prior to submitting a purchase proposal to Mr. Baring, however, he would have to line up commitments for the entire $10 million funds needed.

It was clear that the noncash component of the purchase price would have to be met by issuing notes with a market value of $2 million to Mr. Baring. In order to maintain the maximum amount of flexibility and borrowing capacity for raising financing from outsiders, Mr. Brooks had proposed that Mr. Baring take 4%, junior subordinated, non-amortizing notes. After some negotiation, Mr. Baring had expressed his willingness to accept a $3,000,000 non-amortizing, 4% five-year note which would be junior to all other debt

---

[1] Letter stock is unregistered stock. Such stock may not be sold to the public without registration under the Securities Act of 1933, a costly and time-consuming process. Because letter stock is restricted in its transferability, it represents a relatively illiquid investment and generally sells at a discount below the price that registered stock would command in the public securities markets. When letter stock is issued in an acquisition, the acquirer generally specifies that the stock cannot be registered for a certain period of time.

obligations of the newly formed corporation. The members of the management group as well as the corporate acquirer would have to endorse the note. It was agreed that covenants on the note would include: (1) no additional debt or leases except debt incurred in the acquisition of Harrington, short-term seasonal borrowings, or debt incurred to retire the five-year note; (2) no dividends and maintenance of at least $1.5 million in working capital; (3) no changes in management or increase in management compensation; (4) no sale of Harrington shares by Messrs. Brooks, Darby, Jackson, or Sloane so long as the five-year note was outstanding. If the borrower should default on any terms of this note or of any other indebtedness, the junior subordinated notes would become immediately due and payable. If not promptly paid, ownership of the shares held by the management group would revert to Mr. Baring. The note could be retired before maturity in whole or in part in accord with the following schedule of discounts:

Year	% of Face Value
1	58 %
2	71
3	81
4	96
5	100

In his efforts to line up financing from outside sources, Mr. Brooks had succeeded in obtaining a tentative commitment for a $3,000,000 term loan from a large New York City bank known for its aggressive lending policies. This loan would be amortized over a maximum period of six years through annual installments. The rate would be two points above floating prime, and the borrower would have to maintain average compensating balances of 20% of the outstanding principal amount of the loan. The amount of $3 million was the maximum the bank would commit for on a term basis. Lending officers of the bank had emphasized that any additional term indebtedness incurred in the acquisition of Harrington would have to be effectively subordinated to this loan. Exhibit 6 presents an abstract of the provisions that the bank term loan would bear. Exhibit 7 presents Mr. Brooks' forecast of Harrington's cash flows over the next six years.

Having negotiated the bank commitment, Mr. Brooks was still left with the problem of raising an additional $4.75 million. He thought that he would have to turn to venture capital sources to raise the rest of the funds needed. Based on his experience in venture finance, Mr. Brooks knew that a venture capitalist would expect to earn about 20–25% on his funds. He also knew that most venture capitalists preferred to place their funds in the form of debt securities rather than common stock. The venture capitalist could generally exercise more effective control over his investment through the covenants on a debt obligation than through the voting power on stock. Principal on debt also provided a mechanism for a tax-free recovery of capital; this might not be possible with stock until the company had gone public. Mr. Brooks expected to have to pay an 8–9% coupon rate on any debt funds obtained from a venture capital source. The venture capitalist would probably attempt to realize the rest of his return by taking warrants to buy shares in the new corporation at $1.00, the same price initially paid by the management group. The venture capitalist would probably insist on having the option of exercising the warrants in either cash or Harrington debentures.

Exhibit 1

HARRINGTON CORPORATION

CONSOLIDATED INCOME STATEMENTS

(In thousands)

	1966	1967	1968	1969	1970
Net sales	$4,870	$5,022	$5,974	$6,985	$7,630
Cost of sales	2,918	2,824	3,497	4,152	4,649
Gross profit on sales	$1,952	$2,198	$2,476	$2,833	$2,981
Selling and administrative expenses	1,108	1,036	1,235	1,511	1,637
Other income and (expense)—net	20	54	36	64	60
Profit before income taxes	$ 864	$1,216	$1,277	$1,386	$1,404
Federal income taxes	408	486	460	471	421
Net profit	$ 456	$ 730	$ 817	$ 915	$ 983

Exhibit 2

HARRINGTON CORPORATION

CONSOLIDATED BALANCE SHEET AS OF DECEMBER 31, 1970

(In thousands)

ASSETS		LIABILITIES AND SHAREHOLDERS' EQUITY	
Current assets:		Current liabilities:	
Cash and marketable securities	$2,881	Accounts payable	$ 327
		Accrued expenses	183
Accounts receivable	1,270	Accrued income taxes	123
Inventories at lower of cost or market	294		
Prepaid expenses	54		
Total current assets	$4,499	Total current liabilities	$ 633
Property, plant, and equipment—net	1,055	Shareholders' equity:	
Miscellaneous assets	37	Common stock ($1.00 par value)	100
Total assets	$5,591	Retained profits	4,858
		Total liabilities and shareholders' equity	$5,591

Exhibit 3

HARRINGTON CORPORATION

Ten-Year Summary of Operations

(In thousands except per share data)

	1961	1962	1963	1964	1965	1966	1967	1968	1969	1970
Net sales	$3,844	$4,178	$4,263	$4,395	$4,675	$4,870	$5,022	$5,974	$6,985	$7,630
Net profit	319	334	371	374	379	456	730	817	915	983
Dividends	300	100	140	140	220	220	240	610	687	740
Earnings per share	3.19	3.34	3.71	3.74	3.79	4.56	7.30	8.17	9.15	9.83
Net profit margin	8.3%	8.0%	8.7%	8.5%	8.1%	9.4%	14.5%	13.7%	13.1%	12.9%

Exhibit 4

HARRINGTON CORPORATION

Monthly Working Capital Balances, 1970

(In thousands)

	Jan.	Feb.	Mar.	Apr.	May	Jun.	Jul.	Aug.	Sep.	Oct.	Nov.	Dec.
Cash	$2,768	$2,857	$2,698	$2,392	$2,164	$2,049	$1,177	$ 383	$1,025	$1,915	$2,867	$2,881
Accounts receivable	740	380	367	402	359	302	1,716	3,052	3,082	2,161	1,199	1,270
Inventories	562	833	1,105	1,376	1,647	1,919	1,377	835	263	294	304	294
Current liabilities	(593)	(610)	(621)	(573)	(711)	(672)	(536)	(608)	(587)	(692)	(670)	(633)
Net working capital	$3,477	$3,460	$3,549	$3,597	$3,459	$3,598	$3,734	$3,662	$3,783	$3,678	$3,700	$3,812

Exhibit 5

HARRINGTON CORPORATION

COMPARATIVE DATA ON SELECTED COMPANIES IN RELATED LINES OF BUSINESS

	Dow Jones Industrial Average	*Standard & Poor's 425 Industrial Stocks*	*Linden-Johns, Inc.**		*Kane Co.†*		*Granger, Inc.‡*		*Harrington Corp.*	
Trading market			OTC		OTC		OTC		—	
Current market price			$22¼		$14¾		$29¼		—	
Indicated dividend yield			5.5%		8.7%		3.7%		—	
Price-earnings ratio										
1970	14.6	16.4	8.7		7.2		10.5		—	
1969	14.0	15.7	6.4		5.0		10.2		—	
1968	16.3	18.6	10.8		11.9		13.8		—	
Price range										
1970			24⅝–16¼		14⅞–8⅛		33⅛–26½		—	
1969			18½–12⅛		11½–5⅛		19¾–12⅞		—	
Earnings per share (E) and index (I)			(E)	(I)	(E)	(I)	(E)	(I)	(E)	(I)
1970			$2.48	110	$1.62	82	$2.98	177	$9.83	216
1966			2.26	100	1.97	100	1.68	100	4.56	100
Sales (S) (in thousands) and index (I)			(S)	(I)	(S)	(I)	(S)	(I)	(S)	(I)
1970			$16,427	142	$12,223	108	$18,608	160	$7,630	157
1966			11,568	100	11,317	100	11,630	100	4,870	100
Net earnings (N) (in thousands) and index (I)			(N)	(I)	(N)	(I)	(N)	(I)	(N)	(I)
1970			$1,051	117	$501	84	$1,656	178	$983	216
1966			902	100	600	100	930	100	456	100
Net profit margins										
1970			6.4%		4.1%		8.9%		12.9%	
1966			7.8		5.3		8.0		9.4	
Profit/net worth										
1970			16.6%		6.0%		16.9%		19.8%	
1969			14.2		5.7		15.0		19.0	
1968			15.4		8.8		14.7		19.2	

Exhibit 5—Continued

Book capitalization (dollar figures in thousands)	Dow Jones Industrial Average	Standard & Poor's 425 Industrial Stocks	Linden–Johns, Inc.* 12/31/70		Kane Co.† 12/31/70		Granger, Inc.‡ 12/31/70		Harrington Corp. 12/31/70	
Long-term debt................			$3,995	38.7%	$1,822	18.0%	$4,173	29.9%	$ —	—%
Common stock and surplus.....			6,318	61.3	8,298	82.0	9,783	70.1	4,958	100.0
Total.........			$10,313	100.0%	$10,120	100.0%	$13,956	100.0%	$4,958	100.0%
Total market value (in thousands)........			$9,456		$4,573		$16,234		$ —	
Shares outstanding (in thousands)........			425		310		555		100	

* Producer of desk top accessories, advertising specialty calendars, office stationery.
† Producer of advertising specialty calendars.
‡ Producer of broad line of office paper products and desk accessories.

Exhibit 6

HARRINGTON CORPORATION

EXCERPTS FROM SUMMARY OF LOAN AGREEMENT FOR BANK TERM LOAN

Description of the Loan

Amount: $3,000,000

Rate: Prime rate plus 2%, floating.*

Term: 6 years.

Repayment: Annual payments equal to the greater of $500,000 or the sum of net profit plus amortization of goodwill and debt discounts less $100,000.

Prepayment: Permitted in whole or in part at any time without penalty. All prepayments to be applied to the outstanding principal balance of the loan in inverse order of maturity.

Compensating Balances: Borrower must maintain average annual deposit balances equal to at least 20% of the outstanding principal amount of the loan.

Conditions Precedent

Prior to the making of the loan described above, borrower must have satisfied the following terms and conditions:

Incorporation: Borrower must be a duly incorporated corporation authorized to undertake this borrowing and all other transactions associated with this borrowing.

Purchase Agreement: Borrower must have entered a contract to purchase 100% of the Harrington Corporation.

Financing: Borrower must have arranged firm commitments for the financing of this transaction in a manner consistent with the terms of this loan agreement.

Equity Purchase: Messrs. Brooks, Darby, Jackson, and Sloane must have committed not less than $250,000 to the purchase of common stock in the newly formed corporation which will purchase Harrington.

Affirmative Covenants

During the life of this loan, borrower will adhere to the following terms and conditions:

Financial Statements: Quarterly financial statements must be provided within 60 days of the end of the first three quarters. Audited financial statements bearing an unqualified opinion from a public accounting firm must be provided within 90 days of the end of borrower's fiscal year.

Accounting Changes: Borrower will make no changes in its method of accounting.

Negative Covenants

During the life of this loan, borrower will not do any of the following without written consent of the lender:

Continuation of Management: No changes in management. Aggregate compensation to Messrs. Brooks, Darby, Jackson, and Sloane not to be increased by more than 5% in any year, present compensation to serve as a base for this computation.

Negative Pledge: No assets to be pledged or otherwise used as collateral for any indebtedness.

Sale of Assets: No sale of a substantial portion of the assets of the borrower. Borrower will not merge with or be acquired by any other entity.

Acquisitions: Borrower will not acquire any other entity.

Capital Expenditures: Not to exceed $150,000 in any one year.

Dividends: In any one year restricted to after-tax profits minus all principal repayments on outstanding indebtedness.

Working Capital: Not to decline below $1,500,000.

Additional Indebtedness: No additional debt (including leases) with a term exceeding one year, unless subordinated to this loan. Any short-term debt must be retired for a period of at least 30 consecutive days in every year.

Senior Debt: Senior debt, including all short-term indebtedness, may not exceed $5 million plus all earnings retained in the business after Dec. 30, 1971.

Exhibit 6—Continued

Events of Default

In the event of default, this loan plus accrued interest will become immediately due and payable. The following will constitute events of default:

—Failure to pay interest or principal when due.
—Violation of any affirmative or negative covenant on this loan.
—Bankruptcy, reorganization, receivership, liquidation.
—Commission of an event of default on any other indebtedness.

* At present the prime rate is 5¼%.

Exhibit 7

HARRINGTON CORPORATION

CASH FLOW FORECASTS

(In thousands)

	1972	1973	1974	1975	1976	1977
Net sales........................	$8,012	$8,422	$8,843	$9,285	$9,749	$10,236
Earnings before interest and taxes*...	1,516	1,636	1,717	1,804	1,894	1,988
Interest expense†.................	637	585	523	454	400	400
Profit before tax..................	$ 879	$1,051	$1,194	$1,350	$1,494	$ 1,588
Taxes..........................	137	182	220	278	330	357
Profit after tax...................	$ 742	$ 869	$ 974	$1,072	$1,164	$ 1,231
Add back noncash charges..........	120	130	142	150	155	170
Cash flow from operations.........	$ 862	$ 999	$1,116	$1,222	$1,319	$ 1,401
Less: Increase in working capital....	78	81	85	90	95	100
Less: Capital expenditures.........	60	67	71	75	233	300
Available for debt retirement.......	$ 724	$ 851	$ 960	$1,057	$ 991	$ 1,001
Planned debt retirement:						
Bank loan...................	$ 724	$ 851	$ 960	$ 465	$ 0	$1,001
Baring's note.................	0	0	0	592	2,383‡	0
Subordinated loan.............	0	0	0	0	0	0
Debt as % of total capital.........	89%	80%	70%	58%	47%	35%

* Reflects elimination of Baring's salary.
† 9% coupon on subordinated loan of $3 million; 4% coupon on seller's note of $3 million; 7¼% rate on bank term loan; 6¼% rate on seasonal loan.
‡ Baring's note is retired from cash flow and a $1.4 million new bank term loan in 1976.

BECTON, DICKINSON AND COMPANY

∧∧∧

In mid-June, 1968, Douglas Brash and Harry Mosle of F. Eberstadt & Co. (FE & Co.), a New York investment banking firm, were involved in setting the final terms for a $25,000,000 issue of convertible subordinated debentures of Becton, Dickinson and Company (B-D). Most of the detailed features of the issue had been worked out with B-D over the preceding three months in preparation for the offering, which was planned for June 18. A general understanding had been reached with the company on the coupon rate for the debentures, the conversion premium above the current price of the common stock, and the underwriters' spread; but the final terms were to be set only at the last minute and would be based upon market conditions just before the offering date. A meeting between the top management of FE & Co. and B-D had been called for the afternoon of June 17, after the close of the market; and Douglas Brash was expected to recommend the final terms of the issue at that time.

Ben Harter, B-D's vice president for finance, had called on Ferdinand Eberstadt early in March, 1968, for advice and assistance in raising between $15 and $20 million later in the year. He said that on the basis of the company's current projections, B-D would need at least $15 million and perhaps as much as $25 million for new capital within the next two years. The bulk of the funds would be used to finance expansion of domestic manufacturing and distribution facilities, and the remainder would be needed for additional working capital, principally to carry increased inventories and accounts receivable. He asked for Mr. Eberstadt's views on the various ways in which B-D might raise these funds. Mr. Eberstadt said immediately that B-D should consider as one alternative the possibility of a convertible subordinated debenture, and indicated that his firm would come up with a specific recommendation as soon as a detailed analysis could be made. He indicated that because the firm was so familiar with B-D and its needs, he believed that a concrete proposal could be developed promptly.

Mr. Harter said that he had been in touch recently with the insurance company that held its 5⅛% promissory notes due in 1982. These notes had been placed privately in 1962 with the assistance of the Eberstadt firm. He told Mr. Eberstadt that the insurance company had indicated that it would lend B-D $20 million for 20 years, nonrefundable for the first 10 years, with interest at 7%. He said that in addition to the possibility of straight long-term debt, the company had been considering as alternatives another common stock issue, or arranging a revolving-term loan credit agreement with commercial banks.

F. Eberstadt & Co. had arranged six earlier financings for B-D. The first of these had been a private placement of $7 million of notes in 1958. Since that date it had placed privately another $9 million issue of notes and had handled four common stock issues for the company. The stock issues were all public offerings. Three were combined offerings of the company and certain selling stockholders; the fourth was entirely a registered secondary offering. The selling stockholders were members of the Dickinson and Becton families as well as other substantial holders who had acquired B-D stock through acquisition of their companies by B-D. The most recent issue had been a common stock offering of more than 500,000 shares just a year before; hence the financial affairs of B-D were well known to the firm. (See Exhibit 1.)

THE COMPANY

Becton, Dickinson and Company was incorporated under the laws of New Jersey in 1906 to succeed to a partnership established in 1897. The company and its subsidiaries are engaged principally in the manufacture and sale of a broad line of medical, surgical, laboratory, and diagnostic products used by doctors, hospitals, laboratories, pharmaceutical companies, medical schools, dentists, and veterinarians. The company also manufactures and sells gloves and mittens for industry, farm, home, and recreational uses and electronic and electromechanical products and engineered subassemblies primarily for industrial customers. It also engages in custom contract packaging and the leasing of packaging machinery. In its fiscal year ended September 30, 1967, approximately 75% of its sales were attributable to health care products.

The original business of the company was the manufacture and sale of clinical thermometers. Over the years B-D had diversified its activities and added many product lines, primarily in the medical, surgical, and laboratory areas, both through its own development activities and through acquisitions. It had become one of the leading companies in the expanding health care field. B-D's broad product line provided valuable diversification to lessen the possible impact of any adverse technological or competitive development relating to any one product. Moreover, this diversification across wide areas of medical activity meant that B-D would be exposed to most of the new product opportunities that were likely to develop. Therefore, the company, which had strong research and product development capabilities, could be expected to continue to participate significantly in the expanding health care field.

The company manufactures and sells several thousand individual items within its various product lines. Approximately 92% of its sales are currently derived from items of its own manufacture; the remaining products are made for it by others, generally to its specifications. The company's products include both reusable and disposable items. In recent years there had been substantial growth in the demand for disposable items, and currently they accounted for about 70% of the company's sales of medical, surgical, and laboratory products.

The company has, throughout its history, laid great emphasis on quality control and on biological safety. Particular care is exercised in the control of disposable medical devices, especially in the areas of sterility, toxicity, and pyrogenicity, to ensure that its products are not harmful, when used as indicated, in the care of human beings. B-D's standards for quality and safety have assumed even greater significance with the increased sales of sterile products and products for human implant.

Research and development

The company is actively engaged in the development of new products and in devising new and improved methods of manufacturing existing products. It carries on its research and development activities both at the corporate level and in each of the seven operating divisions.

The corporate research and development group is concerned primarily with areas of investigation not related to the company's existing products. It attempts to satisfy the needs of the medical profession for new and improved instrumentation through research and development. In addition, the corporate research and development group coordinates research and development activities among the various operating units of the company. It is B-D's general policy to delegate as far as possible research and development work relating to the products of an operating facility to that facility. This includes both immediate and advanced product development, as well as extension of product lines and improvement of existing products.

The company owns numerous domestic and foreign patents and is licensed under patents owned by others. It does not believe that any of its patents or licenses give it a substantial competitive advantage with respect to any of the activities in which it is engaged, or that its patents or licenses are of material importance to the overall success of its business. The company relies primarily on the development and manufacturing ability of its technical and engineering staffs rather than upon patents.

Competition

The company is faced with substantial competition in all areas in which it is active, in most cases from companies which provide competition for only a part of B-D's product lines. Some of the company's competitors have greater financial resources and sales than those of B-D. In recent years there has been a tendency on the part of some firms engaged in the distribution of medical products to become manufacturers as well. In addition, the company is faced with competition from products manufactured abroad, particularly reusable hypodermic syringes and needles, clinical thermometers and disposable needles. The rapid progress of medical technology means that new methods or techniques can render B-D's current products in some fields obsolete and, therefore, the company stresses its research and development programs and the orderly introduction of new products.

Property

The executive offices of the company are located in East Rutherford, New Jersey. Principal domestic manufacturing units, some with research and significant warehousing facilities, are located in California, Connecticut, Illinois, Indiana, Louisiana, Maryland, Massachusetts, Michigan, Nebraska, New Jersey, New Mexico, New York, and Ohio. Sales offices and distribution points are also located in other sections of the United States.

The company owns approximately 1,800,000 square feet and leases approximately 800,000 square feet of floor space at its various locations in the United States. Its manufacturing equipment consists in large part of specialized machinery for the precision grinding, processing, shaping, sewing, forming, marking and sealing of glass, rubber, fabric, plastic, and metal. In many instances this machinery has been specially designed by its technical staff and manufactured in its machine shops. Of particular importance to the company because of the nature of its products are various types of sterilization and testing equipment. B-D owns all of its machinery and equipment except for certain items, not of significance, which are furnished by customers in connection with contract business or leased from others.

Major plant facilities are currently being used at or near full capacity. The company has a continuing program for expansion of its plant facilities. The capital expenditures of the company and its consolidated subsidiaries, net of retirements, for property, plant, and equipment for the five fiscal years ended September 30, 1967, were approximately as follows:

1963	$ 5,273,000
1964	6,126,000
1965	8,247,000
1966	8,504,000
1967	10,910,000

Financial data

A statement of consolidated income of B-D for five fiscal years ended September 30, 1963, to 1967 and for the six-month periods ended March 31, 1967, and 1968 is set forth in Exhibit 2. Consolidated balance sheets on September 30, 1967, and March 31, 1968, appear in Exhibit 3.

The common stock of B-D has been listed on the New York Stock Exchange since September 25, 1963. The holders of the stock have noncumulative voting rights and do not have preemptive rights. The range of sale prices of the common stock, from 1964 to June 17, 1968, adjusted for a 1 for 1 stock distribution in November, 1966, is as follows:

	High	Low
1964	19¾	13⅝
1965	32	17⅞
1966	40⅜	26⅝
1967	63	39½
1968 (through June 17)	71⅞	55¼

SELECTING THE SECURITY

A second meeting with B-D officials took place on March 15 to discuss the form of financing that was to be recommended by the Eberstadt firm. The recommendation was that B-D finance its needs by a public offering of convertible subordinated debentures. The approximate terms suggested for such an issue were a $4\frac{1}{2}\%$ coupon, convertible at about 15% above the stock price at the time of issue, and a gross spread no higher than $1\frac{1}{2}\%$, all terms being subject to market conditions.

In the discussion that followed, three alternatives to the convertible debenture were also discussed—a long-term straight debt issue, a revolving-term loan with banks, and a common stock offering. In regard to the possibility of a common stock offering, concern was expressed about the potential dilution involved in such an issue. B-D was now considering an issue of $25 million. An equity issue to raise this amount would involve a substantial number of shares, and the announcement of such a large offering would almost certainly cause the market price of B-D's stock to decline. Depending on the extent of the market reaction, an offering of as many as 500,000 shares might be required. Despite the fact that the resulting capital structure after such an issue of common stock would provide advantageous flexibility for future financings, the potential adverse effect on the company's stock price was believed to be too substantial. A rights offering to minimize the effects of dilution had also been considered, but the idea had been discarded. A substantial amount of the outstanding stock of the company was still in the hands of the Becton and Dickinson families and their interests, and such holders could not be expected to subscribe for additional stock. They had been reducing their holdings through the earlier secondary offerings in order to diversify their investments. Consequently, a rights offering was not considered a realistic alternative.

As indicated earlier, B-D was also reluctant to assume the relatively high cost involved in a long-term, straight debt placement such as had been suggested by the insurance company holding its 1962 debt issue. B-D did express an interest in bank debt, however, with perhaps a five-year term. The Eberstadt representatives, however, thought it unwise to consider relatively short-term bank financing of long-term capital requirements, especially during a period of current and prospective rapid growth of the company.

In regard to a long-term straight debt issue, the Eberstadt people were also concerned about the lack of flexibility inherent in the tight repayment schedule as well as the high interest rate that would be required, whether the debt was offered publicly or placed privately. The repayment provisions were considered to be especially important, because of B-D's desire to retain a maximum amount of earnings for reinvestment in the company rather than for debt repayment. On a long-term straight debt issue the sinking fund would probably commence no later than the beginning of the sixth year and thereafter the entire amount would have to be repaid in approximately equal installments. The FE & Co. representatives also pointed out that long-term straight debt would require call protection for at least 5 and perhaps as many as 10 years, which would reduce B-D's freedom to refinance in the event that interest rates declined. Finally, they expressed concern over B-D's flexibility for future financings if it issued straight debt now. Its debt ratio and interest coverage now were excellent, but both would be reduced with an additional issue of $25 million of senior debt. This would have an adverse impact on whatever rating the bond services would put on B-D's debt securities in the future, and thus make future debt financings more expensive.

The Eberstadt people saw the subordinated convertible debenture as the most attractive alternative at the time. The primary advantage lay in the reduced burden of the security. In the first place the coupon rate would be lower, say $4\frac{1}{2}\%$ as compared with over $6\frac{1}{2}\%$ for a public offering of straight debt. In addition, the indenture would be much less restrictive. Furthermore, the sinking fund would require no repayments at all for 10 years and then the repayment of only half of the issue prior to the final maturity date. At the same time there could be an optional sinking fund for repayments at no premium, which could add additional flexibility to the company's financial planning. Moreover, there might be no need for any repayments because if B-D continued to prosper and grow, its stock price might be expected to rise above the conversion price, leading either to voluntary conversions or to forced conversion in the event the company called the debentures. In either case there would be no required repayments at all for the first 10 years and, to the extent that the conversions took place, required repayments could be further delayed.

In addition, such an issue would be considered as quasi equity and would expand the company's senior borrowing base. And there would be an even clearer case of increased flexibility in future financing after conversion took place. Finally, because of the great interest and enthusiasm for B-D stock as evidenced by its price-earnings ratio above 50, a good conversion premium would be possible, which in turn would minimize dilution. On all these grounds the Eberstadt people believed that a convertible subordinated debenture would best meet B-D's needs at the present time.

As to the tentative terms suggested, these were based on the Eberstadt firm's judgment as to what would be salable in the then current securities market after analyzing the terms of recent convertible issues as of March 12, 1968. Exhibit 4 includes data assembled at that time on eight such issues of industrial corporations which were at least somewhat comparable in size and quality to the proposed B-D issue. Only two of the issuers, Will Ross and Baxter Laboratories, were in the same general industry group as B-D, and both of these companies had high price-earnings ratios and strong growth rates comparable to B-D. On the basis of these figures and the then market conditions, the Eberstadt firm was confident it could sell B-D convertibles at a $4\frac{1}{2}\%$ coupon, 15% conversion premium, and $1\frac{1}{2}\%$ spread.

No decision was reached at the March 15 meeting, but on March 20, B-D's executive vice president, John Simmons, called Douglas Brash to say that B-D's finance committee had decided to proceed expeditiously to raise $25 million through the sale of subordinated convertible debentures. He said that the company would have to hold a special meeting of shareholders to approve the issuance of the recommended securities, but he did not envisage any problem on that score. Mr. Simmons asked the Eberstadt firm to proceed to work out the schedule for the financing and to develop with counsel the detailed covenants for the debentures.

INDENTURE PROVISIONS

On the basis of its experience in designing securities and of a detailed review of the provisions of a number of indentures relating to recent convertible issues by companies of comparable quality, the Eberstadt firm recommended and B-D accepted the following important indenture provisions:

The debentures are to be limited to the principal amount of $25 million being offered hereby, and are to be unsecured obligations of the company. They are to be issuable as definitive registered debentures without coupons in denominations of $1,000, and any multiple of $1,000. Interest will be payable semiannually on June 1 and December 1 of each year (commencing December 1, 1968) to holders of record on the preceding May 15 or November 15, and the debentures will mature on June 1, 1988.

Redemption

The debentures are to be subject to redemption prior to maturity, at the option of the company, as a whole at any time, or from time to time in part, during the respective 12-month period ending May 31 in each of the years set forth in the tabulation below, upon payment of the applicable percentage of the principal amount set forth under the heading "Redemption Price," together with interest accrued to the date fixed for redemption.

Year Ending May 31	Redemption Price	Year Ending May 31	Redemption Price
1969	100% plus coupon rate	1979	
1970		1980	
1971		1981	
1972	Scaled down in equal	1982	
1973	intervals to 100% in	1983	
1974	1986	1984	
1975		1985	
1976		1986	100.00
1977		1987	100.00
1978		1988	100.00

At least 30 days' notice of redemption shall be given by mail to the registered holders of the debentures being redeemed. If less than all of the debentures are to be redeemed, the trustee will select those to be redeemed in any manner it deems fair and appropriate.

The debentures will be redeemable on similar notice through the operation of a sinking fund (optional and mandatory) described below at the principal amount thereof (no premium), together with accrued interest to the redemption date.

Sinking fund

The indenture will require the company to retire $1,250,000 principal amount of debentures on June 1 in each of the years 1978 to and including 1987, subject to credits for debentures converted prior to such June 1 or redeemed or canceled otherwise than through the operation of the sinking fund. In addition, the company may at its option provide cash for the retirement, on June 1 in each of the years 1973 to 1987, both inclusive, of debentures up to a maximum principal amount equal to, but not to exceed, $1,250,000. Such optional right of redemption will be noncumulative and without payment of premium.

Conversion

Any debenture or any portion of the principal amount thereof which is $1,000 or a multiple of $1,000 will be convertible, at its principal amount, into common stock of the company, at any time or from time to time at the option of the holder, on or before June 1, 1988, at the conversion price. The conversion price is to be subject to adjustment in the case of dividends in common stock and in certain other cases, including the issuance or sale of common stock at less than the conversion price then in effect. The conversion price will also be subject to adjustment upon any subdivision or combination of the outstanding shares of common stock, or reclassification of other securities into common stock. No adjustment in the conversion price is to be made with respect to (a) the shares issued upon conversion of the debentures offered hereby; (b) issuance of shares of common stock or securities convertible into shares of common stock in exchange for the assets, or at least 80% of the voting shares, of a going business, or in connection with a merger of another company into B-D; and (c) all shares issued to employees (including officers) under stock options granted under any plan (now or hereafter existing) for the benefit of such employees in connection with their employment. No adjustment in the conversion price will be made until the adjustment formula set forth in the indenture requires a total adjustment per share of 50 cents or more.

Subordination provisions

Upon any distribution of assets of B-D or upon any dissolution, winding up, liquidation, or reorganization of the company, payment of the principal of and premium and interest on the debentures will be subordinated to the prior payment in full of all senior indebtedness. No payment may be made on the debentures while payment of principal of, or interest on, any senior indebtedness is in default or while there is any other default on senior indebtedness which permits its acceleration.

Senior indebtedness includes the principal of and premium, if any, and interest on (a) indebtedness (other than the debentures) of or guaranteed by the company for money borrowed; (*b*) indebtedness of the company evidenced by notes or debentures (other than these debentures) issued under the provisions of an indenture or similar instrument between the company and a financial institution; (*c*) any such indebtedness of another person, firm, or corporation incurred, assumed or guaranteed by the company in connection with the acquisition by B-D of any businesses, properties, or other assets; or (*d*) indebtedness of the company under any deferrals, renewals or extensions of any such foregoing indebtedness, or under any debentures, notes or other evidences of indebtedness issued in exchange for such foregoing indebtedness —unless, in each case, by the terms of the instrument by which the company incurred, assumed or guaranteed such indebtedness, it is expressly provided that such indebtedness is not superior in right of payment to the debentures. (As of March 31, 1968, the principal amount of senior indebtedness was approximately $18,300,000.)

Dividend restrictions

The indenture will provide that no dividend or other distribution (except in stock of the company) may be declared on any stock of the company unless after giving effect thereto, the aggregate amount expended for such purposes since September 30, 1967, does not exceed the sum of (*a*) the consolidated net income of the company earned subsequent to September 30, 1967; (*b*) the aggregate net proceeds of sales after June 1, 1968, of any capital stock of the company; (*c*) the aggregate net cash proceeds of the sales after June 1, 1968, of any indebtedness (including the debentures) of the company thereafter converted into stock; and (*d*) $7,500,000. (If this provision had been in effect on March 31, 1968, approximately $12,250,000 would have been available for cash dividends.)

FINAL TERMS FOR THE ISSUE

It had been estimated that it would require about three months to take all the necessary steps to prepare and file the registration statement, to prepare and mail the proxy statement to obtain the approval of B-D's stockholders, and to have the registration statement become effective. B-D made the first public announcement of the issue on April 8 at the time it filled its preliminary proxy material with the SEC. A second announcement was made when the registration statement was filed on May 14, 1968. After the latter date the Eberstadt firm proceeded to form an underwriting syndicate for the forthcoming issue and, as the red herring prospectuses became available, to ascertain the extent of dealer and investor interest in the debentures.

Interest in the securities was strong and immediate. Invitations to participate in the underwriting went to the investment banking firms which had handled so successfully the previous issues of B-D's common stock under the Eberstadt management. Not only were such invitations readily accepted, but the underwriters generally sought larger participations. In addition, requests for participations came in increasing numbers during the registration period from all across the country as did requests by dealers for selling allotments. A final list of 95 underwriters was submitted to and approved by B-D just after the stockholders had approved on May 21 the issuance of the debentures.

There was no question of the strength of the appetite for the debentures among investors and dealers alike, and the interest seemed to increase as the offering date approached. In addition, the market stayed strong for B-D stock with no significant adverse reaction immediately after the announcement of the issue or later. B-D's stock price strengthened in April and May, and there was no significant weakening as the offering date approached. (See Exhibit 5.)

This was the general situation on Monday, June 17, as Douglas Brash met with Mr. Eberstadt and other top partners of the firm after the close of the market to settle on the final terms of the issue to be negotiated with B-D. To assist them Mr. Mosle had assembled the data appearing in Exhibit 6. He also indicated that the price of B-D's stock at the close of the market was $64⅝. The final terms of the issue to be negotiated later that afternoon with the top officials of B-D included (a) the coupon rate of the debentures, (b) the conversion premium above the current market price or the conversion price itself, and (c) the contemplated gross spread.

Exhibit 1

BECTON, DICKINSON AND COMPANY
CHRONOLOGICAL LIST OF FINANCINGS FOR
BECTON, DICKINSON AND COMPANY
MANAGED BY
F. EBERSTADT & CO.
THROUGH MARCH, 1968

January 22, 1958:   Private placement of:
    $ 500,000 4½% promissory notes due 1963
    $4,500,000 5½% promissory notes due 1978
    $2,000,000 6% subordinated notes due 1983

April 23, 1962:   Registered public offering of 480,000 shares of common
    stock at $25 ($9⅜):*
    200,000 shares for company
    280,000 shares for selling stockholders
    Aggregate prices to public = $12,000,000

December 18, 1962:   Private placement of:
    $9,000,000 5⅛% promissory notes due 1982

May 4, 1965:   Registered public offering of 250,000 shares of common
    stock at $40⅛ ($20¹⁄₁₆)* for selling stockholders:
    Aggregate price to public = $10,031,250

April 5, 1966:   Registered public offering of 368,250 shares of common
    stock at $56.75 ($28⅜):*
    125,000 shares for company
    243,250 shares for selling stockholders
    Aggregate price to public = $20,898,188
    (Joint with White, Weld & Co., Incorporated)

March 22, 1967:   Registered public offering of 526,769 shares of common
    stock at $49.50:
    283,200 shares for company
    243,569 shares for selling stockholders
    Aggregate price to public = $26,075,066

* Stock Prices in ( ) represent adjusted prices to take account of a 4 for 3 stock split in 1963 and a 100% stock dividend in 1966.

Exhibit 2

BECTON, DICKINSON AND COMPANY
STATEMENT OF CONSOLIDATED INCOME
(In thousands, except for per share data)

	Year Ended September 30					Six Months Ended March 31	
	1963	1964	1965	1966	1967	1967 (Unaudited)	1968 (Unaudited)
Revenues:							
Net sales	$88,207	$100,908	$116,001	$140,750	$157,019	$76,507	$85,254
Company's share of undistributed income (net) of unconsolidated subsidiaries	878	1,018	731	845	1,311	439	1,082
Interest and other	695	654	711	836	1,130	375	863
	$89,781	$102,580	$117,443	$142,431	$159,460	$77,321	$87,199
Costs and expenses:							
Cost of products sold	$55,287	$62,175	$69,632	$82,349	$91,349	$44,803	$50,067
Selling, general and administrative, and research and development expenses	24,449	27,697	32,292	39,324	45,040	21,917	25,207
Interest on long-term notes	539	690	850	936	1,003	498	516
Other	147	146	89	109	181	71	88
	$80,422	$90,709	$102,864	$122,718	$137,573	$67,289	$75,878
Income before federal income taxes	$ 9,358	$ 11,872	$ 14,579	$ 19,713	$ 21,888	$10,032	$11,321
Federal income taxes	4,155	5,203	6,612	9,208	9,799	4,731	4,994
Net income	$ 5,203	$ 6,669	$ 7,967	$ 10,505	$ 12,089	$ 5,301	$ 6,327
Net income per share*	$0.55	$0.71	$0.84	$1.05	$1.17	$0.52	$0.60
Dividends per share†	$0.11¼	$0.15	$0.20	$0.20	$0.30	$0.15	$0.15

* Based on the number of shares outstanding at the end of each period (except for the year ended September 30, 1967, and the six months ended March 31, 1967, and 1968 which are based on the average number of shares outstanding for the period) after giving retroactive effect to shares issued in poolings of interests, a 4 for 3 stock split in December, 1963, and a 1 for 1 stock distribution in November, 1966.

† Adjusted to reflect the 4 for 3 stock split in December, 1963, and the 1 for 1 stock distribution in November, 1966.

Figures may not add because of rounding.

Exhibit 3

BECTON, DICKINSON AND COMPANY
CONSOLIDATED BALANCE SHEET
(In thousands)

	September 30, 1967	March 31, 1968 (Unaudited)
ASSETS		
Current assets:		
Cash...	$ 2,307	$ 3,209
Short-term investments at cost (approximate market).........	18,453	10,038
Trade receivables—less allowances of $453,750 ($477,944 at March 31, 1968).....................................	21,359	22,514
Inventories, generally at the lower of cost (first-in, first-out) or market:		
Raw materials and supplies............................	$ 9,996	$ 10,530
Work in process......................................	9,751	11,774
Finished products....................................	15,925	16,495
	$ 35,672	$ 38,800
Prepaid expenses......................................	1,798	1,839
Total current assets....................................	$ 79,590	$ 76,399
Investments and other assets:		
Investments in unconsolidated subsidiaries, including advances of $3,311,444 ($3,170,606 at March 31, 1968).............	13,851	14,677
Other..	1,052	1,101
Property, plant, and equipment—on the basis of cost:		
Land..	$ 3,035	$ 3,583
Buildings...	21,147	23,671
Machinery, equipment, and fixtures.......................	35,044	38,287
Leasehold improvements.................................	861	864
	$ 60,086	$ 66,405
Less: Allowances for depreciation and amortization............	21,247	23,165
	$ 38,839	$ 43,241
Intangible assets (patents, trade-marks, goodwill, etc.)..........	1,138	1,317
Total assets...	$ 134,470	$ 136,735
LIABILITIES AND SHAREHOLDERS' EQUITY		
Current liabilities:		
Trade payables..	$ 4,956	$ 4,115
Salaries, wages, and related items.........................	3,328	4,006
Federal income taxes....................................	8,056	5,194
Other...	3,246	4,173
Current portion of long-term notes payable—Note A...........	1,822	1,821
Total current liabilities...............................	$ 21,408	$ 19,309
Long-term notes payable—Note A..........................	17,404	16,230
Shareholders' equity:		
Common stock—par value $1—authorized 12,000,000 shares (15,000,000 at March 31, 1968); issued 10,749,136 shares (10,783,033 at March 31, 1968) including 90,524 shares in treasury (83,301 at March 31, 1968) and 111,112 shares held by a wholly owned subsidiary............................	$ 18,221	$ 18,255
Capital in excess of par value.............................	25,025	25,778
Retained earnings.......................................	53,435	58,174
	$ 96,681	$ 102,207
Less treasury stock—at cost...............................	1,023	1,011
Total shareholders' equity................................	$ 95,658	101,196
Total liabilities and shareholders' equity....................	$ 134,470	$ 136,735

Exhibit 3—Continued

Note a—Long-Term Notes Payable

	September 30, 1967	March 31, 1968 (Unaudited)
Notes payable to an insurance company and a pension trust:		
5½% promissory notes, due December 31, 1978.	$ 3,600,000	$ 3,300,000
6% subordinated notes, due December 31, 1983.	1,700,000	1,600,000
5⅛% promissory notes, due December 31, 1982.	9,000,000	8,500,000
Notes (5%) payable to banks as trustees and agents, due in		
quarterly installments through October 1, 1985.	1,893,209	1,860,953
6½% term loan (7½% at March 31, 1968) payable to bank		
December 31, 1969, to 1971.	1,163,750	1,163,750
Sundry notes (5% to 6½%), with varied repayments through		
1981.	1,869,011	1,625,610
	$19,225,970	$18,050,313
Less portion included in current liabilities.	1,822,339	1,820,626
	$17,403,631	$16,229,687

Notes payable to an insurance company and a pension trust are subject to fixed sinking fund payments of $900,000 annually. The company has optional prepayment privileges under certain conditions. These notes provide, among other things, that the company and its consolidated subsidiaries will limit: (1) indebtedness for borrowed money; (2) investments in companies other than restricted subsidiaries, as defined; (3) annual rentals under long-term leases, as defined. Such limitations vary with conditions related generally to the growth of the company. The company has agreed to maintain specified amounts of consolidated net current assets, as defined. At September 30, 1967, and March 31, 1968, there was an excess of approximately $36,000,000 and $37,-000,000, respectively, over the then required amounts of consolidated net current assets. In addition, declaration or payment of cash dividends and the acquisition or retirement of the company's capital stock are limited to an amount equivalent to consolidated net income, as defined, subsequent to September 30, 1961. At September 30, 1967, and March 31, 1968, retained earnings of approximately $31,000,000 and $35,000,000, respectively, were unrestricted under such limitation.

The aggregate annual maturities (including sinking fund payments) of long-term notes payable during the fiscal years ending September 30, 1968 to 1972, are as follows: 1968, $1,824,320; 1969, $1,300,478; 1970, $1,431,278; 1971, $1,626,347; 1972, $1,309,874.

Exhibit 4

BECTON, DICKINSON AND COMPANY
DATA ON SELECTED RECENT ISSUES OF SUBORDINATED CONVERTIBLE DEBENTURES AS COMPILED MARCH 12, 1968

Rating	Offering Date	Company	Size of Offering (000)	Coupon Rate	Conversion Price	Market Price at Offering	Conversion Premium
NR	9/06/67	Monogram Ind.	$25,000	4%	$45	41½(2)	8.4%
BB	9/06/67	Will Ross	12,000	4¼	74½	60	24.2
BB	9/14/67	Parker Hannifin	20,000	4	76	65½	16.0
B	11/21/67	Sanders Assoc.	35,000	5	67	60¾	10.3
BB	12/01/67	General Instrument	50,000	5	67	63	6.3
BB	12/05/67	Fischer & Porter	6,000	5½	32⅓	29	11.5
BB	1/17/68	Walt Disney Prod.	40,000	4½	65	56⅞	14.3
BBB	3/05/68	Baxter Labs.	25,000	4½	42	35	20.0
		Becton, Dickinson	25,000				

(1) At the time of the offering, giving effect to the offering.
(2) Adjusted for 3 for 1 split.

		Current Prices			
	Com. Price	Com. Div.	Com. Yield	Deb. Price	Deb. Yield
Monogram Ind. 4s	47	nil	already called		
Will Ross 4¼s	73½	$0.50	0.68%	$111	3.83%
Parker Hannifin 4s	45½	1.20	2.64	84¾	4.72
Sanders Assoc. 5s	47⅛	0.30	0.64	102½	4.88
General Instrument 5s	47⅛	1.08	2.29	92	5.43
Fischer & Porter 5½s	21	0.98	4.67	92	5.98
Walt Disney Prod. 4½s	48⅜	0.30	0.62	98¼	4.58
Baxter Labs. 4½s	36¾	0.16	0.44	105	4.29
Becton, Dickinson	59⅞	0.30	0.50	—	—

Exhibit 4—Continued

1967	1966	EPS 1965	1964	1963	P/E Ratio (1)		LTD as % Total Cap. (1)	Book Value per $1,000 LTD (1)	Market Value per $1,000 LTD (1)
$0.96	$0.52	$0.27	$0.19	$0.09	43.2X	Lehman, Blyth	63.5	$ 575	$ 3,333
1.53E	1.42	1.24	1.07	0.93	39.2X	White, Weld	43.2	1,315	7,966
3.41	3.06	2.23	1.65	1.43	19.2X	Kidder	41.8	1,394	5,165
1.23	0.67	0.70	0.73	0.72	49.4X	Lehman	46.0	1,175	7,727
2.00E	2.27	1.38	0.82	0.46	31.5X	Loeb Rhoades	46.3	1,158	3,857
1.81	1.63	1.54	1.03	0.75	19.9X	Drexel	44.7	1,209	1,907
2.52	3.17	3.04	1.98	1.91	22.6X	Kidder, Lehman	36.1	1,767	5,505
0.70	0.53	0.37	0.27	0.26	50.0X	M.L.P., F.& S.	49.8	1,007	8,736
1.17	1.05	0.84	0.71	0.55			32.8	2,242	15,080

Assume $25 MM Offering

Gross Spread	When Callable	
1.50%	At any time	Usually with 30
1.25	At any time	days' notice
1.25	At any time	Plus various sink-
1.25	At any time	ing fund pro-
1.25	At any time	visions
2.75	At any time	At various pre-
1.25	At any time	miums
1.25	At any time	In whole or in
—		part
		Unless in default

Exhibit 5

BECTON, DICKINSON AND COMPANY
COMMON STOCK PRICES AND VOLUME OF TRADING
MARCH 11 TO JUNE 17, 1968

Date	Closing Price	Volume
March 11	59⅞	3,800
12	58⅞	5,500
13	59⅝	2,600
14	57¼	5,000
15	57¼	7,000
March 18	57¾	14,900
19	57⅞	1,500
20	56⅞	3,100
21	56⅞	2,100
22	56¾	3,900
March 29	59⅞	6,100
April 15	64	7,600
30	64¾	1,300
May 13	69¼	4,300
14	67⅞	3,800
15	67½	1,900
16	67	1,000
17	66⅜	3,300
May 20	65¾	1,300
21	67¼	2,500
22	66⅛	2,400
23	66½	2,100
24	65⅞	8,800
May 27	66½	1,200
28	66¼	12,700
29	66¼	5,400
30	Holiday	
31	68½	2,600
June 3	67	3,800
4	66⅝	3,200
5	66¾	4,300
6	67⅜	3,000
7	67⅞	3,400
June 10	67⅜	1,200
11	66½	3,700
12	Market closed	
13	65¾	4,400
14	66⅛	8,800
June 17	64⅝	5,300

Exhibit 6

BECTON, DICKINSON AND COMPANY
CONVERTIBLE SUBORDINATED DEBENTURES PRICING COMPARISON
(as compiled June 14, 1968)

Rating S & P	Rating Moody	Company	Coupon and Maturity	Size of Issue (Millions)	Date of Issue	Conversion Price	Current Market Price of Stock (1)	Current Market Price of Bond
					1967			
BB	Ba	Will Ross	4¼s '87	12.0	9/6	74.50	90	120
BB	Ba	Parker Hannifin	4s '92	20.0	9/14	76.00	57⅛	90¼
B	Ba	Sanders Associates	5s '92	35.0	11/21	67.00	58¼	111¼
BB	Ba	Fischer & Porter	5½s '87	6.0	12/5	32 33	25	105
BB	Ba	General Instrument	5s '92	50.0	12/01	67.00	53¼	104
					1968			
BB	Ba	Walt Disney	4½s '93	40.0	1/17	65.00	68¼	127
BBB	Ba	Baxter Labs.	4½s '88	25.0	3/5	42.00	51½	134
BBB	Baa	White Motor	5¼s '93	25.0	3/12	54.50	54⅛	112
B	Ba	Sundstrand	5s '93	30.0	4/4	71.00	89¼	132
B	B	Indian Head	5½s '93	25.0	4/10	38.50	37¼	109
BB	B	Lucky Stores	5s '93	28.0	4/23	45.00	45⅝	115
BBB	Baa	Burroughs	3¾s '93	75.0	5/16	253.50	213⅞	102
BB	Ba	Ogden Corp.	5s '93	50.0	6/4	50.00	48¾	108¾
B	Ba	Am. Hoist & Derrick	5½s '93	18.0	6/5	21.50	18½	99¾
BBB	Baa	Becton, Dickinson	— '88	25.0	—	—	65¾	—

(1) Closing prices June 13, 1968.
(2) *Conversion Value*—Current common market price × number of shares into which convertible.

Conversion Value (2) per $1000 Bond	Conversion Premium	Current Bond Yield	Current Conversion Yield (3)	Common Stock Price Range 1967-68	Gross Spread	Yield	Conversion Premium	Managing Underwriter
120.78		3.54	0.56	90–36½	1.25%	4.25%	24.2%	White, Weld
75.18	20.0	4.71	1.75	67¼–38¾	1.25	4.00	16.0	Kidder Peabody
86.97	27.9	4.49	0.40	77¼–26⅝	1.25	5.00	10.3	Lehman—Kidder Peabody
77.33	35.8	5.24	—	37⅛–16⅛	2.75	5.50	11.5	Drexel
79.50	30.8	4.81	—	86–40⅛	1.25	5.00	6.3	Loeb Rhoades
104.97	21.0	3.54	0.36	68½–37½	1.25	4.50	14.3	Kidder Peabody—Lehman
122.62	9.3	3.36	0.28	54⅞–19⅜	1.25	4.50	20.0	MLPFS—White, Weld
99.32	12.8	4.69	3.28	57½–36⅞	0.875(4)	5.25	13.5	Blyth
125.66	5.0	3.79	0.85	90¾–29½	1.25	5.00	16.2	Hornblower—White, Weld
96.74	12.7	5.05	1.43	46–18⅝	1.875	5.50	11.6	White Weld—Blair
101.38	13.4	4.35	2.32	47⅛–16¼	1.75	5.00	13.2	MLPFS—Lehman—Goldman Sachs
84.27	21.0	3.68	0.38	220⅜–80⅞	1.125	3.75	20.5	Kidder Peabody
97.50	11.5	4.60	1.47	52–15¼	1.75	5.00	8.0	Allen—Wertheim
86.04	15.9	5.51	3.26	24⅜–10½	1.50	5.50	10.2	Lehman
—	—	—	—	71⅞–39½	—	—	—	F. Eberstadt & Co.

(3) *Conversion Yield*—Common dividend × number of shares into which convertible as % of bond price.
(4) This issue was combined in a package with an issue of $22 million in common stock.

LING-TEMCO-VOUGHT, INC.

∧∧

In early 1971, Ling-Temco-Vought, Inc. (LTV) faced a serious financial crisis. The company had just completed calendar year 1970 with a loss of about $70 million (line 24, Exhibit 1). This amount, combined with the loss of $38 million reported for 1969, more than wiped out the entire profit earned by the firm from its inception in 1953. By year-end 1970, LTV had a debt/equity ratio of 4.48 (line 26, Exhibit 2), a cash deficit from operations for the year exceeding $15 million (line 11, Exhibit 3) and debt maturities within one year equal to $77 million (line 18, Exhibit 2). While it appeared that this debt could be retired as it matured with cash raised from the sale of assets, it was equally clear that such a move would represent only a holding action at best. To many creditors and investors, LTV's capital structure at the end of 1970 appeared dangerously unbalanced, and they looked to the company for some significant corrective action in the not too distant future.

Corporate structure and business strategy

LTV's corporate structure had always been very complex. In many ways the firm resembled a holding company. As of December 31, 1970, for example, it owned a control position in seven other large and well-known corporations (Exhibit 4). On the other hand, LTV was so active in acquiring and disposing of securities, whole companies, or portions of companies (Exhibit 5) that in some ways it bore a closer resemblance to a mutual fund than to a holding company.

While LTV's corporate structure was complex, its operating strategy as a business enterprise was simple. LTV's business consisted of buying the common stock of large publicly held companies and then "redeploying"[1] the assets of these companies. LTV borrowed very aggressively, and often used this source of cash to finance tender offers made directly to the shareholders of companies it wished to acquire. The companies selected by LTV as acquisition targets generally had (a) low price-to-earnings ratios, (b) substantial unused borrowing capacity, and (c) one or more easily separable operating divisions which competed in industries characterized by relatively higher price-to-earnings ratios.

---

[1] LTV's concept of "redeployment" is explained in the text that immediately follows.

Once a company had been successfully acquired and was wholly owned, LTV would (1) break it up into several different independent firms, usually along the lines of previously separate divisions, (2) have each of these new firms assume a portion of the debt LTV initially used to acquire them (thus reducing LTV's investment), and finally (3) sell a portion (usually about 25%) of the equity in each newly constituted firm to the public in order to return to LTV another large fraction of its investment in the acquisition. The goal of a complete transaction cycle was to leave LTV with a large ownership fraction of some highly leveraged subsidiary companies at no (or very little) cost to LTV. At the conclusion of each transaction, LTV would have the use of an increased reserve of borrowing power generated by its growing portfolio of marketable securities of subsidiary companies. LTV's increased borrowing power could then be used to finance the acquisition of additional and generally larger companies.

This approach to the management of corporate assets was a unique and integral part of the business strategy of LTV and its founder, Mr. James J. Ling. In 1969, Mr. Ling elaborated on his strategy (which he dubbed "Redeployment") and philosophized about the future of LTV as follows:

Thus you see, from my point of view, redeploying assets in this way is building values [in terms of the securities of acquired subsidiaries which LTV retained] and these values are measured on the stock market. And in turn they [the retained securities] are useful financially as the means of building new values.

. . . . .

I personally believe that the best background for corporate life in a company such as LTV is that of a financial analyst working in the Wall Street arena—someone who . . . knows the basic ways of getting good information in and out about companies.

. . . . .

The principles on which we operate—essentially the redeployment concept of managing corporate assets—have general validity for business and are consistent with the general rules of a competitive economy. . . . [But] suppose that for some reason or other [such as Justice Department intervention] the growth of LTV [were] impeded; it might [then] very well benefit all of the underlying LTV companies if LTV disposed of its shares in those companies, and suppose that came to pass. LTV now has no operating connection with any other company. Suppose as a result of our dispositions of our interests in all the underlying companies, we have developed $1.5 billion in assets, and, to simplify the model, let's say that they are in the form of cash in the bank. Now we want to redeploy those assets; at this stage we have the responsibility of building earnings per share—more than we would get from C/D's[2] and the like. And so, hopefully, we purchase control of one of the top twenty corporations on FORTUNE's list of the 500 largest industrials, say a company having a number of major subsidiaries and divisions—one that is suitable for redeployment under our concept of building assets, managing assets (to the best advantage of the shareholders). Having over a period of time ac-

---

[2] C/D's (certificates of deposit) are interest bearing time deposits in banks. [Footnote added.]

complished that, our assets become worth, say $2.5 billion, and we are fenced in again as regards growth. Then, speaking abstractly in terms of the model, we might very well sell out again and buy a bigger company, one, say, in the top ten. Remember, this is all iffy. I believe that we can very well go forward by maintaining the investments that we have in the underlying subsidiary companies. Fenced in or not, we are still in the business of managing assets. That's what, in the multi-industry companies, is really the name of the game.[3]

Creative management of capital structure

While LTV was extremely innovative in the asset management area, the firm was equally creative in its approach to liabilities management. Some of Mr. Ling's views on capital structure follow:

. . . get all the money you can without using equity, or use equity as infrequently as possible. I backed up this thought with a study of the Dow-Jones averages, a personal study. I went back to the last day of December, 1922, the day I was born—I usually think that's far back enough for me to go. I checked the Dow-Jones averages and found that there have been only a few times that the annual averages have been lower than a P/E ratio of 10, and the historical averages have usually been somewhat above that. Money rates, on the other hand, have increasingly risen from 1½ to 2 percent to 3, 4, 5, 6, 7, 8, 9, 10 percent, with intermediate ups and downs. The result is that debentures and bonds that were sold at 2½ percent and 3 percent, and which a lot of banks had and still have in their portfolios, turned out to be the worst investment in the world. Hence the most desirable thing to issue when you buy a company, if you can buy good, solid operating assets and recurring earnings, is debt.

. . . . .

The economic environment we live in demands that we alter capital structure every chance that we get when it's constructive to do so.

. . . . .

As for those [investors] who can't keep up with our changing financial structure . . . we'll use that to our advantage, perhaps by buying in our stock if the P/E remains low enough long enough. Certainly that's an option that we've executed in times past in similar conditions. If the market puts us too high we'll take advantage by selling LTV stock, and if it puts us too low, we take advantage by buying.[4]

Between 1964 and 1968, LTV's operating strategy was extremely successful in terms of the traditional financial measures reported to shareholders. With the aid of several large acquisitions at the parent company level (Exhibit 5), sales grew from $300 million to $2.8 billion;[5] earnings per share rose from $0.91 to $5.01; and the price of LTV common stock moved from $6 to over $100 a share. During this period LTV made three acquisitions of firms in

---

[3] John McDonald, "Some Candid Answers from James J. Ling," *Fortune*, Part I, August 1, 1969, pp. 163–64; Part II, September 1969, p. 185.

[4] John McDonald, *op. cit.*, Part II, pp. 137–38 and 178.

[5] This figure represents consolidated sales. It is derived by adding the sales of all LTV subsidiary companies together and then deducting any sales between subsidiaries.

the $1 billion class.[6] These acquisitions included Wilson & Co. in 1967, Greatamerica Corporation in 1968, and Jones & Laughlin Steel Corporation in 1968. It was this last acquisition and the method used to finance it that ultimately led to LTV's difficulties.

The move into steel

Early in 1968, LTV moved to acquire the Jones & Laughlin Steel Corporation (J&L), a firm larger in terms of earnings than LTV itself. Mr. Ling cited several reasons for his decision to make a major acquisition in the steel industry at that time. His reasons related mostly to the economic and political environment existing in 1968.

Now here we were, early 1968. . . . More and more tenders are being made, and a hostile climate is slowly developing against making them. You are looking at the possibility that there will be clampdowns on acquisitions. This has been coming for a long, long period of time. Thus, we thought, if you want to make not a big terminal acquisition but at least a big one for the time being, this was the time.

. . . . .

At the same time I felt the money market getting tighter and tighter [Exhibit 6] and recognized that we might not be able to borrow 225, 230, 240 million dollars [needed for a tender offer] in three months or six months or nine months. [Any acquisition] had to be a big one. . . . We came down to a choice of going into steel or into capital goods. . . . You look at your ability, hopefully, to recapture part of the cost of buying a company, so that you wind up . . . with a big percentage interest in the company but with no real cost in it. We concluded that we couldn't really do that in some of the capital-goods businesses, but I had an idea of how to do it in the steel industry.[7]

Having made this decision, in May, 1968, LTV tendered for and ultimately received 5 million shares of J&L common stock. For its equity position, which represented 63% ownership, LTV paid $85 a share in cash, a total of $425 million. This was the largest cash tender offer in history, and it was made at a premium of 75% above J&L's pre-tender offer market price of $48.50. LTV financed the tender offer by:

(a) Raising $75 million in cash through the sale of two subsidiary companies acquired in the Greatamerica acquisition,[8] (Exhibit 5),

(b) Selling 5-year notes for $130 million, and

(c) Borrowing $220 million through one-year loans from a group of 25 banks.

---

[6] Measured in terms of sales for Wilson & Co. and Jones & Laughlin Steel Corporation and in terms of assets for Greatamerica Corporation.

[7] John McDonald, op. cit., Part I, pp. 93–94.

[8] The Greatamerica acquisition was financed with $490 million of LTV subordinated long-term debt (Exhibit 5) which did not mature until 1988. The proceeds from this sale of subsidiary companies were not immediately needed for debt retirement, as the related maturities were far in the future.

In the nine months following the successful tender offer for 63% of J&L common stock, LTV made plans for acquiring the rest of the J&L stock in anticipation of a recapitalization that would relieve LTV of its potentially hazardous $200 million short-term debt position (line 16, Exhibit 2). Standing on the LTV parent company balance sheet, the $200 million short-term debt obligation was rather threatening. A "redeployed" J&L, however, could easily have absorbed this amount of additional debt from its LTV parent since at the end of 1968 J&L's debt position was only $230 million versus an equity base exceeding $700 million.

Unfortunately for LTV, in early 1969, the U.S. Department of Justice, after announcing an antitrust suit aimed at requiring complete divestiture of LTV's ownership interest in J&L, forced LTV to agree that:

Pending the final adjudication of this litigation, the business and financial operations of Jones & Laughlin Steel Corporation shall be maintained completely separate and independent from those of Ling-Temco-Vought, Inc.[9]

This action foreclosed any alternative LTV may have had to transfer some of its debt directly into J&L, and left LTV dangerously overextended. The company could not reverse its acquisition of J&L stock (by selling it in the open market, for example) without losing the premium it had paid in the tender offer. This premium represented $182.5 million or 63% of LTV's net worth at the end of 1968; so LTV was not anxious to exploit this alternative. Unfortunately, even though the company could not afford to divest J&L, neither could it afford to continue holding J&L as an essentially dormant asset. As a holding company, LTV had a tiny revenue base, which in the company's recent history had never come close to covering its expenses (lines 4 and 7, Exhibit 3). By 1968, for example, interest requirements of $46.5 million (line 5, Exhibit 3) on LTV's outstanding debt of $950.0 million (line 24, Exhibit 2) had caused the company to incur a $21.8 million negative cash flow from operations (line 11, Exhibit 3). Since LTV was clearly unable to service its interest costs and debt repayments from internally generated cash flow, the firm could look only to the sale of assets or new financings to satisfy its cash needs.

Again unfortunately for LTV, its legal and financial problems emerged just as the economic climate in the United States began showing signs of weakness. Corporate profits began sliding in the fourth quarter of 1968, as did stock market prices (lines 2–3, Exhibit 6). In addition, interest rates began rising precipitously (lines 4–5, Exhibit 6) just as Mr. Ling had predicted. Perhaps worst of all, the profits of LTV's subsidiary companies fell sharply from $81.4 million to $58.5 million between 1968 and 1969 (lines 1–9, Exhibit 1).

The decline in profitability of LTV's subsidiary companies was accompanied by an even faster decline in the market value of their common stocks.

[9] U.S. Department of Justice, Memorandum of Agreement with Ling-Temco-Vought, Inc., March 26, 1969.

This erosion in market values was naturally reflected in LTV's principal asset (its ownership of subsidiary company common stocks) and in LTV's borrowing power against these assets. So sharp was the decline in the stock price of LTV subsidiary companies (Exhibit 6) that between 12/31/68 and 12/31/69 LTV saw the spread between the market value and the cost of its security portfolio move from a positive $300 million to a negative $440 million (Exhibit 7).

The loss of flexibility, then control

The deterioration in LTV's position made it essentially impossible for the company to raise additional capital.[10] This fact coupled with LTV's negative operating cash flow meant that the only way LTV could satisfy its creditors was through the sale of assets or the refinancing of existing debt as it matured. LTV's bank loans were originally scheduled to be completely retired in 1969, but the firm was unable to accomplish this objective. LTV did, however, reduce its bank debt from $201 million to $111 million during 1969. The $90 million reduction was accomplished through the sale of LTV's entire interest in two subsidiary companies and the sale of a large block of Braniff Airways stock (Exhibit 5). By the end of 1969, LTV had managed to extend the maturity on its remaining $111 million in bank loans to January, 1971.

If 1969 could be described as a difficult year for LTV, 1970 could only be called a disaster. There were two major factors contributing to this condition. First, the earnings of J&L, LTV's most important subsidiary, fell from $22.1 million to a deficit of $15.4 million. This profit reversal of $37.5 million dropped LTV's equity in the earnings of all subsidiaries to below $10 million (line 20, Exhibit 1). Second, the market prices of LTV subsidiary company common stocks were hit very hard in the general market decline of 1970 (Exhibit 6). Indeed, if LTV's entire portfolio of securities in these companies had been liquidated at December 31, 1970 prices and LTV's other assets liquidated at book value, the company would have been unable to pay off its subordinated debt at even close to face value (Exhibit 8).

In an effort to further reduce its bank debt and stave off a possible bankruptcy, LTV sold off all its stock holdings in two subsidiaries during the first quarter of 1970, prompting *Forbes* magazine to write:

Want to buy a glamour company at bargain prices? You should have been in Dallas last month. James J. Ling . . . was selling them off at a pace that would make a used car salesman proud.[11]

In May, 1970, Robert H. Stewart, III, chairman of the First National Bank in Dallas, was elected chairman of LTV replacing Mr. Ling, who became

---

[10] The indenture agreement relating to the 5% subordinated debentures used to acquire the Greatamerica Corporation prohibited additional borrowings when LTV's long-term debt exceeded 150% of the sum of book net worth plus the spread between the market value and the cost of its security holdings in subsidiary companies (line 3, Exhibit 7).

[11] *Forbes*, March 15, 1970.

president. LTV's banks were evidently anxious to salvage what they could on their loans, as might be inferred from Mr. Stewart's comment that:

My responsibility to the First National Bank in Dallas will continue foremost in my mind, but I have confidence in the future of LTV and will be pleased to work with its officers and directors.[12]

Fears that LTV's banks might move precipitously in converting the firm's assets into cash (so as to pay off bank loans) led some analysts to question whether LTV's other creditor and investor groups might not fare better if LTV were forced to file a bankruptcy petition.

. . . Bankruptcy . . . does have certain advantages: By keeping the creditors at arm's length, it gives the troubled company time to get its house in order.

What's happening at LTV, by contrast, is that the creditors, mainly the bankers, hold the reins. Whether that's in the best interests of everyone else with an interest in LTV and its subsidiaries remains to be seen.[13]

So serious was LTV's situation in May, 1970, that at one point the market price of the company's 5% subordinated debentures (which had been issued in the Greatamerica acquisition) fell to 15% of their face value (Exhibit 9). At this price, their yield to maturity in 1988 reached 34%.

YIELD TO MATURITY AS A FUNCTION OF PURCHASE PRICE IN 1971 FOR
LTV 5% SUBORDINATED DEBENTURES, DUE 1988

Market Price*	Yield to Maturity
$60	9.5%
50	11.5
40	14.2
30	18.4
20	26.2
15	34.0

* Bond prices are quoted in terms of dollars per $100 of face amount, in spite of the fact that most bonds are traded in minimum multiples of $1,000 face amount.

The financial picture at LTV improves

LTV management was able to stave off bankruptcy in 1970, and by year-end had reduced the company's bank indebtedness from $111 million to $75 million. The maturity of this $75 million had been extended in the early weeks of 1971 from January 31, 1971 to July 31, 1971. This loan was secured by essentially all the assets of the company.

Perhaps the most significant event of 1970 occurred when LTV negotiated an agreement with the Department of Justice relating to its ownership interest in J&L. That agreement permitted LTV to gain operating control of J&L as soon as LTV divested all its holdings in both Braniff Airways and Okonite (Exhibit 4).

---

[12] *The Wall Street Journal*, May 18, 1970.

[13] *Forbes*, "A Fate Worse Than Bankruptcy," August 15, 1970, p. 18.

In order both to comply with the Justice Department agreement and also to reduce its short-term debt, in early 1971, LTV sold off (1) 4.5 million of its 10.5 million Braniff shares for $44 million cash; (2) 1.15 million of its 4.5 million Wilson & Co. shares for $15 million cash,[14] and (3) all of its stock in Okonite for $40.5 million (roughly half of which was paid in cash—Exhibit 5). The cumulative impact of these transactions, had they been completed by December 31, 1970, would have placed LTV in the year-end position shown (on a retroactive basis) in column 5 of Exhibit 2. Following these three transactions, under the Justice Department agreement, LTV had only to dispose of its remaining 6 million shares of Braniff before it could take control of J&L.

The receipts from the three transactions just described provided almost enough cash to get LTV out from under its bank debt in the spring of 1971. In addition LTV was strengthened by an apparent upturn in the economy during the first quarter of 1971 (Exhibit 6). Estimates of LTV subsidiary company earnings for the first quarter were up sharply (Exhibit 1). By the spring of 1971, it appeared that LTV had solved its immediate problem in that bankruptcy had at least been temporarily averted, but the firm now faced the perhaps more difficult problem of assuring its long-run survival and good health. With a debt/equity ratio of 4.2 (column 5, Exhibit 2), its long-term debentures selling in the $30 range, and its common stock collapsed to the $10 area (Exhibit 9), investors had hardly pronounced the LTV crisis at an end.

Some alternatives for strengthening LTV's capital structure

The management of LTV had numerous options for dealing with the company's financial problems as of the spring of 1971. Of the myriad courses of action open, two (representing more or less opposite ends of the spectrum of alternatives) are sketched in the text which follows and in Exhibit 2.

First, the company might have sold its remaining interest in Braniff for cash, and used the proceeds from this transaction to retire debt. If debt with the nearest term maturities were paid down, LTV would have eliminated its problem with debt repayments until mid-1973 (line 20, column 6, Exhibit 2). Under this alternative the company would continue to suffer under a tremendous debt load in relation to its equity base,[15] (line 26, column 6, Exhibit 2) but it would have purchased two years of "breathing room" in which cash pressures would be absent for the first time in many years. A booming economy and substantial improvement in both the earnings record and stock prices of its remaining subsidiaries (should such events have transpired between 1971 and mid-1973) might then have permitted LTV to (1) meet its

---

[14] These shares were purchased by Wilson & Co. at $13 a share. In the two weeks prior to the announcement of the purchase, Wilson & Co. common stock sold in the $23 range. The sale was thus made at a 43% discount from the market.

[15] LTV's equity base would actually be reduced by the Braniff stock sale (line 13, column 6, Exhibit 2) since the market value of Braniff stock was significantly below the price LTV had originally paid to acquire it.

next debt maturity problem in mid-1973 without difficulty, and (2) make whatever long-term alterations in capital structure it deemed necessary away from the crisis atmosphere and low security valuations characterizing LTV's environment in the spring of 1971. Had this approach been chosen, LTV's position on a pro forma basis retroactive to 12/31/70 would have appeared as shown in column 6 of Exhibit 2.

A second alternative, which LTV could have considered in dealing with its financing and capital structure problems in the spring of 1971, consisted of swapping a package of LTV's stock in Braniff plus LTV's own common stock in exchange for a large fraction of the $475 million face value of 5% subordinated LTV debentures which were then outstanding and selling in the public market at a very large discount from face value. A package consisting of 20 shares of Braniff stock and 20 shares of LTV stock had a market value of about $500 as of 3/10/71. If such a package were offered in exchange for each $1000 face value debenture (with a market value of $310 on 3/10/71), a large number of debenture holders might accept the swap.

If LTV were able to attract enough exchanges so as to exhaust its remaining supply of 6 million Braniff shares, the result of the transaction (restated retroactive to 12/31/70) would have left LTV in the pro forma financial position shown in column 7 of Exhibit 2. This alternative, while increasing the number of outstanding LTV shares from 4.3 to 10.3 million, would have immediately moved the company a long way in the direction of strengthening its capital structure.

Exhibit 1

LING-TEMCO-VOUGHT, INC.

INCOME STATEMENTS FOR LTV, INC., PARENT AND SUBSIDIARY
COMPANIES, 1967–71

(In millions of dollars except per share data)

		1967	1968	1969	1970	3 Months 3/31/70	3 Months 3/31/71
	Total Earnings of LTV Subsidiary Companies						
1	Braniff Airlines	4.7	10.4	6.2	(2.6)	(.8)	(1.1)
2	Jones & Laughlin Steel	35.8	27.6	22.1	(15.4)	(1.0)	10.7
3	LTV Aerospace	9.6	15.0	17.0	11.1	3.0	1.1
4	LTV Electrosystems	5.4	3.3	(3.4)	2.9	0.5	0.5
5	LTV Ling Altec	2.9	2.0	(0.3)	—	0.2	0.1
6	Okonite	9.0	6.5	(0.8)	2.0	§	§
7	Wilson & Co.	11.0	10.1	8.3	12.7	1.6	4.0
8	Wilson Pharmaceutical	1.7	1.5	1.8	1.2	§	§
9	Wilson Sporting Goods	4.0	4.4	3.0	3.3	§	§
10	Combined extraordinary items of all... subsidiaries	—	0.6	4.6	(24.5)		
		84.1	81.4	58.5	(9.3)		
	LTV "Equity in Earnings"[#] of Subsidiary Companies						
11	Braniff Airlines	§	7.7†	3.5	(1.5)		
12	Jones & Laughlin Steel	§	2.6†	15.7	(13.1)		8.6
13	LTV Aerospace	7.9	10.6	18.3*	7.7		0.7
14	LTV Electrosystems	4.0	2.6	(2.8)	2.0		0.4
15	LTV Ling Altec	1.0	1.1	(2.8)	(0.7)		—
16	Okonite	7.9	5.5‡	(0.9)‡	1.9	§	§
17	Wilson & Co.	9.0	8.2	3.8	11.3		3.5
18	Wilson Pharmaceutical	1.3	1.2	1.4	§	§	§
19	Wilson Sporting Goods	3.0	3.3	2.3	§	§	§
20	LTV share of earnings from continuing operations of subsidiaries	34.1	42.8	38.5	7.6		13.2
	LTV parent company operations:						
21	Interest expense + debt discount	(6.7)	(46.5)	(63.6)	(66.1)		(15.9)
22	Other non-extraordinary items‖	5.9	30.3	29.4	7.4		4.6
23	Extraordinary items	—	2.8	(42.6)	(18.5)		0.8
24	Net income (loss) of LTV and subsidiaries on consolidated basis	33.2	29.4	(38.3)	(69.6)	(15.3)	2.7
25	Earnings/share per LTV shareholder reports	$ 6.85	$ 5.01	$(10.15)	$(17.09)	$ (3.95)	$0.32

* Includes extraordinary profit equal to 40% of this figure.
† Included for only a portion of year.
‡ After preferred dividends.
§ Not yet acquired by LTV on this date, or sold by LTV prior to this date.
‖ Includes the tax benefits resulting from consolidation (for tax purposes) of 80% or more owned subsidiaries with the LTV parent, and other miscellaneous income statement items which for the sake of convenience have been added together by the casewriter.
LTV's equity in the earnings of each subsidiary was simply equal to its percentage ownership of that subsidiary's common stock multiplied by the subsidiary's profit after taxes.

Sources: (1) LTV annual reports, 1967–70.
(2) Ling-Temco-Vought, Inc., Prospectus, May 21, 1971.
(3) LTV and subsidiary company quarterly reports.

Exhibit 2

LING-TEMCO-VOUGHT, INC.

BALANCE SHEETS FOR LTV, INC. (PARENT COMPANY) FOR 1967–70 PLUS PRO FORMA
BALANCE SHEETS AS OF 12/31/70 FOR SEVERAL RECAPITALIZATION ALTERNATIVES
(In millions of dollars)

		1 1967	2 1968	3 1969	4 1970	5 12/31/70 With Adjust- ment[1]	6 12/31/70 Pro Forma Recapital- ization[1,2]	7 12/31/70 Pro Forma Recapital- ization[1,3]
1	Current assets.............	84.7	107.6	82.1	31.8	31.8	31.8	31.8
2	Investments in subsidiaries...	181.5	987.8	1,020.3	953.8	788.7	656.4	656.4
3	Unamortized debt discount...	0.5	113.2	103.8	93.5	93.6	93.6	41.6
4	Other assets................	45.7	79.6	23.7	13.9	19.6	19.6	19.6
5	Total................	312.4	1,288.2	1,229.9	1,093.0	933.7	801.4	749.4
	Current liabilities							
6	Current portion of long- term debt..............	1.5	0.4	22.7	77.3	28.6	—	28.6
7	Notes payable to banks....	—	201.4	0.1	0.1	0.1	—	0.1
8	Other...................	9.6	36.9	40.0	23.4	23.4	23.4	27.4
	Long-term debt							
9	Due subsidiaries.........	—	76.1	113.0	108.4	94.0	94.0	94.0
10	Due others..............	51.5	672.1	752.6	627.0	599.2	547.8	296.0
11	Reserve for investment losses.	—	—	30.0	65.3	7.5	—	—
12	Other deferrals.............	4.7	12.7	10.9	10.0	10.0	10.0	10.0
13	Net worth.................	245.1	288.6	260.6	181.5	170.9	126.2	293.3
14	Total.................	312.4	1,288.2	1,229.9	1,093.0	933.7	801.4	749.4
	Maturity schedule of debt*							
15	due in 1968...........	1.5						
16	1969...........	2.5	201.8					
17	1970...........	32.5	27.8	22.9				
18	1971...........	2.5	2.9	127.9	77.5	28.8	—	28.7
19	1972...........	2.5	2.8	2.4	2.4	2.4	—	2.4
20	1973.......... ⎫		116.1	115.7	115.7	115.7	66.7	115.7
21	1974.......... ⎪			2.4	2.4	2.4	2.4	2.4
22	1975.......... ⎬ 11.5		598.6 ⎫		24.4	24.4	24.4	24.4
23	1976 and beyond ⎭		⎭	504.2	482.1	454.3	454.3	151.1
24	Total.................	53.0	950.0	775.5	704.5	628.0	547.8	324.7
25	Ratio of earnings to fixed charges...................	.38	.08	.24	.32	.39	—	1.29
26	Total debt†/equity.........	.22	3.29	3.41	4.48	4.22	5.09	1.43

* Includes all amounts shown in lines 6, 7, and 10. Does not include long-term debt due subsidiaries.
† Includes all amounts shown in lines 6, 7, 9, and 10.
Note: (1) Includes the effects of the early 1971 sale of assets (mentioned on page 465) restated as though the sale had been made prior to 12/31/70.
(2) Includes the effects of Alternative 1 (mentioned on pages 465–66)—an early 1971 sale of LTV's remaining shares in Braniff and the use of the proceeds of this sale to retire all debt maturing prior to mid-1973—all restated as though the transaction had occurred prior to 12/31/70.
(3) Includes the effects of Alternative 2 (mentioned on page 466)—an early 1971 swap of LTV's remaining shares in Braniff plus LTV's common stock in exchange for $300 million in LTV debt due in 1988—all restated as though the transaction had occurred prior to 12/31/70.
Sources: (1) LTV annual reports, 1966–70.
(2) Ling-Temco-Vought, Inc., Prospectus, May 21, 1971.
(3) The data in column 6 include some estimates made by the casewriter.

Exhibit 3

LING-TEMCO-VOUGHT, INC.

STATEMENT OF CASH FLOW FOR LTV, INC. (PARENT COMPANY) FOR 1967–70
(Dollar figures in millions)

		1967	1968	1969	1970
	Income:				
1	Dividends from subsidiaries......................	$ 1.9	$ 2.9	$ 8.5	$ 8.8
2	Interest earned...............................	1.5	2.0	9.8	14.4
3	Other..	3.8	3.3	3.6	3.1
4	Total....................................	$ 7.2	$ 8.2	$21.9	$26.3
	Costs and expenses:				
5	Interest and debt discount......................	6.7	46.5	63.6	59.3
6	Other expenses...............................	5.3	5.7	6.8	7.5
7	Total....................................	$12.0	$52.2	$70.4	$66.8
8	Loss before income tax and extraordinary items.......	(4.8)	(44.0)	(48.5)	(40.5)
	Elimination of noncash charges:				
9	Amortization of debt discount plus depreciation.....	2.7	10.0	13.1	11.1
10	Tax payments received*...........................	6.7	12.2	27.1	14.1
11	Cash flow from operations.........................	4.6	(21.8)	(8.3)	(15.3)
	Liabilities management decisions:				
12	Repayment of debts.............................	(2.1)	(2.2)	(90.7)	(84.9)
13	New debt and equity financings..................	66.1	428.5	22.0	—
	Asset management decisions:				
14	Investments in and advances to subsidiaries........	—	(428.5)	(7.7)	(18.8)
15	Proceeds from sale of assets......................	—	18.0	97.0	79.0
16	Dividends.......................................	(7.8)	(9.3)	(5.5)	(2.8)
17	Other items.....................................	1.0	(3.7)	5.7	(8.7)
18	Net increase (decrease) in cash....................	61.8	(19.0)	12.5	(51.5)
19	Ratio of earnings to fixed charges...................	.38	.08	.24	.32

* From carryback of operating losses, and from subsidiaries under tax agreements.
Source: (1) Ling-Temco-Vought, Inc., Prospectus, May 21, 1971.

Exhibit 4

LING-TEMCO-VOUGHT, INC.

LTV PARENT AND SUBSIDIARY COMPANIES AS OF 12/31/70

```
┌─────────────────────────────────┐
│      LING–TEMCO–VOUGHT, INC.     │
│                                  │
│       Parent company with        │
│         majority interest        │
│       in 7 large subsidiaries    │
└─────────────────────────────────┘
```

```
┌───────────────────────────────────┐   ┌───────────────────────────────────┐
│    LTV AEROSPACE CORPORATION      │   │         JONES & LAUGHLIN          │
│                                   │   │         STEEL CORPORATION         │
│   LTV equity ownership: 63%       │   │   LTV equity ownership: 81%       │
│   1970 Sales: $820 million        │   │   1970 Sales: $994 million        │
│  Product: Aircraft, missiles, etc.│   │       Product: Steel              │
└───────────────────────────────────┘   └───────────────────────────────────┘
```

```
┌───────────────────────────────────┐   ┌───────────────────────────────────┐
│       WILSON & CO., INC.          │   │      BRANIFF INTERNATIONAL        │
│                                   │   │                                   │
│   LTV equity ownership: 89%       │   │   LTV equity ownership: 57%       │
│   1970 Sales: $1.4 billion        │   │ 1970 Operating revenues: $325 million│
│       Product: Meat               │   │  Product: Air transportation      │
└───────────────────────────────────┘   └───────────────────────────────────┘
```

```
┌───────────────────────────────────┐   ┌───────────────────────────────────┐
│      THE OKONITE COMPANY          │   │     LTV ELECTROSYSTEMS, INC.      │
│                                   │   │                                   │
│  Wholly-owned LTV subsidiary      │   │   LTV equity ownership: 69%       │
│  1970 Sales: $205 million         │   │   1970 Sales: $199 million        │
│  Product: Electrical cables       │   │ Product: Advanced guidance systems│
└───────────────────────────────────┘   └───────────────────────────────────┘
```

```
┌───────────────────────────────────┐
│       LTV LING ALTEC, INC.        │
│                                   │
│   LTV equity ownership: 73%       │
│   1970 Sales: $43.6 million       │
│   Product: Electronic systems     │
└───────────────────────────────────┘
```

Source: LTV 1970 Annual Report.

Exhibit 5

LING-TEMCO-VOUGHT, INC.

SUMMARY OF LTV, INC. ACQUISITION AND DIVESTITURE ACTIVITY FROM JANUARY 1, 1964 TO MID-1971

Acquisitions
(Companies having assets in excess of $2,000,000)

Name of the Acquired Company	Date of Acquisition	Total Consideration
The Okonite Co.	January 10, 1966	$31,697,127 cash.
	May, 1970	261,976 shares LTV common stock + 224,999 shares of preferred stock issued to eliminate minority interest.
Wilson & Co., Inc.	December, 1966	$81,505,000 cash.
(Later split into Wilson & Co., Wilson Sporting Goods Co., and Wilson Pharmaceutical Co.).	April 27, 1967	1,153,206 shares of $5 series A preferred stock (redemption value $100 per share).
Greatamerica Corp.	February–April, 1968	$489,761,000, 5 percent subordinated debentures due January 15, 1988; 1,632,539 warrants expiring January 15, 1978.
(Later split into Braniff Airways, Inc.; National Car Rental Systems, Inc.; Stonewall Insurance Co.; First Western Bank & Trust Co., Inc.; American Amicable Life Insurance Co., Inc.).		
Jones & Laughlin Steel Corp.	May, 1968	$428,500,000 cash for 63 percent of stock.
	March, 1969	Jones & Laughlin Industries, Inc., issued the following for 18 percent of the stock; $124,040,600, 6¾ percent subordinated debentures, 1,459,301 warrants, 291,862 common shares.

Divestitures
(Over $1,000,000 in stock or assets)

Company	Date Sold	Net Proceeds
Ed Friedrich & Friedrich Refrigerators, Inc. (100 percent).	May 23, 1964	$6,064,000.
LTV Aerospace Corp. (122,570 common shares); LTV Electrosystems, Inc. (122,570 common shares); LTV Ling-Altec, Inc. (122,570 common shares).	May 27, 1965	$3,145,000 (245,140 shares of LTV common at 22⅜ less $9 cash per share).
LTV Aerospace Corp. (500,000 common shares).	March 1, 1966	$11,175,000 (cash-public offering).
Saturn Industries, Inc.	March 30, 1966	None (distributable as dividend to shareholders of LTV; net worth as of date sold: $1,245,000).
LTV Electrosystems, Inc. (400,000 common shares).	April 27, 1966	$5,500,000 (cash—public offering).
Okonite Co. (500,000 common shares).	June 22, 1966	$7,900,000 (cash—public offering).
Wilson & Co., Inc. (1,000,000 common shares).	July 27, 1967	$21,750,000 (cash—public offering).
Wilson Sporting Goods Co. (600,000 common shares).	August 2, 1967	$17,000,000 (cash—public offering).
Wilson Pharmaceutical & Chemical Corp. (350,000 common shares).	August 15, 1967	$5,635,000 (cash—public offering).
Stonewall Insurance Co. (entire LTV interest).	May 9, 1968	$15,000,000 (cash).
First Western Bank & Trust Co. (entire LTV interest).	June 7, 1968	$62,500,000 (cash).
American Amicable Life Insurance Co. (entire LTV interest).	October 25, 1968	$18,000,000 cash and $26,000 face value of notes and warrants.
Braniff Airways (2,456,227 class A special shares); National Car Rental Systems, Inc. (2,456,227 class A special shares); Computer Technology (810,430 common shares). (In addition to the securities of the above companies, 2,701,567 LTV $115 warrants were issued in the exchange offer.)	December 16, 1968	1,947,001 shares LTV common; $14,822,000 principal amount of LTV 6½ percent notes; $5,000,000 principal amount of 6¾ debentures; $15,306,000 principal amount of LTV 5 percent debentures and $1,811,000 principal amount LTV 5¾ percent debentures.
Braniff Airways, Inc. (2,000,000 class A special shares).	February 24, 1969	$33,900,000 (cash—secondary offering to public).
Computer Technology, Inc. (entire LTV interest).	March 28, 1969	$18,169,000 (cash—secondary offering to public).
National Car Rental Systems, Inc. (entire LTV interest).	May 2, 1969	$31,610,000 (cash).
Jones & Laughlin Industries, Inc. (291,862 common shares—issued pursuant to exchange offer).	May 15, 1969	$7,588,400 (based on an assigned value of $26 per share, its estimated value at the time the exchange offer was made).
Whitehall Electronics Corp. (1,800,000 shares).	July 25, 1969 September 23, 1969	$7,500,000 ($6,140,000 cash and $1,359,500 note receivable).
Wilson Sporting Goods (entire LTV interest).	February 22, 1970	$63,000,000 (cash).
Wilson Pharmaceutical (entire LTV interest).	July 10, 1970	$16,000,000 (cash).
Okonite (entire LTV interest).	Spring, 1971	$40,500,000 ($22 million cash and notes).
Braniff Airways (4,500,000 class A shares).	Spring, 1971	$43,856,000 (cash—secondary offering to public).
Wilson & Co. (1,150,000 common shares).	Spring, 1971	$15,000,000 (cash—repurchased by Wilson).

Exhibit 5 is not included for the purpose of generating insight into individual transactions. It is presented instead to show the extent and variety of LTV's acquisition and divestiture activity.

Sources: (1) U.S. House of Representatives, Antitrust Subcommittee of the Committee on the Judiciary, "Investigation of Conglomerate Corporations," June 1, 1971, pp. 335, 337.
(2) Ling-Temco-Vought, Inc., Prospectus, May 21, 1971.

Exhibit 6

LING-TEMCO-VOUGHT, INC.

SELECTED MACRO ECONOMIC DATA AND LTV SUBSIDIARY SECURITY PRICES FROM 12/31/67 TO 3/31/71

	12/31/67	*12/31/68*	*3/31/69*	*6/30/69*	*9/30/69*	*12/31/69*	*3/31/70*	*6/30/70*	*9/30/70*	*12/31/70*	*3/31/71*
1. GNP seasonally adjusted (billions of 1958 dollars)	683.6	716.5	721.4	724.2	727.8	725.2	719.8	721.1	723.3	715.9	729.7
2. Corporate profits (billions of dollars)	80.0	84.7	82.7	80.7	78.0	73.3	69.8	71.5	73.0	69.0	75.5
3. Dow Jones industrial average	905	944	935	873	813	800	786	683	760	839	904
4. Average yield on medium-grade industrial bonds (%)	6.53	6.82	7.44	7.65	8.02	8.58	8.57	9.05	9.29	8.92	8.18
5. Bank prime rate of interest (%)	6	6¾	7½	8½	8½	8½	8	8	7½	6¾	5¼
PRICE/SHARE OF LTV SUBSIDIARY COMPANY COMMON STOCKS											
6. Braniff Airlines	15½*	21⅛	17⅞	14½	13⅝	10⅛	9¼	8¼	7½	8¼	9½
7. Jones & Laughlin Steel	27⅞*	38¼	29⅝	27¼	31½	17⅝	17⅝	11½	11½	9⅝	12
8. LTV Aerospace	44⅞	41¾	36	24	22½	15⅜	12⅝	7¾	10⅜	7⅜	10
9. LTV Electrosystems	35½	19½	13⅜	10	8⅝	5⅛	5¼	5⅜	5⅜	3⅞	6⅝
10. LTV Ling Altec	22	13½	10¾	7¼	5⅝	2⅜	3⅞	2½	2⅝	1¾	2¾
11. Okonite	30⅛	27⅜	21½	15⅛	10⅝	8	8¾	†	†	†	†
12. Wilson & Co.	28	37⅛	29½	24¼	20	19¼	16	9½	14	16¾	26⅛
13. Wilson Pharmaceutical	18⅝	19⅛	13⅛	11½	9	8⅝	8⅞	6⅛	6¼*	6¾*	9½*
14. Wilson Sporting Goods	26⅛	20	18	14¼	9⅞	10⅝	16¼*	13⅞*	13¾*	14½*	14⅝*

* Not yet acquired by LTV on this date, or sold by LTV prior to this date.
† Security not publicly traded.
Sources: (1) U.S. Department of Commerce, *Survey of Current Business*.
(2) *Bank and Quotation Record*, William B. Dana Co.
(3) U.S. Board of Governors of the Federal Reserve System, *The Federal Reserve Bulletin*.

Exhibit 7

LING-TEMCO-VOUGHT, INC.

MARKET VALUE VERSUS BOOK VALUE FOR LTV'S
PORTFOLIO OF SUBSIDIARY COMPANY SECURITIES

(In millions)

	12/31/67	12/31/68	12/31/69	12/31/70	3/31/71
LTV Investment Portfolio					
1. Market value	$620	$1,320	$ 600	$ 380	$ 480
2. Book* value	170	1,020	1,040	940	940
3. Market-book spread	$450	$ 300	$ (440)	$(560)	$(460)

* Differs from line 2, Exhibit 2 because of miscellaneous items.
Sources: (1) LTV Annual Report—1967.
        (2) LTV Annual Report—1968.
        (3) U.S. House of Representatives, Antitrust Subcommittee of the Committee on the Judiciary
            "Investigation of Conglomerate Corporations," Part 6, April, 1970, p. 79.
        (4) Line 1 data for 12/31/70 and 3/31/71 were calculated by the casewriter.

Exhibit 8

LING-TEMCO-VOUGHT, INC.

ESTIMATED PAYMENTS TO VARIOUS CREDITOR CLASSES IF LTV'S SECURITY
PORTFOLIO HAD BEEN LIQUIDATED AT 12/31/70 PRICES AND THE
COMPANY'S OTHER ASSETS SOLD AT BOOK VALUE

(Dollar figures in millions)

Creditors (In order of priority)	Book Value	Payment in Liquidation	% of Claim Satisfied
Accrued compensation, taxes, etc.	$ 15.4	$ 15.4	100%
Secured debt			
banks	75.0	75.0	100
9¼% notes	27.8	27.8	100
Unsubordinated claims			
borrowed money	227.8	227.8	100
other	4.8	2.7	56‡
Subordinated claims	485.5	184.3	38‡
Preferred stock (liquidation claim)	60.2	—	0
Residual*	196.5	—	0
Total	$1,093.0	$533.0†	

* Includes shareholders' equity and reserves and deferrals less liquidating value of preferred stock.
† Equals the book value of LTV's total assets plus the spread between the market value and the cost of its
security holdings in subsidiary companies (line 3, Exhibit 7).
‡ This calculation might significantly overstate the potential realizations on the lowest level claims, since LTV
had guaranteed (and in one case collateralized) loans of over $100 million to subsidiary companies.
Source: Casewriter's estimates.

1093
- 560
533

Exhibit 9

LING-TEMCO-VOUGHT, INC.

PRICE PERFORMANCE OF SELECTED LTV, INC. SECURITIES
APRIL, 1969–FEBRUARY, 1971

(Month end prices except for May, 1970 data)

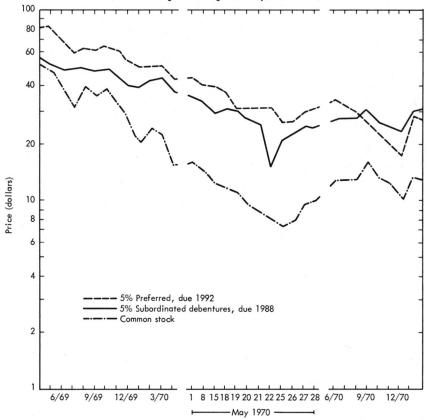

Note: Since these prices are plotted on a semi-log scale, equal percentage price changes are represented by equal vertical distance.
Data for May, 1970 are presented first weekly, then daily.

SYNERDYNE, INC.

∧∧

Henry Middleton, president of Synerdyne, was both surprised and a bit upset. A month earlier, on October 16, 1972, the company had made a tender offer for one million shares of its own stock. Synerdyne was loaded with cash and its stock seemed to be dragging bottom. Repurchase of one million shares at $20 a share seemed certain to benefit stockholders who retained their shares, especially in view of the expected upswing in earnings.

To Middleton's surprise the company was flooded with stock from disenchanted stockholders eager to unload their shares. Eight million shares— over 28% of the total outstanding—were tendered during the 30-day offer period. Although Synerdyne was under no obligation to purchase more than the one million shares tendered for, Middleton's strong inclination was to accept all eight million and be rid of those who did not share his enthusiasm about the company. However, he first wanted to consider carefully all the implications of such a major stock repurchase.

Synerdyne's history[1]

Henry Middleton started Synerdyne in 1960 from scratch. Leaving Litton Industries, Inc., where he had been in charge of the electronic equipment division, Middleton and another Litton alumnus each put up $225,000 to form the company. It was from this humble start—and with the help of a few technical wizards—that Middleton made Synerdyne one of the most impressive conglomerates in the 1960's through one acquisition after another. Touted all over the Street, no conglomerate rode higher. Its sales soared from $4 million in 1961 to $969 million in 1970, and earnings went from an almost invisible 3¢ a share to $1.86—a spectacular average annual compound growth rate of over 70%. Happy investors pinned on it a sizzling price-earnings ratio of 60 at its peak.

The conglomerate movement, of which Synerdyne was a part, originally sprang from several considerations. One was that it allowed businessmen to put together huge corporate entities quickly, through merger. Another element was the possibility of dampening earnings volatility by combining companies

---

[1] The discussion of Synerdyne's history is based, in part, on "The Trouble at Synerdyne," *Dun's Review*, April, 1972, pp. 66 ff. The discussion of the conglomerate movement is based, in part, on John Brooks, *The Go-Go Years* (New York: Weybright & Talley, 1973), pp. 180–81.

with offsetting cyclical swings. Finally, there was the theory of synergism—
a way to make two plus two equal five. By wise mergers companies could be
made to yield a better return on a combined basis than they would separately.
For one thing, managerial talent and capital expenditures could be channeled
into growth areas.

Fortuitously, the stock market boom of the mid and late 1960's provided a
means of putting together huge conglomerates almost instantly. Avid investors
were bidding up the stocks of "growth" companies—those with rapidly rising
earnings per share—regardless of the quality of earnings. Acquisition-minded
companies were able to buy up solid, old-line firms with stock and convertible
securities. And the simple mathematical fact was that any time a company
with a high multiple bought one with a lower multiple a kind of magic came
into play. Earnings per share of the new, merged company in the first year
of its life came out higher than those of the acquiring company in the previous
year even though neither company did any more business than before. (See
Exhibit 1.)

Synerdyne was no exception to this pattern. After a slow start, acquisition
activity rose from three companies in 1962 to sixteen companies in 1966 and
to thirty-eight in 1968. The resultant tenfold increase in earnings per share

Number of Acquisitions by Synerdyne

1961	1962	1963	1964	1965	1966	1967	1968	1969	1970	1971
1	3	9	6	6	16	18	38	10	0	0

pushed the stock price from $4 in 1963 to a high of $60 in 1968. The high
price-earnings multiple relative to the prices paid for acquired companies
provided built-in earnings per share which in turn helped to sustain the high
stock price. (See Exhibit 2.)

In less than four years, however, all that changed. The start of the decline
can be dated. By 1967, Litton Industries had become the pacesetter among
conglomerates—its reputation impeccable, its stock soaring, its earnings
rising steadily as they had been doing for a decade. But that January, when
Litton's top officers met at the company's Beverly Hills headquarters, a totally
unanticipated state of affairs was revealed. Several of the divisions were
discovered, apparently for the first time, to be in serious trouble; and as a
result profits for the quarter ending January 31, 1968 would fail to rise at all
and in fact were headed substantially down.

When the public earnings announcement was made—21¢ profit a share
against 63¢ for the same quarter of the previous year—it was, as a Wall
Street pundit put it, the day the cake of Ivory soap sank. Litton stock dropped
18 points in a week and within a month or so it had lost almost half of its
1967 value. Gulf & Western Industries, Inc. and Ling-Temco-Vought, Inc.
slumped in apparent sympathy and the first tremors of panic shook the whole
conglomerate world.

Plagued by flat sales and earnings, Synerdyne also lost its glamour. In early 1970 Middleton announced the end of the acquisition era at Synerdyne. Investors, to be sure, had given him good reason to do so. Mirroring the general disenchantment with conglomerates, they had swiftly downgraded Synerdyne's multiple to a low of ten—hardly an attractive grist for the acquisition trading mill. So henceforth, Middleton said, the company would grow from within.

The result was that in fiscal 1970 Synerdyne's sales slipped for the first time in its history. Then in fiscal 1971 the company's earnings—Middleton's own primary measure of success—also fell for the first time, declining 14% to $44 million, or $1.58 a share. Sales fell another 9% to $880 million. The acquisition spree was over and now that all the Synerdyne companies were on the line to produce, the caliber of some of them seemed questionable.

To begin with, a number of Synerdyne's major commercial markets were particularly hard hit during the business slowdown in 1971. Added to that, Synerdyne's government business—one third of total sales—was hard hit by cutbacks in government spending. The company took its biggest lumps in two of its most technically advanced and supposedly fastest growing areas: aviation and electronics, and specialty metals. Net income in aviation and electronics fell 61%; in specialty metals, 42%. Of the other three major groups, industrial products fell 13%; consumer products, 30%. Only insurance and finance showed an increase. (See Exhibit 3.)

The 15 Synerdyne companies encompassed tool steels, refractory metals, super-alloys, and exotic metals. Many of the markets for these metals simply shriveled up during 1970–71. Especially hard hit were sales of dies and tool steels for the machine-tool market.

A far greater impact, however, was felt in the company's aviation- and industrial-engine business, which depended on a strong economy. Synerdyne's Waukegan Motors supplied about half of all private aircraft piston engines in the United States and a major segment of the liquid- and air-cooled engines used in industrial plants and various off-the-road vehicles. Both markets slipped sharply during the 1970–71 mini-recession.

At the same time the United States was upsetting Synerdyne's electronic-systems business. First Synerdyne lost a major contract to provide guidance systems for the U.S. Navy's Cheyenne helicopters in 1970. The company was stunned again in early 1972 when a military avionics contract it was expecting went instead to Lear Siegler, Inc. Fortunately, these disappointments were offset by a strong performance by Synerdyne's biggest company, Phillips Aeronautical Company. Contributing well over $80 million a year in revenues, Phillips monopolized the military market for pilotless jet target aircraft. Military men, pleased with the results of unmanned surveillance aircraft in Vietnam, envisioned a variety of new uses. Phillips, with the technological edge developed in recent years, was in a good position to gain a healthy share of the market when it developed.

Finally, the limping consumer economy had restrained the growth of Synerdyne's line of television sets and high-fidelity speakers.

Slumping sales and earnings, coupled with investor wariness of conglomerates, triggered a sharp sell-off of the stock from its 1968 high of $62 to only $16 in October, 1972. For Henry Middleton, with personal holdings of over 500,000 shares, the decline represented a paper loss of $23 million. It also represented an opportunity for the company to repurchase shares at the lowest price-earnings multiple since the founding of Synerdyne and at a time when a cyclical rebound of earnings seemed imminent. (See Exhibit 2.)

On October 16, Synerdyne advertised its tender for one million shares of its stock at $20—a $3½ premium over the closing price on the previous day. Management planned to use funds raised by the sale of its holdings of marketable securities to finance the stock repurchase. (Synerdyne's financial condition is shown in Exhibit 4.)

To Middleton's surprise, stockholders tendered eight million shares during the 30-day period of the tender offer. Acceptance of all shares tendered would increase the company's earnings per share by 21–27%, depending upon its future level of profitability. (See Exhibit 5.) It would also cost $160 million and would necessitate new debt financing. Several banks and insurance companies had already agreed to loan Synerdyne $140 million on terms outlined in Exhibit 6. While troubled by the tight loan restrictions, Middleton believed that the company could service the additional debt, especially if the sinking fund payments were spaced appropriately, and could meet the loan restrictions. (See Exhibit 7.) However, it was feared that a recapitalization of the magnitude under consideration might damage investor confidence in Synerdyne's securities. (Exhibit 8 provides financial information on other conglomerates.) Clearly, a final decision could be reached only after a thorough review of these factors.

Exhibit 1

SYNERDYNE, INC.

IMPACT OF ACQUISITIONS ON EARNINGS PER SHARE

I. Example where company with a high multiple stock acquires a company for a low price.

	Acquired Company	Acquiring Company	Combined Companies
Net income	$ 80	$200	$280
Number of shares		100 →	110
Earnings per share		$2.00	$2.55 +28%
Price-earnings ratio		40	
Market price		$ 80	
Acquisition price (10X)	$800		
Number of shares issued for the acquired company		10	

II. Example where company with a low multiple stock acquires a company for a low price.

	Acquired Company	Acquiring Company	Combined Companies
Net income	$ 80	$200	$280
Number of shares		100 →	140
Earnings per share		$2.00	$2.00 +0%
Price-earnings ratio		10	
Market price		$ 20	
Acquisition price (10X)	$800		
Number of shares issued for the acquired company		40	

Exhibit 2

SYNERDYNE, INC.

SUMMARY OF OPERATIONS AND FINANCIAL CONDITION FOR FISCAL YEARS ENDING SEPTEMBER 30, 1963–72

	1963	1964	1965	1966	1967	1968	1969	1970	1971	1972
Operations (In millions):										
Sales	$ 26	$ 30	$ 70	$ 206	$361	$643	$1,032	$969	$880	$969
Income before interest and taxes	$1.66	$2.97	$6.01	$19.6	$ 36	$ 74	$ 109	$106	$ 80	$ 87
Interest expense	0.45	0.59	0.81	1.9	4	11	18	18	15	16
Income before taxes	$1.21	$2.38	$5.20	$17.7	$ 32	$ 63	$ 91	$ 88	$ 65	$ 71
Taxes	0.62	1.23	2.47	8.2	15	30	43	37	21	26
Net income*	$0.59	$1.15	$2.73	$ 9.5	$ 17	$ 33	$ 48	$ 51	$ 44	$ 45
Per Share:										
Market price	4–7	4–10	5–15	10–27	16–60	39–62	26–49	12–36	14–32	15–28
Earnings per share	0.16	0.27	0.41	0.75	1.02	1.47	1.84	1.86	1.58	1.60
Dividends per share	0	0	0	0	0	0	0	0	0	0
Price-earnings ratio (PER)†	34	26	24	25	37	34	20	13	15	13
PER as % of Dow Jones Industrial PER	189%	137%	134%	167%	217%	212%	143%	90%	91%	84%
PER as % of conglomerate index PER	170%	162%	141%	167%	205%	162%	118%	72%	100%	118%
Financial Condition:										
Long-term debt as % of total capital	53%	53%	36%	33%	43%	50%	47%	36%	31%	30%
Times interest earned	3.6	5.0	7.4	10.2	9.1	6.5	6.1	6.0	5.4	5.4

* Of the $45 million of net income in 1972, $18 million represented Synerdyne's equity in the net income of unconsolidated subsidiaries. The low average tax rate in 1969–71, reflected the inclusion of the equity in the net income of unconsolidated subsidiaries, which is included in Synerdyne's income statement on an after-tax basis. Thus, Synerdyne's income before taxes from *consolidated* subsidiaries was $53 million in 1972 ($71 million minus $18 million). After provision for taxes of $26 million, income after taxes from *consolidated* subsidiaries was $27 million. The reported net income of $45 million was the total of the $27 million from *consolidated* subsidiaries plus the $18 million equity in the net income of unconsolidated subsidiaries. (The unconsolidated subsidiaries were active in the finance and insurance businesses and could not be consolidated under existing generally accepted accounting principles.)

† Based on average of the high and the low market price.

Exhibit 3

SYNERDYNE, INC.

CONTRIBUTION TO AFTER-TAX PROFITS OF VARIOUS
SYNERDYNE OPERATIONS, 1968–72

(In millions)

	1968	1969	1970	1971	1972	% of Total
Industrial products and services	$ 9.5	$13.9	$14.3	$12.4	$13.6	26%
Aviation and electronics	8.5	14.7	14.4	5.6	7.2	14%
Specialty metals	9.1	11.7	10.8	6.3	7.0	13%
Consumer products	6.0	6.2	5.4	3.8	1.0	2%
Total of consolidated subsidiaries	$33.1	$46.5	$44.9	$28.1	$28.8	55%
Unicoa (insurance)	N.A.	N.A.	6.9	8.0	9.6	18%
Argonaut (insurance)	N.A.	N.A.	6.9	14.5	13.2	25%
Other	N.A.	N.A.	1.3	1.4	1.4	2%
Total of unconsolidated subsidiaries	$ 4.9	$10.5	$15.1	$23.9	$24.2	45%
Total net income*	$38	$57	$60	$52	$53	100%

* Total net income *before* interest expense.

Exhibit 4

SYNERDYNE, INC.

CONSOLIDATED BALANCE SHEETS AS OF SEPTEMBER 30, 1971–72

(In millions)

	1971	1972
ASSETS		
Cash	$ 43	$ 39
Marketable securities	6	30
Accounts receivable	126	131
Inventories	148	149
Prepaid expenses	10	9
Total current assets	$333	$358
Investments in unconsolidated subsidiaries	265	304
Net property and equipment	220	229
Other	42	39
Total assets	$860	$930
LIABILITIES AND NET WORTH		
Accounts payable	$ 39	$ 42
Accrued liabilities	59	69
Accrued income taxes	6	2
Current portion of long-term debt	4	18
Total current liabilities	$108	$131
Other long-term liabilities	35	34
Long-term debt*	122	121
Subordinated debentures†	100	100
Common stock‡	495	544
Total liabilities and net worth	$860	$930

* Sinking fund payments are scheduled as follows for the years 1973 through 1977, respectively (in millions of dollars): $18; $14; $14; $7; $5. Fifty million dollars of the subordinated debentures are convertible into common stock at $52.40 per share.
† Sinking fund payments are scheduled to start in 1977 at a rate of $8 million per year.
‡ Outstanding shares of common stock were 27,782,409 and 28,037,125 at year-end 1971 and 1972, respectively.

Exhibit 5

SYNERDYNE, INC.

IMPACT OF REPURCHASE OF EIGHT MILLION SHARES OF STOCK ON EARNINGS PER SHARE

(Dollar figures in millions except per share data)

	EBIT = $87 Million		EBIT = $120 Million	
	Without Repurchase	With Repurchase	Without Repurchase	With Repurchase
Earnings before interest and taxes.....	$87	$ 87	$120	$120
Interest on existing debt............	16	16	16	16
Interest on new debt (first year)......	—	11	—	11
Profit before taxes.................	$ 71	$ 60	$104	$ 93
Taxes*.........................	26	21	42	37
Profit after taxes..................	$ 45	$ 39	$ 62	$ 56
Millions of shares outstanding.......	28	20	28	20
Earnings per share................	$1.61	$1.95	$2.21	$2.80
		+21%		+27%

* The relationship of taxes to profit before taxes is explained in the footnote to Exhibit 2.

Exhibit 6

SYNERDYNE, INC.

TERMS OF THE PROPOSED $140 MILLION FINANCING

Amount: $140 million promissory notes
Date: November 18, 1972
Purpose: Repurchase of Synerdyne common stock
Maturities: (*a*) $50 million loan from commercial banks due on 8/15/76. Loan may be prepaid in part or in whole without penalty.
(*b*) $90 million loan from life insurance companies due in ten equal annual payments commencing in 1977.
Interest Rate: (*a*) On $50 million bank loan: 7% interest and compensating balances equal to 15% of the bank loan outstanding.
(*b*) On $90 million life insurance loan: 8%.
Restrictions: (*a*) Dividends on Synerdyne common stock are limited to 30% of the cumulative consolidated net income subsequent to the date of this agreement.
(*b*) Consolidated net worth must be maintained at not less than $340 million through September 30, 1973, $375 million thereafter through September 30, 1974, and $400 million thereafter.
(*c*) The ratio of consolidated current assets to consolidated current liabilities must be maintained at not less than 1.75 to 1.
(*d*) The ratio of (i) all consolidated liabilities (exclusive of subordinated debentures) to (ii) the sum of consolidated net worth plus subordinated debentures, may not exceed 1.2 to 1. The $140 million promissory notes would be included in consolidated liabilities.
(*e*) Unconsolidated subsidiaries may not increase the ratio of (i) all liabilities (exclusive of subordinated debentures) to (ii) the sum of their net worth plus their subordinated debentures, from the level that existed on September 31, 1972.
(*f*) Subsidiaries may not be sold for other than cash.
(*g*) Cash acquisitions are prohibited.
(*h*) Unconsolidated subsidiaries may not be sold and are prohibited from repurchasing shares of their own stock.
(*i*) Total cumulative dividends to Synerdyne from unconsolidated subsidiaries subsequent to September 30, 1972 may not exceed 50% of Synerdyne's cumulative equity in the net income of its unconsolidated subsidiaries subsequent to September 30, 1972.

Exhibit 6—Continued

SYNERDYNE, INC.

PRO FORMA BALANCE SHEETS AS OF SEPTEMBER 30, 1972–77

(Dollar figures in millions)

	Actual 1972	Pro Forma 1972	1973	1974	1975	1976	1977
ASSETS							
Cash and equivalent................	$ 69	$ 49	$ 45	$ 45	$ 45	$ 45	$ 45
Accounts receivable...............	131	131	139	152	165	177	191
Inventories.......................	149	149	161	174	188	203	219
Prepaid expenses..................	9	9	9	9	9	9	9
Total current assets............	$358	$338	$354	$380	$ 407	$ 434	$ 464
Investment in subsidiaries...........	304	304	320	336	352	368	384
Net property and equipment.........	229	229	228	229	232	237	246
Other............................	39	39	39	39	39	39	39
Total assets..................	$930	$910	$941	$984	$1,030	$1,078	$1,133
LIABILITIES AND NET WORTH							
Accounts payable..................	$ 42	$ 42	$ 45	$ 49	$ 53	$ 57	$ 62
Accrued liabilities.................	69	69	75	81	87	94	102
Accrued taxes.....................	2	2	2	2	3	3	4
Bank loan........................	0	0	0	0	0	6	0
Current portion of long-term debt...........................	18	18	14	14	32	22	22
Total current liabilities........	$131	$131	$136	$146	$ 175	$ 182	$ 190
Other long-term liabilities...........	34	34	34	34	34	34	34
Long-term debt....................	121	261	240	218	176	162	148
Subordinated debentures............	100	100	100	100	100	92	84
Common stock....................	544	384	431	486	545	608	677
Total liabilities and net worth....	$930	$910	$941	$984	$1,030	$1,078	$1,133
COMPLIANCE WITH LOAN RESTRICTIONS							
a. Consolidated net worth...................		$384	$431	$486	$ 545	$ 608	$ 677
b. Ratio of consolidated current assets to consolidated current liabilities............		2.6	2.6	2.6	2.3	2.4	2.4
c. Ratio of consolidated liabilities (exclusive of subordinated debentures) to the sum of consolidated net worth plus subordinated debentures...............................		.9	.8	.7	.6	.5	.5

Exhibit 7

SYNERDYNE, INC.

FORECAST OF SALES, EARNINGS, AND FINANCING NEEDS INCLUDING IMPACT OF THE PROPOSED STOCK REPURCHASE

(In millions)

	Actual 1972	1973	1974	1975	1976	1977
Income Statement						
Net sales	$969	$1,080	$1,160	$1,240	$1,320	$1,410
Profit after taxes from consolidated subsidiaries	27	32	38	40	42	44
Equity in net income of unconsolidated subsidiaries	18	20	22	24	26	28
Net income before interest on new debt	$ 45	$ 52	$ 60	$ 64	$ 68	$ 72
After tax interest expense on $140 million new debt		5	5	5	5	3
Net income (including impact of stock repurchase)		$ 47	$ 55	$ 59	$ 63	$ 69
Financing Need						
Profit after taxes from consolidated subsidiaries		$ 32	$ 38	$ 40	$ 42	$ 44
Non-cash charges		30	32	34	35	37
Cash potential from consolidated operations		$ 62	$ 70	$ 74	$ 77	$ 81
Dividend from unconsolidated operations*		4	6	8	10	12
Total sources		$ 66	$ 76	$ 82	$ 87	$ 93
Less:						
Cash dividends on common stock		0	0	0	0	0
Additions to working capital		7	16	16	16	16
Investment in plant and equipment		29	33	37	40	46
Sinking fund payments on existing debt		18	14	14	7	13
Total		$ 54	$ 63	$ 67	$ 63	$ 75
Available to service $140 million new debt		$ 12	$ 13	$ 15	$ 24	$ 18
Less:						
After-tax interest expense on $140 million new debt		5	5	5	5	3
Sinking fund payments on $140 million new debt		7	8	10	25†	9
Total		$ 12	$ 13	$ 15	$ 30	$ 12
Financing (shortfall) excess		$ 0	$ 0	$ 0	$ (6)	$ 6

* Only the dividend from the unconsolidated subsidiaries would be available to Synerdyne for debt service. The remainder of the net income of the unconsolidated subsidiaries would be reinvested in the subsidiaries.

† The last $25 million of the bank loan must be paid off in 1976 according to the terms of the loan.

Exhibit 8

SYNERDYNE, INC.

FINANCIAL SUMMARY ON EIGHT CONGLOMERATES

	Avco	Colt	Gulf & Western	Kidde	Litton	Signal	Textron	Synerdyne
1971 Operations:								
Net sales (in millions)	$1,117	$637	$1,566	$703	$2,342	$1,315	$1,604	$880
Net income (in millions)	$28	$13	$55	$27	$50	$27	$72	$44
% sales	2.5%	2.0%	3.5%	3.8%	2.1%	2.1%	4.5%	5.0%
Return on equity	8%	5%	9%	10%	6%	5%	14%	9%
Return on capital	5%	4%	5%	8%	5%	4%	11%	7%
Per Share:								
1972 estimated earnings	$2.00	$1.60	$3.31	$2.90	$(2.29)	$1.80	$2.25	$1.60
1971 earnings	.97	1.27	2.61	2.44	1.21	1.19	2.06	1.58
1966 earnings	2.88	2.15	1.68	2.20	1.87	3.08	1.94	.75
% increase: 1966-72	(31%)	(26%)	97%	32%	—	(42%)	16%	113%
1971 cash dividends	$0	$0.80	$0.50	$0	$0	$0.58	$0.90	$0
Market price on 11-16-72	$15	$17	$33	$27	$13	$19	$32	$16
Price-earnings ratio on 11-16-72*	8	11	10	9	—	11	14	10
1971 Financial Condition:								
Long-term debt as % of total capital	56%	38%	63%	35%	41%	39%	22%	31%
Times interest earned	1.23	3.4	2.1	8.0	2.8	2.4	13.2	5.4
Bond rating								
Senior debt	—	BBB	BBB	NR	BBB	BBB	A	BBB
Subordinated debt	B	—	B	NR	BB	BB	BBB	BB

* Based on 1972 estimated earnings.

EQUITABLE CAPITAL FUND

∧∧

Jim Richek, manager of the Equitable Capital Fund, had one more day in which to act on the offer of Gulf & Western Industries, Inc. to exchange a package of cash and debentures for its common stock, up to a total of one million shares. The offer would expire on September 30, 1974. Equitable Capital Fund held 100,000 shares of Gulf & Western common stock, purchased at an average cost of $30 during 1972 and 1973. The stock had subsequently sagged, along with the general market, to a price of only $19⅜ as of September 29, 1974. At this level, the offer to exchange $7 cash plus $24 principal amount of a 7% debenture for each share of common stock seemed appealing. Nevertheless, Mr. Richek was hesitant to part with a stock that was selling at less than four times earnings and was strongly recommended by several advisory services. (See Exhibit 1.)

Gulf & Western's history

The story of Gulf & Western Industries, Inc. began in 1956 with a little company called Michigan Bumper Corporation. Michigan Bumper common stock, with only 220,000 shares outstanding, was selling well below book value. It was the only thing around that Charles Bluhdorn[1] could afford, and selling at $3¼ with a book value of about $9½, the stock looked attractive.

Only after gaining control did Mr. Bluhdorn discover that Michigan Bumper's only valuable asset was a contract to make the rear bumper of the Studebaker automobile. A visit to the plant in Grand Rapids convinced him that sometimes one ought to look at something besides book value. Mr. Bluhdorn decided that there was only one thing to do, and that was to sell the assets. However, that was not easy. As a matter of fact, it was impossible.

At one point, Mr. Bluhdorn thought he finally had a buyer. He has said:

I practically locked the door and wouldn't let him out of the room. And I told him he could have the whole thing for five hundred thousand dollars. He gave me a sort of hopeful sign. And I thought that maybe I had him. But then I found I didn't. So I said, well, all right. If you want it, you can have it for a hundred

---

[1] Charles Bluhdorn immigrated to the United States during World War II and, after an apprenticeship with a commodities firm, started his own export-import business. Michigan Bumper represented the first piece of what was to become Gulf & Western Industries.

thousand dollars a year, payable over five years. But when he didn't accept the offer, I decided, well, we'd better go to work.[2]

In the next 17 years, Mr. Bluhdorn built Gulf & Western from a one-line automotive business with sales of $8 million to a diversified organization with sales in excess of $2 billion, with more than 70,000 employees and 1,700 offices and plants throughout the world.

The company became a favorite of Wall Street during the go-go years of the 1960's. In the five-year period ended 1968, Gulf & Western made over 50 acquisitions—ballooning its outstanding debt from $12 million to $918 million. Earnings per share climbed rapidly from $0.60 in 1964 to $3.00 in 1968 and the market price of the stock, touted by Wall Street, increased nine-fold from $7 to a high of $64. During the heyday of conglomerates, Gulf & Western's stock sold at price-earnings multiples of 21–25 times.

The fortunes of Gulf & Western were battered suddenly in early 1968, however. Litton Industries—the pacesetter among conglomerates—announced that several of its divisions were in serious trouble and that profits for the quarter ending January 31, 1968 could fail to rise at all and in fact were headed substantially down. When the public earnings announcement was made—$0,21 a share against $0.63 for the same quarter of the previous year—Litton stock dropped 18 points in a week. Within a month or so it had lost almost half of its peak 1967 value. Gulf & Western slumped in apparent sympathy and the first tremors of panic shook the whole conglomerate world.

With its price-earnings multiple depressed and its financial position strained, Gulf & Western entered a five-year period of consolidation. The pace of acquisitions slowed substantially and efforts turned to improving internal efficiency. After a sharp decline to $2.15 in 1969, earnings per share gradually recovered to $3.30 in 1972 and the price of the stock rose from its low of $10 in 1970 to $45 in early 1972. (See Exhibit 2.)

The solid price performance of the stock was short-lived, however. No sooner was the new year 1973 ushered in than the stock market fell upon difficult times. A brief rally in the early fall ended abruptly with the October Arab–Israeli War and the curtailment of oil shipments to the United States. The selling pressure gathered momentum as the annual rate of inflation hit double digits, fueled by the 400% increase in oil prices and agricultural shortages. Yields on single A bonds rose sharply from 7.53% in January, 1973 to 10% by late September, 1974, as investors sought compensation for the loss of purchasing power that inflation entailed. The combination of high interest rates, severe strains on both domestic and foreign financial institutions, and virulent inflation drove the Dow Jones Industrial Average from its high of 1052 in January, 1973 to only 607 on September 30, 1974. (See below.) During the same period the price of Gulf & Western stock fell from $36

---

[2] "The Road Back to Confidence," address by Charles G. Bluhdorn, Chairman of the Board of Gulf & Western Industries, Inc., before The Newcomen Society in North America, New York City, June 7, 1973.

to $19⅜. On September 29, 1974, the stock was selling at less than four times estimated earnings per share of $5.70.

	1973			1974	
	January 31	*June 30*	*December 31*	*June 30*	*September 30*
Dow Jones					
Industrials.............	1052	927	851	860	607
AAA rated					
corporate bonds........	7.15%	7.37%	7.68%	8.58%	9.32%
A rated					
corporate bonds........	7.53%	7.71%	8.11%	9.17%	10.01%
B rated					
corporate bonds........	10.32%	10.46%	11.06%	12.13%	14.00%

In 1974, Gulf & Western conducted its business through eight semi-autonomous groups. Its various operating groups, including such well-known companies as Paramount Pictures Corporation and Consolidated Cigar Corporation, contributed to sales and operating income as follows: (See also Exhibit 3.)

	Percentage of Sales	*Percentage of Operating Income*
1. Automotive replacement parts............................	10%	6%
2. Leisure time group (theatrical films, 43% of sales; television series and motion pictures, 18%; theater operations, 24%; other, 15%)............................	14	19
3. Manufacturing (highly diversified).......................	37	12
4. Consumer products (traditional cigars, 75% of sales; small cigars, 20%; allied products, 5%)...................	10	7
5. Natural resources (pigments and metal powders, 65% of sales; zinc metal, 28%; chemicals and minerals, 7%)........	7	6
6. Paper and building products (pulp, paper, and paperboard, 45% of sales; towels, tissues, and food service disposables, 13%; folding cartons, 14%; building products, 25%; matches, 3%)...	15	8
7. Food products (raw and refined cane sugar, 71% of sales; molasses and furfural, 11%; fruit and vegetable produce, 18%)...	7	18
8. Financial services (financing, 58%; casualty insurance, 26%; life insurance, 16%)...............................	0*	24

* Sales are unconsolidated.

The exchange offer

On September 3, 1974, Gulf & Western advised holders of its common stock that it was offering to issue $24 principal amount of its 7% subordinated debentures due July 1, 2003 and to pay $7 in cash in exchange for each share of Gulf & Western common stock. The debentures would be nonconvertible and would include no sinking fund. The entire issue would be due in 2003 and would be callable on 30 days' notice at 100.

The exchange offer was scheduled to expire on September 30, 1974 and

Gulf & Western would accept for exchange any and all duly tendered common stock up to one million shares. There were 15,552,786 shares of common stock outstanding.

Jim Richek was intrigued by the exchange offer, although he had some question as to the value of the package that was being offered. Gulf & Western's aggressive use of debt during its period of rapid growth had reduced its interest coverage to less than three times. At this level, it seemed likely that the new 7% subordinated debentures would be rated only single B—well below Equitable Capital's usual quality standards.

Mr. Richek also questioned the advisability of exchanging the stock at a time when it was selling at its lowest multiple in a decade. The stocks of all conglomerates had suffered in the inflation-ravaged market of 1974 and were selling well below their earlier levels. (See Exhibit 4.) There seemed no doubt that the market was oversold by any measure. The decline in prices in recent weeks had taken some technical indicators down to the oversold extremes of 1970. In fact, many of these indicators, which usually oscillated between two fairly well-defined levels, were still far below their normal bottom areas. However, the story of stock prices over the past two years had been a sad tale of failed rallies. Hopes had been raised sufficiently each time to tempt a few investors into the market only to have them disillusioned by the next down-wave.

Exhibit 1

EQUITABLE CAPITAL FUND

RECOMMENDATIONS OF SEVERAL INVESTMENT ADVISORY SERVICES

"Given the operating results that Gulf & Western has recorded during the past four years, we feel that its common stock, currently priced at approximately four times estimated fiscal 1974 year's fully diluted earnings, represents an excellent investment opportunity which should more than outperform the market during the coming twelve months."

"Future growth is likely to come from efforts to increase the earning power of existing broadly diversified operations, and additional acquisitions can be expected. The reasonably valued common stock merits retention as a long-term speculation."

"The company has increased the dividend steadily in recent years and has room to increase it substantially. At four times our current year estimate, we continue to view Gulf & Western shares as undervalued and recommend purchases."

Exhibit 2

EQUITABLE CAPITAL FUND

FINANCIAL SUMMARY OF GULF & WESTERN INDUSTRIES, INC.

	1964	1965	1966	1967	1968	1969	1970	1971	1972	1973	1974 est.
Operating Data (In millions)											
Sales	$ 130	$ 277	$ 519	$1,189	$1,331	$1,564	$1,630	$1,566	$1,670	$1,927	$2,300
Net income	4.2	11.4	22.8	59.1	67.7	51.0	49.8	55.3	69.4	89.2	N.A.
Common Share Data											
Earnings per share	$0.60	$1.26	$1.68	$ 2.60	$ 3.00	$ 2.15	$ 2.26	$ 2.61	$ 3.30	$ 4.60	$ 5.70
Dividends per share	0	0.12	0.17	0.23	0.28	0.45	0.43	0.50	0.60	0.63	1.04
Price range	7–9	9–31	17–39	28–59	38–64	18–50	10–21	19–31	28–45	21–36	19–29
Price-earnings ratio	12–15	7–25	10–23	11–23	13–21	8–23	4–9	7–12	8–14	5–8	3–5

Exhibit 3

EQUITABLE CAPITAL FUND

SUMMARY OF OPERATING DIVISIONS OF GULF & WESTERN INDUSTRIES, INC.

(In millions)

Revenues				Group	Operating Income*			
1970	1971	1972	1973		1970	1971	1972	1973
$ 357	$ 372	$ 390	$ 444	Financial services..................	$ 35	$ 50	$ 54	$ 48
129	141	163	188	Automotive replacement parts......	7	8	10	13
72	84	100	132	Food products....................	18	24	28	36
166	178	187	200	Consumer products...............	10	12	12	13
236	279	291	277	Leisure time.....................	—	20	31	39
711	606	604	716	Manufacturing...................	45	21	16	25
105	77	102	131	Natural resources.................	2	4	7	12
206	204	226	288	Paper and building products........	4	9	9	16
5	(3)	(3)	(4)	Corporate.......................	(4)	(16)	(20)	(25)
$1,987	$1,938	$2,060	$2,372					
				Less: Financial services				
(357)	(372)	(390)	(444)	revenues.......................	N.A.	N.A.	N.A.	N.A.
$1,630	$1,566	$1,670	$1,927	As reported.....................	$117	$132	$147	$177

* Operating Income is defined as earnings from operations before dividends and before deduction of interest expense, minority interest, and income taxes except that for the Financial Services Group it is defined as operating earnings before income taxes.

Exhibit 4

EQUITABLE CAPITAL FUND

COMPARATIVE ANALYSIS OF SELECTED CONGLOMERATES

(Sales figures in millions)

	Bangor Punta	Gulf & Western	Indian Head	ITT	LTV	Teledyne	Textron
Sales: 1973	$ 341	$1,927	$ 551	$10,183	$4,151	$1,456	$1,858
1968	240	1,331	370	4,724	2,770	875	1,725
% Increase	+42%	+45%	+49%	+116%	+50%	+66%	+8%
Earnings per share: 1974*	$0.75	$ 5.70	$3.85	$ 4.30	$ 4.00	$ 3.00	$ 2.85
1969	1.44	2.15	2.86	2.65	deficit	1.73	2.14
% Increase	−48%	+165%	+35%	+62%	—	+73%	+33%
Dividends per share–1974	0	$ 1.04	$1.00	$ 1.52	0	0	$ 1.10
P/E ratio: 1974 (September)	3.7	3.3	3.9	3.7	2.1	3.4	4.5
1973	2–10	5–8	4–8	6–14	2–4	4–8	6–13
1972	9–19	8–14	7–10	13–17	14–23	9–17	13–16
1971	16–33	7–12	9–13	13–20	—	9–20	12–16
1970	—	4–9	5–10	10–19	—	7–21	8–14
Long-term debt as % of capital†	52%	67%	42%	45%	65%	55%	28%
Interest coverage	1.7	2.9	6.0	4.0	1.7	4.0	12.8
Bond rating:							
Senior debt	BB	BB	—	A	—	BB	A
Subordinated debt	B	B	BB	—	CCC	B	—

* Estimated.
† Year-end 1973.

ELECTRICIRCUIT, INC.

^^^

In late May, 1964, Mr. Vito Rappasadi, treasurer of Electricircuit, Inc., was considering the company's future investment and financing program. Anticipated normal growth, introduction of a new product line, and modification of the company's present inventory control system together would require substantial external financing. The opportunities for such financing were severely restricted, however, by the company's financial condition.

Company background information

Electricircuit, Inc., had been founded on Long Island and incorporated in New York in 1954 by four young electrical engineers. At the outset, stock in the company had been wholly owned by this group of four. Later, stock options had been granted to three particularly desirable managers as an inducement to join the company. These options had been exercised, and in 1964 the entire equity was owned by the seven men, in approximately equal blocks. The seven also held all of the top-management positions and constituted the board of directors.

In the period from formation through 1963 Electricircuit had enjoyed considerable success. The product line had been expanded from one original product to include several lines of proprietary items sold as components for digital systems. In the form of packaged circuits (modules), these products performed decision control, storage, and ancillary functions as components of digital systems. They were primarily produced for off-the-shelf sale to customers who used them in systems of their own design and manufacture. Company profit came principally from the sale of these proprietary products.

As the company had expanded, it had also begun the manufacture-to-order of a variety of special-purpose systems, which applied digital techniques to computing, information handling, control tasks, and data processing. The systems were used in space equipment, navigation and positioning systems, signal processing, data converters, and a variety of other end uses associated directly or indirectly with government expenditures for military and nonmilitary purposes. This business accounted for roughly one fourth of Electricircuit's billings. The company profited from the inclusion of its products in these systems, but little, if any, additional profit had been gained from the provision of engineering services.

493

Electricircuit's proprietary products were subject to a high rate of obsolescence in an extremely competitive market. Although protected by patents, these items were always exposed to the competition of alternatively engineered products performing the same function. Typically the company's new products had achieved about three fourths of their highest sales level in the year in which they were introduced. Peak volumes had been reached and maintained in the second and third years, but these years normally had been followed by steep decay and virtual worthlessness by the sixth or seventh year. This six- to seven-year cycle had been cut short by competitive developments for about 10% of the new products that the company had introduced during the past 10 years, and on those occasions Electricircuit had been forced to absorb substantial inventory write-offs.

Thus, the danger of being leapfrogged technically was a very real one. It had been met by unstinting expenditures on research and development to improve existing product lines and add new ones. Company officials had been successful in recruiting and holding a strong research group, and this group, supported by ample budgetary allocations, had created enviable market respect for the quality of the company's products. The seven owner-managers were determined to maintain that reputation.

Over the years continuing expansion had led to a number of changes in Electricircuit's internal organization. Sales outlets had been established in southern California, and late in 1962 a plant had been constructed there for the design and production of systems for the West Coast space industry. Earlier, production of proprietary products had been shifted from Long Island to a wholly owned subsidiary in North Carolina, largely because of the availability in that area of a low-wage labor force. Production operations at the subsidiary consisted almost entirely of hand assembly and wiring of modules and allied components. Other managerial offices remained at the original site on Long Island.

In the period after 1960, rapidly widening product acceptance had almost trebled the company's sales (Exhibit 1), and its investment in current assets had expanded accordingly (Exhibit 2). Short-term loans, secured by the pledge of receivables, had been obtained from Electricircuit's Long Island bank to support this growing requirement. With isolated exceptions, the bank had been willing to lend 85% of the face amount of the receivables, and this banking arrangement had proved generally satisfactory until early 1964. At that time an officer of the bank had made it clear that Electricircuit had reached the limit of the credit line that the bank was willing to extend in the absence of some improvement in the company's capital structure. New equity or junior debt financing would qualify Electricircuit for a larger loan, if the company so desired and the requisite security was available, but the loan limit would continue to be set in terms of the ratio of bank debt to junior claims (equity plus subordinated debt, if any) that existed at the end of 1963. This assumed no deterioration in earnings or financial condition.

As 1964 had worn on and sales had continued to increase, the company had been forced to cut its cash balance sharply to meet its growing financing needs. Positive earnings had been realized in approximately the same proportion to sales as in 1963, but the retention of these earnings had failed to alter the bank's stand on additional financing. When approached in April, the loan officer had been reluctant to extend additional credit on the basis of unaudited interim statements, but more importantly, he had pointed out that the growth of equity had produced only a modest change in the company's debt/equity ratio. Moreover, about one half of the earnings had been invested in highly specialized equipment, and to that extent the bank had not benefited either from replenishment of the company's deposit balance or, as a creditor, from the increased protection that investment in more liquid assets might have provided.

Growth prospects

In late May, Mr. Rappasadi prepared the following forecast of Electricircuit's year-end current asset position, to help in assessing the company's immediate financing problems.

Cash.....................................		$ 135,000
Receivables.............................		2,720,000
Inventory:		
Raw materials........................	$436,000	
Work in process......................	529,000	
Finished goods.......................	311,000	1,276,000
		$4,131,000

The forecast assumed a year-end sales rate of $13.6 million and a corresponding cost of goods sold figure of $8.1 million. Actual sales for the year were estimated at $12.0 million. These estimates had been employed with some confidence in projecting working capital requirements, since sales in recent months and impressions of customers' production plans for the rest of the year pointed unmistakably toward continued growth. Receivables had been estimated at 20% of sales, and raw materials and work in process at a four-week rate of usage. Finished goods, on the other hand, had been projected at little more than a two-week supply.

During preceding months finished goods inventory had been deliberately reduced in relation to sales as other cash requirements had mounted. Mr. Rappasadi believed that continued curtailment of investment in finished goods inventory was likely to be costly, but lacking other immediate sources of funds, he also felt that the stock of finished goods would have to be held to the projected level if the company was to avoid an acute cash emergency. As it was, cash had been projected at merely its current level.

Beyond 1964, the marketing manager had estimated that sales of the company's current products would reach $16 million in 1965. Without major product innovation, he thought that sales could probably be maintained at that level in 1966, but if past patterns prevailed, he expected that the following year would see a decline, which might amount to as much as $4 million or $5 million. The exact forecast for 1965 was based primarily on the marketing group's knowledge of government appropriations for ongoing defense and space programs. It could be upset by project cancellations, but that was considered highly unlikely for the projects concerned. On the other hand, the plateau and descent pattern of the more distant estimates emphasized the importance of maintaining Electricircuit's technical preeminence.

Investment possibilities

Mr. Rappasadi saw two possible opportunities for investment that might improve the projected sales pattern and its profit consequences in the future. One involved the introduction of a major new product line and the other, a revision of the company's finished goods inventory control system.

The new product line, which had been under development for the past two years, performed comfortably to military specifications and was believed to possess technical qualities that would give it significant competitive advantages. All of the items making up the line were in a late stage of development, and the line was currently scheduled for introduction at the turn of the year. Market reception was difficult to estimate with any degree of precision, but the marketing manager was confident that the line would contribute sales of at least $2.0 million in 1965 and a further increment of at least $0.5 million in 1966. The line would be priced to give the same coverage of costs as was provided by the company's other proprietary products.

To put the line into production in the North Carolina plant would require about $100,000 for specialized equipment. That plant had been built to accommodate more growth than had yet been realized, and therefore no additional outlays were anticipated for production facilities. However, the marketing manager had estimated that a budget allocation of $35,000 would be needed to introduce and promote the line if it was to achieve its full potential.

The second investment possibility—that of increasing stocks of finished goods—grew out of widespread feeling that economizing in that direction had already been pushed far beyond justifiable limits. Expediting had become commonplace in juggling production schedules, with costly consequences, and orders had been lost to competitors with disturbing frequency when customers had been notified of long but necessary delivery delays. Mr. Rappasadi, therefore, had ordered a review of the company's entire inventory control system.

The area of concern, as a result of that study, had been narrowed to the finished goods segment of total inventory. Some improvements seemed possible in balancing raw material stocks, but it was not thought that this would lead to any appreciable change in the relationship of total raw material inventory to production volume. Lead time required by the purchasing department and limited interchangeability of parts among product lines combined to fix the required total at roughly a four-week supply level. Work in process inventory seemed similarly intractable. Allocation of shop labor, timing of lot starts, schedules, and so on, were already being decided on grounds of optimum production arrangements, as the production manager saw them. Technical changes, necessitating work stoppages, often had to be introduced during the in-process stage, and therefore the production manager, and the engineering group as well, attached considerable value to the flexibility allowed by a four-week production period.

By contrast with its approval of current raw material and in-process control practices, the report recommended complete revamping of the system being used to determine finished goods inventory levels. The current system, in brief, was based on specific item-by-item sales forecasts for the coming quarter. Given those forecasts, goods were scheduled into production in quantities that would raise the level of existing stocks to the anticipated sales requirement. Recently, as noted above, financial circumstances had made it necessary to cut stocks below the target levels that would have been set in more normal circumstances, but the report's condemnation of the system was independent of that experience.

Its basic criticism centered on the system's dependence on quarterly sales forecasts and the invariable inaccuracy of such estimates. Replacement demand could be predicted with tolerable margins of error, but the same was not true of new orders. They were typically received at erratic intervals. Moreover, they constituted a large part of the total demand for most products.

To cope with the problem the report urged adoption of a system of buffer stocks, which would be set with more careful regard to the costs, returns, and risks associated with inventory maintenance. To that end data had been compiled on five possible inventory-sales levels representing substantially different inventory policies (Exhibit 3). In each case the lost-sales estimate had been derived from computer simulations (using appropriate reorder points and reorder quantities) of the demand experience of major product lines.

Since Electricircuit was currently operating with lower finished goods stocks than those contemplated by any one of the five policies, Mr. Rappasadi was particularly impressed by the magnitude of the lost-sales figures. On the other hand, he was also impressed by the inventory investment required to cut those losses by appreciable amounts. Any significant change in inventory policy would therefore tend to enlarge the financing problems that already lay ahead.

Financing alternatives

As noted earlier, those problems had come to a head at the beginning of 1964, when Electricircuit's bank had refused to increase its line of credit in the absence of some prior strengthening of the company's capital structure. That development had not been completely unanticipated. In 1963 Mr. Rappasadi had begun to explore the possible issuance of subordinated long-term debt with several investment bankers and representatives of lending institutions. The discussions had all been unsuccessful, however, and as a result Electricircuit had been forced to finance the acquisition of a new headquarters building and its West Coast plant with sale-and-leaseback financing. The two buildings together had been constructed at a cost of $950,000 and had been leased by Electricircuit for a 10-year period at a combined annual rental of $280,000. The leases contained 10-year renewal options at the same annual rentals, but no repurchase option. Mr. Rappasadi, at the time, had estimated that the two plants probably would be worth half their original cost at the end of 10 years and little or nothing at the end of 20 years. Both deals had been arranged with a private group of wealthy New York investors.

The same group had also indicated its willingness to lend the company an additional $500,000 to $1,000,000 at any time at an annual interest rate of 18%. While the loan would be subordinated to bank debt and would permit an increase of the type of secured financing that the bank was currently providing, it would not be without its own restrictive covenants:

1. Cash dividend payments and company purchase of its own stock would be prohibited.
2. No additional debt would be allowed other than bank borrowing and other short-term liabilities arising in the normal course of business, or long-term debt specifically subordinated to this loan.
3. Current assets would have to exceed the sum of current liabilities and all long-term debt by at least $800,000.
4. Default on any provision would automatically accelerate the due date of principal and accrued interest to the date of default.

Interest payments would be payable semiannually, but the principal would not become due for five years. Prepayment in full would become permissible at the end of three years at a penalty of 10% and at the end of four years at 6%, but only with funds from operations.

Concern about weakening of control and earnings dilution made a public sale of common stock seem highly questionable to some of the company's owner-managers. They felt that earnings would continue to improve and cited the company's recent growth record as evidence of the possible cost of bringing in outside shareholders at an inopportune point in the company's development. On the other hand, Mr. Rappasadi had found that underwriters repeatedly expressed the opinion that Electricircuit's only hope for adequate long-term financing was additional common stock. That meant a public offering since none of the current stockholders had additional funds to invest.

Increasingly tight financial straits during 1964 had pressed Mr. Rappasadi to pursue the subject. Expressions of interest had been obtained from several underwriters, but only one, Bayles and Bayles, had expressed willingness to underwrite a stock issue. After many conversations, company visits, and a preliminary study of Electricircuit's financial records, the senior partner of Bayles and Bayles had indicated to Mr. Rappasadi that an issue of common stock to net the company up to $1,000,000 would probably be feasible in early autumn. Offering price to the public would be about $10.50 a share. The brevity of Electricircuit's history of good earnings would be a drawback, but Mr. Bayles explained that he counted on the company's unusual growth record to make that price attainable. The net proceeds to Electricircuit, however, would be closer to $8. The spread between the two prices would cover the underwriter's compensation and risk and all costs of preparing the issue. In addition, the company would agree to sell warrants to Bayles and Bayles for $10,000 to purchase 10,000 shares of stock. The warrants would be exercisable after one year at a price of $13.50 a share.

If the terms of a deal were finally agreed on, Bayles and Bayles would attempt to assemble a syndicate for which it would act as lead underwriter. The syndicate would be organized to provide wide geographic dispersion and insure a distribution of shares that would pose no threat to existing management. For a period of a year or so after the sale Bayles and Bayles would make an informal market for Electricircuit's stock in limited quantities. Although the firm was not an active over-the-counter dealer, it sometimes made an "after market" in issues it had originated, largely for the benefit of customers who might be forced to dispose of their stock in emergency circumstances.

Mr. Rappasadi found it difficult to evaluate the terms of this offer. Inquiries addressed to acquaintances in the financial community uncovered some opinion that the company should hold out for a higher price. These sources cited a number of recent growth issues that had sold in the 30 times price-earnings range. In addition, they noted that the economy showed strong signs of extending its longest postwar boom and that the stock market was currently at a record high.

Although Mr. Rappasadi realized that of all the firms approached Bayles and Bayles had been the only one to express any interest in underwriting a new issue, he decided to review the opinions above with Mr. Bayles. While Mr. Bayles agreed that both the economy and the stock market were unusually strong, he interpreted these developments as cause for apprehension concerning the new-issues market. He was uncertain about how long these favorable conditions could continue, and foresaw a possible break in the market at any time. In a sharply falling market an unseasoned over-the-counter stock such as Electricircuit's was apt to fare much worse than average. In pricing Electricircuit's proposed issue, the underwriter therefore had tried to allow both for some immediate capital appreciation and for the fact that it would be selling the issue to its customers at or near the top of a particularly strong market. Bayles and Bayles was particularly mindful of the second fact because of its agreement to maintain an informal market for Electricircuit common stock. As for the price of so-called comparable issues, the firm disagreed with the critics. The issues referred to were generally smaller, often had a small cash dividend to provide downside price support, and had been sold two or three months earlier in quite different market conditions. For all of these reasons, Bayles and Bayles declined to reconsider the offering price.

An alternative to external equity financing was continued reliance on the plowback of earnings with no payment of dividends. Mr. Rappasadi thought that the outlook for expansion and the profitability of contemplated funds commitments probably threw doubt on the wisdom of that policy, but he was uncertain about the amount and type, or types, of outside financing to recommend to his fellow shareholders.

Exhibit 1

ELECTRICIRCUIT, INC.

INCOME STATEMENTS FOR YEARS ENDED DECEMBER 31, 1961–63

(Dollar figures in thousands)

	1961	1962	1963
Net sales	$3,616	$5,544	$10,637
Cost of goods sold*	2,368	3,758	6,325
Gross profit	$1,248	$1,786	$ 4,312
Research and development expense	422	529	1,097
Selling, general, and administrative expense†	782	1,105	2,376
Interest expense	30	40	93
Income from operations	$ 13	$ 112	$ 746
Other income	2	7	20
Other deductions	(7)	(9)	(92)
Income before tax	$ 8	$ 110	$ 675
Federal income tax	3	45	329
Net income	$ 5	$ 65	$ 346

* Included in cost of goods sold:

	1961	1962	1963
Depreciation, amortization, and maintenance	$31	$ 52	$117
Rental charges	40	80	210
State and local taxes (excluding payroll)	1	1	4
Total	$72	$133	$331

† Included in selling, general, and administrative expense:

	1961	1962	1963
Depreciation, amortization, and maintenance	$11	$ 18	$ 40
Rental charges	19	39	101
State and local taxes (excluding payroll)	10	17	66
Total	$40	$ 74	$207

Exhibit 2

ELECTRICIRCUIT, INC.

BALANCE SHEETS AS OF DECEMBER 31, 1961–63

(Dollar figures in thousands)

ASSETS		1961		1962		1963
Cash...................................		$ 279		$ 303		$ 347
Accounts receivable........................		693		1,260		2,255
Inventories:						
Raw materials............................	$128		$337		$372	
Work in process.........................	187		373		537	
Finished goods...........................	244		311		407	
Total inventory.......................		559		1,022		1,317
Prepaid expenses............................		8		13		24
Total current assets.....................		$1,539		$2,598		$3,943
Gross fixed assets.........................	$212		$298		$537	
Less: Accumulated depreciation............	72		120		155	
Net fixed assets......................		140		178		382
Total assets......................		$1,679		$2,776		$4,325
LIABILITIES						
Notes payable*............................		$ 541		$1,072		$1,804
Trade accounts payable.....................		159		401		484
Accrued expenses..........................		129		246		240
Provision for taxes.........................		9		56		383
Other....................................		20		102		160
Total current liabilities.................		$ 858		$1,876		$3,072
Common stock, stated value 50 cents........		$ 318		$ 328		$ 360
Paid-in surplus............................		486		489		464
Retained earnings..........................		17		83		429
Total stockholders' equity...............		$ 821		$ 900		$1,253
Total liabilities and capital.............		$1,679		$2,776		$4,325
Number of shares outstanding...............		636,086		655,122		719,746

* Secured by the pledge of all receivables.

Exhibit 3

ELECTRICIRCUIT, INC.

SELECTED FINANCIAL DATA ON POSSIBLE INVENTORY POLICIES

(Dollar figures in thousands)

Alternative	Ratio of Inventory to Cost of Goods Sold*	Total Investment in Finished Goods Inventory*	Annual Sales Loss because of Stockouts	Annual Combined Setup, Warehouse, Handling, and Insurance Costs†
A	4.9% (18 days' sales)	$ 381	$495	$21
B..............	6.5 (24 days' sales)	505	301	25
C..............	8.9 (32 days' sales)	692	150	30
D..............	11.8 (42 days' sales)	917	56	35
E..............	14.2 (51 days' sales)	1,103	17	37

* Based on forecast annual cost of sales rate of $8.1 million. Inventory valued at direct cost.
† Interest expense and/or other financing costs are not included.

Exhibit 4

ELECTRICIRCUIT, INC.

BALANCE SHEET, AS OF APRIL 30, 1964, UNAUDITED

(Dollar figures in thousands)

ASSETS

Cash..		$ 135
Accounts receivable................................		2,510
Inventories:		
Raw materials.................................	$410	
Work in process...............................	506	
Finished goods................................	310	1,226
Prepaid expenses..................................		30
Total current assets............................		$3,901
Gross fixed assets.................................	$612	
Less: Accumulated depreciation....................	168	
Net fixed assets.............................		444
Total assets................................		$4,345

LIABILITIES

Notes payable*.....................................	$1,795
Trade accounts payable.............................	530
Accrued expenses..................................	246
Provision for taxes†...............................	245
Other..	143
Total current liabilities........................	$2,959
Common stock, stated value 50 cents................	$ 360
Paid-in surplus....................................	464
Retained earnings.................................	562
Total stockholders' equity......................	$1,386
Total liabilities and capital....................	$4,345
Number of shares outstanding......................	719,746

* Secured by the pledge of receivables.
† Tax liabilities as of April 30 reflect a large, first-quarter adjusting payment. At year-end, "Provision for taxes" normally equals the federal corporate income tax for the year just ended, plus approximately $75,000 state and local tax accruals.

WINCO DISTRIBUTION COMPANY

∧∧

In early June, 1965, the directors of Winco Distribution Company were faced with two major financial decisions that would have a long-run impact on the future of the firm. The first was the possible acquisition of Taylor Markets, Inc. The second was a major overhaul of the long-term capital structure of the company.

The first part of this case will present in summary form background information about Winco Distribution Company, stressing its growth and financing in the years immediately preceding 1965. Thereafter the information relevant to the acquisition of Taylor Markets and to alternative methods of reconstructing Winco's long-term capital structure will be summarized.

Growth of Winco Distribution Company

Winco was founded in 1907 to sell supplies to cotton plantations in the vicinity of Memphis, Tennessee. Through the years it expanded and underwent several changes in the nature of its business. By the end of World War II it had evolved into a grocery wholesaler with headquarters in Memphis servicing grocery stores in 10 states; it also owned and operated a chain of 18 retail food stores in Nashville, Tennessee.

Winco grew steadily from 1945 until 1965. The number of affiliated stores increased from 300 in 1945 to 1,350 in 1965 (Exhibit 1). This growth was also reflected in its operating statements and balance sheets for recent years (Exhibits 2 and 3). By 1965 the company's distribution system had expanded from the original single warehouse to a network of eight distribution points and three marine terminals from which it supplied ships calling in port.

In 1965 Winco was by far the larger of the two independent wholesale grocers in Memphis. It provided a wide range of ancillary services for affiliated retail stores. Stores could operate under their own names with standard brands or under a wide variety of advertising groups sponsored by Winco. Winco's staff was available to help plan all aspects of store operations from advertising to insurance and renovations. Financial support was also available to its retail associates. This support was given in the form of direct loans to 180 stores; of guarantees by Winco of liabilities of affiliates or suppliers; and of leases for prime store space signed by Winco and then sublet at cost to its retail affiliates. Management believed that these arrange-

503

ments were basically quite secure and that they did not expose Winco to major financial risks.

Despite heavy competition from national chains such as A&P, Kroger, and National Tea, Winco's management believed that the sales volume of its own stores and its affiliates was equal to or larger than that of any chain or similar wholesale group in its area of operation. Independent studies by brokerage houses confirmed the ability of Winco and several large grocery wholesalers in other parts of the country to compete effectively with the national chains.

Background information on acquisitions prior to 1965

Part of the rapid expansion of Winco during the 1961–65 period was accounted for by acquisitions rather than by internal growth.

Certain assets of the Henstock Company, a wholesale grocery business operating in southeastern Texas and southwestern Louisiana, were acquired in July, 1962, for $700,000 in cash and common stock of Winco valued at $1.4 million (108,655 shares with a market price at the time of acquisition of about $13). Henstock's after-tax earnings were about $175,000 in the most recent year before acquisition. The book value of the assets acquired, after the deduction of certain liabilities assumed, was $1.7 million. The financial statements for Winco shown in Exhibits 2 and 3 have not been adjusted for the years prior to fiscal year 1963 to show the operations of the combined companies because the transaction was a purchase of assets rather than a merger.

In May, 1964, Winco acquired the principal operating assets of the Warrilow Corporation, a closely held wholesale grocery business and retail store chain operating in Nashville, Tennessee, and nearby areas. Winco paid the owners of Warrilow slightly over $12 million. Payment was made in three parts: (1) $4.8 million in cash; (2) $5 million of 6% cumulative preferred stock (described in more detail in the next section); and (3) the assumption by Winco of $2.4 million of the liabilities of Warrilow. The price paid was estimated by Winco's management at approximately 13 times Warrilow's earnings after taxes. The assets purchased had been carried on Warrilow's books at about $2 million less than the net price Winco paid for them. Most of this amount was assigned to individual asset accounts on Winco's books on the basis of an independent professional appraisal of the acquired assets. The remainder was carried as goodwill.

Financing in connection with the Warrilow acquisition

As previously indicated, Winco issued $5 million of 6% cumulative preferred stock to the owners of the Warrilow Corporation as partial payment for this acquisition. The terms of the preferred stock provided for the retirement of the entire issue in May, 1968, although Winco was given the right to call at par part or all of the issue for retirement prior to that date. If the preferred stock were not retired by May, 1968, the preferred stockholders would be entitled to elect a majority of the board of directors. Furthermore, the holders of the preferred stock could require redemption of their shares on 30 days'

notice if the paid-in surplus and retained earnings of Winco should fall below
$5.5 million.

The management of Winco did not expect to be able to generate funds from
its own working capital position to cover all the $4.8 million cash payment
and the $2.4 million in increased liabilities assumed in the Warrilow Corpora-
tion purchase. It did anticipate, however, that a smaller amount of current
assets would be required to operate the combined businesses than the sum of
their current assets before the acquisition. Inventory duplications could be
eliminated, and other efficiencies were expected to reduce somewhat the need
for working capital. Because the Winco management was uncertain about the
exact amount of funds required to finance the expanded scale of operations, it
decided to seek interim financing rather than longer term debt.

The cash required for the Warrilow acquisition was therefore raised
mainly through an intermediate-term loan negotiated in June, 1964, with
banks in Memphis and Nashville. The banks gave Winco a revolving line of
credit at $5\frac{1}{4}\%$ in addition to the balance outstanding on a $5\frac{1}{4}\%$ loan
previously made to Winco in 1963. The new loan was granted with the
understanding that it would be paid off or replaced by longer term debt when
a more precise estimate of the company's financial requirements could be
made. On June 27, 1964, the end of Winco's 1964 fiscal year, $5 million of the
new line of credit had been drawn down. By the end of fiscal year 1965,
Winco was only borrowing $1.9 million under this arrangement.

Future plans

Except for the possible acquisition of Taylor Markets, Inc., which will be
discussed below, the management of Winco knew of no future possible
acquisitions of retail or wholesale grocery firms. Moreover, in the foreseeable
future the management did not expect to commit funds to integrate operations
backward into processing, packaging, and manufacturing. No major additions
were planned for Winco's physical plant; funds generated from depreciation
charges would be sufficient to cover construction of whatever new fixed assets
might be required. Growth was expected to come primarily from an increased
volume of business in existing market areas. The region served by Winco was
attracting industry at a significant rate; standards of living were rising and
population was increasing. Moreover, as previously noted, the management of
Winco was confident of its ability to compete effectively with the national
chains. It anticipated a probable growth rate of sales of about 13% for the
foreseeable future and set the likely boundaries on the range of this growth
rate as 10% and 16%. The existing physical plant, with relatively minor
additions, was more than adequate to accommodate this rate of growth for
some years to come.

Taylor Markets, Inc.

The management of Winco knew of only one prospect for expansion by
acquisition in the foreseeable future. It had recently learned that the owners
of Taylor Markets, an aggressive retail chain of 10 stores in Memphis, were

willing to sell their chain to Winco if suitable terms could be negotiated. The Taylor chain had grown from a single store opened in 1947 to its current size. An independent market survey conducted early in 1964 indicated that Taylor had 18% of the Memphis food store business.   *— Saving*

Winco had maintained a long and close relationship with Taylor Markets, which had been a member of Winco's voluntary plan since the first Taylor store was opened. The Taylor management had been very impressive, generating sufficient profits to open new stores with a minimum of financial assistance from Winco. Taylor Markets paid approximately $261,000 annually for the properties it leased. Many of these properties had been subleased from Winco and thus were already contingent liabilities of Winco.

The only severe difficulty Taylor Markets had encountered was caused by a labor dispute growing out of an acquisition the chain had made in 1961. As a consequence the company had shown losses for several years, but the issue had been completely resolved by 1965. The management of Winco regarded Taylor Markets' earnings of $220,000 in fiscal year 1965 as reasonably reflecting its true earning power. This figure was also considered a reasonable estimate of Taylor Markets' earning capacity on its existing stores over the next several years. (Recent earning statements of Taylor Markets are shown in Exhibit 4. Its estimated balance sheet for June 26, 1965, is given in Exhibit 5).

The owners of Taylor Markets wished to continue operating the business after its sale. For tax reasons they preferred to sell by means of an exchange of stock rather than for cash. A sale for cash would involve immediate heavy capital gains taxes whereas an exchange of stock would qualify as a taxfree transaction.

A merger with Taylor Markets might be considered as containing seeds of conflict with the independent retail affiliates of Winco. The Winco management, however, had found no ill will generated from its acquisition of the Warrilow stores in Nashville. All retailers, including wholly owned stores, were given the same terms and treatment. Management had concluded that under these circumstances there was little difference between supplying, on the one hand, a wholly owned store and its independent competitor and, on the other hand, two independent retailers who were competing with each other.

Long-term financing

Winco's long-term debt structure as of June 26, 1965, can be summarized as follows:

Current maturities on long-term debt.................................$ 300,000
Balloon maturity due in 1968 on 5¼% note of 1963...................... 2,000,000
Amount outstanding on revolving 5¼% loan in connection with Warrilow
   acquisition.. 1,900,000
Other long-term debt (about half of which was scheduled to mature during or
   prior to 1968)... 1,400,000
                                                                     $5,600,000

In addition to the long-term debt owed by Winco, Taylor Markets had $650,000 outstanding in short-term notes payable. If Taylor was acquired, $650,000 would be required to pay off these notes.[1]

In reviewing its debt position the management of Winco had definitely decided to refinance $5.0 million of its existing debt ($5.65 million if Taylor was acquired). An insurance company had expressed a willingness to share a loan of this size with Winco's banks. The interest rate on the outstanding balance would be between 5% and $5\frac{1}{4}$%. The principal of the loan would be amortized at an even rate over a 20-year period. If the loan was for $5.0 million, the banks would loan $1.25 million and the insurance company $3.75 million. The loan would be paid off at the rate of $250,000 a year, with the full amount going to the banks for the first five years and the remainder to the insurance company for the last 15 years. The covenants on the new loan would be less restrictive than those on the company's existing indebtedness.

Refinancing the $5 million of preferred stock along with the outstanding debt was also under consideration. The lending institutions had indicated that they would be willing to increase the size of the new 20-year loan to a maximum of $7.5 to $8.0 million on the same terms except for a proportionate increase in the annual payments needed to retire the principal of the loan in 20 years. An $8.0 million loan, however, was the maximum amount that they would grant at this time.

In addition to these needs for long-term or equity funds, Winco required seasonal financing each year. Peak needs occurred during the fall months and had amounted to about $1 million in recent years. These funds were borrowed through Winco's Memphis bank, where a 90-day line of credit of $3.5 million was maintained for seasonal financing. No change was expected in this arrangement for seasonal financing.

In its consideration of the restructuring of its long-run financing, Winco's management was considering two other sources of funds to refinance part or all of its needs above the amount that it expected to borrow on a 20-year basis.

Possible issue of common stock

The first was a public issue of common stock. Winco stock, which was traded over the counter, had recently reached an all time high of $28\frac{7}{8}$ a share, bid. (Exhibit 6 shows the range of Winco stock prices to June 10, 1965.) The bid price had only declined to about $28 during the recent softening of the stock market in the second quarter of 1965. During the same period the Dow-Jones average of 30 industrial stocks had declined from 920 to 875.

The company's investment banker had indicated that a new issue of up to $5 million of common stock could probably be sold at a price of about $25 a

---

[1] Winco also had contingent liabilities and lease obligations for its affiliates and suppliers amounting to $900,000, and it leased property in its own name involving annual rental payments of $850,000. Neither of these items was shown on its balance sheet.

share to the public provided that the price of Winco common stock did not decline any further. The management of Winco did not want to price the stock so high as to "crowd the market" for fear that the stock might perform unfavorably thereafter. Fees and expenses were estimated at about 7% of the gross receipts of a $5 million issue and, because of the fixed costs involved, at a somewhat higher percentage of a smaller issue.

Winco common stock had first been made available to the public in July, 1961. At that time the company had sold 115,500 shares to raise funds to retire debt and for general purposes; members of the founder's family had sold 201,000 shares of their personal holdings at the same time. In order to minimize the cash drain from dividends during the first years of public ownership, the family had converted some of the shares they retained into a Class A common stock. The Class A stock was identical with the regular common stock except that it did not participate in dividends. It was convertible share for share into regular common stock according to a fixed schedule. After converting the remaining 109,638 shares of Class A stock on July 1, 1965, the founder's family would own about 437,000 shares of common stock. Other officers and directors owned about 90,000 regular common shares.

Management considered the public stock issue in 1961 a success. It was priced at $12 a share and subsequently rose to a high of $18½ before the stock market decline in April, 1962. At that time the price fell back to about $12.

By 1965 Winco had 1,373 registered stockholders located in 37 states. Some of the stock was held in "street names," the ultimate owner having left the stock in the name of his bank or brokerage house. Some mutual and pension funds had taken positions in the stock. Nevertheless, the number of round lots (100-share lots) held by the public was still small.

An investment banking firm with a special interest in the leading wholesale grocers had noted the limited marketability, the relatively small capitalization, and the lack of listing of these stocks as drawbacks. It expected, though, that these problems would diminish in intensity during the next several years for the larger wholesale grocers such as Winco. Exhibit 7 includes some financial statistics for several large wholesale grocers.

Possible issue of convertible debentures

The management of Winco had also discussed the possibility of issuing a subordinated convertible debenture to the public. Its investment banker had indicated that a company like Winco could raise roughly $5 million by issuing a 15-year or 20-year subordinated convertible debenture bearing interest at a rate of between 4% and 4½%. This rate was lower than Winco could obtain on a straight debt issue because of the potential value of the convertible feature to the lender. The conversion price would be set about 20% above the market price of the common stock at the time the debenture was sold, or at about $34 a share on the basis of the $28 market price. In other words, each $1,000 bond would be convertible into 29.41 shares of common stock. Fees and expenses would be 3½% to 4% of gross funds raised. The banks and insurance company that had offered to lend up to $8 million on a 20-year amortization basis had indicated that they would not object to an issue of convertible debentures provided that these debentures were subordinated to the 20-year loan.

It was normally expected that the price of the common stock of a growing company would rise sufficiently within a few years to make a conversion privilege attractive, thereby enabling the company to force conversion by calling the debenture issue for redemption. Consequently, it was not customary to require a sinking fund for the first few years of a convertible debenture's life. If Winco should issue a 20-year convertible debenture, for example, the repayments on principal would be scheduled to begin after five years and to be sufficient to retire the debt over the remaining 15 years, assuming that it had not been converted in the meantime.

Timing of issue of common stock or convertible debentures

Although an issue of stock or debt could be canceled at the last minute if the market proved extremely unfavorable, a public issue had to be planned several months in advance so that the necessary registration information could be compiled and filed with appropriate authorities. The nature of the information would differ depending on whether management had decided tentatively to issue stock or debt. A decision to shift from one type of issue to the other after planning was well under way would require a substantial revision of the preparatory paper work. The date of issue would be delayed, and an additional investment in management time and in legal and accounting fees would be necessary. For this reason, if a public issue of Winco securities was selected, management was anxious to choose a form of security that would not have to be changed because of moderate changes in stock market conditions during the next several months.

*   *   *   *   *

With the preceding facts in mind, the management of Winco had to decide (1) what action to take with respect to the merger with Taylor Markets; (2) whether to raise more than the $5 million it had already decided to secure by an issue of bonds; and (3) if so, the amount and the source of these additional funds. Management had prepared the forecasts shown in Exhibit 8 as background information for these decisions.

Exhibit 1

WINCO DISTRIBUTION COMPANY

NUMBER OF CLIENT STORES

	Fiscal Year				
	1961	1962	1963	1964	1965
Number of stores, beginning of year	747	767	774	797	1,197
Number of stores added	53	64	41	418*	161*
Number of stores dropped	33	57	18	18	8
Number of stores at year-end	767	774	797	1,197	1,350

* Of the 418 stores added in fiscal year 1964 and the 161 stores added in 1965, 376 and 128 respectively were formerly served by the Warrilow Corporation and became affiliated stores of Winco as a result of the acquisition of Warrilow or by affiliation with Winco after the acquisition.

Exhibit 2

WINCO DISTRIBUTION COMPANY

INCOME STATEMENTS FOR THE FISCAL YEARS 1961–65

(Dollar figures in millions)

Fiscal year ended	June 24, 1961		June 30, 1962		June 29, 1963		June 27, 1964		June 26, 1965 (Preliminary)	
Net sales and service fees*	$74.4	100.0%	$ 86.3	100.0%	$121.4	100.0%	$138.7	100.0%	$211.8	100.0%
Cost of sales less discounts	69.5	93.4	80.6	93.4	112.6	92.8	128.1	92.3	192.0	90.7
Gross profit on sales and service fees	$ 4.9	6.6%	$ 5.7	6.6%	$ 8.8	7.2%	$ 10.6	7.7%	$ 19.8	9.3%
Operating expenses:										
Warehouse and delivery	$ 1.7		$ 1.9		$ 2.8		$ 3.1		$ 4.9	
Selling, general, and administrative	1.9		2.3		3.9		5.2		10.6	
Total operating expenses	$ 3.6	4.8	$ 4.2	4.9	$ 6.7	5.5	$ 8.3	6.0	$ 15.5	7.3
Income from operations	$ 1.3	1.8%	$ 1.5	1.7%	$ 2.1	1.7%	$ 2.3	1.7%	$ 4.3	2.0%
Add: Other income (expenses) net	0.1		0.1		0.1		0.1		(0.2)‡	
Less: Interest	0.1		0.1		0.2		0.2		0.4	
Income before taxes	$ 1.3	1.8%	$ 1.5	1.7%	$ 2.0	1.6%	$ 2.2	1.6%	$ 3.7	1.8%
Provision for income taxes	0.7	1.0	0.8	0.9	1.0	0.8	1.1	0.8	1.8	0.9
Net income after tax	$ 0.6	0.8%	$ 0.7	0.8%	$ 1.0	0.8%	$ 1.1	0.8%	$ 1.9	0.9%
Preferred dividends	...		...		...		...		$ 0.3	
Net income applicable to common shares	$ 0.6		$ 0.7		$ 1.0		$ 1.1		$ 1.6	
Number of shares of common stock outstanding at end of period†	704,411		819,911		928,566		932,901		938,393	
Net income per share†	$ 0.85		$ 0.86		$ 1.07		$ 1.21		$ 1.66	
Dividends per share paid on common shares only	$ 0.04		$ 0.26		$ 0.34		$ 0.41		$ 0.50	
Depreciation (millions)	n.a.		n.a.		$ 0.4		$ 0.5		$ 0.9	

* In fiscal year 1964 includes $10.3 million in sales and a negligible amount in net profits from Warrilow for the period May 4, 1964–June 27, 1964. For the full fiscal year 1965, Warrilow contributed sales of $70.0 million and income from operations of $1.5 million.

† Includes both classes of common stock.

‡ Includes $0.3 million loss on abandonment of equipment in the Warrilow operation.

WRONG!

Exhibit 3

WINCO DISTRIBUTION COMPANY

BALANCE SHEETS AS OF END OF FISCAL YEARS 1961–65

(Dollar figures in millions)

ASSETS	June 24, 1961*	June 30, 1962	June 29, 1963	June 27, 1964	(Preliminary) June 26, 1965
Current assets:	*Sales* 74.9	86.3	121.4	138.7	211.8
Cash	$1.0	$ 1.6	$ 2.4	$ 4.2	$ 2.5
Receivables (net)	1.8 *2.4*	3.3 *3.8*	4.7 *3.9*	8.5 *6.1*	10.2 *4.8*
Inventories of merchandise and supplies	4.3 *5.8*	4.5 *5.2*	7.0 *5.8*	12.7 *9.2*	13.0 *6.1*
Total current assets	$7.1	$ 9.4	$14.1	$25.4	$25.7
Investments, advances to affiliates, and other assets	$1.2	$ 0.5	$ 1.8	$ 1.7	$ 1.8
Property and equipment:					
Property and equipment	$2.2	$ 2.5	$ 3.5	$ 7.0	$ 6.9
Less: Accumulated depreciation	0.7	1.0	1.3	2.1	2.4
Net property and equipment	$1.5	$ 1.5	$ 2.2	$ 4.9	$ 4.5
Goodwill, deferred charges, and other assets	...	...	0.1	0.8	0.8
Total assets	$9.8	$11.4	$18.2	$32.8	$32.8

LIABILITIES					
Current liabilities:	*%*				
Notes payable, bank	$1.5	$ 0.5	$ ...	$ 0.1	$ 0.4
Current maturities, long-term debt	0.1	0.1	0.3	0.3	0.3
Trade accounts payable and other accruals	2.2 *3.0*	2.8 *3.2*	4.7 *3.9*	8.6 *6.2*	10.0 *4.7*
Income taxes payable	0.6	0.6	0.8	0.9	1.4
Total current liabilities	$4.4 *5.9*	$ 4.0 *4.6*	$ 5.8 *4.8*	$ 9.9 *7.1*	$12.1 *5.7*
Long-term debt	$0.9	$ 0.8	$ 4.1	$ 8.8	$ 5.3
Stockholders' equity:					
4% preferred stock, noncumulative	$0.4	$ 0.4	$ ...	$ ...	$ ...
6% preferred stock, cumulative, due 1968	...	...	...	5.0	5.0
Common stock, $1 par value†	0.4	0.5	0.6	0.7	0.8
Common stock Class A, $1 par value†	0.3	0.3	0.3	0.2	0.1
Paid-in surplus	0.5	1.8	3.1	3.1	3.2
Retained earnings	2.9	3.6	4.3	5.1	6.3
Total stockholders' equity	$4.5	$ 6.6	$ 8.3	$14.1	$15.4
Total liabilities and stockholders' equity	$9.8	$11.4	$18.2	$32.8	$32.8

* The statement as of June 24, 1961, has not been restated to allow for certain subsidiaries consolidated in 1962 and subsequent years. The assets of these subsidiaries totalled about $350,000.
† Total number of shares outstanding in each period shown in Exhibit 2.

1.2 %

Exhibit 4

TAYLOR MARKETS, INC.

INCOME STATEMENTS

(Dollar figures in thousands)

Fiscal year ended	June 29, 1963		June 27, 1964		(Preliminary) June 26, 1965	
Net sales	$16,463	100.0%	$18,504	100.0%	$18,162	100.0%
Cost of sales	13,270	80.6	14,833	80.2	14,379	79.2
Gross profit on sales	$ 3,193	19.4%	$ 3,671	19.8%	$ 3,783	20.8%
Operating expenses:						
Direct store expenses	$ 2,041	12.4%	$ 2,203	11.9%	$ 2,176	12.0%
Selling, general, and administrative	1,112	6.8	1,238	6.7	1,100	6.0
Total operating expenses	$ 3,153	19.2%	$ 3,441	18.6%	$ 3,276	18.0%
Income from operations	$ 40	0.2%	$ 230	1.2%	$ 507	2.8%
Other income	19	0.1	46	0.3	3	...
	$ 59	0.3%	$ 276	1.5%	$ 510	2.8%
Other expenses:						
Interest	$ 70		$ 71		$ 66	
Other	15		2		5	
Total other expenses	$ 85	0.5%	$ 73	0.4%	$ 71	0.4%
Net income (loss) before taxes	$ (26)	(0.2%)	$ 203	1.1%	$ 439	2.4%
Provision for state and federal income taxes	...	...	95	0.5	219	1.2
Net income (loss)	$ (26)	(0.2%)	$ 108	0.6%	$ 220	1.2%

Exhibit 5

TAYLOR MARKETS, INC.

PRELIMINARY BALANCE SHEET AS OF JUNE 26, 1965
(Dollar figures in thousands)

ASSETS

Current assets:

Cash..	$ 884
Accounts receivable.....................................	10
Inventory..	600
Prepaid expenses..	116
Total current assets...................................	$1,610
Cash value of life insurance................................	16
Total property and equipment............................$1,659	
Less: Depreciation.................................... 808	
Net property and equipment............................	851
Deferred charges..	1
Total assets..	$2,478

LIABILITIES

Current liabilities:

Note payable...	$ 650
Current maturities, long-term debt.......................	125
Accounts payable and miscellaneous accruals..............	501
Accrued state and federal taxes.........................	219
Total current liabilities.............................	$1,495

Long-term debt:

4% note payable.......................................	$ 42
5% note payable.......................................	130
	$ 172

Stockholders' equity:

Common stock, $100 par, 536 shares outstanding...........	$ 54
Paid-in surplus...	71
Retained earnings	686
Total stockholders' equity	$ 811
Total liabilities.....................................	$2,478

Exhibit 6

WINCO DISTRIBUTION COMPANY

MARKET PRICE OF COMMON STOCK*

Calendar Years	High	Low
1962:		
First quarter	$18½	$16½
Second	15¾	12¼
Third	14¼	12½
Fourth	13½	13
1963:		
First	14	13⅜
Second	17⅝	14¾
Third	17⅛	17
Fourth	17⅜	16⅜
1964:		
First	17	16½
Second	21⅝	19
Third	21½	21⅜
Fourth	24	21½
1965:		
First	25	24
Second (to June 10)	28⅞	24

Handwritten annotations: P/E — 15¾ $16½ } '62 18 — 14⅛ } '63 13 — 17¾ } '64 14.7 — 23¾ } '65 14.3

* Bid price in over-the-counter market.

Handwritten: WRONG!

Exhibit 7

WINCO DISTRIBUTION COMPANY

FINANCIAL STATISTICS, FOUR GROCERY WHOLESALERS

	Winco Distribution Company	Fleming Company	Scot Lad Foods	Super Value Stores
Most recent fiscal year ended	June, 1964	Dec., 1964	June, 1964	Dec., 1964
Most recent fiscal year:				
Sales (millions)	$139	$313	$183	$466
Profit after taxes (millions)	$ 1.1	$ 2.6	$ 1.4	$ 3.2
Gross margin (%)	7.7%	6.6%	11.8%	6.2%
Common dividends as a percentage of profit after taxes	25.5%*	47.5%	21%	43.8%
Stock price, fiscal 1964 range	16⅜–21⅝	22¼–28½	19⅝–27¼	27⅛–35½
Price-earnings ratio (based on average price for fiscal year 1964)	15.7	18.5	12.3	18.3
Yield (fiscal 1964 figures)	2.2%	2.6%	1.7%	2.4%
Quoted bid price, June 11, 1965	$ 28¼	$ 29¾	$ 24¾	$ 33½
Capitalization:				
Long-term debt	38.3%	25.6%	38.5%	22.3%
Preferred stock	21.8	3.4	...	8.6
Common stock and surplus	39.9	71.0	61.5	69.1
	100.0%	100.0%	100.0%	100.0%
Five-year compound growth rate:				
Sales	15.0%	11.6%	21%	17.2%
Profits after taxes	13.3	12.6	28	15.5
Earnings per share	8.4	8.8	18	9.8

* Based on dividends actually paid on the common stock. If dividends at the same rate had been paid on both the regular common and the Class A common stock, dividends would have been 34.8% of profit after taxes.

Exhibit 8

WINCO DISTRIBUTION COMPANY

PRO FORMA PROJECTIONS, FISCAL YEARS 1966 THROUGH 1968*

(Dollar figures in millions)

	Actual 1965	Projected, 1966–68 1966	1967	1968
1. *Sales and Earnings:*				
Sales—13% annual growth	$211.8	$239.3	$270.4	$305.6
Earnings before interest and taxes	4.1	4.4	4.9	5.6
2. *Projected balance sheet data†*				
Current assets and advances to affiliates:				
Cash	$ 2.5	$ 3.6	$ 4.0	$ 4.6
Receivables (net)	10.2	11.0	12.4	13.9
Inventories	13.0	14.6	16.4	18.5
Advances to affiliates	1.8	1.9	2.0	2.1
Total	$ 27.5	$ 31.1	$ 34.8	$ 39.1
Current liabilities:				
Accounts payable	$ 10.0	$ 10.8	$ 12.2	$ 13.7
Income taxes payable	1.4	1.5	1.7	2.0
Other	0.7	0.7	0.7	0.7
Total	$ 12.1	$ 13.0	$ 14.6	$ 16.4
Net working capital and advances to affiliates	$ 15.4	$ 18.1	$ 20.2	$ 22.7
Incremental funds required for NWC and advances to affiliates	...	2.7	2.1	2.5
Cumulative increase in funds required for NWC and advances to affiliates	...	2.7	4.8	7.3
3. *Minimum financial charges following the proposed $5 million refinancing‡:*				
Interest on the $5 million of long-term debt	...	$ 0.25	$ 0.24	$ 0.22
Interest on other remaining long-term debt	...	0.04	0.03	0.03
Debt repayment—$5 million of long-term debt	...	0.25	0.25	0.25
Debt repayment—other remaining long-term debt	...	0.09	0.09	0.09

* Note: The projections in this exhibit do *not* include any adjustments to reflect the possible acquisition of Taylor Markets currently under consideration by the management of Winco.

† The balance sheet data in this section include only current assets and current liabilities with the single exception that "advances to affiliates" is classified here with current assets. As stated in the text, expenditures on fixed assets were expected to be about equal to depreciation expenses.

‡ These charges are computed on the assumption that $5 million of new long-term debt is borrowed at an interest rate of 5% with repayments of principal of $250,000 per annum. If more than $5 million of long-term debt were borrowed, then charges related to long-term borrowings would have to be increased proportionately.

HOLIDAY GREETINGS, INC.

On Tuesday, July 21, 1970, Karl Augspach, president of Holiday Greetings, Inc., met with David Kingston, a friend and financial consultant. They had been discussing the future of Holiday in relation to the research Mr. Kingston had been doing on the firm. Mr. Augspach commented:

> Money is tight and, quite frankly, the cost of financing growth is now so high that I wish we could sit still for a year. But we really can't do that.
>
> If we should start refusing orders from new customers, we would demoralize our salesmen since part of their compensation is based on the volume of orders they generate. Similarly, if we can't respond to increased order sizes from existing customers, these customers might take all of their business to some other company that can meet their needs. Were we to come looking for their business later, they wouldn't let us in the door. You know the record and you saw our growth for last year. We're projecting 20% increases in sales and even larger increases in earnings for next year [see Exhibits 1 and 2 for the company's income statements, projections, and balance sheets]. The momentum we're generating is based mainly on larger orders from existing customers—in fact, already we've seen the size of some orders increase anywhere from 5% to 500% over last year. However, we are keenly aware that growth from this source can't go on forever. Ultimately we will have to expand our customer base and our production operations, not just the size of our orders. If you can come up with some suggestions concerning the financing of our expansion, we can talk about them on Saturday morning; right now I've got to go upstairs to see about the cutting of that new line of round cards, and then look at the Christmas 1971 designs.

With this dismissal from Mr. Augspach, Mr. Kingston left to consider the information that he had collected to date. He knew that he would have to develop some precise recommendations by the end of the week.

INDUSTRY BACKGROUND DATA

In 1968, the greeting card industry consisted of about 215 companies; the "Big Five" (see Exhibits 3 and 4) dominated the scene with an overwhelming market share. Of these five, two were publicly owned (American Greetings and Rust Craft), two were private (Hallmark and Norcross), and one (Gibson) had been purchased by a financial corporation (CIT) in 1964.

The rest of the industry was made up predominantly of small firms, many of which were privately owned and family controlled; 60% of them employed fewer than 20 people and most manufactured seasonal card lines (such as Christmas cards, Valentines, etc.). Growth, however, was most prominent in the larger firms, which had larger, more diversified product lines (as many as 1,200 different cards for Christmas) and more efficient national distribution channels. Smaller companies were often crippled by the expense of setting up a large sales system, of producing a full line and constantly reviewing it, and of designing and preparing new cards. As a result, from 1954 to 1963 the total number of firms in the industry had declined 12%, and from 1963 to 1967 the decline was 15%. Most of this decline occurred within companies of less than 50 employees.[1]

In order to compete successfully, all firms had to deal effectively with high fixed costs. Companies ran large inventory costs because of the necessity of keeping stock for reorders. In addition, many retailers could return unsold or soiled cards to the manufacturer, who would have to bear the expense. Production was costly since long lead times prevented rerunning successful designs.

Because of these high fixed costs and the overall competitiveness of the industry, distribution costs were very important to overall firm profitability. Most large companies used their own sales force to sell directly to various kinds of outlets (see Exhibits 5 and 6); few dealt with supermarkets and little was known about effective marketing strategy in this area. Often, companies would try to increase sales by expanding the distribution network although the policy at Hallmark was to maintain the number of outlets while increasing card turnover. Some firms also marketed different lines for different kinds of stores (such as college versus general drugstores) in order to widen distribution, but the trend appeared to be moving away from this expensive strategy. Sales trends within the industry were quite distinctive; they were often characterized (especially in the case of smaller companies) by seasonal peaks, as most of the actual sales occurred in a short period of time even though cards were in production all year. As an example, for the industry as a whole 37% of dollar sales (and 50% of the total piece volume) occurred at Christmas, with Valentine's Day (7% of sales), Mother's Day (5%), and Father's Day (2%) being other examples where the selling season was short but the revenues were large. Within the industry, companies had been placing

---

[1] Most of these small firms disappeared through failure or merger with other small greeting card firms. The U.S. Department of Justice generally challenged a merger between two firms operating in a highly concentrated industry if these firms' market shares exceeded those shown below:

Acquiring Firm	Acquired Firm
4%	4% or more
10%	2% or more
15% or more	1% or more

Source: U.S. Department of Justice, *Merger Guidelines*, "Enforcement Policy" [for Section 7, Clayton Act], May 30, 1968, p. 13.

an increasing emphasis on variety offering and a rapid replacement of slow sellers to encourage more impulse buying of everyday cards. This had been successful to the extent that in 1954 25% of card volume was represented by everyday sales, and in 1969 this figure was 40%.

Within the industry, trends included a conscious move away from relying solely on greeting card sales. To provide more year-round revenue, firms had been diversifying into different kinds of cards (such as Friendship, Black holidays) as well as related products. Hallmark, for example, also marketed glassware, jewelry, candles, silverware, and giftbooks in its national "Hall Galleries"; American Greetings diversified into gift wrap (16% of sales) and stationery goods (such as playing cards, giftbooks and college study guides—2% of sales). Rust Craft produced art prints, stationery, announcements (wedding, birth, etc.) and owned and operated several TV stations. However, greeting cards still represented 75% of this company's sales in 1968. In a further attempt to even out revenue, the four "giants" had also started licensees and subsidiaries all over the world.

HOLIDAY GREETINGS, INC.

In 1956, four years after coming to the United States, Karl Augspach founded Augspach's Greeting Card Co. in New York City with $1,500. A citizen of Holland, born in Germany, he had decided to enter the business he had learned from his father. In 1961 he acquired the bankrupt Holiday Lithograph Publishing Co. of Reading, Connecticut, and moved his operations to the new plant. A year later Holiday Greetings, Inc., went public through a stock offering at $3 per share.

In the years that followed, Holiday expanded rapidly through internal growth and acquisitions. In general, management policy was to consolidate all production operations at the Reading plant but to keep the acquired facilities and former management to facilitate distribution and to take on extra printing if necessary. Glitter Greetings of Lansing, Michigan, a firm which primarily sold "spoil-proof" acetate wrapped cards to supermarkets, became a wholly owned subsidiary in 1964 in a deal involving both cash and stock. In 1968, Holiday acquired Dorn & Co. (Long Beach, New York) for cash. Dorn was a small company which sold juvenile Valentines through a distribution system that included chain, drug, variety, and discount stores as well as wholesalers, rack jobbers, and supermarkets. Dorn was managed by one of the three brothers who had sold the company to Holiday. The brother, age 66, had spent his entire business career in the greeting card business. Still another market was opened with the acquisition of the California firm "Christmas Cheer," again by means of cash and stock. In 1969 this became "Holiday Artists" and provided the company with a convenient means of West Coast distribution as well as an operation specializing in sales of packaged personalized Christmas cards directly from the warehouse to the retailer.

Holiday operations

Unlike most small companies, Holiday manufactured a full line of greeting cards, i.e., Christmas, Valentines, Birthday, Get Well, Sympathy, Mother's Day and Father's Day, Anniversary, etc.; the 1969 line included 1,200 designs. Approximately 30% of dollar sales was accounted for by Christmas sales and 25% by Valentines, with the remainder made up by everyday and spring holiday cards. Twenty-five percent of total sales were of packaged boxes of cards which were either "title" cards (i.e., Brother's Birthday) or assortments; this helped to cut costs because the manufacturer did not have to supervise racks and reorders of individual cards in every outlet. Returns expense was low here as well, since once the package was sold to a store it was generally not returnable. In addition, the giants of the industry were not as active in packaged sales, concentrating more heavily on the sale of individual cards. At Holiday only Glitter competed heavily in this "counter" market, with 95% of this division's sales being of individual cards in 1969.

None of Holiday's designs were studio cards, which were higher fashion items. Holiday sold primarily to the over 25-year-olds. Mr. Augspach characterized a large part of his market as cost conscious and generally not college educated. He felt that most of the purchasers of his cards would not spend the time or the money in selecting *the* perfect card for each occasion, but would prefer to have the less expensive, more convenient packages at home whenever a card was needed.

Production of all cards and gift wrap was done at the 200-employee plant in Reading. The operation was fully integrated, meaning that all facets were carried out at Holiday from artwork and plate making to printing and packaging. The plant was operating at capacity but much of the printing work could be done by outside printers if necessary.

Mr. Augspach estimated that an individual card that retailed at 25 cents cost him $3\frac{1}{2}$ cents to produce. The largest factors included in this cost-of-goods-sold figure were first, artwork, then envelopes, paper, and boxes.

Eighty percent of the artwork was done by individual artists connected with an independent studio in Cleveland. Besides the individual design costs of $125, color separation and plate making were extremely expensive, making it beneficial to use the design as often as possible. At Holiday the first year a design was used it was used on personalized cards sold in quality department stores; the second year it went into packages to be sold in chain, discount, or variety stores; and the third year it was reworked to be used again. In addition, it was used for gift wrap over its entire life.

Holiday's distribution method

Distribution itself was not a large expense at Holiday; the 15 company salesmen (one third of whom worked on a full commission basis) sold either directly to the central buyers for such stores as Kresge's, Woolworth's, and

Bradlee's or to rack jobbers and wholesalers. This system, however, was a prime factor in the low margins earned by Holiday, for there were often two intermediaries between the manufacturer and the ultimate customer. As a reflection of this, Mr. Augspach estimated that dollar sales of his cards at retail level were three times the sales figures in his income statement.

Operations at Holiday were closely supervised; management included two production and shipping managers, one art director, and a sales manager and an assistant to the president. Besides Mr. Augspach there were nine officers, six of whom were also directors. Mrs. Augspach held the position of secretary and director, but she was the only family member involved. The Augspachs had three daughters, but neither they nor their husbands were interested in entering the greeting card industry. Other officers included the treasurer, the controller, and an executive vice president in charge of Glitter operations.

Financial problems

According to Mr. Augspach, Holiday had never been without financial problems. The business was capital intensive, and Mr. Augspach attributed much of his success to the company's good relations with its banks and suppliers. Its line of credit with a local bank was for $1.5 million, the bank's legal lending limit, and Dorn had a line of credit with a New York bank for an additional million. The company borrowed at 2½ percentage points above the prime rate, with the prime rate being 8% in July, 1970. In addition, several of the company's suppliers extended up to six months' trade credit to the company. After the first 60 days, however, they usually charged 9½% to 10% for this service. Because of the seasonal nature of the industry, Mr. Augspach estimated that the company's peak needs for bank and trade credit, which amounted to $3.1 million in 1969, occurred in December and January. He also stated that the company's low borrowing point following each selling season recurred in April, at which point bank and trade credit was reduced to about 50% of peak needs.

Although the company had a good relationship with its banks, Mr. Augspach had been urged to seek additional equity capital. Holiday's bankers felt uneasy about the extent to which the company was depending on debt capital in financing its operations. Early in 1970 they suggested that when they went along in helping to finance the company through an enormous sales expansion in 1968, they had anticipated a period of consolidation during which sales growth would slow substantially. Under these circumstances growth in the equity account through earnings retentions would have rapidly reduced the firm's debt/equity ratio to the 1967 level, a point substantially below the lofty 5.2 to 1 reached in 1968 (Exhibit 2). Given the firm's performance in 1969 and Mr. Augspach's sales projections (Exhibits 1 and 2), however, a return to the 1967 level in Holiday's debt/equity ratio was at best still several years away. Holiday's bankers therefore insisted that the firm take some action before the 1970 peak borrowing season to make sure that the company would stay safely within two restrictions which the bankers planned to impose on future loans to Holiday.

These two restrictions, which were to become applicable as of the 1970 seasonal peak of borrowing needs, were as follows:

1. The maximum bank loans outstanding at any time could not exceed 80% of Holiday's accounts receivable.
2. Holiday's total liabilities[2] could not exceed three times the book value of the company's net worth. In the event that the company's debt[2] to equity ratio rose to a level of more than three the company's bank loans would become due on demand.

For his own planning purposes Mr. Augspach had decided that to retain some margin of safety within these restrictions he would want to hold Holiday's future debt/equity ratio to a maximum of 2.75 to 1.

DECISIONS CONFRONTING HOLIDAY GREETINGS

Mr. Kingston was familiar with this background information on the greeting card industry and on Holiday Greetings. Mr. Augspach had also referred three other questions to Mr. Kingston:

1. Should Holiday invest in equipment to enable the company to make rather than to buy its envelopes? Mr. Augspach had indicated that he believed such an investment would be profitable but he was concerned about its implications for the company's financing requirements.
2. Should Holiday Greetings acquire Humor Designs, Inc., a small midwestern manufacturer of studio cards?
3. Should Holiday go to the market to raise additional equity capital in order to relieve the pressure on its financial position?

Envelope machine proposal

The cost of envelopes was one of the largest components of total costs. As of mid-1970 Holiday was still purchasing its entire supply of envelopes. During 1969 it had spent $600,000 to purchase the 200 million envelopes used by the company in 1969. Mr. Augspach estimated that he could buy equipment for $200,000 which when operated at full capacity would enable him to manufacture all the envelopes he had used in 1969. He estimated that the envelope-making equipment would have an economic life of about eight years.

Mr. Augspach estimated that seven men would be required to run the envelope-making operation. A two-man team would be needed to operate the machine on each of three daily shifts five days per week. They would each earn $2.50 an hour. One supervisor working only one shift per day would earn $4.00 an hour. Mr. Augspach calculated that paper and glue would cost

---

[2] "Total liabilities" and the "debt" component of the debt/equity ratio are used here as synonymous terms.

about $1.63 per thousand for the 200 million envelopes he had purchased in 1969 for $600,000. Mr. Augspach also estimated that he would need to rent a 25,000 square foot warehouse at a yearly rental of $1.50 per square foot if he manufactured his own envelopes. From these data Mr. Kingston had calculated that the envelope machine project would generate a positive cash flow of $112,500 annually for an eight-year period, disregarding working capital and financing requirements (Exhibit 7).

The additional warehouse space would be needed since if the machine was purchased, the company would be producing envelopes at a level rate substantially in excess of shipments during the spring and summer months of the year so as to build the large inventories needed to meet year-end shipping schedules (Exhibit 8). This inventory situation troubled Mr. Augspach somewhat since he knew that paper manufacturers required payment within 60 days. Under existing arrangements with envelope suppliers Mr. Augspach ordered envelopes on an "as needed" basis, and did not pay for them until about the time he received payment from Holiday's retailers. If he started manufacturing his own envelopes, Mr. Augspach realized that his working capital requirement would be expanded by the amounts shown in Exhibit 8.

Mr. Kingston knew that Mr. Augspach expected a recommendation from him in the immediate future as to whether and when he should establish his own envelope-making capacity. Mr. Augspach wanted to know what rate of return he would make on such an investment, how his earnings would be affected, and what the implications would be for his financing requirements.

Possible acquisition of Humor Designs, Inc.

Mr. Augspach had also been investigating a possible acquisition candidate, Humor Designs, Inc. (HD), a small midwestern manufacturer of studio cards. Humor Designs was privately owned and had sales of about $2 million in 1969 (Exhibit 9). Mr. Augspach had spent considerable time over a four-month period examining the details of HD's operations. He had become convinced that under his management, HD could almost immediately reduce both its cost of goods sold and its other expenses by 5%. He estimated that if Holiday acquired HD during the summer of 1970, HD's sales would remain flat during the year of ownership change, but that beyond 1970 the company would be able to achieve sales increase at about 10% per year as it had done between 1967 and 1969 (Exhibit 9). What particularly interested Mr. Augspach about the potential acquisition was the fact HD's balance sheet (Exhibit 10) was comparatively strong. He felt HD's suppliers would be willing to go a good deal further in providing trade credit than they had in the past, and he knew that the company carried with it substantial unused bank credit lines and other debt capacity. In his discussion with the three present owners of HD, all of whom were approaching retirement age, Mr. Augspach concluded that the company could be acquired for 12 times its 1969 earnings. The principals were willing to take Holiday common stock valued at $6 a share, which would give them a total of 136,000 shares. A check with his public accounting firm convinced Mr. Augspach that the acquisition could be treated as a "pooling of interests" for accounting purposes.

Mr. Augspach had asked Mr. Kingston for a recommendation as to whether he should acquire Humor Designs on these terms. Mr. Kingston knew that he would have to consider the impact of the acquisition on the earnings position of Holiday and also the implications of the acquisition for Holiday's financial position.

Possible sale of new common stock

In order to sustain the projected rapid growth for the next several years and in view of Holiday's extremely tight financial position (Exhibits 1 and 2), Mr. Augspach was aware that he might have to raise additional equity capital. Mr. Kingston knew that Mr. Augspach would be most reluctant to accept a policy recommendation that would force him to curtail the growth in sales projected in Exhibit 1. As already indicated Mr. Augspach believed that if potential increases in orders from new or existing customers were turned down, it would be very difficult and perhaps impossible to regain these customers in subsequent years. Mr. Augspach was also concerned that restrictions on the acceptance of new orders would be demoralizing to his salesmen and perhaps would cause some of his most valuable salesmen to shift to a competing firm.

Mr. Kingston was also troubled by the fact that he knew that mid-1970 was a most difficult and expensive time for any company to raise new equity capital, and especially for a small company like Holiday with unseasoned securities.

Holiday Greetings stock was traded in the over-the-counter market. Volume was light, averaging about 1,000 shares a week. During the past several months the stock price had held at about $6, a low for the year. Earlier in the year the stock had sold as high as $11 a share. During 1968 and 1969 the price of the stock had ranged from a low of $6 to a high of $12 a share. Mr. Kingston knew that Mr. Augspach did not follow the price of his stock "too closely" and that he received relatively few telephone calls from brokers and analysts about the company. Mr. Augspach owned about 55% of the stock currently outstanding. Another 20% was owned by employees and officers of the company. About 25% of the outstanding stock was owned by the public.

Mr. Kingston knew that Mr. Augspach had recently received an offer from a group of West Coast investors who had had a long-term interest in the company. They had offered to buy 100,000 shares of Holiday's common stock at $5 a share. If this offer was accepted, Holiday would have to pay a finder's fee of $25,000, or 5,000 shares, to the individual who had brought this offer to Mr. Augspach's attention.

In considering this offer Mr. Kingston approached Tom Meservey, a friend of his and a partner in the Boston office of the investment banking firm of Stoddard, White & Driscoll, to inquire about the feasibility of a public offering of Holiday stock. Mr. Meservey was not encouraging. He commented:

Now is a tough time to raise equity money, especially for a small company like Holiday. The Dow Jones index of industrial stocks has fallen from 942 in December, 1968, to 732 right now and there's no telling what will happen tomorrow. Unemployment is now over 5% and most predictions are that it will go even higher. This is a bad time for a small company to raise money. The new issue market has badly deteriorated; in fact it has almost dried up.

I hate to say so, but I don't see how we could possibly take Holiday's stock to the market at more than $5 a share, and we could contemplate such an offering only on a "best efforts" rather than an "underwritten" basis. Frankly, I am uncertain how many shares we could sell even at a price as low as $5. In addition, you realize of course that we would have to charge a sizable commission on an offering as risky and problematical as this, and that Holiday would have to bear the legal, accounting, and other fees of preparing and registering a public issue of Holiday's stock. Moreover, it would probably take two to three months, at best, to prepare a prospectus and process it through the Securities and Exchange Commission.

This conversation confirmed Mr. Kingston's initial impression that the only realistic prospect for raising new equity capital was to accept the offer of the West Coast group. This offer would yield $500,000 for 100,000 shares. In addition there would be a finder's fee of 5,000 shares. Legal and administrative costs would be minimal since the transaction would not involve a public issue of stock.

* * * * *

With this background analysis completed, Mr. Kingston sat down to prepare his recommendations for Mr. Augspach. He knew that Mr. Augspach expected a recommendation on whether and when the envelope machine should be purchased, on whether Humor Designs should be acquired, and on whether new equity financing should be obtained. In addition to a recommended course of action Mr. Augspach expected a backup analysis explaining the superiority of Mr. Kingston's recommendations as compared with other feasible courses of action.

Exhibit 1

HOLIDAY GREETINGS, INC.
CONSOLIDATED INCOME STATEMENTS, 1967–69, AND PROJECTED INCOME STATEMENTS, 1970–72*
(Years ending December 31; dollar figures in thousands)

	Actual Data			Projected Data		
	1967	1968	1969	1970	1971	1972
Net sales......................	$3,222	$5,106†	$6,501	$7,800	$9,300	$11,200
Cost of goods sold.............	2,276	3,514	4,216	5,000	5,900	7,000
Gross profit on sales............	$ 946	$1,592	$2,285	$2,800	$3,400	$ 4,200
Expenses:						
Selling, delivery, and warehousing...............	$ 406	$ 717	$ 949	$1,160	$1,390	$ 1,600
General and administrative.....	219	378	450	500	560	650
Total expenses...........	$ 625	$1,095	$1,399	$1,660	$1,950	$ 2,250
Earnings before interest and taxes......................	$ 321	$ 497	$ 886	$1,140	$1,450	$ 1,950
Interest.......................	198	242	305	350§	350§	385§
Income before federal income taxes......................	$ 123	$ 255	$ 581	$ 790	$1,100	$ 1,565
Provision for federal income taxes......................	45	90	307	420	600	850
Net income....................	$ 78	$ 165	$ 274	$ 370	$ 500	$ 715
Earnings per share based on average shares outstanding for the period (in dollars)....	$ 0.29	$ 0.60‡	$ 0.96	$ 1.28§	$ 1.72§	$ 2.47§

* Net sales and net income for 1964–66 were as follows:

	Net Sales (Millions)	Net Income (Thousands)
1964............	$2.2	$21
1965............	2.5	42
1966............	2.8	59

† $600,000 of 1968 sales were from the Dorn acquisition.
‡ $0.13 was from the Dorn acquisition.
§ Based on 290,000 shares outstanding. No allowance is made for additional financing in the form of increased debt or new equity issues in these projections.
Source: Annual reports and management projections.

Exhibit 2

HOLIDAY GREETINGS, INC.

CONSOLIDATED BALANCE SHEETS, 1967–69, AND PROJECTED BALANCE SHEETS, 1970–72

(As of December 31; dollar figures in thousands)

	Actual Data			Projected Data		
	1967	1968	1969	1970	1971	1972	
ASSETS							
Cash	$ 80	$ 148	$ 96	$ 100	$ 100	$ 100	
Notes and accounts receivable	1,168	2,353	2,805	3,354	3,999	4,816	(43% of projected sales)
Inventory	1,000	1,483	2,235	2,652	3,162	3,808	(34% of projected sales)
Prepaid expenses	17	47	77	78	93	112	(1% of projected sales)
Total current assets	$2,265	$4,031	$5,213	$6,184	$7,354	$ 8,836	
Net fixed assets	361	883	973	1,000	1,000	1,000	
Investment at cost	—	40	40	40	40	40	
Goodwill	—	172	172	172	172	172	
Deferred charges and other	74	151	145	150	150	150	
Total assets	$2,700	$5,277	$6,543	$7,546	$8,716	$10,198	
LIABILITIES							
Bank loans	$ 929	$1,740	$2,428	$2,819	$3,253	$ 3,476	(PLUG)
Trade notes payable	348	630	696	1,482	1,767	2,128	(19% of projected sales)
Accounts payable	253	469	528				
Accrued expenses and payroll taxes	90	184	251	312	372	448	(4% of projected sales)
Federal income taxes	43	89	241	336	400	680	
Current portion of long-term debt	47	140	173	173	173	173	
Other	—	75	99	100	100	100	
Total current liabilities	$1,710	$3,327	$4,416	$5,222	$6,065	$ 7,005	
Long-term debt	315	1,101	983	810	637	464	(173,000 retired per yr.)
Total liabilities	$2,025	$4,428	$5,399	$6,032	$6,702	$ 7,469	
Common stock ($0.10 par value)	27	28	29	29	29	29	
Paid-in capital	290	299	319	319	319	319	
Retained earnings	358	522	796	1,166	1,666	2,381	
Total liabilities and net worth	$2,700	$5,277	$6,543	$7,546	$8,716	$10,198	
Equity	$ 675	$ 849	$1,144	$1,514	$2,014	$ 2,729	
Bank loan/receivables	0.80	0.74	0.87	0.84	0.81	0.72	
Liabilities/equity	3.0	5.2	4.7	4.0	3.3	2.7	

Exhibit 3

HOLIDAY GREETINGS, INC.
INDUSTRY PERFORMANCE—1968

Company	Sales* (in Millions)	Income after Taxes (in Millions)	Earnings per Share (in Dollars)	Price- Earnings Ratio
American Greetings	$113.1	$6.9	$1.72	23
Rust Craft	47.5	2.7	2.30	18
Hallmark	150.0	n.a.	n.a.	n.a.
Gibson	65.0	n.a.	n.a.	n.a.
Norcross	20.0	n.a.	n.a.	n.a.
Holiday	5.1	0.2	0.60	10

INDUSTRY GROWTH TRENDS

Company	Annual Percentage Increase in Sales	Annual Percentage Increase in Profits
American Greetings†	13%	13%
Rust Craft‡	7	9
Hallmark†	10–15	10–15
Gibson§	30	n.a.

* Sales include all products of these companies but they consist primarily of greeting cards.
† Annual rate over a 10-year period.
‡ Annual rate after 1962 deficit.
§ Annual rate over five-year period. Gibson's rapid increase in sales reflected a new policy of selling directly to wholesalers and of offering more favorable terms to retailers. It was believed in the industry that profits were lagging because of the high cost of the policy.
Source: "Note on the United States Greeting Card Industry," Intercollegiate Case Clearing House, Harvard Business School, 1969, ICH 14C1R(9-114-001).

Exhibit 4

HOLIDAY GREETINGS, INC.
SALES: INDUSTRY VERSUS HOLIDAY
(In millions)

Year	Industry	Holiday
1963	$332	$2.1
1964	345	2.2
1965	356	2.5
1966	370	2.8
1967	400	3.2
1968	425	5.1

Exhibit 5

HOLIDAY GREETINGS, INC.
INDUSTRY DISTRIBUTION METHODS

Company	Outlets	Salesmen
American Greetings	73,000*	1,000
Hallmark	30,000	n.a.
Rust Craft	16,000	210

* Up in five years from 11,000.

Exhibit 6

HOLIDAY GREETINGS, INC.
INDUSTRY SALES THROUGH DIFFERENT OUTLETS
(Percentage of total sales)

Type of Outlet	Greeting Cards	Gift Wrap
Variety store	25%	35%
Discount house	11	15
Department store	7	25
Drug store	16	5
Food store	5	10
Other*	36	10
Total	100%	100%

* Includes stationery and gift shops.

Exhibit 7

HOLIDAY GREETINGS, INC.
ESTIMATED ANNUAL SAVINGS IN CASH FLOW FROM OPERATION
OF ENVELOPE MACHINE, YEARS 1 THROUGH 8
(In thousands)

Savings: Outlays for envelopes purchased in 1969	$600.0
Incremental expenses from manufacturing envelopes:	
Materials	$326.0
Warehouse	37.5
Labor	36.5
Depreciation*	25.0
Total expenses	$425.0
Increase in profits before taxes	$175.0
Increase in income taxes	87.5
Increase in profit after taxes	$ 87.5
Add back: Depreciation	25.0
Net increase in cash flow from operations	$112.5

* If depreciation were taken on an accelerated basis for tax purposes, as would be possible, the annual increase in cash flows would be larger in the earlier years and smaller in later years.

Exhibit 8

HOLIDAY GREETINGS, INC.
ENVELOPE MACHINE PROJECT—WORKING CAPITAL REQUIREMENTS CALCULATION*

	Feb.	Mar.	Apr.	May	June	July	Aug.	Sep.	Oct.	Nov.	Dec.	Jan.	Feb.	Mar.	Total for Final 12 Months
Shipping level per month:															
(Percent of year's total unit shipments made in month)															
Everyday cards	2.5	2.5	2.5	2.5	2.5	2.5	2.5	2.5	2.5	2.5	2.5	2.5	2.5	2.5	30.0
Spring cards	5.0	5.0	—	—	—	—	—	—	—	—	—	5.0	5.0	5.0	15.0
Christmas cards	—	—	—	—	—	—	—	—	15.0	15.0	—	—	—	—	30.0
Valentine cards	—	—	—	—	—	—	—	—	—	—	12.5	12.5	—	—	25.0
	7.5	7.5	2.5	2.5	2.5	2.5	2.5	2.5	17.5	17.5	15.0	20.0	7.5	7.5	100.0
(In thousands of dollars)															
Production (at cost)†	33.3	33.3	33.3	33.3	33.3	33.3	33.3	33.3	33.3	33.3	33.3	33.3	33.3	33.3	400.0‡
Usage (at cost)†	30.0	30.0	10.0	10.0	10.0	10.0	10.0	10.0	70.0	70.0	60.0	80.0	30.0	30.0	400.0
Cash out for labor	3.0	3.0	3.0	3.0	3.0	3.0	3.0	3.0	3.0	3.0	3.0	3.0	3.0	3.0	36.5‡
Cash out for warehouse	3.1	3.1	3.1	3.1	3.1	3.1	3.1	3.1	3.1	3.1	3.1	3.1	3.1	3.1	37.5‡
Cash out for material	—	—	27.2	27.2	27.2	27.2	27.2	27.2	27.2	27.2	27.2	27.2	27.2	27.2	326.0‡
Total cash out	6.1	6.1	33.3	33.3	33.3	33.3	33.3	33.3	33.3	33.3	33.3	33.3	33.3	33.3	400.0‡
Total cash collected§	—	—	30.0	30.0	10.0	10.0	10.0	10.0	10.0	10.0	70.0	70.0	60.0	80.0	400.0
Monthly cash deficit	6.1	6.1	3.3	3.3	23.3	23.3	23.3	23.3	23.3	23.3	(36.7)	(36.7)	(26.7)	(46.7)	
Working capital required¶	6.1	12.2	15.5	18.8	42.1	65.4	88.7	112.0	135.3	158.6	121.9	85.2	58.5	12.2‡	

* Cycle must begin at positive buildup point to avoid negative inventory; it continues for 14 periods to eliminate "start-up" effect on calculations.

† Cost does not include depreciation.

‡ Figures do not add because of rounding.

§ These figures do not represent anticipated sales revenue, but only that portion of revenue which represents the return of actual cash outlay for the manufacture of envelopes.

¶ The average working capital requirement for the year beginning April 1 and ending March 31 would be $76,000.

Exhibit 9

HOLIDAY GREETINGS, INC.
INCOME STATEMENTS FOR HUMOR DESIGNS, INC. (ACTUAL, 1967–69, AND PROJECTED, 1970–72)
(Years ended December 31; dollar figures in thousands)

	Actual Data			Projected Data		
	1967	*1968*	*1969*	*1970*	*1971*	*1972*
Net sales.............................	$1,670	$1,830	$2,000	$2,000*	$2,200*	$2,420*
Cost of goods sold.....................	993	1,080	1,200			
Gross profit on sales...................	$ 677	$ 750	$ 800			
Expenses:						
Selling, delivery, and warehousing....	420	472	480			
General and administrative..........	112	120	140			
Total expenses..................	$ 532	$ 592	$ 620			
Earnings before interest and taxes.......	145	158	180			
Interest..............................	30	38	40			
Income before federal income taxes......	$ 115	$ 120	$ 140			
Provision for federal income taxes......	58	62	72			
Net income...........................	$ 57	$ 58	$ 68			
Dividends............................	32	32	38			
Retained earnings.....................	$ 25	$ 26	$ 30			

* Projection made by Mr. Augspach.

Exhibit 10

HOLIDAY GREETINGS, INC.
BALANCE SHEETS OF HUMOR DESIGNS, INC., 1967–69
(As of December 31; dollar figures in thousands)

	1967	*1968*	*1969*
ASSETS			
Cash...	$ 27	$ 23	$ 35
Notes and accounts receivable......................	544	613	640
Inventory..	535	620	600
Prepaid expenses.................................	13	22	25
Total current assets..........................	$1,119	$1,278	$1,300
Net fixed assets.................................	436	490	500
Total assets..............................	$1,555	$1,768	$1,800
LIABILITIES			
Bank loans.......................................	$ —	$ 50	$ 100
Accounts payable................................	176	220	200
Current portion of long-term debt..................	15	20	20
Federal income taxes.............................	50	55	65
Other..	121	133	115
Total current liabilities........................	$ 362	$ 478	$ 500
Long-term debt..................................	349	420	400
Total liabilities..............................	$ 711	$ 898	$ 900
Common stock....................................	40	40	40
Paid-in capital...................................	120	120	120
Retained earnings................................	684	710	740
Total liabilities and net worth.................	$1,555	$1,768	$1,800
Equity...	$ 844	$ 870	$ 900
Bank loan/receivables............................	0.00	0.08	0.16
Total liabilities/equity...........................	0.84	1.03	1.00

Appendixes

A. TAX TABLE[1]

∧∧

FEDERAL TAX RATES ON CORPORATE INCOME AND PAYMENT DATES

Income Years	Rate	Income Years	Rate
1940*......................	24%	1954–63..................	52%
1941*......................	31	1964......................	50
1942–45*..................	40	1965–67..................	48
1946–49..................	38	1968–69†.................	52.8
1950......................	47	1970†......................	49.2
1951–53*..................	52	1971–74..................	48

* Excess profits tax also in effect for part or all of year.
† Includes special surcharge.

The 52 percent rate in effect from 1951 through 1963 consisted of a normal tax of 30 percent of taxable income and a surtax of 22 percent of taxable income in excess of $25,000. The 50 percent rate in effect in 1964 consisted of a normal tax of 22 percent and a surtax of 28 percent; and the 48 percent rate in effect from 1965 on consisted of a normal tax of 22 percent and a surtax of 26 percent.

In addition, in 1968 a special surcharge of 10 percent was imposed making the effective rate for that year 52.8 percent. This rate held for 1969, but the special surcharge was phased out gradually by quarters during 1970 so that the overall effective rate for that year was 49.2 percent and by 1971 the rate was again 48 percent.

Recent revenue acts have moved corporate income tax payments close to current payment. Beginning in 1950, payments were gradually accelerated until in 1954 they were brought entirely within the first half of the year following the tax liability. The Revenue Acts of 1954 and 1964 and the Tax Adjustment Act of 1966 set up even more accelerated schedules. Through 1967, all tax liabilities up to $100,000 were payable in equal amounts on March 15 and June 15 of the year following the tax liability. The Revenue

---

[1] This table has been prepared for use in connection with cases in this book. It is not a complete statement of applicable rates, and it should not be used as a reference for general purposes.

Act of 1968 provided for a gradual acceleration of tax payments for corporations with tax liabilities of less than $100,000 as well as for corporations with tax liabilities of more than $100,000. Tax liabilities over $100,000, for companies on a calendar year, were payable according to the following schedule. For 1967 and subsequent years, if the actual tax liability for the year exceeded the amount of estimated tax payments made on this liability during the year, the balance had to be paid in equal installments on March 15 and June 15 of the following year.

Year	Percentage Paid in Income Year*				Percentage Paid in Following Year†			
	Apr. 15	June 15	Sept. 15	Dec. 15	Mar. 15	June 15	Sept. 15	Dec. 15
1949	—	—	—	—	25	25	25	25
1950	—	—	—	—	30	30	20	20
1951	—	—	—	—	35	35	15	15
1952	—	—	—	—	40	40	10	10
1953	—	—	—	—	45	45	5	5
1954	—	—	—	—	50	50	—	—
1955	—	—	5	.5	45	45	—	—
1956	—	—	10	10	40	40	—	—
1957	—	—	15	15	35	35	—	—
1958	—	—	20	20	30	30	—	—
1959–1963	—	—	25	25	25	25	—	—
1964	1	1	25	25	24	24	—	—
1965	4	4	25	25	21	21	—	—
1966	12	12	25	25	13	13	—	—
1967 and subsequent years	25	25	25	25	—	—	—	—

*These are percentages of the estimated tax liability on income of the current year.
†These are percentages of the tax liability on income of the previous year.

B. NOTE ON INVESTMENT TAX CREDIT[1]

∧∧

A tax credit subsidy for business purchases of capital goods was first enacted by the U.S. Congress in 1962. Its purpose was twofold. First, the United States was emerging from a small economic recession in 1961, and it was hoped that the credit would encourage business spending for new plant and equipment. While the prime goal of the credit probably was to bolster a sagging economy, it also promised a substantial secondary benefit. For a number of years trade groups from numerous basic American industries had complained that European producers with lower labor costs and more modern physical facilities were slowly exporting more and more of their production to the United States. It was hoped that a tax subsidy encouraging new investment in capital goods would allow American producers to modernize their facilities and reduce their costs enough to be more competitive in the U.S. market with European producers.

Between 1962 and 1968, the investment credit underwent several revisions. It was "permanently" repealed (there had been a temporary suspension in 1966) by the Tax Reform Act of 1969. Because of a continuing business recession and rising unemployment in 1971 the tax investment credit was re-enacted in the Revenue Act of 1971 under the name "job-development credit." As the law stands after re-enactment, a purchaser of "Sec. 38"[2] property may deduct from his federal income tax liability 7 percent of the cost of new "Sec. 38" property in the year it is purchased, so long as the property has an expected useful life of 7 years or more. For property with a life of from 5 to 7 years the credit is equal to two thirds of this 7 percent, and for property with a useful life of 3 to 5 years the credit is equal to one third of 7 percent. Property with a useful life of less than 3 years does not qualify for the credit. (Under the old investment tax credit repealed in 1969 the required lives were one year longer; i.e., the upper limit was 8 years and the lower limit was 4 years.)

---

[1] This statement has been prepared for use in connection with cases in this book. It is not a definitive statement, and it should not be used as a reference for general purposes.

[2] For purposes of the credit, "Sec. 38" property is defined as all depreciable property (not including buildings) used as an integral part of (a) manufacturing, (b) mining, (c) production, (d) furnishing of services such as transportation, energy, water, and sewage disposal.

With some exceptions the credit is not applicable to foreign-made equipment or to equipment bought for use outside the United States. Public utilities also benefit by the investment tax credit but at the lower rate of 4 percent. Subject to certain limitations, up to $50,000 of the cost of used property may be taken into account in calculating the credit for any one year.

The investment tax credit does not act to reduce the basis for depreciation of equipment; however, the same time span of useful life must be used for calculating the investment tax credit as is used for taking depreciation deductions.

The investment tax credit represents a direct credit against the total income tax liability. For a company in the 48 percent tax bracket, a tax credit of $100,000 can save as much in income taxes as a $208,333 deduction from pretax income. Taxpayers who have a total tax liability of $25,000 or less are allowed to credit up to 100 percent of the liability. For those whose liability exceeds $25,000, the limit on the credit is $25,000 plus $\frac{1}{2}$ of the excess. Pre-1969 limits were the same. Calculations using a flat 50 percent will give results which are approximately correct when dealing with large corporate incomes. Any credit that cannot be used currently may be carried back for 3 years and forward for 7 years.

TAX VERSUS BOOK ACCOUNTING

Internal revenue regulations require corporations to take the investment tax credit in their tax accounting to the maximum allowable amount in the year it arises. In reports of earnings to shareholders, however, public accounting firms permit the credit to be handled by either of two methods. The entire credit can be taken in a single year, as it is for tax purposes, or it can be spread out and taken over the productive lives of the assets giving rise to the credit. The public accounting profession is somewhat divided on the issue, but most accountants favor the latter, the "deferral," approach since it causes less year-to-year distortion of after-tax income. Even so, as of 1974 the American Institute of Certified Public Accountants, in a survey of 600 major companies, found that over 80 percent of these companies adopted the former, the "flow through," treatment.[3] This method results immediately in higher reported earnings.

Exhibit 1 below shows how the accounting convention chosen can affect the after-tax income reported by a corporation to its shareholders.

In 1967, the Accounting Principles Board (APB) of the American Institute of Certified Public Accountants proposed to eliminate the "flow through" option allowing corporations to take the entire amount of the credit in a single year in reports of earnings to shareholders. Instead, corporations would be required to adopt the "deferral" approach and spread the tax saving over the lives of the assets giving rise to the credit. The APB argued that a corporation's after-tax profit as reported to shareholders was subject to great distortion if the entire credit was taken in a single year.

---

[3] AICPA, *Accounting Trends and Techniques*, 28th ed. (New York: 1974), p. 280.

Permitting the investment credit to flow through to net income in the period when the benefit is used to reduce income taxes payable may result in increasing or decreasing reported net income solely by reason of the timing of acquisition, rather than the use, of property. The result is inconsistent with the accepted concept that income results from the use and not from the acquisition of assets. Allocation of the investment credit to those periods in which the property that gives rise to the credit is utilized associates the income effects of the credit with the use of the property, not its acquisition.[4]

In response to the proposed change, the APB was deluged with nearly 1,000 letters concerning the proposal from corporate financial officers, a large portion of whom were critical of the APB's investment tax credit proposal. The officers of those companies whose reported earnings would be affected most (for example, airlines and equipment leasing companies) were the most vocal opponents, but many other businessmen and even government representatives jumped into the fray. The Assistant Secretary for tax policy of the U.S. Treasury Department charged that the board's proposed treatment of the investment tax credit could well blunt its effectiveness as an incentive to modernization and expansion.

Again, when the investment tax credit was re-enacted in 1971, the accounting profession made an attempt to tighten the rules governing the financial reporting of the 7 percent investment tax credit. The APB had the support of the SEC for its ruling that companies would have to report tax savings in income statements over the useful life of the property involved, and the ruling would have specifically disallowed the flow-through accounting method. However, the Senate, with the formal approval of the Nixon administration, vetoed the attempt and in fact inserted into the law a provision that "no taxpayer shall be required to use for the purposes of financial reports . . . any particular method of accounting for the credit allowed by such Section 38." The taxpayer must disclose in his reports the method he uses in accounting for the credit and must use the same method in all financial reports.

Exhibit 1

ACME CORPORATION

	Tax Accounts	Shareholder Reports	
		1 Year Lump Sum	Spread Over 8 Years
Purchases of new "Sec. 38" property............	$2,000,000	$2,000,000	$2,000,000
Profit before federal income tax.................	800,000	800,000	800,000
Federal income tax before credit.................	400,000	400,000	400,000
Less: Investment tax credit.....................	140,000	140,000	17,500
Federal income tax after credit..................	260,000	260,000	382,500
Profit after taxes.........................	$ 540,000	$ 540,000	$ 417,500

---

[4] "Exposure Draft, Proposed APB Opinion: Accounting for Income Taxes," Accounting Principles Board, September 14, 1967, paragraph 58b.

C. PRESENT VALUE TABLES

Table C-1

PRESENT VALUE OF $1

Periods until Payment	1%	2%	2½%	3%	4%	5%	6%	8%	10%	12%	14%	15%	16%	18%	20%	22%	24%	25%	26%	30%	40%	50%
1	0.990	0.980	0.976	0.971	0.962	0.952	0.943	0.926	0.909	0.893	0.877	0.870	0.862	0.847	0.833	0.820	0.806	0.800	0.794	0.769	0.714	0.667
2	0.980	0.961	0.952	0.943	0.925	0.907	0.890	0.857	0.826	0.797	0.769	0.756	0.743	0.718	0.694	0.672	0.650	0.640	0.630	0.592	0.510	0.444
3	0.971	0.942	0.929	0.915	0.889	0.864	0.840	0.794	0.751	0.712	0.675	0.658	0.641	0.609	0.579	0.551	0.524	0.512	0.500	0.455	0.364	0.296
4	0.961	0.924	0.906	0.888	0.855	0.823	0.792	0.735	0.683	0.636	0.592	0.572	0.552	0.516	0.482	0.451	0.423	0.410	0.397	0.350	0.260	0.198
5	0.951	0.906	0.884	0.863	0.822	0.784	0.747	0.681	0.621	0.567	0.519	0.497	0.476	0.437	0.402	0.370	0.341	0.328	0.315	0.269	0.186	0.132
6	0.942	0.888	0.862	0.837	0.790	0.746	0.705	0.630	0.564	0.507	0.456	0.432	0.410	0.370	0.335	0.303	0.275	0.262	0.250	0.207	0.133	0.088
7	0.933	0.871	0.841	0.813	0.760	0.711	0.665	0.583	0.513	0.452	0.400	0.376	0.354	0.314	0.279	0.249	0.222	0.210	0.198	0.159	0.095	0.059
8	0.923	0.853	0.821	0.789	0.731	0.677	0.627	0.540	0.467	0.404	0.351	0.327	0.305	0.266	0.233	0.204	0.179	0.168	0.157	0.123	0.068	0.039
9	0.914	0.837	0.801	0.766	0.703	0.645	0.592	0.500	0.424	0.361	0.308	0.284	0.263	0.225	0.194	0.167	0.144	0.134	0.125	0.094	0.048	0.026
10	0.905	0.820	0.781	0.744	0.676	0.614	0.558	0.463	0.386	0.322	0.270	0.247	0.227	0.191	0.162	0.137	0.116	0.107	0.099	0.073	0.035	0.017
11	0.896	0.804	0.762	0.722	0.650	0.585	0.527	0.429	0.350	0.287	0.237	0.215	0.195	0.162	0.135	0.112	0.094	0.086	0.079	0.056	0.025	0.012
12	0.887	0.788	0.744	0.701	0.625	0.557	0.497	0.397	0.319	0.257	0.208	0.187	0.168	0.137	0.112	0.092	0.076	0.069	0.062	0.043	0.018	0.008
13	0.879	0.773	0.725	0.681	0.601	0.530	0.469	0.368	0.290	0.229	0.182	0.163	0.145	0.116	0.093	0.075	0.061	0.055	0.050	0.033	0.013	0.005
14	0.870	0.758	0.708	0.661	0.577	0.505	0.442	0.340	0.263	0.205	0.160	0.141	0.125	0.099	0.078	0.062	0.049	0.044	0.039	0.025	0.009	0.003
15	0.861	0.743	0.690	0.642	0.555	0.481	0.417	0.315	0.239	0.183	0.140	0.123	0.108	0.084	0.065	0.051	0.040	0.035	0.031	0.020	0.006	0.002
16	0.853	0.728	0.674	0.623	0.534	0.458	0.394	0.292	0.218	0.163	0.123	0.107	0.093	0.071	0.054	0.042	0.032	0.028	0.025	0.015	0.005	0.002
17	0.844	0.714	0.657	0.605	0.513	0.436	0.371	0.270	0.198	0.146	0.108	0.093	0.080	0.060	0.045	0.034	0.026	0.023	0.020	0.012	0.003	0.001
18	0.836	0.700	0.641	0.587	0.494	0.416	0.350	0.250	0.180	0.130	0.095	0.081	0.069	0.051	0.038	0.028	0.021	0.018	0.016	0.009	0.002	0.001
19	0.828	0.686	0.626	0.570	0.475	0.396	0.331	0.232	0.164	0.116	0.083	0.070	0.060	0.043	0.031	0.023	0.017	0.014	0.012	0.007	0.002	
20	0.820	0.673	0.610	0.554	0.456	0.377	0.312	0.215	0.149	0.104	0.073	0.061	0.051	0.037	0.026	0.019	0.014	0.012	0.010	0.005	0.001	
21	0.811	0.660	0.595	0.538	0.439	0.359	0.294	0.199	0.135	0.093	0.064	0.053	0.044	0.031	0.022	0.015	0.011	0.009	0.008	0.004	0.001	
22	0.803	0.647	0.581	0.522	0.422	0.342	0.278	0.184	0.123	0.083	0.056	0.046	0.038	0.026	0.018	0.013	0.009	0.007	0.006	0.003	0.001	
23	0.795	0.634	0.567	0.507	0.406	0.326	0.262	0.170	0.112	0.074	0.049	0.040	0.033	0.022	0.015	0.010	0.007	0.006	0.005	0.002		
24	0.788	0.622	0.553	0.492	0.390	0.310	0.247	0.158	0.102	0.066	0.043	0.035	0.028	0.019	0.013	0.008	0.006	0.005	0.004	0.002		
25	0.780	0.610	0.539	0.478	0.375	0.295	0.233	0.146	0.092	0.059	0.038	0.030	0.024	0.016	0.010	0.007	0.005	0.004	0.003	0.001		
26	0.772	0.598	0.526	0.464	0.361	0.281	0.220	0.135	0.084	0.053	0.033	0.026	0.021	0.014	0.009	0.006	0.004	0.003	0.002	0.001		
27	0.764	0.586	0.513	0.450	0.347	0.268	0.207	0.125	0.076	0.047	0.029	0.023	0.018	0.011	0.007	0.005	0.003	0.002	0.002	0.001		
28	0.757	0.574	0.501	0.437	0.333	0.255	0.196	0.116	0.069	0.042	0.026	0.020	0.016	0.010	0.006	0.004	0.002	0.002	0.001	0.001		
29	0.749	0.563	0.489	0.424	0.321	0.243	0.185	0.107	0.063	0.037	0.022	0.017	0.014	0.008	0.005	0.003	0.002	0.002	0.001			
30	0.742	0.552	0.477	0.412	0.308	0.231	0.174	0.099	0.057	0.033	0.020	0.015	0.012	0.007	0.004	0.003	0.002	0.001	0.001			
40	0.672	0.453	0.372	0.307	0.208	0.142	0.097	0.046	0.022	0.011	0.005	0.004	0.003	0.001	0.001							
50	0.608	0.372	0.291	0.228	0.141	0.087	0.054	0.021	0.009	0.003	0.001	0.001	0.001									

SOURCE: Jerome Bracken and Charles J. Christenson, *Tables for Use in Analyzing Business Decisions* (Homewood, Ill.: Richard D. Irwin, Inc., 1965), except for the data on 2½%, the source for which is *Mathematical Tables from Handbook of Chemistry and Physics* (6th ed.; Cleveland: Chemical Rubber Publishing Co. 1938).

Table C–2

PRESENT VALUE OF $1 RECEIVED ANNUALLY

Periods to Be Paid	1%	2%	2½%	3%	4%	5%	6%	8%	10%	12%	14%	15%	16%	18%	20%	22%	24%	25%	26%	30%	40%	50%
1	0.990	0.980	0.976	0.971	0.962	0.952	0.943	0.926	0.909	0.893	0.877	0.870	0.862	0.847	0.833	0.820	0.806	0.800	0.794	0.769	0.714	0.667
2	1.970	1.942	1.927	1.914	1.886	1.859	1.833	1.783	1.736	1.690	1.647	1.626	1.605	1.566	1.528	1.492	1.457	1.440	1.424	1.361	1.224	1.111
3	2.941	2.884	2.856	2.829	2.775	2.723	2.673	2.577	2.487	2.402	2.322	2.283	2.246	2.174	2.106	2.042	1.981	1.952	1.923	1.816	1.589	1.407
4	3.902	3.808	3.762	3.717	3.630	3.546	3.465	3.312	3.170	3.037	2.914	2.855	2.798	2.690	2.589	2.494	2.404	2.362	2.320	2.166	1.849	1.605
5	4.853	4.713	4.646	4.580	4.452	4.330	4.212	3.993	3.791	3.605	3.433	3.352	3.274	3.127	2.991	2.864	2.745	2.689	2.635	2.436	2.035	1.737
6	5.795	5.601	5.508	5.417	5.242	5.076	4.917	4.623	4.355	4.111	3.889	3.784	3.685	3.498	3.326	3.167	3.020	2.951	2.885	2.643	2.168	1.824
7	6.728	6.472	6.349	6.230	6.002	5.786	5.582	5.206	4.868	4.564	4.288	4.160	4.039	3.812	3.605	3.416	3.242	3.161	3.083	2.802	2.263	1.883
8	7.652	7.325	7.170	7.020	6.733	6.463	6.210	5.747	5.335	4.968	4.639	4.487	4.344	4.078	3.837	3.619	3.421	3.329	3.241	2.925	2.331	1.922
9	8.566	8.162	7.971	7.786	7.435	7.108	6.802	6.247	5.759	5.328	4.946	4.772	4.607	4.303	4.031	3.786	3.566	3.463	3.366	3.019	2.379	1.948
10	9.471	8.983	8.752	8.530	8.111	7.722	7.360	6.710	6.145	5.650	5.216	5.019	4.833	4.494	4.192	3.923	3.682	3.571	3.465	3.092	2.414	1.965
11	10.368	9.787	9.514	9.253	8.760	8.306	7.887	7.139	6.495	5.938	5.453	5.234	5.029	4.656	4.327	4.035	3.776	3.656	3.544	3.147	2.438	1.977
12	11.255	10.575	10.258	9.954	9.385	8.863	8.384	7.536	6.814	6.194	5.660	5.421	5.197	4.793	4.439	4.127	3.851	3.725	3.606	3.190	2.456	1.985
13	12.134	11.348	10.983	10.635	9.986	9.394	8.853	7.904	7.103	6.424	5.842	5.583	5.342	4.910	4.533	4.203	3.912	3.780	3.656	3.223	2.468	1.990
14	13.004	12.106	11.691	11.296	10.563	9.899	9.295	8.244	7.367	6.628	6.002	5.724	5.468	5.008	4.611	4.265	3.962	3.824	3.695	3.249	2.478	1.993
15	13.865	12.849	12.381	11.938	11.118	10.380	9.712	8.559	7.606	6.811	6.142	5.847	5.576	5.092	4.676	4.315	4.001	3.859	3.726	3.268	2.484	1.995
16	14.718	13.578	13.055	12.561	11.652	10.838	10.106	8.851	7.824	6.974	6.265	5.954	5.668	5.162	4.730	4.357	4.033	3.887	3.751	3.283	2.488	1.997
17	15.562	14.292	13.712	13.166	12.166	11.274	10.477	9.122	8.022	7.120	6.373	6.047	5.749	5.222	4.775	4.391	4.059	3.910	3.771	3.295	2.492	1.998
18	16.398	14.992	14.353	13.754	12.659	11.690	10.828	9.372	8.201	7.250	6.467	6.128	5.818	5.273	4.812	4.419	4.080	3.928	3.786	3.304	2.494	1.999
19	17.226	15.678	14.979	14.324	13.134	12.085	11.158	9.604	8.365	7.366	6.550	6.198	5.878	5.316	4.844	4.442	4.097	3.942	3.799	3.311	2.496	1.999
20	18.046	16.351	15.589	14.877	13.590	12.462	11.470	9.818	8.514	7.469	6.623	6.259	5.929	5.353	4.870	4.460	4.110	3.954	3.808	3.316	2.497	1.999
21	18.857	17.011	16.185	15.415	14.029	12.821	11.764	10.017	8.649	7.562	6.687	6.312	5.973	5.384	4.891	4.476	4.121	3.963	3.816	3.320	2.498	2.000
22	19.660	17.658	16.765	15.937	14.451	13.163	12.042	10.201	8.772	7.645	6.743	6.359	6.011	5.410	4.909	4.488	4.130	3.970	3.822	3.323	2.498	2.000
23	20.456	18.292	17.332	16.444	14.857	13.489	12.303	10.371	8.883	7.718	6.792	6.399	6.044	5.432	4.924	4.499	4.137	3.976	3.827	3.325	2.499	2.000
24	21.243	18.914	17.885	16.936	15.247	13.799	12.550	10.529	8.985	7.784	6.835	6.434	6.073	5.451	4.937	4.507	4.143	3.981	3.831	3.327	2.499	2.000
25	22.023	19.523	18.424	17.413	15.622	14.094	12.783	10.675	9.077	7.843	6.873	6.464	6.097	5.467	4.948	4.514	4.147	3.985	3.834	3.329	2.499	2.000
26	22.795	20.121	18.951	17.877	15.983	14.375	13.003	10.810	9.161	7.896	6.906	6.491	6.118	5.480	4.956	4.520	4.151	3.988	3.837	3.330	2.500	2.000
27	23.560	20.707	19.464	18.327	16.330	14.643	13.211	10.935	9.237	7.943	6.935	6.514	6.136	5.492	4.964	4.524	4.154	3.990	3.839	3.331	2.500	2.000
28	24.316	21.281	19.965	18.764	16.663	14.898	13.406	11.051	9.307	7.984	6.961	6.534	6.152	5.502	4.970	4.528	4.157	3.992	3.840	3.331	2.500	2.000
29	25.066	21.844	20.454	19.188	16.984	15.141	13.591	11.158	9.370	8.022	6.983	6.551	6.166	5.510	4.975	4.531	4.159	3.994	3.841	3.332	2.500	2.000
30	25.808	22.396	20.930	19.600	17.292	15.372	13.765	11.258	9.427	8.055	7.003	6.566	6.177	5.517	4.979	4.534	4.160	3.995	3.842	3.332	2.500	2.000
40	32.835	27.355	25.103	23.115	19.793	17.159	15.046	11.925	9.779	8.244	7.105	6.642	6.234	5.548	4.997	4.544	4.166	3.999	3.846	3.333	2.500	2.000
50	39.196	31.424	28.362	25.730	21.482	18.256	15.762	12.233	9.915	8.304	7.133	6.660	6.246	5.554	4.999	4.545	4.167	4.000	3.846	3.333	2.500	2.000

SOURCE: Jerome Bracken and Charles J. Christenson, *Tables for Use in Analyzing Business Decisions* (Homewood, Ill.: Richard D. Irwin, Inc., 1965), except for the data on 2½%, the source for which is *Mathematical Tables from Handbook of Chemistry and Physics* (6th ed.; Cleveland: Chemical Rubber Publishing Co., 1938).

YEAR-END ACCUMULATIONS

Table C–3 shows the year-end accumulation at various effective annual interest rates[1] of $1 received in periodic installments during the year. Observe that fractional interest rates appear at the bottom of the table.

Each period's installment is assumed to be received at the *end* of the period. For example, the entries in the column for a one-half-year period show the accumulation one year from now of two $0.50 payments the first of which is received one-half-year from now, the second one year from now.

The entries in the column for a 0 period show the year-end accumulation of $1 received "continuously" during the year. More accurately, they show the limit approached by the accumulation of $1 received in periodic installments as the period between installments approaches 0.

Example. At 10 percent effective annual interest, $1 received in installments of $0.25 each at the end of each quarter of a year will accumulate to $1.037 at the end of the year.

---

[1] If a single payment of $1 accumulates in one year to $(1 + i)$, the "effective annual" rate of interest is i or $100i$ percent.

Table C-3. YEAR-END ACCUMULATION OF $1

Interest Rate	Period						
	1 year	½ year	¼ year	1 month	1 week	1 day	0
.01	1.000	1.002	1.004	1.005	1.005	1.005	1.005
.02	1.000	1.005	1.007	1.009	1.010	1.010	1.010
.03	1.000	1.007	1.011	1.014	1.015	1.015	1.015
.04	1.000	1.010	1.015	1.018	1.019	1.020	1.020
.05	1.000	1.012	1.019	1.023	1.024	1.025	1.025
.06	1.000	1.015	1.022	1.027	1.029	1.030	1.030
.07	1.000	1.017	1.026	1.032	1.034	1.035	1.035
.08	1.000	1.020	1.030	1.036	1.039	1.039	1.039
.09	1.000	1.022	1.033	1.041	1.043	1.044	1.044
.10	1.000	1.024	1.037	1.045	1.048	1.049	1.049
.11	1.000	1.027	1.040	1.049	1.053	1.054	1.054
.12	1.000	1.029	1.044	1.054	1.058	1.059	1.059
.13	1.000	1.032	1.048	1.058	1.062	1.063	1.064
.14	1.000	1.034	1.051	1.063	1.067	1.068	1.068
.15	1.000	1.036	1.055	1.067	1.072	1.073	1.073
.16	1.000	1.039	1.058	1.071	1.076	1.078	1.078
.17	1.000	1.041	1.062	1.076	1.081	1.083	1.083
.18	1.000	1.043	1.065	1.080	1.086	1.087	1.088
.19	1.000	1.045	1.069	1.084	1.090	1.092	1.092
.20	1.000	1.048	1.072	1.089	1.095	1.097	1.097
.21	1.000	1.050	1.076	1.093	1.100	1.101	1.102
.22	1.000	1.052	1.079	1.097	1.104	1.106	1.106
.23	1.000	1.055	1.083	1.101	1.109	1.111	1.111
.24	1.000	1.057	1.086	1.106	1.113	1.115	1.116
.25	1.000	1.059	1.089	1.110	1.118	1.120	1.120
.26	1.000	1.061	1.093	1.114	1.122	1.125	1.125
.27	1.000	1.063	1.096	1.118	1.127	1.129	1.130
.28	1.000	1.066	1.100	1.123	1.132	1.134	1.134
.29	1.000	1.068	1.103	1.127	1.136	1.138	1.139
.30	1.000	1.070	1.106	1.131	1.141	1.143	1.143
.35	1.000	1.081	1.123	1.152	1.163	1.166	1.166
.40	1.000	1.092	1.140	1.172	1.185	1.188	1.189
.45	1.000	1.102	1.156	1.192	1.207	1.210	1.211
.50	1.000	1.112	1.172	1.212	1.228	1.232	1.233
.55	1.000	1.122	1.187	1.232	1.250	1.254	1.255
.60	1.000	1.132	1.203	1.252	1.271	1.276	1.277
.70	1.000	1.152	1.234	1.290	1.312	1.318	1.319
.80	1.000	1.171	1.263	1.328	1.353	1.360	1.361
.90	1.000	1.189	1.293	1.365	1.394	1.401	1.402
1.00	1.000	1.207	1.321	1.401	1.433	1.441	1.443
.0250	1.000	1.006	1.009	1.011	1.012	1.012	1.012
.0275	1.000	1.007	1.010	1.013	1.013	1.014	1.014
.0300	1.000	1.007	1.011	1.014	1.015	1.015	1.015
.0325	1.000	1.008	1.012	1.015	1.016	1.016	1.016
.0350	1.000	1.009	1.013	1.016	1.017	1.017	1.017
.0375	1.000	1.009	1.014	1.017	1.018	1.019	1.019
.0400	1.000	1.010	1.015	1.018	1.019	1.020	1.020
.0425	1.000	1.011	1.016	1.019	1.021	1.021	1.021
.0450	1.000	1.011	1.017	1.020	1.022	1.022	1.022
.0475	1.000	1.012	1.018	1.022	1.023	1.024	1.024
.0500	1.000	1.012	1.019	1.023	1.024	1.025	1.025
.0525	1.000	1.013	1.019	1.024	1.026	1.026	1.026
.0550	1.000	1.014	1.020	1.025	1.027	1.027	1.027
.0575	1.000	1.014	1.021	1.026	1.028	1.028	1.028
.0600	1.000	1.015	1.022	1.027	1.029	1.030	1.030

Index

INDEX OF CASES